EXAMINING LIVES IN CONTEXT

EXAMINING LIVES IN CONTEXT

Perspectives on the Ecology of Human Development

Edited by Phyllis Moen, Glen H. Elder, Jr., and Kurt Lüscher
with the assistance of Heather E. Quick

American Psychological Association • Washington, DC

First Printing August 1995
Second Printing November 1996

Published by the
American Psychological Association
750 First Street, NE
Washington, DC 20002

Copies may be ordered from
American Psychological Association
Order Department
P.O. Box 92984
Washington, DC 20090-2984

In the UK and Europe, copies may be ordered from
American Psychological Association
3 Henrietta Street
Covent Garden, London
WC2E BLU England

Typeset in Minion by University Graphics, Inc., York, PA

Printer: Data Reproductions Corp., Rochester Hills, MI
Cover Designer: Berg Design, Albany, NY
Technical/Production Editor: Kathryn Lynch

Library of Congress Cataloging in Publication Data
Examining lives in context : perspectives on the ecology of human
    Development / edited by Phyllis Moen, Glen H. Elder, Jr., Kurt
    Lüscher; with the assistance of Heather E. Quick
        p.   cm.
    Includes bibliographical references and index.
    ISBN 1-55798-293-7
    1. Development psychology.   2. Environmental psychology.
    3. Nature and nurture.   I. Moen, Phyllis.   II. Elder, Glen H.
    III. Lüscher, Kurt.
    BF713. E92   1995   95–5704
    155—dc20   CIP

British Library Cataloguing-in-Publication Data
A CIP record is available from the British Library.

Printed in the United States of America

APA Science Volumes

Temperament: Individual Differences at the Interface of Biology and Behavior

Through the Looking Glass: Issues of Psychological Well-Being in Captive Nonhuman Primates

APA expects to publish volumes on the following conference topics:

Attribution Processes, Person Perception and Social Interaction: The Legacy of Ned Jones

Changing Ecological Approaches to Development: Organism–Environment Mutualities

Conceptual Structure and Processes: Emergence, Discovery, and Change

Converging Operations in the Study of Visual Selective Attention

Genetic, Ethological and Evolutionary Perspectives on Human Development

Global Prospects for Education: Development, Culture, and Schooling

Maintaining and Promoting Integrity in Behavioral Science Research

Marital and Family Therapy Outcome and Process Research

Measuring Changes in Patients Following Psychological and Pharmacological Interventions

Psychology of Industrial Relations

Psychophysiological Study of Attention

Stereotype Accuracy

Stereotypes: Brain–Behavior Relationships

Work Team Dynamics and Productivity in the Context of Diversity

As part of its continuing and expanding commitment to enhance the dissemination of scientific psychological knowledge, the Science Directorate of the APA established a Scientific Conferences Program. A series of volumes resulting from these conferences is produced jointly by the Science Directorate and the Office of Communications. A call for proposals is issued several times annually by the Scientific Directorate, which, collaboratively with the APA Board of Scientific Affairs, evaluates the proposals and selects several conferences for funding. This important effort has resulted in an exceptional series of meetings and scholarly volumes, each of which has contributed to the dissemination of research and dialogue in these topical areas.

The APA Science Directorate's conferences funding program has supported 35 conferences since its inception in 1988. To date, 24 volumes resulting from conferences have been published.

WILLIAM C. HOWELL, PHD
Executive Director

VIRGINIA E. HOLT
Assistant Executive Director

Contents

Contributors

Duane F. Alwin, PhD, Professor of Sociology and Program Director, Institute for Social Research, University of Michigan

Jay Belsky, PhD, Professor of Human Development and Family Studies, Pennsylvania State University

Urie Bronfenbrenner, PhD, Jacob Gould Schurman Professor Emeritus of Human Development and Family Studies and of Psychology, Cornell University

Jeanne Brooks-Gunn, PhD, Virginia and Leonard Marx Professor of Child Development and Education, Teachers College, Columbia University

Beverley D. Cairns, AB, Director of the Social Development–Research Unit, Center for Developmental Science, University of North Carolina, Chapel Hill

Robert B. Cairns, PhD, Cary C. Boshamer Professor of Psychology, University of North Carolina, Chapel Hill

Stephen J. Ceci, PhD, Helen L. Carr Professor of Developmental Psychology, Cornell University

Lorna Champion, PhD, Lecturer in Clinical Psychology, Department of Psychiatry, University of Edinburgh, Scotland

John A. Clausen, PhD, Professor Emeritus of Sociology, Institute of Human Development, University of California, Berkeley

Nancy E. Darling, PhD, Assistant Professor of Psychology, Dickinson College

Glen H. Elder, Jr., PhD, Howard W. Odum Distinguished Professor of Sociology and Research Professor of Psychology, Carolina Population Center, University of North Carolina, Chapel Hill

Mary Ann Erickson, MA, Graduate Student, Human Development and Family Studies, Cornell University

Anne C. Fletcher, PhD, Postdoctoral Fellow, Carolina Consortium on Human Development, University of North Carolina, Chapel Hill

Jacqueline J. Goodnow, PhD, Professor of Behavioral Science, Macquarie University, Sydney, New South Wales, Australia

Helene A. Hembrooke, PhD, Postdoctoral Fellow, Human Development and Family Studies, Cornell University

Gerri Jones, BA, Assistant to Professor Bronfenbrenner, Cornell University

Melvin L. Kohn, PhD, Professor of Sociology, Johns Hopkins University

Kurt Lüscher, PhD, Professor of Sociology, University of Konstanz, Germany

Eleanor E. Maccoby, PhD, Professor Emerita of Psychology, Stanford University

David Magnusson, PhD, Olof Eneroth Professor of Psychology and President of the European Academy of Science, University of Stockholm, Sweden

Barbara Maughan, PhD, Career Scientist, Medical Research Council Child Psychiatry Unit, Institute of Psychiatry, London, England

Phyllis Moen, PhD, Ferris Family Professor of Life Course Studies and Sociology and Director of the Bronfenbrenner Life Course Center, Cornell University

Andrew Pickles, PhD, Career Scientist, Medical Research Council Child Psychiatry Unit, Institute of Psychiatry, London, England

David Quinton, PhD, Career Scientist, Medical Research Council Child Psychiatry Unit, Institute of Psychiatry, London, England

Sir Michael Rutter, MD, FRS, Honorary Director, Medical Research Council Child Psychiatry Unit, Institute of Psychiatry, London, England

Laurence Steinberg, PhD, Professor of Psychology, Temple University

William Julius Wilson, PhD, Lucy Flower University Professor of Sociology and Public Policy, University of Chicago

Preface

It is our privilege and pleasure to edit this volume, compiled in honor of someone we are proud to claim as a valued colleague and a close personal friend, Urie Bronfenbrenner. Most developmentalists need no reminder of Urie's outstanding contributions to the enhancement of human development, as a teacher, as a scholar, and as a major contributor to social policy development. His insights and ideas have been recognized, acclaimed, and acted on, not only in the United States, but throughout the world.

We hope this book will serve a variety of readerships: students who seek an introduction to the ecological and life course theoretical approaches; established scholars who want an overview of advances in the field; researchers who are interested in multilevel, multidimensional approaches to human development; and admirers of Urie Bronfenbrenner who want both a tribute to him and an assessment of his contributions. We believe this volume will serve as testimony to Urie's lifetime of work but also as an intellectual challenge to the social and behavioral science community to engage and extend his evolving theoretical paradigm.

Each of the editors has benefited from lively scholarly exchange with Urie Bronfenbrenner over the years. Phyllis Moen has been fortunate to occupy the office across the hall from Urie's office since she came to Cornell in 1978. His was always an open, and welcoming, door. Over the years, she has found her attention to the links between policy and research heightened by Urie's proximity and provocation. Bronfenbrenner has affirmed Moen's comparative approach to social policy, making clear that the United States has much to learn from the experiences of other nations grappling with similar social, economic, and demographic revolutions in their own societies. Urie always reminds her that the ways American society has responded to these challenges differ both in scope and style from the responses of other societies. Bronfenbrenner has also encouraged Moen to investigate the two halves of the life course, a step now begun with her chapter (with Mary Ann Erickson; 6) in this volume.

Glen Elder's intellectual journey with Urie began during his graduate work (circa 1960) at the University of North Carolina, Chapel Hill, and it has continued with growing intensity over more than 3 decades. He visited Cornell during the early 1960s in the fond hope that a faculty post would somehow materialize, and it did, but only after 20 more years—a period in which he devised a life course approach to human development while serving on the faculties of University of California, Berkeley, and University of North Carolina, Chapel Hill. For over 5 marvelous years, he was Urie's departmental colleague and a grateful recipient of his wise counsel and collaboration on teaching ventures, including an unforgettable codirected graduate seminar on human development in the spring of 1984. That was a special moment, but his shared intellectual journey with Urie has provided many others right up to the present. When Glen returned to University of North Carolina, Chapel Hill, and helped to establish (with Robert Cairns) the Carolina Consortium on Human Development, Urie became a founding member of the advisory board and has frequently visited the Consortium proseminar.

Kurt Lüscher first met Urie 30 years ago, at the centennial celebration for Cornell University. A central theme of their ongoing discussions since then, the conceptualization of knowledge and beliefs, is reflected in his chapter (17) in this volume. Lüscher had the great privilege of editing some of Bronfenbrenner's major writings for publication in German, including an edited volume incorporating his intellectual biography published in 1976. Urie was instrumental in introducing Lüscher to the field of childhood socialization and family research, and he encouraged Lüscher to become concerned about social policy for children and families. Bronfenbrenner has served on the Scientific Advisory Committee for the Konstanz Center "Society and Family" since its founding by Kurt Lüscher in 1990.

A key theme in Urie's work is context, and an important context of this book is its origins. Those origins can be traced back to the Second Konstanz Symposium on "Society and Family," held in the fall of 1991, in which all three of us participated. At that time, the three of us came together to discuss how we might best celebrate Urie's distinguished career and intellectual contributions to the field. The seeds planted then have borne an abundance of intellectual fruit, as evident in the quality of the chapters included here.

Early drafts were presented at a symposium in honor of Urie Bronfenbrenner, organized by the Cornell Life Course Institute and sponsored by the Institute, the College of Human Ecology, and the Research Directorate of the American Psychological Association. It was held at Cornell University in September 1993. The symposium and, consequently, the volume offer a reflective assessment and refinement of the ecology of human development. Each contribution builds on Urie's work while at the same time departing from his work to pursue disparate themes.

The symposium furnished the context for each chapter. After long discussions, we agreed to keep the flavor of oral presentations in the chapters. This makes them more interesting to read, engaging the reader in a free flow of thinking. The original contributions to the symposium have been revised by the authors, however, with many of the reformulations sparked by active discussions among the authors. Other chapters were written by invited participants who were unable to attend the symposium but who wished to contribute to the intellectual exchange regarding Bronfenbrenner's work.

Still another context of both the symposium and the volume is the Life Course Institute at Cornell. In 1995, in recognition of Urie's scholarship and leadership in linking fundamental research with social policy, Cornell University renamed the institute the Bronfenbrenner Life Course Center. The creation of the center continues the Cornell tradition, as a land grant university, of combining scientific theory with practice, and basic research with policy analysis, a tradition epitomized by the work of Urie Bronfenbrenner and his legacy of problem-solving research.

We are most grateful to the many people who contributed to organizing the symposium and to editing this volume. First, thanks are due to

Donna Dempster-McClain, Assistant Director of the Bronfenbrenner Life Course Center, who oversaw the myriad of logistic details ensuring the success of the symposium. She was admirably assisted by Heather Quick, Shauna Handrahan, and Irene Pytcher. Heather Quick has also provided valuable assistance in preparing this volume. Thanks also are due to Dean Francille Firebaugh of the College of Human Ecology for her encouragement and financial support and to the American Psychological Association for underwriting this effort.

Support is also acknowledged by the College of Human Ecology at Cornell University, Hatch Funding from the U.S. Department of Agriculture (NYC 321420), the National Institute on Aging (R01-AG05450), National Institute of Mental Health (MH 41327, MH 43270, and MH 51361), a contract with the U.S. Army Research Institute, a grant from the Department of Veterans Affairs Merit Review Program, research support from the John D. and Catherine T. MacArthur Foundation Program for Successful Adolescent Development Among Youth in High-Risk Settings, and a Research Scientist Award for Glen H. Elder, Jr. (MH 00567).

PHYLLIS MOEN, GLEN H. ELDER, JR., AND KURT LÜSCHER

About Urie

Urie Bronfenbrenner is the Jacob Gould Schurman Professor Emeritus of Human Development and Family Studies and of Psychology at Cornell University. Author of the acclaimed *Ecology of Human Development* (Harvard University Press, 1979) and one of the founders of Head Start, he is also the recipient of numerous awards, including the G. Stanley Hall Medal awarded by the American Psychological Association and the Outstanding Achievement Award from the University of Michigan, as well as the James McKeen Cattell Fellow Award for 1993 from the American Psychological Society. He has recently been selected as a foreign member of the Russian Academy of Education in recognition for his "outstanding contributions in psychology and ecology."

He graduated from Cornell University in 1938, receiving a dual degree in psychology and music. He earned his master's in psychology from Harvard University before entering the University of Michigan, from which he received his doctorate in developmental psychology in 1942. After serving as a psychologist in the U.S. Army/Air Force during World War II, Urie returned to Cornell to teach in 1948.

Urie Bronfenbrenner is the author, coauthor, or editor of 13 books and more than 300 articles, most notably *Two Worlds of Childhood: U.S. and U.S.S.R.* and *The Ecology of Human Development.* (See the Appendix for a listing of his published writings.) He is internationally renowned for his cross-cultural studies and is a recipient of honorary degrees worldwide.

Urie has served on innumerable committees dealing with the need for and nature of public policy on children and families in the United States, as well as abroad. Since the early 1960s, when his testimony to committees of the Congress prepared the way for Project Head Start, he has published a continuing series of articles and chapters.

In addition to his intense dedication to his students and his contributions to theory, to more rigorous research designs, and to public policy, Urie counts high among his achievements his 51-year marriage to artist Liese Price Bronfenbrenner. He is the father of 6 children and has, to date, 11 grandchildren.

1

Introduction

Phyllis Moen

The aim of this volume is to bring together the research and thinking of distinguished scholars whose work intersects with that of an internationally renowned behavioral scientist in the field of human development: Urie Bronfenbrenner. His theoretical paradigm, the ecology of human development, has transformed the way many social and behavioral scientists approach, think about, and study human beings and their environments. Bronfenbrenner's ecological model requires behavior and development to be examined as a joint function of the characteristics of the person and of the environment. The former includes both biological and psychological attributes (e.g., an individual's genetic heritage and personality). The latter encompasses the physical, social, and cultural features of the immediate settings in which human beings live (e.g., family, school, and neighborhood), as well as the still broader contemporary and historical contexts in which these settings are embedded (e.g., the society and times into which an individual is born). As Melvin L. Kohn, who studied under Bronfenbrenner 30 years ago, describes him: "Urie was the quintessential person for spurring psychologists to look up and realize that interpersonal relationships did not exist in a social vacuum but were embedded in the larger social structures of community, society, economics, and politics."

In the chapters that follow, the contributors recast, reflect on, and further extend Bronfenbrenner's theoretical framework, the ecology of human development, in the light of their own research and theoretical perspectives. These leading researchers cross borders of discipline, theory, and method toward a common destination in an uncharted terrain. Their common destination: understanding the forces and experiences that shape human development through the life course in a rapidly changing world. What is particularly noteworthy about the architecture of this volume is that it, like Urie's thinking, crosses borders—across theoretical and disciplinary domains, across contexts and environments, across time and space, and out of the past, into the uncharted future. Thus, its scope is both international and interdisciplinary. The work of Urie Bronfenbrenner has perhaps had even more influence abroad than in the United States. In addition, his ecological approach transcends the traditional and typical disciplinary boundaries of developmental psychology. The chapters in this volume reflect his own breadth and ecumenism and provide a forum for a dynamic intellectual exchange—as the authors contemplate, extrapolate from, and even challenge the ecological perspective on human development. Because the authors are introducing ideas on the cutting edge of theory and method, this book makes an important scientific contribution to the study of human development through the life course in a rapidly changing world. Because the authors are communicating across disciplinary borders, they speak a common, rather than technical, language, understandable to a wide audience interested in the intersections between lives, contexts, and change.

MODELS IN PROCESS

The story is told of a visitor to Ithaca who asked an elderly gentleman if he had lived in Ithaca all his life. The amusing but accurate answer was "not yet." Similarly, I believe that Urie Bronfenbrenner would say that his ecological model of human development, first articulated in his 1979 book, is in process but is not yet completed. The chapters in this volume, including two by Bronfenbrenner himself, approach the ecology of human development from distinctive vantage points, drawing on its themes and propositions as points of elaboration. In the final chapter, Bronfenbrenner reflects on and further extends the work of the contributors, as well as his own earlier efforts, in a prospective view of untried theoretical and operational models.

The contributors of these chapters, all outstanding scholars, are not Bronfenbrenner's "disciples." However, their work is clearly relevant in elaborating an ecological approach, articulating in some way with the conceptualizations and main thrust of the ecology of human development. The chapter authors draw on different methods, from experiments to ethnography. Their own work serves as a point of departure in contemplating Bronfenbrenner's framework, challenging its scope and broader utility in the context of their particular substantive and conceptual interests. Because the authors project new ideas not yet tested, they are on the cutting edge of the field, making the volume useful to current scholars and scholars of the next generation.

As Urie is wont to say, "We cannot always define our destination in advance, but we can nevertheless aspire and strive to attain it" (personal communication). What we aspire to is to have this volume both serve as a tribute to Urie Bronfenbrenner's thinking and lifelong accomplishments and provide an intellectual impetus to the social and behavior science community in confronting the challenges, as well as potential, of an evolving theoretical paradigm.

LINKING RESEARCH AND POLICY

As Urie's colleague, with an office across the hall from his, I often have been privy through the years to his sage commentary on science and research. He often refers to the wisdom of his father, who asked him, as he now asks his students, "What do we need to know? The correlation of IQ with the length of the little toe? Why not?" His father's point, and Urie's, is that what we focus on has to matter!

What matters for Urie Bronfenbrenner is theoretically driven research. But equally important to him are the lessons for policy and practice that strong, theoretically grounded research designs can provide. Nothing is more practical, he points out (following Lewin), than a good theory. And he invariably alludes to the lessons that social policy, in turn, can provide for the development and refinement of theory. He contends that science needs policy as much as policy needs science, because "issues of social policy [serve] as points of departure for the identification of significant theoretical and scientific questions concerning the development of the human organism as a function of interaction with its enduring environment—both actual and potential" (Bronfenbrenner, 1974, p. 4).

Most of us have felt the need to make difficult choices between engaging in "applied" or "basic" research (e.g., Moen & Jull, 1995). Bronfenbrenner's life work epitomizes the importance of fundamental science for policy development and vice versa, demonstrating the applied–basic distinction to be a false, and pointless, dichotomy. He stresses the need to systematically examine and apply the implications of research findings in designing, refining, and evaluating programs and policies to further the physical health, psychological well-being, cognitive and socioemotional development, and productive functioning of individuals and families throughout the life course. The work of most of the contributors to this volume stands at the nexus of basic science and social policy, concerned with the ties between research and reality, and the implications of each for the other. As Jay Belsky (chapter 16) points out, Bronfenbrenner and those of us touched by him are concerned with questions of "how" precisely because of the possibilities for intervention that the answers suggest.

Elizabeth Cady Stanton observed that progress is the victory of a new thought over an old superstition. In addition to his many scientific contributions, Urie Bronfenbrenner is perhaps best known for his remarkable ability to draw on social and behavioral research and theory to change the way people think about the problems we confront as a society and to assist in devising new policies and practices that can serve as their solutions.

THE ECOLOGY OF THE LIFE COURSE

Bronfenbrenner's most recent reformulation of his model attends to the interplay between (a) characteristics of the person and (b) the social context in affecting (c) developmental processes (d) over time (chapter 19; Bronfenbrenner & Ceci, 1994). He describes this as the person–process–context–time (PPCT) model, one that defines his emerging bioecological approach to the study of lives. Time, process, and context are also key components of a life course perspective (Clausen, chapter 11; Elder, 1992, chapter 2; Moen & Erickson, chapter 6). Thus, these two formulations unite in their common focus on continuity and change over time and across generations. Both concentrate on the characteristics of individuals and environments that foster healthy development at all stages of the life course. As Magnusson (chapter 2) points out, development always has a temporal dimension, though time is not the same as development. And the Cairnses (chapter 12) emphasize the significance not only of change over time, but also of differences in *rates of change* in persons and in social contexts.

Both the life course and the ecology of human development paradigms underscore the social forces that shape the life course and its developmental consequences. This emphasis builds on Bronfenbrenner's (1979) pioneering consideration of the social embeddedness of individual behavior and his concern with what happens to the individual going through various social trajectories and developmental paths. Most developmental psychologists embracing Bronfenbrenner's approach attend to *development in context,* locating individuals in the context of particular families, schools, or neighborhoods. Some consider developmental trajectories, that is, continuity and change in psychological characteristics of the person over time. Thus, Urie's earlier work (as described by Kohn in chapter 5) considered both context (social class) and change over time (as parental values altered historically). By contrast, *time* is the paramount concern of life course scholars. The life course focus attends to continuity and change in lives, looking at age-graded trajectories and transitions in social roles, relationships, and resources and documenting how these are shaped by social change. For example, life course researchers tend to study the dynamics of entry into and involvement in work, family, schooling, and community roles over the life course. Thus, life course researchers recount the reality imperatives—situational demands, opportunities, and barriers—shaping lives.

Drawing on one of Urie's colorful metaphors, both paradigms are in danger of using a broad brush to paint only half a wall. In this book, we examine where the ecology and life course paradigms intersect, producing an ecology of the life course that acknowledges the lifelong (i.e., over time) interaction between person and context. Individuals are embedded in a changing social, cultural, and economic environment, as well as being products of a life history of events, beliefs, relationships, and behavior. But individuals also construct, and shape, their life as well as their environments. The interweave of life course pathways and developmental trajectories is a recurring focus in Bronfenbrenner's more recent work, as well as in the work of Glen Elder and many of the other contributors to this volume. Bronfenbrenner's most recent model emphasizes *processes*, the mechanisms that produce and sustain stability or change over time, both in individuals and in their environments. (An example of such a process is the "ping pong game" of reciprocal interaction between parent and infant that Urie so frequently describes.)

LINKING THEORY AND RESEARCH

There are four broad components to research: the question or issue to be addressed, the theoretical underpinnings, appropriate data, and methods or procedures of analysis. Bronfenbrenner's ecology of human development paradigm not only furnishes a theoretical model, but also becomes a catalyst, inspiring a redefinition of the problems to be studied. In framing their research designs, he reminds researchers to explicitly acknowledge that individuals and their environments are in constant, reciprocal interplay. The importance of the neighborhood as a neglected context is emphasized by Jeanne Brooks-Gunn (chapter 14) and William Julius Wilson (chapter 15). An outstanding example of this broadening of the research question is provided in the chapter by Laurence Steinberg and his colleagues (chapter 13).

Bronfenbrenner's model also points to the need for data relevant to the substantive questions addressed, including proximal data on processes (e.g., the ping pong interactions between parent and child) and panel data to observe continuity and change over time (e.g., changes in parent–child relations over the years as children move into adolescence and then adulthood). The need for data at more than one point in time is reiterated in the chapters by Glen H. Elder, Jr. (chapter 4), Phyllis Moen and Mary Ann Erickson (chapter 6), John A. Clausen (chapter 11), and Robert B. and Beverley D. Cairns (chapter 12). In data collection, Bronfenbrenner encourages greater attention to the operationalization and measurement of theoretical constructs. All developmental studies provide measures related to characteristics of the individual; some provide measures of the contexts in which the individual lives and grows; a few provide measures of continuity and change over time; and hardly any provide measures of processes of, for example, interchanges between individuals or between the individuals and their environment.

Most recently (1994 and chapter 19), Bronfenbrenner has emphasized the need for methodologies appropriate to the study of development rather than the use of trendy analyses to display technical sophistication. Bronfenbrenner (1994) decries what he calls methodological distortions resulting from the substitution of methodology for science in contemporary psychological research. For example, he is troubled by the exclusive use of averages or central tendencies in describing developmental patterns. Magnusson (chapter 2), Rutter and colleagues (chapter 3), and the Cairnses (chapter 12) echo his concern in arguing for methodologies relevant to the tasks at hand. Kurt Lüscher (chapter 17) refers to another concern of Urie's that also has methodological implications, namely, the relevance of knowledge and beliefs.

The volume highlights the value of Urie Bronfenbrenner as a theory builder, echoing admonitions permeating Urie's lifetime of teaching and writing:

- the fact that there cannot be a theoretical model without a research design, nor can there be a research design without a theoretical model
- the importance of transcending disciplinary boundaries and of passing on ideas and challenges to the next generation
- the need to link research with reality: the implication of research for a changing reality and of basic research for understanding a changing reality
- the primacy of scientific over statistical models

It is very evident that Bronfenbrenner's ecological model touches virtually every aspect of the research process, not only providing theoretical grounding, but also delineating the research questions, the nature of the data, and the procedures of analysis. And he conveys the interactive, dynamic, and evolving nature of science, as scholars learn from, grapple with, and move beyond the theories and findings of their colleagues (Bronfenbrenner, 1986; Bronfenbrenner & Ceci, 1994).

THEMES AND ORGANIZATION OF THE VOLUME

Two overriding and related concepts—development and context—are an integral part of Bronfenbrenner's approach to the human condition. Inquiry into their intersection constitutes the essential plan of this volume. Some of the contributors focus more on *development* in context, others on the *contexts* of development.

What is most conspicuous in Bronfenbrenner's recent work is also what constitutes a common thread throughout many of the chapters that follow: his approach to the temporal aspects of lives, in terms of ongoing processes and their timing, as well as transgenerational relationships and influences. This is a pivotal theme connecting the life course and the ecology of human development frameworks: the importance of *time* in terms of continuity and change in the developmental life course and in the environmental contexts of development.

The first two sections of the volume specifically address various temporal dimensions. In Part One, David Magnusson (chapter 2) underscores the dynamics of development as an unfolding process, and Michael Rutter and colleagues (chapter 3) point to the ways that individuals under certain conditions shape their future development through shaping their own environments over time.

Another temporal dimension involves attention to social change and its implications for development, a theme embodied in Part Two that conveys the importance of historical and social time. Glen H. Elder, Jr. (chapter 4) illustrates the life course principle of the interplay between human lives and their historical times, noting that in times of rapid change individuals from different birth cohorts are exposed to different historical worlds, with different options, opportunities, and imperatives. Melvin L. Kohn (chapter 5) describes his own growing appreciation of the ways in which economic and political changes can alter not only the broader social structure, but also the links between social structure and personality. Phyllis Moen and Mary Ann Erickson (chapter 6) observe how social changes may alter the intergenerational transmission of values, attitudes, and behavior. And Duane F. Alwin (chapter 7) draws out the methodological implications of attending to the temporal dimensions of lives.

The enduring theme most widely associated with Bronfenbrenner's approach has been his attention to the contexts of lives. The focus of Part Three, therefore, is the multiple contexts of human development. Bronfenbrenner's distinctive contribution is to see context not just in terms of variables to be controlled but as ecological niches worthy of investigation. Jacqueline J. Goodnow (chapter 8) describes differences in the social contexts of children's lives, whereas Stephen J. Ceci and Helene A. Hembrooke (chapter 9) ground studies of cognitive intelligence in a contextual framework. Eleanor E. Maccoby (chapter 10) and John A. Clausen (chapter 11) portray an important status characteristic, gender, as a shaper of context at two distinctive stages of the life course.

Bronfenbrenner's foremost effort since his 1979 volume has been to promote research designs incorporating the processes by which contexts, including location in the social structure, can shape individual lives. In defining process as the "exchange of energy between organisms and their environment," he notes a striking omission in most studies in their failure to document the proximal relationships that embody "process." The importance of process is emphasized in Part Four, with Robert B. and Beverley D. Cairns (chapter 12) drawing on and extending Urie's earlier work in describing the mechanisms of development as they unfold in context. Laurence Steinberg and his colleagues (chapter 13) describe an effort to investigate one important process: the ways parents influence their adolescents in different ecologies, emphasizing the proximal influences of family structure and neighborhood settings. Jeanne Brooks-Gunn (chapter 14) examines the process of development in the particularly high-risk environment of poverty. As Bronfenbrenner points out, we need a dynamic model of process, not only of proximal relationships, but also of the changes persons undergo and the choices they make as they pass through life.

The last section of the book, Part Five, looks both backward and forward, with William Julius Wilson (chapter 15) and Jay Belsky (chapter 16) providing reflective and provocative overviews of the ecology of human development. Kurt Lüscher (chapter 17) calls for a new awareness of the implications, for theory and research, of different modes of interpretation, thus interpreting in his own way examples from Bronfenbrenner's writings. Finally, Urie Bronfenbrenner himself provides the biographical context of his own development (chapter 18) and charts a future course for research, drawing on an ecological life course framework (chapter 19). Time and process are important, but too often neglected, considerations in the development of theoretical models and research designs addressing human development over the life course and in a changing world. Those who have been in his classroom or in his audience know that Urie is first and foremost a teacher. How apt it is that he uses the occasion of this volume to continue our education! Those who know Urie will value his enthusiastic and characteristic prospective rather than retrospective stance, probing into the future rather than simply reflecting on his many accomplishments. And those who know him will surely appreciate how appropriate it is for him to have the last word in this volume.

REFERENCES

Bronfenbrenner, U. (1974). Developmental research, public policy, and the ecology of childhood. *Child Development, 45,* 1–5.

Bronfenbrenner, U. (1979). *The ecology of human development.* Cambridge, MA: Harvard University Press.

Bronfenbrenner, U. (1986). Ecology of the family as a context for human development: Research perspectives. *Developmental Psychology, 22,* 723–742.

Bronfenbrenner, U. (1994). Ecological models of human development. In T. Huston & T. N. Postlethwaite (Eds.), *International encyclopedia of education* (2nd ed., Vol. 3, pp. 1643–1647). New York: Elsevier Science.

Bronfenbrenner, U., & Ceci, S. J. (1994). Nature–nurture reconceptualized in developmental perspective: A bioecological model. *Psychological Review, 101,* 568–586.

Elder, G. H., Jr. (1992). The life course. In E. F. Borgatta & M. L. Borgatta (Eds.), *The encyclopedia of sociology* (pp. 1120–1130). New York: Macmillan.

Moen, P., & Jull, P. M. (1995). Informing family policies: The uses of social research. *Journal of Family and Economic Issues 16,* 79–107.

PART ONE

The Dynamics of Individual Development

The Dynamics of Individual Development

Glen H. Elder, Jr.

I n comprehensive theories of human development, the dynamics of individual development are no longer the exclusive province of one discipline, psychology, or even of the psychological sciences in general. Emerging problems at the cutting edge, such as the interplay of social relationships, are typically informed by the insights and scholarship of multiple disciplines, from psychology and psychiatry to anthropology, sociology, and economics. The newly emerging field of developmental science reflects this intellectual breadth and depth.

However, David Magnusson, among other leading developmentalists, has questioned why specialization has not led to more synthetic developments around core problem domains, as in the biological sciences. The relative absence of fruitful integrations among mentalistic, biological, and environmental models represents a potent barrier to scientific advances in the area. The ideal of such integration brings to mind the interdisciplinary fervor of the behavioral sciences during the first third of this century. Jean MacFarlane of the Guidance Study at the Berkeley Institute of Human Development once described her frequent contacts with sociologist Dorothy Thomas, as well as with anthropologists and social economists on the Berkeley campus, University of California. The life record data, collected by projects such as the Guidance Study, reflected this intellectual diversity, though few studies at the time actually crossed disciplinary boundaries.

The recycling of old issues and experiences in terms of contemporary understandings is part of a general trend in developmental studies. The contemporary problems of developmental psychology have "more in common with the field's agenda near the turn of the century than with the agenda of the more recent times of the 1950s and 1960s" (Parke, Ornstein, Rieser, & Zahn-Waxler, 1994, p. 33). This commonality includes renewed interest in the biological bases of behavior, in emotions, in cognition, and in social relationships. It also includes the growing appeal of organismic explanatory models. The aims of theory are now more restricted and pluralistic. Parke and his colleagues (1994) concluded that "the question for the 1990s is to discover which aspects of behavior are likely to be altered by environmental events at specific points in development, and which aspects remain more plastic and open to influence across wide spans of development" (p. 33).

In their respective chapters, David Magnusson and Michael Rutter et al. outline approaches that inform such inquiry and reflect the person–process–context perspective of Bronfenbrenner's ecology of human development. Both assert that the process of individual development is shaped by continuous transactions between ever-changing environments and people. Magnusson makes a persuasive case for the holistic study of individual development, which favors a person- rather than variable-centered design, with links between person and situation over time. In a holistic analysis, the total process cannot be understood by investigating one factor after another, always in isolation from others. The adaptive implications of a personal attribute depend on its relation to other attributes and to the situation itself.

What might a holistic analysis be like? In his chapter, Magnusson provides an example with his longitudinal study of the social development of Swedish girls, a study that links maturation rate, norm-breaking behavior (such as heavy drinking), and social ties with boys. He and his research team found a strong relation between norm-breaking behavior at the age of 14 and early maturation. Early-maturing girls were more engaged in such behavior through their association with older boys. He concludes that the role of biological factors, such as maturation rate, is most fully understood within the context of other personal attributes, mental and social. The chapter provides other examples of biological, psychological, and environmental factors in holistic research designs.

Building on a career of pioneering research on developmental psychopathology, Rutter et al. draw our attention to a critical aspect of development in context—to the variable exposure of individuals to risks, as expressed by individual differences. Risks are unevenly distributed in society. In their chapter, Rutter et al. draw on two longitudinal studies that address in different ways the pathogenic implications of individual attributes that entail a variable exposure to psychosocial risks. Problem behavior in late childhood clearly increases the risk of social disadvantages in young adulthood, and it may do so in part by influencing the social choices people make and the difficulties they have in sustaining rewarding ties with others. One of the studies clearly shows that conduct disorder in childhood increases the prospects of marriage to a socially deviant spouse.

In their instructive chapters, Magnusson and Rutter et al. leave us with a challenging agenda on questions of behavioral continuity and change in ever-changing environments. As Rutter et al. conclude, "there is a long way to go before there can be an adequate delineation of the developmental mechanisms involved in connections between behavior and adult life experiences" (p. 89). How can we account for the large number of children who manage to establish lives of accomplishment by escaping from the limitations of their impoverished childhood? This is a question that Urie Bronfenbrenner has posed to many of us in response to our research.

REFERENCE

Parke, R. D., Ornstein, P. A., Rieser, J. J., & Zahn-Waxler, C. (1994). The past as prologue: An overview of a century of developmental science. In R. D. Parke, P. A. Ornstein, J. J. Rieser, & C. Zahn-Waxler (Eds.), *A century of developmental psychology* (p. 3). Washington, DC: American Psychological Association.

2

Individual Development:
A Holistic, Integrated Model

David Magnusson

A s the title of the chapter suggests, the aim of this chapter is to present and discuss the main elements of an integrated, holistic model for individual functioning and development, which can serve as a general theoretical framework for planning, implementation, and interpretation of empirical research on specific aspects of individual development. The motive for such a model is discussed on the background of an analysis of the present state of affairs, which is characterized more by fragmentation of developmental subfields than by integration, which is a prerequisite for further success.

The old holistic view has got new clothes and an enriched content from three sources during recent decades. The first source is the modern models for dynamic, complex processes, which have meant a theoretical and empirical revolution in disciplines that are concerned with such processes in natural sciences, biology, and medicine. These models emphasize the holistic character of the processes and the need for integration of all operating factors in the theoretical models, which serve as the theoretical framework for planning, implementation, and interpretation of empirical research. The second source is the rapid development in scientific disciplines in which research has contributed knowledge about the role of biological aspects of individual functioning and development: developmental biology, pharmacology, endocrinology, neuropsychology, and other disciplines. The third source is the conceptual analyses of the role of environmental factors, at different levels of organization, for which Bronfenbrenner (1977, 1979a, 1979b, 1993) has been a pioneer.

The chapter is mainly devoted to the presentation of a theoretical outline of a holistic, integrated model for individual development. The research strategy and methodological implications of such a model are far-reaching, and it would lead too far to deal with them more comprehensively in this connection (see Bergman, 1988, 1993; Magnusson, 1988, 1993; Magnusson, Andersson, & Törestad, 1993; Magnusson & Bergman, 1988; Magnusson & Törestad, 1993, for further discussions).

INDIVIDUAL DEVELOPMENT: A DEFINITION

Psychological research on individual development is concerned with individual functioning in terms of thoughts, feelings, actions, and reactions studied across the lifetime of the individual.

Development of living organisms refers to progressive or regressive changes in size, shape, and function during the lifetime. Psychological research on individual development covers this process from conception to death. In this definition, two concepts are essential: change and time. Time is not the same as development, but development always has a temporal dimension. Therefore, if a person's distinctive pattern of characteristics remains unchanged across time, no development has occurred. Consequently, processes that go on in an unchanged manner, within existing structures, do not constitute development. Thus, developmental models should be distinguished from models that analyze and explain why individuals function as they do in terms of their current psychological and biological dispositions. Because the current functioning of an individual is a result of earlier developmental processes in his or her life course and because this current functioning, at the same time, forms the basis for later stages, models for current functioning and developmental models are complementary.

SCIENTIFIC PROGRESS: THE NEED FOR
A GENERAL MODEL OF *HOMO*

In the empirical sciences, one characteristic feature of real scientific progress is increasing specialization. When specialization in a subfield of the natural sciences has reached a certain level, it becomes apparent that further progress lies in integration with what has been achieved in neighboring disciplines. During recent decades, the most important steps forward in natural sciences have been taken by integration within the interface of what earlier had been conspicuously different disciplines. This happened first in the interface of physics and chemistry and recently in the interface of biology, chemistry, and physics. The earlier unambiguous and clear boundaries between subdisciplines have disappeared.

Also in empirical research on individual functioning, specialization takes place. In some areas, specialization has been very productive and has offered important contributions. However, despite the recent indications of more integration among disciplines, for example, between brain research and cognitive psychology, research in behavioral sciences in general is still characterized by what Toulmin (1981) once described as "sectarian rivalry" (p. 267). During the eighties, researchers, discussing the future prospects of psychology, described this lack of integration as one of the main obstacles for further, real scientific progress in behavioral sciences (de Groot, 1990; Thomae, 1988). As a matter of fact, this was also an issue of great concern for Stern (1911) in the beginning of this century.

Thus, fragmentation is still a characteristic of psychological research on individual functioning at all levels, that is, diversification of research in specialties with little or no contact across domains. Fragmentation involves content, concepts, research strategies, and methodology. At a metatheoretical level, it has its roots in the existence of three main explanatory models: mentalistic, biological, and environmental. (The models are, of course, not mutually exclusive; each one is a matter of emphasis.) The distinction between these explanatory models is not only of theoretical interest. Each of them has had and still has a far-reaching impact on fundamental aspects of societies: social welfare, politics, culture, education, the causes and treatment of mental illness, criminal behavior, and alcohol and drug abuse, to mention only a few (see Magnusson, 1988).

According to a mentalistic approach, the main explanation for an individual's way of functioning is to be found in the functioning of the mind and can be discussed and explained in terms of intrapsychic processes of perceptions, thoughts, values, goals, plans, and conflicts. To this approach belong personality theories in general, as well as the mainstream of research on intelligence, cognitive processes, and learning—with repercussions in research on artificial intelligence. A strong representative of this approach is, of course, Piaget.

The biological model identifies biological factors as having primary influence on individual functioning. Its roots can be traced back to the very old notion of individual differences in temperament as dependent on the predominance of one of the four basic body fluids: blood, phlegm, black bile, or yellow bile. When modern biological models of individual development are applied, the major determining guiding factors are genetic and maturational. In its extreme version, this model implies that individual differences in the course of development have their roots in genes, with little role played by environmental and mental factors. This view was characterized by Cairns (1979a) in terms of the organism as a "gene machine" (p. 165). The view was discussed and criticized by Hunt (1961), who characterized the main elements of it in terms of "predetermined development" and "fixed intelligence." Research in behavioral genetics, pharmacology, endocrinology, and neuropsychology during recent decades has strengthened the biological explanation of individual functioning.

The environmental model locates the main causal factors for individual functioning in the environment. It is reflected in theories and models at all levels of generality, from Marxist models for the society to stimulus–response models for very specific aspects of behavior as it is studied in the mainstream of experimental psychology. In developmental research, there are various environmental streams with different sources. A strong and very influential exponent is, of course, behaviorism (cf. Skinner, 1971; Watson, 1930). Another is *psychoanalytic theory*, which refers to early experiences of the environment as guiding forces for the individual's way of functioning later in life. An additional influential line, which strongly influenced developmental psychology during the sixties, seventies, and eighties, is rooted in sociology, in which the basic formulations about the strong environmental impact on individual development were formulated by Durkheim (1897). This view is reflected in the vast amount of research in which individual differences in various aspects of the life course have been studied as the result of differences in upbringing environments (cf. Bronfenbrenner & Crouter, 1983, and their discussion of the "new demography").

An old controversy in developmental research is that between a biological and an environmentalistic view: the *nature–nurture issue*. The debate can be traced back to the early times of our civilization. Plato in his *Republic* discussed the central issue of justice in the perspective of human character as determined by nature [*physics*] and nurture [*trophe*]. In the modern history of psychology, the biological view was formulated and strengthened by the work of Galton and the publication of his influential book *Hereditary Genius* (1869). With respect to intelligence, his line of reasoning was followed in the beginning of this century by Terman, Goddard, and Yerkes, among others, all of whom believed that the intelligence tests that had been constructed at that time actually measured fixed and innate intelligence.

As pointed out by Eccles and Robinson (1985), it was chiefly in the eighteenth century that the thesis of environmentalistic determinism became "official," much influenced by the empiristic psychology of Locke. A view emphasizing the role of environment and the possibilities to influence individual development by environmental factors was advocated by Binet (1909). He strongly argued against the view of intelligence as an inherited, fixed quantity: "We must protest and react against this brutal pessimism. With practice, enthusiasm, and especially method, one can succeed in increasing one's attention, memory and judgement, and in becoming literally more intelligent than one was before" (Binet, 1909, p. 126). Binet also took the consequence of this view and worked out a program of "mental orthopaedics" as a method of improving the intelligence of mentally retarded children (pp. 127–128). A recent contribution to this nature–nurture debate was presented by Bronfenbrenner and Ceci (1994).

A somewhat younger controversy is that between the mentalistic and the environmentalistic perspective, which is reflected in the debate between proponents of a cognitive approach (cf. Piaget, 1948) and propo-

23

nents of a socialization approach (cf. Miller & Dollard, 1941) to social development and behavior. An example drawn from theories of moral development may illustrate the issue. For Kohlberg (1969), moral development is closely related to cognitive development. In contrast, both Marx and Freud, from very different perspectives, regarded conscience, as the base for moral choice, as being instilled from the outside through a process of socialization beyond the individual's control.

Of course, nothing is wrong with each of the three general explanatory models per se. What is wrong occurs when each of them claims total supremacy, and that has been the case to an extent that has hampered real progress both in research and in application.

Now, a basic question to be answered is the following: When research in natural sciences is characterized by the iterative process of specialization and integration, why is behavioral research, including developmental research, on the whole characterized by specialization with only little integration? The reason is probably complex, but let me point to a possible explanation.

One condition that facilitates the iterative process of specialization and integration in natural sciences is the existence of a general theoretical framework, a general model of nature, for theorizing and conducting empirical inquiry. The fact that we lack a corresponding general theoretical framework for the formulation of problems, for the development of a common conceptual space, and for the development and application of adequate methodologies is, in my opinion, an essential obstacle for further real progress in the behavioral sciences. We need the formulation of a general model of homo, which synthesizes and integrates the three metatheoretical models briefly described earlier. A modern, integrated holistic model meets this requirement.

BASIC PROPOSITIONS OF AN INTEGRATED, HOLISTIC VIEW

A modern, integrated, holistic model for individual functioning and development rests on three basic propositions:

1. *The individual functions and develops as a total integrated organism. Development does not take place in single aspects, taken out of context.*

As a general statement, this view is old. It is reflected in the assumption about the four basic temperaments, in the typologies, and in the discussion about an idiographic versus a nomothetical approach and about statistical versus clinical prediction in empirical research. In developmental research, a holistic view was advocated in the beginning of this century (see, e.g., Stern, 1911). During recent decades, it has had its proponents in Block (1971), Cairns (1979a, 1983), Magnusson (1988), Sameroff (1983), Sroufe (1979), and Wapner and Kaplan (1983), among others. In a volume that did not receive the attention it deserved, Cairns (1979a) expressed this view in the following formulation: "Behavior, whether social or nonsocial, is appropriately viewed in terms of an organized system, and its explanation requires a 'holistic analysis' " (p. 325). Sroufe (1979) expressed the same general view: "There is a logic and coherence to the person that can only be seen in looking at total functioning" (p. 835).

In a modern holistic model, individual functioning and development is best described as a series of dynamic, complex processes; that is, many factors are involved and operate simultaneously in an individual, most often in a nonlinear way. For understanding such processes in general, the mainstream models of dynamic, complex processes—chaos theory (Basar, 1990; Gleick, 1987), catastrophe theory (Zeeman, 1976), and general systems theory (Bertalanffy, 1968)—must be considered. They have been formulated in the scientific disciplines concerned with dynamic processes (e.g., meteorology, ecology, biology, brain research, and chemistry) and have had a far-reaching, almost revolutionary influence on theorization and empirical research in these fields (see, e.g., Bothe, Ebeling, Kurzhanski, & Peschel, 1987). A consequence of the formulation of the modern models for complex, dynamic processes has been the development of adequate methodologies for the study of such processes, for example, the revival of nonlinear mathematics and methods for the study of patterns.

These models for dynamic, complex processes have important implications, if adequately applied, also for theorization and empirical research on the dynamic, complex process of individual development. When the methodologies developed for such models are considered in psychology, we have to avoid the mistake we made when we took over models and methods from natural sciences, particularly physics, in the beginning of this century. By doing this without careful analysis of the phenomena that were the objects of our interest and without consideration of these phenomena's characteristics, we applied models and methods from physics in an inappropriate way. Most researchers now agree that this had a hampering effect on real scientific progress in psychological research.

Thus, although it is important to consider the modern models for dynamic, complex processes mentioned above, it is equally important to be careful with their application in research on individual functioning. There are some similarities between the structures and processes studied in natural sciences and the structures and processes investigated in psychological research. But there are also essential differences, particularly when the interest is in the functioning of the total organism. At that level, fundamental characteristics and guiding elements in the dynamic, complex process of individual functioning are intentionality, linked to emotions and values, and lessons learned from experience. This fact must be taken into consideration when methods derived for the study of dynamic, complex processes, which do not have these elements, are applied in planning and implementing of empirical research in psychology.

One basic formulation in modern models for complex, dynamic processes has direct and important application for empirical research on individual functioning. It states that the total process cannot be understood by studying one aspect (variable) after the other in isolation from the other, simultaneously operating elements. The total picture has an information value that is beyond what is contained in its specific parts (the doctrine of epigenesis). This property of dynamic, complex processes has important consequences for the planning, implementation, and interpretation of empirical developmental research.

2. *The individual functions and develops in a continuously ongoing, reciprocal process of interaction with his or her environment.*

This proposition forms the basic feature of classical interactionism. It has been advocated and elaborated for a long time by researchers from very different perspectives, both in research on personality and in research on developmental issues. Baldwin (1895) explicitly discussed ontogenetic and evolutionary development in such terms in the 1890s. And as suggested by Cairns and Cairns (1985), there is a direct line from Baldwin to Piaget and Kohlberg and those who have influenced various areas of developmental research. During the last decades, the role of person–environment interaction for individual development has become accepted by most developmentalists.

Particularly by his theoretical contributions, including the conceptual analyses of the environment and its function, at different levels of organization, in the person–environment interaction process, Bronfenbrenner (1977, 1979a, 1979b, 1989, 1993) has played a leading role in this development.

3. The third basic proposition integrates mental factors, biological factors, behavioral, and environmental factors in a dynamic-process model. As was underlined in the introduction, two models are needed: one for current functioning of the individual within given structures and one for the individual developmental process. Thus, the third basic proposition has two complementary subpropositions: one for current individual functioning (3a) and one for individual functioning in a developmental perspective (3b).

3a. *At each specific moment, individual functioning is determined in a process of continuous, reciprocal interaction between mental factors, biological factors, and behavior—on the individual side—and situational factors.*

The way this process in an immediate situation evolves can be described with reference to Figure 1. The figure gives a simplified (but on the main points correct) picture of what happens psychologically and biologically in a certain situation with specific features. (Note that the figure is only a summarized description of a temporal sequence of events, not a neural network or a neuropathway.)

Assume that an individual encounters a situation that he or she interprets as threatening or demanding. The cognitive act of interpreting the situation stimulates, through the hypothalamus, the excretion of adrenaline from the adrenal glands, which in turn triggers other physiological processes. The cognitive–physiological interplay is accompanied by emotional states of fear, anxiety, or generally experienced arousal. In the next

27

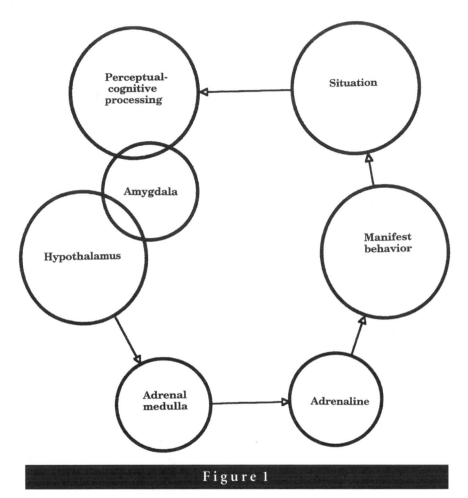

Figure 1

A simplified picture of the interplay of environmental, cognitive–emotional, physiological, and behavioral factors for an individual in a specific situation.

stage of the process, these emotions affect the individual's behavior and handling of the environment. They also influence his or her interpretation of the sequence of changes in the situational conditions and thereby his or her physiological reactions in the next stage of the process.

Thus, the perceptual–cognitive system and the biological system of an individual are involved in a continuous loop of reciprocal interaction. The way this process functions is contingent, among other things, on the environment, as it is perceived and given meaning by the individual. The outcomes of such situation–individual encounters will set the stage for subsequent reactions and actions to psychologically similar situations, as interpreted by the individual in his or her perceptual–cognitive system. In the developmental process, this interaction process affects both the mental system—for example, in the interpretation of certain types of situations and in the response to such situations—and the physiological system. Frequent encounters with stressful situations may affect the immune system and lead to psychosomatic symptoms (Farmer, Kaufmann, Packard, & Perelson, 1987; Öhman & Magnusson, 1987).

3b. *The individual develops in a process of continuous reciprocal interaction among psychological, biological, and environmental factors.*

Stattin and Magnusson (1990) illustrated this process by assessing the implications of biological maturation rate for the developmental process of girls. When the girls were 14 years and 5 months, on average, Stattin and Magnusson found a strong relation between different aspects of norm-breaking behavior (e.g., alcohol consumption) and the age at which each girl had reached menarche. In a follow-up study of the girls when they reached the age of 26, there was no systematic relation between various aspects of social adaptation (e.g., alcohol consumption) and each girl's age at menarche. However, there was a systematic relation between other aspects of adult life (e.g., family, children, education level, and job status) and age at menarche. Further analyses showed that the important mediating factor behind the more advanced social behavior among early-maturing girls was association with older, working boys. Early-maturing girls without this association did not demonstrate socially advanced behavior. The early-maturing girls who associated with older, working boys also differed from girls without this association with respect to mental factors, such as self-perception.

Thus, to understand and explain the role of biological factors, here the rate of biological maturation in the developmental process, we have to consider mental factors, biological factors, behavior, and environmental factors operating simultaneously (Pulkkinen, 1992).

Together, these propositions form the main elements of modern interactionism. What distinguishes modern interactionism from classical interactionism or developmental contextualism is the introduction of biological factors in individual functioning and the ongoing reciprocal interactive processes of biological and mental factors in the individual.

THE MENTAL SYSTEM IN A HOLISTIC PERSPECTIVE

A basic element of an interactionistic, holistic view is that a person is not only a passive receiver of stimulation from the environment, but also an active, purposeful agent in the person–environment interaction process (Endler & Magnusson, 1976). Thus, a guiding principle in the individual's inner and outer life is in the functioning of the perceptual–cognitive system (including worldviews and self-perceptions) with attached emotions, motives, needs, values, and goals. It can be briefly summarized as the integrated mental system.

The dynamic conception of mental processes as activities, rather than as the reception and processing of information, was advocated early by the act psychologists in Europe, such as Brentano (1874/1924) and Stumpf (1883). In the United States, James was a proponent of the same view. The intentional character of the individual's way of functioning was stressed by Tolman (1951), among others, and more recently the individual as an active, purposeful agent has been emphasized in action theory (cf. Brandtstädter, 1993; Strelau, 1983; see also Pervin, 1990).

By selecting and interpreting information from the external world and transforming this information into internal and external actions, the mental system plays a crucial role both in the process of interaction between mental and physiological factors within the individual and in the process of interaction between the individual and his or her environment. Not only does the mental system permit the organism to shape its effective environment, but also it provides a rapid and reversible strategy for organisms to adapt to changing environments. The mental system serves as a leading edge for adaptation in individual development in that it mobilizes neurobiological and physiological modifications and environmental changes.

Congenital factors (including genetic factors) set the stage for the development of an individual's mediating mental system. Within the restrictions, and using the potentialities of these biological factors, the structure and functioning of an individual's mediating mental system are formed. This system changes slowly in a process of maturation and experience that takes place in the continuous, bidirectional interaction between the individual and the environment. Thus, the mediating system is a function of the individual's interaction with the environment in the course of individual development, and it plays a crucial, guiding role in that interaction process at each stage of the developmental process.

In some psychodynamic models of individual development and the functioning of the mental system, the concept of unconscious processes has played a central role. This debate has been given new fuel during the past few decades through the growing interest in and understanding of the parallel processes of controlled (conscious, attended to, and thus subject to critical analysis) versus automatic (out of attentional focus and awareness) processing of information (see, e.g., Bowers, 1981; Brewin, 1986; Greenwald, 1992; Norman & Shallice, 1980). This continuously ongoing processing of signals impinging on the senses subliminally renders new importance to the perceptual–cognitive system; at the same time, it plays down the central role earlier ascribed to its conscious functioning.

BIOLOGICAL FACTORS IN A HOLISTIC PERSPECTIVE

Two lines of research on biological factors are of interest in this connection:

1. As discussed in the introduction, an issue of debate since ancient times has concerned nature versus nurture: the relative role of hereditary and environmental factors in individual functioning, currently and in a developmental perspective.

Since the beginning of the history of differential psychology, the role of genetic factors has been a main issue (Galton, 1869). After a period, starting during the 1960s, in which genetic factors were almost abandoned from the agenda, the development in human genetics has led to a renewed interest. That various aspects of individual functioning are, to some extent, determined by inherited properties of the body is supported by much empirical research (Cairns & Nakelski, 1971; Lagerspetz & Lagerspetz, 1971; Pedersen, 1989; Plomin, Chipuer, & Loehlin, 1990).

The traditional view on the role of genetic factors has been a unidirectional, cause–effect relation. At a most basic level, the onset and course of certain developmental sequences may be determined genetically to the extent that they are common to all individuals. However, even such developmental sequences as the onset of the menstrual cycle in girls and the regulation of growth in height are somewhat modifiable by environmental factors. The individual phenotype develops in the framework offered by the genotype in a reciprocal interaction process with the environment, a process that starts at conception and goes on through the life span. On the scene set by inherited factors, many different plays are possible (Waddington, 1962). Within the limits set by inherited factors, there are large potentialities for change, because of the interplay with environmental factors.

Thus, that there is a hereditary predisposition for a certain type of behavior does not mean that it cannot be changed by environmental influences (cf. Angoff, 1988). Cairns (1979), in his evaluation of the role of heredity and environment in individual differences in aggression, drew the conclusion that the differences obtained by selective breeding show strong environmental specificity and can be modified by environmental social conditions to such an extent that the inherited differences no longer matter. In well-planned longitudinal studies of newborns, Meyer-Probst, Rössler, and Teichmann (1983) demonstrated that favorable social conditions acted as protective factors for later social development among children identified at birth as biologically rich.

In this perspective, current individual functioning is the result of a life history of a person–environment interaction, in which environmental and inherited factors participate in a process for which it is not possible to disentangle their relative role at the individual level. The outcome of the process, at a certain stage of development, depends on the potential resources and limitations of the individual from the start and the properties of the environment with which the individual interacts during the life course.

2. The interaction process in which an individual is involved with the environment can be described in terms of an active adaptation process (Lerner, 1991). In this adaptation process, physiological factors, in constant interaction with cognitive–emotional factors, play an important role. On the biological side of this internal process, the endocrine system, in particular the sympathetic–adrenal and pituitary–adrenal systems, is of special importance. Cannon (1914) pointed to the role of the sympathetic–adrenomedullary system in emergency situations and demonstrated that adrenaline and noradrenaline are released as an effect of sympathetic innervation in response to threatening stimuli, as an adjustment mechanism to prepare the body for fight and flight (see Figure 1 and the discussion under 3a, pp. 27–29).

The rapid developments in neuropsychology, endocrinology, and pharmacology during the last decades have brought new knowledge about the role of physiological factors for the way that people think, feel, act, and react (cf. Magnusson, af Klinteberg, & Stattin, 1993; Rutter & Casaer, 1991; Zuckerman, 1980). Recent research on temperament has demonstrated the biological basis for temperament at an early age (Kagan, 1989, 1994). The relation of thoughts, emotions, and behavior to physiological processes has been elucidated in much recent empirical research (see, e.g., Gunnar, 1986, for a review). The role of individual differences in biological maturation during adolescence was elucidated in the study by Stattin and Magnusson (1990), presented above. That physiological factors are involved in the developmental process has been empirically demonstrated in a number of studies on antisocial behavior (cf. Magnusson, af Klinteberg, & Stattin, 1994).

BEHAVIOR IN A HOLISTIC PERSPECTIVE

As shown in the interactive model presented in Figure 1, behavior in all its manifestations, including verbal and motor behavior, plays an essential role in the total interaction process and, thus, also in individual development. In the interaction process, behavior is influenced by cognitive interpretations of what happens in the outer world (embedded in worldviews, self-perceptions, emotions, values, and needs), by subconscious automatic processing and by physiological processes. At the same time, it has a functional role in the total interaction process in two interrelated respects: first, by activities to reach short-term and long-term goals (Pervin, 1983), such as changing the situational conditions to satisfy personal short-term and long-term needs and to avoid negative cognitive, mental, or biological experiences (Magnusson, 1981) and, second, by adaptation to other individuals' behavior to develop and maintain working social relations (Cairns, 1994). The way the behavioral system of a person functions in a particular situation at a particular stage of the life cycle, and how successfully, is a result of the process of maturation and learning across development.

THE ENVIRONMENT IN A HOLISTIC PERSPECTIVE

In the developmental process of a person, environmental factors play a decisive role (see, e.g., Maccoby & Jacklin, 1983; Radke-Yarrow, 1991). Contact with others is necessary for the development of speech and language as a tool for thought and for communication (Camaioni, 1989; Tomaselli, 1992); for the development of adequate worldviews and self-perceptions (Epstein & Erskine, 1983); and for the development of well functioning, integrated norm and moral systems (Wilson, Williams, & Sugarman, 1967). The importance of contact with others for physical health has been emphasized in the increasing number of reports from research on social networks (e.g., Wills, 1984; Wortman & Dunkel-Schetter, 1987).

The individual and his or her environment do not form separate entities. The individual is an active, intentional part of the environment with which he or she interacts. Individuals meet their environment most directly in specific situations, which, in turn, are embedded in the larger environment with physical, social, and cultural properties operating both directly and indirectly at all levels of specificity–generality in the person–environment interaction (Barker, 1965; Bronfenbrenner, 1977, 1979a, 1979b, 1993; Magnusson, 1981).

The actual, physical environment acts on the individual in important respects that can be reacted to without an intermediate process of interpretation. The view of the environment as a source of stimulation that elicits and releases individual responses was bluntly expressed by Skinner: "A person does not act upon the world, the world acts upon him" (Skinner, 1971, p. 211). This conception of the environment is inherent in much developmental research in which various aspects of the upbringing environment in the home and at schools have been regarded as causes in the developmental process of individuals, with reference to a one-direction cause–effect model.

In a holistic, interactionistic perspective, the main role of the environment in the functioning and development of an individual is to serve as a source of information. This assumption contributes to understanding the way an individual interacts with the environment at various levels of complexity as conceptualized and discussed by Bronfenbrenner in various connections. This view is reflected in modern social learning theory, which assumes that an individual's way of dealing with the external world develops in a learning process in which two types of perceived contingencies are formed: (a) situation–outcome contingencies (implying that certain situational conditions will lead to certain outcomes) and (b) behavior–outcome contingencies (implying that certain actions by the individual will have certain predictable consequences; cf. Bolles, 1972). The formation of situation–outcome and behavior–outcome contingencies constitutes one source for the stability and continuity of individuals' functioning in relation to the environment in current situations and for the development of well functioning mental systems in the individuals.

The environmental influence on the developmental process differs among individuals with respect to size and type of consequences. Of particular interest in this connection is the occurrence of significant single events that may have profound impact on the life course of a person. Some such events occur seemingly randomly, but also as a consequence of the person's readiness for a certain type of action or reaction (e.g., a marriage or a new job) and an opportunity offered by the environment (e.g., meeting a special, matching person or receiving an offer of a new job). In other cases, a significant event may be the result of deliberate action by the person himself or herself or by individuals whose actions influence others.

Significant single events may occur over the whole life span, the character depending on the readiness of the individual, both mentally and physically, to act and react in relation to the opportunities and restrictions offered by the environment.

The effect of significant events is to change the direction of the life course. For example, buying a new house in a certain area with specific characteristics in terms of neighbors, opportunities or jobs, schooling, and cultural and leisure activities—instead of in an area with other characteristics—may have far-reaching effects on the direction of the future life course of all family members. Sometimes the effect is not immediately visible, but grows slowly and ends up having decisive effects on the person's life in a manner that is characteristic of the so-called butterfly effect in chaos theory. In other cases, the effect is more direct and leads to what has been discussed in terms of *turning points* (Pickles & Rutter, 1991).

THE TOTAL PERSON–ENVIRONMENT SYSTEM

The fact that the mental factors, behavior, biological factors, and environmental factors have been discussed separately does not imply that they function as four independent systems, operating interactively in the dualistic sense of a Cartesian view. They represent different aspects of a system of personal and environmental factors, which together constitute an integrated whole and operate as such (see also Schneirla, 1966).

The view reflected in the second proposition (p. 33) concerned with person–environment interaction and referred to as *classical interactionism* has been advocated and discussed by researchers under various headings. For example, Pervin (1968) adopted the term *transactionism,* and Bandura (1978) the term *reciprocal determinism* for individual functioning in a current perspective. Baltes, Reese, and Lipsitt (1980) used the term *dialectic–con-*

textualistic; Bronfenbrenner and Crouter (1983), the term *process–person–context model;* and Lerner and Kauffman (1985), the term *developmental contextualism,* for their view on the person–environment process.

Here and in other connections, I have consistently over the years used the terms *interaction* and *interactionism.* My reason is simple. They are terms well established in all other life sciences to cover the essence of the life processes of living organisms. Recently, a Swedish cell biologist used the title "Life Is an Interaction" for a public lecture on his discipline (Lindberg, 1992). It can only be harmful and detrimental to progress in our own discipline and to collaboration with neighboring sciences if we always try to invent and use new terms instead of adopting concepts well established in sciences with which we want to collaborate.

CAUSALITY: THE CENTRAL ROLE OF DYNAMIC INTERACTION

When I use the term *interaction* here, it refers to lawful dynamic interaction as a basic principle in the process of individual functioning. This meaning of the term has to be distinguished from statistical interaction in experimental designs for the study of individual differences.

An essential common characteristic of the explanatory models, which were briefly described in the introduction, is the view of unidirectional causality for the relation among variables. For a long time, the dominating general view, reflected in the experimental designs in the distinction between dependent and independent variables and between predictors and criteria, has been that biological and environmental factors are causes and that mental phenomena are results. The notion of stimulus–response (S-R) relations has been one of the most influential views in psychology. Many personality models also assume a unidirectional relation between cognitive–emotional factors and behavior.

In contrast to this traditional view, a central element in an interactionistic model is the reciprocal interaction among operating factors (Magnusson, 1990, 1993; Magnusson & Törestad, 1993). Interaction among operating factors is a fundamental characteristic of the processes of all living

37

organisms. (Interaction among elements is also a central aspect of *relational holism* in physics; Zohar, 1990). It is central at all levels of individual functioning, from the functioning of single cells and how they organize themselves into systems in a lawful manner to fulfill their developmental role in the total organism (Edelman, 1987) to the functioning of a person in relation to his or her environment (Endler & Magnusson, 1976). In the interaction process, psychological factors can operate as causal factors, and biological factors can influence psychological phenomena. What starts a specific process and what maintains it vary. A psychological factor can start a biological process that is then maintained by physiological factors, and psychological factors can start and maintain a process that has been triggered by biological factors. Environmental factors influence a person's physical and mental well-being, and at the same time, an individual affects his or her own environment in many different ways.

The example presented in Figure 1 illustrates how the mental, behavioral, and biological systems of a person are involved in a continuous loop of reciprocal interaction in a current situation. The example illustrates how this process is dependent on the character of the specific, proximal situation that the individual encounters, particularly the situation as it is perceived and interpreted by the individual. The empirical example about maturing girls from Stattin and Magnusson (1990) shows how the developmental processes of the girls and their outcomes in the long range were dependent on the psychological and biological dispositions of the girls; the properties of the social, economic, and cultural environments in which the specific situations that the girls encountered were embedded; and the interaction among these factors.

DEVELOPMENTAL CHANGE: LAWFUL PROCESSES IN THE PERSON–ENVIRONMENT SYSTEM

A fundamental characteristic of the developmental process of a person is that the total person–environment system of operating factors—biological, psychological, and social—changes across time (Gottlieb, 1991). In the balance between the built-in resistance to change in the total system and subsystems once established, on the one hand, and sensitivity to factors in the individual and in the environment that work for change, on the other, the total system is in continuous transition into new states across the lifetime. In this process, both individuals and environments change and interact as totalities: individuals as a result of biological changes (e.g., growth or myelinization of the brain), as well as cognitive and emotional experiences, and environments as a consequence of societal changes and of individuals' direct and indirect actions in and on them, among other things. The fact that both persons and environments change across the life span leads to changes in the character of the interaction between them. The interaction process per se will thus precipitate development. For example, the character of the interactive process within a family changes across time.

A consequence of the perspective applied here, with methodological implications, is that changes do not take place in single aspects isolated from the totality. The extent to which different aspects of individual functioning are influenced by environmental factors in this process varies. For example, in sexual development, some features, such as gonadal structure and function, are strongly regulated by biological factors. On the other hand, other aspects of individual functioning, such as choice of peers and type of sexual relations, may be strongly open to experiential influences (Cairns, 1991).

Much debate has been devoted to the issues of stability versus change and continuity versus discontinuity in individual development. Characteristics of most of these studies are (a) that they deal with data for single variables one at a time, for example, aggressiveness, intelligence, and hyperactivity and (b) that they express temporal consistency of single variables in terms of relative stability, that is, in terms of stable rank orders of individuals across time for the variable under consideration (Weinert & Schneider, 1993).

As emphasized above, a fundamental characteristic of individual functioning as a holistic, dynamic process implies, among other things, that individuals do not develop in terms of single variables but as total integrated systems. In this perspective, all changes during the life span of a person are characterized by lawful continuity (Magnusson & Törestad,

1992); the functioning of a person at a certain stage of development is lawfully related to the functioning of the individual at earlier and later stages, but is not necessarily predictable. Each change in the process of human ontogeny is understandable and explainable in the light of the individual's previous life history and the functioning of the environment at the time for the change. This is true even for changes that are so abrupt that they seem to break a stable direction of development; for example, changes that have been characterized as turning points sometimes appear as a result of chance events or significant events. This view makes the dispute about whether individual development is characterized by continuity or discontinuity a pseudoissue in developmental research. The interesting aspect of this issue is what determines abrupt changes in the life course of a person and the kind of mechanisms that underlie such changes.

Individual development is not a process of accumulation of outcomes; it is rather, at the individual level, a process of restructuring of subsystems and the whole system within the boundaries set by biological and social constraints. If one aspect changes, it affects also related parts of the subsystem and sometimes the whole organism. For example, if one of the necessary operating factors in the coronary system totters, the whole coronary system and the whole organism may be affected. At a more general level, the restructuring of processes and structures at the individual level is embedded in and part of the restructuring of the total individual–environment system.

Much developmental research on stability and change has concentrated on stability and change in quantitative terms, and the issue has often been whether individual development is characterized by more of the same in a way that is reflected in statistical stability of rank orders of individuals for the specific variable under consideration. It should be recognized that the process of developmental change in an individual is characterized by both quantitative and qualitative change. The psychological significance of a certain state of a certain variable depends on the context of other, simultaneously operating variables in the system under investigation (i.e., on the pattern of operating factors to which the variable under consideration belongs).

40

These points have the implication—stressed by modern models for dynamic, complex processes, which were briefly referred to above—that the functioning of the total process cannot be understood by the study of single aspects, taken out and studied in isolation from their context with other operating factors. Developmental change does not take place in single variables. It is the total individual that changes in a lawful way across time.

THE PATTERNING OF OPERATING FACTORS

A basic, well-documented principle in the development of biological systems is their ability for self-organization (Barton, 1994; Eigen & Schuster, 1979; Kaplan & Kaplan, 1991; Kauffman, 1993; Nicolis & Prigogine, 1977). From the beginning of the development of the fetus, self-organization is the guiding principle (Hess & Mikhailov, 1994). Within subsystems, the operating components organize themselves in a way that maximizes the functioning of each subsystem with respect to its purpose in the total system. At a higher level, subsystems organize themselves to fulfill their role in the functioning of the totality. We find this principle in the development and functioning of the biological systems of the brain, the coronary system, and the immune system. It can also be applied to the development and functioning of the cognitive systems and manifest behavior.

For the discussion here, two aspects of the self-organizing processes are essential. First, individuals differ in the way operational factors are organized and function within subsystems, such as the perceptual–cognitive–emotional system, the immune system, the coronary system, and the behavioral system. Individuals also differ in subsystem organization and function. These organizations can be described in terms of patterns of operating factors within subsystems and in terms of patterns of functioning, cooperating subsystems. As an example, Weiner (1989) discussed the oscillations produced by natural pacemakers of the heart, the stomach, and the brain in terms of patterns.

Second, the number of ways in which operating factors in a certain subsystem can be organized in patterns, for the subsystem to play its functional role in the totality, is restricted. The goal for empirical research is

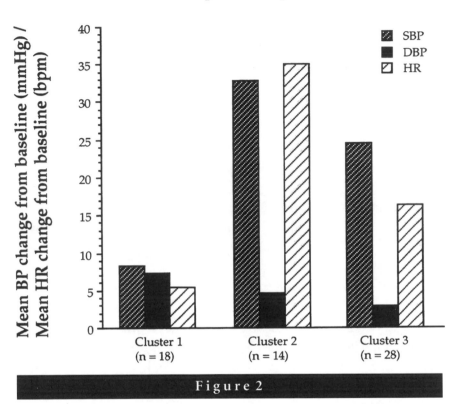

Speech Preparation

Figure 2

Magnitude of systolic blood pressure (SBP), diastolic blood pressure (DBP), and heart rate (HR) reactivity in cardiovascular response clusters during preparation of a speech (from Graber & Huber, 1994).

then twofold: (a) to identify the possible operating factors in the subsystem under consideration and (b) to identify the ways in which these factors are organized (i.e., the actual working patterns of operating factors).

An empirical illustration to this view is presented by Gramer and Huber (1994). In a study of cardiovascular responses in what was assumed to be a stressful situation, they found that the subjects could be classified in three groups on the basis of their distinct pattern of values for systolic blood pressure, diastolic blood pressure, and heart rate (see Figure 2).

These data demonstrate a basic principle in individual development underlying individual differences: The characteristic of individual development is that it takes place in terms of patterns of operating factors. This is true for the operating factors in subsystems such as the coronary system, the immune system, the brain, and the cognitive system. It is also true for the development of the individual as a whole, where the operating subsystems are organized at the top level in terms of patterns.

This view leads to the conclusion that the main individual differences are to be found in the patterning of operating factors within subsystems, such as those I just described, and in the patterning of subsystems in the totality, for example, in the way the cognitive, the behavioral, and the physiological systems function together in the total functioning of the individual.

The view that development takes place in terms of patterns of operating factors forms the theoretical basis for the application of a person approach in developmental research. The person approach is briefly discussed later.

INDIVIDUAL DIFFERENCES

One of the major goals for scientific work is to arrive at generalizations about the lawfulness of structures and processes in the space of phenomena that are the objects of interest. In psychology, one of the roads to this goal has been the systematic study of individual differences (cf. Cronbach, 1957; Eysenck & Eysenck, 1985).

The Variable Approach

Empirical research on individual differences in the area of developmental psychology has three main characteristics. An understanding of these characteristics is important in order to understand and evaluate the relevance of the results.

The first characteristic is the emphasis on variables in the search for lawfulness of structures and processes in individual functioning and development. The focus of interest is on a single variable or a combination of variables, their interrelations, and their relations to a specific criterion. The problems are formulated in terms of variables, and the results are interpreted in such terms. This is the case in such studies as those on the relationships among variables as a basis for factor analysis, on the stability of single variables across time, on the links between environmental factors and various aspects of individual functioning, and on the developmental background of adult functioning. An example is the research focusing on the relation between various aspects of individual functioning and environmental upbringing conditions, on the one hand, and the development of adult alcohol abuse and criminal behavior, on the other.

The second characteristic is that the lawfulness of structures and processes in individual functioning is studied by the application of various regression models, mainly linear regression models. This approach to the search for lawfulness implies the following interrelated assumptions:

1. Individuals can be compared on a nomothetical, continuous dimension in meaningful ways.
2. Individuals differ only quantitatively, not qualitatively, along the dimension for a certain variable.
3. Relationships among variables and their way of functioning in the totality of an individual is assumed to be the same for all individuals. In a multiple regression equation, each variable has the same weight for all individuals and reflects what is characteristic of the average person.
4. The interrelations among variables studied in nomothetic analyses can be used for inferences about how the variables actually function within individuals.

These assumptions are too seldom made explicit and considered in the interpretation of results from variable-oriented studies. Lewin (1931) discussed the limitations of this approach

The third characteristic of developmental research is the fact that many, if not most, of the variables studied in empirical analyses are hypothetical variables. A hypothetical variable is an abstraction aimed at delineating a certain aspect of the total functioning of an individual—such as intelligence, aggressiveness, hyperactivity, attachment, shyness—or sometimes of the environment, such as social class or poverty. What is actually assessed as a measure of such an aspect is, of course, defined by the properties of the procedure used for data collection, independent of the wording of the theoretical definition. Hypothetical constructs, in which developmental psychology abounds, run the risk of reification (i.e., to be regarded as tangible and really existing).

One complication of the traditional variable approach, that is, applying regression models for the treatment of data for hypothetical variables in nomothetic analyses, is the existence of collinearity among variables, expressed in sometimes very high correlations among variables (Darlington, 1968). Statistical collinearity is reflected in sometimes very high intercorrelations among operating variables.

One general aim of traditional, variable-oriented studies in developmental research is to estimate the extent to which a specific variable or a set of variables, regarded as independent variables, contribute to the statistical prediction of a specific criterion, regarded and treated as the dependent variable. A study presented by Magnusson, Andersson, and Törestad (1993) was performed to illustrate the problems connected with this approach, in the perspective presented above.

The study was concerned with early person variables as antecedents of adult alcohol problems. On the basis of an analysis of existing literature, seven variables were chosen: aggressiveness, motor restlessness, concentration difficulties, lack of school motivation, disharmony, peer rejection, and school achievement. The data were collected when the boys were 13 years of age. Data for alcohol abuse were obtained from official registers. Both predictor and criteria data were available with insignificant dropout.

In Table 1, the correlation coefficients are presented for the relationship between each of the independent variables and the dependent variable, obtained as point-biserial coefficients. As expected, each of the independent variables had a significant linear relationship with the dependent variable with one exception: peer rejection. Each of the semipartial coefficients presented in the last column reflects the unique relation between the variable under consideration and the criterion when the role of the other independent variables is partialed out. None of them exceeded the level of .10, which means that data for each of the independent variables shared

Table 1

Point-Biserial Correlations and Semipartial Correlations Between the
Independent Variables and the Dependent Variable:
Registered Alcohol Abuse Age 18 Through Age 24

Independent variable	Correlation	Semipartial correlation
Aggressiveness	.221	.025
Motor restlessness	.236	.036
Concentration difficulties	.262	.048
Low school motivation	.259	.030
Disharmony	.248	.079
School achievement	−.180	−.018
Peer rejection	.055	−.049

less than 1% with the total variance for registered alcohol abuse at adult age, when the variance common with all of the other variables was removed. Thus, the specific contribution of each single variable per se to the prediction of alcohol problems at adulthood was limited.

As illustrated by the entries in Table 1, the specific role of single hypothetical variables in the developmental process is conspicuously overestimated in studies of single variables in isolation from their context of other, simultaneously operating variables. This is overlooked too often because, frequently, the roles of only one or a few independent variables are studied at each time. A good prediction is that it would have been possible to publish at least five studies, independent of each other, demonstrating a significant correlation between early individual functioning and adult alcohol problems.

For a statistician, the figures presented in Table 1 are not surprising, considering the intercorrelations among the independent variables. Nor are the results surprising, if they are interpreted in the perspective of a holistic, integrated model for individual development.

The analysis just presented shows the limitations of a simplistic variable approach as a basis for understanding and explaining the functioning and development of the individual. This does not mean that the vari-

46

able approach can be abandoned in developmental research. It is a useful tool as a first step, in which the goal is to identify possible operating factors in the system that is under consideration as a basis for the application of a person approach.

The Person Approach

As discussed in an earlier section of this chapter, the main characteristics of an individual are in the patterning of structures and functioning of subsystems and cooperating subsystems. A consequence of this view is that the variable approach has to be complemented with a person approach, in which the individual is the basic unit of observation (Bergman, 1988, 1993; Bergman & Magnusson, 1983; Magnusson & Bergman, 1988; Magnusson, Stattin, & Dunér, 1983). In a variable approach, the specific problem under consideration is formulated in person terms and operationalized and studied empirically in terms of patterns of values for variables that are relevant to the problem under consideration. In other scientific disciplines that are concerned with dynamic, complex processes, such as ecology, meteorology, biology, and chemistry, pattern analysis has become an important methodological tool.

The following steps are included in a pattern analysis:

1. Identification of the system to which a pattern analysis is to be applied. This implies specification of the level of analysis, that is, if the interest is in the patterning of variables in a subsystem at a microlevel, such as a subsystem of the brain; in the patterning of variables at a more general level, for example, in the system of manifest behavior; or in the patterning of subsystems forming a system of higher order.
2. Identification of possible operating factors at the specified level of analysis to constitute the pattern to be studied.
3. Application of a statistical method for pattern analysis, for instance, grouping the individuals in categories that are homogeneous with respect to their patterns of values for the variables included in the analysis.

An empirical illustration of a person approach, concerned with the patterning of factors in the cardiovascular system, was presented in Figure 2. Another demonstration, which also offers a comparison with a variable approach, can be obtained from Magnusson and Bergman (1988), who used a person approach to the study of early problem behaviors as precursors of adult adjustment problems, among them, alcohol problems. Thus, the general purpose, the study of early antecedents of adult problems, was the same as that of the study presented by Magnusson, Andersson, and Törestad (1993), referred to above. The result of the pattern analysis is presented in Table 2.

The patterns in Table 2 are based on data for six variables, which cover different aspects of problem behaviors: aggressiveness, motor restlessness, concentration difficulty, low school motivation, underachievement, and peer rejection. Empirical studies indicate that each of them is a possible operating factor in the developmental processes underlying adult maladjustment. Data for each of the variables have been transformed to a scale with values ranging from 0 to 4, reflecting levels of seriousness of problem behaviors for boys at the age of 13. The methodology and results of the pattern analysis were discussed in detail in Magnusson and Bergman (1988). Here, only a few comments, pertinent to the discussion in this chapter, will be made.

Table 2 demonstrates that the boys could be grouped into eight distinctly different groups with reference to their pattern of values for the variables under study. An inspection shows that four out of six problem behaviors did not appear as single problem clusters for the boys at age 13. For example, aggressiveness and motor restlessness, which have been studied extensively in the variable-oriented tradition as separate indicators of maladjustment in both a cross-sectional and in a longitudinal perspective, appear only in combination with other indicators. This result is an illustration of the first basic proposition of a holistic model for individual functioning and individual development: A certain aspect of the total process cannot be finally studied and understood in isolation from its context of other, simultaneously operating factors. A certain factor, say aggressiveness, does not have a significance of its own per se, independent of the context of other factors simultaneously working in the individual.

Table 2

Clusters of Boys at Age 13 Based on Data for Overt Adjustment Problems

Cluster no.	Size	Average coefficient[b]	Cluster mean[a]					
			Aggressiveness	Motor restlessness	Conc. diff.	Low school motivation	Underachievement	Peer rejection
1	296	.12	—	—	—	—	—	—
2	23	.30	—	—	—	—	—	2.4
3	40	.28	—	—	—	—	-2.6	—
4	61	.39	1.3	1.4	—	—	—	—
5	41	.39	—	1.5	2.3	1.9	—	—
6	12	.56	1.7	1.8	2.3	1.9	2.6	—
7	37	.37	2.3	2.3	1.9	1.3	—	—
8	22	.48	2.2	2.7	2.6	2.4	—	1.9
Residue	8	1.5	1.4	1.3	1.3	1.3	2.3	

Note. Conc. diff. = concentration difficulty.
[a]Indicates that the cluster mean of a variable is less than 1 in the 4-point scale coded 0, 1, 2, 3. [b]Average coefficient means average error sum of squares within the cluster.

It gets its significance from its context. This became even more apparent in the follow-up study to the age of 24, which was reported by Magnusson and Bergman (1988). The long-term significance of a certain factor was not in the factor itself, it was in the total pattern in which the factor appeared at the individual level. For example, only when in combination with other severe problem behaviors at the age of 13 was aggressiveness a precursor of adult problems.

A number of methods for pattern analysis have been presented and applied: multivariate P-technique factor analysis (Cattell, Cattell, & Rhymer, 1947), Q-sort technique (Asendorpf & van Aken, 1991; Block, 1971), latent profile analysis (LPA; Gibson, 1959; Magnusson, Dunér, & Zetterblom, 1975), configural frequency analysis (CFA; Lienert & zur Oeveste, 1985; von Eye, 1990), and cluster-analytical techniques (Bergman, 1993). Use of higher order contingency-table techniques, for example, log-linear analysis, seems to be one fruitful way for the study of configurations of individuals' values (see, e.g., Bishop, Feinberg, & Holland, 1975). The methods that are available are mainly applicable to description of patterns and less appropriate for the study of developmental change in process terms (Magnusson & Törestad, 1993). For further scientific progress, development of methods for empirical study of developmental change in process terms is one of the most urgent tasks.

FINAL COMMENTS

A holistic, integrated model for individual functioning and development does not imply that the whole system of an individual must be studied at the same time. The essential function of the model is that it enables us to formulate problems at different levels of the functioning of the total organism, to implement empirical studies, and to interpret the results in a common, theoretical framework. For a long time, the Newtonian view of the physical world has served this purpose in the natural sciences. The implication of the acceptance of that model of nature has never been that the whole universe should be investigated in one and the same study. But it has enabled researchers concerned with very different levels of the total system, for example, nuclear physicists and astrophysicists, to communicate and understand each other. In the same way, an integrated, holistic model for individual development should make it possible for all those concerned with aspects of individual development, from developmental biologists to psychologists focusing on social development, to plan, implement, and interpret research in the same theoretical framework, thus enabling them to communicate with each other effectively.

The complexity of individual functioning and developmental change has brought some researchers to a pessimistic view about the future of psychology as a science (cf. Cronbach, 1975). However, the litmus test of a scientific discipline cannot be whether its phenomena are complex and hard to analyze. The criterion for a science is the appropriateness of the research strategy and methods that are applied in dealing with relevant questions. Whenever processes display order and regularity on the basis of given structures, it is a scientific challenge to map this lawfulness of order and regularity (cf. Bateson, 1978, in press). To do that successfully in research on individual development, a prerequisite for real scientific progress is that we start in careful analysis of the nature of the phenomena that are the objects of our interest; formulate the issues with reference to the result of such analyses; and plan, implement, and interpret the empirical research with reference to a holistic, integrated model for individual functioning and development (Cairns, 1979b, 1986; Magnusson, 1988, 1992; Magnusson & Cairns, in press).

REFERENCES

Angoff, W. H. (1988). The nature–nurture debate, aptitudes, and group differences. *American Psychologist, 43,* 713–720.

Asendorpf, J. B., & van Aken, M. A. G. (1991). Correlates of the temporal consistency of personality patterns in childhood. *Journal of Personality, 59,* 689–703.

Baldwin, J. M. (1895). *Mental development in the child and the race: Method and processes.* New York: Macmillan.

Baltes, P. B., Reese, H. W., & Lipsitt, L. P. (1980). Life-span developmental psychology. In M. R. Rosenzweig & L. W. Porter (Eds.), *Annual review of psychology* (Vol. 31, pp. 65–110). Palo Alto, CA: Annual Reviews.

Bandura, A. (1978). The self system in reciprocal determinism. *American Psychologist*, *33*, 344–358.

Barker, R. G. (1965). Exploration in ecological psychology. *American Psychologist*, *20*, 1–14.

Barton, S. (1994). Chaos, self-organization, and psychology. *American Psychologist*, *49*, 5–14.

Basar, E. (Ed.). (1990). *Chaos in brain function*. Berlin: Springer-Verlag.

Bateson, P. P. G. (1978). How does behavior develop? In P. P. G. Bateson & P. H. Klopfer (Eds.), *Perspectives in ethology: Vol. 3. Social behavior*. New York: Plenum.

Bateson, P. (in press). Design for a life. In D. Magnusson (Ed.), *The life-span development of individuals: Behavioral, neurobiological and psychosocial perspectives*. Cambridge, England: Cambridge University Press.

Bergman, L. R. (1988). Modeling reality. In M. Rutter (Ed.), *Studies of psychosocial risks: The power of longitudinal data* (pp. 354–366). Cambridge, England: Cambridge University Press.

Bergman, L. R. (1993). Some methodological issues in longitudinal research: Looking forward. In D. Magnusson & P. Casaer (Eds.), *Longitudinal research on individual development: Present status and future perspectives* (pp. 217–241). Cambridge, England: Cambridge University Press.

Bergman, L. R., & Magnusson, D. (1983). The development of patterns of maladjustment. In *Report from the project Individual Development and Environment*. Stockholm: Stockholm University.

Bertalanffy, L., von. (1968). *General system theory*. New York: Braziller.

Binet, A. (1909). *Les ideés modernes sur les enfants* [Modern ideas about children]. Paris: Ernest Flammarion.

Bishop, Y. M. M., Feinberg, S. E., & Holland, P. W. (1975). *Discrete multivariate analysis: Theory and practice*. Cambridge, MA: MIT Press.

Block, J. (1971). *Lives through time*. Berkeley, CA: Bancroft Books.

Bolles, R. C. (1972). Reinforcement, expectancy, and learning. *Psychological Review*, *79*, 394–409.

Bothe, H. G., Ebeling, W., Kurzhanski, A. B., & Peschel, M. (Eds.). (1987). *Dynamical systems and environmental models*. Berlin: Akademie-Verlag.

Bowers, K. S. (1981). Knowing more than we can say leads to saying more than we can know: On being implicitly informed. In D. Magnusson (Ed.), *Toward a psychology of situations* (pp. 179–194). Hillsdale, NJ: Erlbaum.

Brandtstädter, J. (1993). Development, aging and control: Empirical and theoretical issues. In D. Magnusson & P. Casaer (Eds.), *Longitudinal research on individual development: Present status and future perspectives* (pp. 194–216). Cambridge, England: Cambridge University Press.

Brentano, F. (1924). *Psychologie vom empirischen Standpunkte. Mit ausführliche Einleitung.* Leipzig: F. Meiner. (Original work published 1874)

Brewin, C. R. (1986). *Cognitive foundations of clinical psychology.* Hillsdale, NJ: Erlbaum.

Bronfenbrenner, U. (1977). Toward an experimental ecology of human development. *American Psychologist, 32,* 513–531.

Bronfenbrenner, U. (1979a). Context of child rearing: Problems and prospects. *American Psychologist, 34,* 834–850.

Bronfenbrenner, U. (1979b). *The ecology of human development: Experiments by nature and design.* Cambridge, MA: Harvard University Press.

Bronfenbrenner, U. (1989). Ecological systems theory. *Annals of Child Development, 6,* 185–246.

Bronfenbrenner, U. (1993). The ecology of cognitive development: Research models and fugitive findings. In R. H. Wozniak & K. Fischer (Eds.), *Development in context: Acting and thinking in specific environments* (pp. 3–44). Hillsdale, NJ: Erlbaum.

Bronfenbrenner, U., & Ceci, S. J. (1994). Nature–nurture reconceptualized in developmental perspective: A bioecological model. *Psychological Review, 101,* 568–586.

Bronfenbrenner, U., & Crouter, A. C. (1983). The evolution of environmental models in developmental research. In P. Mussen (Series Ed.) & W. Kassen (Vol. Ed.), *Handbook of child psychology: Vol. 1. History, theories and methods* (4th ed., pp. 357–414). New York: Wiley.

Cairns, R. B. (1979a). *Social development: The origins and plasticity of interchanges.* San Francisco: W. H. Freeman.

Cairns, R. B. (1979b). Toward guidelines for interactional research. In R. B. Cairns (Ed.), *The analysis of social interactions: Methods, issues, and illustrations.* Hillsdale, NJ: Erlbaum.

Cairns, R. B. (1983). The emergence of developmental psychology. In P. Mussen (Series Ed.) & W. Kassen (Vol. Ed.), *Handbook of child psychology: Vol. 1. History, theories and methods* (4th ed., pp. 41–101). New York: Wiley.

Cairns, R. B. (1986). Phenomena lost: Issues in the study of development. In J. Valsiner (Ed.), *The individual subject and scientific psychology* (pp. 79–111). New York: Plenum.

Cairns, R. B. (1991). Multiple metaphors for a singular idea. *Developmental Psychology, 27*, 23–26.

Cairns, R. B. (1994, June). Socialization and sociogenesis. In *The life-span development of individuals: A synthesis of biological and psychosocial perspectives.* Symposium, Stockholm.

Cairns, R. B., & Cairns, B. D. (1985). The developmental–interactional view of social behavior: Four issues of adolescent aggression. In D. Olweus, J. Block, & M. Radke-Yarrow (Eds.), *The development of antisocial and prosocial behavior.* New York: Academic Press.

Cairns, R. B., & Nakelski, J. S. (1971). On fighting in mice: Ontogenetic and experimental determinants. *Journal of Comparative and Physiological Psychology, 71,* 354–364.

Camaioni, L. (1989). The role of social interaction in the transition from communication to language. In A. de Ribaupierre (Ed.), *Transition mechanisms in child development* (pp. 109–125). New York: Cambridge University Press.

Cannon, W. B. (1914). The emergency function of the adrenal medulla in pain and the major emotions. *American Journal of Physiology, 33,* 356–372.

Cattell, R. B., Cattell, A. K. S., & Rhymer, R. M. (1947). P-technique demonstrated in determining psycho-physiological source traits in a normal individual. *Psychometrika, 12,* 267–288.

Cronbach, L. J. (1957). The two disciplines of scientific psychology. *American Psychologist, 12,* 671–684.

Cronbach, L. J. (1975). Beyond the two disciplines of scientific psychology. *American Psychologist, 30,* 116–127.

Darlington, R. B. (1968). Multiple regression. *Psychological Bulletin, 69,* 161–182.

de Groot, A. D. (1990). Unifying psychology: A European view. In P. J. D. Drenth, J. A. Sergeant, & R. J. Takens (Eds.), *European perspectives in psychology: Theoretical, psychometrics, personality, developmental, educational, cognitive, gerontological* (Vol. 1, pp. 3–16). New York: Wiley.

Durkheim, E. (1897). *Le suicide: Étude de sociologie* [Suicide: A sociological study]. Paris: Alcan.

Eccles, J., & Robinson, D. N. (1985). *The wonder of being human.* Boston: New Science Library.

Edelman, G. (1987). *Neural Darwinism: The theory of neuronal group selection.* New York: Basic Books.

Eigen, M., & Schuster, P. (1979). *The hyper cycle—A principle of natural self-organization.* Heidelberg, Germany: Springer.

Endler, N. S., & Magnusson, D. (1976). Toward an interactional psychology of personality. *Psychological Bulletin, 83,* 956–979.

Epstein, S., & Erskine, N. (1983). The development of personal theories of reality from an interactional perspective. In D. Magnusson & V. L. Allen (Eds.), *Human development: An interactional perspective* (pp. 133–147). New York: Academic Press.

Eysenck, H. J., & Eysenck, M. W. (1985). *Personality and individual differences: A natural science approach.* London: Plenum.

Farmer, J. D., Kaufmann, A., Packard, N. H., & Perelson, A. S. (1987). Adaptive dynamic networks as models for the immune system and autocatalytic sets. In S. H. Koslow, A. J. Mandell, & M. F. Schlesinger (Eds.), *Annals of the New York Academy of Sciences: Vol. 504. Perspectives in biological dynamics and theoretical medicine* (pp. 118–131). New York: New York Academy of Sciences.

Galton, F. (1869). *Hereditary genius: An inquiry into its laws and consequences.* London: Macmillan.

Gibson, W. A. (1959). Three multivariate models: Factor analysis, latent structure analysis and latent profile analysis. *Psychometrica, 24,* 229–252.

Gleick, J. (1987). *Chaos: Making a new science.* New York: Penguin Books.

Gottlieb, G. (1991). Experiential canalization of behavioral development: Theory. *Developmental Psychology, 27,* 4–13.

Gramer, M., & Huber, H. P. (1994). Individual variability in task-specific cardiovascular patterns during psychological challenge. *German Journal of Psychology, 18,* 1–17.

Greenwald, A. G. (1992). Unconscious cognition reclaimed. *American Psychologist, 47,* 766–779.

Gunnar, M. R. (1986). Human developmental psychoendocrinology: A review of research on neuroendocrine responses to challenge and threat in infancy and childhood. In M. E. Lamb, A. L. Brown, & B. Rogoff (Eds.), *Advances in developmental psychology* (Vol. 4). Hillsdale, NJ: Erlbaum.

Hess, B., & Mikhailov, A. (1994). Self-organization in living cells. *Science, 264,* 223–224.

Hunt, J. McV., (1961). *Intelligence and experience.* New York: Ronald Press.

Kagan, J. (1989). *Unstable ideas: Temperament, cognition, and self.* Cambridge, MA: Harvard University Press.

Kagan, J. (1994). *Galen's prophecy: Temperament in human nature.* New York: Basic Books.

Kaplan, M. L., & Kaplan, N. R. (1991). The self-organization of human psychological functioning. *Behavioral Science, 36,* 161–179.

Kauffman, S. A. (1993). *The origins of order.* New York: Oxford University.

Kohlberg, L. (1969). Stage and sequence: The cognitive–developmental approach to socialization. In D. A. Goolin (Ed.), *Handbook of socialization theory and research.* Chicago: Rand McNally.

Lagerspetz, K. M. J., & Lagerspetz, K. Y. H. (1971). Changes in the aggressiveness of mice resulting from selective breeding, learning and social isolation. *Scandinavian Journal of Psychology, 12,* 241–248.

Lerner, R. M. (1991). Changing organism–context relations as the basis of development: A developmental contextual perspective. *Developmental Psychology, 27,* 27–32.

Lerner, R. M., & Kauffman, M. B. (1985). The concept of development in contextualism. *Developmental Review, 5,* 309–333.

Lewin, K. (1931). Environmental forces in child behavior and development. In C. Murchison (Ed.), *A handbook of child psychology* (pp. 94–127). Worcester, MA: Clark University Press.

Lienert, G. A., & zur Oeveste, H. (1985). CFA as a statistical tool for developmental research. *Educational and Psychological Measurement, 45,* 301–307.

Lindberg, U. (1992). *Livet är en interaktion* [Life is an interaction]. Stockholm: Folkuniversitetet.

Maccoby, E. E., & Jacklin, C. N. (1983). The "person" characteristics of children and the family as environment. In D. Magnusson & V. L. Allen (Eds.), *Human development: An interactional perspective* (pp. 75–91). San Diego, CA: Academic Press.

Magnusson, D. (1981). *Toward a psychology of situations: An interactional perspective.* Hillsdale, NJ: Erlbaum.

Magnusson, D. (1988). *Individual development from an interactional perspective.* Hillsdale, NJ: Erlbaum.

Magnusson, D. (1990). Personality development from an interactional perspective. In L. Pervin (Ed.), *Handbook of personality* (pp. 193–222). New York: Guilford Press.

Magnusson, D. (1992). Back to the phenomena: Theory, methods and statistics in psychological research. *European Journal of Personality, 6*, 1–14.

Magnusson, D. (1993). Human ontogeny: A longitudinal perspective. In D. Magnusson & P. Casaer (Eds.), *Longitudinal research on individual development: Present status and future perspectives* (pp. 1–25). Cambridge, England: Cambridge University Press.

Magnusson, D., af Klinteberg, B., & Stattin, H. (1993). Autonomic activity/reactivity, behavior, and crime in a longitudinal perspective. In J. McCord (Ed.), *Facts, frameworks, and forecasts* (pp. 287–318). New Brunswick, NJ: Transaction.

Magnusson, D., af Klinteberg, B., & Stattin, H. (1994). Juvenile and persistent offenders: Behavioral and physiological characteristics. In R. D. Ketterlinus & M. Lamb (Eds.), *Adolescent problem behaviors*. Hillsdale, NJ: Erlbaum.

Magnusson, D., Andersson, T., & Törestad, B. (1993). Methodological implications of a peephole perspective on personality. In D. C. Funder, R. D. Parke, C. Tomlinson-Keasey, & K. Widaman (Eds.), *Studying lives through time: Personality and development* (pp. 207–220). Washington, DC: American Psychological Association.

Magnusson, D., & Bergman, L. R. (1988). Individual and variable-based approaches to longitudinal research on early risk factors. In M. Rutter (Ed.), *Studies of psychosocial risk: The power of longitudinal data* (pp. 45–61). Cambridge, England: Cambridge University Press.

Magnusson, D., & Cairns, R. B. (in press). Developmental science: Principles and illustrations. In R. B. Cairns, G. H. Elder, Jr., E. J. Costello, & A. McGuire (Eds.), *Developmental science*. Cambridge, England: Cambridge University Press.

Magnusson, D., Dunér, A., & Zetterblom, G. (1975). *Adjustment: A longitudinal study*. Stockholm: Almqvist & Wiksell.

Magnusson, D., Stattin, H., & Dunér, A. (1983). Aggression and criminality in a longitudinal perspective. In K. T. van Dusen & S. A. Mednick (Eds.), *Prospective studies of crime and delinquency* (pp. 273–301). Boston: Kluwer-Nijhoff.

Magnusson, D., & Törestad, B. (1992). The individual as an interactive agent in the environment. In W. B. Walsh, K. Craig, & R. Price (Eds.), *Person–environment psychology: Models and perspectives*. Hillsdale, NJ: Erlbaum.

Magnusson, D., & Törestad, B. (1993). A holistic view of personality: A model revisited. *Annual Review of Psychology, 44*, 427–452.

Meyer-Probst, B., Rössler, H. D., & Teichmann, H. (1983). Biological and psychosocial risk factors and development during childhood. In D. Magnusson & V. L.

Allen (Eds.), *Human development: An interactional perspective* (pp. 244–259). San Diego, CA: Academic Press.

Miller, N. E., & Dollard, J. (1941). *Social learning and imitation.* New Haven, CT: Yale University Press.

Nesselroade, J. R., & Ford, D. H. (1987). Methodological considerations in modeling living systems. In M. E. Ford & D. H. Ford (Eds.), *Humans as self-constructing living systems: Putting the framework to work* (pp. 47–79). Hillsdale, NJ: Erlbaum.

Nicolis, G., & Prigogine, I. (1977). *Self-organization in non-equilibrium systems.* New York: Wiley Interscience.

Norman, D. A., & Shallice, T. (1980). *Attention to action: Willed and automatic control of behavior (CHIP Report 99).* San Diego, CA: University of California.

Öhman, A., & Magnusson, D. (1987). An interactional paradigm for research on psychopathology. In D. Magnusson & A. Öhman (Eds.), *Psychopathology: An interactional perspective.* New York: Academic Press.

Pedersen, N. (1989). Some evidence regarding the importance of genes and environments during behavioral development. *ISSBD Newsletter, 15,* 3–4.

Pervin, L. (1968). Performance and satisfaction as a function of individual environment fit. *Psychological Bulletin, 69,* 56–68.

Pervin, L. A. (1983). The stasis and flow of behavior: Toward a theory of goals. In M. M. Page (Ed.), *Personality: Current theory and research* (pp. 1–53). Lincoln: University of Nebraska Press.

Pervin, L. A. (1990). A brief history of modern personality theory. In L. A. Pervin (Ed.), *Handbook of personality: Theory and research* (pp. 3–18). New York: Guilford Press.

Piaget, J. (1948). *The moral judgment of the child.* Glencoe, IL: Free Press.

Pickles, A., & Rutter, M. (1991). Statistical and conceptual models of "turning points" in developmental processes. In D. Magnusson, L. R. Bergman, G. Rudinger, & B. Törestad (Eds.), *Problems and methods in longitudinal research: Stability and change* (pp. 133–166). Cambridge, England: Cambridge University Press.

Plomin, R., Chipuer, H. M., & Loehlin, J. C. (1990). Behavioral genetics and personality. In L. A. Pervin (Ed.), *Handbook of personality: Theory and research.* New York: Guilford Press.

Pulkkinen, L. (1992). Life-styles in personality development. *European Journal of Personality, 6,* 139–155.

Radke-Yarrow, M. (1991). The individual and the environment in human behavioural development. In P. Bateson (Ed.), *The development and integration of behaviour: Essays in honour of Robert Hinde* (pp. 389–410). Cambridge, England: Cambridge University Press.

Rutter, M., & Casaer, P. (1991). *Biological risk factors for psychosocial disorders.* Cambridge, England: Cambridge University Press.

Sameroff, A. J. (1983). Developmental systems: Contexts and evolution. In P. H. Mussen (Ed.), *Handbook of child psychology* (Vol. 1, pp. 237–294). New York: Wiley.

Schneirla, T. C. (1966). Behavioral development and comparative psychology. *Quarterly Review of Biology, 41,* 283–302.

Skinner, B. F. (1971). *Beyond freedom and dignity.* New York: Knopf.

Sroufe, L. A. (1979). The coherence of individual development: Early care, attachment, and subsequent developmental issues. *American Psychologist, 34,* 834–841.

Stattin, H., & Magnusson, D. (1990). *Paths through life: Vol. 2. Pubertal maturation in female development.* Hillsdale, NJ: Erlbaum.

Stern, W. (1911). *Die differentielle Psychologie in ihren metodischen Grundlagen* [Differential psychology in its methodological basis]. Leipzig, Germany: Verlag von Johann A. Barth.

Strelau, J. (1983). *Temperament–personality activity.* New York: Academic Press.

Stumpf, C. (1883). *Tonpsychologie* [True psychology] (Vol. 1). Leipzig, Germany: S. Hirzel.

Thomae, H. (1988). *Das Individuum und seine Welt: Eine Pers onlichkeitstheorie* [The individual and his world: A theory of personality]. Göttingen, Germany: Hogrefe.

Tolman, E. C. (1951). A psychological model. In T. Parsons & E. A. Shils (Eds.), *Toward a general theory of action* (pp. 279–364). Cambridge, MA: Harvard University Press.

Tomaselli, M. (1992). The social bases of language acquisition. *Social Development, 1,* 67–87.

Toulmin, S. (1981). Toward reintegration: An agenda for psychology's next century. In R. A. Kasschau & Ch. N. Cofer (Eds.), *Psychology's next century: Enduring issues* (pp. 264–286). New York: Praeger.

von Eye, A. (1990). *Introduction to configural frequency analysis: The search for types and antitypes in cross-classifications.* New York: Cambridge University Press.

Waddington, C. (1962). *New patterns in genetics and development.* New York: Columbia.

Wapner, S., & Kaplan, B. (1983). *Toward a holistic developmental psychology*. Hillsdale, NJ: Erlbaum.

Watson, J. B. (1930). *Behaviorism* (2nd ed.). New York: Norton.

Weiner, H. (1989). The dynamics of the organism: Implications of recent biological thought for psychosomatic theory and research. *Psychosomatic Medicine, 51*, 608–635.

Weinert, F. E., & Schneider, W. (1993). Cognitive, social, and emotional development. In D. Magnusson & P. Casaer (Eds.), *Longitudinal research on individual development: Present status and future perspectives* (pp. 75–94). Cambridge, England: Cambridge University Press.

Wills, T. A. (1984). Supportive functions of interpersonal relationships. In S. Cohen & L. Syme (Eds.), *Social support and health* (pp. 61–82). New York: Academic Press.

Wilson, J., Williams, N., & Sugarman, B. (1967). *Introduction to moral education*. Baltimore: Penguin Books.

Wortman, C. B., & Dunkel-Schetter, C. (1987). Conceptual and methodological issues in the study of social support. In A. Baum & J. E. Singer (Eds.), *Handbook of psychology and health* (Vol. 5, pp. 33–67). Hillsdale, NJ: Erlbaum.

Zeeman, E. C. (1976). Catastrophe theory. *Scientific American, 234*, 65–83.

Zohar, D. (1990). *The quantum self: A revolutionary view of human nature and consciousness rooted in the new physics.*

Zuckerman, M. (1980). Sensation seeking and its biological correlates. *Psychological Bulletin, 88*, 187–214.

3

Understanding Individual Differences in Environmental-Risk Exposure

Michael Rutter, Lorna Champion, David Quinton,
Barbara Maughan, and Andrew Pickles

U rie Bronfenbrenner (1979, 1989; Bronfenbrenner & Ceci, 1994; Bronfenbrenner & Crouter, 1983) has contributed in many important ways to our understanding of psychological processes, but probably his most important message has been the necessity of considering development in its social context. Growth takes place in a social milieu, and it will, therefore, be influenced by a person's interactions and transactions with that milieu, as well as by within-the-individual organismic factors. Bronfenbrenner's portrayal of these processes has been put in ecological terms: a *biological concept.* One implication is that the impact of particular experiences may vary according to their social context and according to their psychological meaning in relation to a person's previous background and experiences, as well as current circumstances. This consideration focuses on the likely operation of interactions of various sorts, including the possibility that individuals differ in their susceptibility to specific environmental factors. Such interactions are widespread in biology and medicine (Rutter & Pickles, 1991), and they are likely to be so in psychological development, although so far there have been few investigations using methods likely to reveal them.

However, a further essential part of the ecological concept as applied to the process of development concerns the influence of transactions between persons and their environments. That is, not only are individuals shaped by their environments, but so, too, are environments shaped by the individuals within them. That topic constitutes the prime focus of this chapter.

There is now a very substantial research literature on environmental-risk factors for psychopathology. The findings from many well-planned empirical investigations, which used a range of research strategies, provide convincing evidence that environmental-risk mechanisms do indeed play a role in the etiology of psychiatric disorders in both childhood and adult life (Brown & Harris, 1989; Garmezy & Masten, 1994; Goodyer, 1990; Rutter, 1985, 1991a). Most psychosocial researchers have, understandably, been keen to use these data to develop more effective means of preventing psychopathology. Such interventions, designed to counter these environmentally mediated risks, have tended to follow one or another of three main strategies.

First, people have sought to take steps to reduce the prevalence of psychosocial-risk factors (Graham, 1994; Shaffer, Philips, Enver, Silverman, & Anthony, 1989). Thus, there has been a focus on possibilities of ameliorating poor parenting, reducing family discord, and preventing maternal depression. Clearly, this is a worthwhile approach in the case of severe psychosocial hazards, and there are some promising leads on interventions that appear likely to be beneficial. Nevertheless, it is all too apparent that identification of a risk factor is one thing, but that the prevention of its occurrence is quite another (Rutter, 1982).

Despite all the difficulties, it is important that society strive further to improve psychosocial living conditions for both children and adults. The need to do so is apparent from the substantial body of evidence indicating that in both Europe and North America, there has been a considerable rise in the level of psychosocial disturbances in young people over the last half century (Rutter & Smith, 1995). Thus, rates of crime, suicide, drug taking, and depression have all gone up in a most worrying fashion. This adverse trend is all the more striking because this is a time period during which physical health has improved remarkably. Infant mortality has fallen, and life expectancy has greatly increased. An important feature of the analysis of these time trends is that the evidence serves to rule out several of the most well accepted explanations. For example, although all of us accept that poverty and poor living conditions bring with them a host of problems that make effective family functioning more difficult, it is clearly evident that this is not the explanation for the rising rate of disorders in young people. The past 50 years has been a period when living conditions and economic standards have improved considerably for most of the population (at least up until a decade or so ago). Similarly, the worrying rise in the rate of unemployment in most industrialized countries over the last 10 or 15 years cannot be responsible, because the main rise in the rate of disorders occurred before then, when unemployment rates were quite low. It is clear that effective policies are going to have to make careful distinctions between environmental-risk indicators and environmental-risk mechanisms. Poverty and social disadvantage predispose to a range of environmental hazards and are indeed effective indicators for psychosocial risk, but they do not seem to be the variables that directly mediate that risk.

Second, there is the somewhat different enterprise of trying to prepare people better for facing psychosocial stress and adversity. Thus, in recent years, there has been increasing interest in the factors involved in enabling people to show psychosocial resilience (Rutter, 1993), and most recently, there has been a concern to identify possible protective mechanisms. Thus, people have been concerned with what might be done to increase positive self-esteem and self-efficacy (Bandura, 1989). In that connection, it has seemed that the provision of close, harmonious relationships and opportunities for success, accomplishments, and achievements may be helpful (Garmezy, 1985; Rutter, 1992). Once more, this seems a worthwhile endeavor, but of course, the children most at psychosocial risk are just the ones least likely to have such good relationships and opportunities for success.

The third approach focuses on what may be done at the time that people experience stress and adversity. Over the last few decades, there are many examples of well-documented programs that were designed to improve people's social problem-solving strategies (Pellegrini, 1994) and styles of coping with stress situations (Compas, 1995; Consortium on the School-Based Promotion of Social Competence, 1994). There is some evidence that these interventions may be effective. Accordingly, the further development and application of these methods are well warranted. Nevertheless, these personalized interventions are inevitably rather labor intensive, and it would be unrealistic to rely on them as the main method for reducing the psychopathology associated with psychosocial risk mechanisms.

Although seldom studied, or even considered, up to now, a fourth approach requires our attention. One of the very striking features of psychosocial risks is that they are not evenly distributed across the population. Some people grow up in generally advantageous conditions, encountering remarkably little in the way of serious psychosocial hazards. By contrast, others experience a seemingly never ending series of stressors and adversities. It is clear that we need to determine the mechanisms and processes that underlie individual differences in exposure to psychosocial risks (Rutter, 1994b). In the last few years, behavior geneticists have stimulated interest in this question by raising the possibility that genetic influences may play a substantial role in determining, or at least influencing, the environments that people experience (Plomin, 1994; Plomin & Bergeman, 1991; Scarr, 1992; Scarr & McCartney, 1983). They have pointed to the evidence that there are important person–environment correlations and have gone on to suggest that, because people shape and select their environments, genetic forces may underlie much of the variation in environmental-risk exposure. Unfortunately, in our view, some developmentalists have responded to these challenging suggestions with feelings of outrage, as if the very suggestion undermined attempts to improve life circumstances for the many children who continue to be reared in appalling conditions (Baumrind, 1993). This defensive reaction is mistaken on several different counts.

First, it is important to appreciate that the origins of a risk factor and the mode of operation of the risk mechanism have no necessary connection with one another (Rutter, 1986; Rutter, Simonoff, & Silberg, 1993).

Thus, for example, people choose to smoke cigarettes for reasons that reflect social habits, opportunities, and personality features, among other influences. Nevertheless, the risk for lung cancer has nothing to do with any of those causal factors; rather, it derives from the carcinogenic effect of the tars that are present in the inhaled smoke. In the same way, even if it were to be established that individual differences in psychosocial-risk exposure were entirely genetically determined (which is, of course, extremely unlikely) that would not necessarily mean at all that the psychosocial risks are not environmentally mediated with respect to causation of psychopathology.

Second, if we are to intervene effectively, it is crucial that we understand how environmental risks arise. The causal chain of circumstances that give rise to psychosocial risks needs to be studied and understood just as much as the processes and mechanisms by which such risks predispose to psychopathology. If it turns out that genetic factors play an important part in that causal chain, so be it. However, even if that were the case, it does not necessarily mean that interruption of the chain is not open to environmental manipulation. Much depends on the ways in which the genetic factors operate (Rutter, 1994a). As medical geneticists have pointed out recently (Weatherall, 1992), much of the importance of modern genetic research, which uses molecular genetic techniques, is likely to lie in the identification and understanding of environmental-risk mechanisms. That is already happening, for example, in the field of ischemic heart disease, and there is no reason to suppose that psychopathology is likely to prove an exception to this general principle.

Third, however, we need to appreciate that there is very little direct evidence so far that genetic factors in fact do play a major role in the way people shape and select environments (Plomin, 1994). Moreover, it is even more important to recognize that genetic factors are merely one of a much larger series of possible explanations for individual differences in environmental-risk exposure (Rutter, 1991b). Behavior geneticists have done the field a service in raising the question, but it is crucial that the search for explanations extend much more broadly than the identification of the role of genetic factors.

SOME POSSIBLE EXPLANATIONS FOR INDIVIDUAL DIFFERENCES IN ENVIRONMENTAL-RISK EXPOSURE

Exhibit 1 summarizes some of the broad domains of possible mechanisms that need to be considered when examining factors that may underlie individual differences in environmental-risk exposure. The list is not meant to be exhaustive, but rather, it is designed to serve as a reminder of the rather heterogeneous ways in which such individual differences could arise. For example, there is extensive evidence of differences between geographical areas in rates of crime (Reiss, 1995; Rutter & Giller, 1983). The main emphasis in this field of research has been a consideration of what factors in the environment predispose a person to crime. However, with respect to the topic of individual differences in environmental-risk exposure, it is equally relevant that people who live in high-crime areas are going to be much more likely to be victims of mugging, burglary, and vandalism of their property. Similarly, it is well established that there are important occupational differences in job security and stress levels (Rutter & Madge, 1976). Moreover, the research of investigators such as Marmot et al. (1991) has gone on to show that these job-related differences in stress have important implications for physical health. People's level of income, too, is likely to have important consequences in relation to the stresses associated with difficulties in housing, the accumulation of debts, and the many other problems that are associated with reliance on benefits and an income that is barely sufficient for life's needs.

Past experiences also play an important role in determining later experiences. For example, becoming a teenage mother is likely to have adverse economic consequences and will also reduce the chances of a stable, harmonious marriage (Furstenberg, Brooks-Gunn, & Morgan, 1987). People's ethnic background may be important because, regrettably, racial discrimination remains all too prevalent in spite of the fact that discriminatory practices are illegal (C. Brown, 1984). A person's family is likely to be important insofar as the size of the family with which people remain in contact, and the proportion of mentally or physically ill or socially deviant members of that family will influence the stresses that impinge on the in-

66

Exhibit 1

Some Possible Factors Influencing Individual Differences in Environmental-Risk Exposure

GEOGRAPHY e.g., area differences in crime rates

JOB e.g., occupational differences in insecurity and stress level

INCOME e.g., consequences of poverty for housing, debts

PAST EXPERIENCES e.g., teenage pregnancy

ETHNICITY e.g., racial discrimination

FAMILY e.g., size of family and proportion of sick or deviant members

SOCIAL NETWORK e.g., size of network and proportion of sick or deviant members

PERSONAL e.g., disruptive effects of antisocial behavior

---

dividual. In the same sort of way, the size and characteristics of a person's extrafamilial social network are relevant. As Belle (1982) pointed out, being part of a social network can be a mixed blessing. Potentially, a social network is, of course, a source of social support, but in addition, it is likely to mean that there are more individuals who may turn to the person at times of their own stress and difficulties. Finally, personal characteristics are going to be influential because they will play a part in shaping the characteristics of people's interpersonal interactions and the environments that people encounter. Thus, many years ago, Robins (1966) showed that antisocial boys had a much increased risk of experiencing repeated divorce, multiple changes of jobs, prolonged periods of unemployment, and a lack of personal friendships. In one sense, these stressors were part of their continuing personality disturbance. However, they also constitute just the sort of environmental stressors that have been shown to be important in the precipitation of new psychiatric disorders, such as depression.

The topic of individual differences in environmental-risk exposure is an important one. It is apparent from this listing of some of the key possible factors influencing such individual differences that an understanding of the processes involved may well be crucially important in the planning of effective strategies of intervention. In the remainder of this chapter, we refer to two recent studies that exemplify how the question may be investigated. Both focus on the role of personal characteristics, but somewhat similar research strategies could equally well be used to investigate some of the broader societal factors outlined as likely to be also relevant.

CHILDHOOD BEHAVIOR AND STRESS EXPERIENCE IN ADULT LIFE

The first study, undertaken by Champion and her colleagues (Champion, Goodall, & Rutter, in press), was based on a sample of 10-year-old children who attended Local Authority schools in 1970 in a former Inner London borough. The details of the methodology of this epidemiological study, originally designed for comparison with a study done on the Isle of Wight, were described in a series of articles at the time (Berger, Yule, & Rutter, 1975; Rutter, Cox, et al., 1975; Rutter, Yule, et al., 1975). In brief, however, teacher questionnaires (Rutter, 1967) were completed for all children, and the parents were interviewed by means of standardized, investigator-based techniques. For present purposes, the sample was subdivided into those with a teacher questionnaire score of 9 or greater (hereafter referred to as the *behaviorally disturbed* group) and those with scores below the cutoff of 9 (the *nondisturbed* group).

The sample was recontacted when they were in their late 20s. This involved two phases of data collection, undertaken by two separate sets of investigators. The first assessed psychosocial functioning in a range of different domains (e.g., work, marriage, friendships) together with family environmental characteristics (e.g., discord, overcrowding) from childhood onward. The second, conducted between 6 and 12 months after the first, provided a detailed assessment of acute life events (e.g., bereavement or being made redundant) and chronic psychosocial difficulties (e.g., tensions with neighbors) over the 5-year period preceding the interview.

Champion et al. (in press) used the Brown and Harris (1978) Life Events and Difficulties Schedule (LEDS). This is a semistructured interview that provides a systematic coverage of a wide range of stress experiences, each of which is asked about in detail to obtain information, not only on the nature of the event but also on its meaning in the person's own social context. Using a strict set of criteria, each event was rated for long-term contextual threat by a panel trained in the Brown and Harris methods. However, in addition, events were also rated in terms of their "objective" severity, irrespective of social context. Thus, the death of someone close, involuntary loss of a job, divorce, and the experience of assault were all classified as severe stressors. As well as information on stress experiences, systematic data were obtained on the subjects' current social relationships and on the extent to which they planned key life transitions. Complete interview data were available for the majority of the sample, but for a proportion, information was obtained by means of a questionnaire-style structured interview and, in a very few cases, by a mailed questionnaire. In all analyses, careful checks were undertaken to determine if variations in sources of data could have influenced the findings.

The results indicated that the individuals who had shown emotional or behavioral disturbance at 10 years of age experienced twice the rate of severe negative events carrying long-term contextual threat. This was so for all severe events, but as Figure 1 shows, the increased rate included the particularly severe events found by Brown and Harris (1978) as most likely to provoke the onset of psychiatric disorder. However, the increased rate of stressors did not apply to mild events, and it did not apply to the occurrence of challenging, or potentially stressful, normative life transitions. Rather, the increased rate of negative life events was confined to those that were particularly likely to carry long-term contextual threat and, hence, were of a type most likely to provoke psychiatric disorder in adult life.

One of the important methodological advances in the study of the role of life events in the etiology of psychiatric disorder constituted the distinction between events that were independent of a disorder (i.e., they were of a kind that made it quite unlikely that they could stem from the behavioral change associated with the disorder) and those that were non-

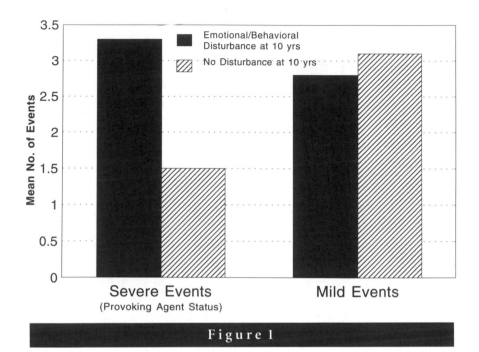

Figure 1

Emotional/behavioral disturbance at 10 years and negative life events in early adult life.

independent. We made a similar distinction, but also broadened the concept of independence to include any type of actions undertaken by the person, irrespective of whether they were brought about by a psychiatric disorder. Thus, a marital quarrel would be regarded as nonindependent, but the death of a loved one from cancer would be regarded as independent. Perhaps somewhat surprisingly, the increased rate of negative life events in adult life that followed emotional or behavioral disturbance at age 10 applied in equal degree to events that were independent of the person and those that were dependent on that person's actions (see Figure 2). The finding is important in its emphasis that in understanding how people's behavior influences their later life experiences, it will be necessary to look beyond mechanisms concerned with the direct provoking of stress experiences (as, e.g., through a propensity to behave in socially disruptive ways).

The next issue concerned the question of whether the increased rate of acute life events arose as a consequence of an increased occurrence of negative experiences or, rather, as an increased likelihood that such experiences would carry long-term threat because of the particular social context within which they occurred. Figure 3 shows the contrast between events that were classified as severe on an objective classification and events that were classified as severe only by virtue of their social context. The findings are clear-cut in indicating that the increase applied in equal degree to events of both kinds. In other words, it seemed that there was both an increased occurrence of objective events and an increased liability for them to be rated as stressful because of the particular social context within which they occurred.

One key aspect of social context, of course, concerns the presence of longer term psychosocial adversities or difficulties. Accordingly, the two groups were compared on the rate of such ongoing difficulties in adult life. Figure 4 shows that the individuals who had exhibited emotional or behavioral disturbance at age 10 were several times as likely as the nondisturbed individuals to have experienced severe psychosocial difficulties in

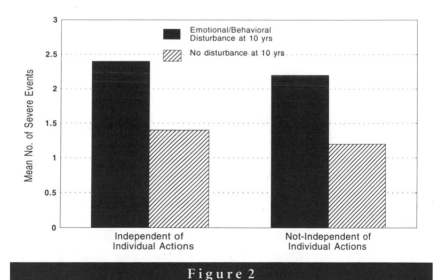

Figure 2

Emotional/behavioral disturbance at 10 years and severely negative events in early adult life, according to independence from individual actions.

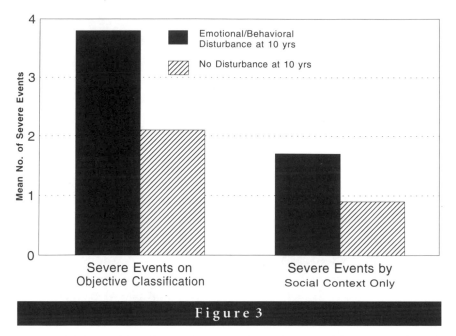

Figure 3

Emotional/behavioral disturbance at 10 years and severely negative life events in early adult life, as influenced by social context.

the 5 years before the follow-up interview in their late 20s. Again, as with acute events, this difference applied only to severe difficulties, there being no increase in the rate of mild difficulties. The pattern was closely comparable in men and women.

As Figure 5 indicates, this increased rate of severe ongoing psychosocial difficulties constituted the key to the increased rate of acutely negative life events. Emotional or behavioral disturbance at age 10 was associated with an increase in severe events only when the events were linked to a chronic difficulty. There was no increase in the rate of severe events that occurred outside that context. In some cases, the acute events arose fairly directly out of the difficulty (e.g., as when a spouse walked out after a quarrel that followed chronic marital discord), but often, the connections were of a much more indirect kind. In many cases, both the acute events and the chronic difficulties were associated with the person's family of origin, and it was clear that many people were part of families in which problems and clashes of various kinds arose in great abundance. Nevertheless, this was only part of the story because the increased rate of events and difficulties applied at least as much to those that were not associated with the family of origin. That is, they involved friends, neighbors, work colleagues, or strangers. However, there was a strong and statistically significant tendency for negative experiences to be particularly frequent in those who lacked a confiding relationship with a cohabiting partner.

One possible mechanism for the increased rate of events and difficulties was that the people who had exhibited emotional or behavioral disturbance at age 10 might be more likely to be living in social disadvantage or residing in high-crime areas in adult life than those who were nondisturbed at age 10. There was some trend in that direction with respect to social disadvantage, but this did not account for the between-groups difference in severe events or difficulties.

Up to this point, behavioral disturbance has been considered without reference to any distinction according to the type of disturbance shown

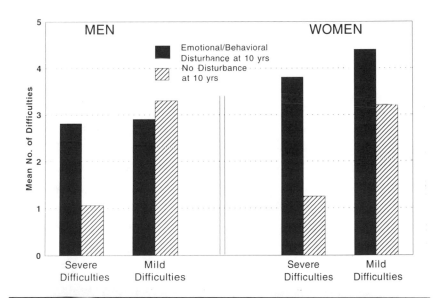

Figure 4

Emotional/behavioral disturbance at 10 years and chronic difficulties in early adult life.

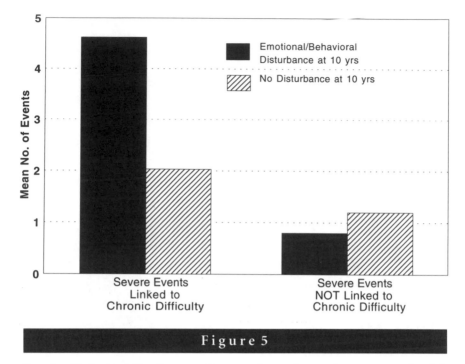

Figure 5

Emotional/behavioral disturbance at 10 years and severely negative events in early adult life, according to presence of chronic difficulties.

in childhood. Figure 6 (which presents the findings for women only, because the diagnostic patterns differed by gender) indicates that the increased rate of negative life events and difficulties was more strongly associated with disturbance of a conduct disorder type than when it mainly involved emotional disturbance of one kind or another. However, there was a significant increase with the latter type of disturbance as well. If the role of childhood behavior in the determination of individual differences in environmental-risk exposure is to be useful in devising effective prevention strategies, it is crucial to find out the factors involved in the relevant developmental processes. That aspect of the study is still underway, but already it is clear that a person's tendency to show planning in relation to key life transitions, choices, and challenges is most important. Figure 7 shows that mean number of severe difficulties was over twice as great in those who lacked planning as in those who showed a definite tendency

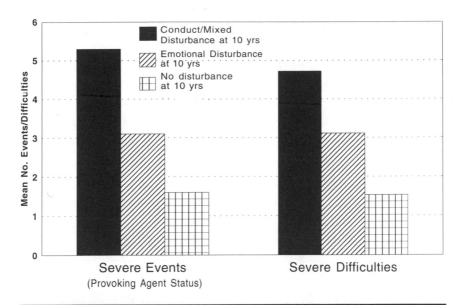

Figure 6

Severe events and difficulties in early adult life and type of disturbance at 10 years (females only).

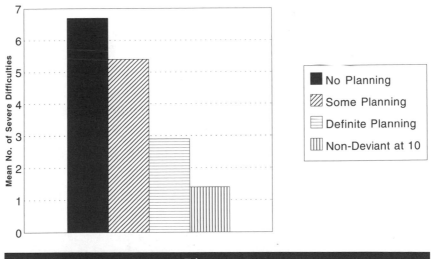

Figure 7

Severe difficulties and planning in domain of committed relationships (females only with investment in committed relationships).

to exert planning in the domain of committed relationships; the same difference applied to severely negative acute life events.

In summary, the findings of this long-term prospective study indicate that children who showed either emotional or conduct problems at age 10 years were twice as likely as those who did not have such problems to experience severely negative life events in the context of ongoing difficulties some 20 years later. It is evident that in some fashion, people behave in ways that shape or select their environments. Thus, we found that severe difficulties were twice as frequent in individuals who tended not to plan their lives when younger. As Elder (chapter 4) points out, people make choices among options that become the building blocks of their evolving life course. Even turning points may come about because individuals act in a manner that either creates or builds on opportunities (see Clausen, chapter 11). As yet, we know remarkably little about the proximal processes (the importance of which is a key feature in Bronfenbrenner and Ceci's, 1994, discussion of the interplay between nature and nurture) that are involved in the shaping and selecting of environments. However, the fact that the association between childhood behavior and negative experiences 20 years later applied to events that were independent of the person's own actions means that the answer cannot be confined to a direct tendency to provoke negative reactions from other people, although that may be part of the story.

CHILDHOOD CONDUCT DISORDER AND ASSORTATIVE PAIRING

The second study focused not on stressors as a whole, but rather on the specific issue of the childhood antecedents of marriage to a behaviorally deviant spouse (Quinton, Pickles, Maughan, & Rutter, 1993). It is a well-replicated research finding that a discordant marriage to a deviant partner (meaning someone who has shown antisocial behavior or drug problems) constitutes an important environmental-risk factor in early adult life and that, conversely, a harmonious marriage with a nondeviant partner exerts a substantial protective influence for adults from a high-risk background or who have themselves shown conduct disorders in child-hood (Laub & Sampson, 1993; Quinton & Rutter, 1988; Sampson & Laub, 1993). The question to be addressed, then, is, what are the pathways by which people end up with a deviant or nondeviant partner?

We used three samples: (a) the same general-population random sam-ple of Inner London 10-year-olds, studied by Maughan and her colleagues, that was used in the first study (Rutter, Cox, et al., 1975); (b) a sample of individuals from Inner London who had been reared in group foster homes, who had been studied by Quinton and his colleagues (Quinton & Rutter, 1988; Rutter, Quinton, & Hill, 1990); and (c) the quasi-random comparison sample for that group (Quinton et al., 1993; Quinton & Rut-ter, 1988; Rutter et al., 1990). Teacher questionnaires (Rutter, 1967) had been available for all samples during their childhood, and all groups were interviewed in their mid-20s with the same standardized, investigator-based interviewing methodology.

It is clear from Figure 8 that there was a very marked tendency for in-dividuals with conduct disorder in childhood to have first cohabiting partners who were deviant in terms of antisocial behavior, persistent drug or alcohol misuse, or marked problems in interpersonal relationships. In

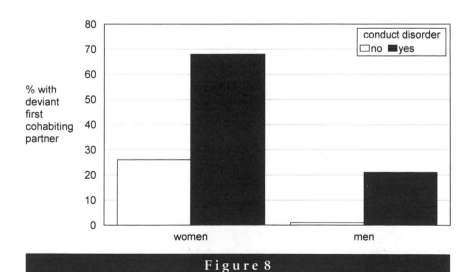

Figure 8

Assortative mating for conduct disorder (combined samples).

this figure, childhood conduct disorder was assessed on the basis of both prospective and retrospective measures. The addition of the latter was helpful in ensuring a measure of conduct disturbance that spanned the years of childhood and adolescence, the contemporaneous measure being available only at one point in time. However, there was still a marked tendency for assortment on the basis of deviance, if the prospective measure alone was used. Because antisocial behavior and drug problems are substantially more frequent in males than in females, women were more likely than men to have a deviant spouse. The main effect on assortment stemmed from conduct disorder in childhood, but there was some slight additional effect deriving from having been reared in an institution.

Sometimes assortative mating is considered as if it necessarily represented a deliberate choice to have a partner of similar characteristics, in this case, marked antisocial and interpersonal difficulties. However, it is clear that many other factors determine whom one chooses to partner (Engfer, Walper, & Rutter, 1994). Thus, the partner is likely to be selected from the social group with which the individual associates. To examine the extent to which this might be the case, we assessed the presence of persistent or pervasive deviance in a person's peer group during the few years after they left school at the age of 16. Deviance was rated if peers were involved in substance abuse, property crimes, or fighting, either persistently or in more than one of these areas. The data clearly indicate that girls who were part of a deviant peer group were very much more likely than other girls to have a deviant spouse (see Figure 9). The effect in males was much weaker.

The next question that had to be considered was what led some individuals to join a deviant peer group, and what protected other individuals from so doing. In the case of girls, the findings (see Figure 10) showed that a disposition to show forethought or planning had a substantial and significant effect in making it much less likely that girls would join a deviant peer group. In order that our measure of planning should be substantively independent from the other variables, it was restricted to planning for work, meaning that the person had given thought to his or her

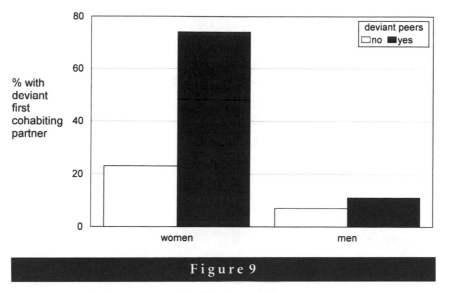

Figure 9

Deviant peers and deviant spouses (combined samples).

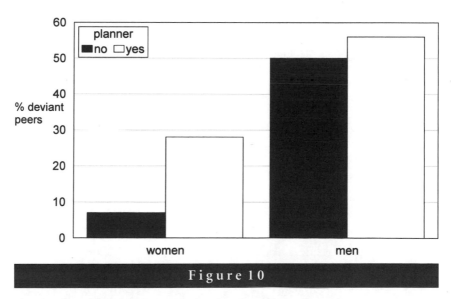

Figure 10

Planning for work and deviant peers (combined samples).

subsequent occupational career in a realistic and practical way (but had not necessarily taken any active steps toward its realization). Interestingly, planning did not have the same beneficial effect in males.

To take delineation of the pathways leading to a deviant spouse further back in the course of development, we examined a range of other variables. Not surprisingly, as Figure 11 shows, conduct disorder was quite strongly associated with a lack of planning for work, especially among women. This was to be expected because antisocial behavior often involves an impulsive quality of living for the moment, without particular concern for the longer term future. Nevertheless, this tendency involved quite a few exceptions, particularly in males, so the question arose as to what other variables might be relevant.

One possible influence concerned the family in which the individuals were living during early adolescence. This was assessed in terms of whether a person was living in a harmonious family or a discordant family or was not in a family setting at all (the last being a common situation among the institution-reared subjects). In both sexes, a lack of family harmony was associated with conduct disorder (see Figure 12). Conduct disorder

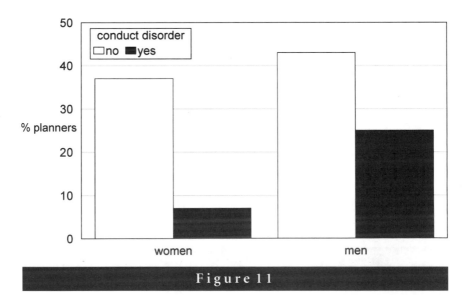

Figure 11

Conduct disorder and planning for work (combined samples).

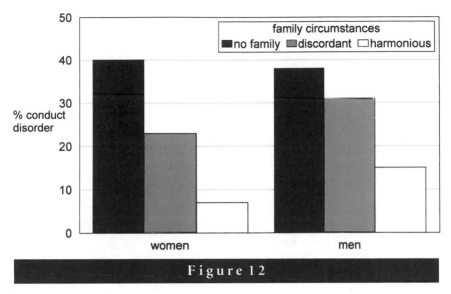

Figure 12

Family harmony and conduct disorder (combined samples).

was most frequent, however, in those individuals not living in a family setting, a reflection of the particularly high rate of conduct problems in the institution-reared group.

In men, but not women, family harmony was quite strongly associated with a tendency to show planning with respect to work and careers (see Figure 13). Why harmonious family relationships were not protective with respect to a planning tendency in girls was not clear. Nevertheless, it was evident that there needed to be a search for other possible influences.

It turned out that positive school experiences were the most important features predisposing females to planning for work. Figure 14 is based on the institution-reared sample and its comparison group, only because the measure of positive school experiences was rather different in the epidemiological sample of individuals followed from age 10. In this connection, *positive school experiences* referred to a range of domains of school life, including sports, arts and crafts, music, social relationships, and positions of responsibility within the school, as well as academic achievements. In fact, in these socially disadvantaged samples, scholastic success was a relatively uncommon experience.

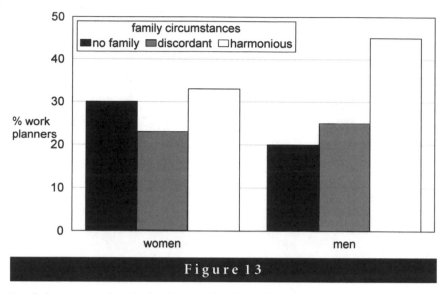

Family harmony and work planning (combined samples).

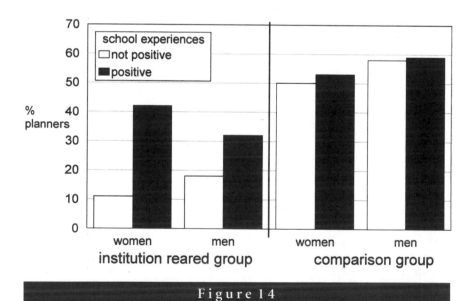

Positive school experiences and work planning (institution-reared study).

A further feature concerned the occurrence of a teenage pregnancy. As shown in Figure 15, teenage pregnancy made it substantially more likely that the first cohabitation would be with a deviant partner.

In the data presented so far, the comparisons have all concerned univariate analyses of one kind or another. However, it was obvious that there was major overlap among the different variables, so multivariate analyses were essential. In addition, it was important to examine the possibility of interaction effects. The results were surprisingly clear-cut. For simplicity of presentation, however, the data are presented graphically for women only, because the overall risk of having a deviant partner was so much greater for them.

Figure 16 shows the proportion of women who had not lived with a deviant partner. The findings are presented in the form of a survival analysis from age 14 to 20 years, with respect to the presence of conduct disorder, planning, and deviant peers. The graph was plotted with respect to that proportion of the sample who had at least one risk factor. Females without conduct disorder or deviant peers, but not showing planning for

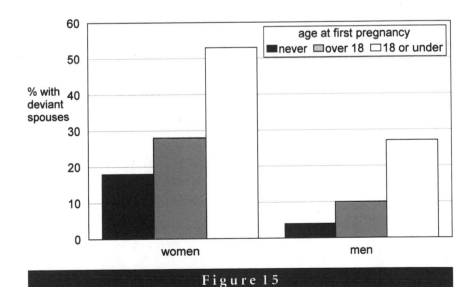

Figure 15

Teenage pregnancy and deviant spouse (combined samples).

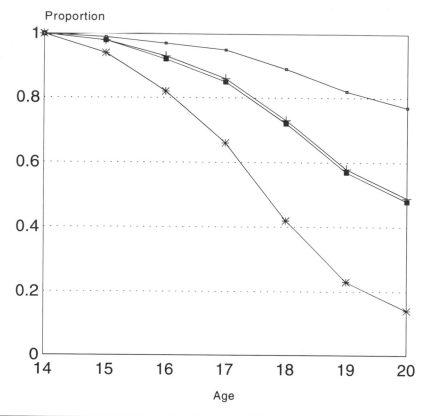

CD=conduct disorder, PL=planner,DP=deviant peers
- CD-,PL-,DP-   + CD+,PL-,DP-
* CD+,PL-,DP+   ■ CD+,PL+,DP+

Figure 16

Proportion of women who had not lived with a deviant man by age, conduct disorder, planning, and deviant peers.

work, had the lowest risk. At the other extreme, those with conduct disorder and deviant peers and a lack of planning had the highest risk; 80% cohabited with a deviant man before the age of 20.

Figure 17 gives a graphical representation of the magnitude of the ef-

Paths of Women to Deviant Men

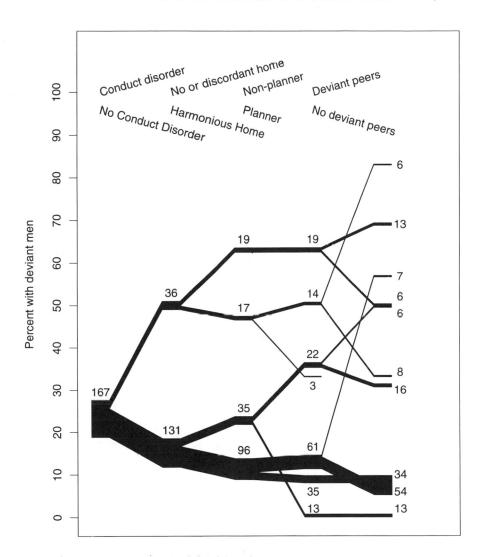

Figure 17

Paths of women to deviant male partners. Frequencies given by numbers and line width.

fects of risk and protective factors in terms of variables arranged as they occurred in time: conduct disorder, quality of home life, planning, and deviant peers. The effect of each factor is shown by the branching of the path at the appropriate point, and the breadth of the lines indicates the size of the proportion of the sample involved in each case. The variables with a frequency of 2 or less are not shown on the diagram. Three main features stand out from the findings. First, the proportions ending up with deviant partners are consistent for all paths, with a protective context or behavior decreasing the probability and a risk factor increasing it. Second, individuals showing conduct disorder experienced disproportionately few of the protective factors. Third, however, the effects of the risk and protective factors were quite strong in all cases for the individuals who experienced them.

A logistic regression analysis was used to model the overall pattern of effects. This differed from the earlier analyses in extending to the presence of marital support, not just the presence of a deviant spouse. This end point was chosen because the literature suggests that this constitutes the most important variable influencing adult social functioning (Laub & Sampson, 1993; Sampson & Laub, 1993). In both sexes, there were substantial protective effects from planning and from a harmonious family, although these were stronger for women than for men. There was an interaction between the two variables by which each had a stronger effect when the other was absent. It was also apparent that an institutional rearing, although not strongly associated with any of the intermediate steps in the chain, did constitute a longer term risk factor for unsupportive intimate relationships. Possibly, this arose because an institutional rearing left people with fewer interpersonal skills for eliciting support; because they were less able to terminate unsatisfactory relationships; and perhaps because they tended to have partners who, though not deviant in the severe sense considered here, nevertheless lacked strengths that were important in a marital relationship.

On the whole, the overall pattern of associations was broadly similar for men and for women, but there were some important differences. For females, the route to marital support lay primarily through the gaining of a first partner who was nondeviant. The risk for conduct-disordered girls lay in the fact that their social group contained so many deviant males. Protection was afforded by stable, harmonious families; by nondeviant peers; and, failing those, by a planning disposition. Conduct-disordered girls frequently lacked those protections.

For men, because there were fewer deviant girls, the risk from poor choices was lower. Conduct-disordered boys, like girls, were more likely to choose deviant first partners, but this applied to a smaller proportion. For men, the main predictors of a lack of marital support involved an institutional rearing and having been a member of a deviant peer group. For them, it may be that the risk operated primarily through the perpetuation of a deviant lifestyle, as reflected in the continuing influence of the peer group, rather than through the direct effects of conduct problems or early poor choices of partner. It appeared that the continuing effect of the peer group was not simply a reflection of the individual's own conduct disorder.

In summary, the findings of this second long-term follow-up study showed that conduct disorder in childhood was associated with a markedly increased tendency some years later to marry (or live with) someone who showed similar antisocial behavior. However, a more detailed analysis of the life course showed that this tendency depended on a complex series of indirect chain effects. Positive school experiences, a tendency to exert planning in dealing with life choices, a lack of a deviant peer group, and a harmonious family environment all made this negative assortative pairing and subsequent marital discord or breakdown less likely. The process starts with the presence of conduct disorder in childhood, but the carryforward of effects into the next generation is dependent on all sorts of intervening circumstances, some of which are outside the individual's control but many of which are, at least partially, open to influence. The message is much the same as in Moen and Erickson's transgenerational approach to resilience (chapter 6): Individuals have an active role in shaping their own life course. As Cairns and Cairns note (chapter 12), peer groups play a key role in this process. Young people choose the groups they join, but having formed part of some group, their subsequent behavior is influenced by social group processes (see Rowe, Woulbroun, & Gulley, 1994). In many respects, the patterns of findings in males and females were similar, but there were some differences. Doubtless, this in part reflects the differences between girls and boys in their social systems and in the ways in which they respond to such systems (see Maccoby, chapter 10).

DISCUSSION

Two main conclusions may be drawn from the findings available so far from these two studies. First, there are surprisingly strong associations between people's behavior in childhood and their experience of psychosocial environmental-risk factors in adult life. The first study showed this with respect to a range of acute and chronic psychosocial stressors and adversities, and the second did so with respect to the presence of a deviant spouse and the lack of marital support in early adult life. To a remarkable extent, the psychosocial factors in adult life that carry a major risk for psychiatric disorders are predictable on the basis of people's behavior and life circumstances in childhood and adolescence. If we are to intervene successfully to prevent psychiatric disorders, it is necessary that we accept the reality of this relative predictability of adult experiences and also that we understand the mechanisms by which this comes about.

In that connection, however, the second main conclusion is that the mechanisms are likely to be multiple in most cases and that the chain of links over time are often indirect, albeit powerful, when the cumulative effects of the chain as a whole are considered. Because the overall connection between childhood behavior and adverse experiences in adult life is direct only to a limited extent, there are many potential opportunities for breaking this chain if the right actions are taken at the right time.

In our introduction, we noted that one cause for the interest in this overall topic stemmed from behavior geneticists' suggestion that genetic factors might play an important role in the shaping and selecting of environments. In studies not considered here, this possibility is being investigated, but the findings are not yet available. The strong, indirect chain effects from the two studies described here suggest that, although genetic factors may well play a part, it is unlikely that they will prove to be strongly determinative. However, it should be emphasized that there is a long way to go before there can be an adequate delineation of the developmental mechanisms involved in connections between childhood behavior and adult life experiences.

In conclusion, it is evident that our findings provide strong support for Bronfenbrenner's emphasis on the need to consider development in terms of ongoing interactions and transactions between individuals and their environments. Until recently, this message has been applied mainly to an understanding of the mechanisms involved in the various ways in which environments influence development. It is apparent that there is a similar need to gain a better appreciation of the ways in which individuals act to shape and select the environments that, in turn, impinge and influence their own later behavior. At the moment, we lack any detailed understanding of the mechanisms involved. Bronfenbrenner and Ceci (1994) emphasized the great need to investigate these proximal processes that are concerned in the interplay between persons and their environments. The research agenda has been set, and it only remains to take up the challenge!

REFERENCES

Bandura, A. (1989). Regulation of cognitive processes through perceived self-efficacy. *Developmental Psychology, 25,* 729–735.

Baumrind, D. (1993). The average expectable environment is not good enough: A response to Scarr. *Child Development, 64,* 1299–1317.

Belle, D. (Ed.). (1982). *Lives in stress: Women and depression.* Beverly Hills, CA: Sage.

Berger, M., Yule, W., & Rutter, M. (1975). Attainment and adjustment in two geographical areas: II. The prevalence of specific reading retardation. *British Journal of Psychiatry, 126,* 493–509.

Bronfenbrenner, U. (1979). *The ecology of human development: Experiments by nature and design.* Cambridge, MA: Harvard University Press.

Bronfenbrenner, U. (1989). Ecological systems theory. In R. Vasta (Ed.), *Annals of child development: A research annual* (Vol. 6, pp. 185–246). Greenwich, CT: JAI Press.

Bronfenbrenner, U., & Ceci, S. J. (1994). Nature–nurture reconceptualized in developmental perspective: A bioecological model. *Psychological Review, 101,* 568–586.

Bronfenbrenner, U., & Crouter, A. C. (1983). The evolution of environmental models in developmental research. In W. Kessen (Ed.), *History, theory, and methods: Vol. 1. Mussen's handbook of child psychology* (4th ed., pp. 357–414). New York: Wiley.

Brown, C. (1984). *Black and White Britain: The third PSI survey.* London: Heinemann.

Brown, G. W., & Harris, T. O. (1978). *Social origins of depression: A study of psychiatric disorder in women.* London: Tavistock.

Brown, G. W., & Harris, T. O. (1989). *Life events and illness.* New York: Guilford Press.

Champion, L., Goodall, G., & Rutter, M. (in press). The relationship between behaviour problems in childhood and acute and chronic stressors in early adult life: A twenty year follow-up of a sample of London school children. *Psychological Medicine.*

Compas, B. (1995). Promoting successful coping during adolescence. In M. Rutter (Ed.), *Psychosocial disturbances in young people: Challenges for prevention* (pp. 247–273). Cambridge, England: Cambridge University Press.

Consortium on the School-Based Promotion of Social Competence. (1994). The school-based promotion of social competence: Theory, research, practice, and policy. In R. Haggerty, L. R. Sherrod, N. Garmezy, & M. Rutter (Eds.), *Stress, risk and resilience in children and adolescents: Processes, mechanisms, and intervention* (pp. 268–316). New York: Cambridge University Press.

Engfer, A., Walper, S., & Rutter, M. (1994). Individual characteristics as a force in development. In M. Rutter & D. Hay (Eds.), *Development through life: A handbook for clinicians* (pp. 79–111). Oxford, England: Blackwell Scientific.

Furstenberg, F. F., Jr., Brooks-Gunn, J., & Morgan, S. P. (1987). *Adolescent mothers in later life.* Cambridge, England: Cambridge University Press.

Garmezy, N. (1985). Stress-resistant children: The search for protective factors. In J. E. Stevenson (Ed.), *Recent research in developmental psychopathology* (pp. 213–234). Oxford, England: Pergamon Press.

Garmezy, N., & Masten, A. (1994). Chronic adversities. In M. Rutter, E. Taylor, & L. Hersov (Eds.), *Child and adolescent psychiatry: Modern approaches* (3rd ed., pp. 191–208). Oxford, England: Blackwell Scientific.

Goodyer, I. M. (1990). *Life experiences, development and childhood psychopathology.* Chichester, England: Wiley.

Graham, P. (1994). Prevention. In M. Rutter, E. Taylor, & L. Hersov (Eds.), *Child and adolescent psychiatry: Modern approaches* (3rd ed., pp. 815–828). Oxford, England: Blackwell Scientific.

Laub, J. H., & Sampson, R. J. (1993). Turning points in the life course: Why change matters to the study of crime. *Criminology, 31,* 301–325.

Marmot, M. G., Smith, G. D., Stansfeld, S., Patel, C., North, F., Head, J., White, I., Brunner, E., & Feeney, A. (1991). Health inequalities among British civil servants: The Whitehall II study. *Epidemiology, 337,* 1387–1393.

Pellegrini, D. (1994). Training in interpersonal cognitive problem-solving. In M. Rutter, E. Taylor, & L. Hersov (Eds.), *Child and adolescent psychiatry: Modern approaches* (3rd ed., pp. 829–843). Oxford, England: Blackwell Scientific.

Plomin, R. (1994). *Genetics and experience.* Newbury Park, CA: Sage.

Plomin, R., & Bergeman, C. S. (1991). The nature of nurture: Genetic influence on "environmental" measures. *Behavioral and Brain Sciences, 14,* 373–386.

Quinton, D., Pickles, A., Maughan, B., & Rutter, M. (1993). Partners, peers and pathways: Assortative pairing and continuities in conduct disorder. *Development and Psychopathology, 5,* 763–783.

Quinton, D., & Rutter, M. (1988). *Parenting breakdown: The making and breaking of inter-generational links.* Aldershot, England: Avebury.

Reiss, A. (1995). Community influences on adolescent behaviour. In M. Rutter (Ed.), *Psychosocial disturbances in young people: Challenges for prevention* (pp. 305–332). Cambridge, England: Cambridge University Press.

Robins, L. (1966). *Deviant children grown up.* Baltimore: Williams & Wilkins.

Rowe, D. C., Woulbroun, J., & Gulley, B. L. (1994). Peers and friends as nonshared environmental influences. In E. M. Hetherington, D. Reiss, & R. Plomin (Eds.), *Separate social worlds of siblings* (pp. 159–173). Hillsdale, NJ: Erlbaum.

Rutter, M. (1967). A children's behaviour questionnaire for completion by teachers: Preliminary findings. *Journal of Child Psychology and Psychiatry, 8,* 1–11.

Rutter, M. (1982). Prevention of children's psychosocial disorders: Myth and substance. *Pediatrics, 70,* 883–894.

Rutter, M. (1985). Family and school influences on behavioural development. *Journal of Child Psychology and Psychiatry, 26,* 349–368.

Rutter, M. (1986). Meyerian psychobiology, personality development and the role of life experiences. *American Journal of Psychiatry, 143,* 1077–1087.

Rutter, M. (1991a). A fresh look at "maternal deprivation." In P. Bateson (Ed.), *Development and integration of behaviour* (pp. 331–374). Cambridge, England: Cambridge University Press.

Rutter, M. (1991b). Origins of nurture: It's not just effects on measures and it's not just effects of nature. *Behavioural Brain Sciences, 14,* 402–403.

Rutter, M. (1992). Psychosocial resilience and protective mechanisms. In J. Rolf, A. Masten, D. Cicchetti, K. Neuchterlein, & S. Weintraub (Eds.), *Risk and protective factors in the development of psychopathology* (pp. 181–214). New York: Cambridge University Press.

Rutter, M. (1993). Resilience: Some conceptual considerations. *Journal of Adolescent Health, 14,* 626–631.

Rutter, M. (1994a). Genetic knowledge and prevention of mental disorders. Background paper for P. J. Mrazek & R. J. Haggerty (Eds.), *Reducing risk factors for mental disorders: Research strategies for prevention.* Institute of Medicine, Committee for Prevention of Mental Disorders.

Rutter, M. (1994b). Stress research: Accomplishments and tasks ahead. In R. Haggerty, N. Garmezy, M. Rutter, & L. R. Sherrod (Eds.), *Stress, risk and resilience in children and adolescents: Processes, mechanisms and intervention* (pp. 354–385). New York: Cambridge University Press.

Rutter, M., Cox, A., Tupling, C., Berger, M., & Yule, W. (1975). Attainment and adjustment in two geographical areas: I. The prevalence of psychiatric disorders. *British Journal of Psychiatry, 126,* 493–509.

Rutter, M., & Giller, H. (1983). *Juvenile delinquency: Trends and perspectives.* Harmonsworth, Middlesex, England: Penguin Books.

Rutter, M., & Madge, N. (1976). *Cycles of disadvantage.* London: Heinemann.

Rutter, M., & Pickles, A. (1991). Person–environment interactions: Concepts, mechanisms and implications for data analysis. In T. D. Wachs & R. Plomin (Eds.), *Conceptualization and measurement of organism–environment interaction* (pp. 105–141). Washington, DC: American Psychological Association.

Rutter, M., Quinton, D., & Hill, J. (1990). Adult outcome of institution-reared children: Males and females compared. In L. Robins & M. Rutter (Eds.), *Straight and devious pathways from childhood* (pp. 135–157). Cambridge, England: Cambridge University Press.

Rutter, M., Simonoff, E., & Silberg, J. (1993). How informative are twin studies of child psychopathology? In T. J. Bouchard, Jr., & P. Propping (Eds.), *Twins as a tool of behaviour genetics* (pp. 179–194). Chichester, England: Wiley.

Rutter, M., & Smith, D. (Eds.). (1995). *Psychosocial disorders in young people: Time trends and their causes.* Chichester, England: Wiley.

Rutter, M., Yule, B., Quinton, D., Rowlands, O., Yule, W., & Berger, M. (1975). At-

tainment and adjustment in two geographical areas: III. Some factors accounting for area differences. *British Journal of Psychiatry, 126,* 520–533.

Sampson, R. J., & Laub, J. H. (1993). *Crime in the making: Pathways and turning
points through life.* Cambridge, MA: Harvard University Press.

Scarr, S. (1992). Developmental theories for the 1990s: Development and individual
differences. *Child Development, 63,* 1–19.

Scarr, S., & McCartney, K. (1983). How people make their own environments: A theory of genotype → environmental effects. *Child Development, 54,* 424–435.

Shaffer, D., Philips, I., Enver, N., Silverman, M., & Anthony, V. Q. (Eds.). (1989). *Prevention of psychiatric disorders in children and adolescents: The project of the
American Academy of Child and Adolescent Psychiatry* (OSAP Prevention Mono-
graph No. 2). Rockville, MD: U. S. Department of Health and Human Services,
Office for Substance Abuse Prevention.

Weatherall, D. (1992). *The Harveian oration: The role of nature and nurture in common diseases: Garrod's legacy.* London: The Royal College of Physicians.

Historical and Social Time

Historical and Social Time

Kurt Lüscher

The four chapters of Part Two can be read as testimonies to the search for a conceptualization of time that would be appropriate to the purposes of social science research. Indeed, Augustine's dictum is still popular wisdom, as it has been over the centuries: "What is time then? If nobody asks me, I know: but if I were desirous to explain it to one that should ask me, plainly I know not." Yet, during the last three or four decades, there has been progress in solving at least some of the puzzles of time, and it is not by mere chance that work in the field of human development has played a central role in this progress.

Perhaps the important first step was taken when social scientists began to think seriously of multiple times and tried to apply this idea in the interpretation of social phenomena and then operationalized it in their designs and instruments. Glen H. Elder, Jr., presents highly informative insights on this process in regard to the study of the life course. This study led ultimately to the formulation of what he correctly calls a new paradigm for the theory of socialization, even to a certain degree replacing this label. He is right in reminding us that early in this century classical authors, particularly W. I. Thomas, already related individual biographies to societal contexts and to historical events. Yet Thomas missed, as Elder correctly observes, the crucial point of attributing sociological, historical, and psychological meanings to age.

However, there is more to this, and Elder's matter-of-fact narrative of his own approach (in the very sense of *approach* as coming closer) to the Berkeley and Oakland data lets the reader reconstruct what was needed: a creative, new perspective by seeing together younger and older children, boys and girls, families from the lower and middle classes, all exposed to the same historical events, yet reacting differently and with different consequences in the course of their later lives. This perspective, which was at first Elder's own view of these different worlds revealed in the wealth of the data, was taken over and adapted by others and so developed into the life course paradigm. There are striking parallels to Urie Bronfenbrenner's thinking and style of working, which range far beyond his sensitivity to temporality.

Melvin L. Kohn's chapter is similar—precise and down-to-earth—and because of this quality a very illuminating account of his search for a solution to the same problem, namely, the reconstruction of the dynamic links between individual and society, or personality and social structure. His harvest consists, so to speak, of a new perspective on one of the oldest themes of sociology, that is, the meanings and the relevance of social class and social stratification. Deeply committed to the discipline of sociology, Kohn has not developed a new paradigm in the sense of giving birth to a new concept, but he has altered the conceptualization, in theory and research, of an enduring paradigm. He, too, invites the reader to reconstruct the flow of his thoughts, nicely embedded in a scholarly dialogue— in part real, in part figurative—with Urie Bronfenbrenner. Kohn demonstrates the values of a strong commitment to logic, to theory, and to methodology, being always open to new advances, especially to techniques of statistical inference. Each of these commitments must be fostered for and cultivated by itself, yet all three need to be balanced continuously. This research strategy makes it possible to describe and to explain the chain of relations extending from the person to the family, to occupational conditions, and to the structure of societies. Recent proof of the fruitfulness of this perspective provided is by Kohn's cross-national studies, which also analyze the impact of recent political transformations in eastern Europe. In doing so, he also relates social time to social space.

A key to the assessment of the temporal organization of society has always been the concept of generations. Karl Mannheim, in his classic essay on "The Problem of Generations," already pointed out that there are—at least—two basic connotations of time contained in this concept. At present, we can observe a renewed interest in the problem of generations. Nowadays, the primary focus is not on the generation as a collectivity of persons, but on the relations between individuals and the relations between groups belonging to two or more generations, for example, individuals and/or groups who, because of their age status, may have experienced the same social events differently. These relations seem crucial for the integration of all kinds of social systems, small and large, in a period of flourishing individualism. What accounts for the integrative power of age status? This question ultimately refers to the relevance of social time for society.

Phyllis Moen and Mary Ann Erickson, in their "Transgenerational Approach to Resilience," clarify a facet of this problem by means of a theoretically and empirically complex and innovative approach. They are able to confirm, in a subtly differentiated way, what they characterize as two basic lessons concerning the implications of early life experiences and the importance of contemporary circumstances. Moreover, they illustrate some of the specificities of mother–daughter relations, again reaching conclusions similar to those that have been reached in other intergenerational studies. However, what gives their study a special flavor and makes for its special value for our understanding of the interconnections between generational relations, personal development, and the development of sociability is their focus on resilience. With this focus, they are able to do more than merely point out the active role of the individual in shaping his or her own life course. Resilience is important not only for the development of the individual but also for society. Thus, resilience can be seen, as it is by the authors, as a resource. In this way, they deftly relate to a major concern of the ecology of human development (in the two senses of personal and societal development) and demonstrate the sensitizing qualities of both the ecological and the life course paradigms. In addition, the two authors show how these two paradigms can be fruitfully interwoven with each other.

Part Two is rounded out by Duane F. Alwin's chapter, which provides, among other things, an overview of the key concepts employed in attempts "to take time seriously" (p. 213). The chapter can thus be used as a reference guide to the major authors in the field and their writings. However, the author's main concern is still another topic that is genuine to the social study of time, namely, the contradictions, the paradoxes, and also the realities of stability and change. Although Alwin was not involved in personal exchanges with him, Urie Bronfenbrenner's ideas turned out to be of special value to Alwin, as Alwin confirms.

4

The Life Course Paradigm: Social Change and Individual Development

Glen H. Elder, Jr.

Human lives carry the imprint of their particular social worlds, and times of rapid change can bring personal disruption and incoherence of one kind or another. In his classic study, *The Little Community*, Robert Redfield (1955) observed that, in times of drastic change, the lifeway of "any one kind of person, man or woman, factory worker or business man, becomes within itself inconsistent and inconclusive . . . the ends of life become obscure" (p. 63). Robert and Helen Lynd (1937) discovered such change when they returned to Middletown during the Great Depression after observing this midwestern community during the prosperous 1920s:

> The city had been shaken for nearly six years by a catastrophe involving not only people's values, but, in the case of many, their very

This chapter was based on a program of research on the life course within the Carolina Consortium on Human Development and the Carolina Population Center. I am indebted to a great many colleagues who read and critiqued the chapter in manuscript form. But my debt is especially large to Urie Bronfenbrenner's mentoring across the years. I also acknowledge support by the National Institute of Mental Health (MH 41327, MH 43270, and MH 48165), a contract with the U.S. Army Research Institute, a grant from the Department of Veterans Affairs Merit Review program, research support from the John D. and Catherine T. MacArthur Foundation Program for Successful Adolescent Development Among Youth in High-Risk Settings, and a Research Scientist Award (MH 00567).

existence. . . . Virtually nobody in the community had been cushioned against the blow; the great knife of the depression had cut down impartially through the entire population, cleaving open the lives and hopes of rich as well as poor. The experience had been more nearly universal than any prolonged recent emotional experience in the city's history; it had approached in its elemental shock the primary experiences of birth and death. (Lynd & Lynd, 1937, p. 273)

The historical record of the twentieth century is filled with monumental changes of this kind: violent swings of the economic cycle, rapid industrial growth, the end of one political regime and the beginning of another, two global wars, many regional conflicts, mass migrations, and natural disasters. Equally important are the long-term developmental transformations through urbanization, industrialization, and political adaptation. Though much continuity persists across this landscape, peak times of change tend to spark fresh concern and thinking about lives over time.

One of the most vivid portraits of late-nineteenth-century America is that of people in search of a more abundant life. In his appropriately titled book, *Drift and Mastery*, Walter Lippmann (1914) observed just before World War II in the United States that "there isn't a human relation, whether of parent or child, husband or wife, worker and employer, that doesn't move in a strange situation" (p. 152). The generations in Middletown of the 1920s also seemed to the Lynds (1937) to be as far apart as they had ever been. They concluded that "the culminating rapidity of recent social change . . . is widening in something resembling a geometrical ratio the gap between the things that were 'right' yesterday and those that make sense to the new generation of today" (Lynd & Lynd, 1937, p. 168).

With such changes in mind, it is not surprising that this century has given birth to a research paradigm that views human lives in their changing worlds, a paradigm generally known by the words *life course*. Life course theory and the ecology of human development (Bronfenbrenner, 1979) share a common interest in explaining how dynamic worlds change people and how people select and construct their environments. Indeed, the two perspectives have evolved and matured through a process of mu-

tual exchange over the past two decades. The temporal dimension, so characteristic of life course studies, is now also characteristic of the ecological
model; whereas ecological studies have been successful in encouraging
more developmental research within a life course framework.

The life course and ecological paradigms have emerged primarily from
the intellectual traditions of different disciplines, sociology and psychology, but they are more broadly shaped by the social, behavioral, and biological sciences. As this chapter makes clear, the paradigms have more in
common today than ever before, and I fully expect this convergence to
continue. Many points of similarity are noted throughout the essay. However, it is also essential to recognize differences.

One of the most important differences concerns the differential
salience of two analytical frames in which problems are specified. The life
course paradigm favors a framing statement that views the sociocultural
environment as a point of departure. A developmental study, guided by
such a frame, would investigate the process by which this environment
makes a difference in children's life and behavior. By contrast, research in
the tradition of an ecology of human development would focus on characteristics of the individual or organism and identify relevant ecological
influences. I discuss these differing models and their analytical implications, along with ways to combine them in the same study. In keeping with
its attention to environmental influences, life course studies place greater
emphasis on the social pathways of human lives, their sequence of events,
transitions, and social roles.

In this chapter, I explore some distinctive principles of the life course
paradigm (Elder, 1994) for understanding how transformed environments
influence lives and developmental trajectories. I begin with the four most
central principles (*lives in time and place, human agency, the timing of lives,*
and *linked lives*) and then focus on the latter two, which provide connections between social change and individual development.

The timing and interdependence of lives are characteristic of different conceptual streams that merged in the 1960s to form the life course
paradigm: temporality as life timing, expressed in studies of age, and linked
lives, from a social relationship tradition that dates back to the nineteenth

century. The relationship tradition includes the pioneering work of W. I. Thomas in sociology and serves as a major source of Bronfenbrenner's (1979) ecology of human development. I discuss these principles and their analytical traditions and then show how both have been central in my efforts to study human lives in their changing worlds.

THE LIFE COURSE PARADIGM AND HISTORICAL CHANGE

Life course theory represents a major change in how we think about and study human lives and development. In this sense, I refer to the life course as an emerging paradigm. Broadly speaking, the change is one element of a conceptual shift that has made time, context, and process more salient dimensions of theory and analysis. As a multidisciplinary field of ideas and empirical observations, the paradigm draws on various conceptual streams, including the generational tradition of life history studies (Thomas & Znaniecki, 1918–1920), the meanings of age in accounts of birth cohorts and age strata (Elder, 1975; Riley, Johnson, & Foner, 1972), cultural and intergenerational models (Kertzer & Keith, 1984), and developmental psychology, both life span (Baltes, 1987) and ecological (Bronfenbrenner, 1979). My perspective tends to stress the social forces that shape the life course and its developmental consequences.

The diversity of these identical contributions is matched in part by some commonalities, such as premises regarding the individual as a biological being. As Magnusson and Törestad (1993) pointed out, "an individual's way of functioning psychologically cannot be understood and explained [satisfactorily] without consideration of the fact that an individual has not only a mind but also a body" (p. 430). The biological course of events and their meaning are core elements of a person's life history, physical attributions and meanings inform cultural accounts of life patterns, and biological timing mechanisms have both social and developmental implications for trajectories of aging and health. Increasingly, analyses are integrating biological factors in accounts of modern interactionism, including general models of the life course. This development, linking processes within and across levels, favors a concept that views behavior in terms of an organized system.

Some Commonalities

There is a coherence to the life course in terms of the individual's total functioning and in crossing multiple levels. These levels range from structured pathways in whole societies (Mayer, 1986; Meyer, 1988), social institutions, and complex organizations to the social trajectories of individuals and their developmental paths. Unfortunately, theories generally exist on one level or another and consequently provide little guidance for life course studies that cross levels, as in efforts to trace the impact of changing economic and political structures through particular locales and family processes to the developmental experience of individuals (Elder, 1974). Bronfenbrenner's (1979) nested levels of social environment represent an important advance in linking macrochange and individual behavior.

In concept, the *social life course* generally refers to the interweave of age-graded trajectories, such as work and family careers, that are subject to changing conditions and future options; and to short-term transitions, ranging from birth and school entry to retirement (Elder, 1985). Empirical examples of trajectories in this volume are provided by Rutter, Champion, Quinton, Maughan, and Pickles (this volume, chapter 3) and by Clausen (this volume, chapter 11). Each trajectory consists of a series of linked states, as in linked jobs in a work history. A change in state, thus, marks a transition, for example, a transition from one job to another. Transitions are always embedded in trajectories that give them distinctive meaning and form. Similar distinctions apply to developmental trajectories, from physical growth in height and weight to the exercise of self-efficacy (Bandura, 1994) and intellectual functioning.

Unlike the single careers, so widely studied in the past, the life course paradigm orients analysis to the dynamics of multiple, interlocking pathways (Moen, Dempster-McClain, & Williams, 1992). Strategies of planning are illustrated in the scheduling of marriage and parenthood and in arranging family events according to the imperatives of a work career.

Interlocking social trajectories are especially prominent across the transition to adulthood. Within a span of 10 years, young people leave home and may return from time to time; they also enter higher education and in some cases complete degree requirements. Some enter the military, vocational certification programs, and colleges, whereas others enter the labor force, marry, and bear children. The challenge from a statistical standpoint is to model these interdependent transitions. Upchurch and Lillard (1994) are making significant headway in this area with econometric models.

For developmental science, the methodological challenge of interlocking processes centers on the relation between social and developmental trajectories. Latent growth curve analysis and hierarchical linear models (HLM) are especially promising for this line of research (Bryk & Raudenbush, 1992) and for more holistic, person-centered approaches, because each study member has one growth curve or developmental trajectory for each variable. Individuals with developmental trajectories can be grouped into common categories and then compared systematically on antecedent and contemporary factors.

Two recent studies have modeled interlocking social and developmental trajectories with this methodology. In a nationwide longitudinal sample, McLeod and Shanahan (1994) found that a poverty trajectory over 6 years significantly increased trajectories of depressed affect and acting out behavior among boys and girls in elementary school, apart from prior (before Time 1 of study) exposure to poverty. Likewise, Ge, Lorenz, Conger, Elder, and Simons (1994) found that a trajectory of negative life events from early to late adolescence significantly increased the level of depressed affect among girls in particular.

Another element of breadth comes from a view of the full life course, its continuities and change. Rutter et al. (this volume, chapter 3) point out that "there is a long way to go before there can be an adequate delineation of the developmental mechanisms involved in connections between childhood behavior and adult life experiences" (p. 89). But with an eye to the two halves of the life course, analysis is necessarily more sensitive to the impact of early transitions for later experience. Indeed, we now see that the implications of early adult choices extend even into the later years of retirement and old age (Clausen, 1993), from the adequacy of economic resources to adaptive skills and activities. The later years of aging and its quality of life cannot be understood in full without knowledge of the prior life course. By seeing human lives as a whole, the analyst is directed to causal pathways across the entire life span. The particular nature of role sequences, whether functionally stable or disrupted (Elder, Shanahan, & Clipp, 1994), clearly matters for subsequent health and adaptation.

Changing Worlds and Human Agency

As noted, a core premise of the life course paradigm asserts that developmental processes and outcomes are shaped by the social trajectories people follow, whether through good times or bad. This premise represents a central component of a core paradigmatic principle on the interplay of *human lives with their historical times and places or ecologies.* Applications of this perspective include chapters by Kohn, Alwin, and Moen and Erickson. Especially in rapidly changing societies, varying years of birth expose individuals to different historical worlds, with distinctive priorities, constraints, and options. Individual lives may well reflect such differences, but to know whether this is so, we must move beyond birth cohorts and their historical context to direct study of the changing environment. The research question should focus on the social change in question and its life course implications. What is the process by which an institutional or political change, such as German reunification, is expressed in particular life patterns?

Historical changes do not occur uniformly across communities, regions, and societies. Consequently, variations in place join variations in historical time as a focal point of life course studies. Within a particular society, it is common to limit analysis to the life course worked out by the individual within a social system of institutionalized pathways. We see the life course as constructed by the individual in terms established by the larger society. Mayer (1986) had these terms in mind when he identified key societal mechanisms "which impose order and constraints on lives" (p. 166), including institutional careers, the cumulative effects of delayed transitions, the collective conditions associated with particular cohorts (e.g., historical circumstances), and state intervention and regulation. The growth of the state in social regulation counters the potential fragmentation of increasing institutional differentiation.

At the individual level,

> the state legalizes, defines, and standardizes most points of entry and exit: into and out of employment, into and out of marriage, into and out of sickness and disability, into and out of formal education. In doing so, the state turns these transitions into strongly demarcated public events and acts as a gatekeeper and sorter. (Mayer, 1986, p. 167)

These are elements of what Buchmann (1989, p. 28) properly called "the public life course." Societies vary greatly on state policies regarding these transition points and on life domains of choice and constraint, as seen in the lack of choice among Chinese during the Cultural Revolution compared with the cafeteria of choices in the Western world.

Initially, the concept of birth cohort seemed to offer a promising way of thinking about lives in a changing society, but the promise depends on originating research questions that link specific changes to the life course. These questions are all too rare. Even when history is substantively important, it may be operationalized as a period or cohort effect that provides no clue as to the precise nature of the influence. To explore this influence, an alternative research design is needed, one that begins with the properties of a particular social change and traces their effects to life experience.

This starting point does not necessarily exclude analyses that investigate attributes of the individual and their social influences. A problem frame that centers on the individual developmental effects of social structures, cultures, and their change does not rule out nested research that conforms to the developmental design preferred by Magnusson and Cairns (in press): "Any significant account of individual processes begins with the developmental status and current functioning of the behaving organism."

Consider the three designs in Figure 1. Model A focuses on characteristics of the individual and identifies relevant influences, in keeping with the Magnusson and Cairns (in press) perspective, as well as Bronfenbrenner's eco-

Model A: Linking Developmental Outcomes to Social Change

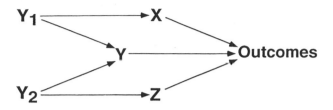

Model B: Linking Social Change to Developmental Outcomes

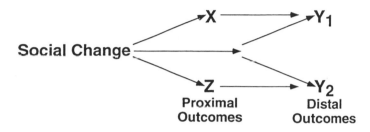

Model C: Putting the Two Models Together: Social Change as the Large Frame

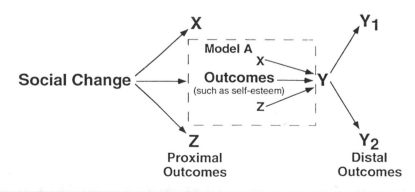

Figure 1

Linking human development to social change.

logical model (1979). For Model C, the individual-centered design of Model A is nested inside the social change framework of Model B, the overall framework of *Children of the Great Depression* (Elder, 1974).

This study traced the effects of Depression hardship through diverse family adaptations, such as a labor-intensive economy and altered family relationships. These adaptations had developmental implications for the child, including a sense of industry and responsibility from the required helpfulness experience of needy households. To fully understand these implications, we can explore other relevant influences, such as rate of maturation and parent behavior. This developmental model is common throughout the project even though the study's general framework is organized around the economy's collapse.

To this view of people in changing environments, the principle of lives in time and place, I add another principle of the life course paradigm: *human agency and self-regulation*. Within the constraints of their world, people are often planful and make choices among options that become the building blocks of their evolving life course. These choices are influenced by the situation and by interpretations of it, as well as by the individual's life history of experience and dispositions. Individual differences and life histories interact with changing environments to produce behavioral outcomes. Human agency and selection processes have become increasingly more important for understanding life course development and aging.

Despite the social regulation of age-graded norms, the agency of individuals and their life choices ensure some degree of "loose coupling" between their actual social transitions and life stage (Elder & O'Rand, 1995). Contrary to the age grading of cultures, people of the same age do not march in concert across major events of the life course; rather, they vary in pace and sequencing, and this variation has real consequences for individuals and society (Hogan, 1981). Entry into a full-time job, completion of schooling, cohabitation and marriage, childbearing—these and other events in the transition to adulthood are not experienced by all members of a birth cohort, and those who experience them do so at widely varied times in life. Even in highly constrained societies, such as Maoist China, individual agency ensures a measure of loose coupling in lived experience.

The role of human agency in shaping the life course is vividly expressed in Clausen's survey (1993; chapter 11, this volume) of nearly 50 years in the lives of Americans who were born during the 1920s in California. Data come from several longitudinal studies that were launched during the 1920s and early 1930s at the Institute of Human Development, Berkeley. Indications of successful aging and personal stability are concentrated among the men and women who entered adulthood with qualities of planful competence. These qualities include an ability to evaluate accurately personal efforts, as well as intentions and responses of others; an informed understanding of self, others, and options; and the personal discipline to pursue chosen goals.

Men with such qualities in adolescence were more accomplished in work and family by the later years. Not all such men did well, of course, nor were the less competent always destined for failure. However, Clausen shows that how one starts out in adult life has much to do with life-shaping choices and with the experience of later life. The planfully competent in adolescence were more likely than other age-mates to find life satisfaction and fulfillment during their last years.

An appreciation for human agency has always been expressed in life-history research, but conceptual trends in the behavioral sciences more generally affirm an agentic view of individuals in shaping development and the life course. They include the cognitive revolution and research on personal efficacy (Bandura, 1994), genetic influences on the selection of environments (Scarr & McCartney, 1983), and the extension of life studies beyond the early years; and the development of Bronfenbrenner's ecological paradigm (1994, p. 203). He writes that an "ecological view of organism–environment interaction . . . takes as its point of departure a conception of the person as an active agent who contributes to her own development."

INTERDEPENDENT LIVES AND THEIR TIMING

No principles of life course study are more central to an understanding of the imprint of changing environments on people's lives than the concepts of *interdependent*, or *linked*, lives and their *timing*. Studies dating back to

Durkheim's (1951) analysis of social integration and suicide and to Thomas and Znaniecki's (1918–1920) research on migration have stressed the interdependence of lives across the generations, in marriage and friendships, and among secondary figures in work and community. The *timing* of lives actually refers to multiple times, based on the meanings of age. Studies informed by age have stressed the historical time of the person, through birth year, and the social timing of events and transitions. I consider each principle in more detail, beginning with *linked lives*.

Linked Lives

The concept of social interdependence conveys the notion of an individual's social embeddedness. Personal actions have consequences for others, and the actions of others impinge on the self. The notion of being counted on by others and a resulting sense of significance are expressions of linked lives. Examples of strong interdependency include children in farm families (Elder, Foster, & Ardelt, 1994) and frontline soldiers in combat units. Single adults generally experience lower levels of interdependence than adults who are married.

Human lives are typically embedded in social relationships with kin and friends across the life span. The social regulation, structuring, and support of human lives occur in part through these multiple, interlocking relationships with their significant others. Processes of this kind are expressed across the life cycle of socialization and behavioral exchange in generational succession, a process well described by Moen and Erickson in chapter 6. The misfortune and opportunity of adult offspring become intergenerational, as well as do personal problems:

> Failed marriages and careers frequently lead adult sons and daughters back to the parental household and have profound implications in shaping the parents' life plans for the later years. Conversely, economic setbacks and divorce among the parents of adolescents may impede their transition to adulthood by postponing leaving home, undertaking higher education or employment, and marriage. Each generation is bound to fateful decisions and events in the other's life course. (Elder, 1985, p. 40)

More generally, the principle of *linked lives* refers to interactive social worlds and networks of relationships over the life span (Hinde, 1979). These worlds or networks connect individuals and their life experience to the broader social changes taking place in society.

A fictive example of this point is based on the experience of two middle-class brothers in the Great Depression. At first glance, the two married brothers seemed to occupy very different worlds. One lost heavily in the economic collapse and held only a part-time job; the other managed to avoid such losses and kept his sales job for a clothier, but he was the oldest son and faced incessant requests for material support from his parents and his wife's more destitute mother. From the perspective of a wider circle of significant others, both brothers were subject to hardships, but in different ways.

Linked lives have particular relevance in understanding the impact of war. Consider two birth cohorts of Japanese men who grew up in the city of Shizuoka, a large metropolis south of Tokyo (Elder & Meguro, 1987). The older men (born 1918–1924) were typically mobilized into military service during World War II, a total of 78%. Nearly two thirds reported family members who had served. Four out of five also experienced an air raid, and over half claimed that their family suffered war damage. Although the younger men (born 1927–1930) were typically too young to serve, they were exposed through family to a high level of personal suffering. They were just as likely to report the military service of family members, the death of a family member, and war damage to the family home.

The younger men were also mobilized out of school for work groups in factories and on farms; thus, an understanding of the war's effect on their life requires knowledge of their workmates and work experience. Just as early work experience can accelerate movement into adult roles, the war-related work of these schoolchildren tended to accelerate their transition to marriage and parenthood. The mobilized men formed families at an earlier age than the nonmobilized, regardless of family background and level of education.

In the lives of California men who served in combat during World War II, stress symptoms during the postwar years had much to do with their loss of one or more comrades (Elder & Clipp, 1988). However, shared losses of this kind also bound the men of a unit together in memory of those who died. Men who reported such losses were more likely to claim enduring ties with service mates as of 1985. These included visits, reunions, and the exchange of letters, cards, and phone calls. The available data suggest that enduring social bonds of this kind also fostered healing through an understanding and supportive community.

This community frequently included an empathic wife who listened and shared. One spouse of a captain in the Marines who had served on Iwo Jima stressed how important his mates had been over the years: "The men are different in so many ways, but the war experience binds them together. When they come together for reunions, they become one as far as their emotions are concerned. They're one person, one thing, one thought" (Elder & Clipp, 1988, p. 193).

The Timing of Lives

The *timing of lives* refers to historical location or time, the social timing of transitions across the life course, the synchrony of individual careers and the lives of significant others, and one's life stage at the point of social change. The timing of an event may be more consequential than its occurrence.

Social timing refers to the incidence, duration, and sequence of roles and to related age expectations and beliefs. Thus, marriages may be relatively early or late, according to demographic patterns and age norms. Options and constraints vary by such timing, including the availability of desirable mates. Thus, teenage brides risk economic disadvantages through marriage to a low-status employee. Marital choices at the other end of the continuum are also limited in number and thus risk permanent single status (Cherlin, 1993). In addition, timing applies to the scheduling of multiple trajectories and their synchrony. Thus, young couples may schedule work and family events to minimize financial, time, and energy pressures, as when children are postponed until the mid- to late-30s.

The timing of encounters with major environmental change in a person's life has much to do with the goodness of fit between lives and new circumstances. In keeping with Bronfenbrenner's (1979) person–process–context model, this *life-stage principle* implies that the effects of a particular social change will vary in type and relative influence across the life course and thus points to the potential complexity of interactions among historical, social, psychological, and biological factors.

With this life-stage distinction in mind, note that children born at opposite ends of the 1920s entered the Great Depression with different prospects (Elder, 1974, 1979). The older ones were 9 to 16 years old during the height of the Depression, too young to leave school and face an unpromising labor market and too old to be highly dependent on the family. By comparison, the younger children were 1 to 8 years old in the economic crisis, ages when they were most dependent on their families under stress and thus at greatest risk of impaired development and life options. Among boys, in particular, these descriptions were borne out in findings that placed the younger boys at greatest risk of developmental impairment.

This age difference may also apply to siblings in a family. Could an economic downturn have different effects on brothers of different ages? Presumably, the nonshared experiences of siblings (Dunn & Plomin, 1990) have much to do with the differential age at which they encounter environmental changes. The age of parents also has rather direct implications for family members. Older and younger fathers faced different consequences from unemployment in the 1930s and the prospect of recovery. Reemployment and economic recovery were more problematic for the older men.

Mobilization for military service in World War II and the Korean War provides yet another illustration of the importance of life stage in structuring historical experience. Time of entry into the armed forces became one of the most powerful influences on how the service affected men's lives in the Oakland and Berkeley cohorts (Elder, 1986, 1987). The Oakland men were born at the beginning of the 1920s; the Berkeley men, in 1928–1929. Early entry, shortly after high school, offered special advantages for life opportunity because it came before family obligations and major work advancements and ensured access to support for higher education on the GI Bill. In both cohorts, disadvantaged youth were more likely to be mobilized shortly after high school than other men. *Disadvantage* refers to a deprived family background in the 1930s, poor school grades, and feelings of inadequacy in adolescence.

By midlife, the inequality of veterans before their war experiences had largely disappeared. Early entry proved to be timely for the Oakland and Berkeley men because it put them on a pathway to greater opportunity, apart from the trauma of combat. One aspect of this pathway involved situational changes that made the early entrants more ambitious, self-directed, and disciplined (Elder, 1986). Military service promoted independence, broadened horizons, and provided a legitimate time-out from the usual career pressures. There was time to think through options, and new people were around to provoke fresh thinking about old issues. A second aspect of this pathway involved access to the GI Bill. In all respects, military service had become a timely developmental experience for a large number of Depression children.

Summary

The interdependence and timing of lives represent two distinctive features of the life course paradigm, as we know it today. In combination, they provide a generative way of thinking about the connections between lives and times, as well as the role of human agency. They also provide a way of connecting lives across the generations, as Moen and Erickson have done (chapter 6). The impact of social change is contingent on the life history that people bring to the new situation, on their life stage at the time, and on the demands of the new situation.

These observations on the life course paradigm refer to developments since the 1960s that are indebted to the merger of analytical traditions that feature social relations and temporality. The relational emphasis dates back in empirical sociology at least to Durkheim and the late nineteenth century. Temporality is linked to the meaning of age and a new version of age-based studies after the 1950s.

HISTORICAL STRANDS: SOCIAL RELATIONS AND TEMPORALITY

The earliest phase of life course studies is typically associated with the pioneering research of Thomas and Znaniecki, published as *The Polish Peas ant in Europe and America* (1918–1920). This two-volume study investigated the transition experience of Polish peasants as they left their rural homeland for major urban centers in Europe and the United States during the late-nineteenth and early-twentieth centuries.

Thomas and Znaniecki (1918–1920) provided an ethnographic and historical account of village and country life in Poland and of the immigrants' settlement in their new urban environments. They did so in part by viewing people's lives over time in a changing world. Continuous life records, typically retrospective, offered such a view, and Thomas soon became an advocate of life-history data and the longitudinal study.

The contributions made by Thomas belong to the social relations strand of the life course paradigm. Over many decades, this includes distinguished studies of social bonding and control, social interaction, socialization, and intergenerational processes, as noted in what follows. Sixty years after Thomas and Znaniecki wrote *The Polish Peasant*, Bronfenbrenner (1979) illuminated the developmental power of interpersonal structures and social roles in his treatise on the ecology of human development. Hartup and Laursen (1991) and Fogel (1993) make a similar point that social relationships are developmental contexts. The relationship-patterned life course is one way that relationships become developmental contexts.

However, the social relations tradition lacked the markers of temporality that place individual lives in historical and lifetime contexts. These markers were provided by the fresh perspectives of sociological age studies during the 1960s and early 1970s. Age has long been studied in anthropology, though not in ways that highlight the problematic relation between an age-graded life course and the actual course of people's lives. The new work on age and the life course gave fresh visibility to the relation between people and their social roles in age-graded trajectories. In this sense, it nicely complemented perspectives based on social relationships.

I begin with the social relations theme and then turn to age in structuring the life course.

Social Relations

The social relations approach views the life course and the impact of changing social structures and institutions through the lens of social ties—familial and other, intimate and more specialized. Over the years, some of the best known research examples have appeared in studies of intergenerational relationships. For example, the concept of life cycle depicts a population process by which one generation is replaced by another through sexual reproduction, social exchange, and socialization.

One of the great strengths of the relationship approach stems from its account of this intergenerational dynamic and the socialization of interdependent lives (Rossi & Rossi, 1990). Kinship ties regulate or constrain choices and options over the life course. Social ties also expose people to the consequences of actions taken by family members (Burton & Bengtson, 1985). A teenage daughter who gives birth shifts her parents into the role of grandparents and her grandparents into the role of great grandparents.

Social change transforms human lives by changing intergenerational relationships and, thus, the nature and effectiveness of socialization, views of self and others, and life course regulation or social control. In their pioneering study of mass immigration from eastern Europe to the United States, Thomas and Znaniecki (1918–1920) viewed the great transition in terms of the breakdown of collective regulation and the rise of individualism. Loss of social control largely stemmed from family disorganization. The behavioral symptoms of youth included sexual promiscuity, vagabondage, and acts of violence. Eventually, disorganization gave way to a period of family reorganization in the new world.

Frazier (1939/1966) followed in their footsteps with a study of Black migration from the South to the great northern cities, a journey that featured exchanges among kin and intergenerational connections. Migration to the North and back to the South occurred within a geographical system of kinship ties and obligations. From the vantage point of the 1930s,

Frazier (1966) forecast a bleak future for rural Black families in the South who would

> continue to seek a living in the towns and cities of the country. They will crowd the slum areas of southern cities or make their way to northern cities where their family life will become disrupted and their poverty will force them to depend upon charity. (pp. 367–368)

The great migration of southern Blacks to northern cities changed the nature of family ties, the content and form of family upbringing and social control, and the availability of social support.

An intergenerational approach to social change also appears in Hareven's (1982) account of the reciprocal flow of French Canadians between textile work in early-twentieth-century Manchester, New Hampshire, and farm employment across the border in Quebec; in Schwarzweller, Brown, and Mangalam's (1971) study of migrants from Kentucky's mountain families, who sought employment in the defense industries of urban centers during World War II; and in Portes and Bach's (1985) analysis of the chain migration of Cuban immigrants to southern Florida. In all three cases, migratory flows occurred within intergenerational systems. They prompted new institutions and the adaptation of existing structures to the social demands of the migrant population.

After World War II, the dramatic growth of school size during the postwar years underscored an impression of young people living in a world of their own. The presumed growth of peer influence prompted concern over the effectiveness of family socialization. By the end of the 1960s, Coleman (1961) and Bronfenbrenner (1970) had explored the relative influence of parents and peers, as well as the unapplauded consequences of peer involvement, ranging from school failure to antisocial behavior.

With its prominence in research at the time, the intergenerational model became a compelling way of viewing student protests across American campuses in the 1960s (Bengtson & Laufer, 1974). Indeed, assumptions regarding a widening generation gap between parents and offspring actually prompted the initiation of Bengtson and Lovejoy's (1973) three-generation study, a pioneering study that is still actively exploring inter-generational differences and similarities in aging. Bengtson and Lovejoy focused on modes of intergenerational solidarity: associational, affec-tional, and value based.

Analysts of student unrest concluded from the intergenerational theory of Davis (1940) that rapid social change increased parent–youth conflict and, thus, the likelihood of student activism and protests. It did so, the analysts believed, by increasing the social–cultural distance between the generations, as in the presumed division between Depression-era par-ents and their postwar children, who grew up in relative affluence. Con-trary to this argument, however, empirical evidence provided no support for the link between generational conflict and student activism (Bengtson & Laufer, 1974). In fact, student activists were typically offspring of par-ents with such beliefs. The picture was more one of intergenerational har-mony and support than of conflict.

Whatever their explanatory limitations, intergenerational accounts of historical change in people's lives usefully directed attention to the mech-anisms of socialization, exchange, and conflict across generational lines. Within a life cycle of generational succession and ties, newborns are so-cialized to maturity, give birth to the next generation, grow old, and die. The web of kinship, generational and collateral (e.g., spouse, siblings, and cousins), identifies a matrix of social influences and support, constraints, and options that give shape to lives lived interdependently over the years. To this web should be added the matrix of nonfamily relations as well— of authority figures, subordinates, friends, friends of friends, and ac-quaintances.

Three interrelated traditions of theory are especially relevant to the relationship approach in studies of human lives and their changing times. They include (a) the interactionist tradition (symbolic interaction and the-ories of self–other relations; Fine, 1992, 1993; Rosenberg, 1981) of Charles Mark Baldwin, W. I. Thomas, Charles H. Cooley, George Herbert Mead, Herbert Blumer, and Leonard Cottrell; (b) a more structural version of role theory in the writings of Merton (1957), Rosow (1974), and Turner (1978); and (c) theories of social networks, of linked social relationships, and of temporal representations of interdependent lives, such as the notion of social convoys (Kahn & Antonucci, 1980) and lifelong associates. Theories of socialization (Brim & Wheeler, 1966; Goslin, 1969) extend across these traditions and the substantive disciplines of the behavioral sciences.

Within developmental psychology, the relationship approach represents one of the primary sources of Bronfenbrenner's (1979) ecology of human development. Each level of this ecology is defined by different types of social relationships: the microlevel of primary relationships; the meso- and exosystems of intergroup and community relationships; and the macrolevel of institutional, interorganizational, and aggregate-type relations.

From the perspective of ecological and life course models, historical change at the macrolevel can eventually transform the developmental experience of children by altering primary relationships within the family and peer group. In line with this formulation, Hinde and Stevenson-Hinde (1987) argued that

> the child must be seen not as an isolated unit, but as a social being, forming part of a network of relationships. Interactions, relationships, social groups, and the sociocultural structure form successive levels of social complexity, each level involving properties not relevant to lower levels. (pp. 1–2)

As noted earlier, the sociologist W. I. Thomas argued for a relationship view of people's lives more than 70 years ago and advocated both life-history data and the longitudinal method when this position was not popular. He urged that priority be given to "the longitudinal approach to life history" (Volkart, 1951, p. 593). Studies should follow "groups of individuals into the future, getting a continuous record of experiences as they occur." Thomas referred to typical "lines of genesis" established by the social order and, with Znaniecki (1918–1920), stressed the human agency of the individual: People are influenced by opportunity, but they also make opportunities.

Remarkably, W. I. Thomas's thinking has much in common with the life course paradigm today, except for one critical deficiency: the neglect of age and its sociological, historical, and psychological meanings. In popular and scientific thought, age has long served as a way of representing the life span and its social stages (Cain, 1964). In anthropology (Kertzer & Keith, 1984), for example, a substantial literature on age grading dates back to the nineteenth century.

Nevertheless, advocates of a relational approach to human biographies and their historical times somehow managed to ignore the temporal insights of age and its multiple meanings. Thomas and Znaniecki (1918–1920), to give one example, did not locate their Polish peasants in historical time through information on birth year, nor did they conceptualize *lines of genesis* in terms of the age-graded life course. Even age at emigration was not discussed in terms of its adaptive implications.

Role theory has also slighted issues of timing. For example, Ebaugh's (1988) contribution to role theory, entitled *Becoming an Ex: The Process of Role Exit*, makes no reference at all to timing. To judge from the analysis, it is not important whether a death involves a child or grandparent, whether divorce occurs in one's 20s or 50s, or whether dismissal from a job comes in one's 30s or at the end of 25 years. The evidence (George, 1993), however, suggests that timing matters in all of these ways, and it does so because we are guided by expectable timetables based on social arrangements and practices, age norms, and age-graded beliefs.

We might note as well that initial statements of Bronfenbrenner's (1979) ecological model also lacked a temporal perspective, a deficiency that has much in common with its roots in Lewinian theory of the psychological field and a social relationship perspective on socialization and human development. Some years later, after making a persuasive case for the person–process–context model, he noted a major lacuna that also applied to "Lewin's original formula—the dimension of time" (Bronfenbrenner, 1989, p. 201). The remarkable growth of longitudinal studies of the life course and human development may have underscored this limitation. The term *ecological transition* had been used in early writings to refer to environmental change that altered the person's social niche or position (Bronfenbrenner, 1979, pp. 26–27), but this did not address developmental change nor the proximal processes that occur in organism-environment interactions. The ecological concept of a *chronosystem* was devised to capture all of these interacting elements over time—the developing person, the nature of the environment, and their proximal processes of interaction. This revision established another base of commonality between the ecological and life course paradigms.

Looking back on the social and behavioral sciences, it is clear that the differential timing of human lives and developmental trajectories remained undeveloped among relationship studies and in the general field of life studies until the 1960s and the emergence of innovative thinking about age in society, history, and human lives. In large part, this thinking came from different quarters in the social and behavioral sciences: from Neugarten (1968) in social and developmental psychology, from Riley et al. (1972) in sociology, and from Ryder (1965) in social demography, among others.

Age and Temporality

Membership in a particular generation typically tells us very little about a particular historical time and its influences. Persons who share a common generational status in the descent hierarchy do not necessarily share a common location in historical time. With a birth range of 30 years or more in a single generation, members of a generation can represent vastly different historical eras.

These observations and their implications are readily observed in a comparison of three generations. Hill's (1970) three-generation study in Minneapolis–St. Paul clearly shows the age diversity of each generation and the way it can obscure the effect of historical change. The age range for the middle, parent, generation extends from 41 to 70. Consequently, some parents married in the 1920s and some in the depressed 1930s, a difficult time in which to have children. Indeed, the 1920s couples ended up with a significantly larger number of children. Moreover, the two groups were found to be sufficiently different in life course to represent different populations, yet they were treated throughout most of the study as one social unit.

The important point in this example is the greater precision of age status in locating people in historical time and in the life course. These distinctions, in turn, enable the analyst to specify more accurately the personal impact of social change. By contrast, a relationship or generational approach does not locate people in precise historical settings, and it also fails to identify the life stage of people in eras of social change. For example, parents with young children may vary in age by 20 or more years and, thus, experience environmental changes at drastically different life stages. As I have noted, such differences can determine how historical change affects life choices, developmental experience, and adaptations.

During the late 1950s and early 1960s, Neugarten and Datan (1973; Neugarten, 1968) developed a normative perspective on the life course that featured a concept of normative timetables and individual deviations from such expectations that are subject to an informal system of sanctions. A *timetable of the life course* refers to social age, as defined by people's expectations or norms regarding events or transitions. In theory, age expectations specify appropriate times for major transitions. There is an appropriate time for entering school, leaving home, getting married, having children, achieving financial independence, and retiring.

These expectations serve as bases of self- and other evaluation, as when a worker concludes that he is not where he should be at his stage of life (see Helson, Mitchell, & Moane, 1984). Generally, marked departures from the usual timetable entail social and psychological consequences, from informal sanctions to lost opportunities and life course disorder. Social relations studies also explore these role transitions in the life cycle, but not in relation to age and matters of timing.

The influence of any social transition depends on when it occurs. There are numerous examples of this observation. Widowhood is an anticipated event during the later years, but not in one's 20s and 30s (Wortman & Silver, 1990). The psychological distress of widowhood is, thus, more severe among women who lose their spouse during the first half of the life course. Younger widows also frequently have the additional burden of child care, along with problems of financial support. Options vary over the life course, such as remarriage, which is more available to younger than to older widows. In the realm of work, periods of work-life instability are more common during the early years of work, and they are easier to surmount than during later life, owing partly to the employer costs of hiring older workers (e.g., retirement benefits).

Timing can also be thought of in terms of life-management strategy and planning. Indeed, the personal scheduling of multiple roles, such as women's work and births, represents a way to balance demands and personal resources over time. Goode (1960) depicted this dynamic in terms of a role-budget system within the family, a budget that favored the synchronization of social roles among members according to available time, labor, and energy. The social stress of life patterns and psychological distress may be due in large measure to the inadequate coordination or synchronization of multiple roles.

Thoits (1983) and others note that coordinated roles and identities in work and marriage can be a source of mental health and resilience. However, multiple roles also entail certain health risks in the sense that they expose people to the problems and worries of others. According to Kessler and McLeod (1984), women experience a higher level of emotional distress than men partly because they are more exposed to the distress of others through greater social ties.

This discussion of age in the life course focuses on two meanings: historical and social. Other interpretations center on biological or maturational age. Social trajectories are frequently not synchronized with the biological timetables of individual children, as in the relation between school structures and the differential maturation rates of students who are age-mates. Turkewitz and Devenny (1993) argued that an understanding of such rates and their behavioral correlates is essential for theories that view development "as the outcome of interactions between a changing organism and changing context" (p. xii).

No single work in the 1960s brought together all of these meanings of age in a synthetic account of social and developmental trajectories, but Riley et al. (1972) authored the most important effort along these lines in a theory of age stratification. This theoretical framework on the macroscopic level relates historical and social age in an account of successive birth cohorts interacting with age-graded social structures of society. Age

125

represents a basis of stratification in historical experience through birth year and in the sequence of social roles across the life course. Birth year or date of entry into the system locates people in the sociohistorical process; with age peers, they are exposed to a particular slice of historical experience in moving through a sequence of social roles over the life span.

Differential birth, death, and migration rates determine the relative size and composition of birth cohorts. Cohorts of small size in an expanding economy offer abundant opportunities (e.g., the 1937 birth cohort), whereas diminished options face large cohorts in a depressed economy (e.g., the late 1950s cohorts; Easterlin, 1980). Within each cohort, socialization and allocation processes connect people and social roles in a lifelong process of aging. Socialization ostensibly develops self-regulation and a sense of responsibility, whereas agents of allocation match people and social roles, as through employee recruitment.

In the 1960s, the two analytical models (on social relations and age) converged and clashed around issues of social change and the life span. The relations tradition entered the decade with a substantial literature on intergenerational relationships, socialization, and role transitions and was immediately put to work on the fast-emerging questions of the decade: on questions concerning intergenerational cleavage, conflict, and social protests relative to historical change and on matters of adult development and aging (Elder, 1980a). However, the conceptual insights of relations studies were limited in both domains.

As noted, generational status could not match the historical precision of a birth cohort. Moreover, studies began to show that the student protests of the decade had more to do with cohort size and problems of succession than with the generations (Elder, 1980a). A perspective based on socialization and social relationships also proved to be incomplete for addressing issues of behavioral continuity and change across the life span. These issues called for an understanding of age grading, with emphasis on the timing of role behavior.

By contrast, age-based models of the life course were limited as well, particularly in terms of social ties and control—a strength of the relationship approach. A life course model based only on the sociology of age tended to understate and neglect the social embeddedness of individual lives and development through linked lives and the ongoing web of social relationships (Watkins, 1980). Attributions of an individualistic bias to life course studies imply such models. Any limitations of the life course perspective for studying collectivities, such as the family and peer group, generally pertain to research that is narrowly focused on age patterns, to the neglect of interlocking relationships.

Both timing and linked lives, with their literatures on age and social relations, are fundamental to a life course theory that connects human lives, development, and social change. The study of age brings historical considerations and insights on age grading and timing to the life course, whereas relationship analysis highlights the given nature of social ties and their social regulation of choices, the interlocking trajectories and relationships of people over the life span, and the cross-generational process by which historical experiences and influences are transmitted.

In the 1960s, I drew on both analytical models and their historical strands in developing my first research on the life course, a study of California children who grew up in the Great Depression (Elder, 1974). The project located children in a birth cohort (birth year, 1920–1921) and followed their lives across age-graded events and transitions into the middle years, but it also addressed their relationships within the family in order to understand how hard times shaped their lives. The basic model traced the effects of the economic collapse through family deprivation and intergenerational processes to the lives of the children.

Over the years since this study, a good many other projects have joined the two analytical traditions in life course research. Examples include Hareven's (1982) historical study of the family and life course in the textile community of Manchester, New Hampshire; Rossi and Rossi's (1990) three-generation study of the relation between individual aging and kin-defined relationships across the life course; and Moen et al.'s (1992) two-generation study of women.

Two additional projects illustrate the analytical power of this perspective. Burton and Bengtson (1985) noted the consequences of a wide disparity between age and generational status among Black mothers of teenagers who had just had a child. A majority of the young mothers refused to accept the child-care burden, and it, thus, fell to the grandmother. The teenagers were too young, or so it seemed. Within a longitudinal sample, Sampson and Laub (1993) showed how attachments to spouse and work played a role in turning the lives of delinquents toward conventional roles in the transition to adulthood. Attachments to conventional pathways fostered conventional behavior.

In my closing observations, I briefly explore some applications in my own work to show how critical the integration of perspectives on social relations and age has been in efforts to link human lives and developmental processes to a changing world.

LINKED LIVES AND THEIR TIMES

Along with many other sociologists, I was trained at the end of the 1950s in the social relations tradition of social psychology, socialization, and social structure. Family socialization provided a way of linking social structures and personality (Elder, 1973). During these years of graduate study at the University of North Carolina, no study interested me more than the ongoing Cornell project of Urie Bronfenbrenner (1961) on parent and peer influences.

My doctoral study of family socialization (Elder, 1980b) was not directly focused on matters of a changing society, and the same could be said for the Cornell project. The literature chapter of the dissertation had *social change* in the title, but I did not have the slightest insight into how to connect changes in society with changes in family socialization and life experience. With much embarrassment, I note that the historical time of the parents and children in the sample did not inform my analysis. Hindsight tells me that a large percentage of the fathers came of age in the Great Depression and served in the armed forces of World War II. Their behavior as a father had much to do with these experiences, if we are to judge from contemporary studies (Elder & O'Rand, 1995).

The social relations model represented my framework when I arrived at the University of California, Berkeley, in fall 1962 for a faculty appointment. Half of my appointment involved research with a distinguished sociologist, John Clausen, at the Institute of Human Development. My initial work entailed the coding of uncoded materials in the longitudinal data archive of the Oakland Growth Study. The study members were born during the early 1920s and participated in a series of follow-ups from the early 1930s to the 1940s. A large percentage had been followed into the fourth decade of life through adult follow-ups. Eventually, the Oakland study members became key figures in *Children of the Great Depression* (Elder, 1974).

The dramatic changefulness of families and lives across the Great Depression underscored for me the relevance of changing family relations for the developmental experience of the Oakland children. In lieu of static notions of family life, I turned to the family economy and its multiple actors as a way of thinking about the economic crisis and its implications for children. Families worked out survival adaptations to their changing economic circumstances. In theory, these included changes in the household economy, in authority and affective relations, and in social and emotional strains. Within the middle and working class of 1929, I compared hard-pressed parents and children with those who were relatively nondeprived across the 1930s and then into the middle years.

Drastic income loss shifted the household economy toward labor-intensive operations involving more productive roles for children and a greater burden for mothers. Girls played a more important role in family chores than did boys. Family deprivation also modified relationships within the family, increasing the centrality of mother as an authority and affectionate figure. In combination, these changes increased the social independence of boys and the family involvement of girls. Heavy income loss also magnified the risk of family discord, disorganization, and demoralization.

Empirical findings from the Oakland study fully document these interrelated family processes as linkages and show, furthermore, that most boys and girls from deprived homes in the middle class generally managed to rise above the limitations of their disadvantaged childhood. Lingering disadvantages were observed among children from hard-pressed working-class families, but these seldom persisted into the middle years. The challenging question was how such life outcomes could arise from prolonged family hardship in the 1930s.

This question underscored for me the importance of the historical time of the generations. When were the parents and children born? How old were they when the economy collapsed? What were the implications of their life stage at the time? In many respects, as I have suggested, the Oakland children were on a relatively protected path through the mine fields of the 1930s. They were too young to experience joblessness, and they were too old to be highly dependent on their unstable families.

To put this "timing" interpretation to a test, I turned to a younger cohort of children in the Great Depression: members of the Berkeley Guidance Study at the Institute of Human Development who were born at the end of the 1920s (Elder, 1979). They were very young when the economy collapsed, and a significant number of their families in the middle and working class lost heavily. Were these younger children more adversely influenced by economic hardship, when compared with the older Oakland children? The Berkeley boys turned out to be the most disadvantaged group overall, owing in large measure to the destructive influence of hard-pressed fathers. The influence was much less adverse among the Berkeley girls, owing partly to the protective role of the mother.

Both sets of distinctions, the linked lives of social relationships and the temporal perspectives of age, were essential in framing this study. The Oakland and Berkeley children entered the Depression era at different stages of life and, thus, were differentially vulnerable to the social and psychological changes in their families. This life-stage principle applies a key proposition in Bronfenbrenner's (1994) ecological model (p. 31). This proposition states that proximal processes that influence development tend to vary systematically as "a joint function of the characteristics of the developing person; of the environment—both immediate and more remote—in which the processes are taking place; and the nature of the developmental outcomes under consideration."

Beyond this life-stage principle, the social meanings of age characterized the adult years in terms of sequential roles and transitions. In a number of instances, Depression hardship altered the salience of adult roles and the timing of key transitions, such as marriage and the establishment of a stable career. Overall, we see that family relationships provided an all-important connection between the large-scale socioeconomic forces of the 1930s and the experience of children, but that the developmental effects of these conditions and processes depended on the age of the child. Subsequent research (Elder, Nguyen, & Caspi, 1985) has identified other instigative characteristics of the child (e.g., physical attractiveness) that determined the Depression experiences of children.

Timing and linked lives also proved to be essential for explaining why so many children of the Depression were able to overcome the limitations of their background. Three factors seemed to make an important difference in turning men's lives around: entry into military service, the initiation of higher education, and marriage (Elder & Caspi, 1990). Over 70% of the Oakland and Berkeley men were mobilized into the service, and those who were had access to higher education through benefits from the GI Bill. In addition, draft pressures tended to accelerate entry into marriage. Beyond these experiences, military service gave men time to think about their future without career pressures, broadened their cultural perspective and understanding, and often gave them the successful experience of coping with challenging circumstances. As noted earlier, the turning point advantages of military service were concentrated among men who entered the armed forces shortly after high school, well before the role pressures and burdens of adulthood—from a full-time career, marriage, and children. Both prospectively and in late-life reflections, the veterans (Elder, 1986, 1987) identified early entry into military service as minimizing the social upheaval or disruptiveness of mobilization and demobilization, entry and exit.

By contrast, these effects should be especially common among the late entrants, who were so common in World War II. Half of all veterans entered after the age of 26. These men were pulled out of major responsibilities to their family and career and then returned to families that had difficulty in accepting them. Hill (1949) and Stolz (1954) showed that a good many marriages and father–child relations remained troubled and unstable in the postwar families of World War II veterans.

These observations about late mobilization do not readily apply to the Oakland and Berkeley veterans because they were in the service by their 25th birthday. All of these veterans faced less disruption and deprivation than men who entered in their 30s. To put the issue of truly late timing to an empirical test, we drew on the unique archival resources of the Stanford–Terman longitudinal study with its sample of some 800 high-ability Californians (Elder, Shanahan, & Clipp, 1994).

The men were first surveyed in 1922. Data collection continued every 5 or so years up to the 1990s. Over 40% of the men entered World War II, even though half were over 29 years of age in 1940. A third of the veterans were mobilized after the age of 32, and another third entered the service between the ages of 29 through 32. Even the youngest Terman entrants were older at time of entry than early joiners among the Oakland and Berkeley veterans.

Truly late mobilization (age 33 and older) for military duty markedly increased the risk of personal and social disadvantages that endured until late life. Though better educated than other veterans, these late entrants ranked higher on divorce, and they were more likely to experience a work life of disappointment, with a permanent loss of income up to old age, especially among the professionals. They also experienced an accelerated decline of physical health, mostly after the age of 50 (apart from combat). And they were less likely to remember the service as a beneficial experience of life. In general, they derived far less from the service than they gave to it.

Here, again, we see the implications of timing and linked lives. The later the military mobilization, the greater the risk of social disruption and impaired health. Though little is known about the actual mechanisms by which social disruption adversely affects health, the nature of social support and the quality of social relationships no doubt play an important role. The challenges faced by the late entrants probably had less to do with military service per se and more to do with the dislocating effect of service time on their postwar life. Some archival materials record deep feelings of resentment about the war's personal effect. Veterans generally faced an unreceptive society on such matters.

In studies of human lives and development amidst economic decline and war, the simple distinctions of timing and linked lives have enabled us to specify processes by which social change affects individual behavior and adaptation. In combination, they alert us to the life histories people bring to a changing world, to the behavioral demands and social supports of the new situation, and to adaptive efforts to regain control over outcomes. As key elements of the life course paradigm, timing and linked lives provide a way of thinking about the social embeddedness and developmental trajectories of human lives and their connection to an ever-changing society.

CONCLUSION

The decade of the 1960s gave birth to interrelated developments that have literally transformed the study of lives within the social sciences. I refer to these developments as an emerging paradigm on the life course and human development, a paradigm that has much in common with Urie Bronfenbrenner's ecological perspective on human development. This chapter describes distinctive features of this paradigm, with emphasis on the timing and interdependence of lives. It surveys a key theoretical integration of two historical strands in research and theory, the social relations and age perspectives on human lives and social change. Both perspectives are essential in thinking about the interaction of lives and society.

Thirty years ago, the life course was not a concept in the social sciences, and those in developmental psychology had yet to take seriously an ecological approach to human development. Today, we find that life course ideas are part of an ecological model of developmental processes and that elements of this model inform life course studies of human development. The mutual possibilities are just beginning to appear in a developmental science that crosses levels and disciplines, but what a journey this has been! It would have been far less rewarding and productive without a nurturing human ecology that featured Urie's intellectual guidance and friendship.

REFERENCES

Baltes, P. B. (1987). Theoretical propositions of life-span developmental psychology: On the dynamics between growth and decline. *Developmental Psychology, 23,* 611–626.

Bandura, A. (1994). *Self-efficacy: The exercise of control.* New York: W. H. Freeman.

Bengtson, V. L., & Laufer, R. S. (Eds.). (1974). Youth, generations, and social change. *Journal of Social Issues, 30,* Part I & Part II.

Bengtson, V. L., & Lovejoy, C. (1973). Values, personality, and social structure: An intergenerational analysis. *American Behavioral Scientist, 16,* 880–912.

Brim, O. G., Jr., & Wheeler, S. A. (1966). *Socialization after childhood: Two essays,* (pp. 1–7). New York: Wiley.

Bronfenbrenner, U. (1961). The changing American child: A speculative analysis. *Merrill-Palmer Quarterly of Behavior and Development, 7,* 73–84.

Bronfenbrenner, U. (1970). *Two worlds of childhood: U.S. and U.S.S.R.* New York: Sage.

Bronfenbrenner, U. (1979). *The ecology of human development.* Cambridge, MA: Harvard University Press.

Bronfenbrenner, U. (1989). Ecological systems theory. In R. Vasta (Ed.), *Six theories of child development: Revised formulations and current issues* (pp. 187–250). Greenwich, CT: JAI Press.

Bronfenbrenner, U. (1994). Ecological models of human development. In T. Hustén & T. N. Postlethwaite (Eds.), *International encyclopedia of education* (2nd ed.). New York: Elsevier Science.

Bryk, A. S., & Raudenbush, S. W. (1992). *Hierarchical linear models: Applications and data analysis methods.* Newbury Park, CA: Sage.

Buchmann, M. (1989). *The script of life in modern society: Entry into adulthood in a changing world.* Chicago: University of Chicago Press.

Burton, L. M., & Bengtson, V. L. (1985). Black grandmothers: Issues of timing and continuity of roles. In V. L. Bengtson & J. F. Robertson (Eds.), *Grandparenthood* (pp. 61–77). Beverly Hills, CA: Sage.

Cain, L. (1964). Life course and social structure. In R. E. L. Faris (Ed.), *Handbook of modern sociology* (pp. 272–309). Chicago: Rand McNally.

Cherlin, A. G. (1993). *Marriage, divorce, and remarriage.* Cambridge, MA: Harvard University Press.

Clausen, J. A. (1993). *American lives.* New York: Free Press.

Coleman, J. S. (1961). *The adolescent society.* New York: Free Press.

Davis, K. (1940). The sociology of parent–youth conflict. *American Sociological Review, 5,* 523–535.

Dunn, J., & Plomin, R. (1990). *Separate lives: Why siblings are so different.* New York: Basic Books.

Durkheim, E. (1951). *Suicide* (J. A. Spalding & G. Simpson, Trans.). Glencoe, IL: Free Press.

Easterlin, R. A. (1980). *Birth and fortune.* New York: Basic Books.

Ebaugh, H. R. F. (1988). *Becoming an ex: The process of role exit.* Chicago: University of Chicago Press.

Elder, G. H., Jr. (Ed.). (1973). *Linking social structure and personality.* Beverly Hills, CA: Sage.

Elder, G. H., Jr. (1974). *Children of the Great Depression: Social change in life experience.* Chicago: University of Chicago Press.

Elder, G. H., Jr. (1975). Age differentiation and the life course. *Annual Review of Sociology, 1,* 165–190.

Elder, G. H., Jr. (1979). Historical change in life patterns and personality. In P. B. Baltes & O. G. Brim, Jr. (Eds.), *Life-span development and behavior* (Vol. 2, pp. 117–159). New York: Academic Press.

Elder, G. H., Jr. (1980a). Adolescence in historical perspective. In J. Adelson (Ed.), *Handbook of adolescent psychology* (pp. 3–46). New York: Wiley.

Elder, G. H., Jr. (1980b). *Family structure and socialization.* New York: Arno Press.

Elder, G. H., Jr. (1985). Perspectives on the life course. In G. H. Elder, Jr. (Ed.), *Life course dynamics* (pp. 23–49). Ithaca, NY: Cornell University Press.

Elder, G. H., Jr. (1986). Military times and turning points in men's lives. *Developmental Psychology, 22,* 233–245.

Elder, G. H., Jr. (1987). War mobilization and the life course: A cohort of World War II veterans. *Sociological Forum, 2,* 449–472.

Elder, G. H., Jr. (1994). Time, human agency, and social change: Perspectives on the life course. *Social Psychology Quarterly, 57,* 4–15.

Elder, G. H., Jr., & Caspi, A. (1990). Studying lives in a changing society: Sociological and personological explorations. In A. I. Rabin, R. A. Zucker, & S. Frank (Eds.), *Studying persons and lives* (pp. 201–247). New York: Springer. (Henry A. Murray Lecture Series)

Elder, G. H., Jr., & Clipp, E. C. (1988). Wartime losses and social bonding: Influences across 40 years in men's lives. *Psychiatry, 51*(May), 177–198.

Elder, G. H., Jr., Foster, E. M., & Ardelt, M. (1994). Children in the household economy. In R. D. Conger & G. H. Elder, Jr. (Eds.), *Families in troubled times: Adapting to change in rural America* (pp. 127–146). Hawthorne, NY: Aldine de Gruyter.

Elder, G. H., Jr., & Meguro, Y. (1987). Wartime in men's lives: A comparative study of American and Japanese cohorts. *International Journal of Behavioral Development, 10,* 439–466.

Elder, G. H., Jr., Nguyen, T. V., & Caspi, A. (1985). Linking family hardship to children's lives. *Child Development, 56,* 361–375.

Elder, G. H., Jr., & O'Rand, A. M. (1995). Adult lives in a changing society. In J. S. House, K. Cook, & G. Fine (Eds.), *Sociological perspectives on social psychology.* New York: Allyn & Bacon.

Elder, G. H., Jr., Shanahan, M. J., & Clipp, E. C. (1994). When war comes to men's lives: Life course patterns in family, work, and health. *Psychology and Aging, 9,* 5–16.

Fine, G. A. (1992). Agency, structure, and comparative contexts: Toward a synthetic interactionism. *Symbolic Interaction, 15,* 87–102.

Fine, G. A. (1993). The sad demise, mysterious disappearance, and glorious triumph of symbolic interactionism. *Annual Review of Sociology, 19,* 61–87.

Fogel, A. (1993). *Developing through relationships: Origins of communication, self, and culture.* Chicago: University of Chicago Press.

Frazier, E. F. (1966). *The Negro family in the United States.* Chicago: University of Chicago Press. (Original work published 1939)

Ge, X., Lorenz, F. O., Conger, R. D., Elder, G. H., Jr., & Simons, R. L. (1994). Trajectories of stressful life events and depressive symptoms during adolescence. *Developmental Psychology, 30,* 467–483.

George, L. K. (1993). Sociological perspectives on life transitions. *Annual Review of Sociology, 19,* 353–373.

Goode, W. J. (1960). A theory of role strain. *American Sociological Review, 25*(4), 483–496.

Goslin, D. A. (Ed.). (1969). *Handbook of socialization theory and research.* Chicago: Rand McNally.

Hareven, T. K. (1982). *Family time and industrial time.* New York: Cambridge University Press.

Hartup, W. W., & Laursen, B. (1991). Relationships as developmental contexts. In R. Cohen & A. W. Siegel (Eds.), *Context and development* (pp. 253–279). Hillsdale, NJ: Erlbaum.

Helson, R. M., Mitchell, V., & Moane, G. (1984). Personality and patterns of adherence and nonadherence to the social clock. *Journal of Personality and Social Psychology, 46,* 1079–1096.

Hill, R. (1949). *Families under stress: Adjustment to the crises of war separation and reunion.* New York: Harper & Row.

Hill, R. (1970). *Family development in three generations.* Cambridge, MA: Schenkman.

Hinde, R. A. (1979). *Towards understanding relationships.* New York: Academic Press.

Hinde, R. A., & Stevenson-Hinde, J. (1987). Interpersonal relationships and child development. *Developmental Review, 7,* 1–21.

Hogan, D. P. (1981). *Transitions and social change: The early lives of American man.* New York: Academic Press.

Kahn, R. L., & Antonucci, T. C. (1980). Convoys over the life course: Attachments, roles, and social support. *Life-Span Development and Behavior, 2,* 253–286.

Kertzer, D. I., & Keith, J. (Eds.). (1984). *Age and anthropological theory.* Ithaca, NY: Cornell University Press.

Kessler, R. C., & McLeod, J. D. (1984). Sex differences in vulnerability to undesirable life events. *American Sociological Review, 49,* 620–631.

Lippmann, W. (1914). *Drift and mastery.* New York: Mitchell Kennerly.

Lynd, R. S., & Lynd, H. M. (1937). *Middletown in transition: A study in cultural conflicts.* New York: Harcourt, Brace.

Magnusson, D., & Cairns, R. B. (in press). Developmental science: Principles and illustrations. In R. B. Cairns, G. H. Elder, Jr., & E. J. Costello (Eds.), *Developmental science: Multidisciplinary perspectives.* Cambridge, England: Cambridge University Press.

Magnusson, D., & Törestad, B. (1993). A holistic view of personality: A model revisited. *Annual Review of Psychology, 44,* 427–452.

Mayer, K. U. (1986). Structural constraints on the life course. *Human Development, 29*(3), 163–170.

McLeod, J. D., & Shanahan, M. J. (1994, May). *Trajectories of poverty and children's adjustment.* Paper presented at the International Stress Conference, Honolulu, HI.

Merton, R. K. (1957). *Social theory and social structure.* New York: Free Press.

Meyer, J. W. (1988). The life course as a cultural construction. In M. W. Riley (Ed.), *Social change and the life course* (Vol. 1, pp. 49–62). Newbury Park, CA: Sage.

Moen, P., Dempster-McClain, D., & Williams, R. M., Jr. (1992). Successful aging: A life-course perspective on women's multiple roles and health. *American Journal of Sociology, 97,* 1612–1638.

Neugarten, B. L. (1968). *Middle age and aging: A reader in social psychology*. Chicago: University of Chicago Press.

Neugarten, B. L., & Datan, N. (1973). Sociological perspectives on the life cycle. In P. B. Baltes & K. W. Schaie (Eds.), *Life-span developmental psychology: Personality and socialization* (pp. 53–69). New York: Academic Press.

Portes, A., & Bach, R. L. (1985). *Latin journey: Cuban and Mexican immigrants in the United States*. Berkeley: University of California Press.

Redfield, R. (1955). *The little community*. Chicago: University of Chicago Press.

Riley, M. W., Johnson, M. E., & Foner, A. (Eds.). (1972). *Aging and society: A sociology of age stratification* (Vol. 3). New York: Russell Sage Foundation.

Rosenberg, M. (1981). *The conceived self*. New York: Free Press.

Rosow, I. (1974). *Socialization to old age*. Berkeley: University of California Press.

Rossi, A. S., & Rossi, P. H. (1990). *Of human bonding: Parent–child relations across the life course*. New York: Aldine de Gruyter.

Ryder, N.–B. (1965). The cohort as a concept in the study of social change. *American Sociological Review, 30,* 843–861.

Sampson, R. J., & Laub, J. H. (1993). *Crime in the making: Pathways and turning points through life*. Cambridge, MA: Harvard University Press.

Scarr, S., & McCartney, K. (1983). How people make their own environments: A theory of genotype–environment effects. *Child Development, 54,* 424–435.

Schwarzweller, H. K., Brown, J. S., & Mangalam, J. J. (1971). *Mountain families in transition*. University Park: Pennsylvania State Press.

Stolz, L. M. (1954). *Father relations of war-born children*. Stanford, CA: Stanford University Press.

Thoits, P. A. (1983). Multiple identities and psychological well-being: A reformulation and test of the social isolation hypothesis. *American Sociological Review, 47,* 174–187.

Thomas, W. I., & Znaniecki, F. (1918–1920). *The Polish peasant in Europe and America* (Vols. 1–2). Urbana: University of Illinois Press.

Turkewitz, G., & Devenny, D. A. (Eds.). (1993). *Developmental time and timing* (pp. xii). Hillsdale, NJ: Erlbaum.

Turner, R. H. (1978). Role and the person. *American Journal of Sociology, 84,* 1–23.

Upchurch, D. M., & Lillard, L. A. (1994, May). *Interdependencies over the life course: Women's fertility, marital, and education experiences*. Paper presented at the Population Association of America meeting, Miami, FL.

Volkart, E. H. (1951). *Social behavior and personality: Contributions of W. I. Thomas to theory and social research.* New York: Social Science Research Council.

Watkins, S. C. (1980). On measuring transitions and turning points. *Historical Methods, 13,* 181–186.

Wortman, C. B., & Silver, R. C. (1990). Successful mastery of bereavement and widowhood: A life-course perspective. In P. B. Baltes & M. M. Baltes (Eds.), *Successful aging: Perspectives from the behavioral sciences* (pp. 225–264). New York: University of Cambridge Press.

5

Social Structure and Personality Through Time and Space

Melvin L. Kohn

I first encountered Urie Bronfenbrenner in the fall of 1948, when I was a beginning graduate student in sociology at Cornell, fresh from a bachelor of arts degree in psychology from that same worthy institution. My education in psychology in a department still in the Titchnerian tradition had taught me more than any sane person could possibly care to know about warm spots, cold spots, pressure spots, and pain spots, but precious little about human personality. The young Urie Bronfenbrenner—he was just beginning his Cornell career at that time—introduced me to Kurt Lewin, Harry Stack Sullivan, and—most important of all—to the thinking and the intellectual vitality of Urie himself.

In the ensuing years, partly by planning and partly by happenstance, Urie and I have often bridged the gulfs of geography and academic discipline to meet and to talk—to talk with an intensity rarely matched in my experience with anyone else. Urie has influenced my thinking in so many ways, and so profoundly, that it would take more time than I have available simply to enumerate them. Our many lively discussions, particularly the many two-person seminars that we managed to have in Ithaca, in Washington, in Berlin, and wherever else we could get together, have been among the intellectual highlights of my life. I have benefited enormously from 45 years of having Urie as teacher—he is still my teacher—my colleague, and my friend.

If you were to look at the defining points of my own intellectual career (my choice of problems and my formulation of those problems), you would have not the slightest difficulty in seeing Urie's influence, particularly if you recognized how Urie's influence had interacted with those of my sociological mentors: Robin Williams, John Clausen, and Bill Whyte. I may not have adopted Urie's terminology—we do, after all, ply our trades in different disciplines—but I have certainly been attuned to his problem formulations and to his theoretical approach.

Because I cannot possibly deal with the whole of Urie's intellectual edifice in this paper, I choose to focus on an early Urie Bronfenbrenner chapter, one that long precedes, but clearly points the way toward *The Ecology of Human Development* (Bronfenbrenner, 1979). I refer, as you have already inferred from the title of my chapter, to his 1958 synthesis and reinterpretation of the research literature on social class and parent–child relations, "Socialization and Social Class Through Time and Space."

From early on, it was apparent to many people that what Urie had done in that paper was an extraordinary intellectual feat. Even so, I doubt that many people realized just *how* extraordinary a feat it was. I was particularly well positioned to appreciate its accomplishment because I had attempted the same task as a prelude to my own research and had failed in the effort. All I could see in the research literature that Urie reviewed was massive inconsistency, an inconsistency of findings, which were based on inconsistencies of conceptualization and of measurement and, in many instances, on abysmal methods. To me, the entire literature added up to nothing more than chaos, to be noted only in passing and then only because of the required academic ritual of "reviewing the literature," but the less said the better, because that literature led nowhere useful.

To Urie, though, the findings of these disparate and often methodologically deficient studies added up, not to chaos, but to orderly change. His was a remarkably insightful analysis. He also demonstrated the validity of a moral and methodological principle too often ignored by most of us, but characteristic of Urie's entire intellectual life: Do *not* dismiss past work for its flaws. Try, instead, to find what is valuable in everyone's past work, and build on that.[1]

I learned more than a methodological lesson, and more even than a moral lesson, from Urie's paper. That paper also taught me theoretical lessons that have helped define the main issues for my own work ever since. Urie, more than anyone else I know, will appreciate that some of those lessons came from the accomplishments of that paper, and some of those lessons came from its shortcomings. And what—I can hear Urie asking as I write this—is more useful than provocative failures, when they open up new issues? Urie will also appreciate that I learned some of the lessons of his paper when I first read it, but that I am only now coming to understand others of those lessons. I rather suspect that the latter will ultimately prove to have the greater impact; certainly, they are central to my current work.

Before pursuing these issues, I want briefly to review what I see as the main thrust of Urie's classic paper, just to refresh your memory, in case you have not reread that paper in recent decades. Then I want to discuss four very important issues that—for me—were posed by Urie's analysis, issues that have been at the heart of my own work ever since: (a) The difference between *parallelism* and *cause*. Urie raised the issue. I have devoted many years to pursuing it. (b) A crucial substantive problem: Why does *education* matter? The question has intrigued me ever since I read Urie's paper—as I have tried to distinguish between education as a precondition for jobs and the direct effects of education itself. (c) As exemplified in the title of Urie's paper, and carried further in his *Two Worlds of Childhood* (1970), the comparative theme of *space* has dominated my research of recent years. (d) The fourth issue is *time*, which is shorthand, in the title of Urie's paper, for the analysis of social change. For some years, I underestimated the importance of this theme, emphasizing stability over change.

---

[1]Some years later, when reviewing and assessing the research literature on social class and schizophrenia (Kohn, 1968), I took Urie's lesson to heart. As stated in the first footnote of that article:

> The *raison d'être* of this review, aside from its being momentarily current, is in its effort to organize the evidence around certain central issues and to make use of all studies relevant to those issues. There are no definitive studies in this field, but most of them contribute something to our knowledge when placed in perspective of all the others. (Kohn, 1968, p. 155)

143

But now the reality of radical social change in eastern Europe has caught up with me, and *change* is at the center of my work.

URIE'S ANALYSIS OF "SOCIALIZATION AND SOCIAL CLASS THROUGH TIME AND SPACE"

Urie's analysis was in two parts: the careful reassembly of past findings, made as comparable as possible and ordered in terms of when the field-work was done—from which a lovely pattern emerged—and the elucidation of the parallels between his findings and earlier findings on changes in advice given to parents by experts.

In the first part of Urie's analysis, he arrayed the findings from all published and some not-yet published studies, including one of my own—attempting to make the data of those studies as comparable as possible, mainly by collapsing all socioeconomic classifications into two broad categories: the middle class and the working class. As he was clearly aware, this classification amounted to settling for the lowest common denominator of the indexes used in the several studies, the distinction between nonmanual and manual employment. It was the only way that he could achieve comparability among the studies, and although a terribly crude classification, it proved fruitful. Urie divided the findings into those that dealt with child-rearing practices vis-á-vis infants and very young children, and those that dealt with child-rearing practices vis-á-vis somewhat older children. What was crucial—indeed, the guiding inspiration of the entire endeavor—was that he arrayed those two sets of findings, not in terms of the dates of publication of the studies, but in terms of when the fieldwork for these inquiries was carried out.

It sounds so simple in retrospect, but it was so imaginative: Urie side-stepped the ideological Sturm und Drang that had characterized this contentious literature; commented on the methodological inadequacies of the studies, but then regretfully acknowledged that there was little he could do about those inadequacies; and performed a reanalysis of the data that surpassed anything that any of the original investigators, or any other secondary analysts, including me, had done.

144

Where I had seen nothing other than inconsistent findings, Urie found a surprisingly consistent picture of orderly change. There had been substantial changes in the child-training techniques used by middle-class parents during the 25 years covered by the research. Similar changes had been taking place in the working class, but working-class parents had consistently lagged behind by a few years. While middle-class parents had once been more "restrictive" than working-class parents, by the late 1950s they had become the more "permissive."

Why the changes?—the second part of Urie's analysis. His interpretation was ingeniously, or ingenuously, simple. He noted that the changes in techniques used by middle-class parents closely paralleled those advocated by presumed experts, and he concluded that middle-class parents had changed their practices *because* they were responsive to what the experts had told them was right and proper. Working-class parents, being less educated and, thus, less directly responsive to printed communication, had followed only later. In support of this interpretation, he cited convincing evidence that middle-class mothers were much more likely to be exposed to current information on child care. In particular, they were much more likely to read books, pamphlets, and magazine articles written by the experts. From this, he inferred that [middle-class] "mothers not only read these books, but take them seriously" (Bronfenbrenner, 1958, p. 411). It was a plausible inference.

PARALLELISM AND CAUSE

Parallelism does not necessarily prove causality. In an article that I submitted to the *American Journal of Sociology* a few years later (published as Kohn, 1963), I questioned the "parallelism" portion of Urie's interpretation:

> Bronfenbrenner is almost undoubtedly right in asserting that middle-class parents have followed the drift of presumably expert opinion. But why have they done so? It is not sufficient to assume that the explanation lies in their greater degree of education. This might explain why middle-class parents are substantially more likely

145

than are working-class parents to *read* books and articles on child rearing, as we know they do. But they need not *follow* the experts' advice. We know from various studies of the mass media that people generally search for confirmation of their existing beliefs and practices and tend to ignore what contradicts them.

From all the information at our disposal, it looks as if middle-class parents not only read what the experts have to say, but also search out a wide variety of other sources of information and advice: they are far more likely than are working-class parents to discuss child-rearing with friends and neighbors, to consult physicians on these matters, to attend Parent–Teacher Association meetings, to discuss the child's behavior with his teacher. Middle-class parents seem to regard child rearing as more problematic than do working-class parents. This can hardly be a matter of education alone. It must be rooted more deeply in the conditions of life of the two social classes.

Everything about working-class parents' lives—their comparative lack of education, the nature of their jobs, their greater attachment to the extended family—conduces to their retaining familiar methods. Furthermore, even should they be receptive to change, they are less likely than are middle-class parents to find the experts' writings appropriate to their wants, for the experts predicate their advice on middle-class values. Everything about middle-class parents' lives, on the other hand, conduces to their looking for new methods to achieve their goals. They look to the experts, to other sources of relevant information, and to each other not for new values but for more serviceable techniques. And within the limits of our present scanty knowledge about means–ends relationships in child-rearing, the experts have provided practical and useful advice. It is not that middle-class parents slavishly follow the experts but that the experts have provided what the parents have sought. (Kohn, 1963, pp. 473–474)[2]

How did Urie react to this questioning of his interpretation? You undoubtedly know how most scholars would react to having their interpretations questioned. Not Urie. The editor of the *American Journal of Sociology* sent the article to Urie for anonymous review. Urie told the editor that he found my rationale convincing, and he recommended publication. He even reprinted the article in a volume he later edited. I would like to believe that under similar circumstances I would be capable of rising to the same moral stature.

Still, my offering and Urie's graciously accepting a plausible alternative interpretation did not necessarily mean that my interpretation was correct. I, too, was putting forth a largely prima facie case, one in keeping with the evidence, but by no means demonstrated.

Nor was I able to do much better in advancing my own central thesis, in *Class and Conformity* (Kohn, 1969), that class differences in values and orientation result primarily from systematically differentiated conditions of life—job conditions, in particular—that profoundly affect people's views of social reality. In support of this thesis, I argued (guess what?) that the evident parallel between class differences in people's job conditions and class differences in their values represented more than just a parallelism; it represented cause.

I began with the observation that

> there is an appealing simplicity to the supposition that the experience of occupational self-direction is conducive to valuing self-direction, off as well as on the job, and to seeing the possibilities for self-direction not only in work but also in other realms of life. (Kohn, 1969, p. 139)

In support of this hypothesis, I demonstrated that statistically controlling the job conditions conducive to, or restrictive of, occupational self-direction greatly reduced the initial correlations between social stratification and values and orientations. And then—the weakest link in the argument—I argued, on essentially a priori grounds, that the correlations of social stratification with job conditions, and of job conditions with values and orientations, could not be entirely a matter of self-directed people selecting and being selected for self-directed jobs and higher educational and occupational statuses. Some part of the explanation for these correlations must be that social stratification affects job conditions, and job conditions affect values and orientations.

The argument was plausible, but hardly definitive. Having questioned Urie's inferring cause from parallelism, I was not doing much better. But it was the best that I could do with cross-sectional data and with the methods of data analysis available at that time.

Later, Schooler and I (Kohn & Schooler, 1973), following the wise advice of Blalock, pushed the analysis one step further by using an econometric technique called *two-stage least squares,* to explore the magnitudes of effects in what we correctly presumed to be the reciprocal relationships between job conditions and personality. These analyses supported the supposition that job conditions actually do affect adult personality. However, it was not until we had collected longitudinal data and used the newly invented methods of confirmatory factor analysis and linear structural equations modeling (Kohn & Schooler, 1978, 1982, 1983) that I could be confident of an actual causal chain: Position in the stratification hierarchy profoundly affects (and is affected by) job conditions; job conditions profoundly affect (and are affected by) personality.

It had taken Schooler and me a quarter of a century of learning and hard work, and we could not have done it without the use of methods that were not invented until a couple of decades after Urie's analysis. What had begun as my questioning Urie's inference of cause from parallelism had become a major part of my own life's work, a persistent effort to go beyond an appealing parallel, to demonstrate an actual causal chain. Is it any wonder that Urie, doing a secondary analysis of published reports of other people's cross-sectional data, years before the invention of LISREL, had to settle for inferring causality from a parallel?

WHY DOES EDUCATION MATTER?

If Urie had not caused me enough trouble by posing the issue of what it takes to demonstrate an actual causal chain, he posed a further perplexing issue by focusing his interpretation on education. Why education, when the studies were based not on the parents' educational levels, but on their occupational status—Urie's primary differentiation being between parents employed in nonmanual and parents employed in manual occupations? To me, what was central about what Urie and I then called *social class* (and what I would now prefer to call *social stratification*) was its occupational, not its educational, component.

In hindsight, we were both half right. Urie was right about the importance of education, but he jumped too quickly to interpreting why education is important. I was right about the importance of occupation, but I was caught in the sociologist's characteristic error of contrasting education with occupational status, even though my own research demonstrated that status was only one component of occupation and by no means its most important component.

When, much later, Schooler and I painstakingly examined the direct and indirect effects of education on personality, we found that half or more of education's effect resulted from educational attainment being a major determinant of job conditions, in particular of the substantive complexity of the work, which, in turn, affect personality. It is not that education and job conditions are competing for importance; they are part of the same process.

If *part* of the explanation of education's affecting personality is that education is a major determinant of job conditions, then what is the rest of the explanation? For many years, Schooler and I puzzled over this question, without being able to do much about it, for our data came from interviews with adults who had long since completed their formal education. We got our chance to pursue the issue when we did a follow-up study of the men in our cross-sectional survey, this time interviewing their wives and selected offspring as well. It was the offspring, most of them still in school, who gave us the opportunity to study the relationship between educational process and personality development for people still in school.

Our underlying hypothesis was that a learning-generalization model—which is to say, an educational model—of how the conditions of work that adults experience in paid employment affect their personalities would apply as well to the conditions of work that adolescents and young adults experience in schooling. To that end, we created a concept, educational self-direction, exactly analogous to occupational self-direction: the use of initiative, thought, and independent judgment in schoolwork. We even asked questions exactly analogous to those for occupational self-direction: measuring the substantive complexity of schoolwork and closeness of supervision by the teachers.

Our analyses of educational self-direction and personality are far from definitive, partly because the indexes of educational self-direction are imprecise. We had to design questions applicable to a wide range of grade levels, from junior high school through graduate school, and, thus, had to ask very general questions. Moreover, the data are cross-sectional, which means *inter alia* that we cannot statistically control earlier measures of students' personality when assessing the effects of educational self-direction on current measures of personality. And because our data come from students scattered across the entire contiguous United States, we lack information about the organizational structure of the school systems, the social structures of the schools themselves, tracking, and all sorts of other important social structural facts. We believe that the lack of information about school structure does not invalidate our findings about educational process, but certainly we do not have as complete a picture as we would like to have. In effect, we examine educational self-direction in a social structural vacuum, whereas we would like to see it in context. Still, we did have one tremendous advantage in this analysis: Because our data come from a study of families, and not only of the students themselves, we are able to statistically control the pertinent dimensions of both parents' personalities when assessing the effects of educational self-direction on students' personalities.

In one set of analyses, Miller, Schooler, and I (K. A. Miller, Kohn, & Schooler, 1985) assessed the reciprocal relationship between educational self-direction and students' intellectual flexibility. We measured intellectual flexibility with a diverse array of indicators, ranging from cognitive questions, to the interviewer's rating of the respondent's intelligence, to an "agree score." It was not meant to be a measure of cognitive *ability*, which I do not think we can measure in any case, but a measure of actual intellectual performance in a non-school situation that seemed to elicit considerable intellectual effort, in short, a measure of the student's flexibility in attempting to cope with the intellectual demands of a complex situation.

With these measures and models, we found that the exercise of self-direction by students in their schoolwork has a decided effect on their intellectual flexibility and that their intellectual flexibility, in turn, has a decided effect on their exercise of self-direction in schoolwork—exactly parallel to our findings for employed adults about the reciprocal effects of occupational self-direction and intellectual flexibility. By slightly modifying the model, we also showed that it is the substantive complexity of schoolwork, not the closeness of supervision by teachers, that matters for students' intellectual flexibility. Moreover, separate analyses of secondary school and college students indicate that the findings apply to both. All these conclusions applied even though we statistically controlled both mother's and father's levels of intellectual flexibility, which means that both family process and genetics were substantially taken into account in our assessments of the effect of educational self-direction on students' intellectual flexibility.

We then extended the analyses (K. A. Miller, Kohn, & Schooler, 1986) to assess the relationships between educational self-direction and noncognitive aspects of personality. Here we used Schooler's and my conceptualization and measurement of two principal underlying dimensions of orientation to self and society (Kohn & Schooler, 1983, chapter 6): self-directedness of orientation versus conformity to external authority, and a sense of well-being versus a sense of distress.[3] We found that greater self-

---

[3] We have measured several distinct facets of orientation to self and society. For many analytic purposes, though, it is preferable to deal with a small number of fundamental dimensions that underlie these several facets of orientation. To do this, we use "second-order" confirmatory factor analyses, which show that there are two principal underlying dimensions: self-directedness of orientation versus conformity to external authority, and a sense of distress versus a sense of well-being. Self-directedness is reflected in not having authoritarian–conservative beliefs, having personally responsible standards of morality, being trustful of others, not being self-deprecatory, not being fatalistic, and not being conformist in one's ideas. Distress is reflected in anxiety, self-deprecation, lack of self-confidence, nonconformity in one's ideas, and distrust.

direction in schoolwork increases students' self-directedness of orientation and decreases their sense of distress. Distress, in turn, negatively affects educational self-direction. We also found that the effect of educational self-direction on self-directedness of orientation mainly results from substantively more complex schoolwork increasing self-directedness of orientation; closeness of supervision does not much matter. Closeness of supervision does matter for distress.

And then, finally, we extended the model to include all three facets of personality. The extended model generally confirmed what the more limited models had shown. In particular, educational self-direction affects all three dimensions of personality. And all three dimensions of personality, in turn, directly or indirectly affect educational self-direction. What is to me the most intriguing finding of all is the complex dynamics of the process. Contrary to my expectations, fully half of the effect of educational self-direction on intellectual flexibility is indirect through self-directedness of orientation: Greater educational self-direction increases students' self-directedness of orientation, and greater self-directedness of orientation increases intellectual flexibility. It is a matter of motivation: Wanting to think for yourself helps you to think.

To put the matter most simply, education matters for personality for much the same reasons as does occupation: People learn from their experiences, and learn most of all from having to cope with complex and demanding experiences. There is more to education than attuning people to the printed page, important though that is.

SPACE

The next challenge that Urie posed for my life's work was what in the title of his paper was simply called "space," but what in his later work, particularly in *Two Worlds of Childhood* (Bronfenbrenner, 1970), was refined to mean comparative, particularly cross-nationally comparative, analysis.

Cross-national research is valuable, even indispensable, for establishing the generality of findings and the validity of interpretations derived from single-nation studies. (See my extended discussions of this theme in

Kohn, 1987, 1989.) In no other way can we be certain that what we believe to be social structural regularities are not merely particularities, the product of some limited set of historical, cultural, or political circumstances. Consider my own research.

From our U.S. studies, my collaborators and I developed a powerful interpretation of the relationship between social structure and personality, an interpretation meant to apply not just to the United States but to all industrialized societies. The main theme of our findings and interpretation is that position in the social structure—in particular, in the class structure and the social stratification hierarchy—has profound effects on personality. A more advantageous class position, or a higher position in the stratification order, affords greater opportunity to be self-directed in one's work, that is, to work at jobs that are substantively complex, that are not subject to close supervision, and that are not routinized. The experience of occupational self-direction, in turn, leads to a higher valuation of self-direction for oneself and for one's children, to greater intellectual flexibility, and to a more self-directed orientation to self and society (Kohn, 1969; Kohn & Schooler, 1983, particularly chapters 5–7).

Being self-directed in one's work even leads to making more intellectually demanding use of one's leisure time (K. A. Miller & Kohn, 1983). Moreover, self-direction in realms other than paid employment—in particular, housework (Schooler, Kohn, Miller, & Miller, 1983) and, as we have seen, schoolwork (K. A. Miller et al., 1985, 1986)—has psychological effects very much like those of self-direction in paid employment. The experience of self-direction is of pervasive importance for linking social structural position to personality.

There have been many replications of this research, both in the United States and in several other industrialized societies. The findings of all of these studies are generally consonant with those of the original U.S. studies (see the review in Kohn & Slomczynski, 1990, chapter 9). The most systematic replications, and the most rigorous cross-national assessments of the interpretation, have been done in comparative studies carried out by Slomczynski and his associates in Poland in 1978 and by Naoi, Schooler, and their associates in Japan in 1979. The intent of these studies was to determine whether the findings and interpretation developed from the U.S. studies applied as well to an "actually existing socialist society," as Poland then was (see Kohn, Naoi, Schoenbach, Schooler, & Slomczynski, 1990; Kohn & Slomczynski, 1990; Slomczynski, Miller, & Kohn, 1981) and to a non-Western capitalist society (see Kohn et al., 1990; Naoi & Schooler, 1985; Schooler & Naoi, 1988).

I do not mean to imply that the United States in the 1960s and 1970s, and Japan in the 1970s, were exemplary of some ideal type of capitalist society, or that in 1978 Poland was exemplary of some ideal type of socialist society (to the contrary: see Wesolowski, 1988). Whether the United States and Japan really were capitalist at those times or some hybrid of capitalism and welfare statism, or whether Poland in 1978 really was socialist or state capitalist or some hybrid of socialism and capitalism is immaterial. The United States and Japan were different from Poland in the crucial respect of how their economies were organized: The United States and Japan had economies in which market forces predominated; Poland had a centrally planned and administered economy.

In most respects, the findings for Poland and Japan are entirely in keeping with those for the United States and support the interpretations that Schooler and I (Kohn & Schooler, 1983) drew from the U.S. data: Social structural position greatly affects opportunities, even the necessity, for occupational self-direction. The exercise of self-direction in work, in turn, increases intellectual flexibility, promotes the valuation of self-direction (in contrast to conformity to external authority) by parents for their children, and facilitates a self-directed orientation to self and others (see Kohn, 1987; Kohn et al., 1990). In short, social structural position has generally similar psychological effects in both capitalist and socialist societies and in both Western and non-Western capitalist societies. Moreover, and much more important, social structural position has generally similar effects for essentially the same reason: because position in the larger social structure profoundly affects people's immediately impinging conditions of life, their job conditions in particular, which affect their values, orientations, and cognitive functioning.

Further comparative analyses of the U.S. and Polish data have extended the interpretative model by showing that the psychological effects of occupational self-direction are as great for older workers as for younger and middle-aged workers (J. Miller, Slomczynski, & Kohn, 1985). These effects even extend intergenerationally: Parents' occupational self-direction affects their own values; their values in turn decidedly affect their children's values (Kohn & Slomczynski, 1990, chapter 7; Kohn, Slomczynski, & Schoenbach, 1986).

There is, then, tremendous interpretive value in knowing that the relationships of social structure and personality transcend the boundaries of a single nation–state—with its particular political and economic structure, its particular culture, and its unique history. Our interpretations can be much more general, and much more certain, when we have such information.

Cross-national research is equally valuable, perhaps even more valuable, for forcing us to revise our interpretations to take account of cross-national differences and inconsistencies that could never be uncovered in single-nation research. As apt an example as any is my collaborators' and my discovery that the relationship between social structure and a sense of well-being versus a sense of distress was radically different for the capitalist United States and for then-Socialist Poland, and different still for Japan. In the United States, managers have a strong sense of well-being, and manual workers are the most distressed social class; in Poland, nearly the opposite; and in Japan, as in the United States, managers have a strong sense of well-being, but it is the nonmanual workers, not the manual workers, who are particularly distressed (Kohn et al., 1990; Kohn & Slomczynski, 1990). Similarly, for the United States, the correlation between social stratification and distress is negative; for Poland, it is positive; and for Japan, it is virtually nil. This single set of findings caused us to do considerable soul-searching about our general interpretive model, not only as it applied to Poland and to Japan but even as it applied to the United States.

Our original analyses of U.S. data (Kohn & Schoenbach, 1983) clearly showed that the relationships of both social class and social stratification with a sense of well-being or of distress paralleled those of class and stratification with all other facets of psychological functioning that we had investigated: The more advantageous their location in the class structure, or the higher their position in the stratification order, the greater is men's sense of well-being, just as the greater their valuation of self-direction, the greater their degree of intellectual flexibility, and the more self-directed their orientations to self and society. Moreover, the explanation for the relationships between position in the social structure and a sense of well-being or of distress seemed to be much the same as that for the relationships between position in the social structure and other facets of personality, with occupational self-direction being the key intervening link between social structure and a sense of well-being or distress.

We were well aware that occupational self-direction does not provide as complete an explanation of the relationship between position in the social structure and a sense of well-being or of distress as it does of the relationships between position in the social structure and other facets of personality.[4] We were also aware (Kohn & Schooler, 1982; 1983, chapter 6) that job conditions other than those directly involved in occupational self-direction are more important for distress than for other facets of personality. But these we regarded as minor variations on a doubly consistent theme: Social structure had consistent effects on all facets of personality that we studied, and the consistent explanation of these consistent effects was that position in the social structure decidedly affected occupational self-direction and that occupational self-direction decidedly affected personality.

The discoveries that the relationships of social structure with a sense of well-being or of distress are dramatically different—nearly the opposite—for Poland, and different still for Japan—meant that we had to reassess our interpretation, not only as it applied or did not apply to Poland

---

[4]That is, statistically controlling the job conditions determinative of occupational self-direction does not reduce the correlations between social structural position and a sense of well-being or of distress to nearly the same degree as it does the correlations between social structural position and other facets of personality.

and to Japan, but also as it applied to the United States. The minor variations on theme no longer seemed so minor.

Perhaps we should have realized this even before we had the discrepant cross-national evidence. But one simply does not focus on what seem to be minor variations in the face of a powerful interpretation that is consistent with all of the evidence at hand and that withstands many competing interpretations. The process of theoretical interpretation necessarily requires one to emphasize main themes and to de-emphasize variations. One does not focus on the variations—that is, unless and until one has reason to think them not so minor. The discrepant cross-national findings provided just that evidence. Only then did we pay serious attention to our interpretation being less powerful for the sense of well-being or of distress than for other facets of personality, and only then did we seriously attempt to integrate our findings for other job conditions into our interpretation of the relationship between position in the social structure and the sense of well-being or of distress. These analyses led to a significant enlargement of our interpretation.

We continue to believe that part of the reason why social structural position affects people's sense of well-being or of distress is that social structural position affects opportunities for occupational self-direction and that the experience of occupational self-direction is conducive to a sense of well-being and ameliorates a sense of distress. What is new in our interpretation is the recognition that social structural position also affects people's sense of well-being or distress through its effects on other job conditions—notably, job uncertainties and protections from those uncertainties—in ways that countervail the effects of social structural position through occupational self-direction.

For example, at the time of our surveys, manual workers in the United States had less opportunity for occupational self-direction than did members of more advantaged social classes, which is the main reason why manual workers were the most distressed social class. But many manual workers have (or, at any rate, *had*) considerable job protections, such as seniority provisions in union contracts, and such job protections ameliorate distress. Manual workers were distressed because they lacked opportunities for occupational self-direction—despite the job protections that many of them, particularly union members, enjoyed. Were it not for these job protections, manual workers would have been even more distressed than they were. Correspondingly, managers—who enjoyed substantial opportunity for occupational self-direction and, hence, had a relatively strong sense of well-being—would have had an even greater sense of well-being if they had greater job protections. Occupational self-direction and job protections have countervailing effects.

Thus, to adequately explain the relationships of social structure to job conditions to distress, we had to enlarge the range of job conditions beyond those directly involved in occupational self-direction, to take account of countervailing influences of other job conditions also associated with social structural position. Whether or not we should have recognized this from U.S. data alone, the fact is that we did not recognize it until we were brought face-to-face with a striking cross-national inconsistency. Only then did we enlarge our model, not only as it applies to Poland and Japan, but even as it applies to the United States. It was precisely because we found cross-national differences that we had to rethink our interpretation of the U.S. data.

Admittedly, this takes us quite some distance from Urie's analysis of "space," but he did point the direction. To understand the relationship between social structure and personality in any one country, for example, the United States, it is essential that we systematically search for comparative evidence. Even if we had no interest at all in other countries for their own sake, it would still be essential to do systematic cross-national comparisons if we want to understand processes internal to our own country.

SOCIAL CHANGE

In his analysis of socialization and social class through time and space, Urie used the word *time* not only to describe his inventive methodology of arraying the studies according to the time when fieldwork was carried out, but also to call attention to social change.[5] Still, he did note that in some respects, there was also great stability over the 25 years encompassed in the inquiries he reassessed. Parental practices had changed, but there was little or no evidence of change in the relationship of social class to parental values or, for that matter, in the relationship of social class to the overall quality of parent–child relations.

In my 1963 discussion of Urie's 1958 paper, I noted the following:

> There is clear evidence that the past quarter-century has seen change, even faddism, with respect to the use of breast-feeding or bottle-feeding, scheduling or not scheduling, spanking or isolating. But when we generalize from these specifics to talk of a change from "restrictive" to "permissive" practices—or, worse yet, of a change from "restrictive" to "permissive" parent–child relationships—we impute to them a far greater importance than they probably have, either to parents or to children.
>
> There is no evidence that recent faddism in child-training techniques is symptomatic of profound changes in the relations of parents to children in either social class. In fact, as Bronfenbrenner notes, what little evidence we do have points in the opposite direction: the overall quality of parent–child relationships does not seem to have changed substantially in either class. In all probability, parents have changed techniques in service of much the same values, and the changes have been quite specific. These changes must be explained, but the enduring characteristics are probably even more important. (Kohn, 1963, p. 473)

With that, I focused my attention for the next quarter century on "the enduring characteristics," assessing the relationship of social structure to

---

[5]In his later work, as several authors in this volume point out, Urie Bronfenbrenner has focused more and more on a third sense of the word *time*, namely, the timing of crucial events during an individual's life course. (See, in particular, Phyllis Moen's introduction to this volume, as well as the chapters by Clausen, Elder, and Moen and Erickson.) Urie is still way ahead of me, for my own work has dealt with the life course only incidentally, mainly in showing that the effects of job complexity on intellective process are as great for the oldest cohort of employed men in the United States and Poland as for the youngest and middle cohorts (J. Miller et al., 1985). This is not quite the type of finding that advocates of the life course perspective especially welcome, but it is, at any rate, an acknowledgment that theirs is an important perspective that I should take into greater account.

personality in what appeared to be stable, albeit very different, societies. I might still be ignoring social change, were it not for the revolutionary events in Poland, and later in the other countries of eastern Europe, that compelled me to attend to the psychological implications of radical social change.

My collaborators' and my past research, and our entire understanding of social structure and personality, have been based on studies conducted under relatively stable social conditions. This is true even for the Polish survey, which was carried out more than a year before the advent of *Solidarnosc*, before there were any decided signs of impending change. The obvious and important question is whether our findings and interpretation apply also in times of radical social change.[6] Will the relationships between social structure and personality remain the same during a period of radical social change, or will those relationships themselves be radically transformed? This is a truly exciting question.

If the generalizations and interpretations developed from studies conducted under conditions of relative stability should apply under conditions of radical social change, this would greatly increase the power of those interpretations. If not, how must past interpretations be modified, either in terms of delimiting the conditions under which they apply or in terms of respecifying the mechanisms through which social structure affects individual psychological functioning? My collaborators and I have developed a new research project to attempt to answer these questions.[7]

The very idea of there being a relationship between social structure and personality implies a dynamic interchange. What we learn about this interchange at times of social stability provides a static slice of a dynamic process.[8] Whether what we learn of that process is typical of the more general process

---

[6]I follow Williams (1970) in conceiving social change as change in the structure of the society, not merely as an eventful or dramatic period in the life of that society: "Change occurs when there is a shift in pattern, when new relationships emerge" (p. 621).

[7]This research is being supported by the National Science Foundation and the National Council for Soviet and East European Research.

[8]Unlike those who see an incompatibility between the concepts of social structure and social change, I think that the concept of structure is entirely consistent with that of change. Built into the definition of social structure is the notion of relatively enduring patterns of behavior, but certainly not of permanence or nonmodifiability (on this point, see Boskoff, 1966).

or is specific to times of social stability is at present an open question. The null hypothesis, so to speak, is that our general interpretation of the relationships between social structure and personality will prove valid even during periods of radical social change. The alternative hypothesis would predict that radical social change might obliterate or, at any rate, greatly modify the relationships between social structure and personality that we have heretofore found. This could happen for any of several reasons:

1. The class and stratification systems of Poland, and of the other countries of eastern Europe, are themselves in the process of change. It is an open question whether the class structures and the systems of social stratification of these societies will be as completely transformed as their political and economic structures. Nevertheless, there is every reason to expect that with marketization and privatization, these systems will be substantially reshaped. For example, in Poland there is almost certain to be a considerable expansion and internal diversification of the class of small- to medium-sized employers; in the former Soviet Union, where there has been no such class, it is now beginning to emerge (sometimes in the form of so-called "cooperatives"). Almost certainly, everywhere in eastern Europe, the stratification hierarchies will become steeper: Inequality will increase. And, of course, with the Communist Party no longer a dominant power, other sources of political power will assume a more important role in shaping the social structure. These and other changes in the class structure and stratification system may bring about corresponding changes in the relationships of these very facets of social structure with personality.

2. In all of our studies, the invariant relationship has been between social structural position and occupational self-direction, a relationship that transcends differences between capitalist and socialist, Western and non-Western societies. (Such cross-national differences as we have found are entirely at the next linkage, that between occupational self-direction and personality.) It is certainly a plausible hypothesis, though, that the relationship between social structural po-

sition and occupational self-direction may be weakened during periods of transformation from one system to another, when the occupational structure is itself in flux. Although one cannot predict the final outcome, it is already clear that as massive, state-run, highly bureaucratized enterprises are dismantled, fewer people will be employed in such enterprises, and more people will be employed as entrepreneurs or as employees in small enterprises and in the secondary and informal economies. Many other changes are likely to be introduced in working conditions, including those attendant on the introduction of new technologies—which, as the history of the United States and of western Europe has shown (Form, 1987; Spenner, 1983), can have both positive and negative, often unpredictable, implications for workers' opportunities for self-direction in their work. The obvious hypothesis is that the heretofore invariant relationship between social structural position and opportunities for occupational self-direction may be weakened or may even disappear under such conditions.

3. The pivotal role of occupational self-direction as an explanatory link between social structural position and personality may well be challenged under the conditions of change and uncertainty presently being experienced in eastern Europe. Job conditions other than those directly involved in occupational self-direction may come much more to the fore. It is certainly a plausible extrapolation from our past findings vis-á-vis distress that conditions of uncertainty, and not only job uncertainty, will have powerful psychological effects. It is a reasonable hypothesis, as well, that non-job conditions of life may play an important bridging role between social structural position and psychological functioning during a period when occupational conditions are in flux. Church, political organizations, neighborhood, family, friendship networks, and even voluntary organizations may come to play a more important role in shaping or buffering the proximate experiences that link position in the social structure to individual psychological functioning. Finally, current conditions of life may play a less crucial role, and people's ex-

pectations about their future prospects a more important role, under conditions of radical social change.

4. There is also the distinct possibility that the experience of radical social change will itself have such wide-ranging psychological consequences as to overwhelm all else. I certainly do expect that the uncertainties attendant on radical social change will increase distress. There is reason to expect, as well, that anything that increases distress will also affect the relationships between social structural position and other facets of psychological functioning. All of the relationships we have studied—those between social structural position and occupational self-direction; those between occupational self-direction and psychological functioning; and, what may be most pertinent here, those between the several different dimensions of psychological functioning—are reciprocal. In our analyses of longitudinal U.S. data (Kohn & Schooler, 1983, chapter 6), Schooler and I found, for example, that distress has a dampening effect on self-directedness of orientation, thus also on intellectual flexibility and on occupational self-direction. Might the distress-inducing conditions of life now being experienced in eastern Europe short-circuit the processes by which advantaged position facilitates a self-directed orientation and intellectual flexibility in more stable times?

5. Finally, even if the interpretation we have drawn from our past research should prove to be generally applicable to the changing circumstances of life in eastern Europe, our map of the actual empirical relationships will have to be modified in its particulars. To take only one striking example, Slomczynski and I found (Kohn & Slomczynski, 1990, Table 8.3) that Polish managers who did not belong to the Polish United Workers (Communist) Party were exceptional in their degree of distress: They were much more distressed than managers who did belong to the Party and also more distressed than members of any other social class. That particular finding cannot be replicated in a Poland where the Party no longer exists. But our more general interpretation—that the non-Party managers were so distressed because their positions entailed uncertainties, risks,

and insecurities greater than those experienced by managers who were members of the Party and greater than those experienced by managers in the less centralized systems of the capitalist countries—could be tested by looking for sources of job insecurities, and job support, in the modified occupational structure of post-Socialist Poland. More than that, the changes currently being experienced in eastern Europe provide an exceptional opportunity for increasing our understanding of the relationships between social structurally based uncertainties and the sense of distress.

How do we learn more about the effects of radical social change on the relationships between social structure and personality? Poland is certainly experiencing radical social change, and for my purposes a restudy of Poland is strategically central. The former Soviet Union offers an attractive contrast for much the same reason that my collaborators and I originally studied Poland and Japan: to differentiate social structural universals from single-nation particularities. A comparative study of Poland and the former Soviet Union would provide an opportunity to study the effects of social change under rather different conditions. The political conditions of the two are, of course, quite different. Poland is also much further along in the transition from a Socialist to some form of post-Socialist economy, and we can foresee the eventual outcome of the process with somewhat greater assurance for Poland than for any of the Republics of the former Soviet Union. Poland evidently is moving toward some form of market economy, the Parliament having long since passed the necessary enabling legislation and the populace being generally, albeit with growing reservations, in favor of such a transformation. For the Republics of the former Soviet Union, there is considerably greater uncertainty about what form their economies will eventually take.

The former Soviet Union as an entirety, however, is too ethnically and linguistically heterogenous, and too complex politically, for my purposes; a study of one of the larger Republics is both more feasible and more strategic. Ukraine is particularly well suited for comparison to Poland, because (by contrast to the other Republics) its culture is relatively similar to Poland's. Poland and Ukraine differ less in culture than in political and economic context. This should make it much more possible to interpret whatever differences we may find than if we were to choose societies that differed in both culture and social structural context. My collaborators and I have therefore conducted surveys of Poland and Ukraine, both of them carried out in late 1992.[9]

For practical reasons, we limit ourselves to the urban populace, but we do include all adults living in urban areas. The changing conditions that Poland and Ukraine are currently experiencing make it essential that we define the pertinent population to include both employed and unemployed men and women. In the process of radical social change, the not currently employed may be the most affected, very likely the most adversely affected. This seems almost self-evident for those who have lost their jobs and are actively seeking new employment, as well as for those who may be too discouraged to seek new employment. Another group who may be adversely affected by social change are the members of a growing social category (in Poland, albeit not yet in Ukraine): women who had been employed but who have become housewives, either because they have lost their jobs and cannot find new employment or because they can no longer afford to be employed, as a result of the dismantling of state child care and other facilities. The study of social structure and personality cannot be limited to the employed populace.

Our new research is thus comparative in three distinct ways: It is comparative over time, in that it compares Poland in late 1992, under conditions of radical social change, to the Poland of 1978, a time of relative stability. It compares Poland to Ukraine, a Republic that is also undergoing radical social change but under rather different political and economic cir-

---

[9]My collaborators in this research are Kazimierz Slomczynski (of the Ohio State University and the Institute of Philosophy and Sociology of the Polish Academy of Sciences), Bogdan Mach (of the Institute of Political Studies of the Polish Academy of Sciences), Krystyna Janicka and Wojciech Zaborowski (of the Institute of Philosophy and Sociology of the Polish Academy of Sciences), and Valeri Khmelko and Vladimir Paniotto (of the National University "Kiev-Mohyla Academy"). For further information about the design of these surveys, and about the questions asked of the respondents, see Kohn, Slomczynski, Janicka, Khmelko, et al. (1992) or Kohn, Slomczynski, Janicka, Mach, and Zaborowski (1992). For a history of the research, beginning with the origins of the original Polish study and continuing through the planning of the current research, see Kohn (1993).

cumstances. And it compares both Poland and Ukraine to the United States and Japan, two relatively stable capitalist societies.

In short, my collaborators and I are pursuing Urie's themes of "time and space" to a fare-thee-well. It has taken us only 35 years to catch up to where Urie Bronfenbrenner was in 1958. Not too bad, by my reckoning, considering the standard by which I am judging our efforts.

REFERENCES

Boskoff, A. (1966). Social change: Major problems in the emergence of theoretical and research foci. In H. Becker & A. Boskoff (Eds.), *Modern sociological theory: In continuity and change* (pp. 260–302). New York: Holt, Rinehart & Winston.

Bronfenbrenner, U. (1958). Socialization and social class through time and space. In E. E. Maccoby, T. M. Newcomb, & E. L. Hartley (Eds.), *Readings in social psychology* (pp. 400–425). New York: Holt, Rinehart & Winston.

Bronfenbrenner, U. (1970). *Two worlds of childhood: U.S. and U.S.S.R.*. New York: Russell Sage Foundation.

Bronfenbrenner, U. (1979). *The ecology of human development: Experiments by nature and design.* Cambridge, MA: Harvard University Press.

Form, W. (1987). On the degradation of skills. In W. R. Scott & J. F. Short, Jr. (Eds.), *Annual review of sociology* (Vol. 13, pp. 29–47). Palo Alto, CA: Annual Reviews.

Kohn, M. L. (1963). Social class and parent–child relationships: An interpretation. *American Journal of Sociology, 68,* 471–480.

Kohn, M. L. (1968). Social class and schizophrenia: A critical review. *Journal of Psychiatric Research, 6*(Suppl. 1), 155–173.

Kohn, M. L. (1969). *Class and conformity: A study in values.* Homewood, IL: Dorsey. (2nd ed., University of Chicago Press, 1977)

Kohn, M. L. (1987). Cross-national research as an analytic strategy: American Sociological Association 1987 presidential address. *American Sociological Review, 52,* 713–731.

Kohn, M. L. (Ed.). (1989). *Cross-national research in sociology: American Sociological Association presidential series.* Newbury Park, CA: Sage.

Kohn, M. L. (1993). Studying social structure and personality under conditions of radical social change: The biography of an ongoing research project (1992

Cooley-Mead Award lecture, American Sociological Association). *Social Psychology Quarterly, 56*, 4–20.

Kohn, M. L., Naoi, A., Schoenbach, C., Schooler, C., & Slomczynski, K. (1990). Position in the class structure and psychological functioning in the United States, Japan, and Poland. *American Journal of Sociology, 95*, 964–1008.

Kohn, M. L., & Schoenbach, C. (1983). Class, stratification, and psychological functioning. In M. L. Kohn & C. Schooler (Eds.), *Work and personality: An inquiry into the impact of social stratification* (pp. 154–193). Norwood, NJ: Ablex.

Kohn, M. L., & Schooler, C. (1973). Occupational experience and psychological functioning: An assessment of reciprocal effects. *American Sociological Review, 38*, 97–118.

Kohn, M. L., & Schooler, C. (1978). The reciprocal effects of the substantive complexity of work and intellectual flexibility: A longitudinal assessment. *American Journal of Sociology, 84*, 24–52.

Kohn, M. L., & Schooler, C. (1982). Job conditions and personality: A longitudinal assessment of their reciprocal effects. *American Journal of Sociology, 87*, 1257–1286.

Kohn, M. L., & Schooler, C. (with the collaboration of Miller, J., Miller, K. A., Schoenbach, C., & Schoenberg, R.). (1983). In M. L. Kohn & C. Schooler (Eds.), *Work and personality: An inquiry into the impact of social stratification.* Norwood, NJ: Ablex.

Kohn, M. L., & Slomczynski, K. M. (with the collaboration of Schoenbach, C.). (1990). *Social structure and self-direction: A comparative analysis of the United States and Poland.* Oxford, England: Basil Blackwell.

Kohn, M. L., Slomczynski, K. M., Janicka, K., Khmelko, V., Mach, B. W., Paniotto, V., & Zaborowski, W. (1992). Social structure and personality under conditions of radical social change: A comparative study of Poland and Ukraine. In H. Mannari, H. K. Nishio, J. Watanuki, & K. Azumi (Eds.), *Power shifts and value changes in the post Cold War world: Proceedings (selected papers) of the joint symposium of the International Sociological Association's research committees: Comparative Sociology and Sociology of Organizations* (pp. 97–111). Kurashiki City, Japan: Kibi International University.

Kohn, M. L., Slomczynski, K. M., Janicka, K., Mach, B. W., & Zaborowski, W. (1992). Social structure and personality under conditions of radical social change: A theoretical approach and research strategy. *Sisyphus: Sociological studies* (Polish Academy of Sciences), *2*(8), 145–159.

Kohn, M. L., Slomczynski, K. M., & Schoenbach, C. (1986). Social stratification and the transmission of values in the family: A cross-national assessment. *Sociological Forum*, *1*, 73–102.

Miller, J., Slomczynski, K. M., & Kohn, M. L. (1985). Continuity of learning-generalization: The effect of job on men's intellective process in the United States and Poland. *American Journal of Sociology*, *91*, 593–615.

Miller, K. A., & Kohn, M. L. (1983). The reciprocal effects of job conditions and the intellectuality of leisure-time activities. In M. L. Kohn & C. Schooler (Eds.), *Work and personality: An inquiry into the impact of social stratification* (pp. 217–241). Norwood, NJ: Ablex.

Miller, K. A., Kohn, M. L., & Schooler, C. (1985). Educational self-direction and the cognitive functioning of students. *Social Forces*, *63*, 923–944.

Miller, K. A., Kohn, M. L., & Schooler, C. (1986). Educational self-direction and personality. *American Sociological Review*, *51*, 372–390.

Naoi, A., & Schooler, C. (1985). Occupational conditions and psychological functioning in Japan. *American Journal of Sociology*, *90*, 729–752.

Schooler, C., Kohn, M. L., Miller, K. A., & Miller, J. (1983). Housework as work. In M. L. Kohn & C. Schooler (Eds.), *Work and personality: An inquiry into the impact of social stratification* (pp. 242–260). Norwood, NJ: Ablex.

Schooler, C., & Naoi, A. (1988). The psychological effects of traditional and of economically peripheral job settings in Japan. *American Journal of Sociology*, *94*, 335–355.

Slomczynski, K. M., Miller, J., & Kohn, M. L. (1981). Stratification, work, and values: A Polish–United States comparison. *American Sociological Review*, *46*, 720–744.

Spenner, K. I. (1983). Deciphering Prometheus: Temporal change in the skill level of work. *American Sociological Review*, *48*, 824–837.

Wesolowski, W. (1988). *Does socialist stratification exist?* (The fifth Fuller bequest lecture). University of Essex, Department of Sociology.

Williams, R. M., Jr. (1970). *American society: A sociological interpretation* (3rd ed.). New York: Knopf.

6

Linked Lives:
A Transgenerational Approach
to Resilience

Phyllis Moen and Mary Ann Erickson

U rie Bronfenbrenner has often remarked that the family is the primary, as well as the most efficient and effective, agent for promoting child development. But how does this come about? From the perspective of the ecology of human development, the psychological and social resources of parents can be important ingredients in fostering their children's healthy development. And we know that potentially stressful transitions and turning points in the family—the death of a family member, divorce, a major move—can transform the very fabric of children's lives. But do these childhood experiences and parental resources have lasting implications, leaving their imprint on the next generation as it moves into and through adulthood?

A key component of healthy development is the cultivation of *psychosocial resilience*. This concept refers to a sense of competency and effectiveness, on the one hand, and to connectedness to the broader community, on the other. Those who possess such resources can best cope with life's inevitable setbacks and challenges. In this chapter, we draw on both the ecology of human development and the life course frameworks to propose a transgenerational approach to resilience in adult children. These

The research reported in this chapter was supported by Research Grant Nos. R01-AG05450 from the National Institute on Aging and Hatch-321420 from the U. S. Department of Agriculture.

169

paradigms share a common focus on continuity and change over time and across generations (Bronfenbrenner, 1979, this volume, chapter 19; Bronfenbrenner & Ceci, 1994; Elder, this volume, chapter 4). Uniting both frameworks is an emphasis on the interdependencies between generations.

How do the characteristics of person (especially parents) and context in the family of orientation play out in promoting optimal development in children as they become adults? The first section of this chapter addresses broad conceptual issues in building a model of transgenerational influences, focusing on both the nature and antecedents of resilience. To actually test an ecology of the life course model calls for a research design including components of person, process, timing, and context and is beyond the scope of this chapter. Indeed, few data sources meet such stringent demands. However, in the second section, we draw on admittedly incomplete data from an ongoing study of mothers and daughters, to at least illustrate how one might investigate intergenerational factors affecting adult daughters' psychological and social resources.

THE NATURE OF RESILIENCE

Resilience can be defined as the capacity to cope with life's setbacks and challenges. As Werner (1990) pointed out, the concepts of *resilience* and *protective factors* are the obverse of *vulnerability* and *risk factors*. Two sets of protective factors promote resilience in the face of adversity: *social resources* and *personal resources* (see Rutter, 1987; Schaefer & Moos, 1992). *Social resources* pertain to social integration or connectedness and consist of social bonds in the form of multiple role occupancy, the presence of a confidant relationship, good relationships with family and friends, and access to support networks. Such social connectedness enables individuals to withstand stressful events and strains. *Personal resources* encompass subjective dispositions such as self-reliance, self-understanding, empathy, altruism, maturity, and basic values and priorities. One important psychological resource is a sense of mastery, involving assessments about how well one can deal with ambiguous or stressful situations (Bandura, 1982, 1989, 1994). These attributes also contribute to an individual's capacity to cope with adversity. Both personal and social resources have been termed *psychosocial resources*, or *coping resources*.

Research has documented the importance of these psychosocial resources in moderating the negative psychological effects of stressful events and ongoing strains (e.g., Bandura, 1989; Betz & Hackett, 1987; Lazarus & Folkman, 1984). For example, research has shown that the effects of stress on depressive symptomatology are lessened in the face of such personal coping resources as self-esteem and mastery (e.g., Pearlin, Lieberman, Menaghan, & Mullan, 1981; Pearlin & Schooler, 1978; Thoits, 1987). Similarly, social integration, in the form of multiple role involvements, has been negatively associated with depressive symptomatology (Moen, Dempster-McClain, & Williams, 1995; Thoits, 1983, 1986). Thus, individuals with high levels of personal and social resources are typically more effective in the face of life stressors and strains than those lacking such assets. In this chapter, we characterize individuals with high levels of personal and social coping resources as *resilient*.

THE INTERGENERATIONAL ANTECEDENTS OF RESILIENCE

What is the developmental course of resilience? Is there congruence across the generations in resilience? Do parents' feelings of well-being and agency (e.g., optimism, self-esteem, and mastery) or their social integration (e.g., multiple role involvements) promote these same resources in their adult children? What are the impacts of family stressors during childhood on subsequent adult resilience? An ecology of the life course model of resilience suggests a number of questions: (a) Are, and under what circumstances, parental coping resources transmitted to adult children? (b) What is the role of the family environment, with its childhood stressors, in shaping children's subsequent resilience as adults? (c) Do current circumstances in adult children's lives moderate the effects of early experiences on their resilience, and how are current circumstances themselves shaped by earlier experiences? Finally, this approach also emphasizes that societal changes may affect the influence of one generation on the next. (d) How do broad social changes in the larger opportunity structure and in societal norms affect the influence of parents on their children?

Current Theoretical Approaches

We begin with two traditional views of intergenerational connections: *socialization theory* and *status attainment*. Much of the research on intergenerational transmission has followed either childhood socialization, social status models, or a combination of the two (Acock, 1984; Acock & Bengtson, 1980; Glass, Bengtson, & Dunham, 1986; Kohn, Slomczynski, & Schoenbach, 1986).

Socialization

Socialization theory suggests the importance of early childhood experiences and social learning, whether in terms of role modeling or verbal exhortations, for the transmission of ideologies, orientations, and behavior across the generations (e.g., Bandura, 1982, 1989). As Caplan (1976) described it, the family is a "collector and disseminator of information about the world" (p. 22). As Haller (1982) pointed out, significant others may be *definers*, who communicate their expectations to the individual, or *models*, who illustrate their own statuses and roles to the individual. This may be consequential for children experiencing family stress during their childhood; what is learned may not be vulnerability, but family strategies of adaptation (Elder, 1974; Moen & Wethington, 1992; Rutter, 1987).

However, socialization models do not address the question as to whether children respond more to what their parents *do* or to what they *say*, especially when the two kinds of messages are contradictory. A traditional homemaker, for example, may be extremely frustrated in that role and consequently encourage her daughter not to identify with or emulate her.

Status Attainment

The status attainment model of educational and occupational achievement underscores the importance of both socioeconomic background and parental encouragement for educational, occupational, and economic success (Blau & Duncan, 1967; Featherman & Hauser, 1978; Sewell & Hauser,

1975). What may matter most for children's resilience as adults is their family of origin's location in the social structure. Socialization may occur less directly, as a function of role modeling or explicit persuasion, than indirectly, in the provision of resources and opportunities during, and following, childhood. Coleman (1988), for example, pointed to the significance of social capital, in the form of cultural advantages and interpersonal resources, as key to the development of human capital in the next generation.

Thus, there is the possibility that parents transmit not so much specific psychological orientations but, rather, access to social, cultural, and economic resources and position in the larger social structure. Parents and children typically occupy the same *social address* (Bronfenbrenner, 1979); that is, they have the same social class, ethnic, and religious background and are likely to attain similar levels of educational achievement. Any congruence in psychological coping resources between the generations may simply reflect the benefits of their family's location in the opportunity structure of society, rather than direct parental influence per se.

Literature on status similarity (e.g., Fischer, 1981, 1986; Glass et al., 1986; Suitor, 1987, 1988) builds on this social address theme, suggesting that parents and children who occupy the same roles or positions within society will be more alike in attitudes and values and emotionally closer than those in different locations in the social structure. Parents, from this perspective, do not socialize their children in terms of transmitting specific coping resources but, rather, provide access to resources and social position that, in turn, shape self-conceptions and social connectedness. And they do so differentially—with, for example, the eldest son getting the farm while the daughters are encouraged to marry within the parents' social circle.

Linking Person and Environment

The sociological focus on family resources in status attainment theory provides a useful lens with which to view parent–child dyads, suggesting that any intergenerational similarities in coping resources may be less a consequence of explicit socialization than of social address, that is, location in the larger social structure. But the process of parenting also matters. Socialization theorists remind us that experiences in childhood play a pivotal role in identity formation with significant people, such as parents, being most influential (e.g., Bandura, 1982, 1989; Chodorow, 1978).

We suggest that both status attainment and socialization processes operate in a complex, interactive way, each modifying the effects of the other. For example, educated parents who are themselves resilient are likely to provide the optimal circumstances for the fostering of resilience in their children. And their parents' socioeconomic status could be particularly salient for children's subsequent social resources, in terms of their own role involvements and achievements in adulthood. It may well be that parents' emotional health is most consequential for their children's psychological coping resources under some circumstances, but not others. We consider both status attainment and socialization in the larger framework of the ecology of the life course.

AN ECOLOGY OF THE LIFE COURSE APPROACH

The life course orientation (Clausen, 1986; Elder, 1985, 1992; Hagestad, 1990) emphasizes the potential importance of *trajectories, transitions,* and their *timing,* whereas the ecology of human development (Bronfenbrenner, 1979, Bronfenbrenner & Ceci, 1994) emphasizes the significance of *context* and of viewing development as a joint function of characteristics of the *person* and the *environment.* In Bronfenbrenner's (1979) book, *The Ecology of Human Development,* the issue of time was conspicuously absent. Since then, Bronfenbrenner has increasingly focused on two important aspects of time: development through the life course and transgenerational transmission (Bronfenbrenner & Ceci, 1994).

Transitions and events experienced in adulthood always occur within the context of ongoing life trajectories (Elder, this volume, chapter 4). Thus, adults confront the stressors of adulthood equipped with differing levels of social and personal resources, rendering them more or less resilient in the face of these stressors. To what degree do childhood experiences promote or inhibit the development of these coping resources?

The child development literature typically focuses on the childhood years; consequently, it has little to say about the factors in parents' lives that relate to children's well-being as they mature into adulthood. However, the life course and developmental psychopathology literatures, along with Bronfenbrenner's ecology of human development perspective, suggest that just such a temporal, transgenerational perspective may provide insights into the antecedents of adult resilience. Quinton and Rutter (1988), for example, examined the reproduction of discordant family life across generations, as well as the pathways away from such continuity in dysfunction. Caspi, Elder, and Bem (1987, 1988) looked at the ties between early antisocial or shy behavior in childhood and similar difficulties in adulthood. Brown and Harris (1978) charted the long-term effects of early life events on women's subsequent depression. And Clausen (1991, 1993) documented the importance of feelings of competence during adolescence in shaping the adult life course. The notion of hardiness (Kobasa, 1987) suggests that psychological resources acquired earlier in life, such as a sense of control and self-worth, serve to promote a fulfilling life and as a buffer to stress.

Although the early years of childhood may well be consequential for fostering resilience in adulthood, we need to understand the *pathways* to adult resilience (see Figure 1). Is it the childhood experience of the parents' own social and personal resources, or stressful family events (e.g., divorce), or ongoing strains (e.g., financial hardship) that matter most in shaping adult children's psychological resilience? Does the quality of parenting matter? Both Elder (1992; Elder & Caspi, 1990) and Bronfenbrenner (1979) underscore the *interdependence* of lives, wherein critical life events in one generation touch the lives of another generation. They also describe the potential for *accentuation* of traits over time. Is there an accentuation process, building on parents' psychosocial resources experienced early in the child's life? The import of the seeds of early childhood socialization for adult resilience may shift with age in conjunction with adult children's own changing roles, responsibilities, and attainments. For example, Bandura (1982) suggested that self-conceptions of competence/mastery are drawn from personal experience, as well as from so-

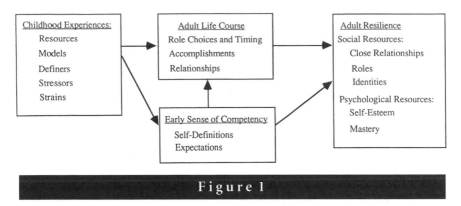

Figure 1

Conceptual model of the pathways to adult resilience.

cialization processes (cf. Downey & Moen, 1987; Rutter, 1987). Does this mean that as children become adults, their own personal experiences in adulthood matter more than their experiences in childhood? If that is the case, then adult children might be less influenced by childhood protective factors (e.g., parents' psychosocial resources) and risk factors (e.g., stressful events in childhood) than they might have been as children or adolescents. Bronfenbrenner emphasizes that developmental growth is not limited primarily to the period of childhood and adolescence, but continues throughout adulthood. The resilience of adult children, then, could well be influenced more by their own circumstances (e.g., occupational attainment, marital status, and parental status) than by the experiences or resources in their family of origin. However, it is important to recognize that these very achievements in adulthood may have been shaped by experiences earlier in life (Kohn, this volume, chapter 5; Rutter, Champion, Quinton, Maughan, & Pickles, this volume, chapter 3; Rutter & Quinton, 1984).

The timing of parental identification may also be important. For example, daughters may not come to identify with their mothers until they, too, are married and mothers of young children, as suggested by status similarity theory. In support of this, Glass et al.'s (1986) findings suggest that the attitudes of parents and their adult children may converge with age.

Tracing cumulative advantage or disadvantage across lives and across generations requires the establishment of pathways linking inherited inclinations with environmental influence and investigating the salience of self-conceptions over the life course, regardless of objective circumstances. For example, Campbell (1981) pointed out that "even low income individuals with a high sense of personal control have a positive outlook on life" (p. 218).

Parental Resources and Responsiveness

Bronfenbrenner (1979) underscored the importance of a strong, mutual, emotional attachment between parent and child for optimal development. Such an enduring emotional relationship promotes motivation, attentiveness, sensitivity, and persistence on the part of both parent and child, contributing to a sustained active orientation toward their environment. Bronfenbrenner suggested that parents' responsiveness plays a key role in the fostering of the development of children; conversely, the absence of parental responsiveness hinders general psychological development in children, particularly among those exposed to stress. Impaired parent–child relationships become a predisposing factor for problem behaviors in children.

From a socialization perspective, parental well-being constitutes a key resource promoting resilience in children, but the social integration or embeddedness of parents may be a consequential resource as well. As Bronfenbrenner (this volume, chapters 18 & 19) and Wilson (this volume, chapter 15) suggest, parental roles and relationships with others expand the child's as well as the parents' social environment; thus, broader parental involvement and activity may promote the effectiveness of parents in fostering the development of their children. This recalls Coser's (1975) notion of roles as promoting autonomy and, consequently, health and well-being (Moen, Dempster-McClain, & Williams, 1989, 1992, 1995). Such a perspective is also congruent with the findings on social support, with effective parents more integrated in a network of friends, kin, and neighbors (Cochran, Larner, Riley, Gunnarsson, & Henderson, 1990; Hetherington & Clingempeel, 1992; Wilson, this volume, chapter 15).

Childhood Stressors

Key to any understanding of the links across generations are the situational imperatives (Elder & Caspi, 1990) that shape that process. Family patterns and transitions (e.g., divorce, death, and moving) representing childhood stressors may be harmful to development precisely because they tend to increase the hecticness, instability, inconsistency, and unpredictability in children's daily lives (Bronfenbrenner & Ceci, 1994). But stress and adversity need not always be a risk factor. As Elder's (1974) work has shown, family stress and adaptive strategies mediate the transmission of orientations and behavior across the generations, providing what are frequently unintentional lessons to sons and daughters on positive, as well as negative, ways of coping with life's exigencies. This legacy of patterns of living can have long-term consequences. Subsequent events may trigger early established vulnerabilities or resiliencies (Brown & Harris, 1978; Forest, Moen, & Dempster-McClain, 1995).

Rutter and Quinton (1984) suggest that the experience of adversity may well present learning opportunities that actually promote resilience. Thus, a limited exposure to adversity during childhood may provide an "inoculation against stress later on" (Rutter, 1987, p. 326). For example, parental divorce has been shown to elicit different outcomes in children, depending in part on other family transitions (Hetherington, 1989).

CONTEXTS AND CONTINGENCIES

An ecology of the life course approach suggests that early childhood experiences need not result in the inheritance of values, attitudes, behaviors, or opportunities from parents. Rather, shifting social, cultural, and economic contexts may serve to contribute new opportunities or compound existing constraints in individual lives (e.g., Brown & Harris, 1978; Quinton & Rutter, 1988). How do events in adulthood, including the taking on of family roles, trigger potentially latent coping patterns or serve to enhance or diminish the significance of resources acquired in childhood (Forest et al., 1995)? One's own life experience, such as occupational achievement or being in a supportive marriage, may alter both life course pathways and coping resources (e.g., Furstenberg, Brooks-Gunn, & Morgan, 1987). Clearly, structural location, as well as the circumstances of adult life, may affect the impact of previous experiences, including their impact on coping resources (Menaghan, 1989; Moen et al., 1989; Wheaton, 1990).

Location in the Social Structure

Our ecology of the life course approach to resilience draws on the status attainment literature discussed above to underscore the importance of *socioeconomic context*, especially in the form of opportunities, resources, and perceptions (cf. Gecas, 1979, 1981). Social class is correlated with material resources as well as power and prestige, all of which should increase mastery and self-esteem (Gecas & Seff, 1990; Mortimer & Finch, 1986). Research documents social class differences in psychosocial distress and mental health (Dohrenwend & Dohrenwend, 1984; Hollingshead & Redlich, 1958; Langner & Michael, 1963), which may reflect differences in personal and social coping resources and how effectively individuals deal with stress.

Thus, a key consideration in intergenerational relationships is social class—with a number of studies finding that working-class families are more kin oriented than middle-class families (Adams, 1968; Young & Wilmott, 1957), that low socioeconomic status reduces opportunities and resources in childhood (Brown & Harris, 1978; Kessler, 1979), and that working-class parents and children may well relate to one another far differently than those in the middle class (Bronfenbrenner, 1986; Kohn, 1969). There is some evidence that mothers and daughters with less education have closer ties than do those with more education (Bott, 1971; Young & Willmott, 1957). But that does not mean that working-class daughters are more likely than those in the middle class to emulate their mother or inherit their psychological or social resources.

Adult Connections and Accomplishments

Resilience, in the form of psychosocial resources, is not a fixed attribute, set in place during childhood, but may be modified by subsequent life experiences. Rutter (1987) suggested that both good relationships and accomplishments promote self-esteem and self-mastery. Experiences in adulthood may serve to shape values, aspirations, and behavior, apart from what might have been learned during childhood socialization. These include opportunities and constraints in the immediate social environment (cf. Jacobs, 1989). Thus, occupational achievement, marriage, and parenthood may modify the effects of childhood experiences. Having emotional support, in the form of a positive marital relationship, may be particularly consequential (Brown, 1987; Rutter et al., this volume, chapter 3; Rutter, Quinton, & Hill, 1990).

GENERATIONAL TRANSMISSION IN TIMES OF TRANSITION

An ecology of the life course approach to resilience also locates generations within the broader *historical backdrop* of social change. As Elder pointed out (this volume, chapter 4), times of dramatic change produce new life-ways, often creating dislocations and disruptions in the lives and outlooks of those experiencing them. Thus, the opening up or closing of opportunities may render the lessons of parents less relevant for their children. For example, over the past 50 years, we have witnessed a major historical change in societal views of women's roles within society (Moen, 1992). These revolutionary societal changes in gender roles and expectations may mean that mothers are less influential shapers of their daughters' orientations and expectations (Moen, Erickson, & Dempster-McClain, 1995). Conventional mothers embracing traditional gender roles may find themselves with daughters who are in the vanguard of the women's movement. Some mothers may even push their daughters to achieve what was impossible for themselves. The fact that mothers and daughters experience historical events and social changes from different age vantage points means that their lives are differentially touched by them and that their perspectives may well diverge (Bengtson, 1989; Elder, 1992; Mannheim, 1952). Mothers and their daughters in the United States in the second half of the twentieth century provide a striking case example for the study of the microlevel individual dispositions both propagating in and emanating from social change. The revolution in women's roles, lifestyles, identities, and values within American society may reduce maternal influence on daughters' resilience. How this revolution of rising and frequently ambiguous aspirations and expectations has touched the lives of individual mothers and their daughters in its midst is a story yet to be told.

AN ILLUSTRATIVE EXAMPLE

The remainder of this chapter draws on a panel study of mothers and their adult daughters, to illustrate the types of studies necessary to explore the relationships between early life experiences and subsequent resilience (or other outcomes) during adulthood. Although we were handicapped by a research design constructed for quite different purposes in the 1950s (Dean & Williams, 1956), our goal was to examine whether there are links between daughters' resources as adults (in the form of personal dispositions and social integration) and their resources and experiences while they were growing up. Their mothers' own coping abilities and responsiveness may have constituted a key childhood asset. On the other hand, family stressors in childhood may reduce, enhance, or no longer be relevant to daughters' coping resources as adults. We investigated whether resources and stressors in the family of orientation relate to two facilitators of adult daughters' resilience: their sense of personal mastery and their social integration into the broader community.

Mothers and daughters have the closest ties across the generations, at all ages (Rossi & Rossi, 1990; Troll, 1987). Moreover, mothers and daughters not only are closer to each other than are other family members, but also tend to identify with each other (Chodorow, 1978). Do daughters, in fact, assimilate the psychological orientations and reproduce the patterns of role involvements of their mother and, if so, under what circumstances? Or do daughters, as adults, chart their own paths and create their own coping strategies, regardless of their childhood experiences?

The Women's Roles and Well-Being Project constitutes an important data source to examine, however imperfectly, any possible congruence between childhood experiences and adult daughters' resilience. It is a two-wave panel study of women who were interviewed in 1956 in an upstate New York community and were reinterviewed 30 years later, in 1986 (Moen et al., 1989, 1992). Their adult daughters were also interviewed in 1988, providing a sample of 246 mother–daughter dyads. We analyzed the relationships between (a) mothers' resources in the 1950s and family stressors while their daughters were growing up and (b) the subsequent resilience of their adult daughters.

Of course, the experiences of these mothers and daughters have been shaped by the very different events each generation has experienced. The mothers in our sample were born between 1906 and 1933; thus, they came to adulthood during the 1930s and 1940s. Their life chances and outlook were greatly affected by the Great Depression and World War II. The daughters of these mothers were born between 1929 and 1964, with a median birth year of 1949. These women reached age 23, then, between 1952 and 1987, with their own life chances shaped by the vast changes in women's roles from the family-oriented 1950s through the revolutionary changes during the late 1960s and 1970s. This disparity in historical context may well influence the kinds of lessons these daughters learned from their mother.

Hypotheses

Socialization theory suggests a direct transgenerational inheritance of the social and personal resources related to resilience and a direct negative effect of early childhood strains. Specifically,

> Hypothesis 1: Daughters who as children experienced mothers' high psychological resources and role involvements are more likely to be highly resilient as adults, whereas daughters who have experienced adversity during childhood are more likely to have lower resilience as adults.

Status attainment theory suggests that location in the social structure should affect the social and psychological resources of adults. Thus,

> Hypothesis 2: Daughters of highly educated mothers are more likely to be highly resilient as adults, in terms of both psychological and social resources.

An ecology of the life course focus on context and contingencies points to possible moderators, or interaction effects. We consider the following:

> Hypothesis 3: Daughters of mothers with higher levels of education are more likely to be highly resilient when they experience mothers' high psychological resources and role involvements as children.

> Hypothesis 4: Daughters who experienced a good relationship with their mother as children, in terms of high maternal responsiveness,

are more likely to be highly resilient as adults, despite childhood stressors, than are daughters who did not experience as positive a relationship with their mother.

Hypothesis 5: Daughters whose current life situation reflects either high occupational achievement or involvement in a close marital relationship are more likely to be highly resilient than are daughters with similar childhood experiences and either low occupational achievement or no close marital relationship.

Hypothesis 6: Given the dramatic changes in gender role expectations, less traditional mothers may be more influential in transmitting resilience to their adult daughters, and more recent cohorts of daughters should be less influenced by their childhood experiences.

Data and Procedures[1]

Dependent variables. We operationalized adult daughters' resilience using two measures of individual resources, one psychological and one social. The psychological component of resilience consists of feelings of control and mastery. *Mastery* refers to beliefs individuals hold about their abilities to act, to shape their own life (Pearlin et al., 1981). We used the Pearlin Self-Efficacy Scale (Pearlin et al., 1981), which is composed of seven statements, such as "There is really no way I can solve some of the problems I have" or "I can do just about anything I really set my mind to." The alpha coefficient for this scale in our sample was .77. Daughters scoring below the median on the scale were classified as low in mastery, whereas daughters scoring at the median or above were classified as high in mastery.

Social resources in the form of connectedness and social integration can also contribute to resilience. As a measure of social integration, we used a count of the number of roles daughters had in 1988. Possible roles include those of club member, employee, close friend, churchgoer, relative, neighbor, and volunteer. Again, daughters scoring below the mean on the scale were classified as low in number of roles, whereas daughters scor-

---

[1]Complete variable descriptions and distributions are presented in the chapter's Appendix.

ing at or above the median were classified as having a high number of roles. Although marriage is itself an important integrative role, we treated it as an adult status that could shape both mastery and other role involvements.

Independent variables. We had a number of variables representing maternal characteristics and childhood experiences that could affect the resilience of adult daughters: mother's education, mother's psychological well-being, mother's social integration, mother's gender role beliefs, maternal responsiveness, daughter's childhood stressors, and family financial hardship. The measures of mothers' psychological dispositions were drawn from the 1956 interviews, at a time when they were actively involved in mothering. The measures of family experiences during daughters' childhood were derived from retrospective life histories of the mother's life, as well as data from the (mother's) 1956 interviews.

Mothers' educational level was operationalized in terms of whether they had attended college by 1956. Mothers' psychological well-being (in 1956) was a composite measure, based on two scales, self-concept and general life satisfaction. Mothers' self-concept was evaluated by mothers' responses to seven statements, such as "I don't feel that I am a very interesting person" and "I have difficulties making decisions." Mothers' general life satisfaction was measured by averaging mothers' responses to three questions: "How often do you find yourself feeling disappointed about the way things turned out for you?"; "All in all, how much happiness would you say you find in life today?"; and, "On the whole, how satisfied would you say you are with your way of life today?" The alpha coefficients for these two scales were .58 and .59, respectively.[2] Mothers who were high (above the median) in both self-concept and life satisfaction were classified as high in overall well-being. Mothers' social resources were measured by the number of roles they occupied in 1956 (with the same components as for daughters' social resources); those above the median were characterized as socially integrated.

The scale of mothers' gender role beliefs was an average of responses to nine questions, such as "Do you think it's all right for a woman to . . ."

---

[2]Although these reliabilities were lower than we would have liked, we were limited to the scales contained in the 1956 survey. We tried to minimize the impact of unreliability by combining responses to both scales in the analyses.

"supervise the work of men" or "get more education than her husband," where the response categories ranged from *all right* (1), to *undecided* (2), to *not all right* (3). Thus, 3 was the most traditional response. The alpha coefficient for the 1956 scale was .75. The indicator of maternal responsiveness was composed of two scales, maternal discontent and maternal detachment. Maternal discontent was evaluated through mothers' responses in 1956 to the following two statements: "I don't enjoy the child(ren) as much as I would like to" and "I would like to spend more time with my child(ren)." Maternal detachment was indicated by mothers' agreement with the following two statements: "I often feel I just have to get away from the child(ren)" and "I feel that I will enjoy life more when the child(ren) are older." Mothers scoring below the median in both discontent and detachment were classified as high in responsiveness.

To capture possible stressors in daughters' childhood, we used two measures: stressful childhood events and economic hardship. We operationalized childhood stressors as potentially disruptive events occurring during daughters' childhood—including parental divorce, geographical moves, parental alcohol abuse, and paternal unemployment.[3] Daughters experiencing one or two of these stressors were classified as having some stress, whereas daughters with three or more incidents of stress were classified as high in stress. Other daughters never experienced any of these stressors. We created a separate indicator of the ongoing strain of economic hardship from each mother's reports of being poor or having a poor financial situation during the time that her daughter was growing up.

Other variables represented daughters' current life situation. Daughters' occupational achievement was measured by whether daughters had held a professional- or managerial-level job, whereas daughters' educational level was measured by whether daughters had any college education. The indicator of involvement in a close marital relationship focused on those daughters who were married and who had a positive response to the question, "How would you describe your marriage these days?" Daughters were rated as having a close relationship if they responded with *very*

[3]Virtually no mothers characterized themselves as unemployed during this period. Most were full-time homemakers who were not seeking a paid job.

happy or *happy*. Thus, those who were in the 0 category included those who were not married as well as those who were unhappily married. This conforms to Rutter et al.'s (this volume, chapter 3) emphasis on the importance of a close, personal relationship.

Methods of Analysis

Given our interest in moderating factors rather than simply linear effects and Bronfenbrenner's admonitions about "controlling" for context, we present our data in the form of higher order interactions, to examine the relationships among variables related to daughters' resilience. To assess possible interactions between maternal characteristics, daughters' early experiences, and daughters' current life situation, we used the logit form of *log-linear analysis* (Knoke & Burke, 1980). Log-linear analysis is a method used to model the sources of association within a group of categorical variables. A log-linear model generates expected frequencies, which can then be compared to observed frequencies to evaluate the fit of the model. In the logit form of log-linear analysis, the researcher designates one variable as the dependent variable and evaluates the contribution of the independent variables to the expected odds of observing the dependent variable.

An advantage to log-linear analysis is being able to test the fit of different models, to choose the most parsimonious model that fits the data. Alternatively, we could have used multiple regression and avoided having to dichotomize any of our continuous variables. However, our aim was to avoid making the invalid assumptions that are inevitable in linear regression analysis about the linearity of effects.[4] We believe that little information was lost by dichotomizing the variables in this case, because we were interested in assessing what combinations of factors might influence daughters' resilience. We also recognize that such data as we had were insufficient to capture the process of intergenerational links; categorizing

---

[4]Of course, by dichotomizing many of our variables, many of the figures seem to imply linearity of effects. Although dividing our variables into more than two points would have eliminated this problem, problems of sample size prevented us from taking this approach.

our variables into dichotomies and trichotomies would nevertheless offer rough measures of the concepts we were seeking to illustrate.

Findings

Hypotheses 1 and 2 were drawn from socialization and status attainment theory and suggested that mothers with greater-than-average psychological well-being, education, or social resources would tend to have daughters with greater-than-average resilience, whereas daughters with more childhood stressors would tend to have lower resilience as adults. Figure 2 and Figure 3 show the means of daughters' mastery and number of roles by mothers' well-being, mothers' educational level, mothers' number of roles, daughters' childhood stressors, and the presence of financial hardship. For mothers' well-being, mothers' education, and mothers' number of roles, the differences in daughters' resilience are generally in the hypothesized direction, but are not statistically significant. Figure 3(a) shows that there was little relationship between the measures of daughters' resilience and level of childhood stressors. Figure 3(b), however, shows a significant negative relationship between the presence of financial hardship in daughters' childhood and daughters' number of adult roles, $t(197) = -2.22, p = .028$. The relationship between financial hardship and daughters' mastery, though positive, was not significant.

The results from Figure 2 suggest that the effects of early experiences on adult resilience may be more complex than simple, bivariate relationships. To investigate possible interactions between the variables of interest, we fit separate logit models for each outcome. We began by using mothers' education, mothers' well-being, mothers' social integration, and daughters' experience of childhood stressors as independent variables in estimating the likelihood of daughters' high adult resilience (in the form of mastery and number of roles occupied). The best fitting model for daughters' mastery included all main effects, as well as interactions between childhood stressors and mothers' education, and between mothers' well-being and mothers' number of roles $\chi^2(14, N = 205) = 20.11, p = .13$. Figure 4 graphs the interaction between number of childhood stressors and mothers' education. For those daughters experiencing few child-

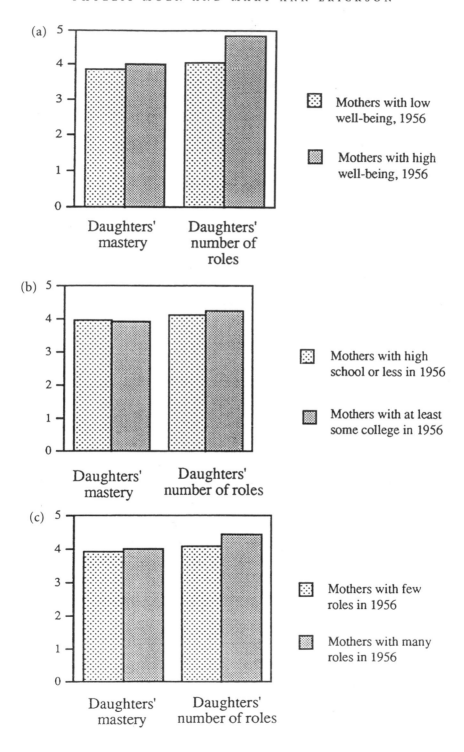

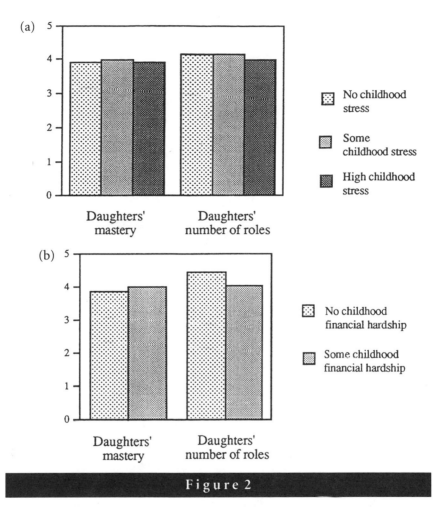

Figure 2

(Facing page)
Adult daughters' sense of mastery and role occupancy as a function of mothers' psychological well-being (2a), education (2b), and role occupancy (2c).

Figure 3

(Top of page)
Adult daughters' sense of mastery and role occupancy as a function of childhood stressors (3a) and childhood financial hardship (3b).

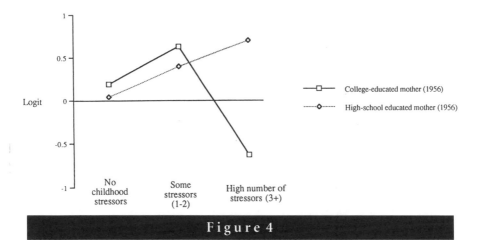

Figure 4

Interaction of childhood stressors and mothers' education for adult daughters' sense of mastery. Positive logit means likelihood of high sense of personal mastery in adulthood (1988).

hood stressors, having a college-educated mother did seem to promote daughters' mastery, but among those having high numbers of stressors in childhood, daughters of high school educated mothers tended to have higher mastery than did daughters of college-educated mothers. It could be that daughters of mothers with only a high school education expected to deal with adversity and have a greater sense of mastery as a consequence (see Elder, 1974).

One particular case illustrates some reasons why seemingly nonoptimal conditions in childhood may lead to improved outcomes in adulthood. One daughter of a high school educated mother in our sample experienced a high-stress childhood, including the death of her biological father, her mother's remarriage, and three major geographical moves. Yet she described her childhood by saying, "There was so much love and caring. Everything was so perfect when I was growing up." Evidently, these seemingly traumatic early events are viewed by this daughter through the lens of a loving relationship with her family. However, being able to overcome difficult times is important for this daughter; she would like her own daughter "to be extremely strong and not depend on anyone but herself

... to learn from hard knocks and learn how to come back." This is re-markably similar to her own mother's wish for her daughter's life: "I want her to be independent, her own woman, and make her own decisions in life and be able to handle all situations." This mother and daughter both value independence and facing up to the challenges of life.

Figure 5 shows the interaction of mothers' levels of psychological and social resources in 1956 (from the same model) for daughters' mastery in 1988. Consider, first, mothers who felt bad about themselves and their life while raising their children, mothers with low levels of well-being. Under these circumstances of low well-being, mothers with high social integration (in the form of number of roles the mother held in the 1950s) were more likely to have daughters with high mastery than were mothers with few roles. For mothers experiencing a high sense of psychological well-being in the 1950s, the number of roles they occupied at that time made less of a difference for daughters' mastery. Indeed, engaging in activities outside the home may have been an effective coping strategy for women who were unhappy at home. One daughter of a mother reporting a low sense of well-being, but higher-than-average social integration, said that

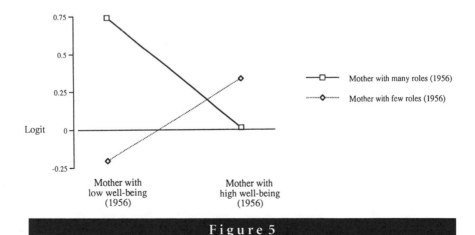

Figure 5

Interaction of mothers' psychological well-being and role occupancy for adult daughters' sense of mastery. Positive logit reflects likelihood of high sense of personal mastery in adulthood (1988).

her mother "used volunteer and other social roles to escape constraints of the home . . . [she] needed the outlet."

Another facet of resilience is daughters' own social integration, in terms of the number of roles the daughters themselves occupy in adulthood. The best fitting model accounting for the daughters' number of roles included main effects of childhood stressors, mothers' education, and mothers' well-being, as well as interactions of both stressors and mothers' education with mothers' well-being $\chi^2(15, N = 205) = 19.49, p = .19$. Figure 6 shows the interaction between level of childhood stressors and mothers' well-being in 1956, as related to daughters' having many or few roles as adults. For mothers who reported low levels of well-being in the 1950s, the number of childhood stressors made less of a difference; however, a moderate number of childhood stressors was associated with the lowest probability of their daughters' having a high number of roles as adults. For mothers with high levels of well-being, however, a moderate number of childhood stressors was associated with the highest probability of a high number of adult roles for daughters, and a high number of childhood stressors led to the worst outcomes for daughters. As in Figure

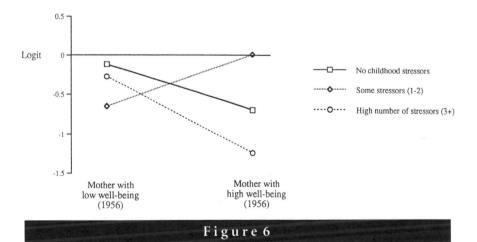

Figure 6

Interaction of childhood stressors and mothers' psychological well-being for adult daughters' role occupancy. Logit reflects likelihood of daughter occupying a high number of roles (5–7) in adulthood (1988).

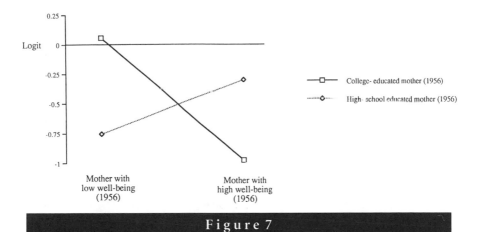

Figure 7

Interaction of mothers' education and psychological well-being for adult daughters' role occupancy. Logit reflects likelihood of daughter occupying a high number of roles (5–7) in adulthood (1988).

4, childhood stress did not necessarily lead to vulnerability but seemed to lead, in some cases, to better adaptation.

Daughters may learn positive, as well as negative, lessons from their mother. This was the case for one daughter, who experienced a moderate number of stressors during her childhood and whose mother felt good about herself and her life in 1956. She speaks positively about her mother's relationship with her children: "She always managed to do everything with and for her children . . . [and] maintained a sense of normalcy despite caring for [a sick child] for eight years." But this daughter also "learned what it takes to have a good marriage through observing the opposite."

Figure 7 shows the interaction of mothers' well-being and mothers' education (both measured in 1956) for their adult daughters' role occupancy in 1988. In the case of mothers reporting low levels of well-being in the 1950s, those having a college education had daughters with higher mastery, suggesting that maternal education was an important resource for daughters whose mothers possessed few psychological resources. At high levels of maternal well-being, however, daughters of high school educated mothers had a greater probability of occupying a high number of roles than did daughters of college-educated mothers. Although this was contrary to our expectations, this result could have been partly due to our measure of social integration. Daughters of college-educated mothers who were psychologically well-off in the 1950s may be especially and exclusively immersed in one role: paid employment.

It may also be that mothers encourage their daughters to embrace different values in response to women's changing opportunities. One daughter of a high school educated mother with few psychological resources seemed to have a great deal of insight into her mother's situation: "I don't think she felt good about herself. Even though all she wanted to be was a good housewife/mother, she felt others judged her harshly for not wanting a career. . . . My father was always supportive, but [her mother] was *extremely* critical." This daughter sees her mother in a "generational" conflict: "Mother never gained her independence from her mother. . . . On the other hand, I was brought up to question everything and make my own decisions." Mothers like these raised their daughters to take advantage of opportunities they never had. Daughters may also want to choose different life paths. As one daughter said, "[I want to be] more independent, more outgoing and active in non-family things."

Next, we considered the effects of maternal characteristics in combination with financial hardship during childhood on daughters' subsequent resilience in adulthood. About half of the daughters in the sample experienced some financial hardship during childhood (as reported in mothers' interviews). The best fitting model included main effects of all five independent variables, as well as an interaction between mothers' number of roles and mothers' education, and three interactions between financial hardship and mothers' well-being, childhood stressors, and mothers' number of roles, $\chi^2(31, N = 205) = 40.31, p = .12$. These findings suggest that financial hardship during childhood may serve to *promote* daughters' sense of mastery in adulthood. For instance, Figure 8 shows the interaction between mothers' number of roles and financial hardship as related to daughters' subsequent mastery. For daughters whose mothers occupied few roles during their childhood, the effect of financial hardship was negligible, but daughters of mothers with greater social integration (in terms of number

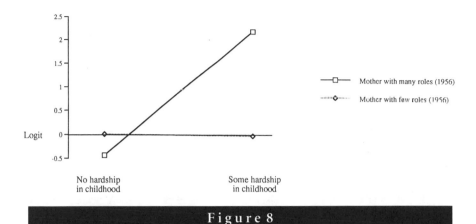

Figure 8

Interaction of mothers' role occupancy and financial hardship for adult daughters' sense of mastery. Logit shows likelihood of high sense of personal mastery in adulthood (1988).

of roles) had a greater chance of having high mastery if they did experience financial hardship in childhood. In fact, the chances of daughters having high levels of mastery as adults rose to about 8.8 from about 1.0. It may be that these daughters benefited from observing the strategies that their mothers used to mobilize their social resources during a time of hardship. This conclusion was supported by statements daughters made when interviewed. One daughter of a single, working mother said she "learned independence and the necessity for self-sufficiency." Another daughter said she "learned to survive through hard times."

A similar effect can be seen in Figure 9, which shows the interaction of mothers' sense of well-being in 1956 and financial hardship during daughters' childhood, as related to adult daughters' mastery. For daughters of mothers with few psychological resources, the experience of financial hardship was associated with somewhat higher levels of mastery, compared with those with no such hardship. But the highest levels of mastery were reported by the daughters of mothers who themselves reported high well-being in the 1950s, along with the experience of financial hardship while their daughters were young. Again, daughters of these mothers may have benefited from observing their mothers deal successfully with finan-

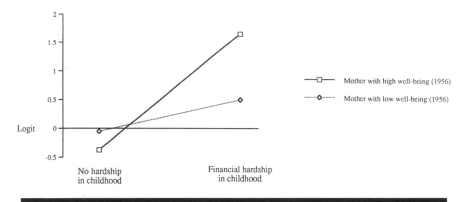

Figure 9

Interaction of mothers' psychological well-being and financial hardship for adult daughters' sense of mastery. Logit reflects likelihood of high sense of personal mastery in adulthood (1988).

cial strain. This suggests the importance of mothers' own resilience as a context in demonstrating the link between the experience of adversity and the development of resilience in daughters (see also Elder & Liker, 1982).

Hypothesis 5 suggests that daughters' current life situation may moderate the effects of childhood models and experiences on daughters' resilience. Although we found no significant interactions for daughters' close marital relationships, we did see a direct effect: Daughters who had a close marital relationship were significantly more likely to have both high levels of mastery, $\chi^2(1, N = 205) = 5.33, p = .02$, and higher social integration $\chi^2(1, N = 205) = 3.40, p = .06$. Moreover, we found that daughters' occupational achievement functioned as a moderating factor on adult resilience. Figure 10 contains the interaction of mothers' number of roles (occupied in 1956) with daughters' adult occupational status, for daughters' adult level of mastery (in 1988). In the case where their mothers reported few social resources (few roles in 1956), those daughters who had a professional or managerial job were more likely to also have higher levels of mastery. Differences were less pronounced among daughters of mothers with high social resources; regardless of whether these daughters had a professional or managerial job, they had a better-than-average chance of having high levels of mastery.

The attainment of professional occupational status may in itself be a response to lessons a daughter learns from her mother's life stories. One daughter who held a professional job and whose mother had reported few roles in 1956 said, "I wanted to be like my mother, but have more money." Another may have absorbed a lesson about the importance of work from her mother, who "always wanted to go back to her career and never did."

Because parental responsiveness is important for children's development, we looked for interactions of our admittedly inadequate measure of maternal responsiveness with our other independent variables. The only significant interaction we found was with mothers' education for daughters' role occupancy as adults. Figure 11 shows that the best outcome was for daughters of college-educated mothers who were highly responsive. This suggests a process of accentuation, in which mothers who respond well to their daughters are able to use their higher social position for daughters' betterment.

We expected to find differences in these transgenerational links by cohort, but no main effects or interactions were significant when we fitted models containing mothers' gender role beliefs, mothers' education, mothers' well-being, and daughters' cohort. This suggests that these links between mothers and daughters operated similarly for the daughters of the

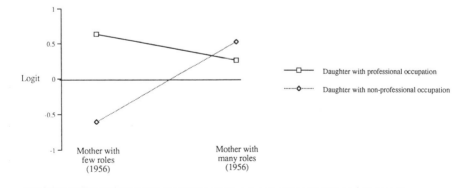

Figure 10

Interaction of mothers' role occupancy and daughters' occupational status for adult daughters' sense of mastery. Logit reflects likelihood of high sense of personal mastery in adulthood (1988).

197

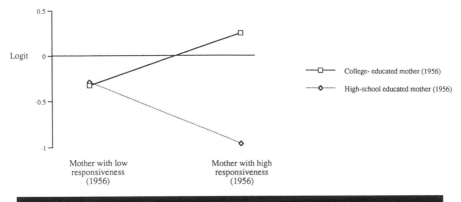

Figure 11

Interaction of mothers' education and responsiveness for adult daughters' role occupancy. Logit reflects likelihood of daughters occupying a high number of roles (5–7) in adulthood (1988).

baby boom and those born before the baby boom and that not age but mothers' and daughters' own characteristics best capture the social changes of this time of transition in gender roles.

DISCUSSION AND CONCLUSIONS

The transgenerational fostering of resilience provides an optimal topic to revisit the issue of intergenerational links from a new vantage point. The interlocking life courses of parents and children mean that events in the parents' lives constitute the backdrop of their children's lives, the resilience of parents becoming a childhood resource for children. How these social contexts play out in children's later life course suggests the importance of an ecology of the life course framework. *Ecology* emphasizes development in context; *life course* emphasizes development over time. Incorporating the life course themes of time and social change (Elder, 1992) into the ecology of human development's emphasis on the interplay between the person and environment (Bronfenbrenner, 1979) suggests a rich research agenda requiring sophisticated research designs.

Although our measures are imperfect and we lack indicators of some important concepts altogether, our illustrative study of mothers and their adult daughters nevertheless points to the utility of incorporating social-ization and status attainment models into an ecology of the life course ap-proach to the links across the generations. We have shown that contexts and contingencies shape the pathway to resilience in complex, and some-times unanticipated, ways.

Other Contexts and Contingencies

In the introduction, we discussed a number of considerations important to our dynamic, contextual approach that could not be incorporated in our empirical example. We mention them briefly here. One important con-sideration is the timing of events. *When* marital transitions, financial hard-ship, or other stressful changes occur may have important implications for the development and experiences of children (Elder, 1974, this volume, chapter 4) Similarly, it may not be the sum of stressors but particular stres-sors that are especially consequential. Both Magnusson and Clausen (this volume, chapters 2 and 11, respectively) point to the importance of chance events or single events that can have tremendous effects on the life course of individuals. Moreover, in our analyses, we were unable to consider the importance of *meaning*, that is, how individuals define their past, present, and future. And yet perceptions or definitions of situations may well play a key role in whether, and how, one generation learns from the previous generation.

We have no real measure of process, a key component in the Bron-fenbrenner paradigm. An adequate gauge of parental responsiveness, sup-portiveness, or parent–child interaction during childhood could help to explain the circumstances in which parents' resilience is passed on to their children. We have little information on fathers, and our sample does not include sons. How gender and paternal influence affect the links across generations are important research topics, as is the study of grandparents and three-generation relationships and influences.

Lessons

Several lessons can be gleaned from our illustrative study of mothers and daughters. The first is that early life experiences have implications for later resources and experience. Resilience in adulthood, in terms of social integration and feelings of mastery, is related to earlier developmental processes. We found that daughters' resilience is promoted not just by having a mother with high psychological or social resources, but by the example of such a mother coping with adversity (Figures 6, 8, and 9). But these apparently beneficial effects of some stress or hardship during childhood for daughters' subsequent resilience in adulthood need also to be placed in context. These daughters are part of, or were born immediately preceding, the baby boom generation. They grew up in the 1950s and 1960s, a time of unparalleled economic growth. Moreover, the mothers and daughters in this sample were members largely of working- or middle-class families living in a relatively homogeneous upstate New York community, with opportunities for employment and upward mobility; thus, they may have been somewhat insulated from severe stresses and hardship experienced in other environments. In this study, a high number of childhood stressors could mean two geographical moves and the father being away in the military. Thus, high stress does not mean severe negative outcomes for daughters, but may represent a number of mild stressors that served as learning opportunities. Similarly, financial hardship was gauged by mothers in relation to other families generally and was not a measure of absolute privation. Magnusson (this volume, chapter 2) points out that the effects of earlier developmental processes in earlier life course on the current functioning is contingent, in part, on the meanings individuals give to their environments and experiences. What we did not have in the Women's Roles and Well-Being Project was any assessment of the subjective meanings for the daughters of the stressors they experienced in childhood.

The second lesson is the importance of contemporary circumstances and the active role of individuals in shaping their own life course. The developmental course of individuals is also shaped by the individuals themselves, in terms of their own achievements and actions (Rutter et al., this volume, chapter 3). For example, Clausen (this volume, chapter 11) reports substantial change in subjective dispositions from adolescence to early adult years, suggesting the importance of the role experiences associated with the transition to adulthood. We find that daughters' happy marital status and professional occupational status contribute directly to their sense of mastery, as well as to the number of roles they occupy. Moreover, professional occupational status moderates the effects of mothers' social resources, so that daughters of mothers with few social resources have a much higher chance of having a strong sense of mastery if they themselves have achieved success in the form of a professional or managerial job. This is in line with earlier findings that daughters' own experiences are more important than their mothers' attitudes or identity in shaping the daughters' work role identity (Moen, Erickson, & Dempster-McClain, 1995). Also, this reinforces the point that developmental growth is not limited to childhood and adolescence, but continues throughout adulthood.

The third lesson is the complexity of capturing the imprint of social and historical change on the lives of individuals. Our rough measure of social change, dividing our sample of daughters into two cohorts, was an inadequate operationalization of the dramatic changes in women's lives over the second half of the twentieth century. But these drastic shifts in gender roles and women's opportunity structure could well have reduced the influence of mothers on their daughters. Consider, for example, the fact that those adult daughters with professional jobs whose mothers had occupied few roles in the 1950s had an odds of having a high sense of mastery of 1.89, versus an odds of only 0.54 for daughters who never had a professional-level job. This suggests that social mobility between the generations, a consequence of the expanding opportunity structure for women, may be an important pathway to resilience.

Models Linking Lives

The proper assessment of intergenerational pathways to adult resilience, or, indeed, behavior and dispositions more generally, requires recognition that parents and children are each progressing along both developmental and life course paths. As Urie Bronfenbrenner has noted, the links between each generation are bidirectional, with the development and experiences of parents and children invariably interdependent and influenced by those of the other. These links are further complicated, as the Cairnses (this volume, chapter 12) remind us, by the very real possibility of different rates of change, both within and across individuals and generations. These interrelated paths, in turn, are embedded in larger contexts of social structure, relationships, and historical change. Future assessments as to continuity or change across generations need to attend to the ecology of the life course to capture the richness, and complexity, of this process.

REFERENCES

Acock, A. C. (1984). Parents and their children: The study of inter-generation influence. *Sociology and Social Research, 68,* 151–171.

Acock, A., & Bengtson, V. (1980). Socialization and attribution process: Actual versus perceived similarity among parents and youth. *Journal of Marriage and the Family, 42,* 501–515.

Adams, B. N. (1968). *Kinship in an urban setting.* Chicago: Markham.

Bandura, A. (1982). The self and mechanisms of agency. In J. Suls (Ed.), *Psychological perspectives on the self* (Vol. 1, pp. 3–39). Hillsdale, NJ: Erlbaum.

Bandura, A. (1989). Regulation of cognitive processes through perceived self-efficacy. *Developmental Psychology, 25,* 729–735.

Bandura, A. (1994). *Self-efficacy: The exercise of control.* New York: W. H. Freeman.

Bengtson, V. L. (1989). The problem of generations: Age group contrasts, continuities, and social change. In V. L. Bengtson & K. W. Schae (Eds.), *The course of later life: Research and reflections* (pp. 25–54). New York: Springer.

Betz, N. E., & Hackett, G. (1987). Concept of agency in educational and career development. *Journal of Counseling Psychology, 34,* 299–308.

Blau, P. M., & Duncan, O. D. (1967). *The American occupational structure.* New York: Wiley.

Bott, E. (1971). *Family and social network: Roles, norms and external relationships in ordinary urban families.* London: Tavistock.

Bronfenbrenner, U. (1979). *The ecology of human development.* Cambridge, MA: Harvard University Press.

Bronfenbrenner, U. (1986). Ecology of the family as a context for human development: Research perspectives. *Developmental Psychology, 22,* 723–742.

Bronfenbrenner, U., & Ceci, S. J. (1994). Nature–nurture reconceptualized in developmental perspective: A bioecological model. *Psychological Review, 101,* 568–586.

Brown, G. W. (1987). Social factors and the development and course of depressive disorders in women: A review of a research programme. *British Journal of Social Work, 17,* 615–634.

Brown, G. W., & Harris, T. (1978). *Social origins of depression: A study of psychiatric disorder in women.* London: Tavistock.

Campbell, A. (1981). *The sense of well-being in America: Recent patterns and trends.* New York: McGraw-Hill.

Caplan, G. (1976). The family as support system. In G. Caplan & M. Killilee (Eds.), *Support systems and mutual help* (pp. 19–36). New York: Grune & Stratton.

Caspi, A., Elder, G. H., Jr., & Bem, D. J. (1987). Moving against the world: Life-course patterns of explosive children. *Developmental Psychology, 23,* 308–313.

Caspi, A., Elder, G. H., Jr., & Bem, D. J. (1988). Moving away from the world: Life-course patterns of shy children. *Developmental Psychology, 24,* 824–831.

Chodorow, N. (1978). *The reproduction of mothering: Psychoanalysis and the sociology of gender.* Berkeley: University of California Press.

Clausen, J. A. (1986). *The life course: A sociological perspective.* Englewood Cliffs, NJ: Prentice Hall.

Clausen, J. A. (1991). Adolescent competence and the shaping of the life course. *American Journal of Sociology, 96,* 805–842.

Clausen, J. A. (1993). *American lives: Looking back at the children of the Great Depression.* New York: Free Press.

Cochran, M., Larner, M., Riley, D., Gunnarsson, L., & Henderson, C. R., Jr. (1990). *Extending families: The social networks of parents and their children.* Cambridge, England: Cambridge University Press.

Coleman, J. (1988). Social capital in the creation of human capital. *American Journal of Sociology, 94,* 95–120.

Coser, R.–L. (1975). The complexity of roles as a seedbed of individual autonomy. In L. A. Coser (Ed.), *The idea of social structure: Papers in honor of Robert Merton* (pp. 237–264). New York: Harcourt Brace Jovanovich.

Dean, J. P., & Williams, R. M., Jr. (1956). *Social and cultural factors affecting role-conflict and adjustment among American women: A pilot investigation* (Progress report). National Institute of Mental Health, Bethesda, MD.

Dohrenwend, B. S., & Dohrenwend, B. P. (1984). *Stressful life events: Their nature and effects* (3rd ed.). New York: Wiley.

Downey, G., & Moen, P. (1987). Personal mastery, income, and family transitions: A study of women heading households. *Journal of Health and Social Behavior, 28,* 320–333.

Elder, G. H., Jr. (1974). *Children of the Great Depression.* Chicago: University of Chicago Press.

Elder, G. H., Jr. (1985). *Life course dynamics: 1960s to 1980s.* Ithaca, NY: Cornell University.

Elder, G. H., Jr. (1992). The life course. In E. Borgatta & M. Borgatta (Eds.), *Encyclopedia of sociology* (pp. 1120–1130). New York: Macmillan.

Elder, G. H., Jr., & Caspi, A. (1990). Studying lives in a changing society. In A. I. Rabin, R. A. Zucker, S. Frank, & R. Simmons (Eds.), *Study in persons and lives* (pp. 201–247). New York: Springer.

Elder, G. H., Jr., & Liker, J. K. (1982). Hard times in women's lives: Historical influences across forty years. *American Journal of Sociology, 88,* 241–269.

Featherman, D. L., & Hauser, R. M. (1978). *Opportunity and change.* New York: Academic Press.

Fischer, L. R. (1981). Transition in the mother–daughter relationship. *Journal of Marriage and the Family, 43,* 613–622.

Fischer, L. R. (1986). *Linked lives: Adult daughters and their mothers.* New York: Harper & Row.

Forest, K. B., Moen, P., & Dempster-McClain, D. (1995). *Cohort differences in the transition to motherhood: The variable effects of education and employment before marriage.* Unpublished manuscript.

Furstenberg, F. F., Jr., Brooks-Gunn, J., & Morgan, S. P. (1987). Adolescent mothers and their children in later life. *Family Planning Perspectives, 19,* 142–151.

Gecas, V. (1979). The influence of social class on socialization. In W. R. Burr, R. Hill, F. I. Nye, & I. L. Reiss (Eds.), *Contemporary theories about the family* (Vol. 1, pp. 365–404). New York: Free Press.

Gecas, V. (1981). Contexts of socialization. In M. Rosenberg & R. H. Turner (Eds.), *Social psychology: Sociological perspectives* (pp. 165–199). New York: Basic Books.

Gecas, V., & Seff, M. A. (1990). Social class and self-esteem: Psychological centrality, compensation, and the relative effects of work and home. *Social Psychological Quarterly, 53,* 165–173.

Glass, J., Bengtson, V. L., & Dunham, C. C. (1986). Attitude similarity in three-generation families: Socialization, status inheritance, or reciprocal influence? *American Sociological Review, 51,* 685–698.

Hagestad, G. O. (1990). Social perspectives on the life course. *Handbook of aging and the social sciences* (3rd ed.). New York: Academic Press.

Haller, A. O. (1982). Reflections on the social psychology of status attainment. In R. M. Hauser, D. Mechanic, A. O. Haller, & T. S. Hauser (Eds.), *Social structure and behavior: Essays in honor of William Hamilton Sewell* (pp. 3–28). New York: Academic Press.

Hetherington, E. M. (1989). Coping with family transitions: Winners, losers, and survivors. *Child Development, 60,* 1–14.

Hetherington, E. M., & Clingempeel, W. G. (1992). Coping with marital transitions: A family systems perspective. *Monographs of the Society for Research in Child Development, 57,* 1–242.

Hollingshead, A. B., & Redlich, R. C. (1958). *Social class and mental illness: A community study.* New York: Wiley.

Jacobs, J. A. (1989). *Revolving doors: Sex segregation and women's careers.* Stanford, CA: Stanford University Press.

Kessler, R. C. (1979). Stress, social status, and psychological distress. *Journal of Health and Social Behavior, 20,* 259–272.

Knoke, D., & Burke, P. T. (1980). *Log-linear models.* Beverly Hills, CA: Sage.

Kobasa, S. C. (1987). Stress responses and personality. In R. C. Barnett, L. Bienor, & G. K. Baruch (Eds.), *Gender and stress* (pp. 308–329). New York: Free Press.

Kohn, M. L. (1969). *Class and conformity: A study in values.* Chicago: University of Chicago Press.

Kohn, M. L., Slomczynski, K. M., & Schoenbach, C. (1986). Social stratification and the transmission of values in the family: A cross-national assessment. *Sociological Forum, 1,* 73–102.

Langner, T. S., & Michael, S. T. (1963). *Life stress and mental health.* New York: Free Press of Glencoe.

Lazarus, R. S., & Folkman, S. (1984). *Stress, appraisal, and coping.* New York: Springer.

Mannheim, K. (1952). The problem of generations. In D. Kecskemeti (Ed.), *Essays on the sociology of knowledge* (pp. 276–320). London: Routledge & Kegan Paul. (Original work published 1928)

Menaghan, E. C. (1989). Role changes and psychological well-being: Variations in effects by gender and role repertoire. *Social Forces, 67,* 693–714.

Moen, P. (1992). *Women's two roles: A contemporary dilemma.* New York: Auburn House.

Moen, P., Dempster–McClain, D., & Williams, R. M., Jr. (1989). Social integration and longevity: An event history analysis of women's roles and resilience. *American Sociological Review, 54,* 635–647.

Moen, P., Dempster–McClain, D., & Williams, R. M., Jr. (1992). Successful aging: A life course perspective on women's multiple roles and health. *American Journal of Sociology, 97,* 1612–1638.

Moen, P., Dempster–McClain, D., & Williams, R. M., Jr. (1995, October). *Women's roles and well-being in later adulthood: A life-course perspective.* Paper presented at the ISA World Congress of Sociology, Bielefeld, Germany.

Moen, P., Erickson, M. A., & Dempster–McClain, D. (1995). *Their mothers' daughters? A study of the intergenerational transmission of gender orientations.* Unpublished manuscript.

Moen, P., & Wethington, E. (1992). The concept of family adaptive strategies. *Annual Review of Sociology, 18,* 233–251.

Mortimer, J. T., & Finch, M. D. (1986). The development of self-esteem in the early work career. *Work & Occupations, 13,* 217–239.

Pearlin, L., Lieberman, M., Menaghan, E., & Mullan, J. (1981). The stress process. *Journal of Health and Social Behavior, 22,* 337–356.

Pearlin, L. I., & Schooler, C. (1978). The structure of coping. *Journal of Health and Social Behavior, 19,* 2–21.

Quinton, D., & Rutter, M. (1988). *Parenting breakdown: The making and breaking of intergenerational links.* Avebury, England: Gower.

Rossi, A., & Rossi, P. (1990). *Of human bonding: Parent–child relations across the life course.* New York: Aldine de Gruyter.

Rutter, M. (1987). Psychosocial resilience and protective mechanisms. *American Journal of Orthopsychiatry, 57,* 316–331.

Rutter, M., & Quinton, D. (1984). Long-term follow-up of women institutionalized in childhood: Factors promoting good functioning in adult life. *British Journal of Developmental Psychology, 18,* 225–234.

Rutter, M., Quinton, D., & Hill, J. (1990). Adult outcome of institution-reared children: Males and females compared. In L. Robins & M. Rutter (Eds.), *Straight and devious pathways from childhood* (pp. 135–157). Cambridge, England: Cambridge University Press.

Schaefer, J. A., & Moos, R. H. (1992). Life crises and personal growth. In B. N. Carpenter (Ed.), *Personal coping: Theory, research, and application* (pp. 149–170). Westport, CT: Praeger.

Sewell, W. H., & Hauser, R. M. (1975). *Education, occupation, earnings: Achievement in the early career.* New York: Academic Press.

Suitor, J. J. (1987). Mother–daughter relations when married daughter returns to school: Effects of status similarity. *Journal of Marriage and the Family, 49,* 435–444.

Suitor, J. J. (1988). Husbands' educational attainment and support for wives' return to school. *Gender and Society, 2,* 482–495.

Thoits, P. A. (1983). Multiple identities and psychological well-being: A reformulation and test of the social isolation hypothesis. *American Sociological Review, 48,* 174–187.

Thoits, P. A. (1986). Multiple identities: Examining gender and marital status differences in distress. *American Sociological Review, 51,* 259–272.

Thoits, P. A. (1987). Gender and marital status differences in control and distress: Common stress versus unique stress explanations. *Journal of Health and Social Behavior, 28,* 7–22.

Troll, L. E. (1987). Mother–daughter relationships through the life span. In S. Oskamp (Ed.), *Family processes and problems: Social psychological aspects* (pp. 284–305). Newbury Park, CA: Sage.

Werner, E. E. (1990). Protective factors and individual resilience. In S. J. Meisels & J. P. Shankoff (Eds.), *Handbook of early childhood intervention* (pp. 97–116). Cambridge, England: Cambridge University Press.

Wheaton, B. (1990). Life transitions, role histories, and mental health. *American Sociological Review, 55,* 209–223.

Young, M., & Willmott, P. (1957). *Family and kinship in east London.* London: Routledge & Kegan Paul.

VARIABLE DESCRIPTIONS AND DISTRIBUTIONS

Description	n	M	SD
Source variables			
Daughters' sense of mastery, 1988[a]	221	3.92	0.60
Daughters' number of roles, 1988[b]	241	4.14	1.38
Mothers' self-concept, 1956[c]	246	2.34	0.44
Mothers' general life satisfaction, 1956[d]	246	2.71	0.34
Mothers' number of roles, 1956[b]	236	4.74	1.16
Mothers' traditional gender role beliefs, 1956[e]	246	1.65	0.47
Mothers' discontent in mother role, 1956[f]	232	1.69	0.77
Mothers' detachment from mother role, 1956[g]	246	1.56	0.81
Daughters' number of childhood stressors[h]	205	1.78	1.61

Description	Categorical variables	Frequency	
Daughters' sense of mastery, 1988[a]	221	High = 52%	
		Low = 48%	
Daughters' number of roles, 1988[b]	241	High = 40%	
		Low = 60%	
Mothers' educational level, 1956	246	Some college = 40%	
		High school or less = 60%	
Mothers' self-concept, 1956[c]	246	High = 56%	
		Low = 44%	
Mothers' general life satisfaction, 1956[d]	246	High = 46%	
		Low = 54%	

(Continues on next page)

Description	n	Frequency
	Categorical variables	
Mothers' psychological well-being, 1956 (high self-concept and high life satisfaction)	246	High = 30% Low = 70%
Mothers' number of roles, 1956[b]	236	High = 26% Low = 74%
Mothers' traditional gender role beliefs, 1956[e]	246	High = 51% Low = 49%
Maternal discontent, 1956[f]	246	High = 44% Low = 56%
Maternal detachment, 1956[g]	232	High = 50% Low = 50%
Maternal responsiveness, 1956 (low maternal discontent and detachment)	246	High = 26% Low = 74%
Daughters' childhood stressors[h]	205	None = 21% Some = 52% High = 27%
Childhood financial hardship[i]	222	Some = 59% None = 41%
Daughters happily married, 1988[j]	246	Yes = 50% No = 50%
Daughters' occupational status, 1988	246	Prof = 52% Nonprof = 48%

Note. Prof = professional, Nonprof = nonprofessional.

[a]*Scale of mastery:*

Five-level response categories for the following seven statements: (a) There is really no way I can solve some of the problems I have; (b) Sometimes I feel that I'm being pushed around in life; (c) I have little control over the things that happen to me; (d) I can do just about anything I really set my mind to; (e) I often feel helpless in dealing with the problems of life; (f) What happens to me in the future mostly depends on me; (g) There is little I can do to change many of the important things in my life.

[b]*Number of roles:*

Sum of seven possible roles; for each component, 0 = no and 1 = yes: (a) Member of any clubs, (b) Currently works for pay, (c) Has really close friends, (d) Attends religious services at least twice a month, (e) Sees relatives at least twice a month, (f) Sees neighbors at least weekly, (g) Currently volunteers.

(*Continues on next page*)

[c]*Self-concept scale:*

Respondents could agree, disagree, or be unsure about the following eight statements: (a) I don't feel that I am a very interesting person, (b) I don't feel sure of myself as a hostess, (c) I feel that I am letting my appearance go, (d) I often act a little bit helpless, (e) I am pleased with myself, (f) I have difficulties making decisions, (g) I have faith in myself, (h) I am attractive.

[d]*Scale of general life satisfaction:*

Three-level response categories for the following three questions: (a) How often do you find yourself feeling disappointed about the way things turned out for you? (b) All in all, how much happiness would you say you find in life today? (c) On the whole, how satisfied would you say you are with your way of life today?

[e]*Scale of gender role beliefs:*

Each of the nine responses in this section were coded with a 1 for *all right,* a 2 for *undecided,* or a 3 for *not all right.* The questions asked, "Is it all right or not all right for a woman to: (a) travel long distances by herself; (b) have many interests outside the house; (c) supervise the work of men; (d) argue with a man not her husband at a social gathering; (e) become an electrical engineer; (f) become a lawyer; (g) take an active part in politics; (h) remain unmarried; (i) get more education than her husband."

[f]*Scale of maternal discontent:*

Three-level response categories for the following two statements: (a) I don't enjoy the child(ren) as much as I would like to; (b) I would like to spend more time with my child(ren).

[g]*Scale of maternal detachment:*

Three-level response categories for the following two statements: (a) I often feel I just have to get away from the child(ren); (b) I feel that I will enjoy life more when the child(ren) are older.

[h]*Scale of childhood stressors:*

For each of three periods in daughters' childhood (birth–age 6, ages 7–12, ages 13–18) add one for any of the following events: death of parent, sibling, or close relative; parental divorce; parental remarriage; family move; parental alcohol abuse; fathers' absence for business or military service; fathers' unemployment; parental illness or accident.

[i]*Financial hardship:* Mothers were asked about the family's financial situation in the life history interview. Daughters were classified as experiencing financial hardship if mothers mentioned being poor or having a poor financial situation during the time her daughter was growing up.

[j]*Marital satisfaction:* Based on daughters' responses to the question, "How would you describe your marriage these days?" Daughters were classified as happily married if they responded "very happy" or "happy" to this question.

7

Taking Time Seriously: Studying Social Change, Social Structure, and Human Lives

Duane F. Alwin

The topic of this chapter was motivated by the suggestion of Mills (1959) that social scientists engage in active examination of the intersection of biography and history, and their joint implications for the shape and content of the structural conditions affecting human lives. Mills urged sociologists to address questions of how the individual and structural positions intersect, and with what consequences. He emphasized the need to study both the biographical processes that bring the person to the position and the historical processes that bring the position to the person. This set of issues is especially relevant to the study of occupations and status attainment (see Featherman, 1980, and Kohn, this volume, chapter 5), but it has a much more general applicability to the study of human development. It is in the spirit of Mills's "dynamic" perspective on the link between individual personalities and social structure that I here discuss

Previous versions of this chapter were presented at the annual meetings of the American Sociological Association, Cincinnati, OH, 1991; and at the meetings of the Research Committee on Social Psychology, World Congress of Sociology, Bielefeld, Germany, July 1994.

The research reported here was based on a project titled "Aging, Personality and Social Change," supported by funding from the National Institute on Aging (R01-AG04743-06).

several issues that come up in the consideration of the study of human lives, which are also relevant to the study of the relation between society and the individual, or what sociologists refer to as *social structure and personality*.

These aims are greatly facilitated by the ecological psychology of Urie Bronfenbrenner (1979, 1986), which conceptualizes the nature of the social environment and underscores the need to consider processes of human development in dynamic terms. The ecological perspective of Bronfenbrenner is unique in the sophistication with which it integrates person and structural concepts. In Bronfenbrenner's (1979) work, the social environment is conceived of as sets of multilayered settings, embedded in one another or linked to one another through networks of interconnections. These environments interact with the individual through a system of roles, relationships, and molar activities. Bronfenbrenner emphasizes the reciprocal interaction between persons and elements of such environments and the potency of the nature of that interaction for optimal human development—optimal in the sense of fulfilling genetic potentials. Patterns of interaction taking place in the context of these environments that create optimal development are called *proximal processes* (see Bronfenbrenner & Ceci, 1994).

The starting point for this chapter is a discussion of the problems with the way in which the relationship between personality and social structure is often conceptualized. Echoing Bronfenbrenner, I consider some advantages of conceptualizing this relationship in dynamic rather than static terms, and in doing so, I argue that changes in both biographical and historical time must be specified in our conceptualization of factors that influence human development, if the link between the person and society is to be understood. I propose an approach to studying one aspect of the link between person and society through the specification of trajectories of molar stability across the life span. Although the application of this framework to preadult development is of crucial importance, as Bronfenbrenner's (1979) work strongly indicates, my eventual focus in this chapter is on issues of continuity and stability of individual differences in adult development.[1] I turn first to some definitions of component concepts of personality and social structure, and their linkage, and then I proceed to the consideration of the conceptual and methodological tools needed to take time seriously, as Mills (1959) proposed we do, in studies of social structural factors shaping human lives.

PERSONALITY AND SOCIAL STRUCTURE

Psychologists generally view personality as regularities in behavior that are more or less stable over time and across situations. Sociologists, on the other hand, see structural patterning of environments as being largely behind the regularities in behavior. Clearly, the origin and maintenance of personality is to some extent dependent on the social environment; thus, most modern developmental theories of personality emphasize the nature of *processes of socialization* through which social environments influence behavioral tendencies and through which individual differences develop. The social environment is generally thought to be responsible not only for the development of regularities in behavior, but also for the medium through which individuals acquire a range of behavioral dispositions, involving language and other symbolic systems, identities, values and goal priorities, beliefs, social norms and ways of behaving, skills, and knowledge.

As suggested by Bronfenbrenner (1979, 1986), traditional ideas about socialization can be shown to be flawed in several ways, including the assumption of unidirectional flow of influence from the environment to the person. By recasting issues of development and socialization within a dynamic framework, that is, one that incorporates time, it is possible to focus on the dual questions of (a) how stable are individuals over their lives? and (b) what are the relative contributions of developmental and environmental factors in shaping those trajectories of stability and change? The examination of these questions requires the integration of psycho-

---

[1]This approach can be applied with equal vigor to preadult development, although there is a general lack of representative data for preadolescent populations of interest that allow for the systematic estimation of molar stability and cohort effects.

logical and sociological conceptions of human life span development. Numerous past efforts have attempted to do this, and although the conceptual sweep of these undertakings is often impressive, they seldom incorporate a commitment to verify existing hypotheses regarding elements of human constancy and change in the empirical record (see Elder & Caspi, 1990; Featherman & Lerner, 1985; Nesselroade, 1990).

This chapter takes the investigation of human constancy and change as both theoretically and methodologically problematic. I begin by reconsidering several of the assumptions underlying current approaches to the study of socialization in the literature on personality development, as well as recent writings in sociological social psychology on the topic of social structure and personality. On the basis of this discussion, I go on to suggest ways in which our understanding of these processes can be enhanced by taking time seriously in formulating the linkage between the person and the society. The contribution of this effort, it is hoped, involves the development of a framework that incorporates the dynamic elements affecting human lives. Before discussing these assumptions and evaluating their overall utility, let me define a few basic concepts.

Personality

As Gilligan, Brown, and Rogers (1990) pointed out, the word *personality* has its origins in the Latin *per*, meaning *through*, and the verb *sonare*, meaning *to sound*. This makes sense when one considers the meaning of the related word *persona*, which was literally the face mask used by the ancient actors on the stage, hence, a character, a person. In modern times, we use the term to refer to the quality or fact of being a person, or a particular person, with a particular set of identities and habits that convey individuality or uniqueness. To some, "the very concept of personality implies a differentiated and organized hierarchy of psychological sets and behavioral dispositions that are manifested as consistent and enduring patterns in denoting the uniqueness of the individual" (Moss & Susman, 1980, p. 73).

Although there is general agreement among psychologists on the meaning of the term, a closer inspection reveals some disagreement. A key issue is whether to include *all* individual differences, regardless of their origins and regardless of their degree of stability. Strelau (1987), for example, pointed out that some traditions of thought distinguish personality from the concept of *temperament*. In psychology, the latter term has come to refer to those relatively stable differences in human behavior that might be explained by biological mechanisms, whereas the term *personality* is reserved for those traits that originate primarily from environmental differences. Strelau (1987, p. 109) pointed out that in biologically oriented theories of personality, the terms *temperament* and *personality* are often used interchangeably (the work of the trait psychologists, phrenologists, and morphologists), whereas other theorists include *temperament*, along with additional traits, such as intelligence, within the more global concept of personality as a set of dispositions. In still other theories, the concept of *temperament* is distinguished from the concept of *personality*, and the two are thought to interact in the production of behavior, as embodiments of the biological and the social, respectively. Strelau (1987), for example, suggested the two concepts be distinguished along the following dimensions (temperament vs. personality): (a) behavior is determined by biology versus determined by social factors, (b) behavior is shaped during childhood versus developed in adulthood, (c) traits applied to both man and animals versus applied only to man, (d) absence versus presence of content-saturated behavior, and (e) the extent to which the construct refers to a central regulating function of humans.

The sociological literature on social structure and personality has avoided the development of a formal definition of personality but has relied on definitions of *personality* as a generic label for "relatively stable and enduring individual psychological attributes (values, attitudes, motives, needs, beliefs, and so forth)" (House, 1981, p. 527).[2] At the same time, to other sociologists (e.g., Berger & Luckmann, 1967; Riesman, 1950), some aspects of human differences are "endlessly fugitive ... always fragile and precarious, and modern man is a chameleon" (Musgrove, 1977, p. 1). The

---

[2]A similar approach is seen in Kohn and Slomczynski's (1990, p. 3) use of the term *personality* interchangeably with attributes of *psychological functioning*.

social environment is where change is lodged, according to many socio-logical views, and some even define constancies in personality in terms of the stability of the person's interpersonal environment (Sullivan, 1953). Thus, although personality may have some constancies, it is also inher-ently flexible and able to take on a variety of different forms over the span of life (see Gergen, 1980).

While I agree to some extent with all of these approaches, I would put less emphasis on distinguishing among traits according to whether they were primarily biologically or socially driven. It is advantageous to study the stabilities of identities and attributes as reflecting dispositional aspects of behavior underlying such phenotypic characteristics, regardless of their origins. In fact, it is no doubt impossible to disentangle the extent of bi-ological versus social influence on behavior; thus, into the domain of per-sonality I would essentially bring potentially *all* human dispositions and behavioral orientations, including concepts such as *temperament*, which are thought to develop early and are closely tied to biological givens. How-ever, this type of "boundaryless" definition of the concept may prove to be more all-encompassing than what may be justified on the basis of cross-disciplinary agreement on what is referred to by the term *personality*. Still, I think it is short-sighted to limit any discussion of personality to just those concepts that have been heretofore considered by personality re-searchers. Because the issues span a much broader terrain, it is my strong preference to include, rather than exclude, dimensions of human orienta-tions. Thus, lacking a better designation for the conceptual domain of fo-cus, for present purposes, I simply equate the term *personality* with indi-vidual differences in predispositions to behave in various ways, regardless of their origins, be they biological, social, or some combination of both. Indeed, part of the overall goal of a focus on human stability is to allo-cate various human characteristics to various realms, as designated by their degree of stability (see Alwin, 1994a).

Where I would take most serious issue with common definitions of personality is in their reference to relatively stable and enduring individ-ual differences of a dispositional nature. There are several things that are problematic about this. First, how stable does a trait have to be for it to be considered "stable and enduring"? At what point or points in the life cycle does a predisposition have to be stable to consider it a feature of personality? To put it another way, what types of life span trajectories of stability will qualify a particular variable as in the domain of personality? As will be clear from the following discussion, there is considerable variety in patterns of stability of traits or dispositions over the life span, and there is probably no strong need to follow House's (1981) approach and make the degree of stability evidenced by a particular characteristic a requirement for considering it an aspect of personality (see Alwin, 1994a; Alwin, Cohen, & Newcomb, 1991). Nesselroade's (1988, 1990) work has done much to clarify the nature of the distinctions between *trait* and *state*, which helps anticipate conceptually the possibility that some characteristics of individuals may be more stable than others across situations and across time.

Social Structure

A few years ago, I sat on a panel of social psychologists discussing the meaning of the concept of *social structure* and the usefulness of a structural social psychology.[3] There was little theoretical consensus on what *structure* was and a confusion of meanings, but virtually everyone agreed that the conceptual apparatus conveyed by the concept of *social structure* was what made a sociological contribution to the study of individual lives a possibility. Although often misunderstood, the concept of *structure* is "one of the most important and most elusive terms in the vocabulary of current social science" (Sewell, 1992, p. 1). The concept is central not only to the classical and neoclassical structural–functionalist perspectives, but also to virtually all streams of social scientific thought. But even as "sociologists find it difficult to do without the concept of structure, they also find it nearly impossible to define it in any adequate way . . . [sometimes] finding it embarrassingly difficult to define the term without using the word 'structure' or one of its variants in the definition" (Sewell, 1992, p. 2).

---

[3]This was on the occasion of the 87th annual meetings of the American Sociological Association, Social Psychology Section Day, Pittsburgh, PA, August 1993.

In this chapter, I use the concept of *social structure* to refer to opportunities and constraints within networks of roles, relationships, and communication patterns, which are relatively patterned and persisting (see Williams, 1960). In this sense, *structure* may refer, on the one hand, to large organic institutional structures, such as bureaucracies, which structure and orient human activities; or it may refer, at the other extreme, to a set of dyadic norms negotiated between two individuals for purposes of social exchange. The concept should be applicable to large structures, as well as small ones, which have some degree of stability. However, even as I find it difficult to insist on stability as an essential defining ingredient of personality, so too is it difficult to think of social structures as unchanging.

This approach is in keeping with definitions of the concept in current use within the literature, although there are a number of difficulties in providing operational definitions to the concept. Researchers who attempt to study the influence of social structure on the individual, usually done under the heading of the study of personality and social structure (e.g., House, 1981; Inkeles & Levinson, 1954; Kohn & Slomczynski, 1990), often reify individual-level variables such as occupational status or educational level as aspects of social structure. Bronfenbrenner and Crouter (1983) referred to such approaches as studying the *social address* of the individual and criticized them for failing to undertake a thorough conceptualization of the link between the individual and the group (see also Bronfenbrenner, 1986). Individual-level properties may be useful indicators of the individual's location in the network of positions that define and constrain social structure, but in terms of measuring structure, as it was defined above, this social address approach hits wide of the mark. In the sense we have defined it here, social structure may be virtually impossible to measure, although we should be able to observe its effects on the behavior of actors. One thing is clear: The social address of the individual is not what sociologists mean by *social structure*. It would also be a mistake to conceptualize the concept of structure purely at the macrolevel, although there are well-intentioned researchers who would argue that structure could only be conceived of at the group level (e.g., dyads, small groups, organizations, and macrosocial level) so that the concept of *structure* refers primarily to group properties. This position, unfortunately, ignores the suggestions of the symbolic interactionist viewpoint, which states that the person and aspects of society cannot be so easily separated (see Stryker, 1981; Wells & Stryker, 1988).

LINKING PERSONALITY AND SOCIAL STRUCTURE

If, as suggested above, we take *social structure* to refer to relatively enduring regularities in social roles, social networks, and communication patterns—and social relationships that condition or constrain predispositions to behave—then we can pursue social structure in one of two ways. First, we can seek out its origins in social experience and try to find evidence of its influence on individual actors. The origins and stability of these regularities are open-ended issues, and many theoretical statements exist regarding the nature of structural development and change. At the simplest level, however, *structure* refers to a set of constraints or differential opportunities that confront the individual, for example, the experience of gender, occupation, schooling, or any set of role relations. This is the dominant approach taken by researchers in the field of personality and social structure, and at a very general level, the approach focuses on how social structure conditions and constrains the nature of the personality. This approach essentially correlates aspects of the social address or positional location within a structure with properties of individuals and attempts to tease out the nature of the causal relationships between the two. Sometimes this is done with longitudinal data, using quite sophisticated statistical techniques, but these models often fall short of a complete specification of sources of individual differences in personality (see Kohn, this volume, chapter 5; Kohn & Schooler, 1983; Kohn & Slomczynski, 1990).

An Emergent View

There is a second approach, less well-developed, but tied in many ways to Bronfenbrenner's (1979) work in ecological psychology. This emergent view is a much more dynamic view of the linkage between the person and the society. Some of the elements of this approach are articulated in the following discussion, and it is important to clarify these in moving toward a justification of a need for a dynamic rather than a static approach to the study of the link between the person and society. It is, therefore, important at this stage in the discussion to emphasize five basic elements that distinguish this approach.

The first element refers to the *principle of reciprocity* in conceptualizing the link between the person and the social environment. It is often assumed that there is a unidirectional pattern to socialization, with influence moving from the environment to the individual. The focus, for example, on parents as agents of socialization, whose characteristics are linked to particular outcomes for children, is a highly visible approach to studying parent–child relationships (e.g., Baumrind, 1989). On the other hand, many now accept Bronfenbrenner's (1979) argument about reciprocal influences between the individual and his or her environment. Theories of socialization cannot ignore the ways in which individuals influence their environments and are not just passive recipients of culture. Otherwise, our theoretical views will present serious limitations to understanding the nature of human learning and human development. There have been several recent efforts to introduce the concept of *dynamic stability* as a way of emphasizing the reciprocal influences between persons and their environments (for discussions of this approach, see Alwin, 1994a; Alwin, Cohen, & Newcomb, 1991; Bronfenbrenner, 1979; Lorence & Mortimer, 1985; Mortimer, Finch, & Kumka, 1982, 1986; Mortimer, Finch, & Maruyama, 1988; Mortimer & Lorence, 1981).

The second element in this approach is the *principle of behavioral individuality*, which recognizes that each individual is unique and that one aspect of this uniqueness is the heterogeneity of experience with the environment. This principle suggests that the linkage between the individual and the social environment varies from individual to individual so that variation exists in the ways in which individuals experience culture or social structure. It is often mistakenly assumed, by those writing on the topic of culture and personality or social structure and personality, that cultural or structural content is unidimensional—that individuals in a given sociocultural niche have the same experiences. This could not be further from reality, because there is incredible within-culture variation in virtually all outcomes of interest. Variation occurs in at least two forms. First, individuals may occupy different niches within the same social address, because there is heterogeneity of experience even within socially constructed common experience. Second, there may be individual differences in reaction to a particular proximal environment, that is, organism–environment interaction (Bronfenbrenner & Ceci, 1994). Thus, by this principle we can assert that even as individuals are unique in the outcomes of development and socialization, so are the linkages between persons and their environments. This element is present in Bronfenbrenner's (1979) ecological psychology, with its emphasis on the social psychological premise that all socially relevant environmental experiences must be viewed from the point of view of the developing individual.

The third element of this approach refers to the *principle of common experience.* Although we allow for behavioral individuality and heterogeneity of experience with the environment, we also assert that some similarities of individuals exist because of common experiences with the environment. The assumption is that one of the ways in which society organizes experience for individuals is by structuring interaction that provides experiences common among individuals, in which the commonality refers to aspects of the social organizational environment. For example, gender is a pervasive social characteristic that produces common experiences differentiated on the basis of sex (see Chodorow, 1978). Race or ethnic status is yet another example. Perhaps the most prominent example used to illustrate the principle of common experience is the study of social class position (see, e.g., Kohn & Slomczynski, 1990). For purposes of the present discussion, common experiences linked to age are of considerable interest, where age-linked experiences are rooted in either biographical or historical time. These dimensions are explored further in the final two principles on which the present discussion is based.

There is an obvious and intended tension between Principle 2 (behavioral individuality) and Principle 3 (common experience), but this does not mean they are not both useful. Principle 2 suggests that experience with the social environment leads to individual differences in developmental trajectories, whereas Principle 3 suggests that social experiences, especially those that are socially structured, may predispose individuals to common developmental pathways. Obviously, tendencies exist in both directions, which may be one of the reasons variables tapping the individual's social address rarely explain very much variation in behavioral differences or predispositions to respond.

It is often assumed that cultural content is constant with respect to time, that what is learned and patterns to learning within specific structural elements at a given time have a certain generality with respect to time. The element of this type of assumption that is perhaps most hidden and that undermines a realistic approach to studying the linkage between personality and social structure is the idea that certain individual characteristics, such as level of schooling and occupational position, or other aspects of the social address are uniformly linked to certain personality variables over time. As is emphasized below, social change clearly operates not only to change what is learned across time in a given society but also to change the relationships between variables over time. In any case, I would invoke the *principle of temporal heterogeneity* to underscore the fact that aspects of human experience change over historical time.

One example of the recognition of this principle can be found in Bronfenbrenner's (1958) classic work on social changes in parental socialization, "Socialization and Social Class Through Time and Space." In that paper, he argued that a kind of *stratified diffusion* (this term comes from Stone, 1977) operates in processes of social change in parental child-rearing techniques. He noted that the linkages of aspects of social class, particularly education, were critical factors in child-rearing approaches. The development of child-rearing approaches in the higher social classes diffuses over time to the lower social classes, and the particular approaches are subject to historical change. Thus, Bronfenbrenner (1958) noted that although middle classes preferred "stricter" regimens of child rearing during one historical era, at another they seemed to adopt a more "permissive" set of child-rearing strategies. These are, of course, empirical issues, and although there may not have been enough time over which empirical studies have been carried out on this issue, there is evidence that parental socialization values have experienced considerable change, with some evidence that the linkage of parental values to socioeconomic variables may have changed in significant ways (see Alwin, 1984, 1986, 1988, 1989a, 1989b, 1990a, 1990b, in press).

Finally, it is often assumed that socialization is a set of experiences that happens primarily to the young and that most of what is learned over the course of life is accomplished by the time of young adulthood, with little possibility of change thereafter (see Musgrove, 1977). This is also an area in which there has been considerable attention to the limitations of this assumption, but very little is known about the stability of human characteristics (see Alwin, 1994a; Alwin et al., 1991; Alwin & Krosnick, 1991a; Cohen & Alwin, 1993; Mortimer et al., 1982, 1988; Mortimer & Lorence, 1981). Here it is important to specify the *principle of life-span dynamics* to refer to the fact that the link between the person and society, the link between personality and social structure, is not necessarily invariant over biographical time. It therefore becomes necessary to approach the study of human lives from a perspective that encourages attention to the nature of these differences over the life course.

INDIVIDUAL STABILITY OR ENVIRONMENTAL STABILITY

Theoretical conceptions of human development differ in (a) their assumptions about the nature of the individual, (b) their specification of the potency of influences of social environments on the individuals inhabiting them, (c) conclusions about the timing of those influences, and (d) conclusions about the persistence of their effects. Sears (1981) recounts the story told about the Jesuits, who believed that they could control a person's thinking for life if they were able to control their education up to the age of 5 years. This view is compatible with theoretical perspectives that assume there are critical stages in which the environment has an impact on the individual and that the earliest experiences are the most powerful in terms of their lasting influences. Other perspectives also stress critical stages but place the molding of human tendencies later in life. One picture of human development, which allows for several possibilities, suggests that the relative receptivity to change is mediated by life stage and the relevance of social events to development (see Stewart & Healy, 1989). One such possibility is represented by the classic view that establishes some aspects of human personality rather later in life, not until age 30 or 35 years, but then it is thought to be "set like plaster" (James, 1890/1950, p. 121) throughout the remainder of the life span.

These contrasts suggest that theories of life span development of personality can be grouped into several distinct types of perspectives. One regards personality as a set of stable predispositions, acquired relatively early in life or early in adult life and reflected in a number of consistencies or regularities in identities and behavior. This is in keeping with the concept of personality as a set of behavioral dispositions that are manifestly consistent and enduring, attesting to the uniqueness of the individual. Another perspective views personality in terms of systematic changes that result from traversing an ordered sequence of epigenetic stages, but within which there is considerable continuity of psychological processes and functions but not necessarily stability of psychological structures and behavior. As Asendorpf (1992) suggested, in this sense, stability and continuity are confounded. A third perspective is one that views personality as having some constancies, but also as inherently flexible and able to take on a variety of different forms over the span of life (see Gergen, 1980). This *aleatoric* account of human stability calls attention to the inherent potential for adjustment and adaptation to changes in the social environments to which individuals are exposed. Indeed, as I suggested above, this view would pay as much attention to the stability of a person's interpersonal environment as it would individual attributes alone.

To introduce some clarity to this theoretical variegation in views of the stability of personality and its sources, we can distinguish between two complementary sources of stability and change of individuals over time, noting that factors leading to stability or change may reside both in the person and in the environment. Individuals may differ in their susceptibility to change, that is, there may be something inherently different among individuals in their predispositions to stability. Age, for example, is often thought to be a factor that conditions the nature of the individual's flexibility or ability to change (Musgrove, 1977). Or, among persons of the same age, individuals may differ in their malleability with respect to social influence. Individuals may also differ in the opportunities for change presented by the social environment, and these may vary over the life course, as well as over historical time. We may, thus, contrast explanations of human stability and change that rely on *personological* factors, implicating differential tendencies of individuals to resist or incorporate change, with those *sociological* explanations that target differences in environmentally based experiences in accounting for change and stability (see Alwin, 1994a; Alwin et al., 1991; Elder & Caspi, 1988, 1990; Wells & Stryker, 1988).

DYNAMIC ASPECTS OF HUMAN LIVES

In this part of the chapter, I introduce the basic elements of a dynamic approach to the study of personality and social structure. I discuss three aspects of time, which give meaning to the idea that this approach is in fact dynamic. First, I discuss the importance of incorporating notions of *historical time* into the conceptual link between the person and the society. Second, I review the importance of the dimension of time that spans the lives of individuals, *biographical time*, illustrating why it is important to conceptualize the linkage between human lives and society along this temporal dimension. Finally, I review the *intersection* of these two time lines, the embeddedness of individual biographies in historical time. The following discussion is intended to further clarify the meaning of these various influences and to interpret what Mills (1959) meant when he urged sociologists to study the intersection of biography and history in social structure.

Historical Time

For reasons that are not completely clear, social and behavioral scientists often conceive of the influence of society and social processes as static, in the sense that there are more or less universal laws or principles governing the relation of personality to social structure. Historical influences, or changes in the nature of the social environment or the set of sociohistorical events experienced by individuals, have been increasingly viewed as a factor relevant to the development of personality. For example, Elder's (1974) study of the influences of the Great Depression on one small Oakland, California, birth cohort ($N = 167$, born 1920–1921) provided a laboratory for the discussion of historical influences on the development of aspirations and expectations for the future. Of course, because of the inherent limitations of small, single-cohort studies, as Elder acknowledged, social change cannot be fully studied by reliance on such types of designs. Rather, the kind of repeated cross-sectional studies in which questions are replicated over time, as, for example, in the General Social Surveys or in the National Election Studies, is an important vehicle for studying the effects of history in producing social change (see Alwin, 1992). Elder's work is nonetheless extremely valuable in emphasizing the importance of historical factors in individuals' lives (see, e.g., Elder, 1980; Elder, Caspi, & Burton, 1988; Elder & Hareven, 1993; Elder, Modell, & Parke, 1993).

Biographical Time

As indicated above, there is a duality to the timelines that can produce events and experiences that affect human development: biographical time, as well as historical time. Within the past three decades, considerable attention has been paid to issues of human stability over the life span (Brim & Kagan, 1980). These issues are of particular importance to students of human development and aging, but they are also important for the student of social change. In fact, theories of social change relying on cohort notions—specifically, the concepts of cohort differences, cohort effects, and cohort succession—usually make some assumptions about the stability of individuals over time (see Ryder, 1965).

How stable are individuals? To what extent is there truth to the widely held cultural belief that individuals stabilize in most of their characteristics by early adulthood? There is a wide array of opinion and judgment on these matters, depending on the subject matter—ranging from *aleatoric* views, positing extreme levels of plasticity and adaptability throughout the life span, to *persistence* views, suggesting that humans are usually flexible and susceptible to influence in their earliest years, but become increasingly stable after early adulthood. There has been some research aimed at the overall stability of various human characteristics over various parts of the life span, but there are a number of methodological difficulties that need to be surmounted to achieve an answer to this question (see Alwin, 1994a).[4]

Generations and Cohorts

In contemporary industrial societies, as well as traditional ones, each generation experiences life differently. Each has its "unique themes and problems, [regularly facing] situations vastly different from those that confronted their parents" (Clausen, 1986, p. 7). Still, as Inkeles (1955) observed, the parental generation is often responsible for mediating the influences of social change on their children, so the role of the elder generations in promoting adaptation to social change must be acknowledged. Used in this way, the concept of *generation* refers to the intersection of individual lives with historical time, with new generations replacing older ones through time. Within families, however, the replacement of generations over time does not correspond in any neat manner to the historical process, because the temporal gap between generations is variable across families.

Despite the popularity of the term *generation* in theorizing about the influences of cohort turnover on social change, this term is somewhat less precise than might otherwise be desirable. The term *generation* has several meanings, referring variously to kinship status (e.g., parental generation), to a unit of time separating members of kinship groups (a generation is often thought to be about 30 years), as well as to groups of persons affected uniquely by particular historical periods (e.g., the Vietnam gen-

---

[4]Briefly, what is needed is an approach that is able to distinguish measurement error from true change, an approach that can assess differences in stability between occasions of measurement in studies differing in the remeasurement period, and an approach that allows the comparison of estimates of stability across concepts, or content domains of personality. Elsewhere I have developed an approach that solves these three problems (see Alwin, 1994a).

eration). Obviously, because human species do not replace themselves according to any regular cycle, there can be no exact equivalence between *generations* in the sense of kinship relationships and *cohorts* (see Blau & Duncan, 1967, pp. 82–90). Given the difficulties of establishing the definitional and interpretive aspects of designating generations in the sense referred to by Mannheim (1952), it is perhaps best simply to use the term *birth cohort* or *cohort*, rather than *generation*, to refer to the placement of differential socialization experiences in historical time.

Therefore, social scientists have come to prefer the more precise concept of *birth cohort* to refer to a group that moves through the life course together, experiencing events in historical time at the same point in their lives. Within this context, the concept of *generation* is sometimes used to refer to sets of contiguous birth cohorts, but again it is often difficult to decide when one generation begins and another one ends, and as pointed out above, cohort effects often interact with other variables. Whether there are such interactions with culture or social structure, theories emphasizing cohort replacement give attention to the potency of historically linked socialization experiences that produce different parental orientations as a result of cohort membership. This can be visualized with respect to Figure 1, which depicts the intersection of biographical and historical times in the lives of four hypothetical cohorts.

Stated compactly, the assumptions of the theory of cohort replacement in this context are twofold: (a) Because each cohort experiences a unique slice of history during their youth, presumed to be the critical period for the acquisition of values, attitudes, and beliefs, distinctive cohort differences exist in the value orientations relevant to parental approaches to socialization; and (b) cohort differences endure over time, owing principally to the stability inherent in the life span trajectories of individuals, which typically "crystallize" into stable value orientations during midlife. These two assumptions combine, then, to form a picture of social change driven primarily by the natural processes of *social metabolism*, wherein the passage of historical time results in the replacement of old cohorts, and their ideas, with new ones (Ryder, 1965).

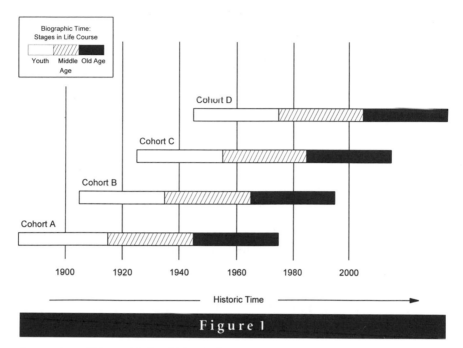

Figure 1

Intersection of biographical and historical time.

The plausibility, thus, of this type of interpretation rests on two things: (a) the potency of unique historical influences on each cohort or set of cohorts, so that cohort differences can be said to exist, and (b) a set of assumptions about the nature of individual stability over the life course. The latter poses a particularly interesting set of issues, as the assumption about the stability of individuals over most of their life span is critical. Thus, distinct historical experiences may exist and distinguish cohorts for a time, but if individuals are not stable after some early point in their life cycle, such intercohort differences may not persist through time. Humans are often thought to be susceptible to change in their early life, but to become increasingly stable in important respects with age, remaining relatively resistant to change throughout most of their adult life. But this may not be the case, and there is an emergent view of the adult life course as essentially *open-ended*, in which human life reflects a lifelong openness to change rather than growing stability and resistance to change (see Gergen, 1980).

With respect to the historical process and social change, these concepts are useful in conjunction with some notion of *the formative years*, a period in biographical time (see earlier section of this name) during which socialization experiences are thought to be critical in shaping the nature of lives in ways that may affect the nature of society. The assumption that there are unique influences within historical time that help shape the lives of sets of cohorts early in their lives, the assumption of formative years which leave an indelible mark on the characteristic modes of thought and experience, forms the basis for theorizing about *cohort effects* and the progression of social change through *cohort succession.*

Cohort effect is a term that is used to refer to differences in the formative experiences of members of different cohorts/generations, which endure throughout the life span. Thus, if particular periods in history have distinct effects on members of cohorts undergoing formative experiences that will shape them for life, it is then possible to imagine that social change comes in part from the succession of cohorts (see Mannheim, 1952; Ryder, 1965). According to White (1992), cohorts only become "actors" when they cohere enough around historical events, in both their own and others' eyes, to be called "generations." In this sense, we would distinguish between *cohorts* and *generations*, in that the former refers simply to year of birth, whereas a *generation* (in the nonkinship sense) is a "joint interpretive construction which insists upon and builds among tangible cohorts in defining a style recognized from outside and from within" (White, 1992, p. 31). Through such mechanisms, cohort effects are given life through these interpretive and behavioral aspects.

Social scientists often turn to repeated cross-section surveys for purposes of identifying cohort effects (e.g., Campbell, 1992; Campbell, Abolafia, & Maddox, 1985). However, because cohort membership is perfectly confounded with age even in these designs, it is impossible to identify such effects in any purely exploratory fashion. One needs to turn to supplementary types of data, invoking theory and common sense to produce what Converse (1976) called *side information*, assumptions about the nature of certain historical and generational processes. Ordinarily, the types of data available to social scientists to distinguish cohort effects from the effects of aging are not adequate, and other steps must be taken. I return to this issue briefly below.

If one can make strong theoretical assumptions about the nature of certain influences, for example, setting either cohort, aging, or period effects to zero, or arguing that one or the other source of influence is so small that it can be ignored, it is possible to creatively interpret survey data in service of the goal of identifying cohort phenomena when they exist. But replicated cross-sectional surveys can only estimate net changes in the aggregate and at the level of the cohort. Panel data are needed to ascertain information on gross rates of constancy and change (see Alwin, 1994b).

Personality, Cohorts, and Social Change

The idea that social change occurs, at least in part, by a process of cohort succession, with each new cohort being exposed to a unique climate of ideas and eventually replacing older ones in the overall composition of society, is an extremely important one (Ryder, 1965). In a recent article regarding social change in Western democracies, Lesthaeghe and Surkyn (1988) argued that the long-term trends toward individualism and away from institutional control are due to cohort differences and processes of cohort replacement (see also Inglehart, 1990). Their research shows that for a number of important indicators from the 1981 European Values Survey, including measures of values regarding parental emphasis on the autonomy and obedience of children, there are tangible cohort differences. Compared with older cohorts (born in 1936 or before), the younger cohorts (born after 1936) showed greater preference for an emphasis on the imagination and independence of children and lesser preference for social conformity and obedience to traditional institutional authority. Lesthaeghe and Surkyn argued that these intercohort differences resulted from a historical process tied to different generational experiences of the type referred to in theories of cohort replacement (see Mannheim, 1952; Ryder, 1965). These changes resulted, they argued, from a permanent ideational or cultural imprinting that arose from unique cohort experiences, which generate a momentum of their own. Thus, as my research regarding historical changes in child-rearing values indicates, each new set of cohorts potentially possesses its own particular set of orientations to children (see Alwin, in press).

The alternative to this model of social change is that societal-level changes are reflections not of cohort differences, but of individual-level changes occurring within cohorts. Two classes of factors influence individuals, causing them (and their cohorts) to change: factors tied to the life cycle or aging and factors tied to historical or period influences. Due to either, or both, life cycle/aging factors or period factors, there will be substantial intracohort change rather than change due just to cohort turnover or replacement. Regardless of the source of the within-cohort change, this is a very different model for how social change occurs than one that relies solely on cohort replacement ideas.

How do these social factors introduced to explain social change operate to produce the observed changes? What are the effects of social change on individuals? What is the linkage between life span developmental trajectories of individuals and the nature of social change? These questions have been addressed both in general and with specific aspects of social change, for example, changes in political preferences (Inglehart, 1990; Krosnick, 1991; Krosnick & Alwin, 1989), political party identification (Alwin et al., 1991; Alwin & Krosnick, 1991a), changes in orientations to the family (Alwin, in press), changes in national standardized test scores (Alwin, 1991; Glenn, in press), and changes in human dispositions more generally (Glenn, 1980).

Social changes in identities, attitudes, beliefs, values, knowledge, skills, and other human dispositions can all happen through one or both of two types of social processes: *cohort replacement* or *intracohort change* (Ryder, 1965). These types of processes are not mutually exclusive, because both may be happening simultaneously. However, theories of social change tend to emphasize one or the other process in explaining why social values, attitudes, and beliefs change over time. It may also be the case that these processes may interact with other factors, such as cultural or structural variables, wherein one or another process may be apparent within some subgroups of society but not in others (see Alwin, in press).

STABILITY OF PERSONALITY OVER THE LIFE SPAN

The considerations just discussed lead us back to one of the central questions raised at the outset, specifically, how stable are individuals over their lives? If we can successfully address this question, then we can more productively address the question of the potential for changes in the relationship between the social environment and the individual. To confront this issue in terms of the available empirical record, I recently engaged in an exploration of varieties of stability in individual differences in psychological characteristics, including personality, intelligence, identities, self-image, and social attitudes (Alwin, 1994a). This research was aimed at integrating psychological and sociological conceptions of human life span development. As noted above, numerous past efforts have attempted to do this, and although that work is certainly impressive in its scope and aims, it has seldom incorporated a commitment to empirically verify existing hypotheses regarding elements of human constancy and change. This research takes the investigation of human constancy and change as theoretically and empirically problematic, focusing on a wide range of human dispositions.

With this purpose in mind, I presented a theoretical rationale for studying levels of stability over sequential periods of the life span, and I developed an approach to gauging patterns of stability over time. The approach taken to estimating rates of change/stability solves several problems that have plagued past researches on the study of life span trajectories of human change and stability. First, the research uses an approach that directly addresses the unconfounding of measurement errors and true change in longitudinal studies of the same individuals. Second, the approach is used to assess differences in stability between occasions of measurement, where the reinterview period varies from study to study. The models used to articulate this framework are particularly useful in conjunction with a synthetic cohort approach, as molar stability estimates can be generated across several cohorts, varying in age. Third, not only does this approach allow a method by which we can compare estimates of stability and change across cohorts differing in age, but also it makes it possible to compare molar stability estimates across concepts, or content domains of personality, as well as across studies using remeasurement designs. By thus standardizing rates of change in various human characteristics, one is eventually in a position to be able to develop inferences about the trajectories of constancy and change in specifiable characteristics over the entire life span.

The theoretical framework for this research focuses explicitly on the introduction of the concept of *molar stability*, the persistence of behavior or behavioral orientations as expressed in age-homogenous rates of change over specified periods of time. This concept was introduced as a means of organizing empirical information on human constancy and change, and of comparing raw stability estimates across studies having different remeasurement intervals and across different concepts (Alwin, 1994a). Molar stability is defined as $\beta^{j/k}$, where β is the cohort-specific or age-homogenous stability observed empirically, k is the number of years over which raw stability is assessed, and j is the number of years selected to express molar stability. In my research to date, for example, I have chosen j to equal 8, but this is governed in part by the nature of the remeasurement interval and the amount of expected change (see Alwin, 1994a). The goal is to obtain raw stability estimates and convert them into the standardized units of molar stability.

In this research, stability is estimated as the extent of true over-time correlation among single variables within groups that are relatively homogenous with respect to age. This type of stability is sometimes referred to as *differential stability* (see Alwin, 1994a; Caspi & Bem, 1990; Costa & McCrae, 1980). However, it is a mistake to estimate stability of individual differences over time using simple observed correlations between time points. This is the case because over-time correlations confound true change/stability with measurement imprecision (Heise, 1969). Due to the confounding involved, it becomes necessary to separate unreliability of measurement from true instability to precisely estimate stability.[5] This is particularly important when measurement errors are correlated with age (see Alwin & Krosnick, 1991a, 1991b). In short, any analysis of the stability of individual differences over time must take into account random errors of measurement.

There are several approaches to doing this, but the one that has proven itself to be the most useful in our research is the calculation of raw stability estimates from simple, single-variable simplex models (see Alwin, 1988, 1994a). Such models are characterized by a series of measures (a minimum of three) of the same variable separated in time. The models posit a Markovian (lag-1) restriction to account for change and stability in the underlying latent or "true" variable, which is a highly robust assumption in most change processes. This type of model has been useful in analyzing individual development or change while simultaneously taking random errors of measurement into account. These models are the basic building blocks of a research program aimed at comparing aspects of personality in their trajectories of stability at various stages or points in the life span.

Using this approach, six different phenotypic models of human stability were introduced—(a) the persistence model, (b) the lifelong-openness model, (c) the increasing-persistence model, (d) the impressionable-years model, (e) the midlife-stability model, and (f) the decreasing-persistence model—and their descriptive applicability to various domains has been investigated. These models are depicted graphically in Figure 2. The aim of my research up to this point has focused on the question of which models of human life span stability are most applicable to particular domains of personality and psychological functioning (see Alwin, 1994a). A key question focused on the question of whether persons tended to be more or less stable over their lives once they have experienced a critical stage of socialization in their young lives or early in their adulthood (Alwin et al., 1991).

---

[5]There is some recognition in the psychological literature of the need to deal with measurement errors (see Block, 1977, 1981; Epstein, 1980; Rushton, Brainerd, & Pressley, 1983). Although the solutions proposed move in the right direction, they do not accomplish the separation of errors or measurement from true change that I advocate here.

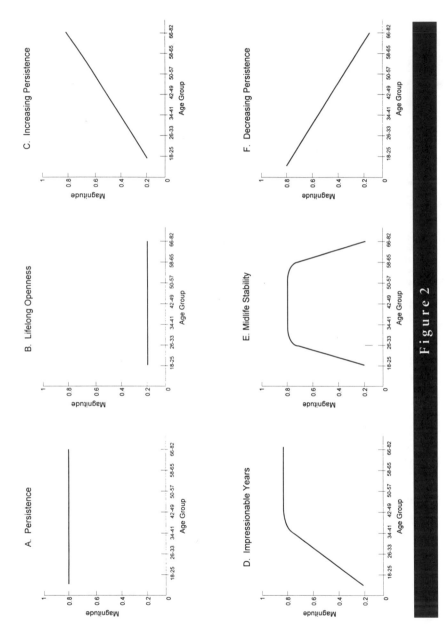

Figure 2

Models of human stability over the adult life span.

Except perhaps for personality and intellectual, there is considerable evidence in support of the notion that youth is a particularly impressionable time, in which the lowest levels of stability are experienced. I found that for many characteristics, such as cognitive and intellectual skills, identities, and some aspects of personality traits, there is a strong basis for assuming high levels of stability after adolescence or early adulthood. For others, primarily social attitudes, self-images, and political orientations, there is only a weak basis for the assumption of stability in human traits over the adult life span. The main findings can be summarized as follows: Personality and intellectual traits reveal relatively high levels of persistence from early adulthood to old age, whereas extant evidence on the stability of sociopolitical identities, self-conceptions, and attitudes appears to follow either the generational/persistence or midlife-stability models, in which constancies in behavioral orientations are substantially lowest in young adulthood, but reach a peak in midlife and from there either persist or decline in stability through the mature years of old age.

The degree of stability is, thus, not uniform across the life span, nor does it necessarily follow the same pattern for all human traits. Although young adulthood seems to be a particularly unstable period of the life course, most traits grow in stability with age; however, for many traits, old age is likely to be a time of change as well (see Alwin, 1994a). Despite this highly impressionable character of many aspects of human behavior and functioning, most achieve relatively high levels of stability soon after young adulthood, with midlife typically being the apex of assessed stability. By age 35, most characteristics have reached their highest stability. After midlife, however, the trajectories of human stability are quite variable across domains. Some traits continue to increase in stability, whereas others decline. Still others remain quite persistent until old age, where detectable declines in stability are witnessed for many human traits. Little support was found for the lifelong-openness model of human stability and change.

Note that the estimated trajectories of human stability are "average" estimates, in the sense that they describe the "typical" individual and represent a "normative" pattern of stability. Clearly, there is wide variability over human lives in the nature of change and stability, which is all the more reason to obtain average estimates. Still, this variability in human stability and change should be recognized, and although there may be a temptation to find in these results a basis for a pattern that represents "normal" life cycle development, akin to assumptions about some types of "normative" stages in life, there is considerable risk in generalizing too much from what we now know. Specifically with regard to the estimation of molar stability, it is not possible to obtain useful empirical assessments in many areas of behavioral functioning, and in some cases, the age range investigated in extant research was not a sufficient basis for drawing any conclusions.

The Stability of Intellectual Abilities

An example of the basic approach to the study of human stability that I am advocating is the development of intelligence in adulthood. In addition to personality, one of the most stable components of human behavior seems to be the domain of intellectual abilities or cognitive skills. Considerable evidence exists that many cognitive and intellectual variables, although quite unstable in infancy and childhood (see McCall, 1979), tend to stabilize in early adulthood. Bloom's (1964) pioneering work demonstrated a high degree of stability in intelligence scores even before early adulthood. In adulthood, measures of intellectual variables are highly stable over most of the adult life span, with changes in intellectual functioning due to differential aging only very late in the adult years. For example, Schaie (1983) concluded that "reliably replicable age changes in psychometric abilities of more than trivial magnitude cannot be demonstrated prior to age 60" (p. 127). His results are based on a 21-year longitudinal study of Seattle adults, and his conclusions are supported by other longitudinal studies (e.g., Cunningham & Owens, 1983).

One of the early demonstrations of the stability of intelligence scores in the preadult years is Nesselroade and Baltes's (1974) study of the stability of scores on the Thurstone and Thurstone (1962) Primary Mental Abilities battery in a sample of 1,849 students from three West Virginia counties in a three-wave panel design, with 1-year intervals between occasions of measurement. Those test scores contained measures of six primary factors: Verbal Meaning, Number Facility, Letter Series (reasoning), Work Grouping (reasoning), Number Series (reasoning), and Spatial Relations (Nesselroade & Baltes, 1974). Their examination of correlational data for these intellectual factors suggested that ability measures were systematically more stable with age, assessed over four graduating cohorts.

In a reanalysis of these data, using simplex models, I found considerable support for the Nesselroade and Baltes (1974) conclusions (see Alwin, 1994a). These results, reproduced here in Figure 3 support the dual observations that very high levels of stability in intelligence scores are reached during late adolescence, and that the stability of intelligence test scores increases systematically with age during this period. Stability esti-

Magnitude

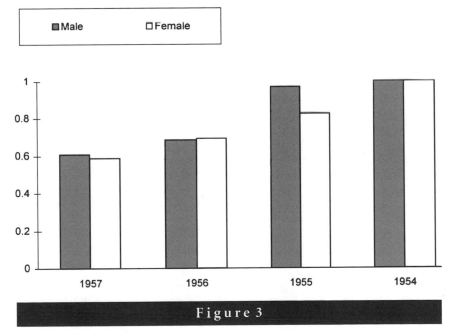

Figure 3

Stability of intelligence.

Magnitude

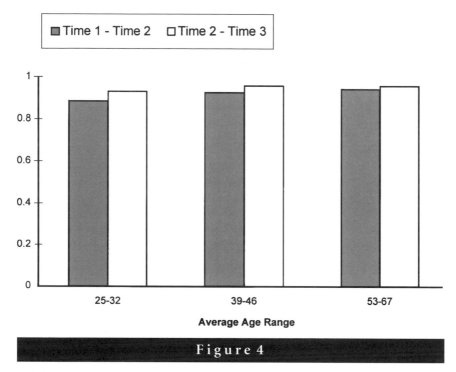

Figure 4

Stability of intelligence.

mates during adulthood bear out these conclusions. On the basis of the Seattle study of Schaie (1983) mentioned earlier, in which the same Thurstone and Thurstone (1962) battery of primary mental abilities, on which the Nesselroade and Baltes (1974) results given here are based, Hertzog and Schaie (1986) reported an analysis of stability over a 14-year period for three age groups: young (25–32 years of age), middle-aged (39–46 years of age), and old (53–67 years of age). Converted into units of molar stability, as shown in Figure 4, the Hertzog–Schaie results show very high levels of stability from young adulthood through old age and some growth in stability with age, this despite the very high levels of stability already reached in young adulthood. On the basis of these two studies, which are admittedly limited in representation of national populations, there is little question that intellectual abilities are highly stable from early adulthood.

These results may seem to pose a serious threat to sociological interpretations arguing that socialization or learning affecting basic intellectual abilities continues well into adulthood. On the other hand, if one argues that stability is a function of constancies of person–situation or linkages of person–structure, then continuities over time may be viewed as reflections of the stability of human locations in social structure and interpersonal ties. If one can argue further that such demonstrated stabilities reflect (at least in part) the stability of socially structured experience, then the proper adjudication of the issue of whether a sociological interpretation exists for the stability of intellectual abilities would have to focus on the segment of populations who experience change in social locations at different points in the life cycle, so that life course linkages to changes in socially structured experiences could be determined.

Schooler's (1987) analysis of the development of intellectual flexibility over the life span through exposure to changes in the complexity of the environment represents one attempt to apply theories of social structure and personality to human development (see Kohn & Schooler, 1983; Kohn & Slomczynski, 1990), but data from this research program have not been adequately organized to reflect life span variations in stability. On the other hand, sociological investigations aimed at the examination of cohort differences in verbal skills have found the role of "aging" or "life cycle" contributions to verbal skills beyond early adulthood to be negligible (see Alwin, 1991).

Patterns of Intercohort Stability

As I argued earlier, patterns of molar stability are linked to models of social change, as unique cohort experiences at critical stages, for example, the period of youth, may play a strong role in shaping behavior and behavioral orientations (Sears, 1981). Thus, one component of individual-level stability is the stability of intercohort influences on dispositional traits. It is therefore necessary to examine patterns of intracohort change and stability, and a vast amount of research has been undertaken to estimate the existence of cohort effects. Using a vast array of measures from repeated, longitudinal cross-sections, recent research has examined the two components of cohort stability and change, which are the essential ingredients in social change: patterns and cohort replacement and patterns of intracohort change. New approaches for estimating the components have been implemented, and results are available in several domains. Recent results in a number of different areas of human functioning have isolated evidence of cohort processes in a wide range of psychological attributes, for example, in racial attitudes (Firebaugh & Davis, 1988), sex role attitudes (Mason & Lu, 1988; Scott, Alwin, & Braun, 1994), intellectual skills (Alwin, 1991), parental values (Alwin, in press), political goals (Inglehart, 1990), political attitudes (Alwin, 1992, 1993b), and material expectations and satisfaction (Alwin & Carson, 1993; Easterlin, 1980).

Although further analysis and refinements to the empirical estimates are needed, the following conclusions are emerging from the study of cohort stability. First, there is considerable evidence of differences in cohort experiences and cohort replacement effects across many domains. These patterns strongly suggest a stability to behavioral orientations, in keeping with the previous treatment of the topic, due both to socialization influences in the formative years and to tendencies toward stability at the individual level. Second, these effects are, however, counterbalanced by patterns of intracohort change, the latter reflecting processes of aging and life cycle change and influences of historical, or period, effects (Alwin, 1992). Third, although there is variability across domains and it is difficult to draw general conclusions about cohort processes from these results, there is general support for the usefulness of the framework introduced here for studying the link between processes of social change and processes of individual change.

The Life Cycle and Opportunities for Change in Personality

In the foregoing, I raised the confounding of individual and environmental change, noting that processes of social and individual change are inexorably intertwined. I also pointed out that the concept of stability introduced here was not meant to convey information about, simply, the stability of individuals, but a complex mixture of environmental and personality stability and change. In effect, what is being assessed is the relative stability of individuals within particular environments, and at particular times or at particular life cycle stages, so that estimated stability coefficients summarize the stability of both persons and their environments at a particular intersection of biographical and historical time. Although there has been some attention to the issue of the relative stability of psychological traits, there has been much less attention to questions of the stability of the elements of environments that persons inhabit.

It is highly relevant in this context to consider the classic study of the American occupational structure by Blau and Duncan (1967), in which they argued that the processes that link occupational experiences, their causes and their consequences, are very much conditioned by life cycle stage. For present purposes, we consider occupational experiences to be a distinct aspect of the environment. Figure 5 contains a causal diagram representing the synthetic cohort model introduced by Blau and Duncan—synthetic because it results from a series of longitudinal assessments across persons of different ages rather than from data on a single cohort followed throughout their entire life span (see Blau & Duncan, 1967, pp. 177–188). This example illustrates very nicely some of the potential dynamics of life cycle variations in stability/change in aspects of the environment, although here again, it is difficult to disentangle stabilities associated with the nature of the occupation (an environmental attribute) and the nature of the personality or a particular individual-level attribute. The model can potentially be expanded to do this, as I argue below (see Figure 6), but that should come later.

The key outcome variable in this model is *occupational status*, which is usually defined as the "relative standing" of a particular occupational group in the society. As Blau and Duncan (1967) argued, occupational status is very closely related to the dimension of *occupational complexity*, or how intellectually demanding a particular job is (see Duncan, Featherman, & Duncan, 1972). This means that in some ways, occupational status can be thought of as measuring occupational complexity as well as status (but

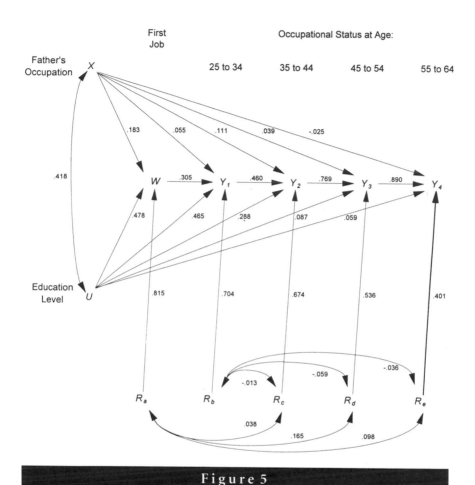

Figure 5

Synthetic cohort interpretation of the achievement of occupational status.

see Kohn & Schooler, 1983; Kohn & Slomczynski, 1990). Although there are clearly differences in the concepts of occupational status and complexity, they are very highly correlated. One study (Alwin, 1989a) reported a product–moment correlation of .816 in a sample of persons, based on a detailed set of questions regarding occupational complexity of the nature of the job. Using occupational titles instead of persons, Duncan et al. (1972) reported correlations in the range of .9 for measures of occupational prestige and the intellectual demandingness of the

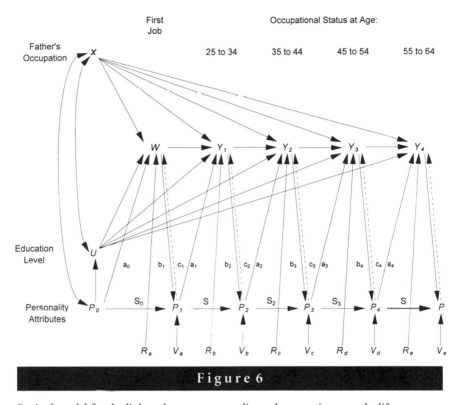

Figure 6

Revised model for the linkage between personality and occupation over the life span.

occupation.[6] There is, then, reason to believe that these two variables measure the same thing.

This admittedly oversimplified version of the Blau–Duncan (1967) model for the attainment of occupational success argues that two primary determinants of a person's occupational status are family origins, represented here by parental occupation (for sons, especially father's occupation) and the individual's level of schooling. Other parental status characteristics, such as father's and mother's educational levels or parental

---

[6]Using the simple logic that measurement error tends to attenuate relationships among variables, this correlation would be even higher if we were to allow for even small amounts of unreliability. By most accounts, the reliability of occupational status is in the neighborhood of .9, suggesting that a similar level of reliability of occupational complexity would yield a true correlation between these variables very close to .9 (for a discussion of the logic of corrections for attenuation, see Lord & Novick, 1968).

income levels are not represented in the model, either because they are re-dundant with respect to the occupational dimension (in the case of in-come) or because they operate indirectly through the educational level at-tained by the child (see Sewell & Hauser, 1975).[7] In this model (see Figure 5), father's occupation affects the nature of a person's first job but has lit-tle or no effect on attainment subsequent to the earliest adult achieve-ments. By contrast, the person's educational level has strong direct effects on the nature of one's first job, as well as independent effects on job com-plexity through midlife, and then little detectable influence thereafter. Sta-tus origins and educational resources, thus, operate very differently in their effects on the individual across the life course. Educational resources have continuing influences beyond the earliest strivings, whereas advantages from one's family background directly influence the person's initial posi-tioning in the adult occupation hierarchy, but have little influence after that. Obviously, without taking the life cycle into account, as the Blau–Duncan synthetic cohort model does, it would not be possible to have detected this different set of causal effects. And if such effects were assessed in a sample that is heterogenous with respect to age, the estimates would be some unknown admixture of quite different patterns of influ-ences (see Campbell, 1984).

This set of results suggests that the progression of *exposure to occu-pational experiences* (assessed as occupational status, but highly correlated to the intellectual requirements/demandingness of jobs; see Duncan et al., 1972, pp. 75–79) becomes increasingly stable over time. They demonstrate that exposure to occupational complexity increases in stability over the life cycle, obeying the increasing-persistence model discussed earlier. Com-plementing this process, as shown in Figure 5, is the diminished influen-tial role of factors associated with the family of origin and educational ex-periences. In other words, factors associated with the past become less important over biographical time, whereas the experiences tied to the na-

---

[7]To appreciate the nature of the causal dynamics that this exercise requires it is important to understand the technique of path analysis (Alwin & Hauser, 1975). Nontechnical discussions of the logic of this type of causal modeling are perhaps also useful (see Alwin, 1994b).

ture of one's occupation increase in importance in perpetuating themselves. The stability of the occupational career increases over biographical time, whereas both proximal and distal causes of events promoting change recede in importance. Occupational status attainment becomes an increasingly stable phenomenon, and as such it gains a momentum of its own.

If one takes these results seriously, it should be obvious from this exercise that it would be a mistake to ignore life cycle variations on these experiences in attempting to assess their causes and consequences. Indeed, these results should provide a cautionary set of guidelines to those who would seek to know the relationships between such variables, or even assessments of the causal impacts of variables as in this case, involving the causes and consequences of social experience, without taking life stage into account. Clearly, the linkage between experiences tied to the family of origin, or the level of schooling, or presumably countless other aspects of social experiences, depends intimately on the person's location in biographical time. In concrete terms, it would no doubt be a mistake to draw conclusions about the causes and consequences of occupational experiences without examining such models within a framework that allows for changes in these relationships over time.

Consideration of Preadult Experiences

Earlier, I indicated that the discussion would focus primarily on adult development, although the realities of occupational attainment are much more complicated. However, our general observations about the importance of life cycle factors would also apply to more complicated models. For example, the Blau–Duncan (1967) model of status attainment was modified and extended in significant ways by Sewell, Hauser, and their colleagues (Sewell & Hauser, 1975), who argued that (a) the concept of intellectual ability should be added to the set of exogenous predictors, because intellectual factors may directly influence early occupational involvement, (b) the influences of family origin on a person's educational level operate primarily through variables such as mental abilities, motivation, aspirations, and the influence of significant others and role models, and (c) the overall influences of socialization outcomes during the pre-adult years must be incorporated and controlled to specify the influences of later attainments on later embodiments of those same outcomes of development and socialization.

What then of studies that ignore life cycle variation in occupational experiences, when assessing their effects on psychological outcomes? And what of those studies that ignore, and do not control for, preadult embodiments of later adult personality development? In one famous study, Kohn and his colleagues (most notably Schooler and Slomczynski) have been for more than 30 years advancing an interpretation of the processes by which structural factors condition and constrain psychological functioning in adulthood. Kohn and his colleagues (see Kohn, this volume, chapter 5; Kohn & Schooler, 1983; Kohn & Slomczynski, 1990) have been interested in why men and women's positions in the social structure are correlated with aspects of psychological functioning (value orientations, intellectual functioning, and authoritarianism, among other things). Their argument is distinctly causal in nature: They believe that conditions of work directly influence or otherwise affect, through learning and socialization experiences, individual differences in psychological functioning, and yet they ignore preadult experiences of the type Sewell and Hauser (1975) argue are important.

The critical factors identified in the research of Kohn and his colleagues as psychologically relevant to social structure are circumscribed by the extent of control over the conditions of lives, specifically the extent to which a person's job provides opportunities and constraints with respect to the development of self-direction. Clearly, such opportunities and constraints are linked to family of origin and preadult experiences, not captured by measures of schooling alone. Kohn and Schooler (1983) used the term *occupational self-direction* to define the relevant aspects of occupational experiences that encourage or inhibit outcomes of human development, and they allow for the possibility that jobs explicitly select on preadult factors of relevance. These occupational experiences are theorized to affect, through learning processes, personality and other aspects of psychological functioning. These effects could just as easily have been attributed to other socioeconomic experiences, for example, educational level. In Bronfenbrenner's (1979) words, "The further one goes in school, the more likely one [is] to experience freedom from close supervision, nonroutinized flow [of work], substantively complex work, and the opportunity for self-direction" (p. 248). Using model-based empirical estimates of the effects of educational attainment and reciprocal parameters linking job experiences and personality, Kohn and his colleagues have established an empirical relationship between schooling and aspects of occupational experience, on the one hand, and several aspects of psychological orientations, on the other. They argue that they have identified the key processes involved. These models involve a two-ply argument that (a) there is selection into occupations on the basis of psychological orientations, and (b) occupational experiences, in part, account for the relationships. Note, however, that in their results, education has a more powerful set of influences than job experiences, suggesting that the socialization impact of educational structures may be much more influential in people's lives than those of occupational structures.

It can be argued that the Kohn–Schooler (1983) models misspecify the link between the person and the position by not, at a minimum, taking life cycle variation in occupational experience into account. Campbell (1984), for example, argued that one should not ignore the specification of differing causal effects of job conditions on personality, and vice versa, at different stages in the life cycle:

> Ideally, to study how job conditions affect psychological functioning, one would study a cohort of young people as they enter the labor force. In the present case [the Kohn–Schooler et al. case], we have estimates based on men who are in their first years in the labor force and men who are about to leave it. One has to believe that the impact of job conditions on men who have been working for 30 years is different from their impact on new workers. (p. 595)

Furthermore, not including preadult levels of personality variables in their model, as well as other aspects of family origins, eliminates consideration of critical factors.

Job Complexity and Personality: Taking Time Seriously

We can illustrate these problems for present purposes by imagining another variable in the Blau–Duncan model (1967) discussed above, a variable representing an aspect of personality, or individual differences, depicted as P in Figure 6, assessed at each of several stages in the life course. The specification of a model such as this would correspond to an interest in estimating the reciprocal effects of occupation and some aspect of personality at various stages in the life cycle while taking developmental processes and life cycle factors into account. Given what we know about most aspects of human stability, there is strong reason to believe that the parameters describing these reciprocal relationships would vary across stages in the life span. This model allows for these possibilities.

The P depicted in this diagram could be any aspect of personality of interest, but the most relevant one in this case is intellectual functioning, given that intelligence is an aspect of personality and is known to directly influence early occupational attainment (Sewell & Hauser, 1975). Furthermore, the consideration of preadult levels of intellectual functioning is important, given that intellectual flexibility is one of the key variables that Kohn and his colleagues argue is reciprocally related in a causal sense to occupational experiences (see Kohn & Schooler, 1983). We have depicted all of these parameters in the model shown in Figure 6. Specifically, a_0 represents the impact of preadult intellectual functioning on first job, b_1 represents the influence of first job on intellectual functioning later on, and c_1 reflects the possible reciprocal influence of intelligence on first job status, net of P_0 (preadult level of intellectual functioning). In general, the a_t parameters describe the "selection" into levels of occupational complexity on the basis of intellectual functioning at each successive stage in the life cycle. Similarly, in general, the b_t parameters describe the influence of occupational complexity on P_t, and c_t reflects the simultaneous feedback influence of P_t on occupational complexity (see Kohn & Slomczynski, 1990). In addition, the s_t parameters represent the stability of intellectual functioning across the life span. Note that there is no lagged effect of occupation on personality over time.[8]

The role of early intellectual functioning in directly affecting early job experiences is one of the factors taken into account by prior models of occupational attainment (see Sewell & Hauser, 1975), which is omitted in the Kohn–Schooler (1983) research. Thus, to the extent that a_0 and s_0 are nonzero and positive, estimates of b_1, c_1, and a_1 are biased as a result. The extent of the bias would, of course, depend on the seriousness of the omission, which, in turn, depends on the magnitudes of the omitted parameters. This involves the issue of the stability of the aspect of personality, P, under investigation. If it is a highly stable characteristic, then it would be relatively immune to disturbing influences for later adult experiences, for example, the experience of changes in levels of occupational complexity. In the case of intellectual functioning, the existing evidence, as reviewed above, suggests that individual differences in test scores achieve extremely high levels of stability in late adolescence and persist at very high levels over time (Alwin, 1994a; Hertzog & Schaie, 1986; Nesselroade & Baltes, 1974).

There is less evidence of a direct effect of intellectual factors on occupation, once education is controlled. Specifically, in an age-homogenous sample of 1957 Wisconsin high school graduates, Sewell and Hauser (1975, p. 65) estimated the relevant reduced-form path coefficient to be .32, so there appears to be some basis for concern. At the same time, they noted that the bulk of this effect of preadult intelligence on later occupational attainment operates primarily through level of schooling, so there may not be any direct effects of intelligence on status attainment to contend with, contrary to naive notions that intelligence strongly determines occupational status (Herrnstein & Murray, 1994). To the extent that it does influence one's position in the occupational hierarchy, the Sewell and Hauser (1975) results suggest that it is largely indirect through the amount of schooling attained.

These conclusions are also strongly buttressed by Duncan's (1968) effort to determine the independent effects of intelligence on early status

---

[8]This specification is given primarily for illustrative purposes. Clearly, there are alternative causal specifications that would be in keeping with the reciprocal relationship between job and person.

strivings in a large sample of White army veterans, men aged 25–34 in 1964. His results showed that (a) measures of intelligence are highly stable after early adolescence, (b) early intelligence does not directly affect occupational attainment, but does so through its effects on education and on later embodiments of intelligence, and (c) aspects of later intellectual functioning only marginally affect occupational attainment directly (a path coefficient of .10).

The grounds for caution, therefore, in evaluating current approaches to the estimation of the mutual effects of job experiences (social structure) and psychological functioning (personality) clearly exist. The conclusions here are in part based on conjecture, but the intellectual exercise is valuable because it suggests the need to take time seriously in the specification of the link between aspects of personality and social structure. Moreover, the framework provided by the model in Figure 6 for examining the relationship between aspects of personality (e.g., intellectual functioning) and aspects of the social environment (e.g., occupational conditions) encourages the analysis of this relationship in biographical and historical time. It is hoped that future researchers will consider these possibilities, and the knowledge available about the dynamic processes of human development, before engaging in the estimation of models that are clearly misspecified.

Historical Factors in Environmental Opportunities

The previous example of life cycle patterns of status attainment give weight to two types of conclusions. One is that experiences that occur quite early in the life cycle (family origins and length of schooling completed) continue to affect later attainments throughout the life course, even into older age. Second, the results suggest that the effects of both types of factors (social origins and educational achievement) decline in their relative influence over time. This means, in part, that the occupational career tends to stabilize into a set of patterns that become increasingly less penetrable by past events and experiences. Individuals tend to settle into a set of occupational choices and experiences that do not change. Changing even relatively immediate or proximal environmental conditions has little effect on occupational conditions later in life.

These conclusions, however, must be understood in a historical context, because the opportunities for occupational mobility (up or down) may be quite different across historical time. Elder's (1974) research on the Great Depression gives strong testament to the potential disruptive effects of changes in a family's economic circumstances, and several other writers (e.g., Easterlin, 1980; Levy, 1987) argued that there may be cohort differences in early labor force experiences. It is, therefore, important to underscore the necessity of viewing all social processes as time dependent, in the sense that the results may not be generalizable across cohorts and time periods. Featherman and Hauser (1978) provided the most complete analysis to date of changing status attainment opportunities, analyzing age-specific intercohort differences in occupational stratification (see also Featherman, 1980). Their analysis suggested that in more recent cohorts, there is a decreasing tendency for men to have current occupations like those of their fathers. Across successive cohorts, educational attainments, Featherman and Hauser argued, became more equally distributed and had less dependence on socioeconomic background. The returns on investment in schooling, such as occupational and economic attainments, appear to be stronger in more recent cohorts, and the stratification system experienced by younger cohorts is less rigidly stratified by social origins. Thus, it is clear from these types of observations that any conclusions about the causes and consequences of occupational experiences, as an embodiment of position in the social structure, must be carefully considered in a manner that recognizes potential historical trends and processes.

CONCLUSIONS

Social scientists are constantly confronted with issues that relate to change—changes in both biographical and historical time. In the course of people's life, they experience, for example, changes in aspects of the family and household, changes in roles and interpersonal relations, changes in intergenerational relations, changes in the economy, changes in government and politics, and changes in social structure and social organization. An approach to the study of the link between the individual and society, the link between personality and social structure, which ignores the nature of biographical and historical change, will provide only a limited understanding of that connection. An approach to the study of human lives in the context of social change must be able to conceptualize the person, or personality, and the structural aspects of the social environment, within a dynamic framework that incorporates such possibilities of change. In this chapter, I tried to articulate a distinctly dynamic view of human personality development conceived of in terms of the stability of several components of the relationship between the individual and the social environment. The concepts of *personality* and *social structure* are used, respectively, to conceptualize (a) the individual and (b) the sociostructural elements that influence and constrain the individual and her or his behavioral settings. Within this framework, human development is conceptualized in terms of the reciprocal relationship between the person and the environment—in which the person is an active participant in shaping her or his environment while at the same time key elements of the environment (interpersonal relations, roles, and molar activities) provide the potential for transforming the individual.

This set of issues focuses attention on the question of stability of personality and the stability of the social environment. By addressing the question of variation in life span stability of personality, the question of the linkage between personality and social structure has been placed within a dynamic framework, allowing for variation in human stability across both biographical and historical time. In this sense, the notion of the stability of personality has been recast as one of *dynamic stability*, a concept that can be used to productively view the reciprocal relationship between persons and their social environments (Bronfenbrenner, 1979; Mortimer et al., 1982). Consequently, we can better capture the processes by which the person is the recipient of influences from the environment while at the same time functioning as an active agent in the shaping of that environment.

REFERENCES

Alwin, D. F. (1984). Trends in parental socialization values: Detroit, 1958 to 1983. *American Journal of Sociology, 90*, 359–382.

Alwin, D. F. (1986). Religion and parental child-rearing orientations: Evidence of a Catholic–Protestant convergence. *American Journal of Sociology, 92*, 412–440.

Alwin, D. F. (1988). From obedience to autonomy: Changes in traits desired in children, 1924–78. *Public Opinion Quarterly, 52*, 33–52.

Alwin, D. F. (1989a). Changes in qualities valued in children in the United States, 1964 to 1984. *Social Science Research, 18*, 195–236.

Alwin, D. F. (1989b). Social stratification, conditions of work, and parental socialization values. In N. Eisenberg, J. Reykowski, & E. Staub (Eds.), *Social and moral values: Individual and societal perspectives* (pp. 327–346). Hillsdale, NJ: Erlbaum.

Alwin, D. F. (1990a). Cohort replacement and parental socialization values. *Journal of Marriage and the Family, 52*, 347–360.

Alwin, D. F. (1990b). Historical changes in parental orientations to children. In N. Mandell & S. Cahill (Eds.), *Sociological studies of child development* (Vol. 3, pp. 65–86). Greenwich, CT: JAI Press.

Alwin, D. F. (1991). Family of origin and cohort differences in verbal ability. *American Sociological Review, 56*, 625–638.

Alwin, D. F. (1992). Aging, cohorts, and social change: An examination of the generational replacement model of social change. In H. A. Becker (Ed.), *Dynamics of cohort and generations research* (pp. 53–95). Amsterdam: Thesis.

Alwin, D. F. (1993a). Cohorts, family change, and intergenerational solidarity. In H. A. Becker & P. L. J. Hermkens (Eds.), *Solidarity of generations* (pp. 149–174). Amsterdam: Thesis.

Alwin, D. F. (1993b). Socio-political attitude development in adulthood: The role of generational and life-cycle factors. In D. Krebs & P. Schmidt (Eds.), *New directions in attitude measurement* (pp. 61–93). Berlin: de Gryter.

Alwin, D. F. (1994a). Aging, personality and social change: The stability of individual differences over the adult life-span. In D. L. Featherman, R. M. Lerner, & M. Perlmutter (Eds.), *Life-span development and behavior* (Vol. 12, pp. 135–185). Hillsdale, NJ: Erlbaum.

Alwin, D. F. (1994b). Quantitative methods in social psychology. In K. Cook, G. Fine, & J. House (Eds.), *Sociological perspectives in social psychology.* New York: Allyn & Bacon.

Alwin, D. F. (in press). Parental socialization values in historical perspective. In C. Ryff & M. M. Seltzer (Eds.), *The parental experience at midlife.* Chicago: University of Chicago Press.

Alwin, D. F., & Carson, T. (1993). Cohorts, economic change, and perceptions of material well-being. In H. A. Becker & P. L. J. Hermkens (Eds.), *Solidarity of generations* (pp. 351–383). Amsterdam: Thesis.

Alwin, D. F., Cohen, R. L., & Newcomb, T. M. (1991). *Political attitudes over the life-span: The Bennington women after fifty years.* Madison: University of Wisconsin Press.

Alwin, D. F., & Hauser, R. M. (1975). The decomposition of effects in path analysis. *American Sociological Review, 40,* 37–47.

Alwin, D. F., & Krosnick, J. A. (1991a). Aging, cohorts and the stability of socio-political orientations over the life-span. *American Journal of Sociology, 97,* 169–195.

Alwin, D. F., & Krosnick, J. A. (1991b). The reliability of survey attitude measurement: The influence of question and respondent attributes. *Sociological Methods and Research, 20,* 139–181.

Asendorpf, J. B. (1992). Continuity and stability of personality traits and personality patterns. In J. B. Asendorpf & J. Valsiner (Eds.), *Stability and change in development* (pp. 116–154). Newbury Park, CA: Sage.

Baumrind, D. (1989). Rearing competent children. In W. Damon (Ed.), *Child development today and tomorrow* (pp. 349–378). San Francisco: Jossey-Bass.

Berger, P. L., & Luckmann, T. (1967). *Social construction of reality: A treatise in the sociology of knowledge.* New York: Doubleday.

Blau, P. M., & Duncan, O. D. (1967). *The American occupational structure.* New York: Wiley.

Block, J. (1977). Advancing the science of personality: Paradigmatic shift or improving the quality of research. In D. Magnusson & N. S. Endler (Eds.), *Psychology at the crossroads: Current issues in interactional psychology* (pp. 37–63). Hillsdale, NJ: Erlbaum.

Block, J. (1981). Some enduring and consequential structures of personality. In A. I. Rabin, J. Aronoff, A. M. Barclay, & R. A. Zucker (Eds.), *Further explorations in personality* (pp. 27–43). New York: Wiley.

Bloom, B. (1964). *Stability and change in human characteristics.* New York: Wiley.

Brim, O. G., Jr., & Kagan, J. (1980). *Constancy and change in human development.* Cambridge, MA: Harvard University Press.

Bronfenbrenner, U. (1958). Socialization and social class through time and space. In E. Maccoby, T. Newcomb, & E. Hartley (Eds.), *Readings in social psychology* (pp. 400–425). New York: Holt, Rinehart & Winston.

Bronfenbrenner, U. (1979). *The ecology of human development.* Cambridge, MA: Harvard University Press.

Bronfenbrenner, U. (1986). Ecology of the family as a context for human development: Research perspectives. *Developmental Psychology, 22,* 723–742.

Bronfenbrenner, U., & Ceci, S. J. (1994). Nature–nurture reconceptualized in developmental perspective: A bioecological model. *Psychological Review, 101,* 568–586.

Bronfenbrenner, U., & Crouter, A. C. (1983). The evolution of environmental models in developmental research. In P. H. Mussen (Series Ed.) & W. Kessen (Vol. Ed.), *Handbook of child psychology: Vol. 1. History, theory, and methods* (4th ed., pp. 357–414). New York: Wiley.

Campbell, R. T. (1984). Ramifications of work experience. *Science, 224,* 594–595.

Campbell, R. T. (1992). Longitudinal research. In E. F. Borgatta & M. L. Borgatta (Eds.), *Encyclopedia of sociology* (pp. 1146–1158). New York: Macmillan.

Campbell, R. T., Abolafia, J., & Maddox, G. (1985). Life-course analysis in social gerontology: Using replicated social surveys to study cohort differences. In A. S. Rossi (Ed.), *Gender and the life course* (pp. 301–318). New York: Aldine de Gruyter.

Caspi, A. (1987). Personality in the life course. *Journal of Personality and Social Psychology, 53,* 1203–1213.

Caspi, A., & Bem, D. J. (1990). Personality continuity and change across the life course. In L. Pervin (Ed.), *Handbook of personality theory and research* (pp. 549–575). New York: Guilford Press.

Chodorow, N. (1978). *The reproduction of mothering: Psychoanalysis and the sociology of gender.* Berkeley: University of California Press.

Clausen, J. A. (1986). *The life course: A sociological perspective.* Englewood Cliffs, NJ: Prentice-Hall.

Cohen, R. L., & Alwin, D. F. (1993). The Bennington women of the 1930s: Political attitudes over the life course. In K. Hulbert & D. Schuster (Eds.), *Women's lives through time: Educated American women of the twentieth century* (pp. 117–139). San Francisco: Jossey-Bass.

Converse, P. E. (1976). *The dynamics of party support.* Beverly Hills, CA: Sage.

Costa, P. T., Jr., & McCrae, R. R. (1980). Still stable after all these years: Personality as a key to some issues in adulthood and old age. In P. B. Baltes & O. G. Brim, Jr. (Eds.), *Life-span development and behavior* (Vol. 3, pp. 65–102). New York: Academic Press.

Cunningham, W. R., & Owens, W. A., Jr. (1983). The Iowa state study of adult development of intellectual abilities. In K. W. Schaie (Ed.), *Longitudinal studies of adult psychological development* (pp. 20–39). New York: Guilford Press.

Duncan, O. D. (1968). Ability and achievement. *Eugenics Quarterly, 15,* 1–11.

Duncan, O. D., Featherman, D. L., & Duncan, B. (1972). *Socioeconomic background and achievement.* New York: Seminar Press.

Easterlin, R. (1980). *Birth and fortune: The impact of numbers on personal welfare.* New York: Basic Books.

Elder, G. H., Jr. (1974). *Children of the Great Depression.* Chicago: University of Chicago Press.

Elder, G. H., Jr. (1980). Adolescence in historical perspective. In J. Adelson (Ed.), *Handbook of adolescent psychology* (pp. 3–46). New York: Wiley.

Elder, G. H., Jr., & Caspi, A. (1988). Human development and social change: An emerging perspective on the life course. In N. Bolger, A. Caspi, G. Downey, & M. Moorehouse (Eds.), *Persons in context: Developmental processes* (pp. 77–113). New York: Cambridge University Press.

Elder, G. H., Jr., & Caspi, A. (1990). Studying lives in a changing society: Sociological and personological explorations. In A. I. Rabin, R. A. Zucker, R. A. Emmons, & S. Frank (Eds.), *Studying persons and lives* (pp. 201–247). New York: Springer.

Elder, G. H., Jr., Caspi, A., & Burton, L. M. (1988). Adolescent transitions in developmental perspective: Sociological and historical insights. *Minnesota Symposium on Child Psychology, 21,* 151–179.

Elder, G. H., Jr., & Hareven, T. K. (1993). Rising above life's disadvantages: From the Great Depression to war. In G. H. Elder, Jr., J. Modell, & R. D. Parke (Eds.), *Children in time and place* (pp. 47–72). Cambridge, England: Cambridge University Press.

Elder, G. H., Jr., Modell, J., & Parke, R. D. (1993). Studying children in a changing world. In G. H. Elder, Jr., J. Modell, & R. D. Parke (Eds.), *Children in time and place* (pp. 3–21). Cambridge, England: Cambridge University Press.

Epstein, S. (1980). The stability of behavior: II. Implications for psychological research. *American Psychologist, 35,* 790–806.

Featherman, D. L. (1980). Schooling and occupational careers: Constancy and change in worldly success. In O. G. Brim, Jr., & J. Kagan (Eds.), *Constancy and change in human development* (pp. 675–738). Cambridge, MA: Harvard University Press.

Featherman, D. L., & Hauser, R. M. (1978). *Opportunity and change.* New York: Academic Press.

Featherman, D. L., & Lerner, R. M. (1985). Ontogenesis and sociogenesis: Problematics for theory and research about development and socialization across the lifespan. *American Sociological Review, 50*, 659–676.

Firebaugh, G., & Davis, K. E. (1988). Trends in anti-Black prejudice, 1972–1984: Region and cohort effects. *American Journal of Sociology, 94*, 251–272.

Gergen, K. J. (1980). The emerging crisis in life-span developmental theory. In P. B. Baltes & O. G. Brim, Jr. (Eds.), *Life-span development and behavior* (Vol. 3, pp. 32–65). New York: Academic Press.

Gilligan, C., Brown, L., & Rogers, A. (1990). Psyche embedded: A place for body, relationships and culture in personality theory. In A. I Rabin, R. A. Zucker, R. A. Emmons, & S. Frank (Eds.), *Studying persons and lives* (pp. 86–147). New York: Springer.

Glenn, N. D. (1980). Values, attitudes and beliefs. In O. G. Brim, Jr., & J. Kagan (Eds.), *Constancy and change in human development* (pp. 596–640). Cambridge, MA: Harvard University Press.

Glenn, N. D. (1994). Television watching, newspaper reading, and cohort differences in verbal ability. *Sociology of Education, 67*, 216–230.

Heise, D. R. (1969). Separating reliability and stability in test–retest correlation. *American Sociological Review, 34*, 93–191.

Herrnstein, R. J., & Murray, C. (1994). *The bell curve: Intelligence and class structure in American life*. New York: Free Press.

Hertzog, C., & Schaie, K. W. (1986). Stability and change in adult intelligence: I. Analysis of longitudinal covariance structures. *Psychology and Aging, 1*, 159–171.

House, J. S. (1981). Social structure and personality. In M. Rosenberg & R. H. Turner (Eds.), *Social psychology: Sociological perspectives* (pp. 525–561). New York: Basic Books.

Inglehart, R. (1990). *Cultural change: The impact of economic and political change on culture, and the impact of culture on economics, society and politics in advanced industrial society*. Princeton, NJ: Princeton University Press.

Inkeles, A. (1955). Social change and social character: The role of parental mediation. *Journal of Social Issues, 39*, 179–191.

Inkeles, A., & Levinson, D. (1954). National character: The study of modal personality and social systems. In G. Lindzey (Ed.), *Handbook of social psychology* (pp. 975–1020). Cambridge, MA: Addison-Wesley.

James, W. (1950). *The principles of psychology*. New York: Dover. (Original work published 1890)

Kohn, M. L., & Schooler, C. (1983). *Work and personality: An inquiry into the impact of social stratification.* Norwood, NJ: Ablex.

Kohn, M. L., & Slomczynski, K. M. (1990). *Social structure and self-direction: A comparative analysis of the United States and Poland.* Cambridge, MA: Basil Blackwell.

Krosnick, J. A. (1991). The stability of political preferences: Comparisons of symbolic and nonsymbolic attitudes. *American Journal of Political Science, 35,* 547–576.

Krosnick, J. A., & Alwin, D. F. (1989). Aging and susceptibility to attitude change. *Journal of Personality and Social Psychology, 57,* 416–425.

Lesthaeghe, R., & Surkyn, J. (1988). Cultural dynamics and economic theories of fertility change. *Population and Development Review, 11,* 1–45.

Levy, F. (1987). *Dollars and dreams: The changing American income distribution.* New York: Norton.

Lord, F. M., & Novick, M. L. (1968). *Statistical theories of mental test scores.* Reading, MA: Addison-Wesley.

Lorence, J., & Mortimer, J. T. (1985). Job involvement through the life course: A panel study of three age groups. *American Sociological Review, 50,* 618–638.

Mannheim, K. (1952). The problem of generations. In P. Kecskemeti (Ed.), *Essays in the sociology of knowledge* (pp. 276–320). London: Routledge & Kegan Paul.

Mason, K. O., & Lu, Y. H. (1988). Attitudes toward women's familial roles: Changes in the United States, 1977–1985. *Gender and Society, 2,* 39–57.

McCall, R. B. (1979). The development of intellectual functioning in infancy and the prediction of later IQ. In J. D. Osofsky (Ed.), *Handbook of infant development* (pp. 707–741). New York: Wiley.

Mills, C. W. (1959). *The sociological imagination.* New York: Oxford University Press.

Mortimer, J. T., Finch, M. D., & Kumka, D. (1982). Persistence and change in development: The multidimensional self-concept. In P. B. Baltes & O. G. Brim, Jr. (Eds.), *Life-span development and behavior.* New York: Academic Press.

Mortimer, J. T., Finch, M. D., & Kumka, D. (1986). *Work, family, and personality: Transition to adulthood.* Norwood, NJ: Ablex.

Mortimer, J. T., Finch, M. D., & Maruyama, G. (1988). Work experience and job satisfaction: Variation by age and gender. In J. T. Mortimer & K. M. Borman (Eds.), *Work experience and psychological development through the life-span.* Boulder, CO: Westview Press.

Mortimer, J. T., & Lorence, J. (1981). Self-concept stability and change from late adolescence to early adulthood. In R. G. Simmons (Ed.), *Research in community and mental health* (Vol. 2, pp. 5–42). Greenwich, CT: JAI Press.

Moss, H. A., & Susman, E. J. (1980). Longitudinal study of personality development. In O. G. Brim, Jr., & J. Kagan (Eds.), *Constancy and change in human development* (pp. 530–595). Cambridge, MA: Harvard University Press.

Musgrove, F. (1977). *Margins of the mind.* London: Methuen.

Nesselroade, J. R. (1988). Some implications of the trait–state distinction for the study of development over the life span: The case of personality. In P. B. Baltes, D. L. Featherman, & R. M. Lerner (Eds.), *Life-span development and behavior* (pp. 163–189). Hillsdale, NJ: Erlbaum.

Nesselroade, J. R. (1990). Adult personality development: Issues in assessing constancy and change. In A. I. Rabin, R. A. Zucker, R. A. Emmons, & S. Frank. (Eds.), *Studying persons and lives* (pp. 41–85). New York: Springer.

Nesselroade, J. R., & Baltes, P. B. (1974). Adolescent personality development and historical change: 1970–1972. *Monographs of the Society for Research in Child Development, 39*(1, Serial No. 154).

Riesman, D. (1950). *The lonely crowd: A study of the changing American character.* London: Yale University Press.

Rushton, J. P., Brainerd, C. J., & Pressley, M. (1983). Behavioral development and construct validity: The principle of aggregation. *Psychological Bulletin, 94,* 18–38.

Ryder, N. B. (1965). The cohort as a concept in the study of social change. *American Sociological Review, 30,* 843–861.

Schaie, K. W. (1983). The Seattle longitudinal study: A 21-year exploration of psychometric intelligence in adulthood. In K. W. Schaie (Ed.), *Longitudinal studies of adult psychological development* (pp. 64–135). New York: Guilford Press.

Schooler, C. (1987). Psychological effects of complex environments during the life span: A review and theory. In C. Schooler & K. W. Schaie (Eds.), *Cognitive functioning and social structure over the lifecourse.* Norwood, NJ: Ablex.

Scott, J. L., Alwin, D. F., & Braun, M. (1994, July). *Sex-role attitude change in Britain, the United States, and Germany.* Paper presented at the 13th World Congress of Sociology, Bielefeld, Germany.

Sears, D. O. (1981). Life-stage effects on attitude change, especially among the elderly. In S. B. Kiesler, J. N. Morgan, & V. K. Oppenheimer (Eds.), *Aging and social change* (pp. 183–204). New York: Academic Press.

Sewell, W. H., Jr. (1992). A theory of structure: Duality, agency, and transformation. *American Journal of Sociology, 98,* 1–29.

Sewell, W. H., Sr., & Hauser, R. M. (1975). *Education, occupation and earnings achievement in the early career.* New York: Academic Press.

Stewart, A. J., & Healy, J. M., Jr. (1989). Linking individual development and social changes. *American Psychologist, 44,* 30–42.

Stone, L. (1977). *The family, sex and marriage in England 1500–1800.* New York: Harper & Row.

Strelau, J. (1987). The concept of temperament in personality research. *European Journal of Personality, 1,* 107–117.

Stryker, S. (1981). Symbolic interactionism: Themes and variations. In M. Rosenberg & R. H. Turner (Eds.), *Social psychology: Sociological perspectives* (pp. 3–29). New York: Basic Books.

Sullivan, H. S. (1953). *An interpersonal theory of psychiatry.* New York: Norton.

Thurstone, L. L., & Thurstone, T. G. (1962). *SRA Primary Mental Abilities.* Chicago: Science Research Associates.

Wells, L. E., & Stryker, S. (1988). Stability and change in the self over the life course. In P. B. Baltes, D. L. Featherman, & R. M. Lerner (Eds.), *Life-span development and behavior* (pp. 191–229). Hillsdale, NJ: Erlbaum.

White, H. (1992). Succession and generations: Looking back on chains of opportunity. In H. A. Becker (Ed.), *Dynamics of cohort and generations research* (pp. 31–51). Amsterdam: Thesis.

Williams, R. M., Jr. (1960). *American society: A sociological interpretation* (2nd ed). New York: Knopf.

PART THREE

The Multiple Contexts of Human Development

The Multiple Contexts of Human Development

Kurt Lüscher

Human development is, following an axiom of Bronfenbrenner's eco-logical theory, always development in contexts. The fruitfulness of this idea results from its manifold heuristic, theoretical, methodological, and practical implications, which can be seen from the contributions to this volume and especially in this section.

On the heuristic level, the primary concern is to probe the different meanings of the notion of context. One may be tempted to say, and Clausen points in this direction, that the ultimate interest lies in the "*con-text,* from which the *text*" emerges, that is, in the script from which the individual life narrative emerges. This can be studied by assessing "the per-son's own report of his or her life: his or her perceptions of the influences on it as these have been experienced" (p. 367).

Clausen conceives context primarily in the spatial or geographical sense of the word. His data demonstrate, among other things, the signif-icance of moving from one location to another, especially in the lives of women. Maccoby enlarges the concept by offering a systematic account of the "life worlds" in which males and females typically grow up. Goodnow favors an even broader notion of the concept. She proposes to characterize context not only in a physical–spatial sense but also in regard to the forms of face-to-face interaction that are possible in different life sectors and, finally, in regard to benefits and obligations. In this way, she captures the moral force or moral power exercised in and through social contexts. In other words, contexts are characterized by the moral meanings they confer on social relations or with which social relations are interpreted. Ceci and Hembrooke's point of departure is perhaps the most fundamental. Referring to the old problem of nature versus nurture, they take a firm stand that differs from the well-known dichotomous positions insofar as they consider "context to be a basic ingredient of intellectual development"(p. 303).

Indeed, on a theoretical level, contexts must be related systematically to development. Ceci and Hembrooke pick up the idea of proximal processes, which they demarcate as the mechanism translating genotypes into phenotypes. Although their primary concern is to offer a compelling alternative to biological reductionism, and consequently, they refer to and discuss primarily the literature that relates psychological and biological findings, especially on the topic of heredity, their own approach is open to the views of social psychologists and even sociologists, as can easily be deduced from their distinction of four types of contexts and from the experiments that they discuss.

Clausen, who in his rich oeuvre, himself integrates social psychology and sociology in a unique way, unfolds his arguments on the basis of an approach that is located just on the borderline of these two disciplines, namely, role analysis. Roles are expressions of behaviors related to positions in the social structure. Clausen combines this view in an innovative way with the concept of *turning points*. In this way, he manages to combine spatial or structural orientation with the experience of personal development. This idea has the additional advantage that it facilitates empirical operationalization.

Maccoby's arguments also derive their plausibility from role-analytical considerations. But there is an interesting difference between the two authors in view of their disciplinary association. Maccoby, the psychologist, asks us to concentrate more on structural aspects. Clausen, the sociologist, aims through a reconstruction of turning points to clarify the emergence of the self or of personal identity. Both authors have in common that they look at all phases of personal development. Clausen emphasizes that we should pay attention, within the ecological approach, to later adulthood, and he has good reasons for this. Partnership and marriage are entered into during this period: New meanings and gender differences between partners acquire greater prominence. Maccoby's analysis demonstrates the central importance of the middle phases of childhood, at least for youngsters growing up in Western societies.

The very fact that these authors transcend disciplinary boundaries is typical of the interdisciplinary spirit created by the ecology of human development. This spirit can also be recognized in Goodnow's contribution. She tries to integrate reflections that are emerging within the contemporary sociology of knowledge. Ceci and Hembrooke's chapter stands for still another facet of interdisciplinary work.

The different notions of context discussed in Part Three throw light on the empirical qualities or features of contemporary societies. Maccoby's analysis points to societal stability. Looking at gender relations, one is impressed by their continuity despite constant societal change. The binary structure of gender is the feature that determines its impact as an organizing dimension of social identities and social interactions, and it could well be that this binary structure limits the possibilities for variation, as she suggests. However, one may ask what this means for the debate on inequality.

Problems of normative and moral dimensions are emphasized by Goodnow. She points to a certain instability, not so much in regard to gender, but to intergenerational relations. To what extent are these influenced by the way mutual services are rewarded or even purchased? Do the kinds of rewards provided even influence the constitution of personal identity? It is obvious, even though not explicitly stated, that Goodnow's analysis could be seen in the horizon of *Zeitdiagnose*, that is, as an evaluation of our present time, in which individualism is a central value. Clausen's research also demonstrates the importance of individualism. Several passages quoted from interviews underline the fact that judgments made about turning points depend on whether they have led to a more profound self-understanding. The quest for self-understanding is sometimes very difficult and, consequently, also difficult to reconstruct. A precise methodology is required, and in keeping with his work in general, Clausen pays considerable attention to methods; if his approach is further developed, it may well serve to overcome some of the limitations of retrospective surveys.

Turning points also refer to the structural contingencies of context in contemporary society, in other words, to their aleatory qualities, because personal lives and careers cannot be completely predicted or planned. This is especially difficult if two "trajectories of personal development" must be combined, as in contemporary partnership or marriage. Thus, whenever contexts are considered in regard to contemporary societies, their pluralistic and highly complex character must be accounted for, and this requires a theoretical orientation, such as the ecology of human development, which allows increasing degrees of differentiation. Ceci and Hembrooke rely on studies—partly ones made at Cornell, partly ones reported in the literature—which may be seen as experiments in context. In this way, they take up a strong concern of Urie Bronfenbrenner, namely, the search for a pragmatic synthesis between the two contexts, in the laboratory and in the real-life setting.

8

Differentiating Among Social Contexts: By Spatial Features, Forms of Participation, and Social Contracts

Jacqueline J. Goodnow

S ome time ago, Urie Bronfenbrenner took a diffuse concept, *social context*, and broke it into a set of nested sectors (macrosystem, ecosystem, microsystem, and mesosystem). Accompanying that differentiation was a range of proposals—proposals about the way these sectors differed from one another, were related to one another, influenced the development of individuals, and were open to change over historical time or over the lifetime of a person (e.g., Bronfenbrenner, 1979, 1988; Bronfenbrenner & Crouter, 1983).

There is no need for me to describe the revitalizing effect that this work had on research on "persons in context," to take the title of an earlier Cornell conference based on Bronfenbrenner's approach (Bolger, Caspi, Downey, & Moorehouse, 1988). Instead, my goal is to return to a first step in Bronfenbrenner's position: the ways in which sectors differ from one another. These dimensions, I argue, shape the way we think about other issues related to contexts: our ideas, for instance, about the links between one sector and another, about the nature of development in context, or about appropriate forms of intervention.

The broad argument overlaps the chapters by Lüscher (this volume, chapter 17) and by Magnusson (this volume, chapter 2). With both, I share the view that a critical step in the process of understanding consists of becoming aware of the assumptions, the perspectives, and the models that we use in everyday life or as formal psychologists.

The content area that I target in this chapter, however, differs from theirs. Lüscher's primary concern is with the individual's "knowledge and beliefs" and with their impact on the individual's interpretations and actions. Parents' knowledge and beliefs about the nature of development, for example, shape their interpretations of a child's behavior and the ways in which they respond to that behavior. Magnusson's primary concern is with the models that researchers hold about the interactions between people and contexts—models that shape the research questions that are asked and the interpretations that biologists or social scientists give to human behavior.

In this chapter, I start at a level similar to Magnusson's. The models I consider, however, are not the same as his. Instead of models of interactions between people and contexts, I examine researchers' models of contexts: models of the way contexts differ from one another and are linked to one another. At a later point, however, I turn to asking how these models are represented in the ideas held by individuals and how they can be used to explore the ideas that individuals hold about the ways in which contexts, such as family and not family, or home and paid work, are related to one another or should be related to one another.

Less broadly, my analysis of the features that distinguish one environmental setting from another is by way of two steps. The first goes back to the original distinctions and indicates where these have led. In essence, these distinctions were in terms of what I call *spatial features* (e.g., proximal or distal) and, more dynamically, in terms of the opportunities for face-to-face interaction or participation. My primary aim here is to bring out the way these dimensions lead to particular questions about links between contexts, forms and sources of development, and forms of intervention.

In the later part of the chapter, I propose a further dimension. Sectors of the environment, I suggest, differ from one another in the *social contracts*—the expectations of rights and obligations—that are attached to them. Those rights and obligations—specifying what should or should not be done—add a *directive, imperative,* or *motivational* quality to any description of the environment. They also, I propose, prompt new questions about links between contexts, change over time, and intervention. To show how some of those questions may be turned into empirical research, I draw from a series of studies addressed primarily to the analysis of obligations.

An emphasis on distinctions in terms of social contracts may seem an odd departure from a strong theme in my comments at the earlier Bronfenbrenner-based symposium. At that time, I was much taken by the way the proposal for separated sectors prompted questions about access— questions, for instance, about access routes or options, as they were structurally defined and as they were perceived by individuals at various times (Goodnow, 1988). I have not lost that interest, but I have come to feel that it is far from being a complete account of how sectors differ from or are related to one another. In particular, it did not seem to provide a comfortable way of covering a number of observations about contexts. Because those observations prompted both my return to the original proposals and the wish to add to them, let me place several of them up front. Let me also preface them all with the question, What do events or possibilities like these say about the way various parts of an environment—state, school, mother, father, and child—differ from and are related to one another?

- The state has the right to remove children from parents, to make children wards of the state, if the parents are judged, by some particular agents of the state, to be incompetent or irresponsible.
- Parents (in Australia at least) can ask that children be made wards of the state if the children can be shown to be uncontrollable.
- Children (in the United States at least) can now "divorce" their biological parents, if they can prove that continued union, or reunion, would be detrimental to their health or welfare.
- Compulsory education, in both Australia and the United States, was once argued against on the grounds that it was an intrusion on the rights of the parents. Now most parents regard the provision of schooling as a right on their part and an obligation on the part of the state.

- Parents and teachers often disagree over the domains of knowledge that should be the province of parents. Parents, for instance, often argue for control over sex education; school representatives often reply that parents have "abdicated" their role in this respect.

Those several examples may easily be multiplied. They suggest that the web connecting children, parents, and the state is in part a web of rights and obligations. Moreover, that web is not static. The nature of the rights and obligations, and the grounds used to justify them, changes over time. They are also often contested; that is, not everyone agrees on the rights and obligations that should apply, and different interpretations often compete with one another.

The examples I have given, however, all have to do with connections among children, parents, and the state. Any feature worth its salt should also apply to connections among people within a setting. Let me then add a few that are within households:

- Within couples, the current expectation, in Australia at least, is that a wife will contribute financially to the cost of a household, at least until the time that children are born. An obligation once felt strongly—the obligation to delay marriage until a man could support a wife—has lost its strength and has been transformed.
- Within families, the expectation that women will have sole responsibility for the day-to-day rearing of children or the running of a household is under review in many countries. Moreover, an old justification, "women's work," is losing its force. In the words of many of the Australian women we have interviewed (Goodnow & Bowes, 1994), "I don't see why I should do it *just* because I'm a woman."

Taken as a whole, what do these examples imply? They say to me, first, that people hold expectations about the way parts of a social world should be connected with one another—expectations that often deal with the rights and obligations of various parties. Second, these expectations are usually accompanied by justifications as to why people should act in a certain way or why a past "natural order" should no longer hold. Third, these expectations and justifications change over time, providing us with one way of adding a dimension of time to what may appear otherwise to be a static picture. Fourth, these expectations have a great deal to do with the extent to which people feel satisfied or dissatisfied with the contributions being made by other people or other sectors of the social world. Fifth, these expectations provide a way of meeting the problem that D'Andrade and Strauss (1992) emphasized as crucial for accounts of the social world in terms of the ideas people hold: linking such ideas to actions.

In short, describing contexts in terms of associated rights and obligations supplies us with a way of adding directives, moral imperatives, or motives to accounts of the social world. I have placed that possibility squarely at the front of this chapter because it represents a shift in the way we usually view environmental sectors. Their place in accounts of social context, however, is best appreciated if one starts from dimensions that do not have a "should/should not" quality to them. I accordingly delay exploring directive aspects until I have first considered the two dimensions that Bronfenbrenner emphasized and the kinds of questions those dimensions provoke.

DIFFERENTIATION BY WAY OF SPATIAL DIMENSIONS

In what ways is any part of one's environment, micro or macro, like or unlike any other? I start from that question for two reasons. One is that it is difficult to talk about questions of influence or interconnection among sectors or settings if we do not first specify how they differ from one another. The other is a reason noted earlier: The dimensions we use to differentiate parts of the environment shape the questions we are prompted to ask.

In Bronfenbrenner's original proposal and in others that are similar to it, spatial features are often emphasized, with attention drawn both to sites—the physical space occupied by a particular sector—and to *boundaries* between these sites. That emphasis is perhaps not surprising when the starting point is essentially a geographical metaphor: the "ecology" of social contexts. The same type of emphasis, one should note, occurs also in Barker and Wright's (1955) description of homes, schools, and clubs as different "habitats" and in Super and Harkness's (1986) description of "developmental niches." One feature of such niches is their location in spaces or settings that are to some extent physically separate from those meant primarily for adults.

The notion of differences in the space occupied has certainly been productive. It has prompted, first of all, questions about *transitions* from one site to another. How, to take an example from Bronfenbrenner (1979), do children come to make the transition from home to school? Are they accompanied by someone who knows the route well? Do they have, from a sibling or a parent, a description of the terrain that will serve as a map of what to expect?

Questions about the separateness of spaces and the nature of the route or the transition become even more productive if one converts physical to social spaces. To go back again to Barker and Wright (1955), one may ask if there are, on the route to adulthood, halfway houses for children: clubs, for instance, where the level of adult control is less than at home or in school, but still greater than when one is fully adult. There are also changes in social space that occur when one becomes an "expert" rather than a "novice" or "apprentice," when one's socioeconomic status goes up or down, when one moves from being "single" to being "married," or when one moves from being one of the "big kids" in primary school to being at the bottom of the heap in high school. School transitions, in fact, blend a change in physical setting with a change in social space and have led with particular clarity to questions about whether the effects of a transition—effects on self-esteem, for instance—stem from the total number of transitions being made at one time or from one aspect of change more than another (e.g., Simmons & Blyth, 1987).

Spatial dimensions prompt also questions about access: to physical spaces, social spaces, or—to add a third form of space—domains or areas of knowledge. The notion of access to areas of knowledge or skill may come less readily to mind than access to physical or social space. There are, however, areas of knowledge to which most children (and many adults) have limited access: areas to do, for instance, with sex or with family money. Moreover, these lines of access may vary by gender. Mathematics, to take one example, is a content area in which some of the structural restrictions to females acquiring knowledge have been removed. Access is still restricted, however, by the stereotype that this content area is less relevant, less natural, or less easy for females than it is for males.

Finally, an ecological picture of contexts promptly opens up questions about the boundaries that mark or seal off one site or space from another. Boundaries were prominent in Lewin's (1936, 1951) topological theory of contexts and of mind—a theory that Bronfenbrenner also has admired—in the form of an emphasis on the extent to which sectors were separated from one another by walls or boundaries that were more versus less permeable. The "compartmentalized mind" is an example I have carried forward. As a counter to the way my examples of access may promote the idea that all will be well if sectors are open and access is easy, let me take this time to cite examples that suggest a positive value to the presence of barriers or boundaries. (I am tempted to borrow from Rutter and to add examples of *buffers* to this set, but the metaphor underlying buffers is slightly different from that of boundaries and deserves separate recognition.)

A first example of the way in which attention to boundaries prompts a particular way of describing social contexts is interest in the phenomenon of *spillover*. Spillover essentially refers to the extent to which there are firm or permeable boundaries between one area of living or one area of concern and another. Under the labels of *spillover* or *contagion*, the concept has given rise to an interesting series of studies exploring connections between family life and paid work: the carryover of work or worries from home to work site, or work site to home (e.g., Bolger, deLongie, Kessler, & Wethington, 1989; Crouter, 1984; Piotrkowski, 1979; Pleck, 1977). These studies, as the names of the authors suggest, have often had a Cornell base. In a less well known series of studies, Finch (1983) has drawn attention to the way some occupations are especially likely to invite spillover. Being a clergyman, or a clergyman's wife, is one of these (especially if the home is the rectory). Being a policeman in a country town, or again a policeman's wife, is another (again, the physical site—the home provided—invites a lack of division to the day or to one's roles).

A second example of the use of boundaries comes from analyses of communication. One of the difficulties presented to politicians by national radio and television is that the walls between several audiences suddenly disappear. Delivering different messages to different groups—messages that are incompatible—is no longer a feasible strategy (Meyerovitz, 1990). Classrooms, Cazden (1993) suggested, may involve a similar problem. Present in the one place are one's peers and one's teacher. How can a student impress both, especially if these two audiences normally admire different styles or "voices"? The skill called for in such situations, Cazden (1993) argued, is skill in *multivocalism*—a term that, borrowing from Bakhtin, refers both to the ability to use different voices for different audiences and to skill in blending these voices when audiences that are usually separate are now present at one and the same time.

I have said enough to indicate that spatial descriptions have provided, and continue to provide, a productive base for describing the nature of a social context and some of the ways in which one part of the social world is related to another. Now let me indicate what else is possible.

Spatial Dimensions, Cognitive Development, and Forms of Intervention

In a volume based on an earlier Cornell conference, the editors—Bolger et al. (1988)—outlined a series of tasks that followed from Bronfenbrenner's ecological proposals. One of those had to do with specifying the nature of the link to development: What aspects of development were likely to be affected by what aspects of the environment, and by what process? A further challenge—one clearly dear to Bronfenbrenner's heart—was the use of environmental descriptions to construct forms of intervention.

My last comments on the benefits of working from spatial dimensions are related to those challenges. Where links to development are concerned, one of the conceptual difficulties is that, as researchers, we frequently change vocabularies in the process of testing for connections (Goodnow, 1987). We start, for instance, with spatial descriptions of the social environment and ask whether these are related to the level of a child's logical structures—an approach that allows no easy overlay of the descriptions of context and of cognition. We can, however, avoid that difficulty if we change our description of what develops. For instance, we can propose that part of cognitive development is the understanding of features of the environment, the knowledge and the perception, for instance, of routes and boundaries—physical, social, or cognitive. To take one example, part of cognitive development lies in coming to know or to believe that there are particular "escape routes" from a disadvantaged position, for example, getting education, marrying, emigrating, or finding a patron. One may designate changes in such perceptions as somehow less developmental than changes in logical structures. The fact remains that they are a significant part of the view of the world that people hold and a significant part of what changes from one time to another.

The step to intervention may seem less obvious. Let me give two examples. One comes from the area of gender and school achievement. In this area, intervention has often been directed toward structural change. In Australia, for instance, one drive for change has been directed toward providing access routes: providing girls in single-sex high schools with classes that go beyond the first level of education in mathematics or in the natural sciences. A second aspect of that drive, however, has been directed toward changing the perceptions of these access routes—toward persuading females that entry into, and success in, these areas of knowledge is both useful and compatible with being "feminine" (cf. Willis, 1989).

The second example I know about only from hearing it described by its Norwegian developer: Hundeide (personal communication, 1993). His experience in Third World countries has led him to argue for, and to put into practice, forms of intervention that start from first discovering what the community sees as the escape routes out of disadvantage. Compatibility with the local perceptions, he insists, is the critical first step toward the acceptance and the effectiveness of any intervention. Hundeide's solution may not be effective when the local community's perceived escape route is unacceptable to the larger community—is, for instance, illegal. The general argument, however, fits neatly with Bourdieu and Passeron's (1977) concern with the question, Who is most likely to perceive schooling as the optimal or only escape route from poverty? That perception, they argue, is particularly strong among France's petit bourgeoisie, but even there is displaying some change over time.

Summary

This will be by way of two questions: Does the spatial metaphor need to imply a nested hierarchy? And is there any need for any further dimension, one that is not spatial?

On the first score, let me draw attention to a nonnested description. The notion of a triangle—child, parent, and community, for instance, or child, parent, and state—does not require the notion of nested sectors (Goodnow, 1988). It also has several advantages to it. One now begins, for instance, to think more readily in terms of the child's direct access to the world outside the family, without parents as the gatekeepers or the conduit. Parents may hope to limit that access (a hope expressed in the description of television as "the uninvited guest"), but the fact remains that direct access exists. Children can bypass parents, just as the state may also bypass parents when it reaches past them to take control of children. As a further advantage, the notion of triangular arrangements prompts one to think in terms of possible competition and, as in Heider's attribution theory, of some dynamic tension, some form of balance that requires that the nature of the connection between any two parts of a triangle will alter the connections each has with other parts (e.g., Heider, 1944).

On the second score, the possibilities of a nonspatial dimension, let me start by asking, Is anything further needed? After all, here I have a way of differentiating among sectors, of describing their links to one another, of picturing the nature of development, of describing change over time, and of thinking about interventions. What more could be needed? What more could there be? There is, in fact, more within Bronfenbrenner's work itself. Let me then take up a second proposal from Bronfenbrenner.

DIFFERENTIATION BY FORMS OF
INTEGRATION AND PARTICIPATION

For Bronfenbrenner, one way in which the microsystem differs from the exosystem and the macrosystem has to do with the extent to which there is an opportunity for face-to-face interaction (e.g., Bronfenbrenner, 1979). For the child, for example, the home and the school allow face-to-face interactions. The parents' workplace, however, is an exosystem for the child. He or she has few, if any, possibilities for face-to-face interaction with the people in this world, even though this is a world that influences the child's development and that the child influences at least indirectly (e.g., by influencing parents' participation in paid work).

What are the advantages to this second way of differentiating among sectors of the environment? Some of the questions provoked overlap with those generated by thinking about the nature of access. To some extent, in fact, interaction may be thought of as a part of access. Certainly one needs to know who is accessible, who to go to and how to do so, for interaction to occur or to occur effectively. There are, however, sufficient differences in the questions provoked that I treat interaction separately from the more spatial dimension of access.

A first advantage consists of the ease with which considering the dimension of face-to-face interaction leads to considering questions of participation. Epstein (1983), to take one example, described both families and schools in terms of the extent to which each allows scope for participation and decision making. The highest independence scores and the highest achievement scores are held by pupils who come from a high–high combination: high-participatory families and high-participatory schools. In contrast, among the lowest in school grades are pupils who want participation (they are high in independence), but who encounter both families and schools that are low-participatory in style.

I chose Epstein (1983) as an opening example for a double purpose. One was to highlight the importance of participation, as well as interaction. The other was to take up a challenge that faces any account of differentiated sectors: finding a means to describe the ways in which sectors support, reinforce, or undermine one another. We know that interconnections of this kind exist. We also know that they are of concern to a number of people with an interest in contexts. Within developmental theory, for instance, Dix (1991, 1992) has begun to ask how far any new sector (e.g., a nursery school or a group of peers) makes it more or less likely that a parent's goals will be achieved—an interesting extension concerning the effects of parents agreeing on the messages they deliver to children (e.g., Cashmore & Goodnow, 1985). In everyday life, to speak from personal experience, parents consider the extent to which a child's school or a child's street life will "undo all their good work"—will expose a child to a message that differs from a parent's or that directly attacks a parent's message.

It is difficult, however, to get to interconnections in the form of support or interference if one restricts the analysis of environments to spatial features. In contrast, the move is easier if one starts from attention to the kinds of interaction and participation that are feasible or are fostered in different environmental sectors. It becomes easier, for instance, to accommodate findings of the kind reported by Nicolopoulou and Cole (1993). One computer game, they find, brings with it different levels of achievement in two settings. Placed in an after-school club, the game attracts frequent and wide participation, but for short bursts of time. The presence of attractive competing activities is not conducive to working one's way through the difficult parts of the problem that mark the transition from one level of understanding to another. In contrast, the same game placed in a library does produce a higher level of understanding, but the number of children participating at all is less (and the library's interest in having the game on their premises is less).

A second advantage to considering sectors in terms of the forms of interaction and participation they allow or invite can be illustrated by a finding from research by Alexander and Entwisle (1988). The impact of a child's repeating a grade in the early years of school, they reported, differs with the parents' own level of education. The difference, Alexander and Entwisle proposed, lies in the extent to which parents regard the school as a *monolithic* structure: one that allows little scope for a parent's participation or influence. The more schooling one has, the more likely is the perception of the school wall as having breaks within it—as made up of people, some of whom are more approachable than others. The more likely also is the perception that one has a right to ask questions and to attempt to influence decisions.

In effect, thinking in terms of participation helps one to avoid the sense that the macro level is "faceless." The structure of the school system, or of law and order, may be faceless for those who occupy particular social positions. The school, however, is far from faceless for those who feel at ease with teachers and are skilled in recognizing the differences between one and another. In similar fashion, "the law" is far from faceless to those who have, say, friends in the judiciary or among those who are often arrested. Individuals of this kind have a knowledge of the law as it actually operates that is likely to allow opportunities for interaction and persuasion that do not exist for those who do not know, from "above" or "below," the people who implement or make the decisions that are part of a macro social structure.

One last advantage to thinking in terms of interaction and participation is that there is no loss of potential links to the nature of intervention, of change over time, or of development. Intervention can now be cast in terms more of empowerment than of creating access. Historical change occurs in one's right to participate (the right to vote or the right to claim access to a document once classified as "secret") or in one's right to decline participation (one's right to remain silent or to refuse to be drafted). Individual development can now be seen as the acquisition of knowledge about participation and of a sense of self that makes it feasible to act on that knowledge. To use Lave and Wenger's (1991) graphic phrases, change may be thought of as a move from *peripheral* to *central* participation, and perhaps from illegitimate participation (by way, say, of eavesdropping) to participation that is formally approved.

Nonetheless, the notion of contexts as varying in the forms of interaction and participation that they allow or invite is nowhere nearly as well developed as the description of spatial features. Before one decides on a heavy investment in this way of differentiating among social contexts, however, let me sketch out a third way of differentiating, one that overlaps with the dimension of interaction and participation, but is by no means identical with it. This is the dimension that I label *differentiation by social contracts, by rights and obligations*. It is not a dimension that Bronfenbrenner treats explicitly. It is, however, certainly compatible with his interest in the nature of the interactions that occur in various contexts and with his pervasive interest in the way people should treat one another.

DIFFERENTIATION BY SOCIAL CONTRACTS: BY RIGHTS AND OBLIGATIONS

I shall introduce this notion somewhat indirectly. D'Andrade (1981) once criticized most of cognitive psychology for not taking into account the social pressures that exist toward acquiring some skills or some forms of knowledge rather than others. Some we are firmly expected to acquire: We will be punished, judged incompetent, if we do not do so. Others we may acquire if we wish. And a few others are "taboo": They are the preserves only of the priests or of the initiates. Psychologists' usual emphasis on logical capacities or logical structures, D'Andrade (1981) pointed out, leaves little room for such differences among content areas or for the operation of social pressure. Valsiner (1984) made a similar point in his analysis of parents' actions within the zone of proximal development, based on observing mothers' responses to their young children's moves toward independence in feeding and in exploring parts of the home. Parents do encourage some moves toward independence, he pointed out. They also prohibit others and make it clear that still others are barely tolerable. Part of cognitive development, he implied, must then consist of the child's coming to understand which moves toward being independent will be accepted by the parent and when this will be the case.

For both D'Andrade's (1981) criticism of cognitive research and Valsiner's (1984) analysis of parental actions, I felt an instant sympathy. They both fitted neatly with my own concerns about the extent to which descriptions of the environment in cognitive theories are extraordinarily neutral in tone. These descriptions proceed as if everyone agrees on what being intelligent means, as if knowledge or skill were there for the taking (a "free market" assumption), as if all teachers were willing to teach and all learners were eager, as if learners always sought increasing knowledge rather than—an equally arguable goal—strategic ignorance (Goodnow, 1976, 1990a, 1990b).

Recognizing that pressures exist toward holding some ideas rather than others or toward being knowledgeable in some areas and ignorant in others, however, is only a first step. The more general problem is one of finding a way to incorporate some sense of this directiveness into one's accounts either of cognition or of context.

This is the problem that D'Andrade and Strauss (1992) underlined when they argued for attention to both "human motives and cultural models," for the need to ask, Where does the affect associated with models come from? How do ideas come to function as directives, organizing action and generating emotion? One way to meet that larger problem, they proposed, is to argue that schemas in themselves serve as goals or contain statements of goals. They serve then to direct not only our interpretations of the world, but also our actions within it (D'Andrade, 1992).

My own concern with the larger problem has led toward ideas that contain the implication "this should be done"—ideas that have some moral force to them. These ideas, to pick up an argument from Lüscher (this volume, chapter 17) are likely to highlight the evaluations we make of events in addition to the interpretations of what things are. Ideas about the way things should be, it seems to me, are also particularly likely to be associated with affect. They can also vary from one person to another and can involve the possibility, a possibility emphasized also by D'Andrade and Strauss (1992), of both acceptance and resistance or contest. That last possibility, I must admit, was of particular importance to me. Part of my attraction to an analysis of contexts in terms of the directives they contain about what one should or should not do is that this kind of analysis provides a base for considering the presence of resistance to the messages that many contexts present. In the course of psychologists' concern with socialization and internalization, the phenomenon of resistance—like the phenomenon of deliberate or strategic ignorance—seems to have become hidden to the point of near invisibility (Goodnow, 1990a).

One way forward, I felt, was to take a conceptual step: to incorporate the recognition of directive aspects into descriptions of development in context and into differentiations among contexts. The second was to take the empirical step of asking, How can I specify the nature of these directive aspects and the opportunities they may offer for distinguishing one context from another?

I begin with the conceptual step, leaving the empirical steps to the section that follows. The starting point is the proposal that social contexts contain social contracts. More precisely, social contexts have patterns of rights and obligations attached to them or expected to apply to them. In Western countries, for example, the state has the obligation to provide education and the right to compel children's attendance at school from one specified age to another. Parents have the obligation to bring their children to school and the right to negotiate some alternatives related to schooling (e.g., schooling at home, the choice of school, or the possibility of late entry or early release). In most Western countries, the state also has the obligation to provide some form of care for the ill, the old, or the homeless. These individuals, however, are often expected to take on themselves the obligation of avoiding dependence on the state where possible: They are expected, for instance, to insure themselves against illness, and in a variety of ways, they are rewarded for doing so.

In all social contexts, there is also an *ethos*: a set of justifications for the pattern that is followed or expected. One might call this ethos an *ideology*. I use instead a term from Backett's (1982) analysis of family life, a *fabric of explanation*. Family divisions of labor, she commented, are usually accompanied by a stock of explanations that are seldom examined and that sustain a sense of being in communication with others. Women take on the major part of child rearing and household work, to quote some of the comments offered by the parents she interviewed, because "young children need their mother more than their father," because "men don't know how," or because "this arrangement is only temporary." The words may have different meanings to each party (*sharing* is Backett's prime example), but the use of common terms keeps the parents feeling that they are meeting a major goal: communication with each other. The availability of these terms generates also a sense that there are good reasons for what is sometimes felt by the women to be painful: the discrepancy between the belief that it is important to share and the reality of their carrying the major load.

Does that kind of proposal allow one to relate a view of context to a view of development and to proposals for intervention? We can certainly say that part of development consists of coming to know the usual definitions of rights and obligations and of coming to accept, reinterpret, or resist these. Part of development will also consist of coming to know, and to accept or resist, the usual pattern of justifications, the usual fabric of explanation (Backett, 1982). In similar fashion, a link to intervention presents no great difficulty. Basically, intervention now takes the form of attempts to change the picture that people hold of rights and obligations, a form of persuasion that could easily accompany changes in a content area previously mentioned: the perception of possible participation and influence. Parents may now, for instance, come to see themselves not only as able to participate and persuade when questions arise about a child's schooling, but also as having a right to do so and perhaps an obligation to do so on behalf of their children.

In short, the conceptual possibilities are attractive. The more difficult steps came when I asked, How shall we study the nature and the developing perception of rights and obligations? And what evidence is there that expected rights and obligations provide a way of differentiating one social context or one sector of an environment from another? I take up those questions in the next section.

STUDYING OBLIGATIONS

It is one thing to propose that sectors of our social environment can be described and distinguished from one another in terms of the *social contracts*, the patterns of rights and obligations, that are expected to apply to each. It is another to ask, How can we determine the nature of these rights and obligations? And can we do so in ways that can be applied across sectors—be relevant, for instance, to patterns among members of a family and also among children, family, and state? Unless we can find dimensions that cut across sectors, it will not be possible to compare one with another.

To approach such questions, my colleagues and I have started from the nature of obligations. How, we have asked, can we specify the nature of obligations and the difference between those that are likely to occur in one sector as against another? To focus the question further, we have begun with an emphasis on the way people perceive obligations within the family and, to a lesser extent, within schools. We have by now completed several studies (Goodnow, in press, provides a review). Cutting across these is a concern with three routes to specification. These have to do with (a) the expected spirit of a contribution, (b) the limits of responsibility, and (c) the medium of exchange (in particular, the involvement of money).

The Spirit of a Contribution

We have increasingly come to recognize that the ideal for many Australian mothers, and for adults in a couple relationship, is a contribution of work that is outside the regular schedule, that is not prompted (i.e., no reminders and no nagging), and that shows some awareness of the other's needs or preferences (Goodnow & Warton, 1991).

That observation has to do with the way one hopes others will make their contributions. What can be said about the way one hopes one's own contributions will be accepted? To quote a man interviewed for a study of couples who share household work, "I enjoy doing it for her as a bit of a treat, when she doesn't expect it" (Goodnow & Bowes, 1994). Gifts need to be appreciated and, in most cases, returned. Making something as a gift also says that it should not be expected to occur regularly (it is not a right that the other may come to rely on). It should not be looked at too closely. As a 14-year-old in one of our studies commented, "If it's a favor, they can't be too picky" (Goodnow & Warton, 1992b). Above all, any action kept in the gift category can be withheld at the discretion of the giver.

The obligation to be careful about inspecting gifts emerged with particular clarity in a study of what adolescents thought should happen after one sibling agreed to do a job that the asker normally did. The asker, children and adolescents tell us, should check that the job is done, but the checking needs to be done with tact (Goodnow & Warton, 1992b). More precisely, it must be done in ways that avoid implying that the other is forgetful, lazy, unwilling, or incompetent. "It's not the Army," in the words of one 18-year-old boy interviewed for this study. "You can't just stand over them and watch them do it"—a comment that brings to the surface one distinction between settings that are "family" and "not family."

Our first awareness of people feeling the need to be cautious in the treatment of gifts came from considering families. Is the sense of work as a gift, we then began to ask, one of the ways in which people distinguish between one context and another? Does a concern with the way gifts should be treated at least surface outside contexts that involve close relationships? "In the Army," work may not be contributed as a gift. Within the profession of teaching, however, we found considerable concern with the way in which gifts of work should be treated. The topic came up in the course of interviews with teachers at a time of industrial action (Warton, Goodnow, & Bowes, 1992). These teachers had voted to "work to rule" for a month as a mark of their dissatisfaction with some policies introduced by a new minister for education. We were curious to know about the specific sources of dissatisfaction with the new policies. Also, we were curious to know what parts of their teaching they felt they could not do, as against those they felt they had to retain.

On the first score, the causes of dissatisfaction, it turned out that teachers distinguished between *mandatory* and *discretionary* parts of teaching. The latter parts, in the teachers' explicit terms, were *extras* or *gifts*. They were also what made teaching satisfying. A teacher, it was pointed out, had to be at school for certain hours and had to be in the classroom teaching at certain times. It was not mandatory, however, to see students at lunchtime, to supervise sports after school, to consult with parents in the evening, to take work home, or to put one's own time into developing new ways of teaching, especially if these meant assignments that called for extra marking. One of the major sources of annoyance with the new minister was that he had attempted to make mandatory what was the teacher's discretionary gift, requiring—to take one example—attendance before

9:00 a.m. and for a specified time after 3:00 p.m. The implication, many teachers commented, was that they were lazy or "in the job only for the short hours." These issues, we soon discovered, are not unique to Australia. There are, for instance, North American studies that illustrate precisely the same waves of concern and industrial action when a move is made to convert what is discretionary, even if frequently or regularly done, into a mandatory part of one's job (Corwin, 1970; Kerchner & Mitchell, 1988).

On the second score, what the teachers set aside when they "worked to rule," it might be expected that they would simply discard all of the discretionary activities. To a large extent that is what they did. They worked only the prescribed hours; they did not take work home; almost everything that was extracurricular was dropped. These divestments, however, were carried out more often in high school than in primary school (the final year of high school was an exception), for one month only (the union's recommendation), and in a particular manner (stories to the press and to parents emphasized that the goal was to let the public and the minister know how much the teachers did beyond what they were legally required to do).

These several ways of proceeding, it turned out, stemmed from the need to sustain a reasonable working relationship with one's pupils and with their parents. Pupils, especially in primary school, do not understand why a concert or an excursion might be canceled or their homework not marked. Parents are important allies when teachers are fighting with their own bureaucracy. Small wonder then that all teachers agreed that "work to rule" in all schools could not be continued indefinitely and that any task related to teaching in the last year of high school, the year of a competitive statewide examination, was to be an exception. Gifts may clearly be seen as within one's discretion. Equally, withdrawing some gifts—in particular, those that others are accustomed to receive and see as the necessary mark of one's commitment—can be unwise.

In effect, the distinction between gifts and enforced tributes is not unique to the home setting. The presence or absence of the distinction will not differentiate between home and not home. The critical distinctions, it now appears, are likely to be perceptions related to what the content of a gift should be, who should control what is offered, and what the probable benefits and costs will be if a gift is withheld.

The Limits of Responsibility

The limits of responsibility provided for us a further way of pinning down the nature of rights and obligations and of exploring the use of this kind of feature as a way of distinguishing one context from another. We have explored this aspect of obligations in two ways. One is by asking when responsibility ends. The other, the more extended exploration, has to do with the extent to which a task may be moved from one person to another.

When Does Responsibility End?

Our exploration of this issue has been based on interviews with adolescents and young adults, although we could well ask parents about what they see as the end of their responsibility for their children. Suppose, we said, you had asked a brother or sister (always a real person in this study) to do for you a job that you normally did, and they agreed. Would it be your job to check that the work was done, or theirs to do it without your checking? Should you give a reminder, or should they remember? Should you anticipate problems and describe what needs to be done if they occur, or should they think ahead?

The strong majority of the Australian teenagers in this study (14- and 18-year-olds) agreed that all these actions were part of their job. (The minority held the firm view that "once they agree, it's their problem.") Moreover, they were easily able to give examples of reasonable and unreasonable ways to follow through after a request—to give reminders or to check that the job had been done. Finally, most of them agreed that, in paid work, expectations and practices related to how one should give reminders or follow through on a delegated job would be different from expectations and practices within the family. (The question was asked only of the 18-year-olds, who had direct experience with paid work.) This majority, however, contains a gender difference. Males regarded the two work sectors as different from one another more often than females did (the women were more inclined to assert that, in both settings, feelings and relationships would be important; Goodnow & Warton, 1992b). The manner of exercising a responsibility, then, rather than the responsibility itself may be what distinguishes one context from another.

What Can Be Moved From One Person to Another?

In a further effort to pin down what is meant by *responsibility* or *obligation*, by terms such as *your job*, we turned to questions about whether a task could be moved from one person to another. It is easy to say that *your job* means that you should do it, but that definition of possession actually does not take us very far. Does it mean, for instance, that no one else can be asked to do it? What happens if you do not do it? Can you ever dissociate yourself from your job—stop doing it, declare it finished, simply walk away from it?

Within households, we have explored questions of that type in a variety of ways. We have asked mothers what would happen if a child did not do his or her regular job. Would she insist (the job stays with the child), do it herself, or ask—on more than an occasional basis—a sibling to take over the job? The answer is that the mother's action depends on whether the job is of a *self-care* or an *other-care* kind. Putting away what you have used, cleaning up after yourself, making your own bed—these are everyday examples of self-care. These are the jobs most likely to attract phrases such as "just looking after yourself," "just looking after your own stuff," or "just cleaning up after yourself." Preparing a meal that others will also eat (or helping do so), setting or clearing a table, watering plants, cleaning up or helping clean up family space (beyond one's own room)—these are everyday examples of the jobs we labeled *family-care* or *other-care*.

Other-care jobs can be freely asked of another child. Self-care tasks are seldom asked of the other (the mother either insists or "takes the job back"). The mother's reasons are twofold: "It would not be right" to ask anyone else to do self-care work, and "it would be useless—they'd object: 'I didn't take them out,' 'they're not mine,' etc."(Goodnow & Delaney, 1989). The reason why "it would not be right" to ask one child to make another's bed has to do with a principle we have come to call a principle

290

of *causation* (Warton & Goodnow, 1991). If you have created the need for this work, made this "mess," caused this problem, then you have a particular obligation to take care of the consequences or to take part in doing so. To ask someone else to do so is a particular favor. To expect someone else to do so, without any signal that this is a special request, is to put them in the position of someone paid to do the job or in a status lower than that of the person who leaves the job to be done. Small wonder, then, that many Australian mothers use phrases that explicitly say to children that there is a difference between what can be expected within the family and outside it. "This is not a hotel, guest house, laundromat, cafeteria, restaurant"—these are familiar refrains (Goodnow & Delaney, 1989; Goodnow & Warton, 1991).

We have now come to have a healthy respect for the importance of causation and for the extent to which Australian mothers teach both the principle and its limit (e.g., "yes, but we're a family"; "they'd do it for you"; "we're in a hurry"; "I need it to be done"). We have also come to have a healthy respect for the extent to which the application of the principle of causation can distinguish among contexts, between, for instance, family and contexts in which people are paid to clean up after you (e.g., hotels). We did not know, however, whether this kind of distinction was drawn outside parent–child interactions. Does it, for instance, have any impact on what adults feel obliged to do or to avoid asking others to do?

A positive answer to that question came through clearly in a study of the household jobs that adults share and do not share (Goodnow & Bowes, 1994). When couples share household work, we asked, are there some jobs that are less likely to be shared than others? Two jobs stood out in this respect. They were the care of cars and ironing. Close to half of this sample divided these jobs in terms of "to each their own." The one who drove the car or wore the clothes got the job, with acts of generosity thrown in by the other in cases of particular need. "Expecting me to do work that is mainly for your benefit, or that you have created the need for, is unreasonable (the expectation places me in the category of servant). My involvement must be regarded either as a withdrawable gift or as part of an agreed-on division of a set of tasks, balancing something that you do."

Nor need one limit examples to households. There is, in fact, no shortage of settings in which the potential movement of a task from one sector to another brings out varying perceptions of rights and obligations. Proposals to shift the care of the elderly from the family to the state, or of the mentally ill from the state to the care of the community, provide one set of examples. Proposals to shift the costs of a service from the state to the user provide a further set. "User pays," for that matter, is essentially a version of obligation defined by direct causation, similar to the household objection, "I didn't take that stuff out" or "I didn't leave this mess."

For a specific and telling example, I am indebted to Judith Cashmore, whose current research project is concerned with what happens to children who have been wards of the state but, at the age of 16 years, can or must leave the institutions or foster homes that have been the site of care up until then. In some ways, the government agency concerned with the care of wards can, and does, argue that its responsibility has ended. Responsibility should now be taken over by the agencies that are concerned with refugee shelters, unemployment benefits, supports for educational training, and so on. These agencies, however, can—and do—argue that the original department still holds an obligation and that the once-upon-a-time wards are entitled to some continuing care or assistance, both legally and morally. That debate, at the level of the state, is essentially the same as the debate within households over the issue of what can be moved from one person to another and on what grounds. In short, debates over the ending of responsibility and the moveability of an obligation are far from being limited to households. They also hold considerable promise as ways of exploring the distinctions people draw between one setting and another.

The Medium of Exchange: The Place of Money

Money is clearly a currency used to define a variety of expectations about rights and obligations. The use of money is also a feature that has been proposed as differentiating between family and nonfamily sectors and as changing over time in its acceptability as a currency.

Let me draw some examples from Zelizer's (1985) historical analysis of changes within one country (the United States) over the period between the 1890s and the 1930s. (I offer a historical example with special pleasure, given Bronfenbrenner's insistence that contexts need to be considered in historical terms.) During the period that Zelizer (1985) considered, major changes occurred in the size of monetary compensations awarded, by the courts, to parents for the loss of a child through negligence on the part of someone outside the family (e.g., the driver of a motor car or a streetcar). The amount awarded, Zelizer (1985) documented, was once determined by the amount of income that the child could have been expected to contribute to the family. Increasingly, it became—and has remained—a compensation for the emotional loss, despite the sense that no amount of money could wipe out the loss. Even though the economic basis for money as the form of compensation has disappeared, money somehow remains—perhaps uneasily—the medium by which loss or damage is sought. The same period of time, Zelizer (1985) documented, also saw the rise of a lively debate, in parents' magazines, about pocket money for children and about the money that child film stars should earn or have access to.

Why should arrangements concerning money involve any hesitation? Why should money not be the basis for all forms of restitution, compensation, and expressions of appreciation for a job well done or expressions of disapproval for a job that falls below the expected standard? If children—to take one specific example—are ultimately the responsibility of the state, if the state has an interest in the welfare of children, why should the state not pay parents or fine parents according to how well they do their job? Why should anyone think twice about the statement, "In the future, if society wants children, it will have to be prepared to reduce the costs it expects individual women to bear" [by providing affordable child care] (Letter to the Editor, *Sydney Morning Herald*, September 2, 1993)?

The answer, I suggest, lies in a tendency to use the involvement of money as a basis for distinguishing the responsibilities of one part of the world from those of another. Fathers provide money; mothers provide love. That is one stereotype. Parents provide loving care; the state provides money for some of the services parents need, but does not pay parents directly. That is another. We seem, in a variety of situations, to be concerned that money will mark a relationship as being based on strict exchange rather than being based on responsiveness to the needs of others (Clark, 1984). Money will give rise to a confusion between "the principles of the home . . . and the principles of the shop" (to quote a phrase cited by Zelizer, 1985, p. 104). Money will turn a "gift relationship" into a commercial exchange (to take a phrase from Titmuss's, 1970, analysis of people's feelings about blood being donated as against being purchased).

In short, it is as if we hope to make a neat separation between contexts that involve money and those that do not. How then does money ever come to be involved in any transaction within the family? Money is certainly part of the pattern of expected rights and obligations within many families. Moreover, the provision of money by one person seems often tied to the provision of work or services by another. What has happened to the promisingly neat distinction between home and shop?

For the exploration of such apparent anomalies, we took as a specific case the provision of pocket money to children. On the one hand, pocket money appears to involve the expectation that children are entitled to some financial provision by their parents. That expectation seems, in fact, to be so strongly held by children that Australian adolescents reduce the blame assigned to others for shoplifting if "their parents haven't given them what they need" (Jeannette Lawrence, personal communication, 1994). On the other hand, there appears to be, at least among many parents in the United States, a sense that the money given to children is not an entitlement, but is essentially earned—is a return for the children's work contributions to the family (Miller & Yung, 1990).

We decided to interview a group of Australian parents (mothers and fathers of 9- to 16-year-olds; Goodnow & Warton, 1992a; Warton & Goodnow, in press). To cut a long story short, there were no differences in the extent to which pocket money came from mothers or fathers and small differences only in the extent to which a parent would reduce an agreed-on amount if a job was not well done (the mothers, to our surprise, were the tougher on this score). All parents disapproved of the practice of paying specific amounts for specific jobs. But only 10% refused to link jobs to money in any fashion. The vast majority were prepared to have some link be made, either by way of paying for extra jobs (the most common pattern) or by threatening to reduce pocket money if the child's overall job performance had been poor that week.

Why do most parents not say unequivocally that the home is a place in which work and money are separate from one another, as distinct from the business world? Why do they send an apparently mixed message? One reason, it turns out, is that the separateness of work and money is regarded as an ideal that is not always attainable. To avoid the worst outcome, the child making no work contribution at all, parents need to keep money as a reserve incentive or a reserve threat: "as a last resort, it's OK" or "when they're young and don't understand why they should do it, that's okay." A further reason is that the parents we interviewed actually endorsed two principles. One was that household jobs and money should be separate. The other was that, "if they're getting money, they should be doing something in return." The ideal might be one of families offering financial support that responds only to children's needs and is not linked in any way to the work they do. Into that ideal, however, comes also an expectation that is explicit and completely acceptable in contexts outside the family: an expectation of some return for the money one expends.

Most parents, one might say, adopt toward children an attitude similar to the attitude that the state adopts toward its citizens. The state's message is that we expect you to be good citizens, to voluntarily contribute to the state what you should contribute. We expect that as part of your membership of the state and as a return for the services we provide. But we hold in reserve some extrinsic rewards and sanctions in case your intrinsic motivation or your gratitude turn out to be insufficient. In large terms, one might say that the ideal is phrased in terms of an *enlightenment ideology*: An informed and fairly treated citizenry will do the right thing. That ideal, however, is accompanied by a belief in regulatory power, to be used when enlightenment fails to produce good citizenship. Under such circumstances, it is unlikely that we will find completely clear and constant distinctions between one context and another. The result, as Bronfenbrenner would expect, is one of some degree of fuzziness at the edges, some degree of overlap in people's expectations of what should occur in one context and another.

SUMMARY

I began this chapter with an expression of interest in Bronfenbrenner's description of the social environment as made up of differentiated sectors and in the question, How shall we describe the difference between one sector and another? The answers to that question, I proposed, shape ideas and research related to the way sectors are linked to one another, the nature of change over time, and the nature of development in context.

Starting from that position, I turned to two proposals contained in Bronfenbrenner's first ecological description. One of these emphasized spatial features. Sectors of the social context differ from one another, for instance, in the extent to which they occupy different physical spaces or are proximal rather than distal in relation to the child. That type of proposal quickly gives rise to questions about access routes, escape routes, the quality of barriers, and the knowledge or perceptions people hold about these aspects of their social world.

A second way of differentiating among *sectors* (and I use that term to differentiate among the people in a single physical setting, e.g., mothers and fathers) turns attention to the forms of face-to-face interaction and participation that are possible or are encouraged. The approach again opens questions—questions, for instance, about the extent to which people see participation as possible or perceive structures outside the family as "faceless" and about the extent to which participation includes opportunities to decline or to refuse to participate.

A third approach, one I currently see as warranting particular attention, consists of describing sectors in terms of the rights and obligations that are expected to operate. This approach, I have proposed, has two main advantages. First, it supplies a directive quality to the earlier descriptions of social contexts. These descriptions now move toward a concern with what should happen. Contexts may now be perceived as exercising a certain moral force, and development may be perceived as the internalization of the moral precepts that describe each person's rights and obligations. Second, the approach can be accompanied by a variety of research questions and procedures. We have, in fact, followed through with some of these research possibilities, asking about the ideas people hold about obligations and the principles—the principle of "direct causation," for instance, or the principle of "nothing for nothing"—that underlie these ideas. The difference between one social context and another, and the course of development, I suggest, may now be viewed in terms of the way obligations are defined and in terms of the relative strengths of such principles.

I end with a disclaimer. The three descriptions I have offered are far from being the only ways by which one may differentiate one social context from another. One could start, for instance, by considering the extent to which a social context allows for heterogeneity or insists on "the one right way"—a feature of contexts that might well be expected to influence the extent to which individuals acquire experience in taking the perspective of others or come to reflect on their own viewpoints. One could also start from the view that various sectors form different kinds of systems or occupy different places within an overall system. That type of approach readily gives rise to questions about the extent to which one part of a system can substitute for another. When a family loses one parent, for example, do other members of the family fill in—take on all or part of the role that this parent once occupied? That type of approach could also give rise to a more general goal: the merger of systems theory (e.g., family systems theory) with descriptions of the social environment in ecological terms. I have not attempted the grand task of bringing together systems descriptions and ecological descriptions, but I would like to see it attempted. Within any description, however, or within any merger, I would argue for attention to the directive aspects of contexts: to the way they specify both the rights and obligations of the individuals, groups, agencies, and structures that make up our social world and to the justifications that accompany claims for what one should give or be given. As we begin to explore such ways of describing and distinguishing among contexts and as we begin to consider the implications of any form of description—by spatial features, by the nature of interactions, or by the pattern of rights and obligations that makes up a social contract—we shall begin to make progress on the task that Bronfenbrenner set us: to build an account of contexts and of development in context.

REFERENCES

Alexander, K. L., & Entwisle, D. D. (1988). Achievement in the first two years of school: Patterns and processes. *Monographs of the Society for Research in Child Development, 53* (Serial No. 218).

Backett, K. (1982). *Mothers and fathers.* London: Macmillan.

Bakhtin, M. M. (1981). *The dialogic imagination: Four essays.* Austin: University of Texas Press.

Barker, R. G., & Wright, H. F. (1955). *Midwest and its children: The psychological ecology of an American town.* New York: Harper & Row.

Bolger, N., Caspi, A., Downey, G., & Moorehouse, M. (Eds.). (1988). *Persons in context: Developmental processes.* Cambridge, England: Cambridge University Press.

Bolger, N., deLongie, A., Kessler, R. C., & Wethington, E. (1989). The contagion of stress across multiple roles. *Journal of Marriage and the Family, 51,* 175–183.

Bourdieu, P., & Passeron, J.-C. (1977). *Reproduction in education, culture, and society.* Beverly Hills, CA: Sage.

Bronfenbrenner, U. (1979). *The ecology of human development: Experiments by nature and by design.* Cambridge, MA: Harvard University Press.

Bronfenbrenner, U. (1988). Interacting systems in human development: Research paradigms. Present and future. In N. Bolger, A. Caspi, G. Downey, & M. Moorehouse (Eds.), *Persons in context: Developmental processes* (pp. 25–49). Cambridge, England: Cambridge University Press.

Bronfenbrenner, U., & Crouter, A. C. (1983). The evolution of environmental models in developmental research. In P. H. Mussen (Series Ed.) & W. Kessen (Vol. Ed.), *Handbook of child psychology: Vol 1. History, theory, and methods* (4th ed., pp. 357–414). New York: Wiley.

Cashmore, J., & Goodnow, J. J. (1985). Agreement between generations: A two-phase approach. *Child Development, 56,* 493–501.

Cazden, C. (1993). Vygotsky, Hymes, and Bakhtin: From word to utterance to voice. In E. A. Forman, N. Minick, & C. A. Stone (Eds.), *Contexts for learning: Sociocultural dynamics in children's development* (pp. 197–212). New York: Oxford University Press.

Clark, M. (1984). Implications of relationship type for understanding compatibility. In W. Ickes (Ed.), *Compatible and incompatible relationships* (pp. 119–140). New York: Springer-Verlag.

Corwin, R. G. (1970). *Militant professionalism: A study of organizational conflict in high schools.* New York: Appleton-Century-Crofts.

Crouter, A. C. (1984). Spillover from family to work: The neglected side of the work–family interface. *Human Relations, 27,* 425–442.

D'Andrade, R. C. (1981). The cultural part of cognition. *Cognitive Science, 5,* 179–195.

D'Andrade, R. G. (1992). Schemas and motivation. In R. G. D'Andrade & C. Strauss (Eds.), *Human motives and cultural models* (pp. 23–44). Cambridge, England: Cambridge University Press.

D'Andrade, R. G., & Strauss, C. (1992). (Eds.). *Human motives and cultural models.* Cambridge, England: Cambridge University Press.

Dix, T. H. (1991). The affective organization of parenting: Adaptive and maladaptive processes. *Psychological Bulletin, 110,* 3–25.

Dix, T. H. (1992). Parenting on behalf of the child: Empathic goals in the regulation of responsive parenting. In I. E. Sigel, A. M. McGillicuddy-deLisi, & J. J. Goodnow (Eds.), *Parental belief systems* (pp. 319–346). Hillsdale, NJ: Erlbaum.

Epstein, J. L. (1983). Longitudinal effects of family–school–person interactions on student outcomes. In *Research in sociology of education and socialization* (Vol. 4, pp. 42–68). Greenwich, CT: JAI Press.

Finch, J. (1983). *Married to the job: Wives' incorporation in men's work.* London: Allen & Unwin.

Goodnow, J. J. (1976). The nature of intelligent behavior: Questions raised by cross-cultural studies. In L. B. Resnick (Ed.), *The nature of intelligence* (pp. 169–188). Hillsdale, NJ: Erlbaum.

Goodnow, J. J. (1987). Cultural conditions and individual behaviours: Conceptual and methodological links. *Australian Journal of Psychology, 38,* 231–244.

Goodnow, J. J. (1988). Children, families and communities: Ways of viewing their relationships to one another. In N. Bolger, A. Caspi, G. Downey, & M. Moorehouse (Eds.), *Interactive systems in development* (pp. 51–76). Cambridge, England: Cambridge University Press.

Goodnow, J. J. (1990a). The socialization of cognition: What's involved? In J. Stigler, R. Shweder, & G. Herdt (Eds.), *Culture and human development* (pp. 259–286). Chicago: University of Chicago Press.

Goodnow, J. J. (1990b). Using sociology to extend psychological accounts of cognitive development. *Human Development, 33*, 81–107.

Goodnow, J. J. (in press). From household practices to parents' ideas about work and interpersonal relationships. In S. Harkness & C. Super (Eds.), *Parents' cultural belief systems.* New York: Guilford Press.

Goodnow, J. J., & Bowes, J. A. (1994). *Men, women, and household work.* Sydney, New South Wales, Australia: Oxford University Press.

Goodnow, J. J., & Delaney, S. (1989). Children's household work: Task differences, styles of assignment, and links to family relationships. *Journal of Applied Developmental Psychology, 10*, 209–226.

Goodnow, J. J., & Warton, P. M. (1991). The social basis of social cognition: Interactions about work and lessons about relationships. *Merrill-Palmer Quarterly, 37*, 27–58.

Goodnow, J. J., & Warton, P. M. (1992a). Contexts and cognitions: Taking a pluralist view. In P. Light & G. Butterworth (Eds.), *Context and cognition* (pp. 85–112). Oxford, England: Oxford University Press.

Goodnow, J. J., & Warton, P. M. (1992b). Understanding responsibility: Adolescents' concepts of delegation and follow-through within the family. *Social Development, 1*, 89–106.

Heider, F. (1944). Social perception and phenomenal causality. *Psychological Review, 51*, 358–374.

Kerchner, C. T., & Mitchell, D. E. (1988). *The changing idea of a teachers union.* New York: Falmer Press.

Lave, J., & Wenger, E. (1991). *Situated learning: Legitimate peripheral participation.* Cambridge, England: Cambridge University Press.

Lewin, K. (1936). *Principles of topological psychology.* New York: McGraw-Hill.

Lewin, K. (1951). *Field theory in social science: Selected theoretical papers.* New York: Harper.

Meyerovitz, J. (1990). *No sense of place.* New York: Oxford University Press.

Miller, J., & Yung, S. (1990). The role of allowances in adolescent socialization. *Youth and Society, 22*, 137–159.

Nicolopoulou, A., & Cole, M. (1993). The fifth dimension, its play-world, and its institutional contexts: The generation and transmission of shared knowledge in the culture of collaborative learning. In E. A. Forman, N. Minick, & C. A. Stone (Eds.), *Contexts for learning: Socio-cultural dynamics in children's development* (pp. 283–314). New York: Oxford University Press.

Piotrkowski, C. (1979). *Work and the family system.* New York: Free Press.

Pleck, J. (1977). The work–family role system. *Social Problems, 24,* 417–427.

Simmons, R. G., & Blyth, D. A. (1987). *Moving into adolescence: The impact of pubertal change and school context.* Hawthorn, NY: Aldine de Gruyter.

Strauss, C. (1992). Models and motives. In R. G. D'Andrade & C. Strauss (Eds.), *Human motives and cultural models* (pp. 1–20). Cambridge, England: Cambridge University Press.

Super, C. M., & Harkness, S. (1986). The developmental niche: A conceptualization of the interface of child and culture. *International Journal of Behavioral Development, 9,* 545–569.

Titmuss, R. I. (1970). *The gift relationship: From human blood to social policy.* London: Allen & Unwin.

Valsiner, J. (1984). Construction of the zone of proximal development in adult–child joint action: The socialization of meals. In B. Rogoff & J. Wertsch (Eds.), *Children's learning in the zone of proximal development* (pp. 65–76). San Francisco: Jossey-Bass.

Warton, P. M., & Goodnow, J. J. (1991). The nature of responsibility: Children's understanding of "your job." *Child Development, 62,* 156–165.

Warton, P. M., & Goodnow, J. J. (in press). Money and children's household jobs: Parents' views of their interconnection. *International Journal of Behavioral Development.*

Warton, P. M., Goodnow, J. J., & Bowes, J. M. (1992). Teaching as a form of work: Effects of teachers' roles and role definitions on working to rule. *Australian Journal of Education, 36,* 170–180.

Willis, S. (1989). *"Real girls don't do maths": Gender and the construction of privilege.* Geelong, Australia: Deakin University Press.

Zelizer, V. A. (1985). *Pricing the priceless child: The changing social value of children.* New York: Basic Books.

9

A Bioecological Model of Intellectual Development

Stephen J. Ceci and Helene A. Hembrooke

Traditional accounts of intellectual development have virtually ignored the role that contextual factors assume as various cognitive operations unfold in the developing organism. Although most orientations recognize that context exerts some influence in this process, its influence has been minimized in relation to biological–genetic mechanisms. In this chapter, we outline an alternative approach to intellectual development and cognition. The *bioecological* perspective that we offer here is one that considers context to be a basic ingredient of intellectual development. This is not to deny the role of biological factors, as will be seen, but it is to argue that context differentiates and actualizes biological potential.

Traditionally, context has been perceived as little more than an annoyance—noise or variance masking the "truth," or signal, a variable to be controlled or covaried. In so doing, our understanding of intellectual development has been truncated. By limiting our research to include only that which we can understand, we never really progress beyond the limits of our current understanding. As is usually the case, the very thing that we have tried so desperately to ignore has come back to haunt us. Within the last decade, the cognitive–developmental literature has been inundated with examples of the contextually dependent nature of cognition. Current theories have proven inadequate in their ability to explain or predict such findings. It is clear that we can no longer avoid the issue of context: Our models no longer provide the best fit, and so we must adapt them. Including context as an integral component of our models is one such adaptation.

In this chapter, we first describe both the assumptions and the limitations inherent in traditional psychometric and biological models of intelligence. We then provide an alternative framework, the bioecological theory of intellectual development. In some detail we consider the major assumptions of the bioecological approach, focusing primarily on the interactive relationship between biology and the environment.

Admittedly, this approach is, as yet, untested. Even at this point in its construction, the bioecological theory seems able to account for more of the critical biological, contextual, and statistical data than its competitor theories of intellectual development crafted by structuralists, geneticists, and information-processing researchers. The ability of the bioecological theory to withstand the rigors of scientific inquiry remains to be seen. What is becoming clear, however, is that theories of cognitive development must accommodate the recent research findings and extend context the attention it not only deserves, but demands.

ASSUMPTIONS OF TRADITIONAL PSYCHOMETRIC MODELS

The traditional psychometric models (e.g., Humphreys, 1962, 1979; Jensen, 1979; Marshalek, Lohman, & Snow, 1983; Spearman, 1904) contain three major assumptions. First, there is a singular, pervasive ability called *general intelligence, g,* which subsumes and dictates performance abilities in a variety of cognitive domains. The consistent performance of individuals across a diverse battery of tests, which measure seemingly different abilities, is taken as evidence for this assumption. It is reasoned that consistent performance across tasks that purport to measure distinct, independent abilities—such as verbal reasoning, cultural knowledge, and spatial abilities—can only reflect the fact that each test is saturated with a common factor, namely, g.

The second assumption of traditional psychometric models is that this general intelligence is biologically based. Many researchers have reached this conclusion because measures of g are correlated with h^2 and other constructs of heritability, as well as with a variety of physiological measures—such as cranial blood flow, evoked potential recordings, central nerve conductance velocity, and oscillation (e.g., Eysenck, 1989; Hendrickson & Hendrickson, 1980; Jensen, 1992; Schafer, 1987). Recently, Plomin and his colleagues have attempted to provide the missing piece of construct validation for the claim that heritability estimates are not simply epiphenomenal, but rather reflect the biological substrate responsible for intellectual functioning. Their approach has been to show that DNA markers, from genes thought to be relevant to neural functioning, taken from children who differ in IQ, have different allelic associations. Specifically, the allelic frequency for two genetic markers appears to be different for high- and low-IQ individuals, thus supporting the notion of a direct link between IQ and its heritability (see Plomin & McClearn, 1993). This is exciting work and promises to open up the debate over nature–nurture to new levels of analysis. Presently, however, it is a promissory note that will require far more research to document, as Plomin and his colleagues noted.

The third assumption of traditional psychometric models is that IQ tests are good measures of this biologically based general intelligence, which permeates most intellectual endeavors, from verbal reasoning, reading comprehension, and cultural knowledge to quantitative, spatial, and mechanical abilities. Construct validation research has attempted to show that IQ tests are more potent predictors of a range of outcomes such as job success, school grades, and training scores than are measures of specific cognitive abilities, motivation, or relevant background experience (e.g., Barrett & Depinet, 1991; Gottfredson, 1986; Hunter & Schmidt, 1982; Hunter, Schmidt, & Rauschenberger, 1984). It is argued that there are lower correlations with these specific factors because they are less perfect markers of g than are IQ tests, which are alleged to be highly saturated with g.

Taken together, these three categories of evidence have persuaded many to view psychometric test scores as reflections of a singular, biologically based resource pool that permeates virtually all intellectual feats and that is responsible for individual differences in many real-world outcomes. However, there are alternative ways to interpret such evidence. Compelling arguments have been made against the issues of generality and biology (Ceci, 1990a, 1990b; Detterman, 1986). Suffice it to say here that the evidentiary basis that underlies traditional assumptions about them is open to different interpretations; that is, both psychometric test performance and intellectual development appear to result from a concatenation of cognitive, social, and biological factors (e.g., Sternberg, 1985, 1990) rather than from a singular gene system.

LIMITATIONS OF TRADITIONAL MODELS—THE CONTEXT-DEPENDENT NATURE OF COGNITION

The most serious limitation of theories of intellectual development is that they focus on the unfolding of basic psychological processes at the expense of the equally important role of unfolding contexts. As mentioned earlier, the message of structuralist, psychometric, information-processing, and behavioral genetic theories is that, if one is to get at the essence of age-related changes and chart the trajectories of various psychological processes, then context is a form of noise to be controlled, deleted, or otherwise purged from the data. As a result of this processing emphasis, these theories have misconstrued the essence of intellectual development. The latter can be captured only by building context into our models of the way basic processes unfold. To adumbrate our conclusion, intellectual processes are ecologically dependent, and their development and concurrent efficiency cannot be assessed independent of their context.

This point is best exemplified by some of the research outside the field of intellectual development. In the past decade, many researchers in the area of cognitive development have begun to recognize the importance of context. They have discovered that aspects of the physical, mental (e.g., the contents and organization of the memory representation), historical, and social contexts contribute to many cognitive attainments that were once thought to be the result of age-related changes in basic cognitive or biological processes. Recognition of the power of context on cognition can be seen in several areas of cognitive–developmental research; for example, Keil (1984) argued that metaphorical reasoning was context specific, occurring much earlier in some content domains than in others, and Chi and Ceci (1987) suggested that many types of problem solving were under the direct influence of the structure of the mental representation, that is, the mental context the child brings to the problem-solving task.

Perhaps the area that has received the most attention in this regard has been that of memory development. It is here that researchers studying both human and animal developmental processes have seen the need to acknowledge the importance of context. Both the physical milieu and emotional/affective environment are considered to be inextricable aspects of cognition:

> There is a "new look" in memory development research, and it is decidedly contextual. The crux of the current view, in fact, is that memory processes cannot be adequately understood or evaluated acontextually: To think about memory without considering the contexts that lead children to remember is akin to thinking about smiles independently of the faces on which they appear. Different contexts not only evoke different strategies to aid recall, but they also differentially shape an individual's perception of the recall task itself. Depending on the context in which remembering takes place, children may recall everything or nothing; their level of performance speaks as much to the power of context as to their native mnemonic processing capacity. (Ceci & Leichtman, 1992, p. 18)

Related to this, another limitation of traditional models is that they provide no mechanism(s) for the expression of intellectual potential. Although these other theories recognize that the environment exercises a mediating role in the development of cognitive abilities, primacy is reserved for biological factors. Thus, the traditional interactionist view is that genes encode phenotypes and that the eliciting power of the environment releases phenotypes. In contrast, the bioecological view departs from this preformationist view of the genotype and gives the environment a far more significant role. Genes do not encode phenotypes, but rather they manufacture proteins and enzymes that influence the expression of neighboring genes, as well as interacting among themselves. If this view is correct (i.e., that the proteins and enzymes that are produced interact among themselves)—and there is every reason to believe that it is—this implies that such interactions are governed by physical and chemical laws independent of the strand of DNA from which they originated (Subtelny & Green, 1982). A model of the translation of genotypes into phenotypes requires that we consider not just the proteins that genes manufacture but also the developmental role such proteins play, because most of the hormones, inducers, and inhibitors are connected in complex ways with the activity of multiple gene systems. Thus, the resultant morphology is only indirectly related to genes, making it impossible to explain phenotypes or morphological change exclusively or even primarily in terms of genes. As the evolutionary biologist, Alberch, wrote,

> even if we knew the complete DNA sequence of an organism, we could not reconstruct its morphology. We need to know about the epigenetic interactions that generated the phenotype. (Alberch, 1983, p. 862)

The bioecological theory was developed by Bronfenbrenner and Ceci (1994; Ceci, 1990a) with these limitations in mind. The environment, including the physical, mental, social, and historical context, assumes a pivotal role in the development of cognition. In addition, bioecological theory assumes that within each one of these different contexts, the interactions that transpire between the child and other people, objects, and symbols are what unleashes the unactualized potential contained within. In other words, these reciprocal interactions, referred to as *proximal processes,* are the mechanisms by which genotypes are translated into phenotypes. Furthermore, it is the absence or presence of these proximal processes, either at the time of initial acquisition or during later attempts to reinstate a particular process, that explains the differences both within the individual across different contexts and between individuals with comparable abilities as measured by standard IQ tests. These, and other assumptions that underlie the bioecological theory, are discussed in more detail below. It seems prudent, however, to first describe more explicitly what is meant by *context* and to provide the reader with recent research that illustrates the contextual specificity of cognitive functioning.

The Nature of Context

It is possible to distinguish among at least four types of context: (a) the physical context, (b) the social context, (c) the mental context, and (d) the historical context. Each of these can exert powerful influences on the efficiency of the developing organism's cognitive ability. As will be seen later, a given physical context may elicit strategies that are not elicited by another. Or, to take another example, the context in which a cognitive attainment is made can subsequently serve as an elicitor of that attainment, whereas a similar context that was not associated with its acquisition cannot. This is because, initially, most cognitive attainments are tied to the contexts in which they are acquired and, as a result, the child benefits from context reinstatement when trying to solve a problem. Thus, 3-year-old children have a contextually limited understanding of the "halving rule," which states that half of any entity results from its division by 2. To them, the halving rule applies only to a limited set of small, edible, concrete items. For example, a 3-year-old knows that, if you cut an apple in half you get two pieces, and if you cut an orange in half, you get two pieces. But when asked how many pieces will result from cutting a boulder in half, a 3-year-old will frequently reply in a manner that demonstrates the importance of the acquisition context (e.g., by claiming that it depends on how large the boulder is). This is because 3-year-olds' rule for halving may not extend beyond the category of small, edible, concrete objects; therefore, they do not extend the rule to large or nonconcrete entities (e.g., "work," "horsepower," or "volume"). With development, some individuals learn to extricate some mental operations from the contexts of their original acquisition, though the degree to which we as adults are truly context independent is less than many believe (Ceci, 1993).

Finally, alteration of the social valence of a task (e.g., by reversing its sex role expectation or by changing the incentive value for its successful completion) can lead to pronounced differences in outcomes, even though the cognitive processing demands of the task have not changed (e.g., Ceci, Baker, & Bronfenbrenner, 1987; Ceci & Bronfenbrenner, 1985; Ceci, Bronfenbrenner, & Baker, 1988). One social context may elicit a higher level of processing efficiency than another, even though the same process is ostensibly operating in both.

The previous examples all concern physical and social notions of context. There are two other types of context that matter when it comes to intellectual development, mental and historical contexts. The manner in which an individual mentally represents a problem is a type of mental context, and it is intimately linked to cognitive performance—as the literature on expertise amply demonstrates (e.g., Chi, Hutchinson, & Robin, 1989; Means & Voss, 1985). An elaborate knowledge representation in a specific content domain allows for more sophisticated solutions in that domain because it determines how the problems are coded, as well as the type of strategies that will be deployed (e.g., Staszewski, 1989; Walker, 1987). In fact, Rumelhart (1991) uses the term *re-presentation* instead of *representation* because he believes that an elaborated mental context represents the problem at hand; that is, a range of problems is already present in the representation of an expert, and this creates a mental context for understanding the problem at hand.

The final type of context to consider is the historical epoch during development. We have relatively little to say about this context here, except to note that the era in which one is born can be a powerful determinant of a broad range of intellectual outcomes, as shown in the fascinating and trail-blazing life course analyses of Elder and his colleagues (e.g., Elder, Hastings, & Pavalko, 1991). Historical epochs are associated with political ideologies, values, and cultural resources that can be potent determinants of school attendance, modes of cognizing, and so on. Social dynamics are set in motion by historical changes, and these dynamics may result in cognitive developments because they create situational imperatives. To give one example of how this can come about, consider the most famous of all longitudinal analyses of intellectual development, the Terman study of genius. Most readers probably assume that Terman's high-IQ youngsters went on to eminent careers, earning more money than their less intellectually able peers, as this is the received wisdom in developmental textbooks (see Ceci, 1990b, for review of texts on this study). However, there was tremendous variability among Terman's subjects. The most important difference between the high-IQ children who became successful in adulthood and their high-IQ peers who did not can be located in the historical contexts in which they were born. Specifically, those children born between 1904 and 1910 faced a more difficult set of situational imperatives than those born just a few years later. They graduated from college when the U.S. was in the throes of a cataclysmic depression. After years of struggling to get established in their livelihoods, they were mobilized for military service in World War II, which often disrupted their career trajectories. In short, being in one's 20s during the 1930s was a double whammy! In contrast, Elder et al. (1991) reported that the younger cohort, who were born between 1911 and 1917, were able to use college to buffer them from the worst years of the depression. Following college, many were able to use World War II service to practice their skills as engineers, doctors, and technical specialists or to use the service-related benefits to later launch careers in business or education. Lest we give the impression that the historical context is solely economic, similar examples can be given for the importance of cultural opportunities that appear at various times in a society (e.g., educational television or museums), social and political values that a culture adopts (e.g., toward different kinds of schooling), and so on.

So these four types of context (physical, social, mental, and historical) play powerful roles in intellectual development, simultaneously limiting and facilitating performance, creating at times continuities and at other times discontinuities in mental development, to the extent that these four types of context are consistent across tasks, settings, and epochs. The bioecological theory of intellectual development makes explicit contact with all four types of context, both during the initial acquisition of a cognitive attainment and subsequently during its instantiation. We say more about this later when we describe the theory's main tenets.

Having thus stated the problem, we turn now to a description of the research conducted both here, in the United States, and in South America on contextual influences on cognitive development.

North American Research on Context

In the series of experiments to be discussed next, children and adults were asked to solve problems in two different contexts. A complete description of our procedures and findings is beyond the scope of this article, but the interested reader can consult Ceci (1990a, in press), Ceci and Bronfenbrenner (1985), Ceci and Ruiz (1992, 1993), Ceci et al. (1987, 1988), and Ceci and Roazzi (1994) for details. Here we provide only a synopsis of what we have done.

Capturing Butterflies

The moderating effects that context exerts on processing efficiency are illustrated nicely in an experiment that was conducted in three parts. In the first phase, 10-year-olds were asked to anticipate the direction a geometric shape would migrate. The shape (circle, square, or triangle) always appeared in the center of the screen, but would migrate to some other location. Children were instructed to point to the location on the screen where they thought the shape would migrate. Children were not informed of the algorithm that determined where the shape would migrate. Shape, color, and size of the geometric form were the dimensions used in the algorithm to indicate left/right directionality, up/down directionality, and distance, respectively. This would be an example of a *main effects* algorithm, wherein one needs only to add a shape's features to determine where it will migrate. A large, dark circle, for instance, should move upward, leftward, and a short distance from the center. On each trial, children indicated where they thought a shape would migrate, and we placed a cursor at that location, so they could judge how far off the mark they were from where it actually migrated (and also measure in screen pixels the distance for our analysis).

In this acontextualized task, 10-year-olds were not very proficient at figuring out the algorithm that drove the shapes. Even after 750 trials, they were only slightly above chance. Their performance indicated that they had been successful in memorizing a few specific combinations of features, but that they had no understanding of the independent, additive values associated with color, shape, or size after 750 trials.

In Phase 2 of the experiment, the context was altered. Animals (birds, bees, and butterflies) were substituted for the three geometric shapes, and sound effects were added, thereby enhancing the meaningfulness of the context. The algorithm that drove the event was unchanged. Children were challenged to capture the animals by placing a cursor that looked like a net at the spot where they thought the animal would migrate.

This contextual change resulted in nearly perfect performance after 300 trials. We have repeated this experiment with a variety of algorithms, including complex sine functions, and the result has been the same: Children solve the same algorithm in this video game context far better than they solve it in the disembedded geometric shape context.

In Phase 3 of the study, we investigated whether the children could transfer the knowledge gained in the video game context to the more abstract geometric shape context. The answer seems to be that they can do so, but only if the laboratory context is presented within a few hours of solving the video game context and then only if the testing context is physically unchanged (i.e., if the same room, the same computer, and the same mouse are used). Thus, the generality of their reasoning is context bound. Similar boundaries have been observed in the adult literature whenever transfer between contexts is found (Nisbett, Fong, Lehman, & Cheng, 1988; Schooler, 1988).

Baking Cupcakes—Charging Batteries

The previous study provides a demonstration of how modifications in the context can alter the efficacy with which a process may function. In the current series of studies, deployment of cognitive strategies is similarly impacted by differences in context.

Ceci and Bronfenbrenner (1985) asked 10- and 14-year-old children to either charge a motorcycle battery or bake cupcakes for exactly 30 min. While they waited to remove the battery cables from the motorcycle or the cupcakes from the oven, the children were allowed to play a video game that was positioned so that each time they checked the clock to see if the 30 min had elapsed, the experimenter could record it. Some children were asked to charge the battery or bake the cupcakes in their home; others were asked to do so in a laboratory.

Results indicated that children who performed these tasks in their homes exhibited a U-shaped pattern of clock checking during the 30-min waiting period. This pattern of clock checking reflected an early calibration strategy. Initially, these children would check the clock every few minutes during the early part of the period. This vigilant checking served to confirm their subjective assessments of the passage of time, allowing them to "set" their mental clocks accordingly. Running on "autopilot," they could then immerse themselves in the video game without interruption until the waning minutes, when they would check incessantly. Support for this interpretation was obtained in a follow-up study, in which the clocks were programmed to run faster or slower than real time. Again, the same U-shaped function was obtained.

In contrast, children who performed these tasks in the laboratory exhibited a completely different pattern of clock checking, one that was ascending and linear over the 30-min period. These two patterns of clock checking reflect different cognitive strategies and different efficiencies. The U-shaped pattern of clock checking resulted in 30% fewer clock checks without any sacrifice in punctuality. In addition, the U-shaped pattern allowed the children to invest all of their resources to improve their video game scores, instead of worrying about time. Thus, a coefficient representing the U-shaped quadratic was associated with superior video game performance.

In summary, the home context allowed children to engage in a relaxed, yet strategic form of time monitoring that had significant advantages. If we had observed the children only in the laboratory context, there would be no evidence that they possessed such a strategy.

A Day at the Races

Perhaps the strongest evidence for the argument that the efficiency of information processing is domain specific comes from results of studies that compare specific cognitive skills of experts and novices. A series of ongoing experiments (Ceci & Liker, 1986a, 1986b, 1988; Ceci & Ruiz, in press-b) describes a unique group of men, harness racetrack experts. The sample comprised 14 experts and 16 peers (matched on years of daily attendance at the racetrack, IQ, and education). On average, the men had attended races on an almost daily basis for the past 16 years. Experts and nonexperts were both very knowledgeable about racing facts, but the experts were far more able to accurately estimate post time odds and other racing tasks that are important in pari-mutuel wagering. Both groups of men were asked to handicap 25 hypothetical races.

The findings indicated that expert handicappers used a complex, multiplicative model involving multiple interaction effects. The regression of 25 racetrack variables on experts' assessments of odds showed that simple, additive models of handicapping races failed to account for the complexity of their decisions. Experts not only took into consideration more variables when handicapping a race, but they did not simply add up this information. Rather, they developed implicit algorithms that gave varying weight to different types of information. And each type of information changed the way they thought about the other types. A seven-way interaction term was highly predictive of experts' superiority over nonexperts in the estimation of odds, and we argued that this interaction term was a surrogate for cognitive complexity at the racetrack.

The correlation between an expert's IQ score and the unstandardized regression coefficient weight for the seven-way interactive term was $-.07$. This means that, even though the greater use of complex, interactive thinking was causally related to success at predicting odds, there was no relation between such complex thinking at the racetrack and complex thinking on an IQ test. Because of this, assessment of the experts' intelligence on a standard IQ test was irrelevant in predicting the complexity of their thinking at the racetrack (Ceci & Liker, 1986a, 1988). Within either group (experts or nonexperts), IQ was unrelated to handicapping complexity. Between groups, however, there was an invariant finding: Even experts with low IQs always used more complex, interactive models than did nonexperts with high IQs, and their success was due in large part to the use of these complex interactive models. IQ was unrelated to how complexly these experts reasoned and the number of variables they considered interactively in their judgments.

Interestingly, experts' success at making these computations depended on their skill at doing mental arithmetic and, in particular, at subtractions that cross fifths boundaries. Yet this skill was unrelated to their scores on the mental arithmetic subscale of the IQ test, too. For example, although the Wechsler Adult Intelligence Scale—Revised (WAIS-R) asks arithmetical questions that require subtractions that cross tens boundaries (e.g., "If John has 14 newspapers and sells 9, how many will he have left?"), performance on such questions was not related to mental arithmetic in the racetrack context. For example, questions such as, "If a horse ran the first three fourths of a mile in 1:313 (i.e., 1 min, $31^3/_5$ s), and he finished the race in 1:592, how fast did he run the final quarter mile?" require mental subtraction of the final speed from the penultimate speed (answer: $57^4/_5$ s). This type of mental subtraction was unrelated to the type on the WAIS-R.

Stocks and Bonds

It could be argued that IQ is still a valid predictor of intellectual functioning, despite the failure to find it correlated with reasoning complexity or arithmetic in the racetrack context. After all, the participants in the racetrack study attended the races nearly every day for 16 years, and perhaps those with high IQs developed the complex understanding needed to reason so complexly long before those with low IQs. By subjecting two of these individuals to a new task that was novel for both of them, but which depended on a seven-way interaction term similar to the one they used at the racetrack, it was possible to assess whether the man with a higher IQ would be quicker at reinventing the complex algorithm to succeed at this new task. There were no data on such a question, and this effort represented a rather crude first attempt.

Two men who had participated in the racetrack study agreed to participate in an analog of it that entailed a similar type of reasoning, but in the context of a stock market simulation. One man was a 46-year-old self-employed businessman with a master's degree in mathematics education and an IQ of 121. The other man was a retired, 74-year-old dock worker with an IQ of 81 and a fifth-grade education. Both were rated as comparable experts in racetrack handicapping in the previous study (they were Subjects 20 and 29, respectively, in the Ceci & Liker, 1986b, study), and both had exhibited comparable use of the complex multiple interaction term in their decisions (see Table 6 of Ceci & Liker, 1986b, for these subjects' scores).

Neither of these men had prior experience in the stock market before participating in this simulation or claimed to know anything about the variables that influence actual market forces or to have played stock market games such as Millionaire. On this quiz, designed to assess basic understanding of the stock market, neither man achieved an above-chance score answering questions about basic stock market mechanisms.

Both men were presented with 600 trials of a stock market game that required them to estimate which of two stocks would have the best future earning-to-price ratio, or P/E ratio (a stock's price divided by its earnings per share). One of the two stocks was always listed at the market average, and the other was a stock that was to be evaluated against the average, by estimating the probability that it would yield a higher P/E ratio than the average.

The two men were informed that the information presented about stocks was fictitious and that the task was a game to see whether they could determine the rule that predicted P/E ratios. They were informed that the information to be presented was prepared in a manner so that the P/E ratio could be inferred, but it was not obvious how this was done, and it was their job to figure out the rule. Some of the information to be presented was sufficient to predict which stocks would have the most favorable future P/E ratio, but not all information presented would be useful (which is also true of racetrack information). Finally, even among those categories of information that were useful in determining the P/E ratio, not all were of equal importance to determining the P/E ratio. Each of 18 variables were explained to the participants, and examples were provided until they indicated that they understood what the variables stood for. In addition, a glossary of the meaning of all 18 variables was available throughout the study.

The rule to establish whether a particular stock's P/E ratio would rise or fall above the market average was precisely the same one used by these men to establish post time odds at the racetrack. In short, it was a seven-factor equation, with multiple interaction effects.

In the course of the presentation of the 600 trials, these 7 variables were systematically related to the P/E ratio prediction task. This was done through the use of an algorithm that was written to generate the stock market data. The task for the men was to infer the nature of the algorithm and the seven-factor interactive term that determined the P/E ratios. These 7 variables were weighted by the algorithm to provide deterministic outcomes. Thus, as in harness race handicapping, occasionally irrelevant independent variables might be associated with changes in the dependent variable (P/E ratio), but over the long haul, only the 7 variables interacted to consistently determine P/E ratios. The men were not informed of the similarity between the rule governing P/E ratios and the one that they routinely used at the racetrack. The goal of presenting these trials was to see if these two individuals would realize, on the basis of the 600 feedback trials, that (a) only 7 of the 18 independent variables that were presented were deterministic of P/E ratios, (b) simple main effects and lower level interactive models were inadequate for determining P/E ratios, and (c) they would be able to construct more complex models akin to those they had already demonstrated in another context (harness racing).

Although the stock market context was structurally similar to the racetrack context, there were several important differences. First, and foremost, there was no actual financial risk or gain involved in this task, unlike the racetrack task. Second, participants were not provided with the same extensive experience on this task that they had with the racetrack-handicapping task. And within this less extensive period of experience, they were presented the actual trials much less frequently than they had experienced them at the racetrack. That is, in contrast to their 16 years of experience at the track, these men were provided only about 18 months of experience at the stock market task. To handicap the comparable number of races ($N = 600$) would take approximately 12 weeks (10 races/day $\times$ 5 racing days/week), whereas these 600 stock market trials were spaced over

18 months. Finally, the level of motivation, although seemingly high, could not be equated with that involved in harness racing for these men. The latter enterprise was a fundamental aspect of their adult life, one that had not waned over more than 16 years of almost daily attendance.

Although the men's accuracy at predicting stock P/E ratios after 600 trials was considerably better than chance (50%), the two men were far from adept. At the end of 600 trials, both men had acquired part of the complex seven-way interactive model that drove the simulation, to roughly similar degrees.

To analyze the implicit algorithms that the men developed to guide their P/E ratio decisions, a modeling procedure that was based on Ceci and Liker (1986b) was used. This is a modification of the general linear procedure, so that parameters can be estimated without fully crossing all levels of each variable with those of the others. The analytical approach was to assess whether the nonadditive combination of variables (the seven-way interaction term) had a unique net effect on the participants' decisions about P/E ratios, not the simple additive effects of the individual variables. Therefore, this interactive term was added after all of the variables were first entered into the model, to determine whether this interaction term resulted in a reduction of the sums of squares error independently of the variables' additive effects.

After 600 trials, their implicit algorithms had become stable at the time of the final trial, and it is unlikely that they would have continued to change with increased experience. At the 600th trial, they were using different variables and different strategies. Interestingly, the lower-IQ man actually used a higher order interaction term than the higher-IQ man, though this finding must be considered with caution in view of the special reliability risks of a case study.

After the 600th trial, the men were told that the same model they used at the racetrack could be used to predict P/E ratios in this task. Following this hint, the men were given 25 additional trials to see if they could apply it in this context. When given this information, both men quickly figured out what the seven relevant variables were, how much relative weight to assign to each of them, and how to combine them in an interactive model. They reached ceiling levels of accuracy within the next 25 trials.

Finally, after the men had reached ceiling, relative weights of the seven variables were altered to make sure that the men were using the same algorithm they used at the racetrack. If they were using the same algorithm, then altering the weights could be expected to reduce their accuracy to chance. This is essentially what happened, though due to a fortuitous association of some of the altered weights on Trials 625 to 650, performance actually dropped below chance when the alterations were made.

In short, these two gamblers behaved just like graduate students who, after failing to solve a statistics problem in one context, are then told that it is the same problem that they had already solved in another context (see Ceci, in press, for examples). They can immediately solve the new problem, but only after a hint makes the transferability of contexts salient! Detterman (1992) noted that this is the rule, not the exception, in studies of cognitive transfer, even when the new context is highly similar to the original context:

> The amazing thing about all of these (reasoning and problem-solving) studies is not that they don't produce transfer. The surprise is the extent of similarity it is possible to have between two problems without subjects realizing that the two situations are identical and require the same process. (p. 13)

South American Research on Context

Like their North American counterparts, Brazilian researchers have shown that solutions to a wide variety of arithmetical and logical problems are context specific. Piagetian tasks such as conservation of liquid, length, and quantity all have been shown to be highly susceptible to slight changes in the instructions or in the explicitness of the task demands (e.g., for reviews, see Ceci & Roazzi, 1994; Roazzi & Bryant, 1992). Solutions to everyday kinds of proportional reasoning are also highly context specific (see Schliemann & Carraher, 1992, for review). Below, we describe five Brazilian studies in some detail, as they provide clues to the causal mechanisms involved.

To Measure or Not to Measure

Schliemann and Magalhaes (1990) gave unschooled Brazilian maids proportional reasoning problems in familiar contexts (e.g., cooking or purchasing foods) and unfamiliar contexts (mixing medicinal herbs). They found that initially solving problems in the familiar food-purchasing context improved the maids' ability to solve similar problems in the familiar cooking context, as well as in the unfamiliar medicinal herbs context. This becomes understandable when one considers the contexts themselves. Purchasing food requires an exactness that is not true of cooking and mixing medicinal herbs. Thus, when asked, "If 2 kilograms of rice cost 5 cruzados, how much will you have to pay for 3 kilograms?" these maids frequently exhibited exact proportional reasoning, whereas when they were given isomorphic problems having to do with how much water to add to a recipe, they usually estimated answers—the same way they do when actually cooking. As a result, their answers on cooking questions gave no evidence that they could engage in accurate proportional reasoning. When the purchasing problems preceded the cooking and medicinal herbs problems, proportional reasoning accuracy was significantly greater because it alerted the maids to the isomorphism between the tasks. In Detterman's (1992) framework, placing the purchasing task immediately before the cooking and herbs tasks "rigged" the results by making the contextual isomorphism so salient and obvious. Nevertheless, these studies of transfer across contexts may hold a clue as to how more distal transfer may be nurtured. The use of proximal examples and explicit instructions may be a necessary first step to inculcating transfer, at least for most people.

In the remainder of this section, we describe studies concerned with the manner in which cognitive abilities are affected by contextual factors across social classes. Where much of this research has been conducted, in Recife (the capital of Pernambuco, in northeast Brazil), approximately half of the population of 2 million dwell in urban shanty towns, called *favelas*. The management of money is one of the most pressing problems faced by favela families. Generally, the basic wages earned by the parents of favela children are insufficient to cover even the most basic daily subsistence needs, let alone to save for unexpected emergencies. Thus, many informal activities are used within favela families to meet their financial needs, for example, providing all sorts of services or preparing food. These informal activities are carried out in the neighborhood by most of its members to ensure the flow of resources. In addition, favela children are forced to go out to work at a very early age to aid the family. These children work at a range of unskilled occupations, such as selling fruits or peanuts at the market; selling ice cream or suntan oil on the beach; selling sweets, coffee, needles, naftaline (mothballs/insect repellant), postcards, coconuts, corn-on-the-cob, or other items at sidewalk stands; watching over parked cars in front of restaurants and shops for a tip; collecting choice bits of garbage or begging for leftover food from door to door for themselves or for their chickens, pigs, or other domestic fowl at home in the backyard; shining shoes in the town center; cleaning windshields and selling popcorn at the traffic lights; and gathering disposal paper, plastic containers, metal, and other waste products that can be sold for scrap. Even when they do not go outside to work, favela children are expected to help their mother with domestic chores. They will skip school whenever the economy of the household needs them, and a sizable number of them do not attend school at all beyond first grade. Generally, the number of children who quit school rises precipitously around 10 to 11 years of age, a period in which a large number start working to contribute to the family financially (Ceccom & Oliviera, 1982). Only 12% of children who attend the first year of school finish the last year of so-called compulsory education.

The first study investigated street vendor children from favelas as they were engaged in solving arithmetical problems. Some of these problems were embedded in academic tasks, and others were embedded in everyday contexts that the children confront in their jobs. In the next two studies that we describe, performance on two common Piagetian tasks is compared between poor and middle-class children as a function of the context and the instructions provided.

Mathematics in the Street and in the School

Schliemann and Magalhaes (1990) carried out a study of daily uses of mathematics by 9- to 15-year-old Brazilians working in commercial activities. In the course of their daily jobs as street vendors, their work required them to carry out mental subtraction, addition, multiplication, and sometimes division. An intriguing observation is that despite their limited formal education—in general, these children attend school for fewer than 5 years—they can easily calculate how much certain goods cost and how much change a customer should receive, given a certain amount of money.

Carraher, Carraher, and Schliemann (1985) compared performance on mathematical problems embedded in real-life situations with context-free isomorphs. The results indicated that problems presented in the context of customer–vendor transactions (e.g., "If a large coconut costs 76 cruzeiros, and a small one costs 50 cruzeiros, how much do the two cost together?") were solved much more easily than the same problems presented without such a context (e.g., "How much is 76 + 50?"). In fact, 98% of the problems presented in the customer–vendor context were correctly solved by these uneducated street vendors; on the other hand, they correctly answered only 37% of the decontextualized questions. At an intermediate level of context, there were problems that provided some descriptive setting for the subject, but were not couched in the rich language or contents of their specific jobs (e.g., "If an orange costs 76 cruzeiros and a passion fruit costs 50, how much do the two cost together?"). The rate of correct answers on these intermediate problems was 74%. Clearly, children bring different aspects of their knowledge to bear in different problem-solving contexts.

How is it possible that subjects are able to solve a computational problem in a natural context and yet fail to solve the same problem when it is disconnected from that context? A qualitative analysis of the children's verbal protocols indicated that the problem-solving routines used may have been different in the various contexts. In the two more familiar contexts, children tended to reason by using what could be termed *convenient groupings*, whereas in the disconnected setting, school-taught routines were used frequently, although not exclusively.

Thus, mathematical ability is highly dependent on the context in which it is elicited. The context specificity of unschooled children's arithmetic is not unique: Schooled children also often fail to solve isomorphs of school problems when they are couched in nonschool language and content (Schubauer-Leoni & Perret-Clermont, 1980).

In summary, the findings of Carraher et al. (1985) suggest that, when we try to appraise practical capacities that may be enhanced by everyday life experiences, it is necessary to consider the context carefully, not only as a general setting for development, but also as an elicitor of the specific ability in question. The way in which individuals tackle intellectual problems may change radically with alterations of the social context.

Class Inclusion

The study that was just discussed suggests that a discrepancy between formal and informal testing exists when comparing children from diverse social backgrounds. To explore this further, Roazzi and his colleagues (Roazzi, 1987; Roazzi & Bryant, 1992; Roazzi, Bryant, & Schliemann, 1988) examined variations in instructions on two popular Piagetian tasks: class inclusion and conservation.

In the first study, Roazzi (Roazzi, 1987; Roazzi & Bryant, 1992) analyzed the performances of 60 poor and middle-class 6- to 9-year-old children on class-inclusion problems, first in an informal context and then in a formal one (Roazzi, 1986a).

Street vendor children unknowingly participated in the research during the normal course of a customer–vendor interaction. Children received two versions of a class-inclusion problem. In the first (referred to as the *informal test*), instructions were modified to reflect the context these children were most versed in. The interviewer, posing as a casual purchaser, searched among the goods for two classes of items of the same price per unit (e.g., mint gum and strawberry gum). Then the interviewer divided four units of one subclass (i.e., mint chewing gum) and two units of the other subclass (i.e., strawberry chewing gum) and asked, "Do I pay more for the mint chewing gum or for the strawberry chewing gum? Why?" "For you to get more money, is it better to sell me the mint chewing gum or is it better to sell me the chewing gum? Why?"

Afterwards, the same children were given a formal test (called Formal Test 2), similar to that described by Piaget and Inhelder (1969), which has the same logical structure as the informal test ("Are there more yellow balls, or are there more balls? Why?").

In addition, middle-class children were tested in the same way in these two kinds of class-inclusion tests. The informal test now was called Formal Test 1 because, in spite of the same questions, for these children the context was not one in which they met their daily challenges. As part of a game context, these middle-class children were invited to pretend they were chewing gum vendors and the examiner was a purchaser. After giving the children chewing gum to sell, the same series of questions was asked as in the informal test.

Results showed a significant interaction between social class and context. Differences between poor and middle-class children were found in each of the contexts. Street vendor children were more successful at the class-inclusion task in the natural (informal) context than in the formal one; middle-class children, on the other hand, were more prone to success in the classical (formal) version of the task than in the so-called informal version, which entailed unfamiliar vending roles. Furthermore, a comparison of poor and middle-class children in the two kinds of tests, Formal 2 and informal (for poor children) and Formal 1 (for middle-class children), indicated that the superiority of the informal context was disproportionately greater for the poor children.

A second experiment was conducted to examine middle-class children's performance in a context that would represent an informal test for them. Consequently, in this new experiment, a special effort was made to make one of the two class-inclusion tasks as natural as possible for the middle-class children. This was achieved by having middle-class children repeatedly role play as vendors and the examiner role play as a customer in a gamelike context. The first five sessions were preparatory for the actual testing. This informal test followed the identical procedure of the informal test that was used with poor street vendors above. The formal test was the same Formal Test 2 used in the above experiment.

A comparison of this experiment with the one that was discussed earlier revealed that the performance of the middle-class children in the informal condition in the second experiment showed no difference from the performance of poor children in the first experiment. These findings demonstrate that context is as relevant for middle-class children as it is for poor ones. Thus, the contextual differences make it difficult to infer competence directly from a single performance in a single setting. Inferences about cognitive differences between a class of children for whom a context is more familiar than it is for another group are problematic (Roazzi, 1986b, 1987).

Conservation

The final study examined conservation ability across social classes (Roazzi & Bryant, 1992; Roazzi et al., 1988). This work suggests that wrong answers on the traditional conservation task may be due to a misinterpretation of the crucial conservation question by the poor children (i.e., due to a lack of explicitness) rather than to a delayed acquisition of logical ability.

In the traditional conservation task, children are first asked to compare two quantities that are identical in appearance. After the children judge them to be equal, the perceptual appearance of one of the quantities is transformed, and the child is asked to compare the two quantities again. Preoperational children usually claim that the two quantities are now unequal, a finding exacerbated among economically disadvantaged and culturally different children. An incorrect response on this task led Piaget to claim that children have not grasped the principle of invariance of quantity and, therefore, they wrongly treat a mere perceptual change as a genuinely quantitative change.

This conservation procedure can be criticized for not making it clear to subjects that the judgment they are being asked to make is quantitative as opposed to perceptual. In the traditional form of the task, children are first simply asked to look at and compare two quantities that are identical both quantitatively and perceptually. That the two quantities also look perceptually alike may mislead the child into thinking that the initial, pre-transformation question and also the question asked after the transformation are about the perceptual appearance of the two quantities (e.g., height of beakers) and not about their quantitative amounts. So, when the experimenter transforms the appearance of one of the quantities in front of the child, the child, seeing that they are different and thinking the question to be a perceptual one, answers that they are no longer the same. If correct, then the standard Piagetian context may lead to a misinterpretation of children's logical ability. If the traditional sequence of questions leads children to incorrectly assume that what the examiner wants is a perceptual and not a quantitative comparison, then stressing the quantitative comparison from the beginning should lead to more conservation answers, especially among economically disadvantaged children, who do so poorly on this task.

In the study by Carraher et al. (1985), 4- and 5-year-old children were given either the standard Piagetian instructions, establishing the equality between the quantities through perceptual comparison, or a modified version of the task where, instead of a perceptual comparison, the child was first asked to make a quantitative comparison between the two quantities. Results revealed a significantly higher performance in the modified version among 5-year-olds (60% and 45% conservation answers for discrete and continuous quantity, respectively, in the modified version vs. 27% and 0% in the traditional version).

Roazzi (1987) compared Brazilian children of different social classes in two types of conservation tasks: liquid and length. In the conservation of liquid task, where the traditional perceptual comparison of the two quantities was asked in the first phase of the task, middle-class Brazilian children performed much better than their poorer peers. In the length conservation task, however, which laid more emphasis, from the beginning, on a quantitative comparison, no social class differences were found. The fact that the poor children did not differ from middle-class children when the quantitative aim of the task was made explicit from the beginning suggests that the social class differences that are usually found may be due to misunderstandings about what it is that the examiner wants rather than to a deficit in logical reasoning.

On the basis of these two studies, Roazzi et al. (1988) conducted a third study to determine whether differences between social classes in the conservation task could be explained in terms of differences in the need for explicitness. This study provides a clue to one of the sources of poor performance among poor children.

Poor and middle-class 5-, 6-, 7-, and 8-year-old children were studied in liquid conservation tasks under three conditions: control, quantity, and money. In the control condition, the initial comparison was made through a perceptual estimate. In the quantity condition, the child was not allowed to make a perceptual comparison. The initial comparison to establish the equality between the two glasses was obtained through measurement. The instructions were more explicit about the quantitative nature of the task than was the case in the control condition and involved measurement in the initial part of the problem. In the quantity condition, the children were explicitly asked to put four ladles of lemonade into each glass. One of the two glasses was covered to preclude a perceptual comparison. The child had to judge the two amounts as equal on the basis of having put the same number of ladlefuls into each glass. Thereafter, the procedure was exactly the same as in the control condition.

The money condition was exactly the same as the quantity condition, except that the child was told that she or he would have to sell the lemonade and that each ladleful was worth one cruzeiro. The child was asked to put four cruzeiros' worth of lemonade in each glass. So the emphasis here was as much on the price as on the number of ladlefuls.

Children were divided into the usual Piagetian categories: nonconservers, intermediate conservers (i.e., children who were either inconsistent or who gave the correct answer, but could not justify it), and conservers (i.e., children who gave the correct answer and produced the correct explanation for it). The differences between social classes reached significance only in the control condition. Social class differences in the other two measurement conditions disappeared. Thus, these data indicate that it is not a question of having or not having a logical ability that differentiated poor and middle-class children, but a difference in the ability to detect without confusion the communicative message of the experimenter and the procedures he or she was using.

BRONFENBRENNER'S THEORY OF PROXIMAL PROCESSES: TRANSLATING GENES INTO COGNITIVE PHENOTYPES

Earlier, it was argued that one of the limitations of traditional models of intellectual development was that none make any provision(s) for the mechanism of the behavioral expression of genetic potential. The bioeco-logical view departs from traditional behavioral genetic models regarding the nature and meaning of h^2. According to the bioecological view, h^2 re-flects the proportion of actualized genetic potential, leaving unknown and unknowable the amount of unactualized genetic potential (Bronfenbren-ner & Ceci, 1994). According to the bioecological view, nothing can be said about a person's potential for success or failure without knowing about the level of proximal processes and more distal resources that exist in the child's environment.

Proximal processes involve reciprocal interactions between the devel-oping child and other persons, objects, and symbols in its immediate set-ting. To qualify as proximal processes, these interactions must be enduring and lead to progressively more complex forms of behavior. Appropriate proximal processes differ as a function of the developmental status of the organism (e.g., during infancy, a proximal process might be an activity be-tween a caregiver and an infant that serves to maintain the infant's atten-tion or encourage her or him to slightly exceed her or his proximal zone of potential). As we argue below, proximal processes are the engines that drive development; they are the mechanisms that translate genes into phenotypes (Bronfenbrenner & Ceci, 1994). If there are insufficient proximal processes in one's life, then h^2 will reflect only that portion of one's potential that can be brought to fruition by the limited level of proximal processes.

On the basis of the reanalyses of two different data sets, Bronfen-brenner and Ceci (1994) argued that, when proximal processes are at high levels in a child's environment, then heritability estimates are high; yet, at the same time, individual differences may be attenuated. The first part of this claim is no different from that of many in the psychometric commu-nity (e.g., Herrnstein, 1973; Humphreys, 1979), because it has long been recognized that genetic variance becomes relatively greater as a conse-quence of decreasing environmental variance, which is where the second part of the claim comes in: High levels of proximal processes decrease en-vironmental variance because they serve to supply interactive experiences to children who otherwise might not have them. This has the effect of not only increasing h^2 but also leveling group differences.

According to the bioecological view, it is also important to assess the dimensions of the child's ecology or environment, because in two ways it provides limits on the efficiency of proximal processes. First, the environment contains the resources that need to be imported into proximal processes for the latter to work maximally. For example, it is not enough for parents to engage their adolescents in reciprocal interactions that sustain the latter's attention while studying algebra (an example of the proximal process called *monitoring*), if the parents themselves cannot effectively explain the relevant algebraic concepts to their children. Thus, the larger environment can sometimes set limits on proximal processes' efficacy.

A second reason for the importance of the larger environment is that it provides the stability necessary to benefit from proximal processes. A large literature (see Bronfenbrenner & Ceci, 1994) illustrates that regardless of social class, ethnicity, or ability levels, the less stable the environment, the worse the developmental outcome. Frequent changes in daycare arrangements, stepparents, schools, or neighborhoods, for example, are associated with adverse outcomes, and this is presumably independent of the level of proximal processes. Measures of heritability are extremely sensitive to secular trends, generally dropping during times of economic scarcity and climbing during times of plenty. This is in keeping with the view that the ecology brings to fruition differing levels of genetic potential, and h^2s will fluctuate by a factor of three in conjunction with economic fluctuations. We assume that, in times of economic scarcity, the levels of proximal processes are reduced because caregivers' attention is deployed elsewhere.

The Bioecological Theory of Intellectual Development

We turn now to a discussion of some major characteristics of the bioecological model. Although we have discussed two of the major tenets of the theory in some detail already, there are other assumptions that the theory makes that have not yet been introduced. To give the reader a full, cohesive understanding of the theory, what follows is a complete description of all of the assumptions on which the theory is founded, including a brief reiteration of the contextually related propositions discussed earlier.

According to the bioecological view, the data on intellectual development necessitate a four-pronged framework for their explication, namely, (a) the existence of not one type of intellectual resource, but multiple, statistically independent resource pools, (b) the interactive and synergistic effect of gene-environment developments, (c) the role of specific types of contexts (e.g., interactions, called *proximal processes,* as well as more distal environmental resources, such as family educational level) that influence how much of a genotype gets actualized in what type of an environment, (d) the role of motivation in determining how much of one's context aids in the actualization of his or her potential. We briefly review these four prongs next.

First, on the basis of the research and arguments presented in the previous section, intelligence is viewed as a multiple-resource system. Making this assumption gets around the thorny problem of domain specificity and low-cross-task correlations when the same cognitive operation is involved (e.g., low correlations between memory for textual material and memory for digits). It also accords with the analyses by Detterman and his colleagues, showing that independent cognitive processes make unique predictions to g-based measures (e.g., Detterman, 1986).

Second, the bioecological view is inherently developmental and interactionist. Like all interactionist perspectives, the bioecological view asserts that, from the very beginning of life, there is an interplay between biological potentials and environmental forces. To understand how individuals could begin life possessing comparable intellectual potentials, but differ in the level of intelligence they subsequently manifest, the bioecological view posits an interaction between various biologically influenced cognitive potentials—such as the capacity to store, scan, and retrieve information—and the ecological contexts that are relevant for each of their unfoldings. At each point in development, the interplay between biology and ecology results in changes that may themselves produce other changes, until a full cascading of effects is set in motion.

Although biology and ecology are interwoven into an indivisible whole, their relationship is continually changing, and with each change a new set of possibilities is set in motion until soon even small changes produce large effects. Hence, developmental change is not always or even usually linear, but rather is synergistic and nonadditive. A small environmental influence on a protein-fixing gene may initially result in only tiny changes, but over time the chain of events may produce a magnification of effects on other processes. In addition, certain epochs in development can be thought of as sensitive periods during which a unique disposition exists for a specific cognitive muscle to crystallize in response to its interaction with the environment. During such periods, neurons within specific compartments rapidly *overarborize* (spreading their tentaclelike synaptic connections to other neurons). Even though some of the arboreal connections laid down during these periods of brain spurts will not be used at that time, they can be recruited to enable future behaviors to occur, provided they are not "pruned" because of atrophy or disuse. Siegler (1989) concluded that "the timing of the sensitive period seems to be a function of both when synaptic overproduction occurs and when the organism receives relevant experience" (p. 358). It appears that whereas some neural processes are more fully under maturational control, others are responsive to the environment, and synapses are formed in response to learning, which may vary widely among humans. Similar contextual roles have also been found in the case of various animals' cognitive skills (e.g., Lickliter & Hellewell, 1992; Smith & Spear, 1978).

The traditional additive behavioral genetic model assumes that different genotypes have different norms of reaction and that the phenotypic differences are potentially greatest when environmental resources are also greatest. In Figure 1, this is exemplified in the regression lines associated with Genotypes A and C; they both increase by similar amounts in their phenotypic expression as a linear function of the increasing value of the environment. However, it is not only possible, but probable that the norms of reaction are nonmonotonic, with the error about the regression line being heteroscedastic rather than homoscedastic, a point made recently by Bors (in press): "The same maximum mean phenotypic values for all geno-

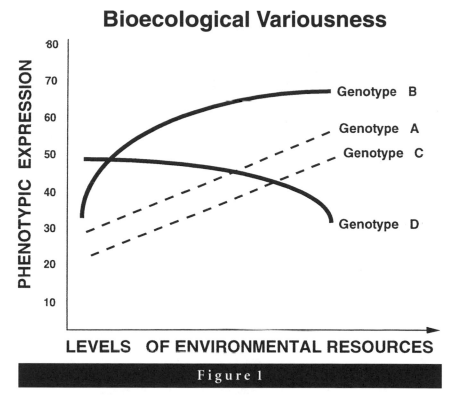

Bioecological Variousness

Figure 1

Hypothetical depiction of four different genotypes unfolding in response to increasing levels of environmental resources.

types could be produced by different intersections of multiple environmental parameters". Thus, a demonstration that different phenotypes are produced by the same environment does not minimize the importance of the latter, because, as can be seen in Figure 1, the maximal phenotypic expression for each of the four genotypes is related to a different level of environmental resources. Differing phenotypic expression in the same environment is no more difficult to reconcile with an important role for the environment than the same phenotypic expression in differing environments is to reconcile with an important role for genetics. There may be multiple gene systems, each with its own norms of reaction and developmental trajectories that are responsive to environmental resources.

Fourth, the bioecological view incorporates motivation as a key ingredient in its explanation of empirical findings. Briefly, an individual must not merely be endowed with some biological potential for a given cognitive resource or merely be exposed to an environment that facilitates the expression of this cognitive resource; the individual must also be motivated to benefit from exposure to such an environment. Men in Ceci and Liker's (1986b) study who demonstrated highly complex forms of reasoning at the racetrack did not exhibit the same degree of complex reasoning in other domains. Had they been exposed to environments that were conducive to, say, learning science or philosophy, and motivated to take advantage of such environments, they would have undoubtedly acquired the ability to think as complexly in those domains as they did at the racetrack, given the isomorphism that was built in between the type of reasoning needed to handicap a race and to reason scientifically in that experiment.

Now that we have briefly described the basic features of the bioecological view of intellectual development, it can be contrasted with the biological, environmental, and psychometric views of intelligence on four grounds. First, the bioecological view proposes multiple cognitive abilities, rather than one pervasive general factor, and these multiple abilities are at best only imperfectly gauged by tests of so-called general intelligence.

Second, the bioecological view differs from traditional nature–nurture interactionist views in the conception of the interaction between biological and environmental factors. Earlier, we discussed the traditional interactionist view, which asserts that biological factors are primarily responsible for releasing the genetic materials that are ultimately observed as intelligence. A bioecological perspective considers environmental forces as the catalysts for unlocking intellectual potential.

Third, like other interactionist views of development, the bioecological view argues that the efficiency of cognitive processes depends on aspects of the context. However, according to Ceci (1990b), context is not an adjunct to cognition, but a constituent of it. Unlike traditional cognitive science, which has assumed that context is merely a background for cognition, the bioecological view regards context as an inextricable aspect of cognitive efficiency. Here, context is defined broadly to include not only external features of the near and far environment and their motivational properties, but internal features of the organism's mental representation, such as the manner in which a stimulus or problem is represented in memory. Thus, speed in recognizing letters and numerals depends on how those stimuli are represented in memory, with more elaborate representations leading to faster recognition rates (Ceci, 1990a). This explains why the same cognitive ability, no matter how basic, often operates inconsistently across diverse contexts (Ceci, 1990b). The same individuals who are slow at recognizing a stimulus in one domain may recognize it in another domain more quickly if its representation in the latter domain is more elaborate. In short, cognition-in-context research has shown that context, including the mental representation or mental context of a task, helps determine the efficiency of cognition.

Fourth, the bioecological view assumes that there are noncognitive abilities that are highly important for subsequent intellectual development and that are inherited. For example, a child may inherit various types of temperament (e.g., restlessness or impulsiveness), physical traits (e.g., skin color or facial shape), and *instigative characteristics* (e.g., Bronfenbrenner's, 1989, "reward-seeking" type) that may influence later learning and development. Whereas these traits are themselves influenced by gene systems and can be shown to exert direct as well as indirect effects on subsequent IQ performance and school success, they are not cognitive in nature. So, these noncognitive characteristics and abilities can account for heritability patterns (e.g., IQs that run along consanguinity lines) without claiming that this is a consequence of the inheritance of a central nervous system with a determinate signal-to-noise ratio that limits processing capacity. Family members that share these characteristics may perform similarly as a result of their noncognitive dispositions rather than because they share the same rate-limiting nervous systems (cf. Lehrl & Fischer, 1988, 1990). Accounts of rate-limiting cognitive functioning that are based on electroencephalogram power spectral density measures (e.g., Weiss, 1990a, 1990b), blood glucose levels in the brain, central nerve conductance velocity and oscillation (Jensen, in press), and heritability analyses (e.g., Pedersen, Plomin, Nesselroade, & McClearn, 1992) cannot distinguish between cognitive (i.e., inherited limits on central nervous system functioning) and noncognitive bases of performance. This is not to deny the importance of genes in intellectual performance, but merely a caution that just as it is not the case that everything that is intellectual is genetic in origin, neither is it the case that everything that is genetic is intellectual in nature.

INTELLIGENCE AS IT UNFOLDS . . . IN CONTEXT

Figure 2 is a partial schematic of the bioecological trajectory through which genes are transformed into intellectual phenotypes. As can be seen, the flow starts at the bottom, with parental genes giving the child its early impetus and direction, ultimately influencing various forms of cognitive processing that are fairly independent of each other (depicted as three independent arrows emanating out of the child). The manifestations of these multiple, gene-based resource pools are influenced by multiple forms of activities that caregivers engage in with children. One such activity, namely, proximal processes, is postulated to actualize genetic potentials. Thus, variations in the level of resources in the environment (dichotomized for ease of illustration) along with variations in the level of proximal processes lead to different levels of h^2.

Several things are not apparent in Figure 2. One is that proximal processes are more than expressions of parental genetics, otherwise there would be no basis for making differential predictions about the size of h^2, because all that we would need to know is the parental genotype. Yet, we have made differential predictions about the size of h^2s that will be found within the same levels of consanguinity when the levels of proximal processes differ (see below).

Second, the central arrow of this figure is broken rather than solid, to emphasize a core principle underlying the bioecological model, namely, the influence of genetics and environment are never wholly separable.

THE BIO-ECOLOGICAL MODEL

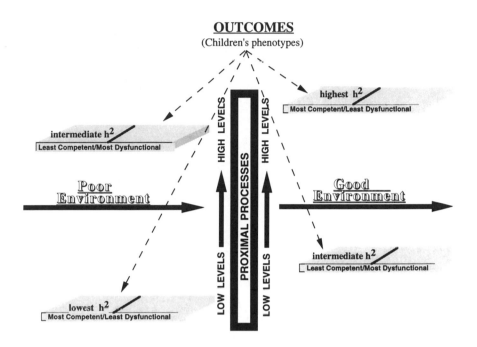

![Figure 2]

The bioecological model. Distances between platforms represent the differential effects of proximal processes and more global environmental resources (e.g., SES) on both absolute levels of competence attained and heritability.

From the moment of conception, the actualization of inherited cognitive dispositions for embryological development does not occur in a vacuum but is differentially responsive to the intrauterine environment (as well as the intercellular environment, including interactions among hormones, inducers, enzymes, and proteins). This power of inherited propensities is not diminished after birth, because as the child interacts with persons, symbols, and objects in his or her environment, the latter becomes genetically loaded, as the active organism selects, changes, and hence constructs his or her own environment.

Finally, illustrated in Figure 2 is the stipulation that proximal processes are the engines of intellectual development, with higher levels of proximal processes associated with increasing levels of intellectual competence. Thus, these processes not only increase h^2 and reduce group differences, but they produce more competent organisms across the board.

Figure 2 further portrays some of the major predictions regarding the inclusion of proximal processes into a theory of intellectual development. An implication of this view is that proximal processes are posited to exert a more potent influence on the various cognitive operations than does the larger environment (e.g., socioeconomic status [SES]) in which they operate. Accordingly, the differences in intellectual outcomes (and their corresponding h^2 estimates) between poor and good environments are expected to be systematically smaller than the differences that are associated with low versus high levels of proximal processes. (This prediction is revealed in the comparison of the distances in the figure; distances between good and poor processes are greater than between good and poor environments.) In addition to the prediction that the highest magnitudes of h^2 are to be found under good–high conditions (i.e., high proximal processes–good environmental resources), the bioecological model makes a corollary prediction: The largest differences in the magnitudes of h^2 for competent outcomes are to be found between children in the high–good condition and the low–poor condition. Hence, in the figure, this is indicated by the largest physical distance between these two conditions. And, again, when it comes to environmental comparisons, the bioecological model makes the claim that the influence of proximal processes is relatively more determinative of the absolute magnitudes of both h^2 and the absolute level of competence achieved than is the larger environment's resources. This is indicated by the greater distances within the high versus low proximal process levels than within good versus poor environmental levels.

Elsewhere, we have attempted to provide a limited test of these predictions with available data. For example, nearly 20 years ago, Bronfenbrenner (1975) reanalyzed the then available data on monozygotic (MZ) twins reared apart. Although there were no measures of proximal processes available, the resources in the environment probably differed markedly as a function of the ecologies in which the twins were raised. Bronfenbrenner reported that the intraclass correlations for IQ reached the high .80s when separated twins were reared in similar ecologies, but plummeted to .28 when they were reared in vastly different ecologies (e.g., agricultural/mining towns vs. manufacturing towns). These data are consistent with the bioecological model's prediction that h^2 will be both far higher and far lower than previously reported when the level of proximal processes and environmental resources are systematically varied.

An implication of the foregoing is that the greater the genotypic dissimilarity, the greater will be the impact of proximal processes in increasing phenotypic dissimilarity. That is, proximal processes will have their greatest impact in making those who are genetically dissimilar even more different, and in making those who are genetically similar phenotypically similar, hence, increasing the value of h^2. This is why the difference between the dizygotic (DZ) and MZ intraclass correlations are almost always greater in good environments than in poor ones (see Bronfenbrenner & Ceci, 1993a). Thus, the bioecological view of the reason that h^2 is so high in studies of identical twins is not because the cognitive phenotypes of MZ pairs are unaffected by the environment, but because the cognitive phenotypes of the DZ pairs are so affected by the environment (e.g., Fischbein, 1982). Thus, the bioecological model finds support for the interplay between ecology and biology in some of the very findings that have served as cornerstones of the behavioral genetic and psychometric traditions.

The results of reanalyses with more recent data are also in keeping with predictions from our bioecological model, though, clearly, much more needs to be done before this can be accepted as definitive (Bronfenbrenner & Ceci, 1993b). If we are correct about the critical role of proximal processes, then under differing levels of proximal processes, the size of the heritability estimate will change, possibly dramatically, because h^2 reflects only the proportion of actualized genetic potential, leaving unknown the amount of genetic potential that remains unactualized due to limited proximal processes. One piece of evidence that this is true can be shown by examining the correlations for MZ and DZ twins' IQ scores. Contrasting 100% (MZ) versus 50% (DZ) of genetic similarity permits a simple calculation of h^2 (doubling the difference between the intraclass rs associated with MZ's and DZ's IQs). If Bronfenbrenner and Ceci were correct in their depiction of proximal processes and distal environmental resources as important in the actualization of genetic potential, then it should be possible to show that h^2 goes up not because MZs become more alike in their IQs, but because DZs become less alike—as the environment allows them the opportunity to make manifest their genetic differences. In other words, if a family has twins who share half their segregating genes in common and the family has economic resources to allow the twin with the musical talent to take piano and composition lessons and the twin with the art talent to attend art camp, then the twins' genetic potentials become manifest. Conversely, in a poor environment, these twins' potentials would remain only that—potential, latent, never expressed.

In summary, current research on intelligence and intellectual development points in a direction that emphasizes the role of context in the formation and assessment of an individual's manifold cognitive potentials. Although traditional measures of general intelligence possess good predictive validity in school, job, and training situations, this does not necessarily reflect the fact that a singular resource pool underpins a significant portion of the prediction, that the size of heritability estimates reflects the amount of variation due to purely genetic processes, or that only cognitive factors are involved. Thus, prediction and explanation can be fundamentally disjunctive enterprises in science. The bioecological view of intellectual development aims to fulfill the promissory note of the interactionist perspective by taking cognizance of the biological and cognitive findings that have been reported throughout this century, but re-casting them in a new developmental–contextual light.

REFERENCES

Alberch, P. (1983). Mapping genes to phenotypes, or the rules that generate form. *Evolution, 37*, 861–863.

Barrett, G. V., & Depinet, R. L. (1991). A reconsideration of testing for competence rather than for intelligence. *American Psychologist, 46*, 1012–1024.

Bronfenbrenner, U. (1975). Nature with nurture: A reinterpretation of the evidence. In A. Montague (Ed.), *Race and IQ.* New York: Oxford University Press.

Bronfenbrenner, U. (1989). Ecological systems theory. In R. Vasta (Ed.), *Annals of child development: Six theories of child development. Revised formulations and current issues* (pp. 185–246). Greenwich, CT: JAI Press.

Bronfenbrenner, U., & Ceci, S. J. (1993). Heredity, environment, and the question "How?": A first approximation. In R. Plomin & G. McClearn (Eds.), *Nature, nurture, and psychology* (pp. 313–325). Washington, DC: American Psychological Association.

Bronfenbrenner, U., & Ceci, S. J. (1994). Nature–nurture reconceptualized in developmental perspective: A bioecological model. *Psychological Review, 101,* 568–586.

Carraher, T. N., Carraher, D., & Schliemann, A. D. (1985). Mathematics in the streets and in the schools. *British Journal of Developmental Psychology, 3,* 21–29.

Ceccom, M., & Oliviera, R. (1982). *A vida na escole e a escola da vida.* Petropolis, Brazil: Vogle.

Ceci, S. J. (1990a). *On intelligence . . . more or less: A bio-ecological treatise on intellectual development.* Englewood Cliffs, NJ: Prentice-Hall.

Ceci, S. J. (1990b). On the relationship between microlevel and macrolevel cognitive processes: Worries over current reductionism. *Intelligence, 14,* 1–19.

Ceci, S. J. (1991). How much does schooling influence cognitive and intellectual development? *Developmental Psychology, 27,* 703–722.

Ceci, S. J. (1993). Contextual trends in intellectual development. *Developmental Review, 13,* 403–435.

Ceci, S. J. (in press). Is less really more? Using microlevel sensory and cognitive measures to predict macrolevel cognitive outcomes. *American Journal of Mental Retardation.*

Ceci, S. J., Baker, J., & Bronfenbrenner, U. (1987). Memory development and ecological complexity: The case of prospective memory. In M. Perlmutter & F. Weinert (Eds.), *Individual differences and universal changes in memory development research* (pp. 156–182). Hillsdale, NJ: Erlbaum.

Ceci, S. J., & Bronfenbrenner, U. (1985). Don't forget to take the cupcakes out of the oven: Strategic time-monitoring, prospective memory and context. *Child Development, 56,* 175–190.

Ceci, S. J., Bronfenbrenner, U., & Baker, J. (1988). Calibration and context in prospective memory. In M. M. Gruneberg, P. Morris, & P. Sykes (Eds.), *Practical aspects of memory* (Vol. 2, pp. 244–262). London: Wiley.

Ceci, S. J., & Leichtman, M. (1992). "I-know-you-know-I-know": Recursive awareness in 3-year-olds. In S. J. Ceci, M. Leichtman, & M. Putnick (Eds.), *Cognitive and social factors in early deception* (pp. 16–25). Hillsdale, NJ: Erlbaum.

Ceci, S. J., & Liker, J. (1986a). Academic versus everyday intelligence: An experimental separation. In R. J. Sternberg & R. K. Wagner (Eds.), *Practical intelligence: Origins of competence in the everyday world* (pp. 119–143). New York: Cambridge University Press.

Ceci, S. J., & Liker, J. (1986b). A day at the races: A study of IQ, expertise, and cognitive complexity. *Journal of Experimental Psychology: General, 115,* 255–266.

Ceci, S. J., & Liker, J. (1988). Stalking the IQ-expertise relation: When the critics go fishing. *Journal of Experimental Psychology: General, 117,* 96–100.

Ceci, S. J., & Roazzi, A. (1994). Conduct and cognition: Postcards from Brazil. In R. Sternberg & R. K. Wagner (Eds.), *Intellectual development* (pp. 26–49). New York: Cambridge University Press.

Ceci, S. J., & Ruiz, A. (1992). Abstractness, transfer and intelligence. In D. Detterman & R. Sternberg (Eds.), *Topics in human intelligence* (pp. 168–191). Norwood, NJ: Ablex.

Ceci, S. J., & Ruiz, A. (1993). The role of context in everyday cognition. In M. Rabinowitz (Ed.), *Applied cognition* (pp. 164–183). New York: Springer-Verlag.

Chi, M. T. H., & Ceci, S. J. (1987). Content knowledge: Its role, representation, and restructuring in memory development. In H. W. Reese (Ed.), *Advances in child development and behavior* (Vol. 20, pp. 91–142). Orlando, FL: Academic Press.

Chi, M. T. H., Hutchinson, J., & Robin, A. (1989). How inferences about novel domain-related concepts can be constrained by structured knowledge. *Merrill Palmer Quarterly, 35,* 27–62.

Detterman, D. K. (1986). Human intelligence is a complex system of separate processes. In R. J. Sternberg & D. Detterman (Eds.), *What is intelligence?* (pp. 57–61). Norwood, NJ: Ablex.

Detterman, D. K. (1992). The case for the prosecution: Transfer as an epiphenomenon. In D. K. Detterman & R. J. Sternberg (Eds.), *Transfer on trial: Intelligence, cognition, and instruction* (pp. 1–24). Norwood, NJ: Ablex.

Elder, G., Hastings, T., & Pavalko, E. (1991, August). *Adult pathways to greater distinction and disappointment.* Paper presented at the Life-History Research Society meetings, Montreal, Quebec, Canada.

Eysenck, H. J. (1989). The biological basis of intelligence. In S. Irvine & J. Berry (Eds.), *Human abilities in cultural context* (pp. 87–104). New York: Cambridge University Press.

Fischbein, S. (1982). IQ and social class. *Intelligence, 4,* 51–63.

Gottfredson, L. S. (1986). Societal consequences of the g factor in employment. *Journal of Vocational Behavior, 29,* 379–410.

Hendrickson, A. E., & Hendrickson, D. E. (1980). The psychophysiology of intelligence. In H. J. Eysenck (Ed.), *A model for intelligence* (pp. 151–228). New York: Springer-Verlag.

Herrnstein, R. J. (1973). *IQ and the meritocracy.* Boston: Little, Brown.

Humphreys, L. (1962). The organization of human abilities. *American Psychologist, 17,* 475–483.

Humphreys, L. (1979). The construct of general intelligence. *Intelligence, 3,* 105–120.

Hunter, J., & Schmidt, F. (1982). Fitting people to jobs: The impact of personnel selection on national productivity. In M. Dunnette & E. Fleishman (Eds.), *Human performance and productivity* (pp. 33–91). Hillsdale, NJ: Erlbaum.

Hunter, J., Schmidt, F., & Rauschenberger, J. (1984). Methodological, statistical, and ethical issues in the study of bias in psychological tests. In C. R. Reynolds & R. T. Brown (Eds.), *Perspectives on bias in mental testing* (pp. 41–97). New York: Plenum.

Jensen, A. R. (1979). g: Outmoded theory or unconquered frontier? *Creative Science Technology, 2,* 16–29.

Jensen, A. R. (1980). *Bias in mental testing.* New York: Free Press.

Jensen, A. R. (1992). Commentary: Vehicles of g. *Psychological Science, 3,* 275–278.

Keil, F. (1984). Mechanisms in cognitive development and the structure of knowledge. In R. Sternberg (Ed.), *Mechanisms in cognitive development* (pp. 81–100). New York: Freeman.

Lehrl, S., & Fischer, B. (1988). The basic parameters of human information processing: Their role in the determination of intelligence. *Personality and Individual Differences, 9,* 883–896.

Lehrl, S., & Fischer, B. (1990). A basic information psychological parameter for the reconstruction of concepts of intelligence. *European Journal of Psychology, 4,* 259–286.

Lickliter, R., & Hellewell, T. B. (1992). Contextual determinants of auditory learning in bobwhite quail embryos and hatchlings. *Developmental Psychobiology, 17,* 17–31.

Marshalek, B., Lohman, D., & Snow, R. (1983). The complexity continuum in the radex and hierarchical models of intelligence. *Intelligence, 7,* 107–127.

Means, M., & Voss, J. (1985). "Star Wars": A developmental study of expert and novice knowledge structures. *Memory & Language, 24,* 746–757.

Nisbett, R. E., Fong, G., Lehman, D., & Cheng, P. (1988). *Teaching reasoning.* Unpublished manuscript, University of Michigan, Ann Arbor.

Pedersen, N. L., Plomin, R., Nesselroade, J., & McClearn, G. E. (1992). A quantitative genetic analysis of cognitive abilities during the second half of the life span. *Psychological Science, 3,* 346–353.

Piaget, J., & Inhelder, B. (1969). *The psychology of the child.* New York: Basic Books.

Plomin, R., & McClearn, G. E. (Eds.). (1993). *Nature, nurture, and psychology.* Washington, DC: American Psychological Association.

Roazzi, A. (1986a). Implicacoes methodologicas na pesquisa transcultural: A influencia do contexto social em tarefas logicas. *Arquivos Brasileiros de Psicologia, 38,* 71–91.

Roazzi, A. (1986b). Social context in psychology. *Ricerche di Psicologia, 4,* 24–45.

Roazzi, A. (1987). Effects of context on cognitive development. In J. F. Cruz, R. A. Goncalves, P. P. (Eds.), *Psicologia e educao: Investigacao e intervencao* (pp. 91–115). Porto: Associacao dos Psicologos Portugueses.

Roazzi, A., & Bryant, P. (1992). Social class, context, and cognitive development. In P. Light & G. Butterworth (Eds.), *Context and cognition: Ways of learning and knowing* (pp. 141–163). London: Harvester Wheatsheaf.

Roazzi, A., Bryant, P., & Schliemann, A. D. (1988, September). *Context effects on children's performance of conservation tasks.* Paper presented at the Annual Conference of the British Psychological Society, Developmental Section, Wales.

Rumelhart, D. (1991, October). *Neuroscience and education.* Paper presented at the Assistant Secretary for Education's Conference on Teaching, Washington, DC.

Schafer, E. W. P. (1987). Neural adaptability: A biological determinant of g-factor intelligence. *Behavioral and Brain Sciences, 10,* 240–241.

Schliemann, A. D., & Carraher, D. W. (1992). Proportional reasoning in and out of school. In P. Light & G. Butterworth (Eds.), *Context and cognition: Ways of learning and knowing.* (pp. 47–73) London: Harvester Wheatsheaf.

Schliemann, A. D., & Magalhaes, V. P. (1990). *Proportional reasoning: From shops, to kitchens, laboratories, and hopefully, schools.* In Proceedings of the XIV International Conference for the Psychology of Mathematics Education, Oaxtepec, Mexico.

Schooler, C. (1988). Social structural effects and experimental situations.: Mutual lessons of cognitive and social science. In K. W. Schaie & C. Schooler (Eds.), *Social structure and aging: Psychological processes* (pp. 162–194). Hillsdale, NJ: Erlbaum.

Siegler, R. S. (1989). Mechanisms of cognitive development. *Annual Reviews of Psychology, 40,* 353–379.

Smith, G. J., & Spear, N. E. (1978). Effects of home environment on withholding behaviors and conditioning in infant and neonatal rats. *Science, 202,* 327–329.

Spearman, C. (1904). General intelligence objectively determined and measured. *American Journal of Psychology, 15,* 206–221.

Staszewski, J. (1989). Exceptional memory: The influence of practice and knowledge on the development of elaborative encoding strategies. In W. Schneider & F. Weinert (Eds.), *Interactions among aptitudes, strategies, and knowledge in cognitive performance* (pp. 145–164). New York: Springer-Verlag.

Sternberg, R. J. (1985). *Beyond IQ: The triarchic theory of intelligence.* New York: Cambridge University Press.

Sternberg, R. (1990). *Competence considered.* New Haven, CT: Yale University Press.

Subtelny, S., & Green, P. B. (1982). *Developmental order: Its origin and regulation.* New York: Alan R. Liss.

Walker, C. H. (1987). Relative importance of domain knowledge and overall aptitude on acquisition of domain-related information. *Cognition and Instruction, 4,* 25–42.

Weiss, V. (1990a). From short term memory capacity toward the EEG resonance code. *Personality and Individual Differences, 10,* 501–508.

Weiss, V. (1990b). The spatial metric of brain underlying the temporal metric of EEG and thought. *Gegenbauers Morphology Jahrb. Leipzig, 136,* 79–87.

10

The Two Sexes and Their Social Systems

Eleanor E. Maccoby

In the mid-1950s, when Ted Newcomb and I set about organizing the third edition of the *Readings in Social Psychology* (Maccoby, Newcomb, & Hartley, 1958), we invited Urie Bronfenbrenner to do a chapter on socialization, asking him to put the issues in a larger context than the usual intrafamilial one. That chapter was in some ways a starting point for the themes that Urie presented in his influential book on the *Ecology of Human Development* (1979). I have had many spirited conversations with Urie, as well as exchanges of letters, before and after that book was published, and I can say with some confidence that the ecology book, even though it occupies a central place in Urie's theorizing, represents only one segment of his larger intellectual agenda. In that book, he placed individual behavior and family functioning in a nested set of sociocultural contexts, something that much needed to be done. But he strives to understand organism–environment interaction in a more comprehensive sense: to understand how an ecological point of view can be integrated with the driving forces of individual growth and development. Effective contexts change with devel-

Parts of the empirical groundwork for this chapter were presented in two previous papers (Maccoby, 1990; Maccoby & Jacklin, 1987); additional documentation will be included in forthcoming work.

opment, not only because individuals at different stages take different things from the same environment, but because they create and select different social networks by which they are then affected. When we consider social environments, we know that individuals are subject to the demands and constraints of significant other persons at every point in the life cycle, but also that individuals exercise their own influence on those who are making these demands and setting these constraints. In other words, the bidirectional perspective is especially important for thinking about social ecology.

What I want to discuss relates to Urie's more comprehensive agenda. I want to consider the social environments that are constructed by, and constructed for, children of the two sexes and, in turn, the way these distinctive social environments shape the interpersonal relationships of male and female persons as they progress through several stages of the life cycle.

Sex, of course, is both a biological and social characteristic. Although hermaphrodites exist, biological sex is almost completely binary; so is *social sex*—that is, the gender label that is given by others to an individual child. In the vast majority of cases, biological and social sex coincide. I suspect it is the very fact that sex is binary that helps to make it so powerful as an organizing dimension for social identity and social interactions. However, the relevance of an individual's sex to that individual's social networks is not a constant through the life course. The relevance of an individual's gender waxes and wanes at different points in development (see also Cairns & Kroll, 1994). And, although we do not have good research evidence on the continuity of sex typing from one period of development to another, I will take it as a given that there is continuity in this sense: The experiences that an individual has as a member of a gender-differentiated social network at one period will have an impact on the way that individual functions within the social networks that are formed at subsequent periods of time.

INFANCY AND TODDLERHOOD

I want to focus now on the succession of social networks within which individuals of the two sexes live their lives as they progress from infancy to mature adulthood. In the first 2 or 3 years of life, the social system of greatest importance to the child is the nuclear family. For many children, it is the only social system within which the child's daily life is enacted at this early time. True, the parents are usually part of several more extensive social systems, but from the standpoint of the child, it is the network of relationships between the child and the parents and siblings that constitute the child's social world. For the majority of children, the network includes both a mother and a father; for a minority, only one parent.

We are accustomed to thinking that the social networks of boys and girls take on a different quality even from the first few months of life. The developmental literature is replete with claims of differential treatment of male and female infants by their parents, or differential responses by children of the two sexes to their parents' socialization efforts. I want to claim that, on the contrary, the social relationships experienced by male and female children within the nuclear family during the first 2 years of life are remarkably similar. Of course, the nuclear family is seldom a gender-neutral structure, if one considers the different roles of the two parents. But from the standpoint of the children, the roles of young boys and girls in the family structure appear to be much the same. We know that boys and girls develop the same kinds of attachments to their parents in early childhood and that their attachments serve the same functions. The child's sex may seem important to the parents, and they may have different expectations regarding the future of a male or female child. But when it comes to day-to-day interactions, they treat children of the two sexes very much alike. The only well-documented differences are that boys are handled somewhat more roughly, and girls are talked to about emotions—their own and others'—more frequently. But parental responsiveness, total amount of interaction with a child, the standards set for the child's behavior, the restrictions and controls imposed, and the modes of discipline—all these aspects of socialization vary considerably from one family to another, but are essentially unrelated to whether a parent is dealing with a young son or daughter. Of course, it is possible that young boys and girls react differentially to the same parental input. But the evidence to date does not reveal any strong or consistent Sex $\times$ Environment interactions of this kind. During infancy and toddlerhood, then, male and female children can be seen as functionally equivalent members of the nuclear family, and we see only pale foreshadowings of the differentiation that will take place in the ensuing years.

CHILDHOOD

Whether the nuclear family continues to be a structure that is gender neutral (from the standpoint of the child's position in it) depends, I think, on how early children are inducted into sex-differentiated work and patterns of deference (Edwards & Whiting, 1988). Whenever young boys are taken by their father to join men in herding large animals, for example, the boys begin to become part of a male social structure; whenever young girls are recruited by their mother into female domestic work or agricultural field work not assigned to boys or whenever girls are taught to defer to and wait on their father and brothers and other older males, the nuclear family becomes a different social structure for male and female children. In modern Western societies, however, this kind of differentiation of boys' and girls' roles within the family is rare. The social positions of boys and girls in the nuclear family are probably somewhat more differentiated than they were in the first 2 years of life, but still are primarily similar.

It is when children become part of the new social structures created by peers that the social experiences of the two sexes truly diverge. The years from age 3 to about age 12 are a crucial, highly active time from the standpoint of gender differentiation. Let me now set out the major themes that seem to me to emerge from the vast literature on boys and girls in this age period:

1. In some cultures, children have many opportunities to spend unstructured time with age-mates; in others, they have very few. The relative influence of peers probably depends on how much unstructured time children spend with their age-mates.
2. When with peers in situations not structured by adults, children tend to segregate themselves by sex, selecting same-sex playmates. In the early preschool years, there is a considerable amount of play in

mixed-sex groups, but by age 5 or 6, gender segregation is strongly in place (Maccoby & Jacklin, 1987).

3. The social structures that emerge in male and female peer groups are different. Male groups tend to be larger and more hierarchical. The modes of interaction occurring in boys' and girls' same-sex groups become progressively differentiated, and the different styles appear to reflect different agendas (see Maccoby, 1990, for summary). Boys are more concerned with competition and dominance, with establishing and protecting turf, and with proving their toughness, and to these ends they are more given to confronting other boys directly, taking risks, issuing or accepting dares, making ego displays, and concealing weakness. Among boys, there is a certain amount of covert sexy (and sexist) talk, as well as the elaboration of homophobic themes (Thorne & Luria, 1986). Girls, though of course concerned with achieving their own individual objectives, are more concerned than boys with maintaining group cohesion and cooperative, mutually supportive relationships. Their friendships are more intimate than those of boys.

4. Boys are more oriented toward their same-sex peers than are girls. In saying this, I do not mean to imply that girls' peer relations are in any sense less important to them than are boys' peer relations to them. I mean rather to imply two things: Boys' groups are more gender differentiating than those of girls, and boys distance themselves more from adults—not only from their nuclear families, but also from teachers and other adults. Boys strongly reject girls and girlish activities and become relatively unresponsive to influence attempts from girls (at least, if other boys are watching). Girls are more gender neutral in their activities and interests, and there is some evidence that they are equally responsive to influence attempts from male and female peers. Boys' stronger peer orientation appears to involve a certain indifference to and distancing from adults (particularly female adults), whereas girls remain oriented toward both adults and female peers. For example, Grant (1985), while observing 6 first-grade classrooms, reported the number of teacher contacts

and peer contacts for each child. In each class, the boys had more contacts with peers than teachers, whereas the pattern for girls was usually the reverse. Thus, the agendas of male peer groups are more incompatible with maintaining a simultaneous orientation to adults than are those of girls.

The age period of 3 to about 12 is unique in many ways. There is no other time of life when gender segregation is so extreme, and the social structures of the two sexes so different, as in middle childhood. Sroufe and colleagues (Sroufe, Bennett, Englund, Urban, & Shulman, 1993) listed the rules that children appear to maintain concerning which kinds of cross-sex contacts are allowable and which are not. For example, contact is acceptable if it is clearly accidental, if a child is acting under instructions from adults, or if a child has recruited a same-sex partner to go along when speaking to a child of the other sex. These rules, which children monitor rigorously among themselves, are not what children observe in their home or among adults in other settings. Children have their own culture. It would seem obvious that the social behavior of male and female children of this age cannot be regarded as merely derivative reflections of the gender arrangements of adult society.

From where then do these distinctive behavior patterns come? It is not possible to present and discuss here the several relevant theories and evidence. My own conclusion is that although we do not understand the etiology very well, what we do know points to a complex causal nexus—including some biological predispositions that differ by sex and have a specifiable time course, some differential social pressures applied by adults to children of the two sexes, and a large component of self-socialization on the basis of gender cognitions, that is, on clusters of attitudes, knowledge, and expectations that make up a gendered self system that has a developmental trajectory. For our present purposes, the main point is that the social structures of middle childhood provide the foundation for those that develop at subsequent points in the life cycle.

So far, I have depicted the nuclear family—and adults more broadly—as playing a rather minor role in the gender differentiation of childhood and have argued that same-sex peer groups are much more powerful. This has not always been so. In many patriarchal societies, men manage and control the life of boys in their groups (witness boys' boarding schools or segregated male living quarters in some preliterate societies). In socialist societies, peer groups may be co-opted by adults to become avenues for socializing children into the communal values of the adult culture (witness Bronfenbrenner's, 1970, report on Russian youth groups in *Two Worlds of Childhood*, and the functioning of the Little Red Soldiers in China). In these two settings, youth groups were usually composed of both boys and girls. In other settings, adult-managed youth groups are gender segregated. But we in modern Western societies have cut youthful peer groups free from adult involvement and influence to an extraordinary degree. The gender differentiation I described above is what happens under conditions of minimal adult involvement, in the context of a larger society with a rapidly changing pattern of sex-role differentiation.

ADOLESCENCE

In adolescence and young adulthood, there is progressive disengagement from the nuclear family and progressive movement toward involvement with opposite-sex peers. In many settings, early cross-sex contexts occur in the context of mixed-sex groups of young people who have not yet explicitly paired off. The rate at which pairing off occurs for youth of the two sexes, of course, depends greatly on the social organization of the society of which the young person is a member. Also, the fact that girls reach sexual maturity at an earlier age than boys is relevant, but more relevant in some societies than in others. In traditional societies, girls were married soon after they reached puberty, often to men considerably older than themselves—men who commanded resources permitting them to support a family. In societies in which marriage was delayed beyond the girl's puberty, various social customs and arrangements were in place to keep the sexes apart; girls were sequestered and chaperoned, and in many parts of the world, fathers and brothers had the responsibility of protecting the girl's virginity until her marriage. Thus, a girl was kept closer to her nuclear family than were boys and young men.

In the modern world, there are progressively fewer restrictions on the social activities of adolescents. What then is happening to the nature of the social networks of which they are a part? In terms of the adolescent's position in the nuclear family, Youniss and Smollar (1985) and Steinberg, Darling, and Fletcher (this volume, chapter 13) have noted that *disengagement* is probably not the right word to use. Rather, what happens is a shift from hierarchical parent–child relationships to more egalitarian ones. Young people continue to live at home even after they have been "emancipated" from parental control to a considerable extent and, in many cases, after they have become sexually active.

The relationships of adolescents with their parents continue to be quite similar for youth of the two sexes, with certain modifications. Youniss and Smollar (1985) noted one respect in which the social relationships are not the same for the two sexes: Fathers seem to distance themselves somewhat from daughters who have reached sexual maturity, whereas this does not happen with sons. In view of the fact that girls, but not boys, are at risk for pregnancy, one might expect that girls would be more closely monitored than boys. The evidence that this is so is, so far, surprisingly weak and contradictory. I am prepared to believe that, in modern Western societies, girls are probably still monitored somewhat more closely than their male counterparts. On the whole, however, it would appear that, in modern Western societies, the nuclear family continues to be a social structure that functions in largely the same way for male and female adolescents.

From about age 12 till the time they leave home, adolescents spend progressively less time in joint activities with their parents and more with their peers. In adolescence, young people continue to congregate largely with same-sex peers and only gradually build up relationships with the opposite sex (Larson & Richards, 1991). Interaction with same-sex peers shows considerable continuity with the styles developed in middle childhood: Interactions among males in their peer groups and between pairs of male friends continue to be qualitatively different from those among adolescent girls, and one sees considerable continuity with the patterns that were apparent in middle childhood. What changes is that there is progressively greater variation among the peer groups of a given sex. Young people find and congregate with others with similar interests and goals. Individuals become known as members of distinctive groups or cliques: the "jocks," the "brains," and the "nerds" (Brown, 1990; Steinberg et al., this volume, chapter 13). There are youth subcultures in which boys lose respect among their peers if they show softness or romantic interest toward girls; instead, they gain points through sexual exploits that do not involve intimacy. (See Anderson's, 1991, book, *Streetwise*, and recent revelations concerning the Spur Posse in the White, middle-class community of Lakewood, CA; "Where 'Boys Will Be Boys,' " 1993.) In other youth subcultures, a young man's special relationship with his girlfriend is understood and respected, even though in other respects the male group may endorse exploitative attitudes toward women. In other words, membership in certain male subcultures is incompatible with forming an intimate, reciprocal, egalitarian relationship with a girl, but this is by no means true for all (probably not for most) male peer groups. Membership in a female subculture is almost always compatible with the formation of an intimate relationship with a male.

When youths of the two sexes encounter each other in adolescence and begin the exploration toward romantic bonds, we can see the process as the formation of a new kind of social structure. Many young people are understandably wary at first, and not altogether comfortable with the other sex. But as members of male–female pairs continue to spend time together, their relationships become progressively more intimate, and I believe that the majority of boys establish relationships with their female partner that are much more intimate and reciprocal—less guarded—than those they have had with male friends. For girls, cross-sex relationships can also achieve deep intimacy, but for both sexes, the intimacy is of a qualitatively different kind than they have known before. Of course, the sexual element in cross-sex relationships is of enormous importance, but the requirements of forming a smooth cross-sex relationship go much beyond negotiating sexuality.

What is also necessary is to find a way to integrate the two different interaction styles that the new partners have brought with them from their childhood history of interaction with same-sex partners. Girls' reciprocal, socially supportive style may put them at something of a disadvantage in dealing with boys' more direct, confrontational style, but couples vary greatly with respect to who is dominant in the relationship. Students of family relationships have found it very difficult to identify which member of a couple has more power. The relationship that any individual couple will construct, of course, depends on a myriad of factors: the temperament and physical attractiveness of each person; each person's history of earlier failed or rewarding cross-sex relationships; and the images, scripts, and messages each person has absorbed from television and other culturally available sources.

In addition to these factors, I think that there are two kinds of interpersonal experiences at earlier points in the life cycle that have an impact. Children construct internal representations of their parents' relationship, and even though these representations probably have little relevance to the same-sex interactions of middle childhood, they no doubt do come into play as couples construct their new cross-sex relationships. I suggest that the nature of cross-sex relationships will be strongly affected by the models presented in the nuclear family of each member of the youthful pair, concerning how adult male and female partners can and do relate to one another. Up until now, I have been arguing that because children of the two sexes are exposed to pretty much the same models of family interaction in childhood, they ought not to be affected differentially by the environment provided in the nuclear family environment. And to some extent, I think that even with respect to relationships with the other gender, the nuclear family continues to be a fairly gender-neutral source of influence. That is, experiencing in childhood a model of harmonious interparental relationships can foster the potential of both young men and women to construct similar relationships with their own romantic partners. In addition, however, there is the question, do young men and women adopt primarily the stance of their same-sex parent? The implication would be that the son of an abusive father will become abusive toward his wife or girlfriend or that the young woman who has watched her mother submit to a dominant husband will be disposed to do the same. It is an easy and common assumption that these continuities prevail, but I think we have not considered sufficiently the possible influence of the cross-sex parent. Both boys and girls can learn nurturance and intimacy from observing whichever parent most displays these qualities and nagging or abusiveness from either parent. I think we should question the assumption that boys and girls identify mainly with the same-sex parent with respect to these matters.

More gender differentiating, I believe, are each person's experiences within the same-sex peer groups of childhood. Peer group experience is probably more uniform within sexes, and more different between sexes, than is nuclear family history. Not only is it true that certain interpersonal styles developed and consolidated within segregated peer groups carry over into cross-sex adult relationships but probably also that some of the attitudes and beliefs concerning the other sex that pervade childhood peer groups are carried over as well. In any case, there is enough variation in both nuclear family experience and peer group experience to produce an almost infinite variety in the nature of the interpersonal solutions that are arrived at by different couples.

CHILDLESS YOUNG ADULTHOOD

The social structure formed by a young, adult, heterosexual couple who live together and do not yet have children can be an extraordinarily powerful one. In Western middle-class societies, such couples spend almost all of their nonworking time together, either at home or in the company of other couples. Although they retain connections with their two sets of parents—perhaps somewhat closer connections with the woman's parents—these connections with the earlier generation fade into the background and have little impact on daily life.

The same-sex social groupings that prevailed before the couple came together become relatively weak. In the words of the old song, "wedding bells break up old gangs," and the bachelor party the night before the wedding is meant to symbolize the end of the carefree days of male companionship and the beginning of a new spousal way of life. In the modern world, both men and women, of course, spend a great deal of time at work outside of the home during the childless young adult period. Working relationships sometimes develop into friendships and become a work-related social network that offers social support to its members. These networks are largely same-sex groupings, either because the workplace itself is gender segregated or because men and women who work together usually maintain a somewhat guarded stance toward one another if they do not want their work relationship to develop overtones of sexual attraction.

Whether or not childless young adults are part of a same-sex work group, the pair bond is their primary social structure in modern societies. The roles of the two persons within this structure need not be greatly differentiated, although many couples do adopt a gender-related division of labor within the household. But joint activities, interests, and goals are the predominant mode of this period. Within this framework of relative undifferentiation, however, there do persist differences in interactive style, which carry forward the distinctions seen in childhood and adolescence.

PARENTHOOD

Some couples feel that the birth of a child brings them closer together: They now have a new joint agenda, a new major enterprise that calls for new kinds of cooperation. However, the usual experience is that even for couples who attempt to maintain equal roles and responsibilities, the birth of a child seems to force a greater division of labor—a greater differentiation of the roles of the two adults—than had been the case before childbearing began. This pull toward differentiation seems to be based on at least four major forces:

1. *The biology of reproduction.* Probably the primary biological distinction between the sexes in mammalian species is that females gestate fetuses and give birth to infants whereas males do not. There has been considerable debate concerning whether this basic biological fact implies any sort of difference between mothers and fathers in terms of the power of parental instincts or the readiness to bond with infants and respond sensitively to them. Lactation adds a further biological element: When mothers breast-feed, it provides a

unique form of interaction with infants that no doubt contributes to the intimacy of the mother–infant bond. Work with nonhuman primates certainly points to a biological element in the more nurturant behavior of females toward the young, but it also indicates that males have a potential for competent nurturance of the young, which can be called into play under exceptional circumstances.

2. *Human culture and social expectations.* Every known society assigns more child-rearing responsibility to women than to men, and girls everywhere grow up with the expectation that they will carry this responsibility if they have children. If we look at the parental roles of the two sexes cross-culturally, we see that there is a great deal more variation among men than among women in terms of their involvement with infants: Women are primary caregivers for infants and young children in every known society. Modern experience shows us that men can become equally competent, committed caregivers for infants and toddlers, but in most societies they seldom do so. It is as though cultures respond to the universal biological role of women in childbearing and lactation by setting up universal cultural arrangements that place women and children together, not only during infancy, but beyond. Thus, societies reinforce women's primary role in childbirth and early nurturance with a network of cultural expectations and demands. Societies have usually assigned different kinds of parenting responsibilities to fathers and to mothers, but expectations for paternal behavior have been changing radically over the past two centuries in the modern industrialized world (see Griswold's 1993 book: *Fatherhood in America*). Paternal roles are cross-culturally highly variable and currently very much in flux.

3. *The economics of family support.* The practicalities of earning a living create pressures for differentiation of maternal and paternal roles. Even for couples in which both have been working full-time, the men usually earn more than the women, often considerably more. When children are born, it usually becomes necessary for one parent to cut back on work time to care for young children (unless, of course, the family can afford a full-time nanny). It makes eco-

nomic sense that it be the lesser earner who stops working or goes to part-time work. Also, complications of pregnancy sometimes dictate that a mother cut back on work hours before a child is born, and time is needed to recover from childbirth. All these factors imply that childbearing will take a greater toll on a woman's out-of-home work life than a man's.

4. *Male and female interaction styles.* A fourth element contributes to a differentiation of parenting functions: the interaction styles that males and females developed at earlier points in their developmental history. As we all know, mothers usually become the managers in the family, setting up time schedules for children's baths and sleep and for meals, household chores, recreation, and out-of-home child care. When both parents are home, fathers often play with the children, but they usually leave to the mothers the job of directing the child through the routines of the day. This would suggest that mothers are, on average, more directive than fathers, and from one standpoint this is true. Certainly the old "instrumental–expressive" distinction with which Parsons (1955) sought to characterize paternal and maternal roles does not come close to fitting the realities of family life. Fathers are at least as warm and affectionate with their children as mothers are (Collins & Russell, 1991). Yet observations of mothers and fathers in family situations show that fathers use more imperatives when dealing with the children, whereas mothers use more suggestions and inductions. Interchanges between mothers and children are more reciprocal and less hierarchical.

Youniss and Smollar (1985), in their study of several large samples of adolescents, give a clear description of the way mothers and fathers relate to their adolescents, noting how different these relationships are:

> The modal relation with fathers appears to be an extension of the structure of unilateral constraint that was in place at the end of childhood. . . . Fathers seem to have a narrow view toward their sons and daughters, thinking of them as potential adults and caring most about their progress toward productive adulthood. As a result, fa-

thers share only a small part of adolescents' here and now interests. . . . Mothers, no less than fathers, hold adolescents to performance standards that refer ultimately to impending adulthood. . . .
But this aspect of the relationship is only one aspect of its full character and it is communicated in a different style than is common in
the paternal relationship. . . . Mothers maintain regular contact with
their sons and daughters. . . . Mothers engage themselves in adolescents' interests, whatever they might be. Mothers closely monitor
their sons and daughters. . . . Mothers do not solely take the role as
authorities, but serve as confidantes who share experiences—with
the end result being empathy. Mutuality enters the relationship. . . .
The mark of the mother–adolescent relationship is conversation for
its own sake—the kind of conversation in which ideas and feelings
are exchanged, not instructional episodes that are designed to influence or persuade. (pp. 89–91)

To my mind, the parallels between the way parents behave with their
children and the way they behaved in their peer groups when they were
children are unmistakable. At each of these life stages, it is the females who
seem to work from a dual agenda: to maintain a norm of reciprocity and
positive affect while at the same time working to achieve the instrumental objectives of the moment. For males, the instrumental objective is foremost, and the authority aspect of the parental role is a natural extension
of the male–male confrontational, didactic interaction style. Mothers are
more likely to listen to a child's point of view, and children, for their part,
seem to feel more free to negotiate with their mother. It is not surprising,
then, that Youniss and Smollar have found that, by the time children become adolescents, they feel closer to their mother and feel that their mother
knows them better, even though they love and respect their two parents
equally. In keeping with this literature, we (Buchanan, Maccoby, & Dornbusch, 1992), too, in our studies of divorcing families, have found that
adolescents report feeling closer to custodial mothers than to custodial fathers.

It is not my intention to suggest that one of these parental styles is
better for children than the other. My intuition is that children of both

sexes benefit from being exposed to both styles. But true to the Bronfenbrenner tradition, what I am trying to do is to focus our attention on a neglected aspect of the social ecology of childhood. I think that, in trying to understand adult sex roles and adult gender differentiation, we have relied too heavily on an individual-differences perspective, thinking about gender as an aspect of the individual personality rooted in individuals' interactive histories within their nuclear families. We need to expand our horizons by giving greater attention to categorical membership, with its roots in both the gender-segregated peer groups of childhood and the categorical perceptions and conceptions that govern so much of our thought and behavior.

No doubt, many of you will already have identified a weakness in the argument of this chapter to date. It is too static. Elder (this volume, chapter 4) has alerted us to the importance of historical time: Large societal events and climates have an impact on the way social contexts such as families and peer groups affect children's development. Furthermore, biological time matters, too: Societal events have a different impact depending on the age of a child at the time they occur. My guess is that the forces of segregation in childhood are so powerful that they are not likely to be cancelled out by large societal events, though they may be modified. (A question: What is the gender composition of the street gangs of homeless children in Brazil? Do the pressures of hunger and homelessness take precedence and make gender irrelevant to social relationships in such groups?) Considering adolescents, it must surely be the case that the widespread availability of contraceptives and the revolution in sexual mores that has taken place in the last several decades in Western societies have profoundly changed the processes of mate selection and cross-sex relationships in young adulthood. We do not know what implications this has for any continuities growing out of the events of the middle-childhood period. It is to be hoped that the next phases of gender research will give us some answers.

Much of what I have said about the sequence of gendered social systems may seem obvious—that is, may be part of the growing consensus among developmental scientists. However, I hope I may have issued at least a few invitations to controversy. If I have, this too would be in the Bronfenbrenner tradition.

REFERENCES

Anderson, E. (1991). *Streetwise.* Chicago: University of Chicago Press.

Bronfenbrenner, U. (1958). Socialization and social class through time and space. In E. E. Maccoby, T. M. Newcomb, & E. L. Hartley (Eds.), *Readings in social psychology* (3rd ed., pp. 400–424). New York: Holt.

Bronfenbrenner, U. (1970). *Two worlds of childhood: U.S. and U.S.S.R.* New York: Russell Sage Foundation.

Bronfenbrenner, U. (1979). *The ecology of human development.* Cambridge, MA: Harvard University Press.

Brown, B. B. (1990). Peer groups and peer cultures. In S. S. Feldman & G. R. Elliott (Eds.), *At the threshold: The developing adolescent* (pp. 171–196). Cambridge, MA: Harvard University Press.

Buchanan, C. M., Maccoby, E. E., & Dornbusch, S. M. (1992). Adolescents and their families after divorce: Three residential arrangements compared. *Journal of Research on Adolescence, 2,* 261–291.

Cairns, R. B., & Kroll, A. B. (1994). A developmental perspective on gender differences and similarities. In M. Rutter & D. Hay (Eds.), *Development through life: A handbook for clinicians.* Boston: Blackwell Scientific Publications.

Collins, W. A., & Russell, G. (1991). Mother–child and father–child relationships in middle childhood and adolescence: A developmental analysis. *Developmental Review, 11,* 99–136.

Edwards, C. P., & Whiting, B. B. (1988). *Children of different worlds.* Cambridge, MA: Harvard University Press.

Grant, L. (1985). Gender, status, classroom interaction and children's socialization in elementary school. In Wilkinson & Marrett (Eds.), *Gender influences in classroom interaction.* New York: Academic Press.

Griswold, R. L. (1993). *Fatherhood in America.* New York: Basic Books.

Larson, R., & Richards, M. H. (1991). Daily companionship in late childhood and early adolescence: Changing developmental contexts. *Child Development, 62,* 284–300.

Maccoby, E. E. (1990). Gender and relationships: A developmental account. *American Psychologist, 45,* 513–520.

Maccoby, E. E., & Jacklin, C. N. (1987). Gender segregation in childhood. In H. Reese (Ed.), *Advances in child behavior and development* (Vol. 20, pp. 239–287). New York: Academic Press.

Maccoby, E. E., Newcomb, T. M., & Hartley, E. L. (Eds.).(1958). *Readings in social psychology* (3rd ed.). New York: Holt.

Parsons, T. (1955). Family structure and the socialization of the child. In T. Parsons & R. F. Bales (Eds.), *Family socialization and interaction process* (pp. 35–131). Glencoe, IL: Free Press.

Sroufe, L. A., Bennett, C., Englund, M., Urban, J., & Shulman, S. (1993). The significance of gender boundaries in preadolescence: Contemporary correlates and antecedents of boundary violation and maintenance. *Child Development, 64,* 455–466.

Thorne, B., & Luria, Z. (1986). Sexuality and gender in children's daily worlds. *Social Problems, 33,* 176–190.

Where "Boys Will Be Boys" and Adults Are Bewildered. (1993, March 29). *The New York Times.*

Youniss, J., & Smollar, J. (1985). *Adolescent relations with others, fathers, and friends.* Chicago: University of Chicago Press.

11

Gender, Contexts, and Turning Points in Adults' Lives

John A. Clausen

In *The Ecology of Human Development*, Urie Bronfenbrenner (1979) elaborated many types and aspects of context that have developmental consequences. He focused primarily on the early years, because that was both where his own work was concentrated and where most of the research data on contextual effects were to be found. I concentrate here on some effects in the adult years, particularly as the two genders are differentiated.

Urie and I have been close friends for nearly 60 years. It will come as no surprise that my own thinking has been much influenced by our discussions over the years and by some of our mutual experiences. When I first met Urie at Cornell, I was an economics major in my junior year, and he was a freshman. He became a psychologist, and I a sociologist. When I entered graduate school 3 years later, we took one course in common that influenced both of us: Lauriston Sharp's introductory anthropology. This then-young assistant professor gave us an appreciation of the power of culture, and through course readings, he introduced us to a concept that has come to link our interests even as it links the individual and society, that is, the concept of *role*. Role expectations are a part of culture, within what Urie calls the *macrosystem*, and they influence other contextual systems in one way or another. They become shapers of personality all along the life course. Moreover, role expectations change with time; thus, they are part of the historical context, too.

Drawing on the data of the Berkeley longitudinal studies, I examine gender's influence on various role expectations and experiences in the lives of men and women studied over the 60-year period of the research and touch on effects on their children in the more recent past. For the past 33 years, I have had the opportunity to work with the data of the longitudinal studies of Berkeley's Institute of Human Development. Three distinct studies with somewhat different objectives were begun between 1928 and 1932. The subjects were followed up with intensive interviews on three occasions—1958, 1970, and 1982—with increased merging of the studies beginning in the 1960s. Supplementary data from questionnaires were obtained on several occasions, most recently in 1990–1991. Parents, spouses, and offspring have been included in some data collection. In 1991, I secured data from more than 350 of the offspring, now mostly in their 30s and 40s. Much of the story of our study members has been compressed in the 600 pages of *American Lives: Looking Back at the Children of the Great Depression* (Clausen, 1993), but far more remains to be told.

Since the completion of *American Lives*, I have been reading, thinking, and doing a number of analyses focusing on personality change over the life course and on ways that individuals look back at their own life. If one examines individual personality profiles as they change from one age period to another, there is very little difference in relative personality stability or change between boys and girls, men and women. There is considerable continuity for both genders in the childhood years and from early to middle adolescence (Block, 1971; Clausen & Jones, 1995; Haan, Millsap, & Hartka, 1986), substantial change from adolescence to the early adult years, and then increasing stability in the middle decades of life. However, the respects in which men and women change are quite different, as are their perceptions of the turning points and sources of satisfaction in their lives.

The life course is to a considerable degree a personal construction, but it entails selective processes and a sifting and sorting of persons into and out of various contexts. There is a danger of thinking of contexts only as they impinge on a person after that person has entered a particular contextual niche or relationship. Society exists as a shifting structure of groups and of positions to be occupied, a structure that is differentiated along a number of dimensions: socioeconomic, ethnic, age level, gender, and lifestyle. That differentiation has its effects from the prenatal period on, but one's position is initially largely assigned by the family's position. As Maccoby observes in this volume, chapter 10, in adolescence, the sifting and sorting of young people lead to differentiation on the basis of interests and goals. In adolescence, personal choice becomes a major factor in determining where one will fit, or seek to fit, in the larger social system. The individual's purposive choices may be rewarded or frustrated. External, often chance, events and circumstances exert their influence on the developing person. The interaction of persons in contexts with varied features—expectations, demands, rewards, and stresses—at any period may strengthen commitments or lead to changes in patterns of association and to sequences of action that disrupt previous behavioral tendencies. The analysis of such sequences is enormously complex, because we must confront continuing contributions from all of the systems that Urie Bronfenbrenner has labeled as part of the ecological order. Opportunities and obstacles are encountered in each of these systems, as Rutter, Champion, Quinton, Maughan, and Pickles documented in this volume, chapter 3. Some systems reinforce the effects of others; some have countervailing effects. We get some sense of these processes through intensive retrospective interviewing or through the use of longitudinal data, but it is obviously impossible to monitor anyone's behavior closely enough to build up more than a clinical summary for the individual subject, let alone for an adequate sample of persons.

For an understanding of interpretive and decision processes, we must rely, then, on the person's own report of his or her life: his or her perceptions of the influences on it as these have been experienced. Certainly such reports are subject to retrospective bias and even to falsification, but if we are fortunate enough to have data that include the perceptions of others, we can analyze these reconstructions of the past.

TRANSITIONS AND TURNING POINTS

Perhaps the most fruitful way to study lives in context would be to focus on the transitions that most people make in the course of their development.[1] From home to school, from school to work, from singlehood to marriage or autonomous adulthood, to parenthood, to retirement, and to widowhood—these transitions offer a framework for analyzing the life course. Unfortunately, this perspective was not yet developed when the early longitudinal studies started, and we do not have the kind of systematic data on preparation for each transition and the adaptations entailed that one would like to have. We can go after such data retrospectively, but some transitions are too deeply buried in the dustbin of memories to be recovered. However, for many people, certain transitions stand out in the memory; they were for one reason or another far more salient than others. Some will be seen as having constituted turning points in the life course. Turning points tend to have considerable salience for the individual, though they are not always recognized as such when they occur. However, other periods have salience as well, whether they were part of a transition or simply part of a continuing period of great satisfaction or intense dissatisfaction. Often, it is a particular role or relationship that is most important; almost always, contextual influences from the past have led to expectations and interpretations that help to explain the salience of the events or circumstances that are focused on by our study members.

My interest is not in turning points as such so much as in achieving an understanding of the developing person in a changing society over time. The various settings that constitute the mesosystem in childhood and adolescence are enormously multiplied in the adult years. Their impacts on development depend to some degree on whether contexts are chosen or assigned and on whether they are opportunities for meaningful contribu-

---

[1]This approach is illustrated in Lowenthal, Thurnher, and Chiriboga (1975).

tions to the well-being of self and others or serve as means of escape from other settings and relationships that are unrewarding. There may be limits to the number and diversity of such settings that one can participate in without damage to the major responsibilities that adult life entails. A wide variety of roles may be enriching in certain respects, as Bronfenbrenner suggests it to be in childhood (see also Coser, 1975; Moen, Dempster-McClain, & Williams, 1989), but too diverse a variety may also lead to the attenuation of one's sense of identity.

Turning Point as a Concept

The meaning of the term *turning point* when applied to a human life seems at first mention to be obvious. The movie that bore that name told the story of a would-be ballet star who chose to marry and have a baby rather than pushing on to become the premiere danseuse. Until that point, she had striven since childhood toward a clearly perceived goal, one that would require a superbly disciplined body, many years of training, a certain flair, and constant devotion to the pursuit of excellence. Suddenly, that trajectory was aborted; marriage and motherhood removed her from the company, and it was her friend who became the star. However, subjective perceptions of discontinuity do not necessarily entail a change in direction. As I illustrate, discontinuities often do prove to be turning points in the life course, but sometimes continuity *accentuated* is seen as a turning point.

In the past decade, there has been a substantial growth of interest among psychologists in what has been called the *narrative approach,* in which one examines people's stories of their own lives (Cohler, 1982; Gergen & Gergen, 1987; McAdams, 1985, 1989; Sarbin, 1986). The Gergens observed that "a self-narrative may be viewed as the individual's account of the relationship among self-relevant events across time, or, in brief, his or her self-history" (Gergen & Gergen, 1987, p. 124). There seems to be general agreement that we tend to formulate our lives in terms that make them coherent, at least to ourselves. The life story then reflects our sense of who we are. Indeed, McAdams (1989) stated that "identity *is* a life story—an internalized narrative integration of past, present, and anticipated future which provides lives with a sense of unity and purpose (p.

161)." If this is so, perceived turning points become a means of bridging continuities and discontinuities in a way that makes sense to the individual.

Securing Data on Turning Points

In the Berkeley studies, the question was first asked as part of a life review section of a structured interview when our respondents were in their mid-50s or early 60s. The respondents were to have before them a life chart in which they had plotted on a year-by-year basis their basic life satisfaction from early childhood to the present. They were asked, "As you look it over, can you pick out any point or points along your life course that you would call 'turning points'—where your life *really* took a *different* direction?" They were then asked to talk about the turning points—the change that had occurred and what had caused it—starting with the most important turning point. Because of time constraints, the interviewer often did not use the life chart, and sometimes the chart had not been completed. The respondents were then confronted with the request to review their whole life and, in an instant, to pick out their most important turning point. It quickly became apparent that we could say very little about the relative importance of turning points from the order in which they were reported. These first efforts became a point of departure for later questioning.

Let me illustrate the varied ways in which a single respondent viewed the stimulus term *turning point,* drawing on a fairly long interchange between a female study member, age 55, and an interviewer, who probed appropriately:

"My first turning point was when I became a teenager. I'd always been very obedient and so on, and then I just went off in the other direction. That was fun! I enjoyed being a teenager. I sort of, you might say, overcame my shyness. That was one turning point. When I became a teacher, that was a turning point, certainly. And getting married and having my children."

"Was becoming a teacher something you had not expected to do?"

"I didn't know what I wanted to do. I went off to college . . . and then I got a job as a playground director and I discovered children and I realized that that's what I wanted, so then I went into it. I was probably about

22, and then I had about two more years of college to go through to get my credential. I knew I didn't want to do any kind of office work. I wanted it to be active, outdoors, and so on. Be a lady forest ranger or something like that. Becoming a teacher made me very fulfilled; it still does. It was very gratifying."

"Then you mentioned marriage. How unexpected was that?"

"Unexpected? I don't know quite what you mean by that."

"The intent of the question was to get at turning points that were unexpected changes in direction rather than transitions which were part of the plan."

"You mean, was I looking for somebody to get married to? Well, I was expecting to get married sometime, yes. And I certainly wanted to get married, and I did. It came at just the right time."

She went on to say that her children were both planned, so having children was not unexpected, but that did not make having children any less a turning point.

This respondent reacted to the stimulus *turning point* in several different frameworks: (a) the acquisition of a new sense of who she was (overcoming shyness), (b) deciding on an occupational goal, (c) making commitments to expected roles that involved new activities and new discoveries, and (d) her sense of becoming fulfilled as an adult. It is immediately clear that one's life does not have to take a different direction for a person to feel that a turning point has occurred. But one must have a feeling that new meanings have been acquired, whether or not life experiences are much changed. Note that in this instance all of the reported turning points were self-initiated choices that led to increased life satisfaction.

In retrospect, it was not realistic to attempt to secure an adequate review of turning points in a single structured interview that dealt with almost all aspects of the respondent's current situation in late middle adulthood. There was less probing than was required and no attempt to assess why events previously reported as crucial influences, events that the interviewer might have interpreted as major turning points, were often not mentioned. Subsequently, I selected a random subsample of 60 subjects living within 50 miles of Berkeley for further questioning about aspects of the life history—among them, turning points. This time, the life chart was used, and the study member had a chance to review the highs and lows charted earlier or, if there had not been a life chart, to produce one before discussing turning points. Very few respondents reported no turning points in their life. Most reported a number, and indeed that number could almost always be increased if the interviewer probed and asked about sharp turns in the life chart itself. The more people review their past history, the greater the number of occasions in which they recognize that there was a change in the way they viewed themselves, in their opportunities, or in their relationships—a change that made a difference.

Collecting adequate data on turning points requires much more intensive interviewing than even my life history interview. Developing adequate codes to handle such data is an equally daunting task. I am still working on this task, but for the present, I have to rely largely on the very inadequate classifications that were made on the basis of early interview returns. My basic classification was along two sets of categories: (a) the major role affected (e.g., educational, occupational, marital, or parental) or the kind of event that caused the turning point (e.g., illness, death of a family member, a geographical move, or a religious conversion); (b) the nature and extent of change, ranging from expected transitions to wholly unanticipated life crises, but also with categories for changes in self-conception, life satisfaction, or interests and goals. In the coding of the extent of change for the full sample, a single turning point—the one deemed most important by the coder—was selected. Reliabilities were relatively poor when several turning points were mentioned, but regardless of which one was chosen, we got an idea of the degree to which there was a sharp turn in the life course.

FINDINGS ON TURNING POINTS

More than half of the so-called "turning points" were role transitions, and of these, more than two thirds were expected transitions, such as entering an occupation, marrying, or becoming a parent—transitions that entailed

Table 1

Initial Responses to Question on Turning Points and Responses After Reinterview of Subsample

Type of turning point	Original frequencies				Reinterview	
	Full sample		Subsample		Subsample	
	M	F	M	F	M	F
Occupational event or circumstance	47	24	48	20	66	50
Marriage	37	35	32	33	56	57
Military service	36	0	30	0	34	0
College or educational experience	23	9	27	13	31	21
Childhood event	17	15	22	15	22	11
Divorce	16	14	18	10	28	14
Parenthood	10	13	5	7	28	35
Own illness or injury	9	7	13	7	19	18
Death of family member	7	12	8	10	9	32
Psychological crisis	5	7	7	7	9	11
Move to another community	NA	NA	NA	NA	9	36
Illness of spouse	NA	NA	NA	NA	0	11
Quest for identity	NA	NA	NA	NA	6	14
Departure of children	NA	NA	NA	NA	0	12
Other	21	38	20	45	28	49
n	124	144	32	28	32	28

Note. M = male, F = female, NA = category not used in initial coding.

some reorientation of one's priorities and activities, but no substantial change from the direction in which one had been heading. Table 1 gives the frequency of mentions by role or event in the structured interview for the full sample, for the subsample later reinterviewed, and then for the subsample on the life history interview. In recoding the subsample, several categories were added, categories that proved to be more relevant to women's lives than to men's. The increased frequency of mention in most categories is a clear indication of how a sharper focus and more probing can make a difference, though relative saliences do not change markedly except for parenthood and for deaths and moves in the case of women.

It is obvious that the two major role sets of adulthood—work and family—were the contexts in which turning points were seen as most salient. What seemed at first surprising was that women mentioned the occupational sphere almost as often as men. A closer look is required.

Occupational Turning Points

For men, the two most frequent occupational turning points entailed a reevaluation of goals (often early in the career) and a change of employers or of fields because of greater opportunities or a feeling of being trapped. A fourth of the men who reported an occupational turning point said that health problems or the bankruptcy or curtailment of jobs by their employer forced a shift. Of those who did not report an occupational turning point, a third mentioned that there had been a *decision point,* in which they decided not to make a change when offered an opportunity by a different employer.

Consider the rather full statement by a man with very high occupational attainment:

> Going back to school after I returned from the army was a definite turning point because I went into a different profession. There were a lot of job-related turning points. One was a move to the East Coast from the West Coast. It was a definite turning point. The job change was a turning point. Two other job changes were turning points, major turning points.
>
> I found out that I was in a line of work that I wasn't going to do for a living. I went from chemistry to chemical engineering [when he returned to college].

Asked about the move from the West Coast to the East Coast, he stated the following:

> It was an executive of the company who told me that I could either move to the East Coast or, as he put it, "I could freeze my ass in that little place in California 'til I died and never get promoted." It was

a high executive of the company that wanted me to move East. I didn't want to move. I turned the job down as a matter of fact because I didn't want to move out of California. He flew me to New York and had this big executive explain the situation. Either you did it or else. I think I told him, "Hell, nobody ever explained that to me before—I guess I better take the job." It was a quantum leap in responsibility and in stature. It exposed me for the first time to the higher management level in the corporation which I had been insulated from. It was a major step in my professional development.

Moving into the higher levels of management was frequently mentioned as a major turning point by men who had been highly competent from adolescence on, whereas feeling trapped in their lower level jobs was far more frequently mentioned by men who had been seen in adolescence as less self-confident, less responsible, and less intellectually involved.

Very few of the occupational turning points reported by men were said to have entailed any sort of crisis, even though the men's past histories and even their recent clinical interviews had sometimes revealed acute crises associated with loss of jobs or problems in self-employment. Such crises were far more frequent among the men who had been less competent in adolescence.

Self-employment often brought problems that, had not been anticipated:

> I bought a restaurant and I had it for five years. It was the biggest turning point of my life. . . . I had no idea of the hours and demands that it takes from a person, seven days a week. The whole family participated.

This man went on to indicate that, before he was able to sell the restaurant, the family was in severe turmoil, and he had become an alcoholic. Other men whose alcoholism had blighted their early careers often simply reported that they changed jobs to enhance their opportunities. Elsewhere, however, they had acknowledged being fired.

Although more than half the men said that their sense of identity had come primarily from their occupations, they tended to discuss turning points in terms of career history and success. Very few of them talked about the effect of the turning point on their sense of who and what they were, except for some professionals who talked about how central the duties and dominant values of the occupation had become to their sense of identity.

Whereas men's occupational turning points very largely dealt with their achievements or their efforts to achieve success, the women's discussion of their occupational turning points indicated that the meaning derived as much from a new sense of worth and identity as from the activities engaged in or the level of attainment achieved. For women, the major occupational turning point was their entrance into the labor force after marriage and having borne children. Roughly two thirds of those who reported an occupational point mentioned this event, which usually took place in their late 30s or their 40s. Most women had worked before marriage, and many indicated that their original entry into the labor force after finishing school had also been a significant turning point. Women who had been in the labor force through much of their adult life more often mentioned changes because of health problems or a search for better opportunities in much the same way that men did.

Typical of many women's feelings when they entered the labor force are the following quotes: "Graduating from high school and going to business school and getting a job in San Francisco. I felt like I was a person on my own." "When I started to work. It was different from just being a child. I became an adult" (this from a woman who had been very dependent on her parents).

More often, the sense of greater autonomy came in the women's middle years. Almost all of the women had married and raised families. They felt mature, but not entirely fulfilled. Many of these women saw their entrance into the labor force as a turning point that affirmed a sense of autonomy and of self-worth. As one woman put it, "[without that] I think I would have been nothing but a bored housewife, and frantically cleaning the house. I would have been an entirely different person." Another said, "It was sort of an ego trip to think I could go back to work . . . and it was just totally amazing to me that I could do this after being home. I had been a scout leader and PTA president and such things, but never on this grandiose a scale." The grandiose scale was becoming president of a state association in her field of work.

Marriage and Family

Both the interviewers and I were at first surprised to find marriage mentioned as a turning point when it was, after all, an anticipated event. The respondents who said, in essence: "How could one's life not be changed by marrying?" were, of course, right! A major role transition inevitably changes the pattern of one's life, whether it be starting kindergarten, beginning to teach, marrying, or retiring, and so it can be considered a kind of turning point. If we examine the consequences of the major transitions in our lives in terms of the way that our days are spent—the persons who become important to us, the values we come to hold, the commitments we make to ourselves and to others, our general level of contentment and satisfaction, and our sense of who we are—it is obvious that major role transitions are places where lives undergo change. Change is often growth, but sometimes it is a matter of becoming trapped or defeated or of escaping from an impossible situation.

Marriage usually entailed a much more profound change for women, particularly if they had been employed for a few years, than it did for men. Almost all of the women had expected to marry; it was the prime goal of women born in the 1920s. Nevertheless, women more often mentioned unexpected aspects of the marriage than did men, perhaps precisely because they had expectations that were not fulfilled. Thus, one woman commented,

> I had always thought that I would quit working when I got married and do all the neat things that women do when they get married, and because my husband had children from a former marriage, I was not able to do that.

Finding that one had married the wrong man, living with in-laws, unexpectedly getting involved in business with their husbands, or finding themselves tied down in caring for their husband's relatives were other unanticipated aspects of some marriages. More often, of course, the marriage was a turning point because it represented a dream come true, at least for a time.

A happy marriage after one that entailed a tension-laden existence marked a special kind of turning point, often more important than the divorce that terminated the initial marriage. "My second marriage was a turning point. I had been married before; it wasn't a positive experience. . . . With Ed, our life together has been just great."

The great majority of the women saw their marriage and family as the chief source of their identity. Men were as likely as women to mention marriage as a turning point, but less likely than women to see their identity lodged primarily in their marriage and family than were women. Nevertheless, many men attested to the crucial role that their wife had played in their life. "When I married Norma, that was the biggest one [turning point]. She's been the really good steadying influence in my life, provided me with wonderful companionship. . . . She gave me ambition to try new things." In general, however, men were less likely to elaborate on the respects in which marriage was a turning point. It was simply mentioned.

In addition to the gender difference in how marriage was seen as a turning point by the study members, there has been a substantial generational change in how marriage is regarded by the daughters of our study members. In 1991, I sent questionnaires to roughly 500 of the offspring, now in their 30s or 40s, and more than 350 responded. A questionnaire is a most inadequate way to get at turning points, but I left a half page to get a crude indication of what they saw as turning points in their life. Again, work and family roles were the contexts of most turning points, but they were viewed somewhat differently.

Women's expectations for marriage and family have changed vastly since our study members were of marrying age—then, their early 20s for the most part. Marriage now comes later and appears to represent a different kind of turning point for many of the offspring of our original study members. Asked about her anticipations of marriage, a 20-year-old reported the following in 1970: "I would live with someone and have a baby, but I would never actually get officially married."

"Why?" she was asked.

She described a friend's experience, recounted to her earlier that very day:

> She's been living with this guy for about three years. And they just got married and she said everything has been horrible ever since. She wanted to get married and so they just got married and now she says they're hardly even friends any more. Because it changed everything. It makes things sort of an obligation than you're doing it because you really want to. It's also security. The security thing. People say, "Well, I'm going to get married." So they know they've got this person forever, you know. But you shouldn't have to say that—this has to be forever. Because people change. And you can't change that. And if it turns out you don't love each other, then you don't. Then you don't have to stay together. You can just leave.

In an era when most young adults live together for a time before marriage, the changes the ceremony brings are much more subtle than they were a generation earlier. The women's movement coupled with much greater sexual license has made marriage itself seem more constricting, yet the ritual commitment actually changes daily routines far less than in the past. Instead of "How could marriage *not* be a turning point?" as several of the original study members asked, the question for many of their offspring seems to be, "Can I marry and not change anything?" Obviously, there are still many for whom marriage is both a major positive turning point and a long-term commitment, but consider this group of responses to my questionnaire request for a description of turning points:

> I knew I could get divorced when I realized my share of the equity in our home would provide a financial cushion until I got a better job—had been married 13 years.

> I realized I'd been living my boyfriend's life instead of my own and started pursuing acting seriously. I don't need a man; I need my life!

> The death of my first husband was a turning point in my life. I was forced to grow up quickly as I was 29 years old and the mother

of two young children. This experience put me in a position to find out who I really was—not my father's daughter, not my husband's wife, not my children's mother—but me. I found out I was OK!

A woman twice married and twice divorced commented with the following:

> Parenting began a process of looking inward. Watching my children face difficulties required me to deal with my own. Recovering from alcoholism and bulimia four years ago significantly changed my life and significantly expanded my visions and options. It also caused me to identify some of the problems in my family of origin.

It is clear that many of the offspring entered marriage with considerable reservations and with the feeling that they could get out of the marriage whether or not they had children. The discussion of their plans for marriage and that of their turning points shows a considerable emphasis on autonomy and finding out who they are. No longer are they content to have their life contingent on the life of their husband, as were their mothers. They express satisfaction when they feel that they have taken control of their life, with or without a husband or a divorce. A detailed analysis of turning points in intimate relationships is contained in Vaughan's *Uncoupling: Turning Points in Intimate Relationships* (1986).

For mothers and daughters, as contrasted with the men in the study, there is far more often an indication that their sense of identity is involved in their turning points. Of the daughters, fully 15% indicated a quest for identity as the essence of at least one of their turning points. The comparable figure for male offspring was 3%. The expectations that exist for women have changed markedly, but they have not made it easier for the daughters of our subjects to know who they are. Men tended to talk about identity and maturity far more when they discussed military experience as a turning point.

Other Types of Turning Points

Strauss (1959) referred to turning points as "critical incidents that occur to force a person to recognize that 'I am not the same person as I was, as I used to be'" (p. 93). Strauss presented a typology of turning points having to do with identity. I shall not attempt to summarize them, but would note that some come about through gradual taking over of a new way of life and some through *transforming incidents*. Transforming incidents often entail playing an important role that one did not expect to be able to handle, and then handling it well. In our data, women more often than men report such incidents. The converse, failing in the performance of a role one thought one could handle with ease, must surely also constitute a turning point. Men qualify more often here, though the data are less adequate.[2] We far more often hear of the positive changes than of the negative ones.

In telling one's life story, the negative experiences are reported largely when they are overcome or when they are ended, as in divorce after a marriage that has gone seriously awry. No one phrased the latter kind of situation more poignantly than the woman who reported the following:

> When my first marriage fell apart, that was the greatest turning point. A turning point because this is when the question came as to who am I? What am I? What am I going to do? Am I anybody or just someone's wife and mother and not anybody in my own right? I think that was the biggest turning point.

That turning point was the product of a long struggle before she had been able to leave her rejecting, abusive, alcoholic husband (whom she had loved), and it took her several more years to become really reconciled to the fact that she had left and would not return.

Women's roles, as defined for our study members born in the 1920s, made their social matrix largely contingent on their husband's life and decisions. Nowhere was this more clearly evident than in the reported importance of geographical moves as a turning point. Among our original study members, women were four times as likely to mention moving to another community as a turning point as were men. Nearly two fifths of the women indicated that, at some point in their life, they had felt up-

---

[2] I earlier found strong evidence of this gender difference in the responses of men and women to a spouse's mental illness (Clausen, 1983, p. 200).

rooted when their husband was reassigned or decided to move to another community. Women who were in the labor force had to give up their own job. Women had to leave their friends and find a new support group, whereas their husbands were more readily incorporated into a relational network that their employment provided. Moreover, in general, women's friendships were far more important in their lives than were men's. And it was the wives who had to contend with their children's problems in making new friends in a new community at the same time that they themselves struggled to find their way. Bronfenbrenner's hypotheses relating to the importance of links between mesosystems nicely serve to explain why family moves resulting from a husband's job transfer are more traumatic for the wife than for the husband.

One of the relatively few men who mentioned a move as a turning point in the 1982 follow-up interview (described earlier) later revealed that there had been three moves that had constituted turning points for him. The first took him out of the study early in his junior year in high school; more important, it took him out of close friendships and into a less attractive neighborhood and a worse school in another community, where his father had gotten a job. A better job in yet a more distant community a year later further complicated the son's life. The second critical move came when he was advised to move from a management job in which he felt there was little future to take a position with a company on the East Coast. There his career took off, and eventually he became president of first one, then another, corporation. But the second presidency entailed another move of more than a thousand miles, and his wife balked. They maintained their home, and he commuted back and forth on weekends for 2 years, a period of much stress and discomfort.

I report the above example in some detail because it illustrates the complexity of analyzing turning points. Each turning point is multifaceted, both in terms of causes and consequences. Having one's father employed during a period of severe depression is good, but being uprooted from friendships and school is not. A move that enhances one's occupational status may be good, but the costs to one's marital and family relationships may be great. The costs and benefits of particular changes of context or particular features of context are not easily disentangled; what seems to be a cost at one period may at times be seen as a benefit later on, and vice versa. Here is an aspect of the ecology of human development that needs much research.

Geographical moves appear to be less of a problem for the daughters of our study members than for their mothers. Such moves are now mentioned as often by male offspring as by female offspring—slightly less than a fifth having indicated this as a significant turning point. Also, we find that more often there are positive aspects to geographical moves as reported by women than as reported by their mothers. To a much greater extent, the daughters have moved to achieve their own goals. Thus, we have a historical change for both genders, but a much sharper change for the women.

Both occupationally and maritally, there are far more disruptions in the lives of the offspring of our study members than were experienced by their parents. To a large extent, they are self-induced disruptions. There is less commitment to career lines, even when they are reported to be satisfactory, and there is obviously less commitment to an enduring marriage. The offspring have far fewer children, and they less often mention parenthood as a turning point in their lives; however, both men and women seem to have considerable commitment to their children.

The basic expectations for their life on the part of the sons and daughters of our study members are more similar to each other than were the expectations of their parents. The cultural context has changed more for women, granting more autonomy and more opportunity in many spheres. Like their parents, those from nonconflicted homes and supportive parents seem to have somewhat fewer turning points that are crises than do their peers from homes beset with conflict and parents who were inattentive, but the life stories that they tell suggest more inner turmoil than was apparent in their parents, who experienced the Great Depression of the 1930s. Both mesosystems and the macrosystem are involved.

Bandura (1982) wrote on the potential importance of chance encounters for life paths. Chance encounters are indeed mentioned by both men and women as leading to the choices they made. Typical examples reported are meeting in strange or unusual circumstances the person who would become one's husband or wife; falling into a job opportunity by accidentally running into the manager looking for someone just like you; or, for several women, entering the labor force and encountering a manager who saw great potential and encouraged its development.

Of course, many of the chance encounters are related to patterns of association. I want to stress strongly that all along the way, choices are made by the person and by those with whom the person associates. As alternative lifestyles multiply, such choices may become more fateful. Some of our study members became heavily dependent on alcohol. Their children were exposed to other drugs as well. If one or both parents had a problem with alcohol, a fourth of their sons from whom we secured data had a serious or significant problem with alcohol or other drugs. If neither parent had a problem with alcohol, less than half as many had a significant or serious problem, and only one sixth as many had a serious problem (i.e., one that essentially incapacitated them). The differences were even greater among daughters. If a parent had a problem with alcohol, fully a third of the daughters reported a significant or serious problem with alcohol or drugs. If neither parent had a problem, 6% of the daughters reported that they themselves had a significant or serious problem. Here we have an effect that is undoubtedly contextual, but that often came about because of seeking outside the home different kinds of encounters, whether as an escape or as a search for new meanings.

The shifting of patterns of association in the course of development into the adult years, the pushes and pulls of particular niches in the ecological order, has not been extensively studied. In a recent book, Sampson and Laub (1993) noted how changing patterns of association and commitment were associated with turning points (i.e., end points) in criminal careers. Critically important were commitments to a wife and family and to a job.

In *The Ecology of Human Development*, Urie Bronfenbrenner's focus of concern was on those contextual arrangements that lead to desirable developmental outcomes—to enhanced cognitive skills and emotional well-being. Desirable outcomes in the adult years share many of the same features—increasing skills, increasing understanding of self and others, making choices based on mindfulness, and increasing ability to attain a balance in one's activities and relationships that will produce a sense of accomplishment and satisfaction with those activities and relationships. Real satisfaction in a relationship demands that there be a large measure of mutual satisfaction.

A major problem with my classification of the roles or circumstances entailed in turning points is that, in itself, it does not permit study of the ways in which roles and contexts interact. Men whose heavy job involvement and efforts to succeed in their careers led them to neglect their families more often see their major turning point as the early attainment of occupational success and less often mention marriage than their peers who were not so heavily involved in their work. The pressure to meet demands of the workplace and family needs was the area of major role conflict for men. It was often a major source of dissatisfaction for women, especially in the period when there were small children and the husband was just getting established in his career. The existence of such a problem at some period of the marriage was reported by three fifths of our male respondents and half the female respondents, and serious consequences for the marriages were reported by roughly a fifth of the men (one third of those who said they had been unavailable) and slightly fewer women. Some marriages were terminated; some wives became alcoholic; and some wives merely complained and tried to cope, but many harbored deep resentments many years later. In instances of couples married more than once, the husbands often reported on their first marriage whereas wives reported on their current marriage, and the higher proportion of men reporting unavailability and serious consequences largely reflected terminated marriages.

Reported turning points seldom revealed such problems, but questions about life satisfaction and family problems over the years brought them to light. We attempted to assess life satisfaction at different periods both by using the life charts on which general level of life satisfaction was plotted from year to year and by asking about chief sources of satisfaction and dissatisfaction in each decade. We also asked about job satisfaction and marital satisfaction at each follow-up. To present our findings in any detail is beyond the scope of this chapter, but two generalizations emerge from the data: (a) Sources of primary satisfaction and dissatisfaction often change greatly from one decade to the next as relationships themselves change and stresses are encountered in major roles; and (b) general life satisfaction is closely linked to satisfaction in the several roles that are most salient for the person, and developments in each of these roles tend to affect performance in and satisfaction with other salient roles.

The number of attributes and circumstances that influence life satisfaction in the adult years is large, and their interrelationships are extraordinarily complex. With a relatively small number of study members, it is not feasible to enter more than four or five variables in a multiple regression, and different combinations of variables produce substantial differences in the magnitude and statistical significance of the contribution of any variable, though a few are always significant. The strongest correlates of our study members' general life satisfaction are marital happiness (highest for women) and the life satisfaction of one's spouse (highest for men). Health has been significant in the years beyond 50, but did not show up earlier, because so few study members were in poor health in the early and middle adult years. Women's satisfaction with their children significantly modifies their general life satisfaction, but this relationship is not found for men. On the other hand, a man's reported satisfaction with his job while still working or with his career, once retired, contributes to the level of his general life satisfaction.

Certain intriguing correlations are found at the zero-order level. A woman's reported life satisfaction was significantly lower if her husband reported watching television many hours a week. A woman's reported life satisfaction was higher in the middle and later years if her husband was well satisfied with his job or, after retirement, his career. Such correlations are, of course, not indications of causal relationships. They reflect personality tendencies and the sifting and sorting of roles, relationships, and activities.

To understand the origins of turning points and how they are defined, we must obtain the person's own story. However, people cannot always tell us what beliefs and experiences led to seeing one kind of change as a turning point, while another that appears to the outsider even more important goes unreported. Asking a person about pathways taken and the course of particular roles is a necessary condition for understanding how that person makes sense of his or her life, but it may not permit us to assess the full meaning or consequences of turning points or the contextual influences involved. To the extent that we have a reasonably full history, alternative interpretations are possible.

I emphasize again that reported turning points tell us not so much how lives have been shaped, but how they have been experienced. It is only in the context of a personal history that we can understand the peculiar importance of escape from a destructive relationship through a geographical move or a sense of peace in a good marriage after years of conflict and a divorce.

SUMMARY

Over the years, Urie Bronfenbrenner has called for research on children in their everyday settings, with attention to proximal processes and the varied contextual effects that exist within the setting and from outside the immediate setting. We need the same kind of attention to the assessment of influences on functioning in adult roles, influences within the role set (the various others with whom one interacts in a given position) and from outside. Urie's basic premise is that both the attributes of the person and those of the setting must be taken into account in trying to explain behavior. What the person brings to new settings and roles by virtue of constitutional makeup and past experiences may be as important as the characterization of the role or setting, particularly in the years beyond childhood. In reviewing lives of persons who have been studied longitudinally over a number of decades, one is struck by the importance of realistic expectations and relevant preparation for major role transitions. Urie has documented how features of the role or setting may increase the likelihood of relevant learning. We have many leads for studying the definitional process as individuals enter new settings and make major role transitions.

In the adult years, there is much scope for choosing the roles and settings in which the person will invest major energies, though the choices are nevertheless strongly influenced by economic conditions, the person's knowledge of available options, and cultural or subcultural norms. Institutional and cultural norms may change even as economic conditions do, and technological advances may induce widespread changes in all ecological systems. As a consequence, reassessment of past choices is almost inevitable.

Three roles seem to be preeminent in people's assessment of their life satisfaction: the occupational, marital, and parental roles. Entry into these roles and changes within them are seen by most men and women as the principal turning points in their life, and the quality of their experiences within these roles makes the greatest contribution to their reported life satisfaction.

REFERENCES

Bandura, A. (1982). The psychology of chance encounters and life paths. *American Psychologist, 37*, 747–755.

Block, J. (with Haan, N.). (1971). *Lives through time.* Berkeley, CA: Bancroft.

Bronfenbrenner, U. (1979). *The ecology of human development.* Cambridge, MA: Harvard University Press.

Clausen, J. A. (1983). Sex roles, marital roles and response to mental disorder. In J. Greenley (Ed.), *Research in community and mental health* (Vol. 3). Greenwich, CT: JAI Press.

Clausen, J. A. (1993). *American lives: Looking back at the children of the Great Depression.* New York: Free Press.

Clausen, J. A., & Jones, C. (1995). *Competence and personality change across the life span.* Manuscript submitted for publication.

Cohler, B. J. (1982). Personal narrative and the life course. In P. Baltes & O. G. Brim (Eds.), *Life span development and behavior* (Vol. 4, pp. 205–241). New York: Academic Press.

Coser, R. L. (1975). The complexity of roles as a seedbed of individual autonomy. In L. A. Coser (Ed.), *The idea of social structure: Papers in honor of Robert Merton* (pp. 237–264). New York: Harcourt Brace Jovanovich.

Gergen, K. J., & Gergen, M. M. (1987). The self in temporal perspective. In R. P. Abeles (Ed.), *Life-span perspectives and social psychology* (pp. 121–138). Hillsdale, NJ: Erlbaum.

Haan, N., Millsap, R., & Hartka, E. (1986). As time goes by: Change and stability in personality over fifty years. *Psychology and Aging, 1,* 220–232.

Lowenthal, M. F., Thurnher, M., & Chiriboga, D. (1975). *Four stages of life.* San Francisco: Jossey-Bass.

McAdams, D. P. (1985). *Power, intimacy and the life story: Personalized inquiries into identity.* Homewood, NJ: Dorsey.

McAdams, D. P. (1989). The development of a narrative identity. In D. M. Buss & N. Cantor (Eds.), *Personality psychology: Recent trends and emerging directions* (pp. 160–174). New York: Springer-Verlag.

Moen, P., Dempster-McClain, D., & Williams, R. M., Jr. (1989). Social integration and longevity: An event history analysis of women's roles and resilience. *American Sociological Review, 54,* 635–647.

Sampson, R. J., & Laub, J. H. (1993). *Crime in the making: Pathways and turning points through life.* Cambridge, MA: Harvard University Press.

Sarbin, T. R. (1986). The narrative as the root metaphor for psychology. In T. R. Sarbin (Ed.), *Narrative psychology: The storied nature of human conduct* (pp. 3–21). New York: Praeger.

Strauss, A. (1959). *Mirrors and masks: The search for identity.* Glencoe, IL: Free Press.

Vaughan, D. (1986). *Uncoupling: Turning points in intimate relationships.* New York: Oxford University Press.

PART FOUR

The Importance of Process

The Importance of Process

Glen H. Elder, Jr.

U rie Bronfenbrenner's concept of social development has always linked the individual to his or her environment, a point very nicely made by the Cairnses in their epigraph to chapter 12, "Social Ecology Over Time and Space." Over half a century ago, Urie asserted that social development "applies not only to the individual but to the social organization of which he is a part" (Bronfenbrenner, 1943, p. 363). This conceptual orientation had much in common at the time with the culture and personality school of anthropology and with sociological assessments of personality and social structure. Although the 1940s psychology of social development had yet to take this perspective seriously, times have surely changed in this respect, owing in large measure to Urie's intellectual leadership.

Also recognized in this early work so well described by the Cairnses is Bronfenbrenner's recognition that a person–context model is not sufficient; it must also address the challenges of delineating and understanding *process*, especially proximal processes. Social development is expressed through the interplay of developing persons in changing environments. As stated by Urie nearly five decades later, the "process–person–context model . . . permits analysis of variations in developmental processes and outcomes as a joint function of the characteristics of the environment and of the person" (Bronfenbrenner, 1989, p. 197). We might amend this statement by adding the word *changing* to the environment and person. Change in the social organization of people can lead to personal change, and the latter, when aggregated, may change the social organization itself. The linking process is reciprocal.

Reciprocal interactive processes of this kind seem basic to an understanding of social development, and yet they have seldom been studied satisfactorily. More often than not, static, cross-sectional measures of the environment are considered sufficient as an index of environmental influences on a behavioral trajectory. In longitudinal studies over 10 to 20 years, a single measure of family social class is commonly regarded as sufficient in assessing the environment's effect. Brooks-Gunn and her colleagues (see chapter 14) would also question the common tendency to ignore economic influences and variations over time. Bronfenbrenner (1989) proposed the concept of *chronosystem* to encompass the evolving interconnected nature of the person, environment, and proximal processes over time. This addition gives temporality its proper place in the bioecology of human development.

The three chapters in this part of the volume address basic elements of Bronfenbrenner's analytical design: process–person–context–time. They do so by giving special attention to nested contexts and explanatory processes. The Cairnses have delineated a multilevel concept of the environment in their research project, from social interactions to social networks, linked networks, and the cultural–ecological–economic context. This is coupled with an integrated processual view of the environment and individual, as expressed in the notion that peers change over the childhood and adolescent years, even though the network or peer culture may remain very much the same.

One of the major directions of developmentally relevant research today involves the investigation of multilevel influences as nested environments. In their respective chapters, Steinberg, Darling, and Fletcher and Brooks-Gunn, with their associates, investigate (among other issues) the effects of neighborhood on child behavior by identifying strategic linking and compositional processes. Steinberg et al. make the important point that parental integration into the neighborhood matters in shaping family influences, but how it matters depends on knowing something about the parenting behavior of the children's parents. The impact of authoritative parenting is particularly strong if it depicts the socialization regime of both one's own parents and one's friends' parents. Brooks-Gunn finds that neighborhood effects depend in large measure on the mix of people who live in the area. The presence of high-status neighbors strengthens the impact of middle-class White parents on children's educational achievement. Both chapters have important observations to make about race–ethnic variations in social influences.

These chapters, like all research initiatives, are steps along a journey of unfinished business. The Cairnses leave us with a challenge that joins attention to the chronosystem and the process by which one generation is succeeded by another. Steinberg et al. and Brooks-Gunn stress the complex task of understanding how geographical and functional communities influence the developmental course of children. In all cases, we must attend to the constantly changing social and physical environment of children, their parents, and their grandparents.

REFERENCES

Bronfenbrenner, U. (1943). A constant frame of reference for sociometric research. *Sociometry, 6,* 363–397.

Bronfenbrenner, U. (1989). Ecological systems theory. In R. Vasta (Ed.), *Six theories of child development: Revised formulations and current issues* (pp. 187–250). Greenwich, CT: JAI Press.

12

Social Ecology Over Time and Space

Robert B. Cairns and Beverley D. Cairns

He believed, and no experience, he knew, would ever make him disbelieve, that one of the great lives of his time had unfolded itself quietly in that little college town.

Wolfe, *Look Homeward, Angel*

Social development applies not only to the individual but to the social organization of which he is a part. Variations occur not only in the social status of a particular person within the group, but also in the structure of the group itself—that is, in the frequency, strength, pattern, and basis of the interrelationships which bind the group together and give it distinctive character. Social status and structure are of course interdependent, but attention must be given to both of these variables if the process of social development is to be properly understood.

(Bronfenbrenner, 1943, p. 363)

This chapter was written to honor the intellectual contributions and personal influence of Urie Bronfenbrenner. The opening quotation expresses how we value his friendship and mentorship.

I n lectures and writing, Urie Bronfenbrenner often identifies an over-looked paper, person, or idea to make insightful points about the present. By example, he reminds us that certain contributions are simply so insightful that they cannot be overlooked. If rediscovered, they demand to be cited with appropriate credit. In that spirit, it seems appropriate to begin by commenting on a remarkable series of articles that was first published 50 years ago (Bronfenbrenner, 1943, 1944a, 1944b). In his first scientific publications, Urie Bronfenbrenner succinctly expressed many of the key ideas basic to the development of modern social ecology.

The need for an integrated developmental science to understand social ontogeny has been recognized for over a century. The vision has become increasingly clear from the contributions of Baldwin (1897), Mead (1934), Bronfenbrenner (1979), and Magnusson (1988) in human social behavior, and Schneirla (1966) and Kuo (1967) in nonhuman comparative study. However, the pragmatics of the new science have not been as easily achieved as the vision. The methods that are required call for inventiveness, creativity, and an enormous investment in careful, laborious, and detailed analysis. It has been easier to adopt the vision than to invent the methods.

This chapter offers some comments on the progress that has been made and the prospects for the future. But it first seems appropriate to take a second look at some of the ideas that were expressed 50 years ago and the technical advances that were achieved in the early work of Urie Bronfenbrenner.

RETROSPECTION: AN OVERVIEW AND CRITIQUE

At the beginning of the first article in the series, Bronfenbrenner (1943) specifies why the social development of individuals cannot be divorced from the social networks in which they are embedded. Virtually all contemporary discussions now acknowledge the integrative nature of social development and adopt the perspective that influences without and within simultaneously affect individual development. Bronfenbrenner's emphasis on the role of social ecology has helped change the face of modern social science. Yet even modern practitioners still have a way to go to catch up with the early science that the young Bronfenbrenner envisioned. There remain today serious gaps in the integration across levels. For the most part, investigators of communities and neighborhoods continue to live in different worlds than investigators of peer groups and social networks, and researchers of individual development still have a hard time reaching beyond the dyad and the family.

There is also the problem of time and timing. In the course of development, individuals inevitably grow, mature, and change. In the same time frame, changes occur in their societies, their communities, their social networks, their families, and their personal relationships. The secrets of social development require the researcher to track these simultaneous developmental changes in persons and social contexts and to determine the interrelations among them.

Overview

Within the articles, Bronfenbrenner (1943, 1944a, 1944b) argued that the questions of social development demand techniques to deal objectively with the measurement, design, and analysis of social groups. Techniques must be created to identify those units that lie beyond the individual, and procedures must be invented to understand the links that exist between observations of these social units over time.

The main theme of the first Bronfenbrenner article (1943), "A Constant Frame of Reference for Sociometric Research," is the need to establish more adequate measures of social groups, to study their properties and their link to the social development of individuals over time. Accordingly, sociometric methods must be extended to include objective mathematical and statistical guides on how to assess social status and coherence and how to track individuals, groups, and their relations to each other over time. In this regard, Bronfenbrenner (1943) observed that the applications of sociometry to that time had been limited to the following:

> the study of status and structure within single social groups viewed
> at a given point in time. . . . The question of change in social status

and structure has been treated principally from the point of view of cross-sectional rather than longitudinal studies. (p. 366)

Without the methods for objective placement of individuals at two time points, sociometric models were necessarily frozen to a snapshot diagram. Hence, the major task of the first article was to solve the statistical issues encountered in determining the probability that an individual was central, average, or peripheral in the social network and how this information on status could be used to study changes over time. A probability analysis, independent of group size and composition, could provide the "constant frame of reference." This article is still admirable in terms of its insights and clarity, and it should be required reading for any investigator in the 1990s who aspires to study sociometric status and social structure.

The second article in this trilogy was entitled, "Part II: Experiment and Inference." It applied the previously described method (i.e., the constant frame of reference) to the "longitudinal study of sociometric status, structure, and development in groups of varying size" (Bronfenbrenner, 1944a, p. 40). The subjects were an entire University of Michigan laboratory elementary school from prekindergarten through the sixth grade, over an academic year. Although Bronfenbrenner adopted standard sociometric questions for the most part, he accentuated the positive and eliminated the negative, as he has done throughout his career. The reasons offered for this modification of common sociometric practice are worthy of note:

> It will be noted that the questions are all phrased positively; that is, the children were not asked to name those whom they would dislike as companions. Despite the fact that they might contribute valuable information concerning the degree and character of social rejection, negative questions were avoided because of their possible effect, by calling attention to the less-favored children in each group, of fostering discrimination and thus causing even more severe social maladjustment. (Bronfenbrenner, 1944a, p. 43)

In the results, we find 24 carefully framed generalizations, including 3 on the nature of social group status (e.g., a distinction between rejected and neglected children) and 4 on the structure of children's social groups (e.g., the nature of gender, age segregation, and group coherence). Among other things, Bronfenbrenner (1944a) concluded that the "classroom groups of older children show greater social solidarity than younger age groups," that in social groups the "sex cleavage becomes very pronounced" as children enter middle and late childhood, and "all of the above developmental trends are interdependent" (p. 74). If this sounds familiar, it should be. This is virtually exactly what Maccoby (this volume, chapter 10) and others (e.g., Cairns & Kroll, 1994; Cairns, Perrin, & Cairns, 1985) have observed in their work on the social groups of children.

To ensure that readers do not miss the point, Bronfenbrenner ended the article with the following summation:

> In sum, the proper evaluation of social status and structure requires the envisagement both of the individual and the group as developing organic units. Piecemeal analysis, fixed in time and space, of isolated aspects is insufficient and even misleading, for the elements of social status and structure are interdependent, organized into complex patterns, and subject both to random and lawful variation. (Bronfenbrenner, 1944a, p. 75)

The third article in this series is a brief methodological note entitled "The Graphic Presentation of Sociometric Data" (Bronfenbrenner, 1944b). One feature of the article is its presentation of a refinement of the sociometric diagram that includes statistical information about status and placement. In sheer appearance, it anticipates the basic Bronfenbrennerian social ecological diagram. The original is reproduced as Figure 1. The center circle represents statistically significant "stardom"; the outer circle represents statistically significant neglect or rejection. The lines that cross the circles indicate links across levels in the social organization, a point that might be generalized to the problems of mediation in social ecology. The article (1944b) also offers a closely reasoned argument for the placement of the lines; namely, the probability that a given individual will be selected beyond chance and the probability that a given individual will be omitted, on the outer fringes, or overnominated, on the inner fringes.

Critique

There is a complementary relationship between Lewin's (1935) topological psychology and Bronfenbrenner's social ecology, which goes beyond their preference for using circles to illustrate people and environments. The models share a concern with the configuration of social forces that

SOCIOGRAM   Grade III

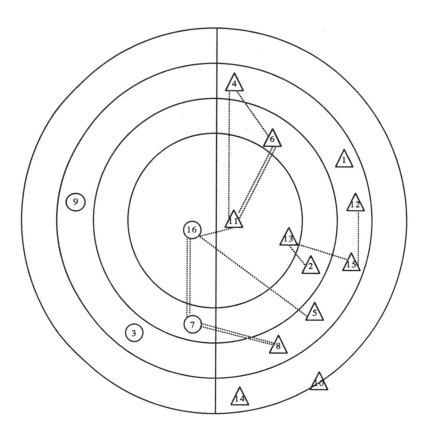

Girls	4
Boys	12
Total	16
Mutuals	13
Isolates	1

Chance likelihood of falling --

within innermost circle	.02 or less
within second circle	.50
outside second circle	.50
outside third circle	.02 or less

operate together and serve as immediate controls for action. As a corollary, they focus on the need for any coherent account of individual functioning and raise doubts about the wisdom of aggregating willy-nilly across persons in the computation of basic statistical descriptions. In Bronfenbrenner's early work, this concern with social action was correlated with a focus on social structure, the individual's placement in it, and the systematic empirical and statistical analysis of individual persons and individual structures. However, Bronfenbrenner's embryonic social ecology provided a significant advance beyond Lewinian dynamic psychology on two basic counts:

1. Bronfenbrenner brought the Lewinian life space into the real world. The article took as a given that there was a pragmatic need to go beyond the person's phenomenology to confront the real world of interactions, relationships, and contexts. Actions then lie at the adaptive interaction between the person and the environment.

2. In addition, all three articles explicitly add the dimension of time for persons and for contexts. Most of the methods and statistics at that time were explicitly designed to get rid of time and developmental change. They still are. One can get rid of development statistically, by standard scores, correlations, covariance, and regression analyses; or experimentally, by the age-controlled selection of sub-

Figure 1

Sociogram of a third grade class redrawn from the original figure in Bronfenbrenner (1944b, Figure C, p. 287). The circles represent females and the triangles, boys. Numbers within the circles/triangles refer to individuals in the third-grade class. The broken lines show constellations of mutual choices over three sets of choices (luncheon, schoolwork, movies); not all choices are shown in the original diagram "since to depict all of these choices would produce a hopelessly confusing diagram. . . . [The concentric circles] delineate differential levels of chance selection [such that] children in the innermost circles [received] a number of choices so great as to be statistically significant (i.e., occurring by chance only two or fewer times out of a hundred). . . . [Similarly] children receiving a number of choices so small as to be statistically significant [in terms of omissions] appear on the outermost right of the target, with isolates shown on the extreme periphery. . . . The second circle designates the 50% or expected value, about which the majority of the subjects are clustered" (Bronfenbrenner, 1944b, p. 288).

jects or matched-control comparison groups. And once it is omitted empirically, it could be omitted theoretically because the developmental variance has been eliminated (Cairns, 1986; Cairns & Valsiner, 1984).

The dilemma of development is illustrated by the omission of time in the classic concentric circle space diagram of social ecology. The different units (circles) of analysis—the person, the family, the social network, the community, the society, and the culture—describe different rates of change. To add time–space to the ecological diagram, one could add a new dimension to each concentric circle. To illustrate these phenomena in a "developmentally sensitive" diagram, the circles should be capable of zooming in or zooming out. Changes occur normally in one's self, in one's friends and families, and in one's society at different rates, yet this everyday experience engenders something akin to methodological and theoretical chaos for conventional models. One shortcoming of modern statistics and research design is that normal changes in persons and social systems overburden most analytical systems.

There is continuity in the development of the science, along with "irregularity in direction and intensity" (Bronfenbrenner, 1944a, p. 74). In 1994 as in 1944, one of the major tasks that confronts students of social development is to figure out how to get persons, social groups, and contexts that are changing over time at different rates into the same system.

SPACE, TIME, AND SOCIAL DEVELOPMENT: THREE EMPIRICAL ILLUSTRATIONS

The remainder of the chapter outlines the scope of the problem that remains and illustrates some steps that are being made toward its solution. The illustrations represent three different levels of the ecological diagram. Accordingly, focus is on the following: (a) how changes at the individual level are linked to development, genetics, and social interactions over time; (b) how changes at the social group level affect and are affected by the individual actions of children and adolescents; and (c) how changes at the societal level and intergenerational level affect social behavior. This coverage is selective rather than exhaustive, in that the illustrations are limited to domains of antisocial, aggressive, and violent actions. In brief, the rest of chapter illustrates some pitfalls and solutions that we have encountered in efforts to incorporate time into the circles of social ecology.

The Individual: Genes, Social Constraints, and Aggression

The proposition that social behaviors may be partitioned into components of nature or nurture has endured for more than a century. At least part of the contemporary debate stems from the fact that different levels of analysis are used in addressing the matter. At one level, the focus has been on the identification of the proximal developmental–genetic mechanisms of influence (Scott, 1977). At another level, the concern has been with the psychometric partitioning of sources of variance that contribute to behavioral characteristics in a specifiable population (Plomin, DeFries, & Loehlin, 1977). The two levels of analyses appear to aspire to a common goal—namely, the understanding of gene–behavior interrelations—but they differ in methods, generate different analyses, and, unhappily, use different conceptual definitions for some of the same terms. Although the assumption that genetic and environmental factors are separate and additive has proved to be productive in the psychometric tradition, it encounters difficulties when social phenomena are conceived as dynamic, reversible, and embedded in the social and cultural matrix.

The results of recent programs to manipulate genetic background experimentally—by selection for aggressive behavior in mice and other non-human mammals—challenge commonly accepted assumptions on the relations among genes, development, neurobiology, and social organization. The challenge to intuition is that a new framework has emerged in which genetic factors cannot be divorced from their proximal controls, developmental functions, and experiential contexts. Rather than complicating the picture, an inclusive developmental perspective clarifies it.

The dissection of the genetic contributors to social behavior has proved to be equally subtle and complex. The first major modern research effort to selectively breed mice for aggressive behavior was initiated by Lagerspetz in the early 1960s. Lagerspetz began with the establishment of aggressive lines of mice through selective breeding, then analyzed for behavioral and physiological mediators. The detailed analysis of between-lines behavioral similarities and differences has proceeded over the past 30 years in the Turku laboratory (e.g., Lagerspetz, 1964; Lagerspetz & Lagerspetz, 1975; Sandnabba, Lagerspetz, & Jensen, in press).

A second research program was initiated in the early 1970s in the United States and focused initially on the interactional and developmental controls of aggression (e.g., Cairns, 1976; Cairns, Gariépy, & Hood, 1990; Gariépy, Hood, & Cairns, 1988; Hood & Cairns, 1988). Once the behavioral determinants were fairly well understood, genetic methods were used to uncover otherwise inexplicable sources of variance in the data. The detailed maps of social interaction were then used in the ontogenetic study of successive generations of animals at the time that new lines were being established through selective breeding. The integration of interactional, ontogenetic, and genetic methods permitted the identification of the likely points of developmental entry for microevolutionary changes.

Despite differences in research strategy, assessment procedures, data coding, and selection programs, the several independent research efforts have yielded convergent answers on key questions about the genetic regulation of aggressive behavior and its relation to social processes. In brief, the findings indicate the following:

1. Genetic lines that differ markedly in aggressive behavior can be produced rapidly, within one to five generations of selective breeding (Cairns, Gariépy, & Hood, 1990). The selection procedures recommended by Falconer (1981) were followed to ensure optimal levels of outbreeding while minimizing the catastrophic effects produced by high-selection pressures. This finding has been replicated in other laboratories and in other subspecies of mice. For this mammalian species, there can now be no question about the magnitude of the genetic effects on aggressive behaviors or about the rapidity by which these effects can be established. This finding

appears to be one of significant generality (see review in R. B. Cairns, Gariépy, & Hood, 1990).

2. Experimental studies show robust effects of rearing, interactional, learning, and social organization on aggressive behavior. These manipulations work, regardless of the genetic background of the animals (e.g., Cairns, 1972; Cairns, Hood, & Midlam, 1985; Cairns, MacCombie, & Hood, 1983; Cairns & Scholz, 1973). Aggressive behaviors can be modified by simple social experiments in both high-aggressive lines and low-aggressive lines, although many of these effects resist manipulation by drugs and neurotransmitters. Stated succinctly: Aggressive behaviors are not fixed by genes or by early experience. Regardless of genetic background, the context and social group in which individual animals are embedded can increase, decrease, or eliminate the level and type of aggressive behaviors that are observed (Cairns, Gariépy, & Hood, 1990). The implications of this robust and repeatedly replicated empirical finding have yet to filter into the contemporary literature on social development.

In any social interchange, including aggression, organisms serve two masters simultaneously. One master is within and reflects the tonic equilibrium that should be maintained among biological subsystems so that organisms can function in an efficient, adaptive fashion (Schneirla, 1966). The other master is without and reflects the constraints of social exchanges. To adapt in concrete settings, organisms must achieve alignment with the actions of others and with the conditions of the broader social and physical environment. Such dual synchrony precludes the reduction of social behavior to any single source of regulation, whether within or without. It also suggests that the biological systems should ultimately be in the service of social constraints rather than vice versa.

This line of reasoning implies that behavior can be reduced to biological structure or environmental influence only in a trivial and misleading sense. Rather, we have noted elsewhere that behavioral adaptations occupy the space between the relatively enduring structures of the organism, on the one hand, and the relatively enduring properties of the physical and social environment, on the other. As such, any behavior that becomes stereotyped or frozen, whether by genes, neurochemistry, or early experiences, will lose its most vital function of flexible and fluid adaptation (Cairns, Gariépy, & Hood, 1990).

3. Those elements of social behavior that are readily manipulated in the course of ontogeny are also the elements of social behavior that are readily manipulated across generations by genetic selection (Cairns, Gariépy, & Hood, 1990). In this regard, Fuller (1967) earlier observed that "behavior most modifiable by variation in experience may also be particularly sensitive to genetic variation" (p. 1647). This empirical generalization provides a new twist to the idea that nature and nurture cooperate rather than compete. It also makes plenty of theoretical and survival sense, in that social patterns that are malleable in the lifetime of the individual should also be malleable across generations. The other counterintuitive finding—that on the rapidity of selection effects—is in keeping with the idea that social behavior is a leading edge of adaptation, and, therefore, it should be highly responsive to changes in social ecology and social context. These changes should then be supported through multiple and correlated mechanisms: genetic, learning, interactional, and cognitive. On this score, we suggested the following elsewhere:

> The rapid adaptation of social behavior by experience in ontogeny may be expected, given the need of individuals to adapt to other individuals and new settings with extreme rapidity. If the change is not rapid, it would be ineffective. By the same reasoning, genes should be able to operate rapidly and selectively upon some features of social behavior across generations. It would also follow that the conditions and contexts for the expression of aggressive, sexual, and attachment behaviors should be more rapidly influenced by genetic selection than the stereotyped expression of the motor patterns. This counter-intuitive proposal implies that genetic mechanisms play an active and dynamic role in the organization and expression of social behaviors. (Cairns, 1993)

In brief, it is proposed that social interactions are more sensitive to biological and genetic biases than are physical features of organisms. Social interactions are also likely to be more sensitive to biases and changes in the social environment during development. The assumption is that social patterns must remain dynamic and responsive to forces both within and without, to serve their distinctive functions in adaptation. From this perspective, the apparent stability of social patterns must be explained. On this score, it has been proposed that stability and continuity in social patterns arise because of the network of correlations between internal and external conditions. These correlations follow directly from the bidirectional influences between actions and the internal states that the actions help produce (R. B. Cairns & Cairns, 1994; Cairns, Gariépy, & Hood, 1990).

This line of reasoning seems consistent with and extends Bronfenbrenner's assertion that "piecemeal analysis, fixed in time and space, of isolated aspects and attributes is insufficient and even misleading" (Bronfenbrenner, 1944a, p. 75). We would add that it is insufficient and even misleading because it leaves out the feedback that exists between behavior and biology, between individuals and peers, and between parents and their offspring. The work underscores that the concept of development should be extended to include developmental changes across generations.

At first blush, this line of research and the results that have been generated may seem to be distant from the major concerns of social ecology. It is true that they have been virtually lost in the space between contemporary sciences. But are the findings really so far removed from social ecology? In this regard, we believe that they constitute one of the most powerful and convincing cases for Bronfenbrenner's (1943) assertion that: "social development applies not only to the individual but to the social organization of which he is a part" (p. 363).

The illustration discussed above concerns the continuity and predictability from an individual level, but it is only about mice. The essential principles that have been identified in these studies are not limited to nonhuman mammals. This point is made clearly in the Bronfenbrenner and Ceci (1994) article on the need to integrate information about social context and opportunities in the theoretical analysis of genetic effects on the adaptations of humans. By way of example, the work of Magnusson and his colleagues shows that the biological effects of early maturation are intimately linked to the nature of social context generated for early- and late-maturing females (Magnusson, 1988; Stattin & Magnusson, 1990). This elegant analysis demonstrates how the effects of maturation are mediated in part by social group influence.

Recent longitudinal studies find reasonably high levels of prediction from childhood to early adulthood in measures of deviance and aggressive behavior (Cairns & Cairns, 1994). Depending on the study and depending on the statistic used, there is roughly a correlation of from .35 to .50 in attenuated predictions over a 10-year period from childhood to late adolescence. Because the focus of the work has been on individuals, explanations have been offered in terms of within-individual factors, including drives, temperament, trait, and genetics. That is impressive, but it surely is not perfect. The failure to assess other correlated influences does not mean that they are irrelevant.

To see what the inclusion of factors outside of the individual information would do, following Magnusson and Bergman (1990b), we computed person analyses in which both individual and social characteristics were considered. The cluster analysis included individual behavioral characteristics (e.g., ratings of aggression, popularity, looks, and academic competence), intraorganismic maturational and physical characteristics (e.g., size, maturational status, and age), as well as social markers (i.e., socio-economic class) into the same clustering model. The idea was to obtain persons who were homogeneous with respect to both personal and contextual characteristics and to determine whether their lives described a common trajectory.

The clusters so derived were effective in predicting school dropout, teenage parenthood, and difficulties. The paradox is that development is supposed to be about change, and we found remarkable consistency. Why? It appears that, when one combines in a predictive equation information about the correlated constraints within the person and within the social context, these processes have a fail-safe quality that holds persons onto trajectory, for good or for ill.

The general picture has been duplicated in many of the high-risk persons that we identified in childhood. There are fail-safe constraints in the self and in society that are time emergent. This is the kind of developmental dynamic that suggests it is not sufficient to intervene at one point in ontogeny and expect that the rest of the system will take care of itself.

The Social Group and Social Network: Stability and Fluidity

The second illustration concerns one of the intermediate circles in the social ecology diagram, the sociometric group, to which Bronfenbrenner (1944a) devoted his early paper. It is almost as if we picked up where he left off, and we had to begin with the same issues of mathematics and statistics (R. B. Cairns, Gariépy, & Kindermann, 1990; Cairns, Perrin, & Cairns, 1985).[1] The problems arise, as Bronfenbrenner (1943) identified, when the research focus shifts the unit of developmental analysis from a person to a group or a network. Curiously enough, despite clear recognition of the problem and guides to its solution by Bronfenbrenner (1943), the task has been attempted only rarely in recent developmental and social studies. This holds despite the strong assumptions in the contemporary social development literature on the effects of peer groups and the power and stability of their influence. And where it has been attempted, the focus has been on the stability of social status rather than the stability of the actual social network and its structure.

Social networks and how they operate over time and space have been a special focus of the longitudinal research program that we have conducted over the past 14 years. The primary 695 subjects have been studied since they were 10 years or 13 years of age (two cohorts were seen). They were seen annually in a multilevel, multimethod analysis, up through 24 years of age. In addition to the subjects, their parents, grandparents,

---

[1]The task, begun 14 years ago, was responsible for our rediscovery of the early articles (Bronfenbrenner, 1943, 1944a, 1944b).

spouses, and children have become part of this ongoing investigation (R. B. Cairns & Cairns, 1994).

We find that networks and groups are remarkably fluid in childhood and adolescence, as are close friendships. As conditions of interchange change, so do friendships and clique affiliations. In one analysis of seventh graders, only 12% of the groups were identifiable after 1 year, even with a loose standard of group identification (Cairns & Cairns, 1994). There was almost as great a turnover in which persons were named as friends. These patterns become more stable with age, but there is still greater than 75% divorce or disaffiliation among teenage parents within 2 years. In any case, close peer relationships as a rule are rather fickle nowadays, no matter how we analyzed our data.

At any one point, the behaviors and attitudes of friends seem to be extremely important for the behaviors and values of children and adolescents. We found high levels of similarity, particularly for deviant, aggressive behaviors. Baldwin (1897) appears to be correct: "So he himself, at every stage, is really in part someone else, even in his own thought of himself" (p. 30). Putting these two findings together yields a puzzling conclusion. At any one point in time, peer influences play a dominant role in behaviors and values, but how can these effects persist when peer groups change so drastically from year to year? The resolution was discovered when we looked carefully at how the social clusters and friendships were reinvented each year. There was selective affiliation—where persons were both accepted by others and attracted to them—in terms of similarity on basic behavioral domains, after factoring out propinquity, gender, and race. There was, in effect, a stability of influence despite changing faces (Neckerman, 1992). This also suggested that the lessons learned carried over to qualify or disqualify individuals for particular groups. The gatekeeping each year was exercised by those recruiting and those being recruited. The outcome is stability of influence in the midst of change. This kind of developmental dynamic permits a continuous updating of behaviors and values through interpersonal synchrony. As Maccoby (1990) clearly described, this can account for the continuous updating of gender-specific attitudes and behaviors, keeping them in line with age-graded roles and expectations. All this is to suggest that there are functions in fickleness.

More generally, as the needs and goals of adolescents change, so should the relationships that are most likely to be productive for themselves and for others with whom they associate. On this count, changes in "best friends" may be, for many persons, adaptive in the course of growing up. The problem, of course, is that changes can be disruptive in the short term, even if they are adaptive in the long term.

The Society: Social Change and Problem Girls

The third illustration addresses the relations between the outermost circle and other units of study in social ecology. There have been significant changes in the way the deviance of girls and women has been viewed over the past century, and these effects can be mediated through individuals, as well as the social networks in which they participate. A case in point is provided by the court records of the juveniles adjudicated in Los Angeles County from 1910 through 1960 (Schlossman & Cairns, 1993). Schlossman obtained permission from the county and state attorney general to analyze all juvenile records over that 50-year period. What came out of the analysis was that sexual promiscuity was a crime for girls, but not for boys during the first half of the twentieth century.

After 1960, charges for incorrigibility and sexual promiscuity did not often appear in the juvenile courts of Los Angeles County. Rather, there was a sharp increase in instances of personal assault and other crimes that males committed. This generational shift in court and school evaluations corresponded to the information from our longitudinal study. In the 1980s, girls were arrested for crimes similar to those of boys in both Los Angeles and North Carolina (Cairns & Cairns, 1994).

In our most recent analysis of Los Angeles data, that of the emergency rooms of UCLA Harbor Hospital, we found high overlap between adolescent boys and girls in the admissions for injuries due to violence (Cairns & Cairns, 1994). For persons in the 15- to 19-year-old group, violence is the leading reason for admission of serious trauma patients. When one projects into the next generation and recognizes that these are likely the persons to be the teenage parents of children in our studies, there is a special futility in blaming irresponsible parents for difficult children. To a significant extent, those parents may be difficult children themselves.

We raise this last illustration because it suggests that focus on the life span is insufficient; development continues from generation to generation, and a systematic analysis must examine those links. It makes good sense, and it is fundamental for prevention strategies.

UNFINISHED BUSINESS: THE MAKING OF DEVELOPMENTAL SCIENCE

Although Bronfenbrenner's early papers on methodology have been virtually lost, the insights on social development reflected in them seem to have gained hegemony in social development. This raises broader questions: Why has empirical progress on basic issues of social development been so hard to achieve, and why has it been so rarely recognized, once the hard-won gains have been made? It is one thing to adopt an overarching framework; it is quite another to go beyond the rhetoric and rigorously assess the logical implications of the orientation.

Few would now debate the assertion that it is folly to proceed with piecemeal analysis that is fixed in time and space. Nevertheless, such piecemeal, variable-oriented research remains dominant in our major developmental journals. If anything, there seems to be less journal space given to integrative study in the 1990s than there was in the 1940s. To be sure, there are implicit and explicit pressures to report findings in terms of multivariate analyses (e.g., multivariate analysis of variance, multiple logistic regression, structural modeling equations [LISREL], and random effect models [hierarchical linear modeling; HLM]). The prevalence of these procedures implies that the problem of integration can be solved by statistical manipulation. That is a myth. The tough tasks of social developmental research must be addressed before analysis: in the research design, measurement, and conceptualization.

Specifically, the challenges confronting social development researchers include the following tasks:

- To formulate procedures for the objective identification of social groups, social networks, and the relations to individuals across time
- To design multilevel research procedures to use across development
- To develop procedures for tracking individuals and maintaining sampling integrity over weeks, months, and years
- To preserve information about persons in context as opposed to information about the individual or information about the context
- To take into account the operation of correlated constraints on behavior at the first level of analysis
- To adopt and perfect methods of person analyses that focus on the patterning and configuration of characteristics and how these may be used in describing behavioral trajectories over time and over generations

These issues of measurement, design, and research execution remain on the table just as they were 50 years ago. Progress has been gradual, as perhaps it had to be, given the nonintuitive nature of the propositions. For every three empirical advances forward, one seems to have been forgotten, and another seems to have been ignored in the beginning. It has been easier to adopt developmental language and concepts than to create developmental measures and methods. But without systematic evaluation, the discipline may be doomed to continue to champion commonsense beliefs that have been dressed up in new developmental rhetoric.

Old ideas about behavior do not always die or fade away; they can be recycled as developmental constructs. Examples include the strict genetic control of behavior (e.g., heritability index,), fixation by early experience (e.g., attachment theory), and freedom of the will (e.g., self-reinforcement and self-efficacy). Social patterns are multidetermined, and any competent research program should be able to identify the piecemeal contributions of genetic, experiential, and social–cognitive factors. The problem of developmental research is to clarify how these influences are woven together in individuals over time to promote social adaptation.

To be sure, there has been substantial progress over the past half century in useful developmental concepts, methods, and substantive findings. Yet much of it has seemed irrelevant to American developmental psychology because it has been accomplished outside the United States or outside the usual confines of child research. In this regard, the maturing of longitudinal studies worldwide provides the field with a data source that never before existed (e.g., Magnusson & Bergman, 1990a). In addition, significant progress has been made in systematic studies of mammalian social development, although its relevance is rarely appreciated by investigators of human socialization.

One criticism that might be raised is that for some kinds of questions, piecemeal analysis may be very appropriate. It depends on the questions that are asked. True, the levels of analysis must be attuned to the issues addressed. But in the study of social phenomena, there can be no substitute for considering the individual in context. Once the interrelations are plotted, the investigator is free—indeed, obligated—to use whatever research methods are appropriate to fully characterize the system of relationships. For example, in the developmental–genetic studies, we used behavioral microanalyses, experimental rearing conditions, hormonal analyses, pharmacological dose–response manipulations, ecological observations, longitudinal observations, interactional controls, short-term learning experiments, cross-foster rearing, and twin control observations, among other research procedures. A holistic orientation to behavioral phenomena can be entirely consistent with rigorous, multilevel analysis. The developmental insight is that the multiple levels are creations of the investigator, not the organism.

A new synthesis on genetic–physiological–social development integration is in the making. As indicated earlier in this chapter, we are currently on the threshold of fully characterizing the development of a significant mammalian social behavior system at all levels: societal, group, interactional, behavioral, physiological, neurobiological, and genetic.

These elements are woven together over development in systems of mutual constraint that simultaneously conserve and promote rapid and effective change. The findings to date point to the elegant simplicity of the integrated system as it operates over development and over generations (Cairns, Gariépy, & Hood, 1990).

One other historical footnote is in order. In addressing the problem of how to measure intelligence, Binet and Henri (1895) argued that, even if one succeeded in splitting the mind into mental elements, one would not know how to put them back together. That insight and the procedures it stimulated paved the way for the various families of intelligence or ability tests, arguably the most influential contribution of psychology to society in the twentieth century. An integrative approach is even more important for social development than for cognitive development, to understand the interdependence of events within and without the individual (Bronfenbrenner & Ceci, 1994; Cairns, Elder, & Costello, in press; Magnusson, this volume, chapter 2).

On this score, critics might argue that there are many problems with any multilevel multidimensional analysis. The developmental model is not neatly accommodated by parametric models that are currently favored. But the problem may lie in the statistical tools that are used, not in the phenomena. This was a main point in Bronfenbrenner's early papers, and it remains accurate today. In this regard, we used configural analyses to address the multilevel, multidimensional dilemma (e.g., Cairns, Cairns, & Neckerman, 1989). Similarly, nonparametric network procedures provide an efficient way to identify units of social analysis beyond the individual and beyond the dyad (e.g., Cairns, Cairns, Neckerman, Gest, & Gariépy, 1988).

The larger problem is that developmental investigators have permitted themselves to be straightjacketed by measurement conventions and statistical procedures that are alien to the phenomena that they aspire to study. Reductionism is but one problem. Another, equally pervasive hazard has been that psychological measurements and designs minimize the variance attributable to age (consider, e.g., such accepted conventions as the IQ ratio, standard scores by age, controlling or matching with respect to age, and covariance adjustments for age). Once the effects of developmental time have been muted or eliminated by methodology, they tend to be ignored by theory.

Given different rates of change in the various segments of social ecology and in persons occurring simultaneously, small wonder that social development appears chaotic. But the chaos may lie in the perceptions of the phenomena and in the limitations of the research strategies rather than in the phenomena themselves. The centrality of socialization and social interactions in understanding biological adaptation and societal organization has been consistently underestimated by the sciences. It is a mild irony that several areas of biology—sociobiology, ethology, and behavioral zoology—appreciate the primacy of social behavior, although the point still remains unrecognized by many in psychology.

Both the society and the science should benefit from an enlarged vision of what can be accomplished within the next decade through intensive developmental study. Part of the vision should be to extend the methods and analyses that capture the integrated nature of social development. Appropriate procedures have already been established; they must now be vigorously exploited (Magnusson & Bergman, 1990b). A related goal should be to determine how these methods, and the ideas that give rise to them, can be used to promote health and prevent chaos in human societies. All this is to suggest that the original statement of Bronfenbrenner on social development (1943) was on target. The discipline needs to enlarge the vision, update the methods, and continue to work on the making of the science.

REFERENCES

Baldwin, J. M. (1897). *Social and ethical interpretations in mental development: A study in social psychology.* New York: Macmillan.

Binet, A., & Henri, V. (1895). La psychologie individuelle. *L'Annee Psychologique, 2,* 411–465.

Bronfenbrenner, U. (1943). A constant frame of reference for sociometric research. *Sociometry, 6,* 363–397.

Bronfenbrenner, U. (1944a). A constant frame of reference for sociometric research: Part II. Experiment and inference. *Sociometry, 7,* 40–75.

Bronfenbrenner, U. (1944b). The graphic presentation of sociometric data. *Sociometry, 7,* 283–289.

Bronfenbrenner, U. (1979). *The ecology of human development: Experiments by nature and design.* Cambridge, MA: Harvard University Press.

Bronfenbrenner, U., & Ceci, S. J. (1994). Nature–nurture reconceptualized: A bioecological model. *Psychological Review, 101,* 568–586.

Cairns, R. B. (1972). Fighting and punishment from a developmental perspective. In J. K. Coles & D. D. Jensen (Eds.), *Nebraska Symposium on Motivation* (Vol. 20, pp. 59–124). Lincoln: University of Nebraska Press.

Cairns, R. B. (1976). The ontogeny and phylogeny of social behavior. In M. E. Hahn & E. C. Simmel (Eds.), *Evolution and communicative behavior* (pp. 115–139). New York: Academic Press.

Cairns, R. B. (1986). Phenomena lost: Issues in the study of development. In J. Valsiner (Ed.), *The individual subject and scientific psychology* (pp. 97–112). New York: Plenum.

Cairns, R. B. (1993). Belated but bedazzling: Timing and genetic influence in social development. In G. Turkewitz & D. A. Devenny (Eds.), *Developmental time and timing* (pp. 61–84). Hillsdale, NJ: Erlbaum.

Cairns, R. B., & Cairns, B. D. (1994). *Lifelines and risks: Pathways of youth in our time.* New York: Cambridge University Press.

Cairns, R. B., Cairns, B. D., & Neckerman, H. J. (1989). Early school dropout: Configurations and determinants. *Child Development, 60,* 1437–1452.

Cairns, R. B., Cairns, B. D., Neckerman, H. J., Gest, S., & Gariépy, J.-L. (1988). Social networks and aggressive behavior: Peer support or peer rejection? *Developmental Psychology, 24,* 815–823.

Cairns, R. B., Elder, G. H., Jr., & Costello, E. J. (in press). (Eds.). *Developmental science.* New York: Cambridge University Press.

Cairns, R. B., Gariépy, J.-L., & Hood, K. E. (1990). Development, microevolution, and social behavior. *Psychological Review, 97,* 49–65.

Cairns, R. B., Gariépy, J.-L., & Kindermann, T. (1990). *Identifying social clusters in natural settings.* Unpublished manuscript, University of North Carolina at Chapel Hill.

Cairns, R. B., Hood, K. E., & Midlam, J. (1985). On fighting in mice: Is there a sensitive period for isolation effects? *Animal Behavior, 33,* 166–180.

419

Cairns, R. B., & Kroll, A. B. (1994). A developmental perspective on gender differences and similarities. In M. L. Rutter, D. F. Hay, & S. Baron-Cohen (Eds.), *Developmental principles and clinical issues in psychology and psychiatry* (pp. 330–372). Oxford, England: Blackwell Scientific.

Cairns, R. B., MacCombie, D. J., & Hood, K. E. (1983). A developmental–genetic analysis of aggressive behavior in mice: I. Behavioral outcomes. *Journal of Comparative Psychology, 97,* 69–89.

Cairns, R. B., Perrin, J. E., & Cairns, B. D. (1985). Social structure and social cognition in early adolescence: Affiliative patterns. *Journal of Early Adolescence, 5,* 339–355.

Cairns, R. B., & Scholz, S. D. (1973). Fighting in mice: Dyadic escalation and what is learned. *Journal of Comparative and Physiological Psychology, 85,* 540–550.

Cairns, R. B., & Valsiner, J. (1984). Child psychology. *Annual Review of Psychology, 35,* 553–577.

Falconer, D. S. (1981). *Introduction to quantitative genetics* (2nd ed.). London: Longman.

Fuller, J. L. (1967). Experiential deprivation and later behavior. *Science, 158,* 1645–1652.

Gariépy, J-L., Hood, K. E., & Cairns, R. B. (1988). A developmental–genetic analysis of aggressive behavior in mice: III. Behavioral mediation by heightened reactivity or increased immobility? *Journal of Comparative Psychology, 102,* 392–399.

Hood, K. E., & Cairns, R. B. (1988). A developmental–genetic analysis of aggressive behavior in mice: II. Cross-sex inheritance. *Behavior Genetics, 18,* 605–619.

Kuo, Z.-Y. (1967). *The dynamics of behavioral development: An epigenetic view.* New York: Random House.

Lagerspetz, K. M. J. (1964). Studies on the aggressive behavior of mice. *Annales Acadamiae Scientiarum Fennicae, 131*(3, Series B), 1–131.

Lagerspetz, K. M. J., & Lagerspetz, K. Y. H. (1975). The expression of the genes of aggressiveness in mice: The effect of androgen on aggression and sexual behavior in females. *Aggressive Behavior, 1,* 291–296.

Lewin, K. (1935). *A dynamic theory of personality.* New York: McGraw-Hill.

Maccoby, E. (1990). Gender and relationships: A developmental account. *American Psychologist, 46,* 513–520.

Magnusson, D. (1988). *Individual development from an interactional perspective.* Hillsdale, NJ: Erlbaum.

Magnusson, D., & Bergman, L. R. (1990a). (Eds.). *Data quality in longitudinal research.* Cambridge, England: Cambridge University Press.

Magnusson, D., & Bergman, L. R. (1990b). A pattern approach to the study of pathways from childhood to adulthood. In L. N. Robins & M. Rutter (Eds.), *Straight and devious pathways from childhood to adulthood* (pp. 101–115). Cambridge, England: Cambridge University Press.

Mead, G. H. (1934). *Mind, self, and society.* Chicago: University of Chicago Press.

Neckerman, H. J. (1992). *A longitudinal investigation of the stability and fluidity of social networks and peer relationships of children and adolescents.* Unpublished doctoral dissertation, University of North Carolina, Chapel Hill.

Plomin, R., DeFries, J. C., & Loehlin, J. C. (1977). Genotype–environment interaction and correlation in the analysis of human behavior. *Psychological Bulletin, 84,* 309–322.

Sandnabba, N. K., Lagerspetz, K. M. J., & Jensen, E. (in press). Effects of testosterone exposure and fighting exprience on the aggressive behavior of female and male mice selectively bred for intermale aggression. *Hormones and Behavior,*

Schlossman, S., & Cairns, R. B. (1993). Problem girls: Some observations on past and present. In J. Modell, R. Parke, & G. H. Elder, Jr. (Eds.), *Children in time and place: Intersecting historical and developmental insights* (pp. 110–130). New York: Cambridge University Press.

Schneirla, T. C. (1966). Behavioral development and comparative psychology. *Quarterly Review of Biology, 41,* 283–302.

Scott, J. P. (1977). Social genetics. *Behavior Genetics, 7,* 327–346.

Stattin, H., & Magnusson, D. (1990). *Pubertal development in girls.* Hillsdale, NJ: Erlbaum.

13

Authoritative Parenting and Adolescent Adjustment: An Ecological Journey

Laurence Steinberg, Nancy E. Darling, and
Anne C. Fletcher, in collaboration with
B. Bradford Brown and Sanford M. Dornbusch

The impetus for much of the research presented in this chapter can be traced to a specific conversation between Laurence Steinberg and Urie Bronfenbrenner in a hotel lobby in Kansas City, at the 1989 meetings of the Society for Research in Child Development.

Earlier that day, our research group had made its first presentation from this project, on the impact of authoritative parenting on adolescent achievement (Mounts, Lamborn, & Steinberg, 1989). Drawing on data collected from a multiethnic, multiclass, multiregional sample of 10,000 adolescents, we had shown that the positive association between parental authoritativeness and adolescent school performance remained statistically significant even after controlling for ethnicity, socioeconomic status, and household composition.

As Urie and I settled into our armchairs, I expected him to tell me how terrific our research was. Ten thousand subjects. Detailed assessment of parenting processes. A multiethnic, multiclass sample of youngsters from different ecologies. I waited for the praise to pour from his lips.

"You know, Larry," he said, "you have a wonderful opportunity with those data to look at some very important questions. It's too bad that what you've done is so dumb."

He went on to explain that it made no sense at all to control for ethnicity, social class, or household composition in an attempt to isolate a "pure" process. No processes occur outside of a context. And if we want to understand context, we need to take it into account, not pretend to control it away.

From that day on, we stopped controlling for context and started taking it into account. This chapter tells the story of what we learned along the way.

In the pages that follow, we illustrate how several aspects of Bronfenbrenner's perspective on the ecology of human development can be incorporated into a program of research. We have been especially interested in examining the role of context in adolescent development at multiple levels. Accordingly, we look at adolescent development in the *microsystems* of the family and peer group, at the intersection of these two microsystems (what Bronfenbrenner calls the *mesosystem*), within the family's social network and community (a level of analysis Bronfenbrenner calls the *exosystem*), and within the broader context of ethnicity (a part of what Bronfenbrenner calls the *macrosystem*).

The study that sparked that auspicious conversation in Kansas City was a 3-year, longitudinal investigation of adolescent adjustment and behavior in a heterogeneous sample, involving over 20,000 U.S. high school students between the ages of 14 and 18. Although the overall program of work permitted us to collect extensive information on several domains of contextual influence, our primary interest—and the focus of this chapter—is on one particular context of development during adolescence: the family. More specifically, we asked whether, and through what mechanisms, parents of high school–age adolescents continue to influence their children to develop in healthy ways. Although the prevailing "wisdom" had been that the significance of parents decreased markedly during the high school years, we believed that this view inhered in an antiquated view of adolescence and of adolescent–parent relationships.

ADOLESCENT DEVELOPMENT IN THE FAMILY

Most research on the influence of the family on adolescent development focuses on early adolescence rather than on development during the high school years (see Collins, 1990; Steinberg, 1990). A small, but growing body of research, however, suggests that high school students who grow up in families characterized by different child-rearing practices show differential patterns of school performance (Dornbusch, Ritter, Leiderman, Roberts, & Fraleigh, 1987) and drug use (Baumrind, 1991b). These studies support the general contention that family relations continue to matter well into the high school years.

Parental influence does not occur in a social vacuum, however. During middle and late adolescence, in particular, the influence of parents is likely to be moderated by forces outside the family, including the adolescent's peer group and the broader community in which the family lives. No complete discussion of the family's role in adolescent development, therefore, can ignore the fact that the norms, expectations, and influences of the family are experienced by the adolescent alongside the norms, expectations, and influences of his or her friends. In some cases, these two agents of influence (the family and the peer group) are likely to have synergistic effects, with support for healthy behavior from peers enhancing the potency of parental support. In other instances, however, the combined effects of family and peer influences may be antagonistic, with one group undermining the best intentions of the other. Without taking peer influences into account, one may end up with an incomplete—or even distorted—picture of the family's significance.

A similar argument can be made in favor of studying parental influences within the context of the broader community. As we demonstrate, the degree to which family factors influence student adjustment varies across ethnic groups and neighborhood contexts. In particular, parental behaviors "known" to positively affect adolescent adjustment are more likely to be associated with adolescent well-being under some conditions than others. Indeed, in some contexts, the adolescent's immediate family does not appear to be an important influence on adolescent behavior and adjustment at all (Dornbusch, Ritter, & Steinberg, 1991; Steinberg, Lamborn, Dornbusch, & Darling, 1992; Steinberg, Mounts, Lamborn, & Dornbusch, 1991).

THE FAMILY IN BROADER CONTEXT

The data we draw on in this chapter present several unique opportunities to study the influence of parents within a broader context. First, because we have extensive data on each adolescent's ethnic background and living arrangements (including each parent's ethnicity, each parent's level of education and employment status, the family's immigration history, patterns of language usage, the parents' marital history, and the number of adults living in the home), we are able to examine parenting practices and adolescent outcomes across environments defined by family structure, ethnicity, and socioeconomic status. Here our work bridges approaches typically found in sociology (in which researchers have asked about differences between demographic groups either in adolescent outcomes or in their family relationships) with those typically found in the field of child development (in which questions have concerned the relation between parenting practices and child outcomes). Instead of treating these demographic variables as controls, however, our approach has been to examine how patterns of relations between parenting and child development vary across demographic groups.

Second, our database allows us to examine the processes through which peers moderate the impact of parents on adolescents at two distinct levels of potential peer influence. First, we have data on each participating adolescent's peer crowd affiliation. (By *crowd*, we refer to the reputation-based groups that structure the social system of the high school, e.g., "jocks"and "druggies.") These peer crowds play an important role in determining norms and values during high school (Brown, 1990; Eckert, 1989). Second, because each adolescent provided us with the names of his or her five closest friends, we are able to examine the influence of each adolescent's immediate social network, or clique.

Finally, we have information about the neighborhood and communities in which the families functioned. In our program of research, *community* was defined both in the sense of residential community (i.e., the neighborhood) and in terms of the family's social network. Far less is known about community influences on adolescent adjustment than is known about familial or peer influences (Steinberg, 1989). The past few years, however, have marked a rebirth in the empirical investigation of community influences on child and adolescent development. Like early work in the field (i.e., Shaw & McKay, 1969; Shaw, Zorbaugh, McKay, & Cottrell, 1929), current community research has been spurred by increasing concern about declining conditions in urban neighborhoods (e.g., Jencks & Mayer, 1988; Wilson, 1987), changes in family structure and functioning thought to weaken informal social bonds (Coleman, 1988; Coleman & Hoffer, 1987), decreasing supervision of children during after-school hours (Dowd, 1991), and recognition that contextual variation in developmental processes is a fundamental part of the study of human development (Bronfenbrenner, 1989). The focus of current community research continues to be on socialization—on the positive side, community socialization toward academic participation, orientation, and performance (e.g., Case & Katz, 1992) and, on the negative side, community influences on the development of delinquency (Sampson & Groves, 1989) and substance use (Esbensen & Huizinga, 1990).

OVERVIEW OF THE RESEARCH
Population

Our sample was drawn from the student bodies of nine high schools in Wisconsin and Northern California. The schools were selected to yield a sample of students from different socioeconomic brackets, a variety of ethnic backgrounds (African-, Asian-, European-, and Hispanic-American), different family structures (e.g., intact, divorced, and remarried), and different types of communities (urban, suburban, and rural). Data for the present analyses were collected during the 1987–1988 and 1988–1989 school years.

Procedure

The use of standard active-consent procedures in research on adolescents and their families (in which both parents and adolescents are asked to return signed consent forms to the appropriate school) may result in sampling biases that overrepresent well-functioning teenagers and families (e.g., Weinberger, Tublin, Ford, & Feldman, 1990). Although groups of participants and nonparticipants generated through such consent procedures may be comparable demographically (the dimension along which investigators typically look for evidence of selective participation), the procedure screens out a disproportionate number of adolescents who have adjustment problems or family difficulties. Because we were interested in studying neglectful, as well as more involved, families in this research and because many of our outcome measures were in the domain of adjustment, we were concerned that using the standard active-consent procedure would bias our sample toward more involved—and, presumably, better functioning—families.

After considering the age of our respondents and their ability to provide informed consent, and with the support of the administrators of our participating schools, the school districts' research review committees, representatives of the U.S. Department of Education (our chief funding agent), and our own institutions' human subjects committees, we decided to use a consent procedure that requested active informed consent from the adolescents, but passive informed consent from their parents. All parents in the participating schools were informed, by first-class mail, of the date and nature of our study well in advance of the scheduled questionnaire administration. (We provided schools with letters in stamped, unaddressed envelopes to be mailed by school officials, to protect the privacy of the families.) Parents were asked to call or write to their child's school or our research office if they did not want their child to participate in the study. Fewer than 1% of the adolescents in each of the target schools had their participation withheld by their parents.

All of the students in attendance on each day of testing were invited to participate in the study and were asked to complete the questionnaires. Informed consent was obtained from all participating students. For each questionnaire administration, out of the total school populations, approximately 5% of the students chose not to participate (or had their participation withheld by parents), approximately 15% were absent from school on the day of questionnaire administration (this figure is comparable to national figures on daily school attendance), and approximately 80% provided completed questionnaires. Each year, approximately 12,000 students participated in the study. We also supplemented these surveys with focused interviews with groups of students in each school: one-on-one interviews with a sample of 600 high-, medium-, and low-achieving students from six of our schools and one-on-one interviews with these 600 students' parents.

The study sample was evenly divided among boys and girls, and among 9th, 10th, 11th, and 12th graders. The sample was quite diverse with respect to other demographic variables: More than 40% of the respondents were from an ethnic minority group, nearly one third were from single-parent households or stepfamilies, and nearly one third came from homes in which the parents had not attended school beyond the 12th grade.

Measures

Adolescent Adjustment

Four sets of outcome variables were examined at various points in the research: psychosocial development, academic competence, internalized distress, and problem behavior.

The three indexes of psychosocial development comprised the Social Competence subscale of the Adolescent Self-Perception Profile (Harter, 1982) and two subscales from Greenberger's Psychosocial Maturity Inventory: Work Orientation and Self-Reliance (Form D; Greenberger, Josselson, Knerr, & Knerr, 1974). The Social Competence measure ($\alpha = .78$) includes five items that ask students whether they perceive themselves as popular, as having many friends, and as making friends easily. The participants were asked to read two alternatives (e.g., "Some teenagers feel that they are socially accepted, but other teenagers wish that more people their age would accept them") and to choose the one that was more like them. The Work Orientation ($\alpha = .73$) and Self-Reliance ($\alpha = .81$) subscales are each composed of 10 items. The Work Orientation scale measures the adolescent's pride in the successful completion of tasks. A sample item, reverse coded, is "I find it hard to stick to anything that takes a long time." The Self-Reliance scale measures the adolescent's feelings of internal control and ability to make decisions without extreme reliance on others. A sample item, reverse coded, is "Luck decides most things that happen to me."

The three measures of school achievement included overall grade point average, the Academic Competence subscale of the Adolescent Self-Perception Profile (Harter, 1982), and a scale developed for this project that assessed the adolescent's orientation toward school. Respondents provided information on their current grade point average, on a 9-point scale ranging from *mostly As* to *mostly Fs*; scores were converted to correspond to a standard 4.0 grading scale. Self-reported grades are highly correlated with actual grades taken from official school records (Donovan & Jessor, 1985; Dornbusch et al., 1987). The Academic Competence subscale (α = .73) includes 5 items regarding the student's perceptions of his or her intelligence in relation to classmates, ability to complete homework quickly, and capability in classwork. The measure of orientation toward school was derived from a set of items that assessed the student's feeling of attachment to school (Wehlage, Rutter, Smith, Lesko, & Fernandez, 1989). Orientation Toward School is a six-item scale (α = .69) that emerged from a factor analysis of the total set of items. A sample item is "I feel satisfied with school because I'm learning a lot."

The set of three measures tapping problem behavior included reports of involvement in drug and alcohol use, school misconduct, and delinquency. The measure of drug and alcohol use tapped the frequency of involvement with cigarettes, alcohol, marijuana, and other drugs (5 items, α = .86; Greenberger, Steinberg, & Vaux, 1981). The measure of school misconduct assessed the frequency of such behaviors as cheating, copying homework, and tardiness (4 items, α = .68; Ruggiero, 1984). The measure of delinquency assessed the frequency of such behaviors as carrying a weapon, stealing, and getting into trouble with the police (6 items, α = .82; Gold, 1970). Although self-reports of deviant behavior are subject to both under- and overreporting (see McCord, 1990), most researchers agree that these provide a closer approximation of youngsters' true involvement in deviant activity than do "official" reports (e.g., police records), and the practice of using self-report data in the study of adolescent deviance is widely established (see Gold, 1970; Jessor & Jessor, 1977; McCord, 1990).

Two measures of internalized distress were derived from a 13-item version of the Depression Scale of the Center for Epidemiologic Studies (CES–D; Radloff, 1977). Results of a factor analysis suggested a Somatic Symptoms scale (7 items, $\alpha = .67$), which included items concerning the frequency of headaches, stomachaches, colds, and so forth, and a Psychological Symptoms scale (6 items, $\alpha = .88$), which included items concerning the frequency of anxiety, tension, and depression.

Parenting Practices

Our battery concerning family relations was aimed primarily at understanding authoritative parenting and its impact on youngsters' development. *Authoritative parenting* is a term coined by Baumrind (1967) to describe a constellation of parenting practices, values, and beliefs that combines warmth, acceptance, and involvement with structure, maturity demands, and firm behavioral control.

The questionnaire we developed contained many items on parenting practices that were taken or adapted from existing measures (e.g., Dornbusch et al., 1985; Patterson & Stouthamer-Loeber, 1984; Rodgers, 1966). On the basis of our previous work (Steinberg, Elmen, & Mounts, 1989), a number of items were selected to correspond with the three dimensions of authoritative parenting identified earlier, and these were subjected to exploratory factor analyses using an oblique rotation. Three factors emerged, corresponding to the dimensions of acceptance–involvement, strictness and behavioral supervision, and psychological autonomy granting. These factors are similar to those suggested in the earlier work of Schaefer (1965) and the recent work of Baumrind (1991a, 1991b). We labeled these scales in ways that both captured the item content of each and emphasized parallels between our measures and those used by other researchers.

The Acceptance/Involvement scale measured the extent to which the adolescent perceived his or her parents as loving, responsive, and involved (sample items: "I can count on her to help me out if I have some kind of problem"; "How often does your family do something fun together?"; 15 items, $\alpha = .72$). The Strictness/Supervision scale assessed parental monitoring and limit setting (sample items: "How much do your parents try to know where you go at night?"; "In a typical week, what is the latest you can stay out on school nights (Monday–Thursday)?"; How much do your parents really know what you do with your free time?"; 9 items, $\alpha = .76$). The Psychological Autonomy Granting scale assessed the extent to which parents used noncoercive, democratic discipline and encouraged the adolescent to express individuality within the family (sample items, reverse scored: "How often do your parents tell you that their ideas are correct and that you should not question them?"; "How often do your parents answer your arguments by saying something like 'You'll know better when you grow up'?"; 12 items, $\alpha = .82$). The items constituting these three dimensions cover a wide variety of topics and index the adolescent's perception of the parents' overall behavior rather than the parents' school-specific socialization practices. For most of the items, students were asked to describe the parent(s) with whom they lived. On those items for which students in two-parent homes were asked to answer separately for their mother and father, scores were averaged before forming composites. (Baumrind, 1991a, reported that there is considerable convergence between mother's and father's ratings.)

We believe that the use of adolescents' reports about their parents is justified on several grounds. Given the size of the sample, it was necessary to rely on questionnaire data, and the difficulties in obtaining data from disengaged parents in particular have already been mentioned. As well, parental self-reports tend to exaggerate both their acceptance and firmness and have been criticized as unreliable (Schwarz, Barton-Henry, & Pruzinsky, 1985). Adolescents, on the other hand, are able to act as knowledgeable informants about parental behaviors (Golden, 1969; Moskowitz & Schwarz, 1982). Moreover, some writers—including Bronfenbrenner himself—have argued that children's perceptions of their parents' behavior may be as important influences on their development as are parents' actual behaviors (cf. Bronfenbrenner, 1979; Schaefer, 1965).

Nevertheless, our findings can be interpreted only to show that adolescents' adjustment is related to the way in which they subjectively experience their parents. Although we recognize that youngsters' reports of their parents' behavior may be colored by a variety of factors, we do not believe that "objective" assessments of family processes (derived in most studies by observing families in contrived and unfamiliar situations in university laboratories) or parental reports provide an inherently superior means of assessing family relationships. Indeed, the few studies that have correlated objective assessments of family life with both adolescents' reports of their parents' behavior and with their parents' reports suggest that adolescents, not parents, are more accurate (e.g., Schwarz et al., 1985). Perhaps more important, our willingness to use adolescents' reports permits us to study a more representative sample than would be the case if parents' participation in the study were required.

Historically, researchers have applied both typological and dimensional approaches to the study of socialization in the family. As we argued elsewhere (Darling & Steinberg, 1993), the two approaches have different theoretical orientations and are based on different assumptions. In the typological tradition, the general pattern, organization, or climate of parenting is of primary interest, and the assessment of specific parenting practices or dimensions (e.g., acceptance or strictness) is done for heuristic purposes, as a means of providing a window on the overall parenting environment. In the dimensional tradition, in contrast, different aspects of the parent–child relationship are assessed to test specific hypotheses about their relation (separately and jointly) to child adjustment. Each tradition has merit, and a decision to use one versus the other should be made on theoretical grounds. We used each approach at various points in the research program.

In analyses in which we used a typological approach, we created four parenting categories by trichotomizing the sample on acceptance and on strictness and by examining families' scores on the two variables simultaneously. Following Maccoby and Martin (1983), *authoritative* families were

433

those who scored in the upper tertiles on both Acceptance/Involvement and Strictness/Supervision, whereas *neglectful* families were in the lowest tertiles on both variables. *Authoritarian* families were in the lowest tertile on involvement, but in the highest tertile on strictness. *Indulgent* families were in the highest tertile on involvement, but in the lowest tertile on strictness. Families who scored in the middle tertile on either of the dimensions were excluded from the typological analysis to ensure that the four groups of families represented distinct categories.

Although we used only the dimensions of warmth and strictness to define our parenting categories, we found that the four types of households differed on other measures of parenting and parent–child relations as well. Thus, authoritative parents were not only warmer and firmer than other parents; they were also more involved in their child's schooling, were more likely to engage in joint decision making, and were more likely to maintain an organized household with predictable routines. Authoritarian parents, in addition to being relatively high in control and relatively low in warmth, were higher in coerciveness than other parents, less involved in their child's schooling, and more likely to make decisions unilaterally. Indulgent parents, in addition to being high in warmth and low in control, scored low in involvement and family organization and were likely to defer decision making to the adolescent. Neglectful families scored poorly on virtually every measure of family functioning we assessed. This sensible patterning of different aspects of family functioning supported the use of a categorical scheme.

In some of the analyses designed to look specifically at the impact of authoritative parenting, we treated authoritativeness as a continuous variable. On the basis of previous work and the theoretical model of authoritative parenting tested in this study, we constructed an ordinal measure of authoritativeness as follows: Families scoring above the sample median on Acceptance/Involvement, Strictness/Supervision, and Psychological Autonomy (authoritative) were assigned an authoritativeness score of 3. Families scoring below the sample median on all three of the dimensions (nonauthoritative) were assigned an authoritativeness score of 0. Families scoring above the sample median on one (somewhat nonauthoritative) or two (somewhat authoritative) of the parenting dimensions were assigned scores of 1 or 2, respectively.

Peer Crowd

Our chief index of peer association was based on the adolescent's membership within a peer crowd. Crowd affiliation was based on the social type rating (STR) procedure (Brown, 1989), an efficient mechanism for identifying adolescents' peer group affiliation, on the basis of their reputation among peers. It is somewhat similar to sociometric ratings by which younger children are classified into comparison groups (e.g., popular, rejected, or neglected; see, e.g., Ladd, 1983), except that the STR ratings take advantage of the more sophisticated social system of adolescents, in which there are commonly shared labels for particular peer groups.

Derived from earlier studies of adolescent peer groups (Clasen & Brown, 1985; Poveda, 1975; Schwendinger & Schwendinger, 1985; Weis, 1974), the STR procedure was a two-step process. In the first step, school administrators were asked to identify a set of boys and girls (within each ethnic group in multiethnic schools) in each grade who represented a good cross-section of the school's student body. These students were interviewed in small groups, composed of students of the same gender, same grade level, and same ethnic group. Through group discussion, each group derived a list of the school's major crowds, then each participant listed two boys and two girls in their grade who were the leaders or most prominent members of each crowd. From these lists, a stratified sample was drawn in each grade (stratified by crowd type, gender, and ethnicity, but with preference given to the most frequently listed students) to become STR raters in the second step.

Each rater, accompanied by a friend of her or his own choosing, was individually interviewed. The raters were presented with the list of crowds derived from the earlier group interviews, then asked to place each student in their grade level into one of the crowds. Raters could indicate that they did not know a student well enough to assign to a crowd. STR ratings continued until each student had been rated by at least 10 STR raters. Because raters could deal with only about 300 names in the time allotted for STR interviews, class lists in the larger schools were partitioned and the number of raters were increased to ensure that all students received the required number of ratings.

Once STR interviews were completed, crowd ratings for each student were collated and analyzed. A student was assigned to a crowd if at least 50% of STR raters knew the student well enough to classify him or her into a crowd and if over 50% of the raters who did classify the student concurred on the student's crowd affiliation. To increase the generalizability of results and our ability to compare findings to previous ethnographic research on adolescent peer groups, we restricted analyses to students associated with one of six crowd types: "jocks, populars, brains, druggies, loners," and "normals." Of the students for whom STR ratings were collected, one third were classified into one of these six crowds. The remaining students were rather evenly divided among individuals in crowds not common to all schools (e.g., farmers, surfers, or ethnically based crowds), individuals whose crowd affiliation was controversial, and individuals not known well enough to be placed in any crowd.

Social Network

We were also interested in the influence of the individuals in the adolescent's immediate social network. Subjects were asked to provide the names of up to five of their closest friends from school. Because these friends also were participants in the study, we were able to match data on parenting practices or adjustment outcomes provided by each respondent with those provided by each of his or her friends. For questions in which we were interested in characterizing peer networks, we limited our analyses to respondents who nominated at least three friends who provided complete information on the variables in question.

Neighborhood

We knew the street addresses of approximately 75% of the youngsters in our sample and used this information to investigate neighborhood effects. In the absence of clear guidelines as to what constitutes a neighborhood, however, we explored these effects at different levels of analysis. In some, we grouped youngsters together by U.S. census tract. The disadvantage of using the census tract as a measure of neighborhood is that a census tract is a good deal larger than a neighborhood—in our sample, the average tract contained about 4,500 individuals. The advantage of using census tracts, however, is that it is possible to match aggregate information compiled by the census about characteristics of a geographical area with information provided by respondents who live in that area.

We are also in the process of "geocoding" our respondents' addresses into real neighborhoods, defined not by the census, but by residents familiar with the community. In some areas, for example, we obtained maps used by city planning offices, realtors, or school districts. These maps provide a breakdown of geographical areas into neighborhoods defined by residents' perceptions and historical, if occasionally unusual, boundaries. Using these maps, we are able to cluster respondents in our sample into neighborhoods on the basis of their street addresses. Not surprisingly, it was a great deal easier to do this in an older, neighborhood-based city, like Milwaukee, than in the sprawling suburbs of Northern California. Nevertheless, despite rumors to the contrary, even Californians can identify neighborhoods in their communities.

RESULTS

We begin our summary of results with our first look at the power of authoritative parenting.

The Power of Authoritative Parenting

Using the fourfold typology of parenting style outlined by Maccoby and Martin (1983), we categorized families into one of four groups—authoritative, authoritarian, indulgent, or neglectful—on the basis of scores on our parenting dimensions. We then contrasted the four groups of youngsters on our four sets of outcome measures: psychosocial adjustment, schooling, behavior problems, and internalized distress. The findings indicated that there are theoretically predictable differences among adolescents raised in authoritative, authoritarian, indulgent, and neglectful homes (for details, see Lamborn, Mounts, Steinberg, & Dornbusch, 1991).

437

For the authoritative and neglectful groups, the findings were consistent across the four sets of outcomes. Adolescents raised in authoritative homes are better adjusted and more competent; they are confident about their abilities, competent in areas of achievement, and less likely than their peers to get into trouble. In sharp contrast, adolescents raised in neglectful homes are consistently compromised, whether the index examined competence, self-perceptions, misbehavior, or psychological distress.

Adolescents in the other two groups showed a mixture of positive and negative traits; the specific pattern was quite interesting, however. As one might expect, adolescents raised in authoritarian homes scored reasonably well on measures of obedience and conformity to the standards of adults; they did well in school, and they were less likely than their peers to be involved in deviant activities. At the same time, however, these youngsters appeared to have paid a price where self-confidence was concerned—both in terms of self-reliance and in terms of their perceptions of their own social and academic abilities. The overall pattern suggested a group of young people who had been overpowered into obedience.

The adolescents from indulgent homes presented an especially intriguing picture. Like their counterparts from neglectful homes, these adolescents were relatively disengaged from school and showed a higher frequency of involvement in certain deviant behaviors, including drug and alcohol use and school misconduct. These are two aspects of deviance that are both peer oriented and, in some circles of adolescents in contemporary America, normative. However, the fact that adolescents from indulgent homes did not score higher than the authoritative or authoritarian groups on the measure of more serious delinquency and the fact that they did score relatively high on measures of social competence and self-confidence suggested a picture of psychologically adjusted youngsters who were especially oriented toward their peers and toward the social activities valued by adolescents, including some activities not especially valued by adults.

Because these analyses were cross-sectional, it is impossible to say with any certainty that the parenting practices examined in fact caused or even preceded the outcomes assessed. It could well be the case, for example, that competent adolescents elicit authoritativeness from their parents or that less well adjusted youth provoke parental neglect (see Lewis, 1981). We, therefore, undertook a series of longitudinal analyses designed to get at this issue more directly.

There are a number of acceptable statistical techniques that one may use in the analysis of short-term longitudinal data. Because preliminary analyses of the data indicated fairly consistent effects of regression to the mean, it was necessary to perform analyses that took this effect into account. One such procedure is analysis of covariance (ANCOVA), in which the dependent variable is the change in the outcome of interest and the covariate is the relevant Time 1 score on the outcome (Laird, 1983). Accordingly, we conducted a series of ANCOVAs, each of which examined the effects of parenting style, ethnicity, and the two-way interaction between parenting style and ethnicity, on changes in the outcome variables of interest. For each analysis, the relevant Time 1 score was used as a covariate. We found that many of the differences observed in the initial cross-sectional analyses were either maintained or increased over time. As a result, over the 1-year period studied, the adjustment gap between adolescents from authoritative and neglectful homes widened.

Let us consider the patterns evinced by each of the four groups in relation to their starting points. In our cross-sectional report, we noted that adolescents reared in authoritative families had advantages over other youngsters on measures of psychosocial competence, academic competence, internalized distress, and problem behaviors. The longitudinal analyses indicated over-time stability in most of these domains, with only two exceptions: academic self-conceptions, which improved, and school misconduct, which declined. Hence, the benefits of authoritative parenting during the high school years seem to be largely in the maintenance of previous levels of high adjustment, rather than in the continued development of competence.

A similar pattern of stability was seen among youngsters from authoritarian homes, with one important exception. Although the disadvantages to adolescent self-confidence associated with authoritarian child-rearing noted in our earlier report were maintained over time, youths from authoritarian homes showed significant increases in internalized distress over the 1-year period. One hypothesis is that the increased levels of psychological and somatic distress reported by these youngsters are tied somehow to their continued exposure to a home environment that is psychologically overpowering and increasingly developmentally inappropriate.

The adolescents from indulgent homes continued to display a psychological and behavioral profile that was mixed. In our cross-sectional report, we had described these youngsters as well-adjusted, but "especially oriented toward their peers and toward the social activities valued by adolescents" (Lamborn et al., 1991, p. 1062). One year later, this description was even more apt: The indulgently reared youth became more positive over time in their academic self-conceptions and reported less somatic distress, but at the same time they showed significant declines in school orientation and significant increases in school misconduct.

It was in the case of neglectfully reared adolescents, however, where we saw the clearest evidence of the impact of parenting on adjustment during the high school years. These youths, already at a psychological and behavioral disadvantage at the time of first assessment, showed continued declines over the 1-year period, with sharp drops in work orientation and school orientation and sizeable increases in delinquency and alcohol and drug use. The overall pattern suggested a group of youngsters on a downward and troublesome trajectory characterized by academic disengagement and problem behavior.

Our ability to demonstrate that the over-time impact of parenting style on adolescent adjustment holds even after controlling for initial group differences was important for several reasons. First, in the absence of a randomized experimental design, the analytical strategy provided at least indirect evidence that authoritative parenting actually precedes—rather than simply accompanies or even follows from—adolescent adjustment. This is not to say that our analyses rule out the possibility that the reverse causal process is operating simultaneously (i.e., that well-adjusted adolescents also provoke authoritativeness in their parents); given past research on the bidirectional nature of socialization (e.g., Bell, 1968), it almost certainly is. What the results provided, however, was evidence that the correlation between adolescent adjustment and parenting style is not solely due to the effect that children have on their parents. At least some of it is due to the impact that parents have on their children.

The covariance analyses also helped to rule out many potential third-variable explanations of the over time association between parenting style and adolescent adjustment, such as those due to genetic transmission. Any such alternative account would necessarily have to posit the existence of a confounding variable that was correlated with the measures of adjustment in the study's 2nd year but was not correlated with the same measures taken in the study's 1st year. Although such variables could, of course, exist, we think it more plausible, given the consistency of our findings and hundreds of other studies in the socialization literature, to accept the conclusion—with all due respect to Scarr (1992)—that what parents do actually does have some effect on their children.

Our consistent findings on the power of authoritative parenting and its various components, such as warmth, strictness, and autonomy, parallel those reported by a number of different investigators, including several of the contributors to this volume (e.g., Moen & Erickson, this volume, chapter 6). Most of these other studies, however, have focused on middle-class, European-American youngsters growing up in two-parent households, and it is not clear from this work whether the benefits of authoritative parenting transcend demographic lines. We had the sample to look at this directly, and this was the next question that we addressed.

Authoritative Parenting: Transcontextual Validity

There are a number of ways to approach the issue of *transcontextual validity* (Weisz, 1978). For developmental psychologists, the conventional approach is to treat factors like socioeconomic status, ethnicity, or family structure as nuisance variables and to take these variables into account through selective sampling or statistical control. In a regression model or an ANCOVA, one would control for these factors and look to see if the relation between authoritative parenting and adolescent adjustment holds after the effects of these demographic factors are taken into account.

Although this is a widely used technique, it does not answer the question that should be of primary interest to the ecologically minded researcher—namely, whether the relation between authoritative parenting and adolescent adjustment is the same for adolescents growing up under one set of circumstances as it is for adolescents growing up under another. The covariance approach may make sense mathematically, but it makes no sense within the ecological perspective. If we believe that context matters, we certainly do not want to control it away. This was the Kansas City lesson.

The size and heterogeneity of our sample permitted us to look at this issue directly. We examined the association between authoritativeness and adolescent outcomes in 16 ecological niches (see Steinberg et al., 1991, for details). Each niche was defined by three variables—ethnicity (four categories: African-American, Asian-American, Hispanic-American, and European-American), socioeconomic status (two categories: working-class and below versus middle-class and above), and family structure (two categories: biological two-parent and nonintact). Crossing these dimensions resulted in ecological niches such as intact, working-class, European-Americans; intact, working-class, Asian-Americans; and nonintact, middle-class, African-Americans. As in previous analyses, families who had scored above the entire sample median on warmth, behavioral control, and psychological autonomy granting were categorized as authoritative. Families who had scored below the entire sample median on any of the three dimensions were categorized as nonauthoritative. (The reliability of each of the three parenting scales was examined and found to be adequate within every ecological niche.)

Adolescents from authoritative and nonauthoritative homes within each niche were then contrasted on four outcome variables, one from each of our outcome sets: grade point average, self-reliance, depression, and delinquency. Although we found that the prevalence of authoritativeness varies across different ecological niches—it is most prevalent among European-Americans, middle-class families, and intact families—the effect of authoritativeness varies much less so. Indeed, the results of the contrasts between authoritatively and nonauthoritatively reared adolescents were remarkably consistent.

Across the 16 ecological groups, and across the 4 outcome variables, youngsters from authoritative homes fared better than their counterparts from nonauthoritative homes. Authoritatively reared adolescents perform better in school, are more self-reliant, are less likely to report feeling depressed, and are less likely to be involved in delinquent activity. Of the 64 contrasts (4 outcomes by 16 niches), 40 were statistically significant, each favoring youngsters from authoritative homes. Of the remaining 24 contrasts, all but 3 were in the expected direction. In no case were youngsters from nonauthoritative homes significantly better off than youngsters from authoritative homes. This consistency is all the more noteworthy because the nonauthoritative group included many adolescents whose parents scored above the sample median on two of the three parenting dimensions.

Our working hypothesis was that authoritativeness would be more strongly related to child adjustment in middle-class, intact, European-American homes. To examine whether the strength of the relation between authoritative parenting and adolescent adjustment varied across the ecological niches, effect sizes were calculated for each contrast. Our hypothesis was only partially borne out, however. When we considered youngsters' psychosocial development, depression, and the likelihood of delinquency, we found that growing up in an authoritative home has comparable benefits, regardless of the family's ethnicity, class, or composition. When we looked at youngsters' school performance, however, we found that European- and Hispanic-American youngsters are more likely to benefit from authoritative parenting than are African- or Asian-American youngsters. That is, within the African- and Asian-American groups, youngsters whose parents are authoritative do not perform better in school than youngsters whose parents are not.

In view of a long history of research on familial influences on school achievement, the fact that we did not find a relation between authoritative parenting and achievement in two of the four ethnic groups we studied came as a surprise. Remember that we had found that authoritative parenting predicts other outcomes in these groups. The puzzling finding was specifically in the domain of achievement. To better understand what was going on, we needed to move our analyses beyond the confines of the family.

Family Influences on School Performance: The Moderating Role of Peers

Many of the items on our questionnaire asked students directly about the extent to which their friends and parents encouraged them to perform well in school. For parents, the questions concerned their involvement in school activities, their performance standards, and their expectations for their child's achievement. For peers, the questions concerned the degree of importance they placed on academic success and the extent to which they supported achievement among their friends. We used these items to calculate the degree to which a student felt he or she received support for academic accomplishment from parents and, independently, from peers and then used these composite indexes of parental and peer support to predict various aspects of the student's attitudes and behaviors toward school. We found, as have others, that, although parents are the most salient influence on youngsters' long-term educational plans, peers are the most potent influence on their day-to-day behaviors in school: how much time they spend on homework, whether they enjoy coming to school each day, and how they behave in the classroom (Steinberg & Brown, 1989).

There are interesting ethnic differences in the relative influence of parents and peers on student achievement and engagement, however (Brown, Steinberg, Mounts, & Philipp, 1990). These differences help to shed light on some of the difficulties we encountered in predicting the school performance of minority youngsters from information on their parents' practices. Our analyses suggested that peers are relatively more potent sources of influence, and parents relatively less potent sources of influence, on school performance among minority youngsters than they are among European-American youngsters. This is not to say that the mean levels of parental encouragement are necessarily lower in minority homes than in majority homes, but that the size of the correlations between parental encouragement and academic success and between peer encouragement and academic success are different for minority than for majority youth. In comparison with European-American youngsters, minority youngsters are relatively more influenced by their peers and relatively less influenced by their parents. This pattern of results suggested that to better understand influences on the school achievement of minority youth, we needed to look less at the family (the traditional focus of research on influences on school achievement) and more closely at the peer group.

The location of an adolescent within the school's social structure is very important, because peer crowd membership exerts an impact on school achievement above and beyond that of the family. Across all ethnic groups, youngsters who are members of academically oriented crowds and whose friends support achievement perform better than their peers, and these effects are over and above the contribution of the family (Steinberg & Brown, 1989). Indeed, an important predictor of academic success for an adolescent is the level of congruence between parent and peer support for academics: Students who receive academic support from both parents and peers perform better in school than those who receive support from only one source. It is important, therefore, to ask how it is that adolescents sort themselves into different crowds. We suspected that one of the key influences on crowd affiliation would be the home environment.

One of our undergraduate research assistants at Temple took on this hunch for her honors thesis (Durbin, Darling, Steinberg, & Brown, 1993). She found that, at least among European-American youth, youngsters from authoritative homes are more likely to belong to peer crowds that encourage academic achievement and school engagement: the "jocks" and the "populars." As a result, middle-class European-American youngsters (who are more likely than their peers to reside in authoritative homes) receive encouragement for school success from virtually everyone important in their life. For these youngsters, authoritative parenting is related to academic achievement not only because of the direct effect it has on the individual adolescent's work habits, but also because of the impact it has on the adolescent's crowd affiliation. Simply put, authoritatively raised adolescents are more likely to run with other youngsters who value school and behave in ways that earn them good grades. Once we realized this,

445

understanding the processes through which the family and peer group are linked during adolescence, and understanding ethnic differences in the nature of this link, became an important component of our research effort.

The Family–Peer Group Linkage

Historically, the implicit assumption has been that the adolescent peer group is a powerful counterinfluence to parental values and expectations, a force over which parents have little control (Gecas & Seff, 1990). (At times, this view has even been espoused by Bronfenbrenner himself [e.g., 1974].) Our data suggest that such an assumption severely underestimates parental influences on adolescents, because it ignores the role that parents play in directing their child to a particular peer group.

Adolescents do not haphazardly fall into one crowd or another and then adjust their attitudes and behavior to the normative pressures of that crowd. Instead, they are "selected into" a particular crowd by virtue of the reputation they establish among peers (Brown, 1990). One does not become a jock by quirk of fate or even simply by honing one's athletic skill and making the basketball team. One must be perceived by peers as acting primarily in "jocklike" ways: being interested in sports, getting fairly good (but not outstanding) grades, exuding self-confidence but remaining compliant with adult authority, shying away from drugs except for alcohol, and so on. There is, to be sure, pressure to conform to crowd norms (Clasen & Brown, 1985; Newman & Newman, 1976) and to select friends from fellow crowd members (Eckert, 1989; Eder, 1985), but these do not direct adolescents to new behaviors as much as they reinforce existing dispositions—dispositions that helped direct the adolescent to a particular crowd in the first place.

The fact that adolescents' crowds are differentiated on behaviors that other studies have shown to be strongly influenced by parenting strategies (e.g., academic achievement, drug use, delinquent activity, self-reliance, or self-esteem) suggests that there is a strong, but indirect, path between parenting practices and adolescent peer group affiliations. In other words, by fostering certain traits in their children, parents direct a child toward a particular peer group. Thus, to the extent that parents can influence characteristics by which adolescents are associated by peers with a crowd, parents can "control" the type of peer group influences to which their child is exposed.

Using our data on parenting practices, adolescent adjustment, and peer crowd affiliation, we developed and tested a model of parental influence on peer group affiliation, a question that focused on context at the mesosystem level (Brown, Mounts, Lamborn, & Steinberg, 1993). Our findings parallel those reported by the Cairnses (this volume, chapter 12) and by Dishion, in their respective studies of the links between home environments and the formation of antisocial cliques (Cairns, Cairns, Neckerman, Gest, & Gariépy, 1988; Dishion, 1990). Specifically, we found that parenting practices predict adolescent personality traits and orientations and that these traits and orientations, in turn, predict youngsters' crowd affiliation. In essence, parents have a direct and primary impact on adolescent behavior patterns—prosocial as well as antisocial. Peer groups serve primarily to reinforce established behavior patterns or dispositions.

The notion that parenting affects personality, which in turn affects peer group selection, seems sensible enough. And, as we demonstrated, the model works very well in predicting crowd affiliation from parenting practices among European-American youngsters. But when we attempted to apply this model to youngsters from minority backgrounds, we were in for a shock (Steinberg, Dornbusch, & Brown, 1992). We found that among African- and Asian-American students, there was no relation between parenting practices and peer crowd membership. Authoritatively raised minority youngsters are no more likely to belong to peer groups that encouraged academic success than are youngsters from less academically oriented homes.

How could this be? Recall that we had found a relation between parenting and personality development among minority as well as majority youngsters. If parents influence adolescent personality, and personality influences peer group selection, why was there no significant relation between parenting and peer group selection among minority youth? The answer, we discovered, is that models of peer group selection that assume an open system, in which adolescents can select into any number of groups as easily as ordering food from a restaurant menu, fail to take into account the tremendous level of ethnic segregation that characterizes the social structure of most ethnically mixed high schools in the United States. The social context of peer group selection for minority youth differs from that for majority youth.

In the course of conducting our interviews that were designed to reveal the social structure of each school, we spoke with students from each ethnic group in each school. For the most part, students from one ethnic group did not know their classmates from other ethnic groups very well. When presented with the name of a European-American classmate, for instance, a European-American student could usually assign that classmate to one of several differentiated peer crowds (e.g., "jocks," "populars," "brains," or "nerds"). When presented with the name of an African-American classmate, however, a European-American student would typically not know the group that this student ran with or might simply say that the student was a part of the "Black" crowd. The same was true for Hispanic- and Asian-American students. In other words, within ethnic groups, youngsters have a very differentiated view of their classmates; across ethnic groups, however, youngsters see their classmates as members of an ethnic group first, and members of a more differentiated crowd second, if at all.

More important, in ethnically mixed high schools, minority youngsters find their choices of peer groups exceedingly restricted. More often than not, Asian-American students have no choice but to belong to a peer group that encourages and rewards academic excellence—for better or for worse, it is extremely difficult for an Asian youngster to become a "jock," a "druggie," or a "preppie." One beneficial by-product of this peer segregation is that Asian-American youngsters report the highest level of peer support for academic achievement. Interestingly, and in contrast to popular belief, Asian-American students' parents are the *least* involved in their youngsters' schooling in terms of attendance at school programs, parent–teacher conferences, and school-sponsored extracurricular activities, and they are among the least authoritative in our sample (see also Dornbusch et al., 1987; Sue & Okazaki, 1990).

African-American students face quite a different dilemma. Although their parents are, as a rule, supportive of academic success (they score among the highest on our measure of parental involvement in schooling), these youngsters, we learned from our interviews, find it much more difficult to join a peer group that encourages the same goal. Just as it is difficult for an Asian-American student to join up with the "jocks," it is extremely difficult for an African-American student to make inroads into the "brains." Our interviews with high-achieving African-American students indicated that peer support for academic success is so limited that many successful African-American students eschew contact with other African-American students and affiliate primarily with students from other ethnic groups. As has been reported by Fordham, in her ethnographic studies of African-American teenagers (Fordham & Ogbu, 1986), we find that African-American students are more likely than others to be caught in a bind between performing well in school and being popular among their peers.

Understanding Asian- and African-American students' experiences in their peer groups helps to account for the finding that authoritative parenting practices, though predictive of these youngsters' psychological adjustment, appear almost unrelated to their school performance. For Asian-American students in nonauthoritative homes, the potential negative effects of these parenting practices on schooling are offset by the homogeneity of influence these youngsters encounter, in favor of academic success, in the peer group. For African-American youngsters in authoritative homes, the benefits of this type of parenting to schooling are offset by the lack of support for academic excellence among their peers.

Authoritative Parenting and the "Functional Community"

In addition to our interest in examining familial influences alongside the moderating influence of the peer group, we have also examined the role of the broader community in which the family lives.

Historically, two very different approaches have been taken in research on community effects. The first, which finds its origins in the Chicago

449

school, was developed initially by sociological or epidemiological researchers (e.g., Shaw et al., 1929). Their focus was on the aggregate characteristics of communities, and they sought to determine, for example, whether neighborhood poverty rates influence overall levels of delinquency or psychiatric disturbance; more recently, they have focused on the impact of neighborhood poverty on family functioning and normal child development, as is nicely illustrated in Brooks-Gunn's contribution to this volume (chapter 14). A second approach to the study of communities has focused on communities as networks of social relations. Researchers such as Ianni (1983) examined the extent to which individuals within a community have strong ties with neighbors and relatives and rely on these significant others for support. Our work falls mainly within this second tradition. We have been interested in examining the role of what sociologist James Coleman has called the *functional community.*

Coleman first introduced the concept of the functional community as a possible explanation for the superior academic performance of students within Catholic high schools (Coleman & Hoffer, 1987). A functional community is characterized both by network closure (nonrelated adults knowing one another) and value consensus (the acceptance of a dominant set of values within the community). In theory, children who develop within a functional community receive consistent messages about their behavior and obligations and are encouraged to behave appropriately by nonfamilial, as well as familial, adults (Coleman & Hoffer, 1987).

What constitutes the functional community for the majority of adolescents? We reasoned that one possibility is the network of families that develops through the child's peer relationships. These relationships are important, because of all nonrelated adults in children's lives, their friends' parents are potentially among those with whom children most often interact. Accordingly, we undertook a series of analyses to investigate whether adolescents are influenced by the parenting practices of their peers' parents (Fletcher, Darling, Steinberg, & Dornbusch, 1993). Specifically, we hypothesized that adolescents would benefit from having friends whose parents are authoritative, over and above the benefits of having authoritative parents of one's own.

In addition to examining whether the parenting practices of friends' parents influence adolescents, we also asked whether such an effect differs according to the home environment of the target adolescent. According to Coleman and Hoffer (1987), the positive outcomes of functional communities may differentially affect children whose own families differ in their internal strength. Interestingly, the authors offered two alternative scenarios for how the presence of a functional community may influence children: *amplification* and *compensation*. In the case of amplification, children who are already advantaged by the human and social capital within their own families are hypothesized to benefit most from residence in a functional community. In contrast, in the case of compensation, the advantage conferred by the social structures of a functional community may benefit more those individuals who have fewer advantages within their own families. In the present study, we asked whether the parenting practices used in the adolescent's peer network amplify or compensate for the practices that the youngster is exposed to at home.

We noted earlier that subjects provided the names of up to five of their closest friends and that these friends also provided information about their own parents' behavior. We were, therefore, able to calculate the authoritativeness of each friend's parents, using the procedure described earlier for assessing authoritativeness as a continuous variable. Target subjects were then classified into one of five levels reflecting the prevalence of authoritativeness among their friends' parents, ranging from *mostly nonauthoritative* (at least half of the reported friends had nonauthoritative parents) to *mostly authoritative* (at least half of the reported friends had authoritative parents).

Our analyses proceeded in two steps. First, we conducted a series of hierarchical regression analyses, in which we first entered a score reflecting the level of authoritativeness in the respondent's home, next entered a score reflecting the prevalence of authoritativeness in the respondent's peer group, and finally entered a term reflecting the interaction between the two parenting measures. The interaction term was tested to examine whether the impact of authoritative parenting in the adolescent's social network is differentially predictive of adjustment among adolescents whose own parents are relatively high versus relatively low in authoritativeness themselves (i.e., whether authoritativeness in the peer network amplifies authoritativeness at home, compensates for nonauthoritativeness at home, or neither).

The second series of analyses were conducted to determine whether any observed association between authoritative parenting in the adolescent's peer network and adolescent adjustment was mediated by the behavior of the adolescent's peers themselves. In these analyses, hierarchical regressions were conducted in which we first entered a score reflecting the level of authoritativeness in the respondent's home, next entered a score reflecting the prevalence of authoritativeness in the respondent's peer group, and finally entered a term reflecting the behavior of the adolescent's peers on the outcome in question. Peer behavior was presumed to mediate the connection between network parenting and adolescent adjustment if a significant association between network parenting and adolescent adjustment diminished to nonsignificance once peer behavior was taken into account.

We found that the prevalence of parental authoritativeness in an adolescent's network of peers is associated with a variety of indicators of healthy adjustment, above and beyond the contribution of authoritativeness in the adolescent's family of origin. Specifically, adolescents whose friends' parents are authoritative earn higher grades in school, spend more time on homework, have more positive perceptions of their academic competence, and report lower levels of delinquency and substance use. In addition, boys whose friends' parents are authoritative are less likely to engage in school misconduct and report lower levels of peer conformity. Among girls, high levels of network authoritativeness are associated with greater psychosocial competence (as indexed by work orientation, self-reliance, and self-esteem) and lower levels of psychological distress, such as depressed affect or anxiety.

Our analyses of whether these network effects tend to amplify versus compensate for the home environment pointed almost always to amplification. In other words, adolescents whose own parents are already relatively more authoritative appear to benefit more from membership in a peer network with other authoritatively reared youngsters than do adolescents in similar networks, but from less authoritative homes. It appears that adolescents need certain "home advantages" to be able to take advantage of the social capital in their social networks.

Our analyses also indicated a mechanism through which authoritative parenting in the adolescent's peer network may operate. We found that the influence of authoritativeness among the adolescent's friends' parents is not direct, but is indirect, transmitted through the friends' behavior. Thus, authoritative parenting promotes adolescent competence, and competent youngsters are attracted to, and influence, each other. On the basis of our analyses of the relation between parenting practices and peer crowd affiliation described earlier, it would appear, then, that well-adjusted adolescents from authoritative homes select similarly competent peers and that experiences within their peer group serve to amplify and maintain their higher level of adjustment. In contrast, less competent adolescents from nonauthoritative homes are more likely to select comparably less competent peers, and their peer group amplifies and maintains their disadvantage.

One exception to this general pattern involves delinquency, however. Here, the relation between network authoritativeness and involvement in delinquent activities remained significant even after controlling for the level of delinquency among the adolescents' peers. Thus, the prevalence of authoritativeness among one's friends' parents may directly influence the likelihood of an adolescent engaging in delinquent activities. We believe that this may be due in part to the higher level of shared social control provided by a network of authoritative parents, an interpretation consistent with research on the impact of parental vigilance on community-wide delinquency (see also Sampson & Groves, 1989). By definition, authoritative parents are careful monitors of their children's behavior; intentionally or inadvertently, they may monitor their children's associates as well.

Growing up in a context in which the nonfamilial adults one knows are authoritative may be beneficial in two ways, then. First, it makes it more likely that one will associate with relatively more competent peers. Second, living in a community that includes authoritative adults other than one's parents may help encourage competence in adolescents directly, by facilitating cross-generational contact between adolescents and effective nonfamilial socialization agents.

Structural Characteristics of Neighborhoods and Their Effects on Parenting

These last findings suggested to us that being immersed in a social network characterized by a high number of friends with authoritative parents is likely to foster the development of the adolescent above and beyond the influence of her or his own family. We next asked whether structural characteristics of the neighborhoods in which families live contribute to adolescent socialization. In our program, neighborhoods differed from social networks in that neighborhoods were defined by geographical boundaries rather than by social ties.

Coleman and Hoffer (1987) argued that two structural properties of neighborhoods facilitate the socialization of adolescents: *value consensus* and *social integration*. Value consensus is the extent to which members of the community share common values and agree about the means to realize those values. Coleman and Hoffer argued that value consensus contributes to the formation of social capital by increasing the likelihood that the different contexts the adolescent is exposed to will reinforce the same values and by allowing agents of socialization (i.e., parents, community adults, and school personnel) to act more freely to socialize adolescents without worrying about social sanction. In addition to these direct benefits, homogeneity of values among parents, community adults, and school personnel will increase the likelihood that an adolescent's peers will share the same values as the adolescent and his or her family, thus further perpetuating the existing social order. Such consensus may also act synergistically, because reinforcement of values in multiple contexts supports, rather than undermines, the influence of each individual context.

Coleman has been interested in a particular form of social integration, what he calls *intergenerational closure*. Intergenerational closure is the extent to which the social networks of neighborhood adults and youth overlap. For example, a neighborhood in which most parents know the friends of their children and those friends' families would be characterized by intergenerational closure. Teachers' knowledge of their students' family members also contributes to intergenerational closure. Coleman and Hoffer (1987) argued that intergenerational closure increases the ability of communities to socialize adolescents in three ways: by increasing social support, by increasing value consensus, and by strengthening the ability of the community to condemn norm violations. Contact with others provides the opportunity to gain instrumental and emotional support and increases the likelihood that agreement will occur. Contact with others also increases opportunities for observing normative behavior as well as the likelihood that norm violations will be criticized. In addition, when neighborhood adults have contact with one another in multiple settings, norm violations in one setting can have implications in others. Similarly, when youths are known not just as individuals, but as members of particular families, norm violations by parents will have consequences for how others perceive and interact with their children.

We were able to examine some of these notions by using the neighborhood as a unit of analysis. As we noted earlier, we plan in the future to use genuine neighborhood codes to undertake this part of the study. For the time being, we have used the census tract as an imperfect proxy for the neighborhood.

The search for neighborhood effects—whatever the level of analysis— is a difficult challenge. To attribute changes in children's behavior to processes operating at the neighborhood level, one needs to separate the influence of communities from the aggregate influence of families (Bronfenbrenner, Moen, & Garbarino, 1984; Jencks & Mayer, 1988; Steinberg, 1989). For example, it is likely that adolescents from a community characterized by high parental monitoring would perform better in school and be less involved in deviance than adolescents from a low monitoring community. This difference cannot necessarily be attributed to the neighborhood, however. The same results would exist if parents in these families influenced their own, and only their own, children. When aggregated at the neighborhood level, family-level effects will result in community-level differences. Documenting neighborhood-level differences is different from documenting neighborhood-level effects, however. Documenting a neighborhood-level effect requires evidence for processes operating outside of the family. In a series of analyses aimed at this, we looked at the effects of social integration and value consensus.

Social Integration

Using a series of questions about parents' contact with their children's friends, about their participation in community and school activities, and about their ties to other families in the neighborhood, we were able to construct a rough index of each family's degree of social integration into the neighborhood. We then used this index in two ways: to characterize individual families (as being relatively more or less integrated into their community) and to characterize neighborhoods (as being composed of a high versus low percentage of socially integrated families; see Darling, Steinberg, & Gringlas, 1993, for details). We refer to these indexes as *family social integration* and *neighborhood social integration*, respectively. We examined the relations between family and neighborhood integration and two specific aspects of adolescent adjustment thought to be influenced at this level: academic performance and deviance. Our working hypothesis was that adolescents who live in families and in communities that are socially integrated will perform better in school and be more likely to stay out of trouble.

As predicted, we found that family social integration was modestly, but consistently, correlated with positive adolescent adjustment. Interestingly, for academic outcomes, this relationship did not appear to be mediated through parenting, but seemed to benefit adolescents directly. In other words, adolescents from families who are integrated into their communities do not perform better in school simply because their family's social integration makes it more likely that their parents will become more involved in academic affairs. Rather, it seems that adolescents benefit directly from the increased exchange of resources allowed by their parents' social integration. On the other hand, the relation between social integration and lack of involvement in deviance dropped below significance once parenting was controlled, suggesting that the impact of family social integration on adolescent deviance is, unlike the impact on academic performance, mediated through parenting practices. Parents who are more socially integrated into the community also are more vigilant about their child's behavior, and this vigilance deters their adolescent from deviance.

These findings support the widely held notion that it is beneficial for parents to be actively integrated into their community. Before we endorse attempts to foster greater contact between families in a neighborhood, however, an important caveat is necessary. We reran these analyses separately in neighborhoods characterized by a high proportion of effective versus noneffective parents. We found that whether family social integration benefits adolescents depends on characteristics of the neighborhood into which parents are being integrated. Social integration benefits only adolescents whose families live in neighborhoods characterized by good parenting. Social integration into a neighborhood characterized by a high proportion of bad parents actually has a harmful effect on adolescents' school performance and behavior.

These findings refer to the integration of the family into the community. Interestingly, we found little support for the notion that neighborhood social integration is beneficial to youngsters above and beyond the level of integration of their own family. That is, living in a neighborhood characterized by a high degree of social integration is beneficial to an individual adolescent only if that child's family is socially integrated. Adolescents growing up in socially isolated families are at a disadvantage, regardless of whether other families in their community are socially integrated. Conversely, adolescents growing up in well-integrated families benefit from their parents' strong ties, regardless of the overall level of social integration among other families in the community. Thus, it is not so much the neighborhood, but the individual family's ties with the neighborhood, that makes a difference. As Brooks-Gunn points out (see this volume, chapter 14) and in keeping with Bronfenbrenner's own perspective, the family is the primary proximal setting through which community influence on children's development is transmitted.

Value Consensus

By aggregating information on various parenting practices and attitudes within members of a neighborhood, we also were able to calculate the degree of value consensus among parents in a given neighborhood. We looked, for example, at the extent to which parents in a neighborhood shared an interest in their children's achievement or practiced similar kinds of monitoring. Here our interest was not in the mean level of parental encouragement or monitoring in a neighborhood, however, but in the correlation that existed between an adolescent's parents' values and those of the other families and in the variability in the values and behaviors of families in a particular area. In other words, value consensus can exist between the family and the community (i.e., whether an individual family's values are consonant with those of other families in the neighborhood) and within the community as a whole (i.e., the general degree of consensus among families in the neighborhood). Our working hypothesis was that adolescents would fare better when the correlation between their parents' values and those of other families was high and when the variance in values among parents in the neighborhood was low.

Our analyses indicated that consensus between the parenting of adolescents' families and neighborhood adults around achievement-related concerns augments the influence of parents on their youngsters—reminiscent of the amplification effect we saw earlier in our analyses of adolescents' social networks. We also find a similar effect for value consensus within the neighborhood as a whole; that is, under conditions of value consensus, parental practices have more of a payoff.

As was the case in our analyses of social integration, however, the impact of value consensus depends on what the consensus is about. High neighborhood consensus augments the association between parenting and adolescent outcomes only when the consensus is around good parenting. High neighborhood consensus around lower standards or less vigilant monitoring, not surprisingly, does not carry a beneficial effect.

We wish to emphasize that our examination of community effects is most informative not when we compare mean levels of functioning among families or adolescents from different communities, but when we examine differences in the correlation between family processes and adolescent outcomes as a function of community context. In looking at our data this way (i.e., comparing correlations rather than comparing means), we have followed Bronfenbrenner's lead that an ecological approach to the study of development requires moving beyond the time-worn practice of relying on measures of central tendencies to describe developmental patterns (see also the chapters in this volume by Magnusson [2], Rutter, Champion, Quinton, Maughan, & Pickles [3], and Cairns & Cairns [12]).

Our analyses of the effects of social integration and value consensus also indicate that the impact of structural features of a neighborhood on any particular adolescent outcome can be assessed only when the content of a community's goals and values are taken into account—a seemingly obvious point that seems to have been overlooked by many researchers interested in neighborhood effects. Although it makes sense to predict that community consensus about high academic standards will be associated with adolescents' positive orientation toward school, there is no reason to believe that community consensus about low standards will be. In other words, it is what parents in a community agree about, not merely whether they agree, that makes a difference. Similarly, although we tend to think of social integration as a desirable endpoint, its desirability depends on the nature of the people that integration brings one into contact with. There are many communities in contemporary America in which it may be more adaptive for parents to be socially isolated than socially integrated. Indeed, some of Furstenberg's (1990) recent work on family life in the inner city of Philadelphia suggests that social isolation is often deliberately practiced as an adaptive strategy by many parents living in dangerous neighborhoods.

CONCLUSION

The findings reported in this chapter should serve to illustrate the complex mechanisms through which the contexts in which adolescents live influence their life and their behavior. They should also serve to illustrate the profound influence that Urie Bronfenbrenner has had on our thinking.

We began with a fairly conventional question within the study of socialization: the relation between authoritative parenting and adolescent adjustment. What we found is, in some cases, old news, reported by Bronfenbrenner some 25 years ago in an obscure, but excellent, volume on the socialization of leadership and responsibility (Bronfenbrenner, 1961). In the 1990s, as was the case in the 1950s, adolescents whose parents are warm, firm, and democratic are better adjusted and more competent than their peers.

I hope that we have expanded on Bronfenbrenner's early insights into the socialization of adolescent competence, however. Our longitudinal analyses suggest that authoritative parenting actually leads to improvements in adolescent adjustment, rather than simply accompanying it, even during the high school years. Also, we have shown that the terrible consequences of parental disengagement continue to accumulate, even as youngsters approach the final years of adolescence. Moreover, our findings suggest that the benefits of parental authoritativeness may not be limited, as has been argued by some, to European-American youngsters from middle-class homes.

Where I think our study may be most important, however—and most tied to the ecological perspective advanced by Bronfenbrenner—is not in what it tells us about what takes place within the family, but in what it suggests about the family's embeddedness in a broader context. The effects of authoritative parenting—or, for that matter, any type of parenting—must be examined within the broader context in which the family lives and in which youngsters develop. The impact of parenting practices on youngsters' behavior and development is moderated to a large extent by the social milieu young people encounter in their peer crowd, among their close friends, within their social network, and in their neighborhood. That, of course, was the moral of the Kansas City conversation. In this chapter, we illustrated how many of Bronfenbrenner's notions about multisetting links, about the embeddedness of proximal contexts in broader ones, and about the links between person, process, and setting can be incorporated into a research program and, more important, how doing so expands our understanding of the course and context of development.

One of the most valuable lessons Urie Bronfenbrenner taught his students was the importance of presenting data in a way that tells a story. It would be remiss, therefore, to conclude this chapter without a strong take-home message. As Urie would invariably ask, "What is the story here?"

We believe that it is this: Although authoritative parenting "works," in the sense that adolescents fare better when their parents behave this way;

it clearly works better in some contexts than in others. Indeed, in certain ecologies, overarching forces, outside the control of parents, may entirely overwhelm the beneficial effects of authoritative parenting in the home. In other contexts, beneficial forces outside the family may offset what otherwise might be disastrous parenting. The ironic lesson we have learned over the past decade, then, is that the key to understanding the influence of the parenting during adolescence inheres in looking beyond the boundaries of the home and at the broader context in which the family lives.

REFERENCES

Baumrind, D. (1967). Child care practices anteceding three patterns of preschool behavior. *Genetic Psychology Monographs, 75*, 43–88.

Baumrind, D. (1991a). Effective parenting during the early adolescent transition. In P. A. Cowan & E. M. Hetherington (Eds.), *Advances in family research* (Vol. 2, pp. 111–163). Hillsdale, NJ: Erlbaum.

Baumrind, D. (1991b). The influence of parenting style on adolescent competence and substance use. *Journal of Early Adolescence, 11*, 56–95.

Bell, R. (1968). A reinterpretation of the direction of effects in studies of socialization. *Psychological Review, 75*, 81–95.

Bronfenbrenner, U. (1961). Some familial antecedents of responsibility and leadership in adolescents. In L. Petrullo & B. Bass (Eds.), *Leadership and interpersonal behavior* (pp. 239–271). New York: Holt, Rinehart & Winston.

Bronfenbrenner, U. (1974). The origins of alienation. *Scientific American, 231*, 53–81.

Bronfenbrenner, U. (1979). *The ecology of human development: Experiments by nature and design.* Cambridge, MA: Harvard University Press.

Bronfenbrenner, U. (1989). Ecological systems theory. In R. Vasta (Ed.), *Annals of child development* (Vol. 6, pp. 187–249). Greenwich, CT: JAI Press.

Bronfenbrenner, U., Moen, P., & Garbarino, J. (1984). Child, family, and community. In R. Parke (Ed.), *Review of child development research* (Vol. 7, pp. 283–328). Chicago: University of Chicago Press.

Brown, B. (1989). *Social type rating manual.* Madison: University of Wisconsin, National Center on Effective Secondary Schools.

Brown, B. (1990). Peer groups and peer cultures. In S. Feldman & G. Elliott (Eds.), *At the threshold: The developing adolescent* (pp. 171–196). Cambridge, MA: Harvard University Press.

Brown, B., Mounts, N., Lamborn, S., & Steinberg, L. (1993). Parenting practices and peer group affiliation in adolescence. *Child Development, 64,* 467–482.

Brown, B., Steinberg, L., Mounts, N., & Philipp, M. (1990, March). The comparative influence of peers and parents on high school achievement: Ethnic differences. In *Ethnic variations in adolescent experience.* Symposium conducted at the biennial meetings of the Society for Research on Adolescence, Atlanta, GA.

Cairns, R. B., Cairns, B. D., Neckerman, H. J., Gest, S. D., & Gariépy, J.-L. (1988). Social networks and aggressive behavior: Peer support or peer rejection? *Developmental Psychology, 24,* 815–823.

Case, A., & Katz, L. (1992). *The company you keep: The effects of family and neighborhood on disadvantaged youths.* Unpublished manuscript, Princeton University, Princeton, NJ.

Clasen, D. R., & Brown, B. B. (1985). The multidimensionality of peer pressure in adolescence. *Journal of Youth and Adolescence, 14,* 451–468.

Coleman, J. (1988). Social capital in the creation of human capital. *American Journal of Sociology, 94,* s95–s120.

Coleman, J., & Hoffer, T. (1987). *Public and private high schools: The impact of communities.* New York: Basic Books.

Collins, W. A. (1990). Parent–child relationships in the transition to adolescence: Continuity and change in interaction, affect, and cognition. In R. Montemayor, G. Adams, & T. Gullotta (Eds.), *Advances in adolescent development: Volume 2. The transition from childhood to adolescence.* Newbury Park, CA: Sage.

Darling, N., & Steinberg, L. (1993). Parenting style as context: An integrative model. *Psychological Bulletin, 113,* 487–496.

Darling, N., Steinberg, L., & Gringlas, M. (1993, March). Community integration and value consensus as forces for adolescent socialization: A test of the Coleman and Hoffer hypothesis. In *Community and neighborhood influences on adolescent behavior.* Symposium conducted at the biennial meetings of the Society for Research in Child Development, New Orleans, LA.

Dishion, T. J. (1990). The peer context of troublesome child and adolescent behavior. In P. E. Leone (Ed.), *Understanding troubled and troubling youth* (pp. 128–153). Newbury Park, CA: Sage.

Donovan, J., & Jessor, R. (1985). Structure of problem behavior in adolescence and young adulthood. *Journal of Consulting and Clinical Psychology, 53,* 890–904.

Dornbusch, S., Carlsmith, J., Bushwall, S., Ritter, P., Leiderman, H., Hastorf, A., & Gross, R. (1985). Single parents, extended households, and the control of adolescents. *Child Development, 56,* 326–341.

Dornbusch, S. M., Ritter, P. L., Leiderman, P., Roberts, D., & Fraleigh, M. (1987). The relation of parenting style to adolescent school performance. *Child Development, 58,* 1244–1257.

Dornbusch, S., Ritter, P., & Steinberg, L. (1991). Differences between African Americans and non-Hispanic Whites in the relation of family statuses to adolescent school performance. *American Journal of Education, August,* 543–567.

Dowd, F. S. (1991). *Latchkey children in the library and community: Issues, strategies, and programs.* Phoenix, AZ: Onyx Press.

Durbin, D., Darling, N., Steinberg, L., & Brown, B. (1993). Parenting style and peer group membership among European-American adolescents. *Journal of Research on Adolescence, 3,* 87–100.

Eckert, P. (1989). *Jocks and burnouts: Social categories and identity in the high school.* New York: Teachers College Press.

Eder, D. (1985). The cycle of popularity: Interpersonal relations among female adolescents. *Sociology of Education, 58,* 154–165.

Esbensen, F., & Huizinga, D. (1990). Community structure and drug use from a social disorganization perspective. *Justice Quarterly, 7,* 691–709.

Fletcher, A., Darling, N., Steinberg, L., & Dornbusch, S. (1993). *The company they keep: Impact of authoritative parenting in the adolescent's social network on individual adjustment and behavior.* Manuscript submitted for publication, Department of Psychology, Temple University, Philadelphia.

Fordham, S., & Ogbu, J. U. (1986). Black students' school success: Coping with the burden of "acting White." *Urban Review, 18,* 176–206.

Furstenburg, F., Jr. (1990, August). *How families manage risk and opportunity in dangerous neighborhoods.* Paper presented at the 84th annual meeting of the American Sociological Association, Washington, DC.

Gecas, V., & Seff, M. A. (1990). Families and adolescents: A review of the 1980s. *Journal of Marriage and the Family, 52,* 941–958.

Gold, M. (1970). *Delinquent behavior in an American city.* Belmont, CA: Brooks/Cole.

Golden, P. (1969). A review of children's reports of parental behaviors. *Psychological Bulletin, 71,* 222–235.

Greenberger, E., Josselson, R., Knerr, C., & Knerr, B. (1974). The measurement and structure of psychosocial maturity. *Journal of Youth and Adolescence, 4,* 127–143.

Greenberger, E., Steinberg, L., & Vaux, A. (1981). Adolescents who work: Health and behavioral consequences of job stress. *Developmental Psychology, 17,* 691–703.

Harter, S. (1982). The perceived competence scale for children. *Child Development, 53,* 87–97.

Ianni, F. A. J. (1983). *Home, school, and community in adolescent education.* New York: Clearinghouse on Urban Education.

Jencks, C., & Mayer, S. (1988). *The social consequences of growing up in a poor neighborhood: A review.* Unpublished manuscript, Northwestern University Center for Urban Affairs and Policy Research, Evanston, IL.

Jessor, R., & Jessor, S. (1977). *Problem behavior and psychosocial development: A longitudinal study of youth.* New York: Academic Press.

Ladd, G. W. (1983). Social networks of popular, average, and rejected children in school settings. *Merrill-Palmer Quarterly, 29*, 353–374.

Laird, N. (1983). Further comparative analyses of pretest–posttest research designs. *The American Statistician, 37*, 329–330.

Lamborn, S., Mounts, N., Steinberg, L., & Dornbusch, S. (1991). Patterns of competence and adjustment among adolescents from authoritative, authoritarian, indulgent, and neglectful homes. *Child Development, 62*, 1049–1065.

Lewis, C. (1981). The effects of parental firm control. *Psychological Bulletin, 90*, 547–563.

Maccoby, E., & Martin, J. (1983). Socialization in the context of the family: Parent–child interaction. In P. H. Mussen (Series Ed.) & E. M. Hetherington (Vol. Ed.), *Handbook of child psychology: Vol. 4. Socialization, personality, and social development* (4th ed., pp. 1–101). New York: Wiley.

McCord, J. (1990). Problem behaviors. In S. Feldman & G. Elliot (Eds.), *At the threshold: The developing adolescent* (pp. 414–430). Cambridge, MA: Harvard University Press.

Moskowitz, D., & Schwarz, J. (1982). A validity comparison of behavior counts and ratings by knowledgeable informants. *Journal of Personality and Social Psychology, 42*, 518–528.

Mounts, N., Lamborn, S., & Steinberg, L. (1989, April). Relations between family process and school achievement in different ethnic contexts. In *Ethnic comparisons of parent and peer influences on adolescent development.* Symposium conducted at the biennial meetings of the Society for Research in Child Development, Kansas City.

Mounts, N., & Steinberg, L. (1992). *Peer influences on adolescent achievement and deviance: An ecological approach.* Manuscript submitted for publication, Department of Educational Psychology, University of Illinois, Champaign.

Newman, P. R., & Newman, B. M. (1976). Early adolescence and its conflict: Group identity versus alienation. *Adolescence, 11*, 261–274.

Patterson, G., & Stouthamer-Loeber, M. (1984). The correlation of family management practices and delinquency. *Child Development, 55,* 1299–1307.

Poveda, T. G. (1975). Reputation and the adolescent girl: An analysis. *Adolescence, 37,* 127–136.

Radloff, L. S. (1977). The CES–D scale: A self-report depression scale for research in the general population. *Applied Psychological Measurement, 1,* 385–401.

Rodgers, R. R. (1966). *Cornell parent behavior description—An interim report.* Unpublished manuscript, Department of Human Development and Family Studies, Cornell University, Ithaca, NY.

Ruggiero, M. (1984). *Work as an impetus to delinquency: An examination of theoretical and empirical connections.* Unpublished doctoral dissertation, University of California, Irvine.

Sampson, R. J. (1992). Family management and child development: Insights from social disorganization theory. In J. McCord (Ed.), *Advances in criminological theory: Vol. 3. Facts, frameworks, and forecasts* (pp. 63–93). New Brunswick, NJ: Transaction.

Sampson, R., & Groves, W. (1989). Community structure and crime: Testing social-disorganization theory. *American Journal of Sociology, 94,* 774–802.

Scarr, S. (1992). Developmental theories for the 1990s: Development and individual differences. *Child Development, 63,* 1–19.

Schaefer, E. (1965). Children's reports of parental behavior: An inventory. *Child Development, 36,* 413–424.

Schwarz, J., Barton-Henry, M., & Pruzinsky, T. (1985). Assessing child-rearing behaviors: A comparison of ratings made by mother, father, child, and sibling on the CRPBI. *Child Development, 56,* 462–479.

Schwendinger, H., & Schwendinger, J. S. (1985). *Adolescent subcultures and delinquency.* New York: Praeger.

Shaw, C., & McKay, H. (1969). *Juvenile delinquency and urban areas: A study of rates of delinquency in relation to differential characteristics of local communities in American cities.* Chicago: University of Chicago Press.

Shaw, C., Zorbaugh, F., McKay, H., & Cottrell, L. (1929). *Delinquency areas.* Chicago: University of Chicago Press.

Steinberg, L. (1989). Communities of families and education. In W. Weston (Ed.), *Education and the American family: A research synthesis* (pp. 138–168). New York: New York University Press.

Steinberg, L. (1990). Autonomy, conflict, and harmony in the family relationship. In

S. Feldman & G. Elliot (Eds.), *At the threshold: The developing adolescent* (pp. 255–276). Cambridge, MA: Harvard University Press.

Steinberg, L., & Brown, B. (1989, March). *Beyond the classroom: Family and peer influences on high school achievement.* Invited paper presented to the Families as Educators special interest group at the annual meetings of the American Educational Research Association, San Francisco.

Steinberg, L., Dornbusch, S., & Brown, B. (1992). Ethnic differences in adolescent achievement: An ecological perspective. *American Psychologist, 47,* 723–729.

Steinberg, L., Elmen, J., & Mounts, N. (1989). Authoritative parenting, psychosocial maturity, and academic success among adolescents. *Child Development, 60,* 1424–1436.

Steinberg, L., Lamborn, S. D., Darling, N., Mounts, N. S., & Dornbusch, S. M. (in press). Over-time changes in adjustment and competence among adolescents from authoritative, authoritarian, indulgent, and neglectful families. *Child Development.*

Steinberg, L., Lamborn, S., Dornbusch, S., & Darling, N. (1992). Impact of parenting practices on adolescent achievement: Authoritative parenting, school involvement, and encouragement to succeed. *Child Development, 63,* 1266–1281.

Steinberg, L., Mounts, N., Lamborn, S., & Dornbusch, S. (1991). Authoritative parenting and adolescent adjustment across varied ecological niches. *Journal of Research on Adolescence, 1*(1), 19–36.

Sue, S., & Okazaki, S. (1990). Asian-American educational achievements: A phenomenon in search of an explanation. *American Psychologist, 45,* 913–920.

Wehlage, G., Rutter, R., Smith, G., Lesko, N., & Fernandez, R. (1989). *Reducing the risk: Schools as communities of support.* London: Falmer Press.

Weinberger, D., Tublin, S., Ford, M., & Feldman, S. (1990). Preadolescents' social–emotional adjustment and selective attrition in family research. *Child Development, 61,* 1374–1386.

Weis, J. R. (1974). Styles of middle-class adolescent drug use. *Pacific Sociological Review, 17,* 251–285.

Weisz, J. R. (1978). Transcontextual validity in developmental research. *Child Development, 49,* 1–12.

Wilson, W. J. (1987). *The truly disadvantaged: The inner city, the underclass, and public policy.* Chicago: University of Chicago Press.

466

14

Children in Families in Communities: Risk and Intervention in the Bronfenbrenner Tradition

Jeanne Brooks-Gunn

It is an honor to contribute to a volume highlighting Urie Bronfen-brenner's central place in developmental psychology. Bronfenbrenner has had far-reaching effects on the theoretical frameworks used to study children, as well as on the intersection of individual, family, and community influences on children. His life work has influenced me profoundly. Though not a student of his in the traditional sense (not having studied at Cornell University), I am, in an intellectual sense, a Bronfenbrenner stu-

The writing of this chapter was supported by foundation grants from the NICHD Child and Family Well-Being Research Network, the March of Dimes, and the Centers for Disease Control. The data sets from which exemplars are drawn were supported by a number of foundations and federal agencies. Their continued interest in children and families at risk is appreciated. The Infant Health and Development Program was funded by grants from the Robert Wood Johnson Foundation, the Pew Charitable Trust, the NICHD, the Bureau of Maternal and Child Health, and the Department of Pediatrics at Stanford University. The Baltimore Study of Teenage Parenthood was supported by the Commonwealth Fund, the Ford Foundation, the Robert Wood Johnson Foundation, the Office of Adolescent Pregnancy (DHHS), and NICHD. The analyses of neighborhood and family effects in the Panel Study of Income Dynamics, the Infant Health and Development Program, and the Children of the National Longitudinal Study of Youth were funded by grants from the Russell Sage Foundation, the Rockefeller Foundation, the W. T. Grant Foundation, and the Smith-Richardson Foundation. Thanks are due to my colleagues Greg Duncan, Kristine Moore, Brett Brown, Pam Klebanov, and Lindsay Chase-Lansdale, Craig Ramey, Cecilia McCarton, Marie McCormick, Ruth Gross, and Ruby Hearn for their collaboration and comments. I would also like to thank the Marx family for their support, and Virginia Marx in particular for her commitment to bettering the lives of young children and their families.

dent. All aspects of my research have benefited from his writings, his wise counsel, and, of course, his lively questioning and critiques.

I first encountered Bronfenbrenner when I was a graduate student, when he presented a seminar at the University of Pennsylvania. My most vivid memory is of Bronfenbrenner beseeching us to go beyond studying individuals to consider context. In this spirit, this chapter is entitled "Children in Families in Communities." Twenty years of the Bronfenbrenner tradition have taught us that children's development may be understood only in context. Whenever the term *children's development* is used, it must stand for children's development in context. Perhaps Bronfenbrenner would retort that the phrase *children in families in communities* is too restrictive. After all, many contexts are excluded, and all of the Bronfenbrenner ecological systems are not represented. However, the phrase captures the spirit of the contextual movement in developmental psychology. My second recollection is of Bronfenbrenner saying how disappointed he was, in that none of the students at the seminar seemed to have the vaguest idea of how to harness developmental theory in the quest to improve the lives of children and families. How could intervention efforts be successful if links to actual life circumstances were not made? And what was wrong with this new generation of developmental psychologists? Clearly, our priorities were wrong or perhaps just muddled.

This essay is dedicated to Urie Bronfenbrenner. It is my fondest hope that perhaps he will revise his 20-year-old prediction. Perhaps my generation's priorities were not really so off the mark. Today, (a) the contextual perspective is taken seriously, (b) more developmentally appropriate interventions are being designed, (c) the effects of interventions are being examined for subgroups of children and families, and (d) the lives of families and children at risk for life difficulties are being studied in a more sensitive and comprehensive fashion.

To tie the four above-mentioned conceptual threads together, a family and community resource framework is used to study children in families in communities. Of particular interest are the effects of the contexts in which children reside (defined, perhaps somewhat narrowly, in terms of resources), particularly those contexts that are often labeled as *disad-*

vantageous. The intersection of context and intervention is also a theme on which the chapter revolves. Three data sets will be drawn on: the Infant Health and Development Program (IHDP), the Panel Study of Income Dynamics (PSID), and the Children of the National Longitudinal Study of Youth (Children of the NLSY).

The IHDP is a multisite clinical trial designed to test the efficacy of providing family and early-childhood-intervention services to low-birth-weight (LBW) premature children, to reduce developmental delays. Services were provided to families randomized into an intervention group. Children received services from their discharge from the neonatal nursery until they were age 3. Home visits were provided throughout the 3 years, while center-based schooling was provided for the second 2 years (age 12 to 36 months). The sample was stratified according to site (eight medical centers) and birth weight (lighter LBW children were 2,000 g or less, and heavier LBW children were 2,001 to 2,500 g at birth). The program is further described in several publications (Brooks-Gunn, Gross, Kraemer, Spiker, & Shapiro, 1992; Brooks-Gunn, Klebanov, Liaw, & Spiker, 1993; Gross, Brooks-Gunn, & Spiker, 1992; Infant Health and Development Program, 1990; Kraemer & Fendt, 1990; McCormick et al., 1991; Ramey et al., 1992). The PSID is an ongoing longitudinal survey of U.S. households begun in 1968 (Survey Research Center, 1984). By following all members of its sample over time, including children as they leave their parents' homes, the PSID maintains a representative sample of the nonimmigrant U.S. populations (which means that Hispanic-American families are underrepresented; however, a new sample of Hispanic-American families was drawn in the last 5 years). Low-income families were oversampled (Duncan, Hill, & Hoffman, 1988; Hill & Duncan, 1987). The NLSY is a nationally representative sample of youth (14 to 19 years of age) drawn in 1979; members are followed yearly. Only the children born to the women in the NLSY are being followed. Child supplements were added in 1986, 1988, 1990, and 1992. The children are not a representative sample because children born to younger mothers are overrepresented. As the NLSY cohort ages, the child sample becomes more representative. African-Americans and low-income European-Americans were oversampled (Brooks-

Gunn, Phelps, & Elder, 1991; Chase-Lansdale, Mott, Brooks-Gunn, & Phillips, 1991).

The chapter is divided into four parts. First, a conceptual framework is described, which draws on economic and sociological as well as developmental theory. The development of a framework taking into account family and community resources has been undertaken with three colleagues from sociology and economics: Greg Duncan, Kristine Moore, and Brett Brown. Perhaps more accurately, we are attempting to inject more developmental theory into the current thinking about family and community resources and their effects on children (Brooks-Gunn, Brown, Duncan, & Moore, 1995). Then, several developmental issues are raised within the context of family resource theory. These include the role of family resources, the accumulation of family resources, the continuity of family resources, the intersection of child characteristics and family resources, and the pathways by which family resources influence children. Next, community resources are discussed vis-à-vis their role in children's development, the accumulation of individual community resources, the intersection of family and community resources, and the pathways by which community resources influence children. Finally, the intersection of early intervention with family and community resources is considered. The role of family and community resources, the intersection between the two, and the pathways by which resources enhance or diminish intervention effects are considered.

Each issue is considered vis-à-vis developmental research on intervention for young children and families. The focus is primarily on children in the preschool years and on children who would be defined as at risk, given biological and environmental characteristics. The biological risk factor under study is birth weight, in that the IHDP was designed to provide services to (and evaluate their efficacy) LBW children. Because children at very low birth weight do less well socially, emotionally, and academically than do children who are low birth weight, but heavier (Klebanov, Brooks-Gunn, & McCormick, 1994a, 1994b; Kopp & Kaler, 1989; McCormick, 1989; McCormick, Brooks-Gunn, Workman-Daniels, Turner, & Peckham, 1992), the IHDP included two groups of LBW children (described above). In Bronfenbrennian terms, birth weight becomes a person characteristic, like gender.

The environmental risk factors under study are subsumed under family resources and include poverty and low maternal education. Although the IHDP sampling frame did not take into account familial characteristics, given links between LBW and maternal disadvantage, the sample has a large number of mothers who are poor and have little education. However, the sample also has mothers who are relatively affluent and have graduated from college, making it possible to consider the effects of maternal and familial characteristics on children's development. The two national studies oversampled low-income families.

FAMILY AND COMMUNITY RESOURCES: A FRAMEWORK

Similar to Bronfenbrenner's ecological model, our group focuses on the different contexts in which children grow up (Brooks-Gunn, Brown, et al., 1995). However, in keeping with our disciplinary differences (sociology, economics, developmental psychology, and social psychology), we have tried to blend microanalytical and macroanalytical perspectives. Borrowing heavily from the work of Haveman and Wolfe (1991, 1994) and Coleman (1988) in the framework, we identified the resources to which children theoretically have access. In very broad terms, four categories of resources in the family are thought to be critical: income, time, human capital, and psychological capital resources. Developmentalists usually focus on the last resource, which in our framework includes parenting behavior, parental attitudes and beliefs, parental emotional health, social support, and the like. Attention is also paid to human capital, in particular parental education and employment. Of interest is how parental decisions about allocation of resources within the family are made, how constraints on resources limit options, how perceptions about the importance of resources might influence parental behavior, and how parental resources influence child outcomes.

Community resources include a variety of contexts—child care settings, schools, peer groups, community groups, and wider societal contexts. On the basis of Coleman's (1988) social capital theory, several dimensions of community resources have been identified: reciprocal relationships and social networks, information, norms and sanctions, opportunity, and stability. Communities (or other contexts) are seen as high in social capital if some of the following characteristics are present: (a) relationships are dense and complex (i.e., overlapping spheres of contact), (b) information networks are easily accessible or are seen as helpful, (c) norms and sanctions about parental or child behavior are relatively clear-cut, (d) opportunity for advancement is believed to exist (i.e., job opportunities and excellent schools), and (e) residence is perceived as quite stable (see Coleman, 1988).

What is missing from the sketch above is a focus on the intersection of resources within the family and the community. In Bronfenbrenner's terms, what may be of most interest is how family resources interact to produce developmental outcomes, or in what circumstances various family resources have direct and indirect effects upon children. If family resources do influence children, what are the pathways by which they exert their influence? The same questions may be asked for neighborhood resources. Additionally, no mention is made of person characteristics that are known to influence the effect of family resources on children and how family resources are allocated (in more developmental terms, reciprocal effects between parent and child, between sibling and child, and so on). Effects of timing are not considered explicitly (individual, family, and historical; Elder, 1974). And more attention needs to be paid to the interaction of family and community resources (Brooks-Gunn, Duncan, & Aber, in press).

These concerns are addressed in the next three sections of the chapter. The concerns just raised (and based on Bronfenbrenner's developmental ecological framework) are addressed vis-à-vis family resources, community resources, and the intersection of intervention and family resources. Research from the data sets briefly described previously will provide exemplars of approaches to understanding the development of and intervention with young children in families in communities.

FAMILY RESOURCES AND YOUNG CHILDREN'S DEVELOPMENT

The Role of Family Resources

Family resources, as defined earlier, include income, time, human capital, and psychological capital resources. Developmentalists have focused more on the second two than on the first two. Human capital would be represented by parental education, as well as parental employment and occupation. Reams of studies report parental education being associated with child outcomes (Bronfenbrenner, 1979; Featherman & Hauser, 1987; Furstenberg, Brooks-Gunn, & Morgan, 1987; Gottfried, 1984; Wachs & Gruen, 1982; Werner & Smith, 1982). Often, developmental studies have not distinguished among these resources, using a composite variable to assess socioeconomic status (SES). Indeed, the term *SES* is a bit of a misnomer, in that very few developmental studies have actually measured economic status directly (e.g., family income or income-to-needs ratio; Duncan, Brooks-Gunn, & Klebanov, 1994). However, the concern for poor children has resulted in an increased interest in income as a resource (Chase-Lansdale & Brooks-Gunn, 1995; Culbertson, 1994; Danziger & Danziger, 1995; Duncan et al., in press; Fitzgerald, Lester, & Zuckerman, 1995; Huston, 1991; Huston, Garcia-Coll, & McLoyd, 1994). Even in these recent compendiums of research, the majority of studies define poverty by proxies such as education, occupation, and employment. We have termed these *poverty cofactors* and do not believe that they may be substituted for income measures (Brooks-Gunn, Klebanov, Liaw, & Duncan, 1995; McCormick & Brooks-Gunn, 1989). Indeed, the combination obscures distinctions among family resources.

We have made a concerted effort to disentangle income and human capital resources, especially parental education, in our analyses of the IDHP, the Baltimore Study of Teenage Parenthood, and the PSID (Baydar, Brooks-Gunn, & Furstenberg, 1993; Brooks-Gunn, Duncan, Klebanov, & Sealand, 1993; Brooks-Gunn, Guo, & Furstenberg, 1993: Brooks-Gunn, Klebanov, & Duncan, in press; Brooks-Gunn, Klebanov, et al., 1995; Chase-Lansdale, Brooks-Gunn, & Zamsky, 1994; Duncan et al., 1994; Klebanov,

Brooks-Gunn, Chase-Lansdale, & Gordon, in press; Klebanov, Brooks-Gunn, & Duncan, 1994). For example, we have examined the relative contribution of income (income-to-needs ratio averaged over the first 4 years of the child's life) and human capital resources (maternal education, single parenthood, and age of mother) to intelligence test scores (Wechsler Preschool and Primary Scale of Intelligence [Wechsler, 1989] and Standford-Binet Intelligence Scale) and behavior problems (Child Behavior Check List; Achenbach, Edelbrock, & Howell, 1987) in over 900 LBW children seen at age 3 and age 5 (Brooks-Gunn, Duncan, et al., 1993; Duncan et al., 1994). Controlling for a variety of other factors (i.e., birth weight, gender, site, and ethnicity), we find that the income-to-needs ratio is the strongest predictor of IQ scores. Of particular interest is that the beta coefficient for the income variable is twice as large as that for maternal education, the factor most often measured in developmental studies. Similar (although somewhat less strong) results emerge in an analysis of the Children of the NLSY. Income-to-needs ratios are highly associated with young children's verbal comprehension scores (Chase-Lansdale, Gordon, Brooks-Gunn, & Klebanov, in press; Korenman, Miller, & Sjaastad, 1995). The comparability of findings from these two studies is reassuring in that the use of an LBW sample is probably not accounting for the IHDP results.

It is also important to distinguish among various measures of income (Brooks-Gunn & Maritato, in press; Duncan et al., 1994; Huston, 1991; Kim, Garfinkel, Meyers, 1994). For example, most of the research on effects of poverty uses family income, or family income adjusted for family size, as the independent variable. Although these analyses are very informative, they do not tell us whether children living below the poverty line are different from those just above the poverty line.[1] That is, do nonlinear effects exist such that children below or near the poverty line have particularly negative outcomes? In analyses using the IHDP data set, we find that income effects on IQ are quite linear; the sample is divided into four

---

[1]The poverty line is based on a number of factors. It can be set higher or lower if the underlying assumptions are changed (Orshansky, 1965; Renwick & Bergmann, 1992; Watts, 1993).

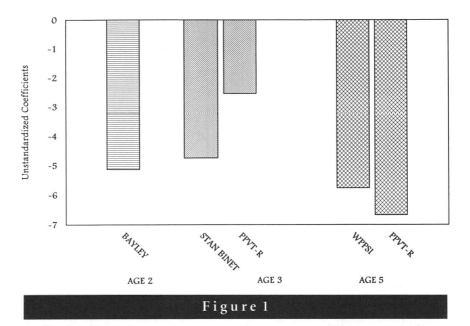

Figure 1

Nonlinear income-to-needs effects on child outcomes at three ages—IHDP: poor families compared with near-poor families. (Unstandardized regression coefficients controlling for child's race, birth weight, age, gender, maternal education, and family structure. Income-to-needs > 1 omitted.) Bayley, Stanford–Binet, and WPSSI are IQ tests; Peabody Picture Vocabulary Test–Revised (PPVT–R) is a verbal comprehension test. Standard deviation on all tests is between 15 and 16 points. IQ differences in figure are about one third of a standard deviation.

groups on the basis of income-to-needs ratio, such that the first group are children whose family income is below the poverty line (poor), the second group are just above the poverty line (between 100% and 150% of the poverty line), the third group is not poor (between 150% and 200% of the poverty line), and the fourth group is affluent (above 200% of the poverty line). Figures 1, 2, and 3 present the adjusted differences in intelligence test score means for three groups of children (the omitted comparison group being the new poor), controlling for human capital and child characteristics (i.e., maternal education, single parenthood, ethnicity, gender, birth weight, and neonatal health; Smith, Brooks-Gunn, & Klebanov, in press). Figure 1 provides the unstandardized coefficients comparing poor and near-poor families, illustrating large IQ differences at ages

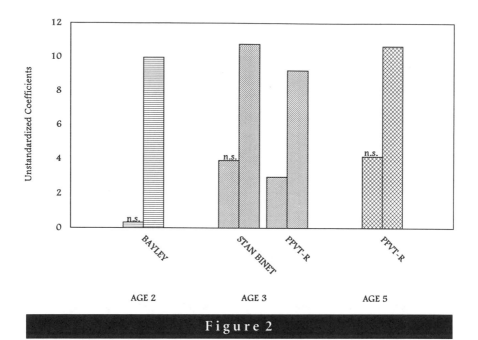

Figure 2

Nonlinear income-to-needs effects on child outcomes at three ages—IHDP: middle-income and affluent families compared with near-poor families. (Unstandardized regression coefficients controlling for child's race, birth weight, age, gender, maternal education, and family structure. Income-to-needs > 1 omitted.) See Figure 1 for explanation.

2, 3, and 5 between these two income groups. In Figure 2, children in near-poor families are compared to middle-income and affluent families: here no differences are seen between near-poor and middle-income families. Such findings could be interpreted by policymakers that whereas increases in family income in all likelihood will increase child functioning, the increments will be similar across the income distribution rather than being more pronounced in poor families. Interestingly, evidence for nonlinear effects is found for internalizing problem behavior (see Figure 4), with the poor and near-poor children both having much higher internalizing problem behavior compared with not-poor and affluent children. Such analyses are more in keeping with Bronfenbrenner's ideas about context—in this case, context being defined in terms of family income. The assumption underlying the separation of families into four income groups is that family organizational functioning may be quite different for poor, near-poor, middle-income, and affluent families. Indeed, not only may family processes differ across these contexts, but the patterns of associations within these contexts may differ as well—a premise advocated by Bronfenbrenner, but not adequately tested. (See Liaw & Brooks-Gunn, 1994, for an exemplar comparing the effects of other familial factors in poor and near-poor families with the effects of the same factors in middle-income and affluent families.)

Single parenthood is a resource associated with time that has been studied extensively, although more by economists and sociologists than by developmental psychologists (Duncan, 1991; Furstenberg et al., 1987; McLanahan, Astone, & Marks, 1991; McLanahan & Sandefur, 1994; McLanahan, Seltzer, Hanson, & Thompson, 1994). Distinctions are now being made between never-married and ever-married single parents, as well as between mothers and fathers who are single parents (Brooks-Gunn, 1995; Chase-Lansdale & Hetherington, 1990; Hernandez, 1993; Thomson,

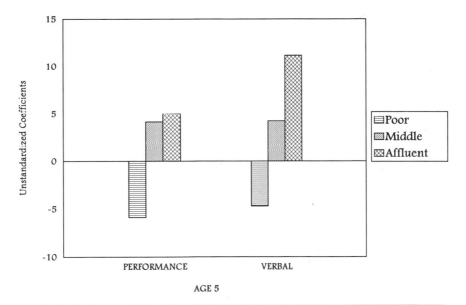

Figure 3

Nonlinear income-to-needs effects on child outcomes at age 5 (WPPSI)—IHDP. (Unstandardized regression coefficients controlling for child's race, birth weight, age, gender, maternal education, and family structure. Income-to-needs > 1 omitted.) See Figure 1 for explanation.

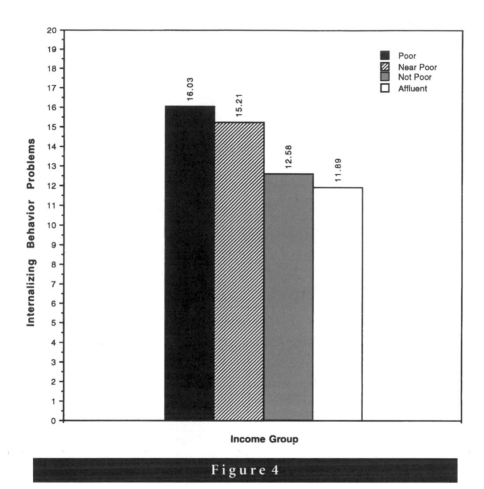

Figure 4

Adjusted mean internalizing behavior problem scores at age 5 by four income groups. Behavior problems are based on maternal report on the Child Behavior Checklist.

Hanson, & McLanahan, 1994; Thomson, Hanson, McLanahan, & Curtin, 1992).

What is of interest here is the relative contribution of single parenthood to child outcomes, over and above maternal education and income. Single-parent families are much more likely to be poor than two-parent families, and mothers in the former are somewhat more likely to have low education (Duncan, 1991; Garfinkel & McLanahan, 1986; Hernandez, 1993). Indeed, the income drop precipitated by divorce seems to account for about one third to one half of the single parenthood effect in studies of adolescent outcomes such as high school dropout, teenage pregnancy, and high school achievement (McLanahan et al., 1991). Less information on single parenthood is available for younger children. However, in the IHDP (and parallel analyses with the Children of the NLSY), single parenthood was associated with child verbal and intelligence test scores, but not as strongly as income or maternal education (Smith et al., in press). Additionally, as might be expected given Bronfenbrenner's focus on timing, effects of parental divorce depend on when it occurs in the young child's life.

Interactions Between Income and Human Capital Resources

The analyses just mentioned beg the question of whether interactions exist among these types of resources. For example, does family income make more of a difference for families with many human capital resources than those with few human capital resources? Almost no studies test such assumptions. In one set of regressions using the IHDP data, interaction terms between family income and a variety of other family resources were entered (Liaw & Brooks-Gunn, 1994). Although few effects emerged, those that did were unexpected: The distribution of low and high family resources made more of a difference for the middle-income and affluent children than for the poor and near-poor children. Perhaps living in poverty exerts such a toll on children that the presence or absence of other resources is less salient than it is for children who are living in more economically secure circumstances.

Psychological Capital Resources

Psychological capital resources include characteristics such as parental emotional and physical health, provision of experiences to the child, parenting behavior, and social support.[2] Developmentalists excel in understanding the interplay of such family resources and child outcomes. In our analyses, we try to estimate the effects of some of these resources, controlling for income and human capital resources. For example, in the IHDP, we added a set of psychological resources to the regressions with

---

[2]Some scholars define social capital as intrafamilial as well as extrafamilial. With such a framework, familial social support would be classified as intrafamilial social capital.

the income and human capital measures. Several measures were selected: report of maternal depression, occurrence of life events, receipt of social support, provision of learning experiences in the home, and ratings of maternal warmth. The physical environment of the home also was assessed (although it is debatable whether physical environment should be considered a psychological resource). Home environment is a strong predictor (see Klebanov, Brooks-Gunn, & Duncan, 1994, for a description of the construction of these three scales from the HOME; Bradley & Caldwell, 1984). Figure 5 (on p. 482) presents the regression for the age 5 intelligence test (in this case controlling for the other human capital and child characteristic data as presented earlier). The other psychosocial measures add little to the regression. Although the family income-to-needs ratio is still significant, its effect is greatly diminished by the inclusion of a home environment measure. The standardized beta coefficient for the income-to-needs ratio drops from .40 to .20 when the psychological resources are entered into the equation.

Results are somewhat different for behavior problems. Figure 6 (on p. 486) illustrates the findings for maternal report of externalizing behavior problems. High maternal depression scores and low home learning scores are associated with more externalizing problems at age 5. Others have found that maternal depression is associated with higher reports of behavior problems, both by mothers and by teachers (Pelligrini, Perlmutter, Galda, & Brody, 1990). Less is known about stimulating learning experiences and behavior problems. The family income effect is not significant after entering the psychosocial resource measures.

In brief, the effects of family income on behavior problems and intelligence test scores are mediated in part by psychological resources (as inferred from the drop in family income beta coefficients when the psychological resources are entered into the equation), all analyses are not shown. We do not see such analyses as very contextually rich (as Bronfenbrenner would no doubt point out). That is, interactions among parents and children are not observed, and reciprocal effects are not modeled. However, these analyses do provide an estimation of effects of psychological resources, controlling for income and human capital resources. Do developmentalists overestimate the importance of psychological resources when little attention is paid to other resources, ones that are known to play a large role in children's development? Alternatively, the effects of poverty may be overestimated when little attention is given to how poor families organize their lives and interactions.

The Accumulation of Family Resources

The approach taken above does not address the issue of what is of paramount importance: specific family resources or the accumulation of resources (or lack of resources). That is, perhaps children are harmed when the number of resources is scanty, irrespective of the nature of the resources. Cumulative risk models have been developed to test this premise, with the work of Sameroff and colleagues (Sameroff, Seifer, Baldwin, & Baldwin, 1993; Sameroff, Seifer, Barocas, Zax, & Greenspan, 1987) being the best example. In the Rochester sample (Sameroff et al., 1993), IQ scores at ages 4 and 13 decreased as the number of familial risk factors increased.

We have borrowed Sameroff et al.'s (1987, 1993) model and extended it to include an examination of the effects of cumulative risks in poor and not-poor children. Given the profound effect of income and poverty on children, our interest was in whether cumulative risks—or multiple, low family resources—would influence children differently as a function of whether they lived in impoverished circumstances. In Bronfenbrennerian terms, the focus was on the interaction of cumulative risk factors and poverty. For these analyses, the outcomes were measured at age 3 (child IQ, child behavior problems, and the three HOME subscales mentioned previously). Thirteen child and family resources were identified in the IHDP data set; they were chosen to be similar to those used by Sameroff and colleagues. They include child characteristics (very low birth weight and poor neonatal health), human capital (unemployed head of household, less than high school education, low verbal ability scores, single parenthood, high density of children to adults, and young maternal age), and psychological resources (life events, depression, and social support), as well as ethnicity, gender, and site.

Families who were poor had, on average, more risk factors than did families who were not poor (defined as 150% above the poverty line when the child was 1 year of age). Expected means (controlling for ethnicity, site, and gender) were 4.5 for the poor group and 2.5 of the 13 risk factors for the not-poor group (Brooks-Gunn, Klebanov, et al., 1995; Liaw & Brooks-Gunn, 1994). Differences between the poor and not-poor families

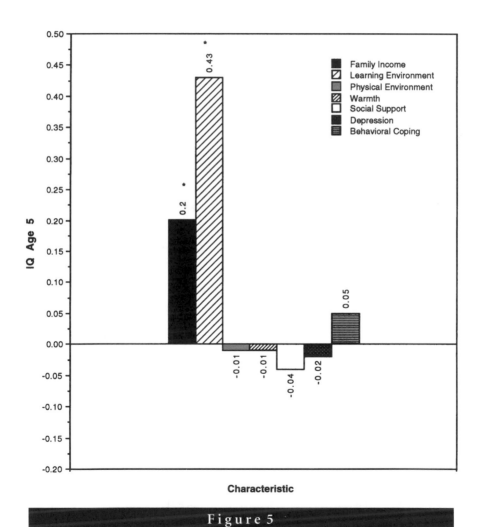

Figure 5

Effects of income, home environment, and maternal characteristics on WPSSI IQ scores at age 5 from the IHDP (standardized regression coefficients). *$p < .05$.

were found for all of the risk factors except the child characteristics (and because the IHDP sample was selected to include only LBW children, no differences would be expected).

As the number of risks increased, the IQ scores declined for both the poor and not-poor children. However, even when poor children had no risk factors, their IQ scores were lower than those of the not-poor children with no risk factors. Of particular interest is that not only were main effects of poverty and cumulative risk found, but also was an interaction between the two, as illustrated in Figure 7 (on p. 487; from Liaw & Brooks-Gunn, 1994). When not-poor children's families had few family resources (i.e., high cumulative risks), their IQ scores were quite similar to those of the poor children with multiple risks (see Figure 7 on p. 487). Such results highlight the importance of considering the context in which risks are experienced—in this case, poverty. In these analyses, context becomes less important when family resources are low.

Poverty and cumulative risk effects were found for learning and physical environment using the HOME. However, an interaction between poverty and cumulative risk was not found for provision of learning experiences or maternal warmth or physical environment (Brooks-Gunn, Klebanov, et al., 1995). As a final example, we have taken seriously Bronfenbrenner's call to look at the interaction between family and neighborhood contexts. My group and Sameroff's group have just completed analyses looking at whether the negative effects of multiple family risks on child IQ are seen in different neighborhood contexts. Preliminary analyses suggest that the number of family risks do not have comparable effects across different neighborhoods, again attesting to the importance of looking at the intersection of family and neighborhood contexts.

THE TIMING AND PERSISTENCE OF FAMILY RESOURCES

The timing and persistence of low family resources are understudied areas. Many studies, being cross-sectional in nature, are unable to explore the effects of the persistence of certain conditions on children. Family resources are often represented in a rather static form, resulting in perhaps an underestimation of family resource effects. Perhaps the best example may be taken from the poverty literature. It is clear that family income and poverty in any given year are associated with less optimal child outcomes. But what about more persistent poverty? A static, single-year measure of income in no way captures the notion of living in poverty. Family income fluctuates yearly, sometimes quite dramatically (Duncan, Smeeding, & Rodgers, 1991; Elder, 1974; McLoyd, 1990). Consequently, great individual variation exists in who is classified as poor in any given year, and only a subset of poor families in any given year will go on to be persistently poor.

In the IHDP data analyses described earlier, we have looked at the effect of being poor in all of the first 4 years of life versus being poor some of the time. On the basis of comparisons with children who were never poor during this time period, those children who were persistently poor had IQ scores that were about 9 points lower, whereas children who resided in more transient poverty conditions had about a 4-point decrement in IQ (controlling for a variety of social and demographic factors; Duncan et al., 1994). The results for externalizing behavior problems were similar, but less pronounced (differences around one third to one quarter of a standard deviation rather than two thirds to one quarter of a standard deviation in the case of IQ).

The untoward effects of persistent poverty have been documented for older children and youth by looking at either income-to-needs ratios or welfare receipt (Baydar et al., 1993; Brooks-Gunn, Guo, & Furstenberg, 1993; Haveman & Wolfe, 1991). An interesting, but not well explored, issue is whether the source of income makes a difference in children's well-being. That is, does receipt of income from Aid to Families with Dependent Children have more negative effects than receipt of income from work, even in families whose income hovers around the poverty line? A few preliminary analyses suggest that receipt from welfare or from work may not make a huge difference if incomes are low (Moore et al., 1993; Smith et al., in press). And does receipt of family income from child support confer positive effects on children, over and above its monetary value?

In other words, even if family income is controlled, do children whose noncustodial parents (typically the father) provide support do so on a consistent basis? Three investigators have shown that child support receipt has beneficial effects on children and youth; these findings are not totally explained by actual family income (Baydar & Brooks-Gunn, 1994; Knox & Bane, 1994; McLanahan et al., 1994). The source of income has effects on family organization and, no doubt, on the meaning of family, salience of parents, and perception of commitment. To date, a more process-oriented look at these issues, which Bronfenbrenner would advocate, has not been attempted (in part, because many of the large-scale natural studies used to examine the issues may be characterized as process poor—that is, little detailed contextual information is available; Brooks-Gunn, Brown, et al., 1995).

The timing of a particular family resource also may be important. Two approaches have been taken to studying the timing of receipt of particular resources. One focuses on the life epoch or developmental stage in which a family event occurs, and the other highlights change and continuity in the occurrence of events. In the first, the timing of a condition, such as poverty, job loss, or welfare receipt, is examined (see Elder, 1974; McLoyd, 1990). In the IHDP, for example, whether poverty occurred in the first or second 2 years of life made no difference on 5-year outcomes. In the Baltimore Study of Teenage Parenthood, welfare receipt in the preschool years was more predictive of grade failure, low literacy, and school dropout than was welfare receipt in the elementary- or middle-school years (Baydar et al., 1993; Brooks-Gunn, Guo, & Furstenberg, 1993). However, the primacy of the preschool years was not replicated in the PSID, looking at high school dropout rates (Haveman & Wolfe, 1991).

Whether the level or quality of family resources is relatively constant or changes is the targeted question using the second approach. An exemplar is the work of Sameroff et al. (1993), who reported that the number of family risk factors remains quite constant over the childhood years (rs of about .70 over a 9-year period). Change may be characteristic only of a subset of families. Even though Sameroff et al. found stability vis-à-vis the overall number of risk factors (or, in our terminology, *low family re-*

sources), changes in some individual resources also may occur. In the Baltimore Study of Teenage Parenthood, for example, if mothers went off welfare after their firstborn's preschool years, their children were less likely to fail a grade in school, even after preschool readiness scores had been taken into account (Brooks-Gunn & Furstenberg, 1987). Similar analyses are

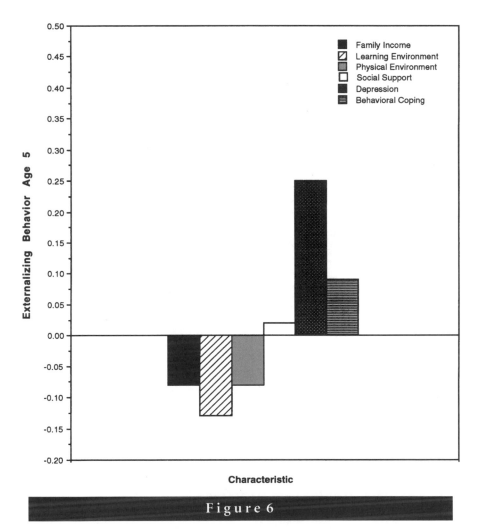

Figure 6

Effects of income, home environment, and maternal characteristics on externalizing behavior problem scores reported by mothers using the Child Behavior Checklist at age 5 in the IHDP (standardized regression coefficients). *$p < .05$.

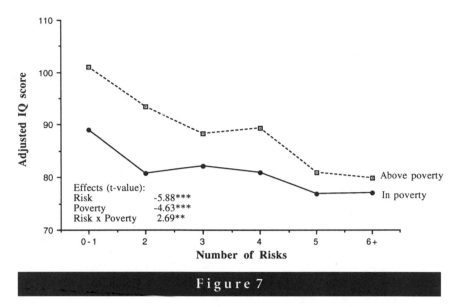

Figure 7

Adjusted IQ scores by risk groups and poverty status: follow-up-only groups. (From "Cumulative Familial Risks and Low-Birthweight Children's Cognitive and Behavioral Development" by F. Liaw and J. Brooks-Gunn, 1994, *Journal of Clinical Child Psychology, 23*, p. 367. Copyright 1994 by Lawrence Erlbaum Associates. Reprinted with permission.) $**p < .01.$ $***p < .001.$

needed for family resources such as maternal education. Do children fare better if their mothers continue their own schooling (and if so, why?). How are family processes altered as the lives of parents change?

Change has been examined vis-à-vis marital and household arrangements. It is clear that marital disruptions (both divorce and remarriage) have negative consequences for children (Hetherington & Jodl, 1995; Hetherington & Clingempeel, 1992). An example is taken from the IHDP: Marital status of the mother was collected at several time points in the first years of life, allowing for a categorization of almost all families into five groups—(a) married when child is 24 and 36 months of age (termed *early*) and married when the child is 60 months of age (termed *late*), (b) single early and late, (c) single early and married late, (d) married early and single late, and (e) single, married, and then single. Figures 8 and 9 illustrate the findings from these analyses for externalization of behavior problems and IQ scores at age 5 (see Duncan et al., 1994). All groups in which the mother was single at some point in the first 5 years of the child's life had lower IQ scores than the always-married group, which was the omitted comparison group. However, the single-parent groups did not differ among themselves. When family income was controlled, not only did the negative effects diminish, but the differences among groups became more pronounced, in that only the always-single mothers had children with low IQ scores (Figure 8 on p. 490). Turning to externalizing problem behavior, a different pattern emerges: Children whose mothers experienced a divorce during their preschool years had higher problem scores, whether or not income was entered into the equation. No negative effects were seen for the group whose mothers were single early but married later in the child's preschool years (Figure 9 on p. 501). In brief, single parenthood seemed to confer a risk in the cognitive arena, whereas marital disruption had more effects on behavior problems (keeping in mind that the use of maternal report of behavior problems is a serious and unfortunate limitation of these results). Again, process-oriented work is necessary to understand why family structure might have different effects on cognitive and emotional outcomes.

The Intersection of Child Characteristics and Family Resources

A glaring omission is reflected in the approaches, and results, just presented. Bronfenbrenner has alerted us to the importance of interactions between the person and the environment, typically studied vis-à-vis family resources. Generally, scholars (including myself) studying poor and at-risk children have paid mostly lip service to his clarion call.

When Person × Environment interactions are targeted, the person characteristics are usually biological characteristics, such as perinatal insults (low birth weight, small for gestational age, and respiratory difficulties; see the classic review by Sameroff & Chandler, 1975). Perhaps most well known is the work of Werner and her colleagues in the Children of Kauai study; perinatal problems were associated with lower IQ scores during the preschool period. This was true of children from families with lower SES but not of children from families with higher SES (Werner, Bierman, & French, 1971; see also Werner & Smith, 1982, for findings from the adolescent years).

Others have talked about the "double jeopardy" that biologically at-risk children face when they are also residing in poor families or in families where the parents have low education (Escalona, 1982; Parker, Greer, & Zuckerman, 1988). However, few scholars have formally tested for interactions between personal characteristics such as low birth weight and familial resource characteristics. Results supporting double jeopardy may not always be found. As an example, McCormick, her colleagues, and I did not find an interaction between birth weight and maternal education on 8-year-olds' IQ scores (McCormick et al., 1992). In our analyses, both low birth weight *and* maternal education contribute to child outcomes. In this sense, children who are low birth weight and have a mother with little education are at double jeopardy in that they have two risk characteristics, but they are not at double jeopardy in that they are disproportionately at risk for poor outcomes over and above the contribution of each risk factor. In the IHDP, too, we are not finding much evidence for disproportionate effects of family resources on very low birth weight infants (keeping in mind that all children are low birth weight).

Liaw and I (1993) took a slightly different approach to this intersection as we have examined patterns of IQ scores at 12, 24, and 36 months using the IHDP sample. The goal was to understand how biological characteristics (person) and family characteristics (environment) were associated with cognitive patterns. Cluster analyses identified five clusters of children (percentages of children in each cluster in parentheses): high stable (16%), high decline to average (30%), high decline to below average (21%), average decline to below average (30%), and very low stable (3%). Figure 10 on pp. 504–505 contains these five patterns (from Liaw & Brooks-Gunn, 1993).

Discriminant function analyses were performed to see if family characteristics (maternal ethnicity, age, and education) and person character-

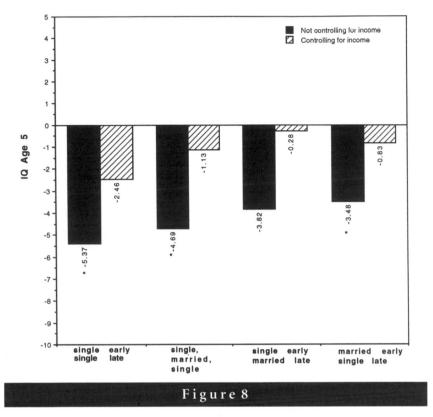

Figure 8

Effects of parental transitions upon IQ scores at age 5. *$p < .05$.

istics (birth weight and neonatal health status) were linked to particular patterns. The very low stable group comprised children who were not healthy; more than one half were very low birth weight, and the neonatal health was very poor. The average decline to below-average group was lighter, but not sicker at birth, compared with the other three clusters. The three clusters of children with higher initial IQ scores had similar biological characteristics to one another; these children were generally healthy at birth. However, the three clusters with higher initial IQ scores differed quite substantially from one another in terms of maternal characteristics. The high stable cluster had proportionately more mothers who had more education and who were older than the high decline to average cluster, which in turn was composed of more educated and older mothers than the high decline to below-average group. One interpretation of these results is that the familial and person characteristics had relatively independent effects on patterns of child IQ over the first 3 years of life.

Maternal characteristics such as depression may operate differently as a function of child characteristics (e.g., gender, birth weight, and neonatal health) or family context. Klebanov and I tested a series of interactions to see how person characteristics might moderate the effect of maternal depression on behavior problem scores at age 3. These analyses were performed for this chapter, in the light of Bronfenbrenner's theoretical writings. We were primarily interested in whether off patterns of association differ for boys and girls, given earlier findings from Bronfenbrenner's work on young children. No effect was found for birth weight or neonatal health. However, maternal depression was associated with reported internalizing behavior for girls, but not boys. Three family contextual characteristics were examined: family income (poor), maternal education, and number of parents in the household. No interactions with maternal depression were found.

Similar analyses were performed, looking at the influence of child characteristics and family context on links between the provision of learning experiences in the home and child intelligence test scores at age 3. Again, birth weight did not moderate the association. However, a significant Gender × Home Learning interaction was found so that home learning was more strongly associated with intelligence test scores for girls than for boys. Family context factors also moderate the learning experience–IQ association: Links between home learning and intelligence test scores were stronger for children of more educated mothers than for children of less educated mothers (less than a high school education).

In brief, gender was highly salient in both examples, following Bronfenbrenner's conjectures. Interestingly, family poverty did not moderate the links between behavior problems and maternal depression on the one hand and intelligence test scores and provision of learning experiences on the other.

COMMUNITY RESOURCES AND YOUNG CHILDREN'S DEVELOPMENT

The Role of Community Resources

Children grow up in contexts larger than the familial contexts (keeping in mind that multiple family contexts exist—family as parents and siblings, family as grandparents, and other relatives). Bronfenbrenner (1986) was a champion of the importance of multiple contexts, even for young children. However, less work has been conducted on the contexts or resources available to the young child outside of the so-called immediate family (the exception being the work on child care, grandparents, and early-intervention programs; Brooks-Gunn & Chase-Lansdale, 1995; Chase-Lansdale et al., in press; Hayes, Palmer, & Zaslow, 1990; Hofferth & Phillips, 1991; Meisels & Shonkoff, 1990). The young child's interactions are more circumscribed than the older child's extrafamilial experiences. Parents make decisions that in large part dictate when, and with whom, the young child interacts. Although parents also influence the everyday experience of their older children and have made choices that bound their children's lives (i.e., by neighborhood residence and school attendance), they do not monitor the interactions outside the home to as great an extent as they do for younger children. However, the community resources available to a family and used by a family (often, these two are quite disparate) have the potential to affect children's lives, and their parents' lives, profoundly. Children may observe or experience neighbors' behavior directly. And parental resources, which are known to affect children, are themselves influenced by the community.

An exciting line of work on the potential effects of neighborhoods on children has arisen recently in large part due to the writing of Wilson (1987, 1991a, 1991b) and Jencks (Jencks & Mayer, 1990; Jencks & Petersen, 1992). Several mechanisms have been postulated to account for how neighborhoods might exert their influence on young children—neighborhood resources, collective socialization, contagion, and social disorganization. All four mechanisms are based roughly on the premise that living in neighborhoods with more affluent neighbors, or with more social capital, would result in better outcomes for children and families. Neighborhood resources include libraries, community centers, high-quality child care, and parks available to families (and easily accessible, well maintained, and safe). Information systems would be in place that would allow parents to learn about services and resources (Brown & Richman, in press). Collective socialization frameworks are based on the premise that norms, sanctions, and reciprocity among neighbors are beneficial to children's growth and to parenting behavior. If neighborhoods have low social capital and are socially isolated, then parents may not be influenced by norms or sanctions for appropriate behavior. Socially isolated neighborhoods—few adults who are employed, a large number of single mothers, few opportunities for work, and a large number of poor people—have also been posited to be low in *collective socialization*. In communities with these characteristics, not only will norms and sanctions not be operating, but family organization, routine parental self-efficacy, and future orientation may be low (Wilson, 1991a, 1991b). Contagion frameworks posit that, when relatively few individuals work in the mainstream economy, certain behavior becomes more likely as more and more individuals act in certain ways (i.e., high school dropout, out-of-wedlock births; Crane, 1991). A general social disorganization framework incorporates aspects of all of the aforementioned mechanisms (Sampson, 1992).

Work on the effects of neighborhoods on young children is just beginning. The IHDP data set has been geocoded to attach neighborhood census tract information to the files. In one analysis, we looked at the effects of a series of community-resource variables on child outcomes (Brooks-Gunn, Duncan, Klebanov, & Sealand, 1993). Residence in neighborhoods with more affluent individuals was associated with high IQ scores, whereas residence in neighborhoods with more poor neighbors had no effect. Other neighborhood-resource variables were associated with child outcome (e.g., proportion of single mothers and proportion of unemployed males), but these resources were not significant after entering proportion of affluent neighbors and proportion of poor neighbors into the equation.

In another set of analyses, five neighborhood factors were identified:

low social class, high social class, male joblessness, ethnic diversity, and concentration of families. Looking at the IHDP and the Children of the NLSY, we found high social class to be important in both data sets (Chase-Lansdale et al., in press; Klebanov et al., in press).

Accumulation of Individual Community Resources

It is possible that the beneficial effects of neighborhoods are really carried by the number of resources available, rather than by any one resource. Few relevant analyses have been carried out. However, in the IHDP and the PSID, the combination of high rates of poverty and low rates of professional workers is associated with poor outcomes (Brooks-Gunn, Duncan, et al., 1993). Crane (1991) talked about a *tipping* phenomenon, in that when a certain concentration of high poverty and low professional workers is reached, neighborhood effects become more pronounced. Our data and Crane's (1991) analysis of the census data provide some support for this premise.

More in-depth analyses of neighborhood resources, often using the social capital network, are beginning. An example is the study of Garbarino (1991), who examined rates of child abuse as a function of neighborhood SES. The author identified neighborhoods that had higher rates of child abuse than would be expected given the SES of the neighborhood, as well as neighborhoods that had lower rates of child abuse than predicted (looking at the slope of the regression line for child abuse and SES and identifying outliers). Those neighborhoods that had lower than predicted rates were high in trust and social networks, probably indicative of high social capital.

The Intersection of Child Characteristics and Community Resources

In a Bronfenbrennerian framework, the interaction of community resources with person characteristics would be examined, given that the individual brings a history to each context into which she or he enters. We have looked at two person characteristics: birth weight in the IHDP and gender in the IHDP and the Children of the NLSY. Birth weight does not seem to alter the links between affluent neighbors and IQ scores in the

IHDP (Brooks-Gunn, Duncan, et al., 1993; Duncan et al., 1994). However, gender does play a role. At age 5, for example, boys but not girls in the Children of the NLSY were influenced by the presence of high-SES neighbors (Chase-Lansdale et al., in press). Much more work is needed to explicate such findings.

The Intersection of Family and Community Resources

Community resources may influence children differently as a function of family resources. Again, such interactions have not been the subject of much investigation (indeed, Bronfenbrenner criticized our working group on neighborhoods, families, and children for not having conducted such interactions in some of our early work). We are finding that the positive effects of affluent neighbors are more pronounced for families with higher resources themselves or that the lack of affluent neighbors is detrimental to children from families with higher resources. Generally, European-American families and families with more income are more likely to be positively affected by affluent neighbors than are African-American families and low-income families (Brooks-Gunn, Duncan, & Aber, in press; Brooks-Gunn et al., 1994; Chase-Lansdale et al., in press).

It is surprising that the effects of affluent neighbors may not exist for poor and for African-American children. Several possibilities for this finding are being explored. The first involves the fact that African-American children are much less likely to live in affluent neighborhoods (Duncan et al., 1994). The second involves the fact that even controlling for family income, African-American children are more likely to have multiple risks (Brooks-Gunn, Klebanov, et al., 1995). Perhaps the lack of neighborhood effects is due to the accumulation of risks, and lack of resources, that characterize so many African-American families today.

Neighborhood residence also affects parenting behavior. The provision of learning experiences in the home is associated with low rates of male joblessness and low rates of poor people in the neighborhood (Klebanov et al., 1994a). We are now exploring the ways in which neighborhood residence might impact on maternal emotional health as well as on social support and coping responses.

EARLY INTERVENTION, RESOURCES, AND
CHILD CHARACTERISTICS

An early-childhood program becomes a new context in which the child
resides, as well as a context that must intersect with the family context. In
this section, the role of family and community resources in the context of
early-intervention services will be explored, specifically (a) the role of family resources, (b) the accumulation of family resources, (c) the intersection of child characteristics and family resources, and (d) pathways by
which intervention effects may be sustained. The IHDP is used as an example of how to incorporate a more resource-based framework into an
understanding of how early intervention affects children, as well as of
which children and families are influenced. A brief description of the findings from the IHDP is presented as a backdrop for the discussion about
resources and child characteristics. The intervention group was offered
home visiting from the time the infant was discharged from the hospital
until the child was 3 years of age (correcting for gestational age). Home
visits were weekly in the 1st year of life and bimonthly thereafter. When
the children were a year of age, they entered a child development center;
the center was open 5 days a week, and transportation was provided. The
curriculum of both the home visits and the center was based on Learning
Games (Sparling & Lewis, 1985), in which a series of activities are presented to the child in the linguistic, cognitive, emotional, social, and physical domains. The activities may be repeated. As children master activities,
they move on to more complex ones (Ramey et al., 1992; Sparling et al.,
1991). Staff were trained to be responsive to children's needs, as well as to
provide developmentally appropriate contexts for learning. Both the intervention and follow-up-only groups were offered referrals and pediatric
surveillance; children were seen 7 times in the first 3 years of life (Brooks-
Gunn, Gross, et al., 1992; Brooks-Gunn, McCarton, et al., 1994; Gross et
al., 1992; Gross & Spiker, in press; Infant Health and Development Program, 1990).

The primary outcome was cognitive functioning, as measured by traditional IQ tests. The reliance on IQ tests as the major measure of efficacy

in this clinical trial is seen by some as unfortunate.[3] The IHDP also gathered data on behavior problems as well as on child social and emotional behavior exhibited during a mother–child interaction sequence (Brooks-Gunn, Klebanov, et al., 1993; Spiker, Ferguson, & Brooks-Gunn, 1993). And a great deal of information was collected on maternal characteristics and outcomes, which may possibly act as mediators or moderators of child outcomes.

The children in the intervention group had higher IQ scores at 24 and 36 months of age than did the children in the follow-up-only group (effect sizes were .59 at both times). They also had lower behavior problem scores at 24 and 36 months of age (effect sizes ranged from −.15 to −.20, using maternal reports on the Child Behavior Scale [Richman & Graham, 1971] and the Child Behavior Checklist [Achenbach, Edelbrock, & Howell, 1987]). On the basis of coding of observational data collected when the children were 30 months of age, the intervention group children had higher scores on enthusiasm and persistence than did the follow-up-only group children (Spiker et al., 1993).

The Role of Family Resources

Provision of enriched learning experiences, availability of a warm and responsive caregiver, receipt of nutrition and health services, opportunity to interact with peers in a structured setting—all might influence children positively. Most evaluation work has focused on the potential effects of the new context on the child. However, as Bronfenbrenner (1986) pointed out, the family context might be influenced by the child's participation in an early-intervention program. With an eye toward our resource model, we might define several areas in which families might be favorably influenced by such services. These include altering (a) income resources in the home; (b) human capital resources, such as increasing maternal education or helping mothers enter the workforce; and (c) psychological resources, such as maternal depression, social support, or parenting behavior. The

---

[3]IQ tests do not tap all aspects of cognitive development, nor do they provide any information on social or emotional functioning.

resource of time spent with the child might be reduced by the child's entering a program. On the other hand, if a program includes a parenting component, parents might spend more time in stimulating activities or in responsive interaction than without a program.

Children whose families have different levels and types of resources may be influenced differently by the receipt of similar early childhood education experiences. Typically, the following question is posed: For whom are early interventions most effective? The premise is that the context in which the child resides sets the stage for how the child will respond to the context of center-based education (and vice versa; see Alexander & Entwisle, 1988, for a discussion of teachers' responses to kindergartners and first graders from various social and economic backgrounds and the links between early teacher treatment and achievement). Few early-childhood programs have examined efficacy vis-à-vis familial context or familial resources. This paucity is due, in part, to the fact that most program evaluations have been based on single-site studies, with a relatively small number of families and a somewhat homogeneous set of families (at least with respect to maternal education, number of parents in the household, and ethnicity). In the IHDP, the efficacy of the intervention as a function of maternal education, age, and ethnicity has been examined. Children whose mothers had a high school education or less were more likely to benefit from the intervention than children whose mothers had attended college (Brooks-Gunn, Gross, et al., 1992). These IQ results were found for both European- and African-American children. Trends in the direction of more of an effect for African-American than European-American children were also found for some of the cognitive test scores (see also Lee, Brooks-Gunn, & Schnur, 1988). In exploring these results further, it seems that the greater benefit for African-American children is due, in part, to the greater incidence of poverty and related factors in African-American families (Brooks-Gunn, Klebanov, et al., 1995).

Another perspective on the influence of maternal education on efficacy of treatment is provided by the research on patterns of cognitive scores (Liaw & Brooks-Gunn, 1993). In the percentage of children in the high stable cognitive cluster, a high percentage had been in the treatment group (well over the expected one third, because one third of the children were enrolled in the intervention group). And maternal education had a strong effect on these findings. Of those children whose mother had less than a high school education, 93% of the children had been in the intervention group; whereas of those children whose mother had a high school education, 66% had been in the intervention group. About 40% of the children whose mother had some college experience were in the intervention group, a little over what would be expected by chance. The odds of having high stable IQ scores over the first 3 years of life were greatly enhanced by the intervention for those children whose mother had a high school education or less.

The Accumulation of Family Resources

The findings just reported led us to think about the accumulation of risks or family resources, as they might influence responses to intervention. Using Sameroff's (Sameroff et al., 1987, 1993) cumulative-risk framework, as described earlier, the intersection of cumulative risks, intervention, and poverty was explored. Results were as follows (Liaw & Brooks-Gunn, 1994): (a) The intervention group had higher mean scores than the follow-up-only group in both poor and not-poor subsamples; (b) the intervention group had higher IQ scores across number of risks in the not-poor subsample, that is, the treatment was equally effective for children with few and with many risk factors, in that the slopes of the two regression lines did not differ (even though the level of IQ was influenced by number of risk factors); (c) in contrast, a larger treatment effect was seen in the poor subsample, who had fewer risk factors (significant Treatment × Number of Risk interaction for the poor group), that is, the slope of the regression lines differed for the intervention and follow-up-only groups of poor children.

One admittedly speculative conclusion from such results is that families with a number of risk factors or very few resources, if also poor in monetary terms, find it very difficult to manage their lives. As Burton (1991) suggested, these families may be attempting to survive, making day-to-day experiences much more variable and tasks much more time-consuming and stressful. Perhaps many of the children from these families have difficulty benefiting from the intervention because of the nature of their life at home. Very different, or at least more intensive, services may be required to assist families with few resources on which to draw, or the nature of the services may not be appropriate. Little work has addressed such possibilities. Indeed, lip service is paid to the concept of individualized services, without much documentation of what services various families need, let alone receive (Brooks-Gunn, Klebanov, & Liaw, 1995). Data such as that from the IHDP provide a very preliminary look at the intersection of family resources and intervention resources. Our findings underscore the paucity of contextually detailed evaluations.

The Intersection of Child Characteristics and Family Resources

Child characteristics also may influence how children respond to early intervention, as well as teachers' responses to them. Almost no early-childhood work has been done on this well accepted premise (see reviews by Brooks-Gunn, 1990; Bryant & Ramey, 1987; Clarke-Stewart & Fein, 1983; Haskins, 1989).[4] Several child characteristics have been examined in the IHDP to test Bronfenbrenner's premises about the Person × Environment interactions in the context of early intervention. These include gender, birth weight, neonatal health, and initial cognitive functioning and behavioral problems. Findings are discussed for the intellectual and behavioral domains.

With respect to IQ scores, no Gender × Treatment interactions were found across age or across cognitive domain (Brooks-Gunn, Gross, et al., 1992; Brooks-Gunn, Klebanov, et al., 1993). Boys and girls were equally responsive to the treatment. The few studies that looked for differential gender effects tended not to find them (Lee et al., 1988; Lee, Brooks-Gunn, Schnur, & Liaw, 1990; McKey et al., 1985). Likewise, children with higher and lower IQ scores at age 12 months were equally likely to benefit from

---

[4]Studies have demonstrated differences in how teachers' react and interact with boys and girls in elementary-school classrooms and the effects of such differences on achievement and possibly self-perceptions of competence (Eccles & Midgley, 1990).

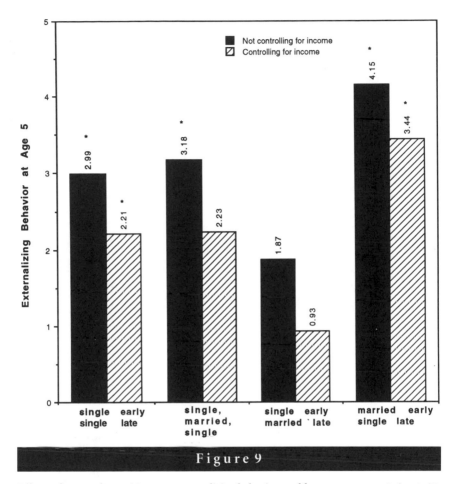

Figure 9

Effects of parental transitions on externalizing behavior-problem scores at age 5. $*p < .05$.

the intervention (see Lee et al., 1988, for similar analyses with children attending Head Start).

However, a Birth Weight × Treatment interaction was found, so that the IHDP was more efficacious for heavy LBW children (2,001 to 2,500 g) than for light LBW children (2,000 g and under). At the same time, treatment effects were seen in both groups, and in the lightest birth weight children (those with birth weights 1,500 g and less; McCormick et al., 1992; see Figure 11 on pp. 507–508). These effects were due to birth weight, not neonatal illness (which was measured as length of stay in the neonatal nursery, independent of birth weight; Infant Health and Development Program, 1990; McCormick, Workman-Daniels, Brooks-Gunn, & Peckham, 1993). We have speculated on the reasons for these differences. Perhaps the set of interventions offered was not as well suited for the lighter LBW children as they were for the heavier LBW children. A related possibility is that some of the lighter LBW infants had biological conditions (concomitants of LBW) that render it difficult to respond to many educational interventions; examples might include cerebral palsy, intraventricular hemorrhage, and respiratory distress syndrome, all of which are more prevalent in very LBW infants. To explore this explanation, our group conducted analyses including and excluding children with cerebral palsy (these children are identified not at birth, but in the 2nd and 3rd years of life). Although the rate of cerebral palsy was the same in the treatment and follow-up groups (as expected), the children with birth weights of 1,500 g or less were more likely to have been diagnosed with one of these conditions (Brooks-Gunn, McCarton, Bauer, Bennett, et al., 1994). Excluding the children with cerebral palsy increases the IQ-treatment effects in the lighter children (Brooks-Gunn, McCarton, et al., 1994). We are also examining links between intraventricular hemorrhage, cognitive scores, and intervention in the very LBW children (McCarton et al., in press).

Perhaps lighter LBW children need more intensive or longer duration of services for early-intervention services of the type offered in the IHDP to show levels of effectiveness seen for the heavier LBW children. One approach to this issue would be to look at the effects of number of days in the center-based schools (dose-related effects) for the treatment group only, to see if the lighter LBW children were more influenced by dosage than were the heavier LBW children (so that the slope of the regression line is steeper for the lighter than for the heavier LBW children). This approach also needs testing.

The behavior problems data are similar in that a trend for larger effects for the heavier than the lighter LBW infants is found (Brooks-Gunn, Klebanov, et al., 1993; Brooks-Gunn, McCarton, et al., 1994). Boys are somewhat (nonsignificantly) more likely to show a larger treatment effect with respect to externalizing behavior problems; this effect is not seen for the overall behavior problems score at 3 years of age (Brooks-Gunn, Klebanov, et al., 1993; Infant Health and Development Program, 1990). The role of maternal perceptions in understanding this possible effect may be substantial (behavior problem data were based on maternal report). That is, boys may be perceived to have higher rates of undercontrolled behavior in the early years of life, and mothers may perceive any changes as more pronounced in boys. Children who were rated as having moderate-to-severe behavior problems at age 24 months were those who benefited most from the intervention between ages 24 and 36 months (see Figure 12 on p. 508; Brooks-Gunn, Duncan, et al., 1993). Such findings underscore the importance of examining the role of person characteristics in the responsivity of children to early intervention.

Pathways by Which Family Resources Influence Children

As Bronfenbrenner stressed 20 years ago, the "engine" of early interventions is the family. It is likely that sustained effects of intervention will be found to be due to the changed context of the family as well as to changes in children's responses to schoollike situations. When outcomes of early-intervention programs are examined into the elementary school years, the often striking IQ effects found at the end of many early-intervention programs are diminished and sometimes disappear altogether by the end of elementary school (Lazar, Darlington, Murray, Royce, & Snipper, 1982; Ramey et al., 1992). Programs that report lasting, but small, IQ or achievement test effects are usually those that included center-based schooling, started in the early years of life, and continued for many years.

At the same time, many more programs report decreases in grade failures and reductions in special education class placement. These effects certainly could be due in part to children in early-intervention programs having more cognitive and emotional self-regulation skills when they enter kindergarten (Lee et al., 1990). These competencies may result in an easier adjustment to school settings (e.g., more attention and understanding of the rules), more rapid learning of reading- and mathematics-related skills, and better treatment by teachers—all of which have the potential of

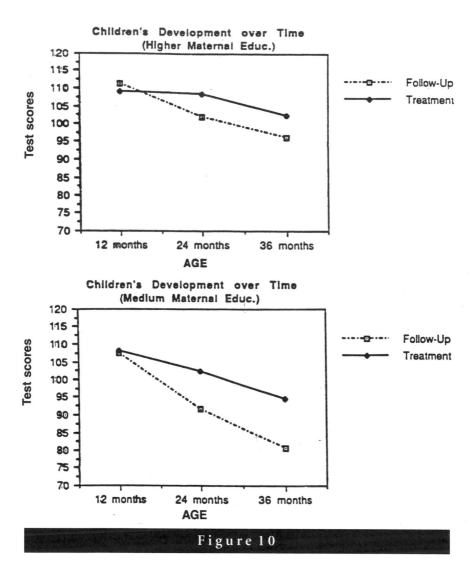

Figure 10

influencing grade retention rates. (See Alexander, Entwisle, & Dauber, 1993, for a discussion of the relative contribution of achievement scores and teacher ratings to grade retention.)

Changes in the family context, familial resources, or distribution of these resources also may play a role in the sustained effects seen. Early intervention programs have been found to influence a number of familial

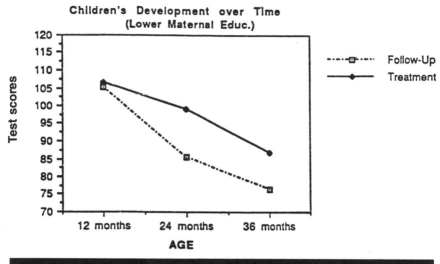

Figure 10 (cont.)

Children's cognitive development over time (12, 24, and 36 months) by maternal education and treatment group.

resources, among them maternal employment and education, provision of home learning experiences, maternal parenting behavior, maternal child-rearing beliefs, and maternal emotional functioning (see review by Benasich & Brooks-Gunn, in press; Benasich, Brooks-Gunn, & Clewell, 1992). It is also believed that early-intervention services may enhance mothers' problem-solving skills, disciplinary styles, and social support networks, although less information is available on these aspects of families. Unlike many earlier studies, the IHDP included measures of all of these family resource or contextual variables.

To date, then, analyses have focused on how families in the intervention group differ from those in the follow-up-only group. Little work has focused on the role of familial resources on child outcome and whether the patterns of associations for those in the intervention group differ from those for the follow-up-only group. That is, the mediated models proposed by Bronfenbrenner as well as others (Woodhead, 1988; Zigler, 1992) have not been tested explicitly. Does participation in early-intervention programs alter the associations between familial resources and child out-

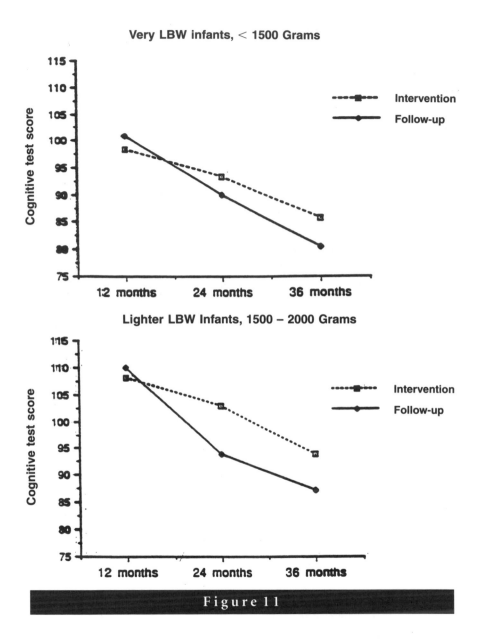

Figure 11

comes? What are the critical familial pathways? Clearly, Bronfenbrenner's call for an understanding of the pathways by which interventions influence families and children, and how changes in the familial context influence children, still remains unanswered (or awaits a more thoughtful research response).

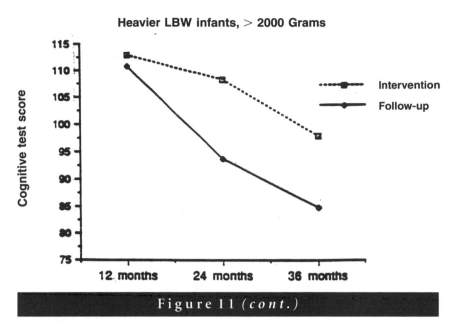

Figure 11 *(cont.)*

Children's cognitive development over time (12, 24, and 36 months) by birthweight and treatment group. From "Enhancing the Development of Low Birthweight, Premature Infants: Changes in Cognition and Behavior Over the First Three Years" by J. Brooks-Gunn, P. K. Klebanov, F. Liaw, and D. Spiker, 1993, *Child Development, 64,* p. 744. Copyright 1993 by University of Chicago Press. Reprinted with permission.

The Role of Community Resources

On the community level, social capital might be enhanced by early intervention. Potential pathways include information, connectedness, and norms and sanctions. Mothers may receive more information, and have more access to information, by means of networks discovered through interaction with parents and staff at a program. For example, a parent who has been connected to an intervention program may know who to contact when his or her child has a behavioral or school problem. The provision of richer and overlapping networks may provide support in times of need. These networks may also facilitate the mother's ability to be an advocate for her child, to obtain resources for the family, and to be engaged in the child's school and community life more generally. Norms and sanctions may be particularly important in terms of parenting behavior and expectancies for

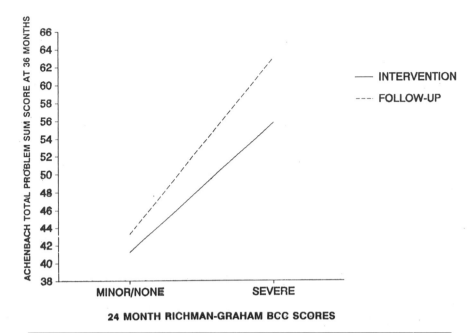

Figure 12

Means for Achenbach Total Problem Sum Score at 36 months by treatment group and 24-month Richman–Graham Behavior Checklist scores. From "Enhancing the Development of Low Birthweight, Premature Infants: Changes in Cognition and Behavior Over the First Three Years" by J. Brooks-Gunn, P. K. Klebanov, F. Liaw, and D. Spiker, 1993, *Child Development, 64*, p. 746. Copyright 1993 by University of Chicago Press. Reprinted with permission.

school performance. A high-quality intervention program may work with families to reduce the use of physical punishment, for example. Altering the norms about harsh discipline styles might be a precondition for individual families to alter practices that they believe are appropriate. Expectancies for school also may be influenced; indeed, many scholars, including Bronfenbrenner, have posited that sustained effects of preschool interventions may be due to motivational and behavioral factors such as expectancies, which themselves may be influenced by social capital in communities.

Little research addresses such possibilities. Indeed, it is unknown how families are selected into community-based programs. For example, only one third to one half of all families eligible for Head Start are currently served by this program. Are these families representative of all eligible families? Two studies suggest that they are not; Head Start seems to serve the poorest of the poor (Hebbler, 1985; Schnur, Brooks-Gunn, & Shipman, 1992). Whether this is true across communities and successive cohorts of children is not known. Also, the process by which some families come to receive a set of services is a relatively unexplored, but important, issue. Do families with certain characteristics seek out services? Or do outreach efforts identify a particular group of families (i.e., staff try to find the poorest of the poor)? Are centers located in the poorest areas of neighborhoods, making it likely that very poor families will attend? Are communities high in social capital more likely to recruit more families, or a certain type of family, into programs?[5]

CONCLUSION

It is clear that Bronfenbrenner has shaped the way in which developmentalists study children in the contexts of family and community. Additionally, his insistence on exploring the intersection of lives and of contexts has provided a guide to more in-depth and rich characterizations of children. Finally, Bronfenbrenner has influenced several generations of scholars who design and evaluate early-intervention programs. I count myself fortunate to be among this group.

REFERENCES

Achenbach, T. M., Edelbrock, C. S., & Howell, C. T. (1987). Empirically based assessment of the behavior/emotional problems of 2- and 3-year-old children. *Journal of Abnormal Child Psychology, 15*, 629–650.

Alexander, K. L., & Entwisle, D. R. (1988). Achievement in the first 2 years of school:

[5]By assigning families to one of two or three groups in randomized evaluation trials, selection bias is controlled. However, which families choose to participate in a trial and which do not is usually not charted, nor are the procedures for recruiting a sample outlined. Consequently, even randomized trials are limited in that it is impossible to estimate whether the families who participate are representative of families in a particular community or with a particular set of characteristics.

Patterns and processes. *Monographs of the Society for Research in Child Development, 53*(2, Serial No. 218).

Alexander, K. L., Entwisle, D. R., & Dauber, S. L. (1993). First-grade behavior: Its short- and long-term consequences for school performance. *Child Development, 64*, 801–814.

Baydar, N., & Brooks-Gunn, J. (1994). The dynamics of child support and its consequences for children. In I. Garfinkel, S. McLanahan, & P. Robins (Eds.), *Child support and child well-being* (pp. 257–284). Washington, DC: Urban Institute Press.

Baydar, N., Brooks-Gunn, J., & Furstenberg, F. F., Jr. (1993). Early warning signs of functional illiteracy: Predictors in childhood and adolescence. *Child Development, 64*, 815–829.

Benasich, A., & Brooks-Gunn, J. (in press). Enhancing maternal knowledge and child-rearing concepts: Results from an early intervention program. *Child Development.*

Benasich, A. A., Brooks-Gunn, J., & Clewell, B. C. (1992). How do mothers benefit from early intervention programs? *Journal of Applied Developmental Psychology, 13*, 311–362.

Bradley, R. H., & Caldwell, B. M. (1984). The HOME inventory and family depression. *Developmental Psychology, 38*, 315–320.

Bronfenbrenner, U. (1979). Contexts of child rearing: Problems and prospects. *American Psychologist, 34*, 844–850.

Bronfenbrenner, U. (1986). Ecology of the family as context for human development: Research perspectives. *Developmental Psychology, 22*, 723–742.

Brooks-Gunn, J. (1990). Identifying the vulnerable young child. In D. E. Rogers & E. Ginzberg (Eds.), *Improving the life chances of children at risk* (pp. 104–124). Boulder, CO: Westview Press.

Brooks-Gunn, J. (1995). Opportunities for change: Effects of intervention programs on mothers and children. In P. L. Chase-Lansdale & J. Brooks-Gunn (Eds.), *Escape from poverty: What makes a difference for children?* New York: Cambridge University Press.

Brooks-Gunn, J., Brown, B., Duncan, G. D., & Moore, K. A. (1995, March–April). *Child development in the context of family and community resources: An agenda for national data collections.* Paper presented at the National Academy of Sciences Conference on Integrating Federal Statistics on Children, Washington, DC.

Brooks-Gunn, J., & Chase-Lansdale, L. P. (1995). Adolescent parenthood. In M. Bornstein (Ed.), *Handbook of parenting*. Hillsdale, NJ: Erlbaum.

Brooks-Gunn, J., Duncan, G., & Aber, J. L. (Eds.). (in press). *Neighborhood poverty: Context and consequences for development*. New York: Russell Sage Foundation.

Brooks-Gunn, J., Duncan, G. J., Klebanov, P. K., & Sealand, N. (1993). Do neighborhoods influence child and adolescent behavior. *American Journal of Sociology, 99*, 353–395.

Brooks-Gunn, J., & Furstenberg, F. F., Jr. (1987). Continuity and change in the context of poverty: Adolescent mothers and their children. In J. J. Gallagher & C. T. Ramey (Eds.), *The malleability of children* (pp. 171–188). Baltimore: Brookes.

Brooks-Gunn, J., Gross, R. T., Kraemer, H. C., Spiker, D., & Shapiro, S. (1992). Enhancing the cognitive outcomes of low-birth-weight, premature infants: For whom is the intervention most effective? *Pediatrics, 89*, 1209–1215.

Brooks-Gunn, J., Guo, G., & Furstenberg, F. F., Jr. (1993). Who drops out of and who continues beyond high school? A 20-year follow-up of Black urban youth. *Journal of Research on Adolescence, 3*, 271–294.

Brooks-Gunn, J., Klebanov, P. K., & Duncan, G. (in press). Ethnic differences in children's intelligence test scores: Role of economic deprivation, home environment, and maternal characteristics. *Child Development*.

Brooks-Gunn, J., Klebanov, P. K., & Liaw, F. (1995). The provision of learning experiences in the context of poverty: The Infant Health and Development Program. *Children and Youth Services Review, 17*, 231–250.

Brooks-Gunn, J., Klebanov, P. K., Liaw, F., & Duncan, G. (1995). Toward an understanding of the effects of poverty upon children. In H. E. Fitzgerald, B. M. Lester, & B. Zuckerman (Eds.), *Children of poverty: Research, health care, and policy issues*. New York: Garland Press.

Brooks-Gunn, J., Klebanov, P. K., Liaw, F. R., & Spiker, D. (1993). Enhancing the development of low-birth-weight, premature infants: Change in cognition and behavior over the first three years. *Child Development, 64*, 736–753.

Brooks-Gunn, J., Liaw, F., & Klebanov, P. K. (1992). Effects of early intervention on low birth weight preterm infants: What aspects of cognitive functioning are enhanced? *Journal of Pediatrics, 120*, 350–359.

Brooks-Gunn, J., & Maritato, N. C. (in press). Growing up poor in the United States: Children, youth, and families. In J. Brooks-Gunn & J. Duncan (Eds.), *Growing up poor*. New York: Russell Sage Foundation.

Brooks-Gunn, J., McCarton, C., Bauer, C., Bennett, F. C., et al. (1994). *Early inter-*

vention in low birthweight, premature infants: Result through age 5 from the Infant Heath and Development Program.

Brooks-Gunn, J., McCormick, M., Shapiro, S., Benasich, A. A., & Black, G. (in press). Effects of early education intervention on maternal employment, public assistance, and health insurance: The Infant Health and Development Program. *American Journal of Public Health.*

Brooks-Gunn, J., Phelps, E., & Elder, G. H. (1991). Studying lives through time: Secondary data analyses in developmental psychology. *Developmental Psychology, 27,* 899–910.

Brown, P., & Richman, H. (in press). Neighborhood effects and state and local policy. In G. Duncan, J. Brooks-Gunn, & J. L. Aber (Eds.), *Neighborhood poverty: Context and consequences for development.* New York: Russell Sage Foundation.

Bryant, D. M., & Ramey, C. T. (1987). An analysis of the effectiveness of early intervention programs for environmentally at-risk children. In M. J. Guralnick & F. C. Bennett (Eds.), *The effectiveness of early intervention for at-risk and handicapped children* (pp. 33–78). New York: Academic Press.

Burton, L. M. (1991). Caring for children in high-risk neighborhoods. *The American Enterprise,* 34–37.

Chase-Lansdale, P. L., & Brooks-Gunn, J. (Eds.). (1995). *Escape from poverty: What makes a difference for children?* New York: Cambridge University Press.

Chase-Lansdale, P. L., Brooks-Gunn, J., & Zamsky, E. S. (1994). Young multigenerational families in poverty: Quality of mothering and grandmothering. *Child Development, 65,* 373–393.

Chase-Lansdale, P. L., Gordon, R., Brooks-Gunn, J., & Klebanov, P. K. (in press). Effects of neighborhood residence upon 5 to 6 year old children's development. In J. Brooks-Gunn, G. Duncan, & J. L. Aber (Eds.), *Neighborhood poverty: Context and consequences for development.* New York: Russell Sage Foundation.

Chase-Lansdale, P. L., & Hetherington, E. M. (1990). The impact of divorce on lifespan development: Short and long term effects. In P. B. Baltes, D. L. Featherman, & R. M. Lerner (Eds.), *Life span development and behavior* (Vol. 10, pp. 107–151). Hillsdale, NJ: Erlbaum.

Chase-Lansdale, P. L., Mott, F. L., Brooks-Gunn, J., & Phillips, D. (1991). Children of the NLSY: A unique research opportunity. *Developmental Psychology, 27,* 918–931.

Clarke-Stewart, K. A., & Fein, G. G. (1983). Early childhood programs. In P. H. Mussen (Ed.), *Handbook of child psychology* (Vol. 2, pp. 917–999). New York: Wiley.

Coleman, J. S. (1988). Social capital in the creation of human capital. *American Journal of Sociology, 94,* 95–120.

Crane, J. (1991). The epidemic theory of ghettos and neighborhood effects on dropping out and teenage childbearing. *American Journal of Sociology, 96,* 1126–1159.

Culbertson, J. L. (Ed.). (1994). Poverty and children [Special issue]. *Journal of Clinical Child Psychology, 23*(4).

Danziger, S. K., & Danziger, S. (Eds.). (1995). Child poverty and social policies [Special issue]. *Children and Youth Services Review, 17*(1).

Duncan, G. J. (1991). The economic environment of childhood. In A. C. Huston (Ed.), *Children in poverty* (pp. 23–50). New York: Cambridge University Press.

Duncan, G. J., Brooks-Gunn, J., & Klebanov, P. K. (1994). Economic deprivation and early-childhood development. *Child Development, 65,* 296–318.

Duncan, G. J., Hill, M. S., & Hoffman, S. D. (1988). Welfare dependence within and across generations. *Science, 1,* 467–471.

Duncan, G. J., Smeeding, T. M., & Rodgers, W. (1991, December). *W(h)ither the middle class? A dynamic view.* Paper presented at the Levy Institute Conference on Income Inequality, Bard College, New York.

Eccles, J. S., & Midgley, C. (1990). Changes in academic motivation and self-perception during early adolescence. In R. Montemayer, G. R. Adams, & T. P. Gullotta (Eds.), *From childhood to adolescence: A transitional period?* (pp. 134–155). Newbury Park, CA: Sage.

Elder, G. H., Jr. (1974). *Children of the Great Depression.* Chicago: University of Chicago Press.

Escalona, S. K. (1982). Babies at double hazard: Early development of biological and social risk. *Pediatrics, 70,* 670–676.

Featherman, D. L., & Hauser, R. M. (1987). *Opportunity and change.* New York: Academic Press.

Fitzgerald, H. E., Lester, B. M., & Zuckerman, B. (Eds.). (1995). *Children of poverty: Research, health care, and policy issues.* New York: Garland Press.

Furstenberg, F. F., Jr., Brooks-Gunn, J., & Morgan, S. P. (1987). Adolescent mothers and their children in later life. *Family Planning Perspectives, 19,* 142–151.

Garbarino, J. (1991). Not all bad developmental outcomes are the result of child abuse. *Developmental Psychopathology, 3,* 45–50.

Garfinkel, I., & McLanahan, S. (1986). *Single mothers and their children: A new American dilemma.* Washington, DC: Urban Institute Press.

Gottfried, A. W. (Ed.). (1984). *Home environment and early cognitive development.* Orlando, FL: Academic Press.

Gross, R. T., Brooks-Gunn, J., & Spiker, D. (1992). Efficacy of educational interventions for low birth weight infants: The Infant Health and Development Program. In S. L. Friedman & M. D. Sigman (Eds.), *The psychological development of low birth weight children: Advances in applied developmental psychology* (pp. 411–434). Norwood, NJ: Ablex.

Gross, R. T., & Spiker, D. (Eds.). (in press). *The Infant Health and Development Program for low birth weight premature infants.* Stanford, CA: Stanford University Press.

Haskins, R. (1989). Beyond metaphor: Efficacy of early childhood education. *American Psychology, 44,* 274–282.

Haveman, R., & Wolfe, B. (1991). Childhood events and circumstances influencing high school completion. *Demography, 28,* 133–157.

Haveman, R., & Wolfe, B. (1994). *Succeeding generations: On the effects of investments in children.* New York: Russell Sage Foundation.

Hayes, C. D., Palmer, J. L., & Zaslow, M. E. (1990). *Who cares for America's children? Child care policy for the 1990's.* Washington, DC: National Academy Press.

Hebbler, K. (1985). An old and new question on the effects of early education for children from low income families. *Educational Evaluation and Policy Analysis, 7*(3), 207–216.

Hernandez, D. J. (1993). *America's children: Resources from family, government, and the economy.* New York: Russell Sage Foundation.

Hetherington, E. M., & Clingempeel, W. G. (1992). Coping with marital transitions: A family systems perspective. *Monographs of the Society for Research in Child Development, 57* (2–3, Serial No. 227).

Hetherington, E. M., & Jodl, K. M. (1995). Stepfamilies as setting for child development. In A. Broth & J. Dunn (Eds.), *Step-parent families with children: Who benefits and who does not?* Hillsdale, NJ: Erlbaum.

Hill, C. R., & Duncan, G. (1987). Parental family income and the socioeconomic attainment of children. *Social Science Research, 16,* 39–73.

Hofferth, S. L., & Phillips, D. A. (1991). Child care policy research. *Journal of Social Issues, 47,* 1–13.

Huston, A. C. (Ed.). (1991). *Children in poverty: Child development and public policy.* Cambridge, England: Cambridge University Press.

Huston, A. C., Garcia-Coll, C., & McLoyd, V. C. (Eds.). (1994). Children and poverty [Special issue]. *Child Development, 65* (2).

Infant Health and Development Program. (1990). Enhancing the outcomes of low-birth-weight, premature infants. *Journal of the American Medical Association, 263*, 3035–3042.

Jencks, C., & Mayer, S. (1990). The social consequences of growing up in a poor neighborhood. In L. Lynn & M. McGeary (Eds.), *Inner-city poverty in the United States* (pp. 111–186). Washington, DC: National Academy Press.

Jencks, C., & Petersen, P. (Eds.). (1992). *The urban underclass.* Washington, DC: Brookings Institution.

Kim, R. Y., Garfinkel, I., & Meyers, D. R. (1994). *Interaction effects of child tax credit, national health insurance, and annual child support.* Madison, WI: Institute for Research in Poverty.

Klebanov, P. K., Brooks-Gunn, J., Chase-Lansdale, P. L., & Gordon, R. (in press). The intersection of the neighborhood and home environment and its influence on young children. In J. Brooks-Gunn, G. Duncan, & J. L. Aber (Eds.), *Neighborhood poverty: Context and consequences for development.* New York: Russell Sage Foundation.

Klebanov, P. K., Brooks-Gunn, J., & Duncan, G. J. (1994). Does neighborhood and family poverty affect mothers' parenting, mental health, and social support? *Journal of Marriage and the Family, 56*, 441–455.

Klebanov, P. K., Brooks-Gunn, J., & McCormick, M. C. (1994a). Classroom behavior of very low birth weight elementary school children. *Pediatrics, 94*, 700–708.

Klebanov, P. K., Brooks-Gunn, J., & McCormick, M. C. (1994b). School achievement and failure in very low birth weight children. *Journal of Behavioral and Developmental Pediatrics, 15*, 248–256.

Knox, V. W., & Bane, M. J. (1994). The effects of child support on educational attainment. In I. Garfinkel, S. McLanahan, & P. Robins (Eds.), *Child support and child well-being.* Washington, DC: Urban Institute Press.

Kopp, C. B., & Kaler, S. R. (1989). Risk in infancy: Origins and implications. *American Psychologist, 44*, 224–230.

Korenman, S., Miller, J. E., & Sjaastad, C. (1995). Long-term poverty and child development in the United States: Results from the NLSY. *Children and Youth Services Review, 17*, 127–156.

Kraemer, H. C., & Fendt, K. H. (1990). Random assignment in clinical trials: Issues in planning (Infant Health and Development Program). *Journal of Clinical Epidemiology, 43,* 1157–1167.

Lazar, I., Darlington, R. B., Murray, H., Royce, J., & Snipper, A. (1982). Lasting effects of early education: A report from the consortium for logitudinal studies. *Monographs of the Society for Research in Child Development, 47*(Serial No. 195).

Lee, V., Brooks-Gunn, J., Schnur, E. (1988). Does Head Start "close the gap"? A comparison of children attending Head Start, no preschool, and other preschool programs. *Developmental Psychology, 24,* 210–222.

Lee, V., Brooks-Gunn, J., Schnur, E., & Liaw, F. (1990). Are Head Start effects sustained? A longitudinal comparison of disadvantaged children attending Head Start, no preschool, and other preschool programs. *Child Development, 61,* 495–507.

Liaw, F. R., & Brooks-Gunn, J. (1993). Patterns of low birth weight children's cognitive development and their determinants. *Developmental Psychology, 29,* 1024–1035.

Liaw, F., & Brooks-Gunn, J. (1994). Cumulative familial risks and low-birthweight children's cognitive and behavioral development. *Journal of Clinical Child Psychology, 23,* 360–372.

McCarton, C., Bennett, F., Donithan, M., Belt, P., Brooks-Gunn, J., Bauer, C., Bernbaum, J., Scott, D., Yogman, M., & Tonascia, J. (in press). Neurologic status at 36 months of age. In R. T. Gross & D. Spiker (Eds.), *The Infant Health and Development Program for low birth weight premature infants.* Stanford, CA: Stanford University Press.

McCormick, M. C. (1989). Long-term follow-up of infants discharged from neonatal intensive care units. *Journal of the American Medical Association, 261,* 1767–1772.

McCormick, M. C., & Brooks-Gunn, J. (1989). Health care for children and adolescents. In H. Freeman & S. Levine (Eds.), *Handbook of medical sociology* (pp. 347–380). Englewood Cliffs, NJ: Prentice Hall.

McCormick, M. C., Brooks-Gunn, J., Shapiro, S., Benasich, A. A., Black, G., & Gross, R. T. (1991). Health care use among young children in day-care: Results seen in a randomized trial of early intervention. *Journal of the American Medical Association, 265,* 2212–2217.

McCormick, M. C., Brooks-Gunn, J., Workman-Daniels, K., Turner, J., & Peckham, G. (1992). The health and developmental status of very low birth weight children at school age. *Journal of the American Medical Association, 267,* 2204–2208.

McCormick, M. C., Workman-Daniels, K., Brooks-Gunn, J., & Peckham, G. J. (1993). Hospitalizations of very low birth weight children at school age. *Journel of Pediatrics, 122,* 360–365.

McKey, R. H., Condelli, L., Granson, H., Barrett, B., McConkey, C., & Plantz, M. (1985). *The impact of Head Start on children, families and communities.* (Final report of Head Start Evaluation, Synthesis and Utilization.)

McLanahan, S., Astone, N. M., & Marks, N. F. (1991). The role of mother-only families in reducing poverty. In A. C. Huston (Ed.), *Children in poverty: Child development and public policy* (pp. 51–78). New York: Cambridge University Press.

McLanahan, S., & Sandefur, G. D. (1994). *Growing up with a single parent: What hurts, what helps.* Cambridge, MA: Harvard University Press.

McLanahan, S., Seltzer, J. A., Hanson, T. L., Thompson, E. (1994). Child support enforcement and child well-being: Greater security or greater conflict? In I. Garfinkel, S. McLanahan, & P. Robins (Eds.), *Child support and child well-being.* Washington, DC: Urban Institute Press.

McLoyd, V. C. (1990). The impact of economic hardship on Black families and development. *Child Development, 61,* 311–346.

Meisels, S. J., & Shonkoff, J. P. (Eds.). (1990). *Handbook of early childhood intervention.* New York: Cambridge University Press.

Moore, K. A., Myers, D. E., Morrison, D. R., Nord, C. W., Brown, B., & Edmonston, B. (1993). Age at first child birth and later poverty. *Journal of Research on Adolescence, 3,* 393–422.

Orshansky, M. (1965, July). Counting the poor: Another look at the poverty profile. *Social Security Bulletin, 26,* 3–29.

Parker, L., Greer, S., & Zuckerman, B. (1988). Double "jeopardy": The impact of poverty on early child development. *Pediatric Clinics of North America, 35,* 1227–1240.

Pelligrini, A. D., Perlmutter, J. C., Galda, L., & Brody, G. H. (1990). Joint reading between Black Head Start children and their mothers. *Child Development, 61,* 443–453.

Ramey, C. T., Bryant, D. M., Wasik, B. H., Sparling, J. J., Fendt, K. H., & LaVange, L. M. (1992). The Infant Health and Development Program: Program elements, family participation, and child intelligence. *Pediatrics, 3,* 454–465.

Renwick, T. J., & Bergmann, B. R. (1992). *Drawing the line—Alternative poverty measures and their implications for public policy.* Washington, DC: Urban Institute Press.

Richman, N., & Graham, P. J. (1971). A behavioral screening questionnaire for use with three-year-old children: Preliminary findings. *Journal of Child Psychology and Psychiatry, 12*, 5–33.

Sameroff, A. J., & Chandler, M. J. (1975). Reproductive risks and the continuum of caretaking causality. In F. D. Horowitz, M. Hetherington, S. Scarr-Salapatek, & G. Siegal (Eds.), *Review of child development research* (Vol. 4, pp. 187–244). Chicago: Society for Research in Child Development.

Sameroff, A. J., Seifer, R., Baldwin, A., & Baldwin, C. (1993). Stability of intelligence from preschool to adolescence: The influence of social and family risk factors. *Child Development, 64*, 80–97.

Sameroff, A. J., Seifer, R., Barocas, R., Zax, M., & Greenspan, S. (1987). Intelligence quotient scores of 4-year-old children: Social and environmental risk factors. *Pediatrics, 79*, 343–350.

Sampson, R. J. (1992). Family management and child development: Insights from social disorganization theory. In J. McCord (Ed.), *Advances in criminological theory* (Vol. 3, pp. 63–93). New Brunswick, NJ: Transaction.

Schnur, E. S., Brooks-Gunn, J., & Shipman, V. (1992). Who attends programs serving poor children? The case of Head Start attendees and nonattendees. *Journal of Applied Developmental Psychology, 13*, 405–421.

Smith, J., & Brooks-Gunn, J. (in press). *Effects of income on child and maternal characteristics.*

Smith, J., Brooks-Gunn, J., & Klebanov, P. (in press). Consequences of growing up poor for young children. In J. Brooks-Gunn & J. Duncan (Eds.), *Growing up poor.* New York: Russell Sage Foundation.

Sparling, J., & Lewis, I. (1985). *Partners for learning.* Lewisville, NC: Kaplan.

Sparling, J., Lewis, I., Ramey, C. T., Wasik, B. H., Bryant, D. M., & LaVange, L. M. (1991). Partners: A curriculum to help premature, low-birth-weight infants get off to a good start. *Topics in Early Childhood Special Education, 11*, 36–55.

Spiker, D., Ferguson, J., & Brooks-Gunn, J. (1993). Enhancing maternal interactive behavior and child social competence in low-birth-weight, premature infants. *Child Development, 64*, 754–768.

Survey Research Center. (1984). *User guide to the PSID.* Ann Arbor, MI: ICPSR.

Thomson, E., Hanson, T. L., & McLanahan, S. (1994). Family structure and child well-being: Economic resource versus parental behavior. *Social Forces, 73*, 221–242.

Thomson, E., Hanson, T. L., McLanahan, S., & Curtin, R. B. (1992). Family structure, gender, and parental socialization. *Journal of Marriage and the Family, 54,* 368–378.

Thorndike, R. L., Hagen, E. P., & Sattler, J. M. (1986). *Stanford-Binet Intelligence Test Scale* (4th ed.).

Wachs, T. D., & Gruen, G. E. (1982). *Early experience and human development.* New York: Plenum.

Watts, H. W. (1993, March). *A review of alternative budget-based expenditure norms.* Paper prepared for Panel on Poverty Measurement of the Committee of National Statistics, National Academy of Sciences/National Research Council.

Wechsler, D. (1989). *Wechsler Preschool and Primary Scale of Intelligence.* New York: The Psychological Corporation.

Werner, E. E., Bierman, J. M., & French, F. E. (1971). *The children of Kauai: A longitudinal study from the prenatal period to age ten.* Honolulu: University of Hawaii Press.

Werner, E. E., & Smith, R. S. (1982). *Vulnerable but invincible: A longitudinal study of resilient children and youth.* New York: Adams.

Wilson, W. J. (1987). *The truly disadvantaged: The inner city, the underclass, and public policy.* Chicago: University of Chicago Press.

Wilson, W. J. (1991a). Public policy research and the truly disadvantaged. In C. Jencks & P. E. Peterson (Eds.), *The urban underclass* (pp. 460–481). Washington, DC: Brookings Institution.

Wilson, W. J. (1991b). Studying inner-city social dislocations: The challenge of public agenda research. *American Sociological Review, 56*(11), 1–14.

Woodhead, M. (1988). When psychology informs public policy: The case of early childhood intervention. *American Psychologist, 43,* 443–454.

Zigler, E. (1992). Early childhood intervention: A promising preventative for juvenile delinquency. *American Psychologist, 47,* 997–1006.

PART FIVE

Reflections and New Directions

Reflections and New Directions

Phyllis Moen

T he chapters in this last section of the volume capture something of the spirit of ecological research. Together, they offer both a synthesis and a challenge to those seeking to understand lives in context.

In his discussion of the importance of neighborhood, William Julius Wilson illustrates the relevance of the broad contexts of the communities in which lives are lived. His case in point, the new urban poverty, exemplifies the utility of Bronfenbrenner's model of the ecology of human development. Unemployment, as experienced in different neighborhood settings, has different meanings and, consequently, different implications. Joblessness is becoming a fact of life in inner-city ghetto neighborhoods in the United States, with profound consequences for self-efficacy, for behavior, and for the socialization of the next generation. Wilson draws on qualitative material from his own program of research to vividly depict the importance of both structure and culture, as well as the differences between the two. Wilson's writings and research findings underscore the need for the concept of *context* to incorporate cultural as well as structural dimensions.

Jay Belsky's chapter summarizes Bronfenbrenner's ecological model, as well as his "style" as a person and a scholar, that is, Bronfenbrenner's ability to make creative and insightful order out of seeming chaos. Belsky reviews three themes that undergird this volume: the processes and pathways of development, the role of context, and, finally, the interplay between developmental processes and context. Most of the questions that this ecological model generates, he maintains, relate to "how": how do contexts shape lives, and how do individuals shape their life contexts? What is missing, according to Belsky, is attention to the "why" questions, the large-scale, biologically grounded "whys" that have to do with the forces of evolutionary history. Belsky proposes that the ecological model be extended to include just such evolutionary considerations.

Kurt Lüscher attends to the key role of knowledge and beliefs in the ecology of human development. He points out that human action is "perspectivistic" (p. 565), that is, individuals come to see themselves and the contexts of their life from a certain point of view. This point of view (interpretation) is generated and sustained by ongoing interactions with others. Lüscher illustrates the central role of interpretation in the process of human development with examples from Bronfenbrenner's own personal and intellectual biography. For example, Lüscher points out that Bronfenbrenner's interpretive talents are displayed in his fruitful melding of the multiple meanings of the very concept of ecology. Culture, in the form of knowledge and beliefs, is crucial to the shaping of lives; that shaping occurs, as Lüscher reminds us, through the process of interpretation.

In the first of his two contributions to this volume, Urie Bronfenbrenner provides insights about his own personal life course. These reflections place this internationally renowned behavioral scientist's life and work in the context of early experiences and lessons learned from parents, peers, teachers, and community. Two influences seem especially powerful: his father's admonitions, anecdotes, and active engagement in life and learning; and Urie's own education—formal and informal—as an undergraduate at Cornell University. His life work as a developmental scientist and as a teacher can better be understood from the perspective of the people, settings, and situational imperatives that shaped Urie's own life course.

I know of no scholar, no human being, more productive than Urie

Bronfenbrenner. We at Cornell, like so many across the nation and abroad, value Urie not only because of his wisdom, his knowledge, and his experience but also because he continues to contribute to the central missions and challenges of the university and society as a theorist, researcher, teacher, and tireless advocate for family, community, and a civil society.

Urie Bronfenbrenner's concluding chapter is both an end and a beginning. So, typically, Urie chooses not to rest on his laurels, but to take the "riskier course of proposing as yet untried theoretical and operational models" (p. 619). He provides elements and examples of his latest thinking about lives in context, formulated as an emerging bioecological paradigm. Urie's goal, as always, is to teach, to inspire the reader to engage in the process of dialogue and discovery, and by doing so, to further advance the field to which he himself has contributed so much.

15

Jobless Ghettos and the Social Outcome of Youngsters

William Julius Wilson

It is a special honor to participate in a symposium honoring one of the truly creative social scientists of our time. As a sociologist, I have appreciated Urie Bronfenbrenner's awareness of the importance of social structure and culture in a child's development. I therefore read with some delight the opening paragraphs in the chapter by Steinberg, Darling, and Fletcher (13), which describe Bronfenbrenner's reaction to a paper that failed to address adequately the problem of social context. According to Steinberg et al., Bronfenbrenner explained that it makes "no sense at all to control for ethnicity, social class, or household composition in an attempt to isolate a 'pure' process. No processes occur outside of a context. And if we want to understand context, we need to take it into account, not pretend to control it away" (p. 424).

As Brooks-Gunn correctly pointed out in her chapter (14), the neigh-

The research for this manuscript was supported by grants from the Ford Foundation, the Rockefeller Foundation, the Carnegie Corporation, the MacArthur Foundation, the Spencer Foundation, the William T, Grant Foundation, the Lloyd A. Fry Foundation, the Woods Charitable Fund, the Department of Health and Human Services. Parts of this chapter are based on a larger study, *Jobless Ghettos: The Disappearance of Work and Its Effect on Urban Life*, to be published by Knopf in 1995.

borhood context has always been deemed important by developmentalists such as Bronfenbrenner. However, in recent years the rapid increase in concentrated inner-city poverty has resulted in an explosion of research examining neighborhood effects on individuals, families, peer groups, and other social networks. An increasing number of scholars, including child development researchers, recognize that neighborhoods matter, but empirical and theoretical discussions of neighborhood effects remain at a rudimentary level. Empirical measures of neighborhood effects are still underdeveloped, and theoretical issues are far from elaborated. This is especially true of the research that measures the effects of neighborhoods on individual outcomes (Elliott et al., 1994).

In this chapter, I would like to build on some of the theoretical issues I have raised in previous writings concerning the effects of neighborhoods on individual outcomes by integrating arguments that feature the concepts *social organization,* and the *new urban poverty.*

THE IMPORTANCE OF NEIGHBORHOOD SOCIAL ORGANIZATION

By *social organization,* I mean the extent to which the residents of a neighborhood are able to maintain effective social control and realize their common values. There are two major dimensions of neighborhood social organization: (a) the prevalence, strength, and interdependence of social networks and (b) the extent of collective supervision that the residents direct and the personal responsibility they assume in addressing neighborhood problems. Both formal institutions and informal networks reflect social organization (Sampson, 1992). In other words, neighborhood social organization depends on the extent of local friendship ties, the degree of social cohesion, the level of resident participation in formal and informal voluntary associations, the density and stability of formal organizations, and the nature of informal social controls. Neighborhoods that integrate the adults by an extensive set of obligations, expectations, and social networks are in a better position to control and supervise the activities and behavior of children and to monitor developments (e.g., the breaking up of congregations of youths on street corners and the supervision of youth leisure time activities; Sampson, 1992).

The connectedness and stability of social networks in such neighborhoods transcend the household because the neighborhood adults have the potential to observe, report on, and discuss the behavior of the children in different circumstances. These networks reinforce the discipline the child receives in the home, because other adults in the neighborhood assume responsibility for the supervision of youth that are not their own (Sampson, 1992).

However, as pointed out by Steinberg et al. (this volume, chapter 13), the norms and supervision imposed on children are most effective when they reflect what Coleman (1990) called "intergenerational closure," that is, the overlapping of youth and adult social networks in the neighborhood. Intergenenerational closure is exhibited in those neighborhoods where most parents know not only their children's friends, but the parents of those friends as well.

A recent study by Furstenberg (1993) provides support for these theoretical arguments. On the basis of the field research of five of his research assistants, which included "extended open-ended interviews with parents and their teenage children residing in five distinct inner-city neighborhoods" (Furstenberg, 1993, p. 234), Furstenberg concluded that family management is profoundly influenced by the neighborhoods in which the families live. "Ordinary parents are likely to have more success when they reside in communities where the burden of raising children is seen as a collective responsibility and where strong institutions sustain the efforts of parents" (Furstenberg, 1993, p. 257).

For example, Furstenberg (1993) reported that regardless of the parenting skills of the parents, residents in a poor, unstable, and socially disorganized neighborhood in North Philadelphia tended to isolate themselves and their children from the surrounding community and were not part of neighborhood institutions. They distrusted local schools, regarded local services suspiciously, and tended to use supportive services that were outside the community. Largely disconnected from the community, the parents had to "manage on their own" (Furstenberg, 1993, p. 243). Accordingly, children not only suffered greater risks because of less supervision and monitoring, but they also did not have the positive experiences of being connected to the wider community through school, job, and friendship ties.

This is in sharp contrast to another neighborhood Furstenberg's (1993) research team studied in South Philadelphia. In this neighborhood, which was poor but nonetheless socially cohesive, Furstenberg's researchers found the same range of parenting skills as in the neighborhood in North Philadelphia, but the youths, despite similar levels of poverty and similar family structures, faced quite different structural constraints. This neighborhood featured shared parental responsibility, informal social control of youths in public spaces, and kinship and friendship bonds that connected local institutions with the family. Youths in this neighborhood could not easily escape the scrutiny of neighborhood adults, and the mutual support of other parents in the neighborhood reinforced the activities of parents inside the home. In other words, children in this South Philadelphia neighborhood were socialized not solely by parents, but also by friends, relatives, and neighbors.[1]

The families in South Philadelphia were socially integrated; those in North Philadelphia were not. As pointed out by Steinberg and his colleagues (this volume, chapter 13), as a general rule, adolescents seem to benefit directly from the exchange of resources produced by their parents' social integration. However, social integration may not be beneficial to adolescents who live in unfavorable neighborhoods, for example, neighborhoods characterized by bad parenting. Steinberg et al. state the following:

Although we tend to think of social integration as a desirable endpoint, its desirability depends on the nature of the people that in-

---

[1]Furstenberg (1993) pointed out that many of our social programs focus solely on improving the material, informational, and psychological resources of parents so that they might manage the task of child rearing. Because the full burden of caretaking is attributed to parents, they receive the full measure of blame when their children do not succeed. However, Furstenberg argued persuasively that if we are committed to strengthening the family, more attention must be given to rebuilding neighborhood centers, recreational services, schools, churches, and other local institutions that support families.

tegration brings one into contact with. There are many communities in contemporary America in which it may be more adaptive for parents to be socially isolated than socially integrated. Indeed, some of Furstenberg's (1990) recent work on family life in the inner city of Philadelphia suggests that social isolation is often deliberately practiced as an adaptive strategy by many parents living in dangerous neighborhoods. (p. 459)

However, in tough inner-city neighborhoods, two kinds of social isolation should be distinguished: (a) families who deliberately isolate themselves from other families and (b) families who lack contact with institutions, families, and individuals in the larger mainstream society, regardless of the level of interaction with neighbors.

Research that we have conducted in Chicago suggests that what many of these tough neighborhoods have in common is a relatively high degree of social integration (isolated from extralocal contacts, inner-city Blacks tend to exhibit higher levels of local neighboring) and a low degree of informal social control. We found a positive relationship between the concentration of disadvantages (poverty, welfare receipt, and joblessness) and the density of local networks and a negative relationship between the concentration of disadvantages and informal social control.[2] To repeat, the structurally disadvantaged inner-city neighborhoods in Chicago feature relatively high levels of local neighboring, but low levels of social control.[3] We need more research on the factors involved in these relationships, but a tentative conclusion would be the following: Not only are children in such neighborhoods adversely affected by the lack of informal social controls, but they are also disadvantaged because the social interaction among neighbors is disproportionately restricted among those who lack the skills, experiences, and resources conducive to healthy child development. I include among these the lack of steady employment, a problem to which I now turn.

---

[2]Informal social control was measured by a four-item scale that tapped the respondent's perception of whether neighbors would intervene if they saw children getting in trouble, a fight, a burglary in progress, or a drug sale. The data are from the Chicago Neighborhood Project at the University of Chicago. This project is part of the Successful Adolescent Research Network of the MacArthur Foundation.

[3]These findings were presented in Sampson (1992).

THE NEW URBAN POVERTY

Many inner-city neighborhoods are plagued by the highest levels of joblessness since the Depression. Indeed, there is a new poverty in our nation's metropolises. By the *new urban poverty,* I mean poor segregated neighborhoods in which a substantial majority of individual adults are either unemployed or have dropped out of the labor force. For example, in 1990 only one in three adults (35%) ages 16 and over in the 12 Chicago community areas with poverty rates that exceeded 40% held a job.[4] Each of these community areas, located on the south and west sides of the city, is overwhelmingly Black. We can add to these 12 high-jobless areas 3 additional predominantly Black community areas, with rates of poverty of 29%, 30%, and 36%, respectively, where only 4 in 10 (42%) adults worked in 1990. Thus, in these 15 Black community areas, representing a total population of 425,125, only 37% of all the adults were gainfully employed in 1990. By contrast, 54% of the adults in the 17 other predominantly Black community areas in Chicago, with a total population of 545,408, worked in 1990. This was close to the citywide figure of 57%. Finally, except for one largely Asian community area with an employment rate of 46% and one largely Latino community area with an employment rate of 49%, a majority of the adults held a job in each of the 45 other community areas of Chicago.[5]

The magnitude of the changes can be seen in the neighborhoods of Douglas, Washington Park, and Grand Boulevard on Chicago's South Side.

---

[4]The figures on adult employment presented in this paragraph are based on calculations from data provided by the 1990 U.S. Bureau of the Census and the *Local Community Fact Book for Chicago, 1950.* The adult employment rates represent the number of employed individuals (14 and over in 1950 and 16 and over in 1990) among the total number of adults in a given area. Those who are not employed include both the individuals who are members of the labor force but are not working and those who have dropped out or are not part of the labor force. The group who is not in the labor force "consists mainly of students, housewives, retired workers, seasonal workers enumerated in an 'off' season who were not looking for work, inmates of institutions, disabled persons, and persons doing only incidental unpaid family work" (Chicago Fact Book Consortium, 1984, p. xxv).

[5]A *community area* is a statistical unit derived by urban sociologists at the University of Chicago for the 1930 census, to analyze varying conditions within the city of Chicago. These delineations were originally drawn up on the basis of settlement and history of the area, local identification and trade patterns, local institutions, and natural and artificial barriers. Needless to say, there have been major shifts in population and land use since then. But these units remain useful to trace changes over time, and they continue to capture much of the contemporary reality of Chicago neighborhoods.

These three neighborhoods were the focus of the ethnographic research in the Drake and Cayton classic study, *Black Metropolis*, published in 1945. In all three areas, a majority of adults were gainfully employed in 1950, but by 1990, only 4 in 10 in Douglas worked, 1 in 3 in Washington Park, and 1 in 4 in Grand Boulevard.

In previous years, the working poor stood out in inner-city ghetto neighborhoods. Today, the nonworking poor predominate in such neighborhoods. Neighborhoods plagued with high levels of joblessness are more likely to experience problems of social organization. The two go hand in hand. High rates of joblessness trigger other problems in the neighborhood, which adversely affect social organization—ranging from crime, gang violence, and drug trafficking to family break-ups and problems in the organization of family life.

Consider, for example, the problems of drug trafficking and violent crime. As many studies have revealed, the decline of legitimate employment opportunities among inner-city residents builds up incentives to sell drugs (Fagan, 1993). The distribution of crack in a neighborhood attracts individuals involved in violence and other crimes. Violent persons in the crack marketplace help shape its social organization and its impact on the neighborhood. Neighborhoods plagued by high levels of joblessness, insufficient economic opportunities, and high residential mobility are unable to control the volatile drug market and the violent crimes related to it (Fagan, 1993; Sampson, 1986). As informal controls weaken in such areas, the social processes that regulate behavior change (Sampson, 1986).

Also, consider the important relationship between joblessness and the organization of family life. Work is not simply a way to make a living and support one's family. It also constitutes the framework for daily behavior and patterns of interaction because of the disciplines and regularities it imposes. Thus, in the absence of regular employment, what is lacking is not only a place in which to work and the receipt of regular income, but also a coherent organization of the present, that is, a system of concrete expectations and goals. Regular employment provides the anchor for the temporal and spatial aspects of daily life. In the absence of regular employment, life, including family life, becomes more incoherent. Persistent unemployment and irregular employment hinder rational planning in daily life, the necessary condition of adaptation to an industrial economy (Bourdieu, 1965). This problem is most severe for jobless families in low-employment neighborhoods. The lack of rational planning among a high number of families without a steady breadwinner in the neighborhood reinforces that condition in any single jobless family.

One way in which joblessness affects the organization of family life is through its effect on the children's future attachment to the labor force. A youngster who grows up in a family with a steady breadwinner and in a neighborhood in which most of the adults are employed will tend to develop some of the disciplined habits associated with stable or steady employment—habits that are reflected in the behavior of his or her parents and of other neighborhood adults. Accordingly, when this youngster enters the labor market, he or she has a distinct advantage over the youngsters who grow up in the typical household in new-urban-poverty neighborhoods—a household without a steady breadwinner and a neighborhood that is not organized around work, in other words, a milieu in which one is more exposed to the less disciplined habits associated with casual or infrequent work both within and outside the family.

The problems of family organization and neighborhood social organization in the new-urban-poverty neighborhoods are mutually reinforcing. The social integration of parents in these neighborhoods may hamper, not promote, healthy child development.

I believe that there is a difference, on the one hand, between a jobless family whose mobility is impeded by the macrostructural constraints in the economy and the larger society, but nonetheless lives in an area with a relatively low rate of joblessness and poverty and, on the other hand, a jobless family that lives in an inner-city ghetto neighborhood that is influenced not only by these same constraints, but also by the behavior of other jobless families in the neighborhood. The latter influence is one of culture—the extent to which individuals follow their inclinations—either through forms of nonverbal action, including engaging in or refraining from certain conduct, or in the verbal expression of opinions or attitudes concerning norms, values, or beliefs—as they have been developed by learning or influence from other members of the community to which they belong or identify. In other words, it is not sufficient to recognize the importance of macrostructural constraints; it is also imperative to see "the merits of a more subtle kind of cultural analysis of life in poverty" (Hannerz, 1969, p. 182).

Let me briefly elaborate on this point with a different example of the kind of cultural analysis I am trying to convey. Joblessness, especially prolonged joblessness, is likely to be associated with or produce feelings of low perceived self-efficacy. In social cognitive theory (Bandura, 1986), *perceived self-efficacy* refers to self-beliefs in one's ability to take the steps or courses of action necessary to achieve the goals required in a given situation. Such beliefs affect the level of challenge that is pursued, the amount of effort expended in a given venture, and the degree of perseverance when confronting difficulties.

As Bandura (1982) put it, "inability to influence events and social conditions that significantly affect one's life can give rise to feelings of futility and despondency as well as to anxiety" (p. 140). Self-efficacy theory identifies two sources of perceived futility. People may seriously doubt that they can do or accomplish what is expected, or they may feel confident of their abilities, but nonetheless, give up trying because they believe that their efforts will ultimately be futile owing to an environment that is unresponsive, discriminatory, or punitive. "The type of outcomes people expect depend largely on their judgments of how well they will be able to perform in given situations" (Bandura, 1982, p. 140).

Weak labor force attachment, I would hypothesize, will tend to lower one's perceived self-efficacy. I would, therefore, expect lower levels of perceived self-efficacy in ghetto neighborhoods—plagued by underemployment, unemployment, and labor force nonparticipation—than in less impoverished neighborhoods. Considering the importance of cultural learning and influence, I would also expect that perceived self-efficacy is higher among those who are weakly attached to the labor force in nonghetto neighborhoods than among their counterparts in ghetto neighborhoods.

In the more socially isolated ghetto neighborhoods, networks of kin, friends, and associates are likely to include a high proportion of individuals who, because of their experiences with extreme economic marginality, tend to doubt that they can achieve approved societal goals. The self-doubts may exist either because of questions concerning their own capabilities or preparedness or because they perceive severe restrictions imposed by a hostile environment. However, because joblessness afflicts a majority of the adult population in the new-poverty neighborhoods, it is likely that problems of self-efficacy among jobless families in low-joblessness neighborhoods may relate more to feelings of low capability because a majority of families in the neighborhood have jobs whereas they do not. As Urie Bronfenbrenner points out (this volume, chapter 19), proximal processes are moderated by "the nature of the development outcomes under consideration" (p. 621).

The central hypothesis is that an individual's feelings of low self-efficacy grow out of weak labor force attachment, and they are reinforced or strengthened by the feelings and views of others in his or her neighborhood who are similarly situated and have similar self-beliefs (e.g., feelings that severe restrictions imposed by a hostile environment hamper their individual progress). The end result, to use a term from Bandura's (1982) work, is a lower sense of *collective efficacy* in the inner-city ghetto.

To repeat, family social integration in a neighborhood plagued by low levels of perceived self- and collective efficacy is not likely to benefit many aspects of child development. Research on the transmission of such views and feelings would represent a cultural analysis of life in poverty. The psychological self-efficacy theory is used here not in isolation, but in relation to the structural problem of weak labor force attachment and the cultural problem of the transmission of self and collective beliefs in the neighborhood.

The transmission of such beliefs is part of what I have called "concentration effects," that is, the effects of living in a neighborhood that is overwhelmingly impoverished (Wilson, 1987). I argue that these concentration effects, reflected in a range of outcomes from degree of labor force attachment to social dispositions, are created by the constraints and opportunities that the residents of the inner-city neighborhoods face in terms of access to jobs and job networks, involvement in quality schools, availability of marriageable partners, and exposure to conventional role models.

The declining proportion of nonpoor families magnifies the problems of increasing and prolonged joblessness in the new-poverty neighborhoods. Basic neighborhood institutions are more difficult to maintain. Stores, banks, credit institutions, restaurants, and professional services lose regular and potential patrons. Churches experience dwindling numbers of parishioners and shrinking resources; recreational facilities, block clubs, community groups, and other informal organizations also suffer. As these organizations decline, the means of formal and informal social control in the neighborhood become weaker. Levels of crime and street violence increase as a result, leading to further deterioration of the neighborhood.

As the neighborhood disintegrates, those who are able to leave depart in increasing numbers, including many working- and middle-class families. The lower population density creates additional problems. Abandoned buildings increase and provide a haven for crack dens and criminal enterprises that establish footholds in the community. Precipitous declines in density also make it more difficult to sustain or develop a sense of community or for people to experience a feeling of safety in numbers (Jargowsky, 1994).

The neighborhoods with many Black working families stand in sharp contrast to the new-poverty areas. Research that we have conducted on the social organization of Chicago neighborhoods reveals that in addition to much lower levels of perceived unemployment than in the poor neighborhoods, Black working- and middle-class neighborhoods also have much higher levels of perceived social control and cohesion, organizational services, and social support. Unlike in the new-poverty neighborhoods, as revealed in our research in Chicago, in the Black working- and middle-class neighborhoods, adolescents seem to benefit directly from the exchange of resources produced by their parents' social integration.

The rise of new-poverty neighborhoods represents a movement from what the historian Spear (1967) called an *institutional ghetto*—which duplicates the structure and activities of the larger society, as portrayed in Drake and Cayton's (1945) description of Bronzeville—to an unstable ghetto, which lacks the capability to provide basic opportunities, resources, and adequate social controls.

In neighborhoods that suffer from a lack of social organization, that is, neighborhoods with weak social controls and weak social monitoring, peer group cultures play a much greater role in shaping the behavior of adolescents, including behavior detrimental to their health, such as alcohol consumption, drug use, gang involvement, and illicit sexual encounters. This is especially true in the new-poverty neighborhoods. Adolescents in the new-poverty neighborhoods not only are influenced by restricted opportunities in the broader society that confront all disadvantaged families (e.g., limited access to employment), but also are influenced by the behavior of other poor individuals and families who face the same constraints.

In my book *The Truly Disadvantaged* (1987), I pointed out that, in poor neighborhoods in which most of the adults are working, perceptive youngsters are more likely to observe individuals regularly going to and from work, see a clear connection between education and meaningful employment, be aware of the presence of many intact families, notice a significant number of nonwelfare families, and recognize that many individuals in their neighborhoods are not involved in the drug trafficking.

However, in the new-urban-poverty neighborhoods, neighborhoods with a paucity of regularly employed families, the chances of children interacting on a sustained basis with people who are employed or with families that have a steady breadwinner are slim. The net effect is that the youths are more likely to see joblessness as normative and perceive a weak relationship between schooling and postschool employment. This environment is not conducive for development of the cognitive, linguistic, and other educational and job-related skills necessary for the world of work in the mainstream economy.

Some of the residents of poor inner-city neighborhoods clearly see and understand the problem facing their youth. The following are quotations from respondents who were interviewed in the Urban Poverty and Family Life Study that I directed at the University of Chicago. Consider the following comments by a perceptive college student who lives in one of the new-poverty neighborhoods on the West Side of Chicago:

> Well, basically, I feel that if you are raised in a neighborhood and all you see is negative things, then you are going to be negative because you don't see anything positive. . . . Guys and Black males see drug dealers on the corner and they see fancy cars and flashy money and they figure, "Hey, if I get into drugs I can be like him."

He made a similar observation when he was interviewed several weeks later:

> And I think about how, you know, the kids around there, all they see, OK, they see these drug addicts, and then what else do they see? Oh, they see thugs, you know; they see the gangbangers. So, who do they, who do they really look, model themselves after? Who is their role model? They have none but the thugs. So that's what they wind up being, you know. . . . They [the children in the neighborhood] deal with the only male role model that they can find and most of the time that be pimps, dope dealers—so what do they do? They model themselves after them. Not intentionally trying to but if, you know, that's the only male you're around and that's the only one you come in close contact with, you tend to want to be like that person. And that's why you have so many young drug dealers.

A 25-year-old West Side father of two who works two jobs to make ends meet raises a similar point:

> They try to find easier routes, uh, and had been conditioned over a period of time to just be lazy, so to speak. Uh, motivation non-existent, you know, and the society that they're affiliated with really don't advocate hard work and struggle to meet your goals, such as education and stuff like that. And they see what's around 'em and they follow that same pattern, you know. The society says, "Well, you can sell dope. You can do this. You can do that." A lot of 'em even

got to the point where they can accept a few years in jail, uh, as a result of what they might do. . . . They don't see nobody getting up early in the morning, going to work or going to school all the time. The guys they—they be with don't do that . . .'cause that's the crowd that you choose, well, that's been presented to you by your neighborhood.

An unemployed Black male, who lives in an impoverished and high-jobless Black suburban community in the Chicago metropolitan area, described how the children in his neighborhood get into drugs and alcohol:

They're in an environment where, if you don't get high, you're square. You know what I'm saying? If you don't get high some kind of way or another. . .and then, you know, kids are gonna emulate what they come up under. . . . I've watched a couple of generations— I've been here since '61. I watched kids, I saw their fathers ruined, and I seen 'em grow up and do the very same thing. . . . The children, they don't have any means of recreation whatsoever out here, other than their back yards, the streets, nothing. . . . The only way it can be intervened if the child has something outside the house to go to, because it is—just go by the environment of the house he's destined to be an alcoholic or a drug addict.

A 40-year-old mother of six, who lives in an extreme-poverty tract on the South Side of Chicago, related the problems of children in her neighborhood to the limited opportunity structure:

There's less opportunities over here: it's no jobs. The kids aren't in school, you know, they're not getting any education, there's a lot of drugs on the streets. So, you know, wrong environment, bad associations. So you have to be in some kind of environment where the kids are more, you know, ready to go to school to get an education instead of, you know, droppin' out to sell drugs because they see their friends, on the corner, makin' money; they got a pocket fulla money, you know. They got kids walkin' around here that's 10 years old selling drugs.

A 37-year-old unemployed Black male from the South Side described the different situation for males and females:

> Some kids just seem like they don't want to learn, but others, they stick to it. Especially the females, they stick to it. The males either become—they see the street life. They see guys out here making big bucks with fancy cars, jewelry and stuff, and they try to emulate them. That's our problem, you know. The males, they're pretty impressionable. That's why they drop out. . . . They see their peers out here, they didn't go to school, they makin' it. But they making it the wrong way.

Ghetto-specific practices such as overt emphasis on sexuality, idleness, and public drinking are often denounced by those who reside in the socially disorganized inner-city ghettos. However, because such practices occur much more frequently there than in middle-class society, owing in major part to social organizational forces, the transmission of these modes of behavior by precept, as in role modeling, is more easily facilitated.

As Prothrow-Stith (1991) argued, in inner-city ghetto neighborhoods plagued by problems of social disorganization, youngsters are more likely to see violence as a way of life. They are more likely to be taught to be violent by exhortation, witness violent acts, and have role models who do not adequately control their own anger. Accordingly, given the availability of and easy access to firearms, adolescent experiments with macho behavior, especially in peer groups that are not subject to neighborhood social controls, often have deadly consequences.

The problems of family management, neighborhood social organization, unsupervised peer groups, and ghetto-specific cultural practices (problems that are enhanced and ultimately shaped by joblessness and poverty) adversely impact the health, health promotion, and development of children. We are just beginning to understand the mutually reinforcing effects of these problems. What is so encouraging is that there are a growing number of developmental psychologists, influenced by the earlier perspectives of Urie Bronfenbrenner, who are now examining these factors.

REFERENCES

Bandura, A. (1982). Self-efficacy mechanism in human agency. *American Psychologist, 37,* 122–147.

Bandura, A. (1986). *Social foundations of thought and action: A social cognitive theory.* Englewood Cliffs, NJ: Prentice Hall.

Bourdieu, P. (1965). *Travail et travailleurs en Algérie* [Work and workers in Algeria]. Paris: Additions Mouton.

Coleman, J. S. (1990). *Foundations of social theory.* Cambridge, MA: Harvard University Press.

Local community fact book for Chicago, 1950. (1953). Chicago Community Inventory, University of Chicago.

Local community fact book Chicago Metropolitan Area, Based on the 1970 and 1980 Censuses. (1984). The Chicago Fact Book Consortium, The University of Illinois at Chicago.

Drake, S., & Cayton, H. (1945). *Black metropolis: A study of Negro life in a northern city.* New York: Harcourt, Brace.

Elliott, D., Wilson, W. J., Huizinga, D., Sampson, R., Elliott, A., & Rankin, B. (1994). *The effects of neighborhood disadvantages on adolescent development.* Unpublished manuscript, University of Colorado, Boulder, and the University of Chicago.

Fagan, J. (1993). Drug selling and licit income in distressed neighborhoods: The economic lives of street-level drug users and dealers. In G. Peterson & A. Harold Washington (Eds.), *Drugs, crime and social isolation* (pp. 99–146). Washington, DC: Urban Institute Press.

Furstenberg, F., Jr. (1990, August). *How families manage risk and opportunity in dangerous neighborhoods.* Paper presented at the 84th annual meeting of the American Sociological Association, Washington, DC.

Furstenberg, F., Jr. (1993). How families manage risk and opportunity in dangerous neighborhoods. In W. J. Wilson (Ed.), *Sociology and the public agenda* (pp. 231–258). Newbury Park, CA: Sage.

Hannerz, U. (1969). *Soulside: Inquiries into ghetto life and culture.* New York: Columbia University Press.

Jargowsky, P. A. (1994). Ghetto poverty among Blacks in the 1980's. *Journal of Policy Analysis and Management.*

Prothrow-Stith, D. (1991). *Deadly consequences.* New York: Harper & Collins Press.

Sampson, R. J. (1986). Crime in cities: The effects of formal and informal social control. In A. J. Reiss, Jr., & M. Tonry (Eds.), *Communities and crime* (pp. 271–310). Chicago: University of Chicago Press.

Sampson, R. J. (1988). Urban Black violence: The effect of male joblessness and family disruption. *American Journal of Sociology, 93,* 348–382.

Sampson, R. J. (1992, August–September). *Integrating family and community level dimensions of social organization: Delinquency and crime in the inner-city of Chicago.* Paper presented at the International Workshop on Integrating Individual and Ecological Aspects on Crime, Stockholm, Sweden.

Sampson, R. J., & Wilson, W. J. (1993). Toward a theory of race, crime, and urban inequality. In J. Hagan & R. Peterson (Eds.), *Crime and inequality* (pp. 37–54). Palo Alto, CA: Stanford University Press.

Spear, A. (1967). *Black Chicago: The making of a Negro ghetto.* Chicago: University of Chicago Press.

Wilson, W. J. (1987). *The truly disadvantaged: The inner city, the underclass, and public policy.* Chicago: University of Chicago Press.

16

Expanding the Ecology of Human Development: An Evolutionary Perspective

Jay Belsky

O ne of the most fascinating things about reading the chapters prepared for this volume is the nature and scope of contributions that are attributed to Urie Bronfenbrenner. If one did not know that everyone had limited space and time to offer testimony, one might think that Bronfenbrenner was an elephant and that all the speakers were blind men, each characterizing Urie's nature and his work in a somewhat different manner. Therefore, it seems appropriate as an invited discussant to take as my first role the job of summarizing and integrating much of what has been said about the man and his work.

At the substantive/conceptual level, we are reminded by many of Bronfenbrenner's emphasis on the social context, and appreciation is repeatedly—and appropriately—expressed for his seminal contribution of dissecting the ecology of human development into its constituent levels of analysis, from micro- to macrosystem (Goodnow, this volume, chapter 8; Steinberg, Darling, & Fletcher, this volume, chapter 13). The role that Bronfenbrenner's time–space distinction has played in our thinking about the nature and consequences of social change has not gone unnoticed either (Elder, this volume, chapter 4; Kohn, this volume, chapter 5), nor has his emphasis on an active organism contributing to his or her own development and, thus, the bidirectional nature of the developmental process (Rutter, Champion, Quinton, Maughan, & Pickles, this volume, chapter 3; Maccoby, this volume, chapter 10). Pointed out, too, has been Bronfenbrenner's seminal insight into the conditions under which child-directed interventions are most likely to exert an enduring impact, namely, when the family environment is itself affected (Brooks-Gunn, this volume, chapter 14).

From a more methodological perspective, Bronfenbrenner's emphasis on context has taught us the costs of statistically controlling for demographic factors like socioeconomic status and ethnicity and the benefits of exploring developmental processes in distinctive ecological niches (Steinberg et al., this volume, chapter 13). Certainly, Bronfenbrenner's concerns for ecological validity and the limitations of the laboratory as a research setting also have had their lasting impact, though this contribution seems to have gone unmentioned.

Then there is the issue of Urie Bronfenbrenner's style, both as a person and as a scholar, which has been commented on repeatedly, though I am not sure that *style* is quite the correct word. It connotes, I fear, too much of a concern for appearances, which I do not think many would attribute to this man. There have been so many times when he has brought to mind, to me at least, the prototype of the absentminded professor, who is far more caught up in the fascinations of whatever scientific concern is confronting him than with any regard for appearances that I wish I had a better word to use than *style*. Nevertheless, with regard to scientific style, Kohn (this volume, chapter 5) most certainly hit the nail right on the head several times, noting in particular Bronfenbrenner's manner of not dwelling on the limits of people's work, but rather always seeming to find what is of value in it and focusing on that. And then there is that truly amazing skill of making order out of chaos. Repeatedly, in Urie Bronfenbrenner's career—be he addressing, as Kohn (this volume, chapter 5) pointed out, social class through time and space (Bronfenbrenner, 1958), or as I will now, Freudian theories of identification and their derivatives (Bronfenbrenner, 1960), or early deprivation (Bronfenbrenner, 1968), or the effectiveness of early intervention (Bronfenbrenner, 1974), to say nothing of the more recent work on the ecology of human development— Bronfenbrenner has been a master of tying pieces together to create mosaics that illuminate and guide where many others have scratched their heads, if not stumbled.

I believe that one of the reasons Bronfenbrenner has been so influential as a scholar is not simply this ability to put pieces together in creative and insightful ways to make coherent wholes, which serve to chart future terrains of inquiry, but also his superb skills as a wordsmith. Even before I encountered Bronfenbrenner as a graduate student, I came to realize as a reader of his work how well he could tell a story. Indeed, I like to say, using the terminology of Piaget, that Bronfenbrenner's synthetic pieces (like those just mentioned) enable readers to assimilate what they would otherwise have to accommodate. That is, he is so good at structuring cognitions, that I have never found—and this should not be read as anything other than admiring—that one had to read Urie more than once. The material just went in and stayed there. It was almost as if Bronfenbrenner himself was that sorcerer of old he referred to when discussing Maccoby's findings of so long ago concerning the detrimental effects of television viewing on family interaction; once he got hold of your intellect—and just through the written word—you were his.

Having endeavored to highlight several features and contributions of Urie Bronfenbrenner that have been mentioned by others and experienced by myself, I turn next to underlying themes that many of the contributions to this volume underscore. After this, I address what I regard as a fun-damental limit of Bronfenbrenner's (1979) model of the ecology of hu-man development and offer a simple, but I think important, expansion of it.

RECURRENT THEMES

At least three themes derived from Bronfenbrenner's thinking are apparent in many of the contributions to this volume. One concerns processes and pathways of development; the second, the role of context; and the third, the interaction of these two.

Beyond Social Address: Pathways/Processes of Influence

There was a time in the study of human development, when explaining a phenomenon—be it parental behavior or some feature of children's functioning, in terms of social class, maternal employment, or even school grade—offered us more understanding of variability in the ecology of human development than we otherwise possessed. Although for a while, Bronfenbrenner himself was enamored with the phenomenon of social class as an explanatory factor, he came to appreciate and speak repeatedly of the limitations of social address variables as explanations of anything. These need to be unpacked, he argued, and in this volume we find much evidence that message has been taken to heart. Brooks-Gunn, in her analysis of the impact of poverty, was not content to settle for discerning statistically significant effects, even of timing, duration, and degree of impoverishment; instead, she sought to understand how—a theme I return to below—poverty comes to exert its pernicious effects on intellectual and behavioral development. This led her, as we saw, to consider, in a very Bronfenbrennerian tradition, the role of the enduring family environment, particularly the learning environment.

Kohn, too, was not satisfied to explain parenting or personality by appeals to education or to social class, but wanted to know what job conditions were, how people got selected into them, and what their specific outputs were. Rutter and colleagues evinced the very same curiosity about developmental process and pathways as they sought to illuminate the mechanisms that led behavioral disorders at age 10 to experiences in adulthood, involving stressful life events and marital dissolution, that are known to increase the risk of psychopathology in adulthood. His exploration of pathways of influence, it will be recalled, took him on an odyssey through schooling experiences, planfulness, and peer groups, as well as harmony in the family setting.

Even Steinberg and colleagues, who never really set out to study a social address per se, because their concern for authoritative parenting reflected a clear interest in a family process, were not content to predict what was presumed to be a developmental output like school achievement with such a simple developmental input. Steinberg, having learned his Cornellian and Bronfenbrennerian lesson, pursued with his colleagues, peer groups and neighborhoods as critical pathways leading from the "social address" of authoritative parenting to school achievement, or lack thereof.

The Role of Context

The second theme to be underscored, that of context, will come as no surprise to anyone who has read this volume or merely knows that the prior conference proceedings had as their central focus the legacy of Urie Bronfenbrenner. Repeatedly, contributors inquired into the role that context played in some feature of development being studied. The context in question might have been a microsystem such as the family, which resulted in Steinberg's studying parenting practices (this volume, chapter 13); or a peer group, which was central to Maccoby's analysis of sex difference in interpersonal styles (this volume, chapter 10) and of Magnusson's (this volume, chapter 2), and the Cairnses' (this volume, chapter 12) analysis of the stability of problem behavior; or the workplace, which led Kohn to investigate specific job conditions (this volume, chapter 5); or it might have been the exosystem, which led Brooks-Gunn to study neighborhoods (this volume, chapter 14); or it might even have been the broader macrosystem context of the society, which led Kohn to contrast Poland and the United States, or that of large-scale social change, which led Elder to study the Great Depression. Although virtually none of the chapter authors seem to rely any longer, if they ever did, on Bronfenbrenner's formal contextual terminology, it is clear and indisputable that his message of a highly differentiated context of development, which needs to be teased apart, has been heard.

Beyond simply drawing attention to context, Bronfenbrenner's longterm concern for this subject has alerted many to the fact, or better yet the possibility, that effects of whatever it is of interest—be it authoritative parenting, poverty, or job condition, to cite just a few examples of topics explored in this volume—might well vary by context. Steinberg et al. discovered this, for instance, on studying the effects of authoritative parenting in various social class, ethnic, and racial subgroups. Kohn also explored this issue in contrasting the effects of job conditions in two nations. And Brooks-Gunn underscored the same Bronfenbrennerian principle that in ecological research, the main effects are likely to be in the interactions, when chronicling the differential effects of poverty and of the Infant Health and Development Project on infants of varying biological vulnerability.

Today we rely on the term *moderator effects* to characterize such contextually conditional impacts of forces and factors that were once considered to exert across-the-board influences. Similarly, rather than speaking about moving beyond social address models, today we speak about mediational processes to describe the pathways of influence that so many of the chapters illuminate. But Bronfenbrenner has encouraged investigators to do more than investigate mechanisms of mediation or moderator effects. Indeed, by appealing to what he refers to as *person–process–context models,* he has essentially led the way in calling for what might be regarded as the interaction of moderators and mediators or, perhaps better yet, moderated mediation. This is the third theme that undergirds many of the contributors to this volume.

Moderated Mediation

What makes an ecological view of development so necessary is not simply that context matters by moderating the effects of certain forces in development. Rather, as this volume demonstrates repeatedly, central to an ecological approach is an appreciation of the fact that mediational processes, that is, developmental pathways, may themselves vary across context. Recall that Steinberg and colleagues (this volume, chapter 13) did not simply find that authoritative parenting had different effects on Whites, Blacks, and Asians but more significantly that the very role of the peer group in mediating family influences on school achievement varied across racial–ethnic group. And Rutter and colleagues (this volume, chapter 3) did not simply demonstrate that the effect of a childhood disorder forecasted experience in young adulthood for males and females alike but rather that the developmental pathway was different for the two genders, with family harmony playing a larger role in the case of boys and planfulness and association with deviant peers playing a larger role in the case of girls. As a final example, Kohn (this volume, chapter 5) did not merely discover that job conditions had different effects sometimes in the United States and in Poland but rather that these same job conditions could operate differentially because of the differential salience of job security in certain occupations in the two nations.

In summary, then, and in the spirit of Bronfenbrennerian ecological research, this volume is testimony to more than advancement beyond social address explanations and to more than evidence that the same developmental agents exert differential influence in different contexts. The legacy of Bronfenbrenner's vision has brought us to the point of appreciating and discovering that pathways through development can operate remarkably differently in different contexts. Processes that may be important to the development of intellectual achievement or psychological disorder in one ecological niche may simply not be operative in another.

EXPANDING THE ECOLOGY OF HUMAN DEVELOPMENT

Reflections on these core themes of the ecology of human development make it clear that perhaps the major fundamental question many developmentalists and contextualists ask in their work is one of "how?" Basically the question being asked in so much of the inquiry presented in this volume concerns "how does development (in context) operate?" Certainly this was the issue central to Maccoby's discussion (this volume, chapter 10) of the origins of gender differences in interpersonal styles; Maccoby pointed out that it was through the peer group rather than through the family that such pervasive differences are likely to emerge, as well as to Elder's analysis of the impact of social change on the life course (this volume, chapter 4). And the question of "how?" was clearly the primary focus of all inquiries concerned with pathways of development and processes of influence. Rutter and colleagues (this volume, chapter 3), after all, wanted to know how early disorder in childhood came to be predictive of troubled adulthoods. Steinberg and colleagues (this volume, chapter 13) wanted to know not simply what were the effects of authoritative parenting, but how these effects come to be realized. Similarly, Brooks-Gunn (this volume, chapter 14) was seeking to find out more than whether poverty was bad for children, because we certainly do not need research to answer that question, but rather how it exerted its detrimental impact. Of course, one of the basic reasons we are so concerned with questions of "how" is that answers to them are presumed to be a necessary step toward effective intervention. This, it should be recalled, was a central point of Rutter et al.'s analysis of the developmental sequelae of disordered behavior in childhood.

It seems to me that this prevailing focus on the issue of "how," however valuable and useful it is, underscores one of the primary limitations of Bronfenbrenner's view of human development and, especially, his model of the ecology of human development, which this volume celebrates. As Bronfenbrenner has noted so often, we all stand on the shoulders of giants as we attempt to make progress in our field, and it is from such a perch that I offer the remainder of my comments. I must note that it remains less precarious way up here than one might suspect because, as Kohn informed us in his chapter, there is little that Urie Bronfenbrenner himself appreciates as much as a critique of his own ideas.

To get directly to the point, it has become ever more apparent to me over the years that one of the things that is missing in Bronfenbrenner's model of the environment, with its nested levels of context, is perhaps the oldest and most fundamental one, namely, that of evolutionary history. At best, in Bronfenbrenner's model, we encounter history in the macrosystem, but here the forces of history, be they reflected in racism or the Great Depression, are those of relatively recent, and certainly recorded, history. When it comes to biology, this plays a role basically in the form of characterizing individual differences in the biological characteristics of the developing child. What seems to be missing is an appreciation of the long-history forces that have shaped not only the human condition but also the very nature of life on earth as we know it.

Whereas developmentalists as well as sociologists like Kohn and Elder are consumed by "how" questions, which will enable us to understand the processes of development and of environmental influence and, thereby, improve our ability to intervene effectively, those who work from an evolutionary perspective are concerned, fundamentally, with a very different but equally important question, namely, that of "why?" Why, for example, are stepparents more likely than biological parents to maltreat their progeny? Why, for example, do males compete, whereas females seem more inclined to cooperate? Why does poverty seem to breed aggression and violence as well as promiscuity?

I submit that asking "why?" questions and thinking more like evolutionary biologists, by adding another circle to Bronfenbrenner's model, would help us immensely. We would discover that, when it comes to the study of that with which Bronfenbrenner has been concerned, namely, children and families, what we are dealing with essentially are issues of reproduction and parental investment and, necessarily, reproductive fitness. After all, the fundamental evolutionary–biological goal of all living things is to have their genetic material replicated for passage on to future generations. By avoiding this fundamental common denominator of all of life, we who study humans, especially children and families, are bound to miss an awful lot and, perhaps even worse, misunderstand what we do discover.

The point to be made is not that we have to or must add another level to Bronfenbrenner's ecological framework, one that incorporates all the others and represents the long-term shaping of life and, thus, the human condition by forces of evolution, but rather that it is useful and helpful to do so. Central to this assertion is a related one that we might glean more insight into how things operate if we had a better understanding of what fundamental job they were trying to get done. Thus, if we ask "why" as well as "how," we might discover not only that what we think is so is actually so for reasons that we did not even begin to realize, but that the "how" questions we do not yet have answers to may be easier to answer if we ask why some developmental or environmental phenomenon might operate the way it appears to.

Throughout the animal kingdom, in fact throughout the entire kingdom of living things, we find organisms diversely, uniquely, and magnificently assembled to get the job of reproduction done. What is not sufficiently appreciated by human ecologists is what behavioral ecologists have learned about habitat and behavior: Many organisms have evolved to adjust their behavior, in response to environmental conditions, in the service of reproductive goals. The lengths to which life goes to get the job of reproduction done are remarkable. My two favorite examples are those of the fish species that actually changes its sex when it becomes more likely that its offspring will survive to reproduce if it is one sex rather than another and of the mountain goat that strategically aborts the fetus it is carrying when the biological father of the fetus is dethroned from his territory by another male. After all, why go to the bother of investing resources into an organism who will be so seriously disfavored by the current dominant male as to be unlikely to successfully survive to reproductive age? A far better bet is to rid oneself of this biological burden so that a more promising offspring can be sired that will receive the support it will need to grow to maturity and reproduce.

Note that in both of these cases, environments—be they conceptualized in terms of the gender ratio of the population or of the biological relatedness of the dominant male to the fetus in question—do not exert a random influence on the functioning of living organisms. Instead, they exert an influence that appears very logical and lawful once the "why" question is asked and issues of evolution and reproductive fitness are entertained, as they currently are not in Bronfenbrenner's ecology of human development. Why would a fish change its sex or a pregnant animal abort its progeny? The answer is terrifically simple and fascinating: Because doing so actually enhances reproductive fitness, whereas doing otherwise detracts from it. For this reason, such behavioral responses to environmental conditions have evolved within organisms.

Now, of course, we humans are not fish capable of changing our gender or, to our knowledge at least, mountain goats inclined to abort a fetus when a new male takes the place of the fetus's biological father, but this does not mean that reproductive fitness considerations have not shaped our development or the way in which we respond to environments. In fact, as I have been arguing, a fundamental limitation of prevailing views of human development, including Bronfenbrenner's view, is that they totally ignore the context of evolutionary history in human development and, consequently, never raise "why" questions or consider issues of reproductive fitness.

In the light of this critique, which is by no ways original to me, many will surely argue, as I once did myself, that this sociobiological or, better yet, behavioral-ecological view may be well and true, but that it has nothing to contribute to what it is that most human developmentalists do. Although I am certain that, to some extent, such a dismissive analysis is not inaccurate, I am absolutely convinced that it is not completely accurate either. Bronfenbrenner is fond of the Lewinian dictum that there is nothing so practical as a good theory; that tends to be my perspective as well. Therefore, in the remainder of this chapter, I highlight two ways in which I have found this view useful. In fact, it is only because I found the intriguing questions that this view has led me to ask—and the uncanny answers that it has generated—that I have become enamored with it.

One "why" question that an evolutionary perspective led me to ask involved why it seemed to be the case that, when it came to the manifestations of behavior problems, boys were more likely to engage in acting-out behavior, whereas girls were more likely to engage in internalizing disorders. From a reproductive fitness perspective, perhaps this was nature's way of regulating the timing of puberty in the service of reproductive goals and in response to the very kind of stressful environmental forces that appear to promote the development of behavior problems in the first place. Why? Possibly because the very contextual stressors related to the development of behavior problems may well be conveying to children that relationships are neither enduring nor trustworthy, so the future is precarious; in consequence, reproduce earlier and more often in hopes of getting any offspring to survive to reproduce (see Belsky, Steinberg, & Draper, 1991, for expanded discussion of this argument). Many plants work this way for reproductive fitness reasons. When nutrients are in plentiful supply, they defer reproduction to gather stores so that seeds are healthy and sizable. But when nutrients are precarious, they go to seed early. Even though seed quality may not be what it might be later, if the plant waits too long and drought continues, there may be no viable seeds at all.

On the basis of such evolutionary, reproductive fitness logic, I advanced the uncanny prediction that stressful childhood experiences would forecast an earlier timing of puberty and that internalizing and externalizing disorders would do the same for girls and boys, respectively. What made these predictions uncanny, of course, was that no other view of human development would generate them. When Steinberg (1988) first endeavored to test the first part of this hypothesis, using a short-term longitudinal design, he, like me, was surprised to discover that family processes did indeed predict the timing of puberty in just the manner hypothesized. And when a larger data set became available, and a full test of the propositions could be made, again support was found for the prediction that indicators of environmental stress would predict—significantly, even if modestly—the timing of puberty; no support whatsoever emerged for the behavior problems part of the hypothesis, however (Moffitt, Caspi, Belsky, & Silva, 1992). Nevertheless, my thoughts about evolutionary history, reproductive fitness, and "why" allowed issues not raised by the prevailing view of the ecology of human development and new possibilities for empirical inquiry to materialize and new findings to emerge. This is not to say that the view advanced is correct, if only because behavioral–genetic alternative explanations of the phenomenon in question have yet to be fully discounted; but rather, the point is that there may be lots of mileage to be gained by adding another ring to Bronfenbrenner's nested model.

There was another place in which I decided to apply the evolutionary perspective and ask a modified form of a "why" question. It involved the issue of infant day care. I reported a number of years ago that early and extensive nonparental care of the kind routinely experienced in the United States today was associated with elevated rates of attachment insecurity, at least as measured in the Ainsworth strange situation (Belsky & Rovine, 1988). This observation, as well as related findings and inferences drawn from it (Belsky, 1988), stirred much controversy (Fox & Fein, 1990). Even critics acknowledge, however, the association between more than 20 hr per week of nonparental care in the first year of life (as we know it and have it in the United States) and elevated rates of insecure infant–mother attachment (Clarke-Stewart, 1990), even though disagreement remains about how to interpret these findings. For the moment, thankfully, that is not the issue.

What became the issue for me went something like this: If, indeed, early and extensive nonparental care carried with it developmental risks, then who would incur such risks? Note that there is a good deal of research, most of if carried out by sociologists, concerning when and why mothers seek employment outside the home in contemporary American society (e.g., Greenstein, 1989; Greenstein & Greenstein, 1985). But I wanted to address this issue from an evolutionary perspective, one informed by reproductive fitness considerations. So, after some reflection, I hypothesized that parents who had more brothers and sisters, and more nieces and nephews, would be more likely to incur the developmental risks that appeared to be associated with relying on nonparental care on a full- or near full-time basis in the first year of life. Why? Because, from an evolutionary perspective, I reasoned, such parents would have more opportunity to have their genetic material passed on to future generations, because they had more siblings (who possessed 50% of their genes), and they would already have more such material passed on in the form of nieces and nephews (who shared 25% of their genes). In other words, because more of these parents' genetic material was already passed on to a future generation (these were all parents of firstborns) and because they had more opportunity for their genetic material to be passed on by siblings, they could more afford to incur risk with their progeny. Needless to say, this was another uncanny, if not crazy, hypothesis. But that is exactly what I was seeking: uncanny predictions derived from a new theoretical viewpoint that would, if confirmed, give me grounds for taking the viewpoint more seriously.

As it turned out, the propositions advanced were again, partially, supported. There was a relation between parents' sibship and their nieces and nephews, and it was in exactly the direction predicted and to a significant or near-significant extent, but it applied only to fathers. That is, as Table 1 shows, infants placed in nonparental care for 20 or more hr per week in their first year of life in this modest-sized sample had fathers who had more brothers and sisters and more nieces and nephews! In point of fact, more careful scrutiny of the data revealed that this finding emerged because children not exposed to early and extensive nonparental care in the first year of life in this central Pennsylvania sample were significantly more likely to be the first grandchildren in the father's lineage (see Table 2).

Table 1

Mean Number of Siblings and Nieces and Nephews as a Function of Extent of Nonparental Child Care

	Extent of child care		
Lineage variables	≥20 hrs/wk	<20 hrs/wk	$F(1, 106)$
Mother			
Siblings	2.33	2.70	*ns*
Nieces and nephews	1.00	1.65	*ns*
Father			
Siblings	2.97	2.33	3.41*
Nieces and nephews	2.44	1.48	4.48**
n	39	69	

ns = nonsignificant. $*p < .06$. $**p < .05$.

It is almost a natural inclination to respond at this time that these findings are in all likelihood an artifact of demographic factors; perhaps lower social class families have larger families and also rely on nonparental child care more. When we examined this competing alternative, it was not supported. But this is not to say that alternative explanations do not

Table 2

Husband's No. of Nieces and Nephews as a Function of Extent of Nonparental Child Care: Actual and Expected Values

	Extent of child care			
	>20 hr/week		<20 hr/week	
Nieces and nephews	Actual	Expected	Actual	Expected
None	6	12.7	43	36.3
≥1	22	15.3	37	43.7

Note. $\chi^2(1, N = 108) = 8.73$, $p < .01$.

Table 3			
Mean Scores of First-Year Social Network Contact and Assistance From Husband's Extended Family			
Social network	First grandchild	Not first grandchild	$F(1, 106)$
Frequency of contact	20.32	19.29	3.04*
Goods and services	21.53	20.45	3.14*
Emotional support	20.55	19.07	6.19**
n	49	59	

*$p < .10.$ **$p < .05.$

abound. In point of fact, an evolutionary perspective, which draws attention to issues of reproductive fitness and parental investment and, ultimately, relies on very distal, ultimate forces to account for human functioning, needs more proximal social and psychological mechanisms of the very kind students of human development typically investigate. Realizing this, I advanced the further hypothesis that perhaps one reason why firstborn grandchildren were less likely to be placed in nonparental child care for 20 or more hr per week was because their parents received more support from the father's lineage. Fortunately, we had gathered such data during the children's first year and so were in a position to discover, fascinatingly, that families rearing firstborn grandchildren tended to have more contact with the paternal grandparents and other relatives, tended to receive more assistance in the form of goods and services, and tended to receive significantly more emotional support than did families not rearing the first grandchild (see Table 3).

In retrospect, of course, these findings, generated by an uncanny hypothesis derived from considering the evolutionary history circle in which I am trying to embed Bronfenbrenner's ecology of human development, seem rather commonsensical. I believe that is exactly what is going to happen when "why" and "how" questions get integrated; that is, when we start taking evolutionary biology and its emphasis on reproductive fitness seriously in studies of human development, especially those concerned with children and families. Fundamentally, evolutionary forces and mechanisms of ultimate causation require more proximal, sociological, and psychological mechanisms of influence if complete explanations are our goal, as I am presuming they are. If evolutionary–biological goals are going to be achieved, they need more proximate mechanisms to serve their ends. An evolutionary perspective is not, therefore, antithetical to the perspective we more typically work from as Bronfenbrennerians of one form or another. In fact, as we have endeavored to show elsewhere, an evolutionary view may give us a great deal of insight into how the environment works (Belsky et al., 1991).

CONCLUSION

In concluding this critique of the model of the ecology of human development, I need to emphasize that the criticism being advanced is not one that leads to throwing the baby out with the bathwater. Central to any viable evolutionary perspective on human development is a need to understand contemporary contexts—in which humans, especially parents and children, find themselves—and a commitment to explore processes of influence and developmental pathways. What is being suggested, though, is that by thinking about what all living things have evolved to do—pass on their genes and promote their reproductive fitness—we may gain more insight into the very concerns that motivate us and issues we seek to investigate. Asking why things operate as they do, especially while considering the biological imperatives that guide all living things, may well enable us to address even better than we are already doing the "how" questions that are central to developmental inquiry. By becoming evolution-oriented human ecologists, and thus, by taking our lead from those in the life sciences who characterize themselves as behavior-oriented ecologists, I strongly believe that we can not only advance our understanding, but in so doing, see beyond the view of the giant whose shoulders we will need to stand on to do so and whose legacy this volume so deservedly celebrates.

REFERENCES

Belsky, J. (1988). The "effects" of infant day care reconsidered. *Early Childhood Research Quarterly, 3*, 235–272.

Belsky, J., & Rovine, M. (1988). Nonmaternal care in the first year of life and security of infant–parent attachment. *Child Development, 59*, 157–167.

Belsky, J., Steinberg, L., & Draper, P. (1991). Childhood experience, interpersonal development and reproductive strategy: An evolutionary theory of socialization. *Child Development, 62*, 647–670.

Bronfenbrenner, U. (1958). Socialization and social class through time and space. In E. Maccoby, T. Newcomb, & E. Hartley (Eds.), *Readings in social psychology* (pp. 400–425). New York: Holt, Rinehart & Winston.

Bronfenbrenner, U. (1960). Freudian theories of identification and their derivatives. *Child Development, 31*, 15–40.

Bronfenbrenner, U. (1968). Early deprivation: A cross-species analysis. In S. Levine & G. Newton (Eds.), *Early experience and behavior* (pp. 627–764). Springfield, IL: Charles C Thomas.

Bronfenbrenner, U. (1974). *Is early intervention effective? A report on longitudinal evaluations of preschool programs* (Vol. 2). Washington, DC: U.S. Department of Health, Education, and Welfare, Office of Child Development.

Bronfenbrenner, U. (1979). *The ecology of human development.* Cambridge, MA: Harvard University Press.

Clarke-Stewart, K. A. (1990). "The effects of infant day care reconsidered" reconsidered: Risks for parents, children, and researchers. In N. Fox & G. Fein (Eds.), *Infant day care: The current debate* (pp. 61–86). Norwood, NJ: Ablex.

Fox, N., & Fein, G. (1990). *Infant day care: The current debate.* Norwood, NJ: Ablex.

Greenstein, T. (1989). Human capital, marital and birth timing, and the postnatal labor force participation of married women. *Journal of Family Issues, 10*, 359–382.

Greenstein, T., & Greenstein, L. (1985). Labor force intentions of mothers with preschool children. In L. Knezek, M. Barrett, & S. Collins (Eds.), *Women and work* (pp. 94–123). Arlington: University of Texas Press.

Moffitt, T., Caspi, A., Belsky, J., & Silva, P. (1992). Childhood experience and the onset of menarche: A test of a sociobiological model. *Child Development, 63*, 47–58.

Steinberg, L. (1988). Reciprocal relation between parent–child distance and pubertal maturation. *Developmental Psychology, 24*, 122–128.

17

Homo Interpretans: On the Relevance of Perspectives, Knowledge, and Beliefs in the Ecology of Human Development

Kurt Lüscher

This chapter is an attempt to pay tribute to Urie Bronfenbrenner and to his program for a general ecology of human development as a fascinating and powerful intellectual achievement. It was my good fortune, in the late 1960s, that Urie served as my mentor, introducing me to American social science. This relationship soon developed into a friendship. Over the years, I came to appreciate his outstanding talents for interpreting the work and texts of others, as well as his own earlier writings. My experiences are a testimony, on a personal level, to the importance of Urie Bronfenbrenner's influence on what has emerged, over the years, as a major theoretical interest in my own work, namely, the appropriate assessment of "the act called interpretation" (to paraphrase the title of an arti-

I would like to thank James Stuart Brice for revising and editing this chapter from a stylistic point of view. Andreas Lange assisted me in reviewing and analyzing the literature on knowledge and beliefs in the context of the "Ecology of Human Development" and discussed with me intensively the arguments developed in this chapter. See also his overview of recent developments in the sociology of the family (Lange, 1994). Glen Elder, Rudolf Fisch, Melvin Kohn, Phyllis Moen, Wolfgang Walter, and Charlotte and Michael Wehrspaun made helpful comments on my drafts.

For a more elaborated attempt to follow Urie Bronfenbrenner's intellectual pathways into the "Ecology of Human Development," see my introduction, "Urie Bronfenbrenners Weg zur ökologischen Sozialisationsforschung" [Urie Bronfenbrenner's Path Toward Ecological Socialization] in Bronfenbrenner (1976, pp. 6–32).

cle by Abel, 1948). I am referring to its role in everyday life, for example, the ways in which people assess and understand each other in their environments, and to the role of interpretations in research and their epistemological qualities.

On this occasion, I focus my argument on the relevance of knowledge and beliefs for the study of socialization processes and their connections with the idea of proximal processes, which received special attention in Bronfenbrenner's recent writings (see this volume, chapter 19; Bronfenbrenner, 1993b).

Knowledge and beliefs occupy a central position in the processes of human development, because human beings, given their anthropological equipment, can and must develop a certain comprehension of the process of caring for their offspring. They can and must attribute certain meanings to their children's and their own behaviors and to the specificities of the relations between generations. In this way, behaviors become actions and relations become interactions.

Theories of socialization must account for this unique feature of human development. This holds true even if one attempts to focus on the biological roots of development. The notion of "proximal processes," as suggested by Bronfenbrenner, is meant particularly to clarify the interplay between the biological equipment and the immediate social situations that frame the interactions between a child and her or his closest caregivers, particularly the mother and father. I suggest that it would be fruitful to incorporate knowledge and beliefs into the conceptualization of proximal processes.

One may be reluctant to do so, because it seems impossible to establish causal links between knowledge and beliefs, on the one hand, and behaviors, on the other. It appears that the human ability to interpret facts and behaviors involves polysemy (e.g., the opportunities and the burdens of a plurality of meanings). However, it is just this potential for openness that gives rise to theoretical and empirical challenges.

To assess the human potential for openness, we may recall, first, the qualities of human communication, particularly of language. However, a more general conceptualization might refer to and elaborate the idea that human action is perspectivistic. In ordinary language, the term *perspectivistic* indicates that we see and comprehend things from a certain point of view. In theory, a perspective can be conceived as the relation of a subject to the world of which he or she is a part. Consequently, in comprehending and expressing their experiences with their environments, with each other and with themselves, human beings—both as individuals and as species, that is, both ontogenetically and phylogenetically—develop notions of how they differ from one another. In becoming aware of the perspectivistic character of their orientations and their acts, and within the same cognitive operation, they may develop notions of their own personal identities (i.e., their self).

Simultaneously, these processes require a minimum of communality, which may be mediated by language and, furthermore, by a common stock of knowledge and beliefs. Processes of interpretation may, thus, be conceived of as ongoing dialogues, queries, and struggles over perspectives as to how socialization tasks may be solved or shaped by processes of influence and the exercise of power to maintain sociality within a family, a community, a state or—ultimately—human societies, that is, human ecologies.

In regard to socialization and with reference to Bronfenbrenner's ecology of human development, I would like to focus here on two kinds of processes of interpretation: the elementary or primary interpretations of immediate actions that people make in concrete situations and the secondary interpretations experts and other observers offer in trying to analyze these actions. Both are to be seen as interwoven with each other and as influencing each other.

Primary interpretations concern micro-orientations of human conduct. They are bound to cognitions and language. They depend for their contents on *culture*, in the broad sense of this term. Secondary interpretations deliberately add an element of reflection, namely, of comparison, which, in turn, requires categorization, theorization, and institutionalization. Thus, the ordinary reasons a mother gives for satisfying most of her child's demands (primary interpretation) may be interpreted by experts as protection or overprotection (secondary interpretation). Furthermore, a mother looking for advice may accept the views of experts and may thereby redefine her own understanding.

I said before that interpretations are bound to perspectives, which in turn may be conceived as identity-related theories. Indeed, the primary interpretations a mother uses may be seen as her own ideas and as a part of her personality. The interpretations of experts, although they may also be seen as having a subjective dimension, are more probably bound to a body of knowledge qualifying a theory, a discipline, a profession, or an organization. They are rooted in collective identities, for example, those of a discipline, such as psychology, or of a subdiscipline or a school of thought within a discipline. Experts' interpretations may also be based on religious or political convictions; they, too, may stand for collective identities. To make matters even more complex, the mother who accepts an expert's interpretation may—at least in part—identify herself as belonging to a group for which the expert's advice holds. This is easily understood if, for example, the expert is a rabbi, priest, or minister. In other cases, the expert's professional status may be less important for mothers, yet it is reasonable to think that it is still important for the expert, for instance, in his or her role as a professional social worker.

There is one final point that is basic to my argument. On one side, processes of interpretation are shaped by influences and power relations; on the other side, they may be genuinely new, that is, they are potentially innovative. This may be assumed for both primary and secondary processes of interpretation. On the microlevel, the close connection between power and interpretation is obvious in everyday interactions where those who exercise authority claim the right to "define the situation" for all persons involved. On the macrolevel, the law and its injunctions serve as strong mechanisms to impose certain forms of knowledge and to frame processes of interpretation. Yet these settings may also offer, deliberately or contingently, opportunities for new thoughts and actions to arise. The reason may be found in the conviction that all processes of interpretation are ultimately framed by the openness characterizing the evolution of the human mind, which is also the exploration of its boundaries.

Taking into account the special occasion that gave rise to this chapter, I frame my argument by starting with some references to Urie Bronfenbrenner's personal and intellectual biography and by closing with a brief coda that takes up these topics again. Indeed, we may easily discover in his origins the roots of his sensitivity to the interplay between the individual and the qualities of his or her physical and social environments. Furthermore, already as a youngster, Bronfenbrenner was exposed simultaneously to two languages and two cultures; this may be the basis for his developing a fine feeling for the potential value of different orientations, perspectives, and identities, as well as for the necessity of interpreting them respectfully and with subtlety. His academic teachers and mentors undoubtedly reinforced these talents, and through the choice of his numerous colleagues, collaborators, and friends in many countries, Urie was able to create a personal ecology of great illumination, which merits its own place in the landscape of contemporary social science.

I begin with a reanalysis of Urie Bronfenbrenner's writings on knowledge and beliefs, relating them briefly to various other approaches. Before this background, however, I present my own propositions on the relevance of knowledge and beliefs, their connections to the idea of proximal processes, and their place within an interpretive, pragmatistic frame of reference for the study of human development.

THE INTELLECTUAL ECOLOGY OF A CREATIVE MIND

Urie Bronfenbrenner's cultural roots are located in European Russia, where he was born (1917 in Moscow), and in America, where he arrived as an immigrant with his family at the age of 6. In the autobiographical material included in the introduction to a German collection of his early articles, documenting the early period of the "ecology of human development" (see Bronfenbrenner, 1976; Lüscher, 1976), he fondly recalls his unique experiences as a child and adolescent in the very special niche of Letchworth Village (New York), where his father was employed as a research pathologist and clinician in a psychiatric hospital.

567

In Urie's formative years as a scholar, Frank Freeman, Fenno Dearborn, psychologists both, and Walter Ulich, a former minister of cultural affairs for Saxony and a humanist and philosopher, were important teachers and mentors, representing the two cultures of academia (science and the humanities), and perhaps already pointing toward the "third culture."

And there was, of course, Kurt Lewin, himself a European immigrant, a philosopher of science, researcher, and practitioner. We can well imagine that he deeply impressed the young Urie Bronfenbrenner, encouraging him to transcend the limits of what are now called established paradigms. Thus, we constantly find references in his writings to Lewin's call for a move from an Aristotelian notion of science toward a Galilean approach. In particular, taxonomic descriptions and linear causal inferences should be replaced by an analysis of the dynamic interplay between organisms (or persons) and their environments and the consequences of this interplay for the development of both. This idea is basic for Bronfenbrenner's models, which all display a triadic structure, most recently expressed in the terms *person–context–process*.[1]

In retrospect, Lewin seems to be the source of Urie's fruitful discontent with developmental psychology in the experimental (strictly positivistic) mode. But it was a long time before he could state with conviction on the first pages of the "Ecology": "Much of developmental psychology, as it now exists, is the science of the strange behavior of children in strange situations with strange adults for the briefest possible periods of time" (Bronfenbrenner, 1979, p. 19).

This critical standpoint is blended, in a sophisticated and constructive way, with energetic and manifold political commitments. Indeed, over the decades, Urie Bronfenbrenner (1979) has become a true disciple of American pragmatism and its classical authors: "Basic science needs public policy even more than public policy needs basic science" (p. 8), he has repeatedly affirmed. This principle reflects a programmatic position that transcends the boundaries separating disciplines and paradigms. It also al-

---

[1]See, in this regard, the novel view of the connections between Lewin's philosophy of science, his theory of the genesis of psychological processes, and his ecological perspective in Lang (1991, 1992a).

ludes to the dialectic between observation and commitment, between knowledge and belief, between detachment and involvement.

THE RELEVANCE OF PERSPECTIVES, KNOWLEDGE, AND BELIEFS

Bronfenbrenner's Interpretations

The synergistic strengths of Urie Bronfenbrenner's interpretive talents are, so to speak, already displayed in the way he combines the different connotations of the concept of *ecology*. In his definition, he shows a deep awareness of the biological origins of the term, as it was originally formulated by Haeckel. Urie Bronfenbrenner also takes into account its etymology: its derivation from *oikos*, the Greek word for household. Finally, in the special meaning he gives the concept, he reorients it toward an innovative view of *human development*. This term, too, in Bronfenbrenner's usage, unites three meanings: the development of the individual, the development of mankind as a species, and the interrelations between the two. This is quite compatible with his own programmatic statement: "From its very beginning, the ecology of human development was defined as a 'scientific undertaking' in the discovery mode . . . The aim was not to test hypotheses, but to generate them . . . the goal was to develop a theoretical framework that could provide both structure and direction for the systematic study of organism–environment interaction in processes of human development" (Bronfenbrenner, 1989, p. 230).

In regard to the conceptual significance of knowledge and beliefs within the "Ecology of Human Development," my point of departure is Urie Bronfenbrenner's own reinterpretation of his seminal 1958 chapter, "Socialization and Social Class Through Time and Space." It was included in the festschrift in honor of his German colleague Hartmut von Hentig, Freedom and Discipline Across the Decades (Bronfenbrenner, 1985). Bronfenbrenner addressed the topic again in his contribution to the Konstanz Symposium on "Intergenerational Relations in 'Postmodern' Societies" (1993b).

The basic argument of "Socialization and Social Class Through Time and Space" is well-known. In Bronfenbrenner's own words, it reads as follows:

> Conflicting findings on social class differences in parental attitudes and practices could be resolved if one took into account the place and date at which the fieldwork for each investigation had been done. . . . Furthermore, a gradual shift, over time, in advice favoring greater permissiveness was being presented to parents in popular magazines, newspaper columns, radio programs, and, especially before World War II, in the widely-circulated successive editions of the manual on Infant Care published by the Children's Bureau. The final step in the argument hypothesized that these sources of advice were more often read and heard by middle class mothers. (Bronfenbrenner, 1993b, p. 62)[2]

What is Bronfenbrenner's own reinterpretation after three decades, and what insights does it suggest for our topic? Turning to this question, we are well advised to note the relevance of at least four categories of knowledge, namely, the knowledge of parents, the knowledge of their advisers (or of experts), the knowledge of the scholars who study the knowledge of parents and advisers, and, finally, the knowledge of the author himself, Bronfenbrenner, in his reinterpretation. The first category corresponds to what I have labeled above *primary* interpretations, whereas the remaining three categories represent *secondary* interpretations.

Bronfenbrenner (1985) emphasized the following aspects of knowledge and beliefs: "The contents of 'knowledge and beliefs' have always been characterized by ambiguity and ambivalence, as far back as Duvall's (1946) typological juxtaposition of 'traditional and developmental families' (pp. 330–333). Blood (1953) changed these terms to *restrictive* versus *permissive* without, as Bronfenbrenner (1985) observed, offering an explicit

---

[2]On the microsocial level, I arrived at a similar interpretation concerning the importance of taking into account time and place for data collected in Switzerland using Bronfenbrenner's well-known Social-Dilemma Instrument. Responses given by pupils were more peer oriented if experiments were carried out in the afternoon, that is, at a time when the ambience was more relaxed than during morning lessons (Lüscher, 1971). I remember how pleased Urie was with this idea; now I see the connection with his more general proposition.

clarification. Sears, Maccoby, and Levin (1957) raised doubts about the positive consequences of permissiveness in the following sentence quoted by Bronfenbrenner (1985): "Not a few parents have developed what almost amounts to a cult of being permissive about aggression" (p. 333).

Baumrind (1967), following Bronfenbrenner (1985, p. 334), resolved the ambiguity by proposing a distinction among three categories of parental styles and knowledge and beliefs related to them: "Authoritarian, characterized by a high level of control and low nurturance; permissive, exhibiting low control with a moderate degree of nurturance, and, finally, authoritative, marked by high levels of both." Thus, the contradiction is overcome by, so to speak, classical means, namely, by the introduction of a third element. Bronfenbrenner pointed out that the authoritative style contains exactly those qualities (listed in detail in the article) that are not included in the original two types.[3] Was he hinting that a more adequate interpretation of the earlier data would have led to the recognition of this third category?

Bronfenbrenner's reinterpretation also implied that ethics and politics are a major concern in the analysis of parent–child relations. This can clearly be inferred from the way knowledge and beliefs are rhetorically related to behavior. Bronfenbrenner illustrated this point, for instance, in paying special attention to Symon's complaint that there is "a tendency to think of children as not quite human beings. . . . Ours is not a child-respecting society" (Bronfenbrenner, 1985, p. 328). Later he stated, "We may infer that good citizens, good scholars, good husbands and wives, and good parents come from homes in which the children are wanted and accepted" (Bronfenbrenner, 1985, p. 330).

What is the basis of this manifest, or in some cases latent, moral dimension? The anthropological arguments ultimately refer to two topics: first, the existential relevance of intergenerational relations for the development of the individual and the community or society and, second, the anthropological openness and even creativity of this development, which are related to the cultural construction of the notion of freedom.

---

[3]For a detailed account of the concept of authoritative parenting and its empirical relevance, see Steinberg, Darling, Fletcher, Brown, and Dornbusch, this volume, chapter 13.

Indeed, in "Freedom and Discipline," Bronfenbrenner (1985) first discussed the validity of Baumrind's (1967) results within a positivistic frame of reference. He then moved on, however. He questioned whether *acceptance*, in Symond's terminology, and *permissiveness*, in Baumrind's, could have the same meaning, because one study dated from the 1930s and the other dated from the late 1960s to the early 1970s. Referring again to his 1958 article, Bronfenbrenner (1985) pointed to the relevance of societal change. The rise in permissive behavior since the 1950s may have disturbed the balance between freedom and discipline, with disruptive consequences for society. However, stated Bronfenbrenner (1985), this hypothesis could not be proved, because the authors' measures of parental practice "cannot be compared" (p. 336). Bronfenbrenner also engaged in a subtle analysis of the meanings of the words used by the different authors. Finally, his own interpretation invited us to extend the chain of interpretation. He also followed such an approach by offering a further alternative. He started from the assumption that everything that happened within the family, including the relationship between freedom and control, depended on the societal systems surrounding the family. Furthermore, he hypothesized that a higher level of instability in social environments would lead to more subordination, aggressiveness, and uncertainty, especially in the later phases of childhood and for male children. This argument was based on parallelism.[4]

However, despite increasing permissiveness on the side of parents, many scholars claim to see advantages in discipline and demand. How do scholars arrive at this viewpoint? It can be inferred from the existence of families cultivating this style, which can be understood as a potential of the family to respond effectively to permissive societal tendencies. "Who shall win out in the end," concluded Bronfenbrenner (1985), "only history can tell" (p. 337).[5] This argumentation certainly is a fine example of cre-

---

[4]On this point, see Kohn's (this volume, chapter 5) arguments concerning "parallelism and cause." Kohn makes a good case for the relevance and the openness of processes of interpretation in academia, and for their perspectivistic character, which ultimately is bound to the personalities of the scholars involved and to the identities of different approaches and disciplines.

[5]This argument is also relevant to the discourse of family and postmodernity. (See Bronfenbrenner, 1993a.) It seems that many contemporary families are touched by the problematization of "personal identity" typical of postmodern culture and society. The question then is whether families are only the victims of these developments or whether they may be the source of new and meaningful forms of socialization. For a further elaboration of these arguments, see Lüscher (1993).

atively interpreting ambiguity and equivocality. It also recalls the struggles over influence and power.

Note how often contradictory or paradoxical findings are pointed to in regard to the functions of knowledge and beliefs, especially in regard to their connection with behavior. For instance, in the reinterpretation of Sigel's (1985) concept of distancing and of Dornbush's survey of parental styles, Bronfenbrenner (1993c) noted that in both cases, these connections seemed not to be very consistent and, in the case of quantitative data (Bronfenbrenner, 1993c, p. 74), the correlations were nonlinear.[6] However, if the triad of person, context, and process is taken into account, many contradictions can be resolved. It is just this paradigm, stated Bronfenbrenner (1992), which allows, even requires, us to determine whether two elements working together produce a synergistic effect greater than the sum of the effects they produce alone.

In his most recent writings on the role of beliefs in intergenerational relations, Bronfenbrenner took the position that beliefs "could exhibit both remarkable stability and dramatic change over historical time" (see full quote below). This apparent contradiction can be resolved if historical developments are separated from the interplay between the beliefs of parents and the opinions of experts in a first step and are related to each other only in a second step. Again we are reminded of what may be called a *chain of interpretations*. This idea is contained in the following propositions (which are quoted here in their full length because they have, at this date, still not been published in English, see 1993b (pp. 64–65).

Proposition 3

Major determinants of the contents and effects of proximal processes are systems of belief (Bronfenbrenner, 1993a), and knowledge (Lüscher, 1982) about human development and how it takes place. These systems exist on three levels. From a developmental perspective, they originate in the broader sociocultural and institutional structures of the larger society, both formal and informal. These sys-

---

[6]Thus, Sigel (1985) wrote the following: "The failures to find consistent relationships between beliefs and behaviors is discouraging."

tems of belief and knowledge are then transmitted, through a variety of pathways, into the more immediate settings of family, school, peer group and workplace, where they exert their direct effects on proximal processes. Finally, through the operation of these processes over an extended period of time, systems of belief are internalized and become characteristics of the developing person, and, as such, influence the course of that person's subsequent development.

This is to be seen in relation to Generational Principle 2.

Generational Principle 2
Continuity and change in development from one generation to the next vary systematically as a function of continuity and change over historical time in the contents of systems of knowledge and belief about human development. Of key importance in this regard is the transmission of knowledge and belief from the broader contexts of the ecological environment to the more proximal settings in which development occurs. The former are of two kinds: (a) the formally organized institutions of the larger society, such as health care systems; educational, religious, and scientific institutions; government agencies; social organizations; and, especially in today's world, the mass media; and (b) the informal structures of class, ethnicity, neighborhood, and social networks. The importance of knowledge and belief systems for cross-generational development is twofold. First, such systems can exhibit both remarkable stability and dramatic changes over historical time; second, they are especially powerful in influencing the content, form, and effectiveness of the proximal processes producing development, both within and across generations.[7]

What, then, is the conceptual status of knowledge and beliefs? Noteworthy is the statement in Proposition 3 that they "originate" in the soci-

---

[7]Because I refer at different points in this chapter to the importance of triadic relationships, it may be worthwhile to note Urie Bronfenbrenner's emphatic pleas for designs which study intergenerational relations over at least three generations.

etal culture and institutional structures of society. In this way, they are to be seen as cultural phenomena (or as culture itself). This conclusion is supported by reference to the well-known fact of their transfer from generation to generation. Proposition 3, concerning continuity and dramatic change, is compatible with the concept of cultural evolution, for instance, development and change in communications and the media.[8]

In addition to the argumentation reconstructed in the previous account, Urie Bronfenbrenner approached the topic of knowledge (and beliefs) in his article on the "Ecology of Cognitive Development" (1993a, p. 6). There, he suggested that we should study cognitions in context. "Thus, it is equally essential for basic science that we understand how encoding operates in learning to read, how memory functions in giving courtroom testimony, or how selective attention operates in the family and the work place, and how such processes develop." The cultural character of systems of cognition is touched on in Bronfenbrenner (1989): "Principle 1: Differences in cognitive performance between groups from different cultures or subcultures are a function of experience, in the course of growing up, with the types of cognitive processes existing in a given culture or subculture at a particular period in its history" (p. 208).

Finally, reference is made in Proposition 3, quoted above (p. 573), to the concept of proximal processes "where they [the 'immediate settings'] exert their direct effects on proximal processes." This remark, even though it is of a somewhat casual character, merits further attention, because it invites reflection on the theoretical and empirical relationship between knowledge and beliefs and proximal processes. Are they best conceived of as independent, yet interrelated? Is it possible, by looking at their interdependence, to further clarify the still somewhat vague notion of proximal processes? Before answering these questions, it seems appropriate to briefly discuss other approaches to the significance of knowledge and beliefs.

---

[8]See, for example, the writings of Walter J. Ong (1967, 1971), who differentiates among three stages: oral culture, alphabets and print, and electronics. He also points "to the rhetorical tradition as one key to understanding much that went on in the past and much that is going on in our own times, as well as much that may come about in the future" (Ong, 1971, p. ix).

Contemporary Conceptualizations of
Knowledge and Beliefs

The questions just raised also provide a link to recent concerns within developmental psychology and socialization theory, where knowledge and beliefs have received increasing attention, and this for good reason. It is a central feature of contemporary (postmodern) societies that people are exposed to an overabundance of information. This is also true in regard to information about the care and education of children, because traditional perspectives, although still widespread, are losing their plausibility. People are looking for new orientations. They are also inclined to develop individualistic justifications for their conduct and to plan their life in terms of personal goals (see also Clausen, this volume, chapter 11).

This is not the place for a lengthy discussion of the literature—even less so now that several reviews have been published recently, including D'Alessio (1990); Goodnow (1984); Molinari, Emiliani, and Carugati (1992); Murphey (1992); Sigel (1985); Sutherland (1983); and Schultheis and Lüscher (1987) for the European literature. In their historical retrospective, Goodnow and Collins (1990) demarcated two periods of increasing interest in knowledge and beliefs in socialization theory. During the 1960s, the first works appeared that dealt with the topic—among them those of Hess and Handel (1959) and Stolz (1967)—without, however, arousing great interest. In the 1980s, there was renewed interest, borne, among other things, by the use of cognitive approaches in developmental psychology and socialization research, as well as by a general interest in everyday life and what were labeled *lay theories, naive theories,* or *everyday life theories* (*Alltagstheorien*). In this period, there appeared, among others, several compilations by Sigel (e.g., 1985) and studies by Goodnow (e.g., 1984). A third phase, which immediately followed this, was characterized by varied empirical research activity, as is documented by recently published overviews. These, however, also showed that there was a need for an overarching conceptualization. Would not the ecology of human development be an appropriate framework for this?

The relationship of knowledge and beliefs to behavior stands in the foreground of empirical research in the tradition of developmental psychology. Murphey (1992) constructed a model for this purpose around which he ordered his overview of the literature: "The model shows parental beliefs, both global and specific, joining parental behavior in mediating child outcomes" (p. 201). The elaboration of the model made it clear that Murphey was, on the whole, very close to viewing beliefs as ultimately the result of interpretive processes.

A useful definitional proposition was offered by Sigel (1985), in his "Conceptual Analysis of Beliefs." He argued that beliefs presupposed the truth of what was believed. Knowledge, in his opinion, was characterized by a dependence on facts, on verifiable information. From this, Sigel concluded that "beliefs are knowledge in the sense that the individual knows that what he (or she) espouses is true or probably true, and evidence may or may not be deemed necessary; or if evidence is used, it forms a basis for the belief but is not the belief itself" (p. 348). Furthermore, "in sum, beliefs are constructions of reality. They may incorporate knowledge of what and of how, but do not necessitate evidential propositions. Beliefs are considered as truth statements even though evidence for their veridicality may or may not exist" (Sigel, 1985, p. 349).[9] Following this lead, I suggest that we conceive of knowledge and beliefs as complementary in regard to action: Incomplete knowledge, in the sense of information, may be supplemented by beliefs. But beliefs may also guide people's sensitivity to factual matters and their selection of information.

Propositions for an Interpretive Conceptualization

Before this background, and with special reference to major concerns within the general program of the "Ecology of Human Development," I propose that we conceptualize knowledge and beliefs as a constituent of proximal processes. If the latter are "the mechanism through which genetic potentials are actualized" (Bronfenbrenner, 1993c, p. 56), or if "genotypes are translated into phenotypes" (Ceci & Hembrooke, this vol-

---

[9]In their discussion of definitional matters, Goodnow and Collins (1990) pleaded for "parental ideas" (p. 12), without, however, giving a formal definition. (See, also, Goodnow's contribution to this volume— chapter 8—which may also be read as an invitation for an interdisciplinary approach.)

ume, chapter 9, p. 308), then knowledge and beliefs stand for the "recognition" of their relevance. In other words, within the ecology of human development, knowledge and beliefs express the meanings that are attributed to the relations between the biological equipment and the environment; these attributions are organized in perspectives proper to the persons, groups, or socialities that originate, influence, and evaluate these meanings.[10] This also implies that proximal processes always go together with interpretations.

Thus, it is assumed that the behaviors that are the focus of the ecology of human development are displayed and can be observed in the realm of nurture, mostly in immediate settings, such as the family, the school, the home, or the university. To analyze human development, it is important to consider the facts of the biological nature of man, not least because they provide a genetic basis for the person's individuality. Yet, what happens in immediate settings is always and necessarily embedded in culture, namely, the world into which man is born, with the properties of general human sociality and the properties of specific socialities, as expressed in the cultural identities of ethnic groups, nations, or subcultures.

My proposition and its underlying assumptions are rooted in a pragmatistic[11] understanding of science, particularly in its implication for a (moderate) social constructivism. It is reasonable (at least for scientific purposes) to consider only those phenomena as real for which we have ideas concerning their effects.[12] This view does not necessarily imply that the ideas must be formulated explicitly, precisely, and consciously or that they need always be socially manifest. They can be latent—contained, for example, in metaphors, in rituals, in customs, or in other forms of symbolic

---

[10] I see a close relationship between this view and Elder's (this volume, chapter 4) statement, "the biological course of events and their meaning are core elements of a person's life history" (p. 104), and with the basic orientation in Ceci and Hembrooke's contribution (chapter 9), although they start from different premises.

[11] Following Peirce, I prefer the term *pragmatistic* over *pragmatic* because the latter may evoke associations with the ordinary language sense of the word, which often restricts itself to the notion of usefulness.

[12] To recall Peirce's doctrine of pragmaticism contained in "How to Make Our Ideas Clear" (orig. 1878): "402. . . . Consider what effects, that might conceivably have practical bearings, we conceive the objects of our conception to have. Then, our conception of these effects is the whole of our conception of the object."

expression. It is the task and the purpose of scholarly analysis to uncover the different meanings lying behind those manifestations and actions.

To state this in general terms within an interpretive framework: Theoretical and empirical research should aim to reconstruct and to reinterpret the processes through which people attribute, deliberately or not, verbally or nonverbally, meanings to their behaviors within given contexts and to uncover the links in the chains of those processes from the micro- to the macrosystems and vice versa.

This also means that proximal processes may be located at the intersection between biology and culture. From the perspective of the bioecological model, as it is sketched out in this volume by Ceci and Hembrooke (chapter 9) and by Bronfenbrenner (chapter 19), an individual's biological potential is realized in concrete microcontexts. The organization of processes can be seen as consisting of selective mechanisms. Simultaneously, this organization requires—in my (sociological) view—acts of interpretation, which may also involve processes of selection, namely, from the stock of knowledge and beliefs available in a given culture and within a given pattern relevant to the social organization of the processes of socialization. In both cases, contingencies allow for new patterns of behavior. Another conceptual approach may be elaborated if knowledge and beliefs are seen as resources at the disposal of the individual and of the society. Such a view parallels Moen and Erickson's (this volume, chapter 6) understanding of resilience.

Furthermore, note that knowledge and beliefs may have a spontaneous and naive character and that they may be the subjects of reflection by acting parents themselves and, even more so, by those observing and analyzing parental behaviors. These persons' knowledge and beliefs are also expressed in advice and instruction.

Thus, the second kind of knowledge and beliefs involves awareness of awareness or, technically speaking, different levels of the reflection of naive knowledge and beliefs.[13] Because nowadays, social reality is highly differ-

---

[13]Such a distinction may be found in several general theories of action, such as Schütz (1963a, 1963b). See also Lenk (1994).

entiated and complex, many more groups of people are engaged in processes of reflecting on knowledge and beliefs concerning the proximal processes of human development. Consequently, we can distinguish a multitude of forms of reflective knowledge and beliefs at different levels of societal organization. Each involves processes of interpretation, both of the basic behaviors and of their spontaneous understanding and existing interpretations. The metaphor of chains of interpretations seems highly appropriate.

As far as the perspectivistic character of knowledge and beliefs is concerned, I add to the remarks made in the introduction draw on Mead's use of the concept of perspective to describe "the world in its relationship to the individual and the individual in his relationship to the world" (Mead, 1938, p. 115). Here, the term *world*, as opposed to *environment*, indicates a reflexive use of a social logic that enables us to include the individual as part of the world. Also significant is the emphasis Mead (1938) places on reciprocity, both quantitatively and qualitatively, and on a plurality of perspectives: "Perspectives have objective existence" (1938, p. 114). Mead continues: "The obverse of this proposition is that the perspective is not subjective. In other words, there is always a perceptual world, that is itself a perspective within which the subjective arises. The subjective is that experience in the individual which takes the place of the object when the reality of the object, at least in some respects, lies in an uncertain future" (1938, p. 114).[14]

I see two good reasons why the idea of perspectivity can be most useful for the theoretical assessment of the relevance of knowledge and beliefs, and even more so within the "ecology." First, the concept assumes the simultaneity of behavior and its re-*cognition*, that is, the simultaneity of conduct and knowledge (or beliefs), and it refers to the necessity to construct a relation between them. In this way, it points out the necessity and the relevance of processes of interpretation and thereby brings in the interpreter. Second, by referring to this triadic operation as fundamental to give meaning to reality, it is a promising attempt to conceive this reality

---

[14]For a lengthier discussion of this concept, see Lüscher (1990).

as permanently emerging, as development, and as embedded, ultimately, in the process of evolution.

I am aware of the abstract character of this argument and of the fact that several steps are needed to prove its usefulness for research. Given the scope of this presentation, I must restrict myself to some considerations that are necessarily incomplete in the logic of their abduction. Nevertheless, they may illustrate what I think to be the fruitfulness of the argument.

Implications for Research

In most instances, knowledge and beliefs are expressed in speech and in writings, for example; they are linguistic phenomena. They stand for observations and for experiences (which may be real, personal, mediated, or fictional), and they refer to processes of personal development (be it that of a child, her or his parents, or their interrelationships) and can be—at least in most cases—traced back to proximal processes.

Thus, to infer their meaning, it may be necessary to analyze their historical and current connotations. To review the history of concepts may be an important prerequisite for research. This may also be important if findings are to be compared and generalized. The history of the concept of "family" is an excellent example of the interplay between tasks and social contents. I also recall Bronfenbrenner's (1985) remarks concerning the recent transformation of "traditional/developmental families" into "restrictive/permissive families" (p. 334). An awareness that the knowledge and beliefs of both subjects and analysts are culture bound, even if it is knowledge concerning proximal processes, reminds us of the limitations of our interpretations and encourages further interpretations. Maccoby's (this volume, chapter 10) essay "The Two Sexes and Their Social Systems" provides, as a whole and in many details, an excellent analysis for the functions of interpretive processes in regard to gender. Clausen (this volume, chapter 11) points out how the reconstruction of turning points may serve to crystalize the interpretation and evaluation of certain situations in view of their impact on personal biographies.

Concrete formulations of knowledge and belief can be conceived as links in chains of interpretation, as conceptions of the tasks of socialization, and as the situations and consequences of the processes of human development. Therefore, it may be appropriate and useful, on one side, to relate the ideas of parents to general notions of human development, of childhood, and of the family and to the understanding of the relationships within and between generations.[15] It may also be important, on the other side, to look for the sources of information that parents use: their reference groups; the media they draw on; and their political, religious, and ideological affiliations. This, of course, is the dominant line of the interpretive argument in Bronfenbrenner's (1958) "Socialization and Social Class Through Time and Space."

In this connection, it may be equally important to look at the histories of cultural ideas on childhood or the child[16] and notions of the family from the view of the social sciences and to analyze examples of social reports on the status of the family, the status of children, or the situation of women.[17] Conceptually, bridges may be built to work on social representations.[18]

However, note also that different levels of interpretation and of generalization may be interrelated in patterns that are not hierarchically organized. Very general notions may be combined with specific experiences. I would like to illustrate this point with an insight from our own studies

---

[15]See as examples of recent German works in this field: Gloger-Tippelt (1991) and Gloger-Tippelt and Tippelt (1986). Moch (1993) showed the relevance of such representations in families that must be restructured and reorganized after a divorce by couples married for 15–20 years.

[16]I have attempted to sketch out the broad outlines of the history of the social role of the child in regard to his or her bearings in an analysis of socialization–knowledge in Lüscher (1975) and recently of the notions of the child contained in propositions concerning social policies for children (Lüscher & Lange 1992).

[17]Still another fruitful approach to analyzing these processes may be seen in the study of counseling processes. See, for example, von Cranach, Thommen, and Ammann (1988).

[18]The concept of "social representations" is grounded in the metaphor of the "thinking society," derived from Durkheimian ideas. Interest is then directed toward the spread of different forms of knowledge (so to speak its "epidemiology"). Furthermore, the focus is not merely on the processing of information, or on the adoption and differential acceptance of hierarchical orderings and corresponding values, but rather on the conflict among them. An analysis of the theoretical and empirical implications of the concept of "social representations" and its possible compatibility with the ecology of human development is still to be made. It may lead to new insights, particularly in regard to socialization knowledge. See, for example, Farr (1993) and Doise, Clemence, and Lorenzi-Cioldi (1993). Billig (1993) and McKinlay, Potter, and Wetherell (1993) try to build a bridge to the study of rhetoric.

of what we called the "everyday conceptions of young mothers" (Fisch, Lüscher, & Pape, 1982). We determined, among other things, that the everyday educational concepts of young parents are characterized by two basic principles: "overarching generalizations and individual peculiarities. The first relates to general conceptions of societal values and norms and not seldom has ideological characteristics; the second rests on individual experience and comprehends a specific conception of individuality" (Fisch et al., 1982, p. 203). We termed this individuality *experienced individuality*, to express the idea that parents do not merely experience their children and themselves as individuals, but as persons, as "Sylvia" or "Mark." This sort of "individuality" is for parents partly the "end" and partly the "ground" of action (Fisch et al., 1982, p. 204).

I would also suggest that we see these complex processes of interpretation as a potential source of new and creative solutions. They concern, first, the tasks of socialization as such, but second, they may also be innovative with regard to more general patterns and contents of culture. Each context may be an instance in which issues—tasks, problems, means, and methods—may be affirmed or altered or even radically changed—in other words, may be interpreted anew. Remember, for example, Bronfenbrenner's reference to both continuity and abrupt change, mentioned in the Generational Principle 2, mentioned above.

At the same time, each link may also be a context of open or hidden tensions; conflicts; or even of struggles over interests, influence, power, or the legitimization of power (*Herrschaft*). Knowledge and beliefs can be the targets of these conflicts or the reason for them, but they may also be merely instruments for settling other issues.[19] Examples may easily be found in debates over family policy or over policies for children, and even—on a secondary level—over the appropriateness of these two kinds of social policy!

The existential importance of proximal processes for the development of the individual person, of groups, and of the society at large; the man-

---

[19]See also Goodnow's (1990) plea for more intensive study of the impact of societal power structures on parental ideas.

ifold possibilities for shaping them; and the unpredictability of future developments give knowledge a certain openness and uncertainty and even
a certain aleatory character, which must be complemented by beliefs and
ultimately by convictions and ideologies. In this connection, the study of
knowledge and beliefs can be related to a new interest in rhetoric. This
particular form of public communication ultimately aims to influence not
only how people act but also how they see and evaluate certain tasks. In
other words, rhetoric also aims, with the use of very special strategies, to
influence processes of interpretation. Thus, family rhetoric may consist of
statements on what the family is or should be and how it should function.
Explicitly or implicitly, many statements of family rhetoric refer to the social organization of proximal processes (e.g., day care or mother–child relations). The study of family rhetoric may also include analysis of the images of the family as well as strategies through which political arguments
are legitimized.[20]

If we return to the idea, implicit in Bronfenbrenner's postulation, of
a connection between knowledge and beliefs and proximal processes, we
may combine this postulate with the notion of chains of interpretation.
Consequently, it may well be worthwhile to insist that core aspects of proximal processes should be seen as points of departure (and also to engage
in a discussion of what these core aspects are). Initially, two come immediately to mind: the development of intelligence, or cognitive ability—a
topic already given high priority by Bronfenbrenner in connection with
the relevance of heredity—and, furthermore, the development of gender
identities, again to be related to the issue of biological potentials. Attention may also be paid to what is called by Bronfenbrenner (1993b) "enhancing functional competence and . . . reducing degrees of dysfunctions"
(p. 34; and to deepening the significance of this juxtaposition both theoretically and empirically).

Finally, within research designs, we may vary the angle of the triadic

---

[20]The analysis of family rhetoric is part of an ongoing program on family and family policy at Konstanz,
Germany. See Lüscher, Wehrspaun, and Lange (1989), Walter (1993), Lamm-Heß and Wehrspaun
(1993), Lüscher (1994), and Ringwald (1994).

structure from which we start. Why should we always take for a given a certain context, such as the family (and perhaps differentiate it into certain subtypes), and then look for its effects on interpretations and behaviors?[21] Why not reverse the order and ask instead why certain behaviors are claimed to fall within the concept of "family"? I am referring here to public debates on what is or should be meant by "family." More generally speaking, such a reversal may guide our search for socialization settings located outside of traditional conceptions—a proposition that may be seen as recalling some of the very early concerns of social science.

Methodological Considerations

How can we properly assess knowledge and beliefs? Is it sufficient to operationalize them in terms of attitudes, of norms, and of values? There can be no doubt about the wealth of information and insights provided by the use of these concepts, which by now are consecrated by their long tradition and are ennobled by the sophistications contained in more and more differentiated methods of measurement. Yet many reviewers and observers agree that there remain some open and disturbing questions. Two of them stand out, namely, the problem of causality and the problem of (ecological) validity, which require new approaches.

In regard to causality, I may quote from Murphey's (1992) review:

> The relationship between beliefs and behavior is one that has bedeviled social psychologists (and opinion survey research in general) for years. In part, this stems from the difficulty of obtaining valid measures of people's beliefs or attitudes, but also from the fact that behavior in almost any situation is determined by multiple factors. . . . It seems particularly likely . . . that parents sometimes act first, and reflect later . . . parents may construct beliefs in order to rationalize or justify the way they already behave." (p. 204)

---

[21]A similar change in point of view (or of perspective) has been proposed by Krappmann (1985) within a set of theoretical considerations for the study of socialization based on Mead's (1938) ideas concerning play and games.

Accordingly, the results of empirical studies can be variously interpreted. In other words, knowledge acquired about parental knowledge is itself in need of interpretation.

> It should be emphasized that any of the correlational findings are subject to alternative interpretations. For instance, beliefs may reflect behavior, rather than the other way round; or, beliefs and behavior may be only spuriously related—for example, when both derive from normative social expectations. (Murphey, 1992, p. 208)

In this context, note Murphey's (1992, p. 210) reference to the critique of the limited discriminatory ability of the Parent Attitude Research Instrument (PARI; Schaefer & Bell, 1958).

Furthermore, parental ideas may display ambiguity and ambivalence. This point is made clear by Goodnow and Collins (1990) in regard to the topic of the relative shares of "heredity and environment" (p. 30), which is especially interesting when we consider the understanding of proximal processes.

A further important aspect that illuminates the interpretive and interpretation-needing character of parental ideas is found in the thesis that these ideas can influence not only the child, but also parents, and are, thus, also ambiguous and reflexive. It seems likely that new solutions to account properly for these ambivalences will be made possible by the help of interpretive techniques in content analysis, which permit the inclusion of different contextual levels.

The idea that an ecological approach requires a differentiated notion of validity is already contained in Bronfenbrenner's definition: "the extent to which the environment experienced by the subject in a scientific investigation has the properties it is supposed or assumed to have by the investigator" (Bronfenbrenner, 1979, p. 29). Recently, various authors have confirmed the need for a differentiated view. The understanding of the task moves away from correcting measurement errors to a reorientation of research in general. Although the point of departure is the methodology of qualitative research, bridges are built to the concerns of quantitative approaches (see Altheide & Johnson, 1994; Cairns & Cairns, this volume, chapter 12; Denzin & Lincoln, 1994), warning against an overestimation of the power of multivariate analysis. Indeed, in the light of the foregoing considerations, it seems desirable, even necessary, to be more explicit. Of special interest is the relationship between the interpretations of the subject and those of the investigator. Not that they are identical, but the mutual translation of one into the other is of crucial relevance. It is well-known that the orientations of subjects, if they are actively involved in the production of data, may influence their behaviors and responses. But theoretical and practical efforts are still required to account for them properly, that is, explicitly, especially if topics as sensitive as knowledge and beliefs are under consideration. Things become even more complicated because of the different agencies involved in the social construction and reconstruction of meanings.

In view of these tasks, it may be useful to turn to the approaches dealt with under the heading of "semiotic analysis," here to be understood and used as a formal and heuristic meta-theory, aimed at developing general propositions on the emergence of signs and the sequential structure of their consequences.

There is a general logic in which "something stands for something to somebody"—a logic that "describes the encounter between two entities from which a third entity results" (Lang, 1992b, p. 116). This logic, which emphasizes the triadic structure of procedural dynamics, is axiomatic for semiotics as a meta-theory, for its use in deriving more concrete theories, and, in particular, as a prerequisite for overcoming the shortcomings of Cartesian logic as applied in the human sciences.

In this case, the label *semiotic* also stands for an invitation to engage in an exchange with pragmatic (or, more precisely, pragmatistic) theories of action (or acting). The latter are conceived of as alternatives to theories of behavior and learning based on stimulus–response mechanisms. Pragmatic theories of action or acting may be called *semiotic*, because they conceive of perceptions and cognitions as phases that guide action. Reflexivity is posited to be permanently preconditioned in any kind of acting (Joas, 1992, p. 232). More generally speaking, acting is seen as embedded in a continuous flow of interpretive processes. The question then arises as to which configuration of context, act, and person evokes conscious and verbal statements of motives, reasons, or goals—in other words, of knowledge and beliefs—and, furthermore, which configurations lead to a search for new ideas. Acting, conceived of on these premises, follows the logic of "abduction," in the sense of Peirce (see, e.g., Peirce, 1970, pp. 365–388).

CONCLUSIONS AND PROSPECTS

Knowledge and beliefs in the ecology of human development, with reference to the notion of proximal processes, are the cultural counterparts of the biological equipment of human beings. Phenomenologically speaking, they may be observable in all kinds of verbal and nonverbal actions and symbols, and they may be analyzed under the assumption that they express the meanings that subjects attribute to the tasks involved in the organization of personal human development (or of socialization). The contents of knowledge and beliefs may be considered as elements of perspectives, which, in turn, represent theories of the relations of subjects to the worlds in which they live and the identities that are constituted by these relations. The worlds and the identities may be located in micro-, meso-, exo-, and macrosystems. Knowledge and beliefs are activated in processes of interpretation through which (or by which) subjects individually and collectively define situations, relying on previous experiences, selecting from the information provided by general stocks of knowledge and beliefs, and taking into account—consciously or unconsciously—representations of themselves and of the socialities to which subjects want or are forced to belong or to which they aspire. In this way, knowledge and beliefs define meanings that change in the course of time, and thus, they can be conceived as parts of chronosystems.

As a consequence, I consider the analysis of the act called interpretation (or should I say, the actions called interpretation) as a strategic part of research on the ecology of human development, as well as a part of related approaches. I see a great potential for directing our attention to this research task, and I would like to close with some general considerations.

The image of man expressed in these considerations is the image of a *homo interpretans*. I suggest this label in reference to an argument elaborated by Lenk (1994). He stressed the point that higher species also have capacities for symbolic communication, which presuppose interpretive skills, and he, therefore, held the view that ultimately the difference might be seen in the ability for meta-interpretation. The crucial difference lies in the capacity, which is at the same time a necessity, to develop an understanding of symbol-making and symbol-using interpretation. The deeper reason may be seen in man's relation to nature. The very fact that, to develop this argument, I can use, but also must use, a term for nature illustrates this point. More generally speaking, the impact of nature, although it is the primary environment of man, is not accessible to him directly and instinctively, but only as mediated through language and thought. There are good reasons to claim that, for humankind, there is no nature without culture.

It is just this idea that underlies my proposition that we see knowledge and beliefs as constituents to the "biological mechanism" to which Bronfenbrenner refers in his delineation of "proximal processes" (1993a, p. 56). Furthermore, knowledge and beliefs may be seen as linked to micro-, meso-, exo-, and macrosystems, and their dynamics can be related to different chronosystems, particularly the temporal developments of personal biographies and of history.

Throughout this chapter, I emphasized the importance of processes of interpretation, and the question may arise as to the difference between explanation and interpretation. On a methodological level, I would like to suggest the following distinction. Explanations are interpretations with reference to a highly differentiated, in many instances even formalized, system of propositions and hypotheses. They are based on (or oriented toward) a binary logic of confirmation or falsification. Ideally, each correct explanation confirms a theory as a whole, whereas each falsification raises questions about at least parts of a theory and, depending on the weight of these parts, may force its revision or abandonment. Thus, explaining, as it is understood here, is a formalized process. Interpreting, in turn, is much more open, dynamic, and innovative. Its rules are less formalized. It is related to the search for meaning.

In regard to theory, and particularly the ecology of human development, this distinction directs our attention to what I would like to call the "paradox of research on socialization." Essentially, it consists of the fact that the image of man underlying most theories of socialization, or human development in one way or another, presupposes an individuality of the subject as a person. This individualtiy includes a genuine unpredictability of his or her actions and biography. Yet the aim of socialization theory is precisely to explain, and consequently to predict, behaviors and developments. This paradox may be solved if we include in our conceptualization modes of reflection, which themselves are open to idiosyncrasies and the emergence of the genuinely new, both in everyday behavior and in its analysis. Ultimately, it is just this quality that may be seen as the difference between interpretations and explanations, or to put it simply: Interpretations transcend explanations.

CODA

In preparing my contribution to this volume elaborating on Bronfenbrenner's ecology of human development, I saw myself engaging in a style of academic work that he himself has mastered and refined to a high degree, namely, the act of interpreting observations, data, and the writings of others and that of reconsidering his own ideas. I became attracted by his increasing interest in knowledge and beliefs and challenged by a certain openness of his notion of proximal processes. Following his characterization of the ecology of human development as a scientific adventure in the "discovery mode" (Bronfenbrenner, 1989, p. 230), I felt confirmed in my belief in the affinity and relevance of pragmatistic orientations to the theoretical foundations of the study of human development. At the same time, I became aware of how deeply Bronfenbrenner's thinking and work are rooted in these traditions, which themselves originated, early in this century, in a differentiated interplay between European and American philosophy and social thought. In Bronfenbrenner's writings, these theoretical foundations are dealt with more implicitly than explicitly, although—as I gradually realized in the course of my discussions with him—he is quite conscious of them. The occasion of the symposium and this resulting volume and the topic of knowledge and beliefs have provided excellent opportunities to remind us of this side of his oeuvre.

As for the fundamental significance of processes of interpretation in everyday life, we may remember one of the opening statements in the "Ecology": "What matters for behavior and development is the environment as it is perceived rather than as it may exist in 'objective' reality" (Bronfenbrenner, 1979, p. 4). In this connection, again and again, Bronfenbrenner displays a fascination for the Thomas theorem: "If men define situations as real, they are real in their consequences" (see Bronfenbrenner, 1979, p. 23). However, in his recent oral commentaries, and in connection with his interest in proximal processes, Bronfenbrenner does not understand the theorem as a law, but rather as a hypothesis whose scope must be empirically explored.

The Thomas theorem expresses in a nutshell, yet not without ambiguities, one of the overarching ideas of American pragmatism. Its founding fathers, such as Peirce, James, Dewey, Mead, and Thomas himself, all worked on the development of a general theory of human action. They elaborated the synchronic interplay between individual and societal development. Is not this concern also very neatly contained in the dimensions of the term *human development* within the project of the "Ecology of Human Development"? We may also remember the broad attention given by Mead (1934) to the biological preconditions for the "conversation of gestures and of the development of the human self" (p. 63). The inclination is strong to relate Mead's thoughts more profoundly to Bronfenbrenner's model of proximal processes. More generally speaking, we are invited to explore the extent to which the formulations of the "Ecology of Human Development" could be seen as empirically oriented successors to Mead's (1934) general theory on the interrelations between "mind, self and society," their biological foundations, their social and cultural expressions, and the policy implications of social scientific research.

REFERENCES

Abel, T. (1948). The operation called "Verstehen." *American Journal of Sociology 54,* 1948–49: 211–218.

Altheide, D., & Johnson, J. (1994). Criteria for assessing interpretive validity in qualitative research. In N. K. Denzin & Y. Lincoln (Eds.), *Handbook of qualitative research* (pp. 485–499). Thousand Oaks, CA: Sage.

Baumrind, D. (1967). Child care practices anteceding three patterns of preschool behavior. *Genetic Psychology Monographs, 75*, 43–88.

Billig, M. (1993). Studying the thinking society: Social representations, rhetoric, and attitudes. In: B. M. Breakwell & D. V. Canter (Eds.), *Empirical approaches to social representations* (pp. 39–62). Oxford, England: Clarendon Press.

Blood, R. O. (1953). Consequences of permissiveness of parents of young children. *Marriage and Family Living, 15*, 209–212.

Bronfenbrenner, U. (1958). Socialization and social class through time and space. In E. E. Maccoby, T. M. Newcomb, & E. L. Hartley (Eds.), *Readings in social psychology* (pp. 400–425). New York: Holt.

Bronfenbrenner, U. (1970). *Two worlds of childhood: U.S. and U.S.S.R.* New York: Russell Sage Foundation.

Bronfenbrenner, U. (1976). Ökologische Sozialisationsforschung [Ecological socialization research] (K. Lüscher, Ed.). Stuttgart: Klett.

Bronfenbrenner, U. (1979). *The ecology of human development.* Cambridge, MA: Harvard University Press.

Bronfenbrenner, U. (1985). Freedom and discipline across the decades. In G. Becker, H. Becker, & L. Huber (Eds.), *Ordnung und Unordnung. Hartmut von Hentig zum 23. September 1985 [Order and disorder. Festschrift for Hartmut von Hentig, September 23, 1985]* (pp. 326–337).Weinheim, Germany: Beltz.

Bronfenbrenner, U. (1989). Ecological systems theory. *Annals of Child Development, 6*, 187–249.

Bronfenbrenner, U. (1992). Child care in the Anglo-Saxon mode. In M. E. Lamb (Ed.), *Child care in context* (pp. 281–291). Hillsdale, NJ: Erlbaum.

Bronfenbrenner, U. (1993a). The ecology of cognitive development: Research models and fugitive findings. In R. H. Wozniak & K. W. Fischer (Eds.), *Development in context: Acting and thinking in specific environments* (The Jean Piaget Symposium Series; pp. 3–44). Hillsdale, NJ: Erlbaum.

Bronfenbrenner, U. (1993b). Generationenbeziehungen in der Ökologie menschlicher Entwicklung [Intergenerational relationships and cross-generational development: An ecological perspective] In K. Lüscher & F. Schultheis (Eds.), *Generationenbeziehungen in "postmodernen" Gesellschaften [Intergenerational relations in "postmodern" societies]* (pp. 51–74). Konstanz, Germany: Universitätsverlag.

Bronfenbrenner, U. (1993c). *Nature–nurture reconceptualized: Toward a new theoretical and operational model*. Ithaca, NY: mimeo.

Bronfenbrenner, U. (1993d). Distancing theory from a distance. In R. R. Cocking & K. A. Renninger (Eds.), *The development and meaning of psychological distance* (pp. 63–77). Hillsdale, NJ: Erlbaum.

D'Alessio, M. (1990). Social representations of childhood: An implicit theory of childhood. In G. Duveen & B. Lloyd (Eds.), *Social representations and the development of knowledge* (pp. 70–90). Cambridge, England: Cambridge University Press.

Denzin, N. K., & Lincoln, Y. (Eds.). (1994). *Handbook of qualitative research* (pp. 485–499). Thousand Oaks, CA: Sage.

Doise, W., Clemence, A., & Lorenzi-Cioldi, F. (1993). *The quantitative analysis of social representations*. New York: Wheatsheaf.

Duvall, E. M. (1946). Conceptions of parenthood. *American Journal of Sociology, 52,* 193–203.

Farr, R. (1993). Theory and method in the study of social representations. In G. M. Breakwell & D. V. Canter (Eds.), *Empirical approaches to social representations* (pp. 168–190). Oxford, England: Clarendon Press.

Fisch, R., Lüscher, K., & Pape, T. (1982). Das alltägliche Erziehungsverständnis junger Mütter [Young mothers' everyday knowledge of child rearing]. *Zeitschrift für Sozialisationsforschung und Erziehungssoziologie, 2,* 189–206.

Gloger-Tippelt, G. (1991). Zusammenhänge zwischen dem Schema vom eigenen Kind vor der Geburt und dem Bindungsverhalten nach der Geburt bei erstmaligen Müttern [Interactions between the first-time mother's image of her unborn child and postnatal maternal bonding]. *Zeitschrift für Entwicklungspsychologie, 23,* 95–114.

Gloger-Tippelt, G., & Tippelt, R. (1986). Kindheit und kindliche Entwicklung als soziale Konstruktion [Childhood and child development as social constructions]. *Bildung und Erziehung, 2,* 149–164.

Goodnow, J. (1984). Parents' ideas about parenting and development: A review of issues and current work. In M. E. Lamb, A. L. Brown, & B. Rogoff (Eds.), *Advances in developmental psychology* (Vol. 3, pp. 193–242). Hillsdale, NJ: Erlbaum.

Goodnow, J. (1990). Using sociology to extend psychological accounts of cognitive development. *Human Development, 33,* 81–107.

Goodnow, J., & Collins, A. (1990). *Development according to parents*. Hillsdale, NJ: Erlbaum.

Hess, R. D., & Handel, G. (1959). *Family worlds: A psychosocial approach to family life.* Chicago: University of Chicago Press.

Joas, H. (1992). *Die Kreativität des Handelns* [The creativity of action]. Frankfurt, Germany: Suhrkamp.

Krappmann, L. (1985). Mead und die Sozialisationsforschung [Mead and socialization research]. In H. Joas (Ed.), *Das Problem der Intersubjektivität* [The problem of intersubjectivity]. Frankfurt, Germany: Suhrkamp.

Lamm-Heß, Y., & Wehrspaun, C. (1993). *Frauen- und Müttererwerbstätigkeit im Dritten und Vierten Familienbericht [Women's and mother's gainful employment as topics of the third and the fourth Germany family report].* Konstanz, Germany: Forschungsschwerpunkt "Gesellschaft und Familie." Arbeitspapier Nr. 4 [Research program Society and Family working paper No. 4].

Lang, A. (1991). *Non-cartesian culture: Steps toward a semiotic ecology.* Bern: Berichte aus der Gruppe Umwelt- und Kulturpsychologie des Psychologischen Instituts der Universität Bern [Report of working group ecological and cultural psychology, Institute for Psychology, University Bern].

Lang, A. (1992a). Die Frage nach den psychologischen Genesereihen—Kurt Lewins große Herausforderung [The problem of psychological genesis—Kurt Lewin's great challenge] In W. Schönpflug (Ed.), *Kurt Lewin—Person, Werk, Umfeld [Kurt Lewin—Person, Work, Context]* (pp. 39–68). Frankfurt. Germany: Peter Lang.

Lang, A. (1992b). On the knowledge in things and places. In M. von Cranach, W. Doise, & G. Mugny (Eds.), *Social representations and the social basis of knowledge* (pp. 112–119). Bern: Hogrefe & Huber.

Lange, A. (1994). *Veränderungen der Familie—Entwicklungen der Familienforschung: ein Trendbericht [Changes in the family—developments in family research. A trend report].* Konstanz, Germany: Forschungsschwerpunkt "Gesellschaft und Familie." Arbeitspapier Nr. 9 [Research program Society and Family working paper No. 9].

Lenk, M. (1994). Interpretationskonstrukte als Interpretationskonstrukte [Interpretive constructs as interpretive constructs]. In J. Simon (Ed.), *Zeichen und Interpretation [Signs and interpretation].* Frankfurt, Germany: Suhrkamp.

Lüscher, K. (1971) Dreizehnjährige Schweizer zwischen Peers und Erwachsenen im interkulturellen Vergleich [Thirteen-year-old Swiss children in role conflicts between peers and adults: A cross-cultural comparison]. *Schweizerische Zeitschrift für Psychologie und ihre Anwendungen, 30,* 219–229.

Lüscher, K. (1975). Perspektiven einer Soziologie der Sozialisation—Die Entwicklung der Rolle des Kindes [Perspectives of a sociology of socialization—The development of the social role of the child]. *Zeitschrift für Soziologie, 4,* 359–379.

Lüscher, K. (1976). Urie Bronfenbrenners Weg zur ökologischen Sozialisationsforschung [Urie Bronfenbrenner's path toward ecological socialization research]. In U. Bronfenbrenner, (Ed.), *Ökologische Sozialisationsforschung* (pp. 6–32). Stuttgart, Germany: Klett.

Lüscher, K. (1982). Familienpolitik und Wissenssysteme [Family policy and systems of knowledge]. In F. X. Kaufmann (Ed.), *Staatliche Sozialpolitik und Familie* (pp. 191–211). Munich: Oldenbourg.

Lüscher, K. (1990). The social reality of perspectives: On G. H. Mead's potential relevance for the analysis of contemporary societies. *Symbolic Interaction, 13,* 1–18.

Lüscher, K. (1993). Generationenbeziehungen—Neue Zugänge zu einem alten Thema [Intergenerational relations—New approaches to an old theme]. In K. Lüscher & F. Schultheis (Eds.), *Generationenbeziehungen in "postmodernen" Gesellschaften* (pp. 17–46). Konstanz, Germany: Unversitätsverlag.

Lüscher, K. (1994). Was heißt heute Familie? Thesen zur Familienrhetorik. [What do we mean by family? Propositions on family rhetoric]. In U. Gerhardt, S. Hradil, D. Lucke, & B. Nauck (Eds.), *Familie der Zukunft. Lebensbedingungen und Lebensformen.* Opladen, Germany: Leske & Budrich.

Lüscher, K., & Lange, A. (1992). Konzeptuelle Grundlagen einer Politik für Kinder: Ansätze und Begründungen aus sozialwissenschaftlicher Sicht [Conceptual foundations of a policy for children: Approaches and justifications from a social scientific perspective]. *Zeitschrift für Sozialisationsforschung und Erziehungssoziologie, 12,* 204–218.

Lüscher, K., Wehrspaun, M., & Lange, A. (1989). Begriff und Rhetorik von Familie [Concept and rhetoric of the family]. *Zeitschrift für Familienforschung, 1, 2,* 61–76.

McKinlay, A., Potter, J., & Wetherell, M. (1993). Discourse analysis and social representations. In G. M. Breakwell & D. V. Canter (Eds.), *Empirical approaches to social representations* (pp. 134–156). Oxford, England: Clarendon Press.

Mead, G. H. (1934). *Mind, self and society.* Chicago: University of Chicago Press.

Mead, G. H. (1938). *The philosophy of the act.* Chicago: University of Chicago Press.

Moch, M. (1993). Subjektive Repräsentationen von "Familie" nach einer Scheidung im mittleren Lebensalter [Subjective representations of the "family" after divorce in middle age]. In K. Lüscher & F. Schultheis (Eds.), *Generationen-*

beziehungen in "postmodernen" Gesellschaften (pp. 215–233). Konstanz, Germany: Universitätsverlag.

Molinari, L., Emiliani, F., & Carugati, F. (1992). Development according to mothers: A case of social representations. In M. von Cranach, W. Doise, & G. Mugny (Eds.), *Social representations and the social bases of knowledge* (pp. 104–111). Toronto, Ontario, Canada: Huber.

Murphey, D. A. (1992). Constructing the child: Relations between parents' beliefs and child outcomes. *Developmental Review, 12,* 199–232.

Ong, J. (1967). *The presence of the word.* Minneapolis: University of Minnesota Press.

Ong, J. (1971). *Rhetoric, romance, and technology.* Ithaca, NY: Cornell University Press.

Peirce, C. S. (1970). Schriften II. [Collected writings] (K. O. Apel, Ed.). Frankfurt, Germany: Suhrkamp.

Ringwald, A. (1994). *Entmachtung durch Idealisierung. Amerikanische Familienrhetorik im 19. Jahrhundert [Deprivation of power through idealization. American family rhetoric in the 19th century].* Konstanz, Germany: Forschungsschwerpunkt "Gesellschaft und Familie." Arbeitspapier Nr. 11 [Research program Society and Family working paper No. 11].

Schaefer, E. S., & Bell, R. Q. (1958). Development of a parental attitudes research instrument. *Child Development, 29,* 339–361.

Schultheis, F., & Lüscher, K. (1987). Familles et savoirs [Families and knowledge]. *L' Année sociologique, 37,* 239–267.

Schütz, A. (1960). *Der sinnhafte Aufbau der sozialen Welt [The meaningful construction of the social world].* Vienna: Springer.

Schütz, A. (1963a). Common-sense and scientific interpretation of human action. In M. Natanson (Ed.), *Philosophy of the social sciences* (pp. 302–346). New York: Random House.

Schütz, A. (1963b). Concept and theory formation in the social sciences. In M. Natanson (Ed.), *Philosophy of the social sciences* (pp. 231–249). New York: Random House.

Sears, R. R., Maccoby, E. E., & Levin, H. (1957). *Patterns of child rearing.* Evanston, IL: Row.

Sigel, I. E. (1985). A conceptual analysis of beliefs. In I. E. Sigel (Ed.), *Parental belief systems* (pp. 345–371). Hillsdale, NJ: Erlbaum.

Stolz, C. M. (1967). *Influences on parental behavior.* Stanford: Stanford University Press.

Sutherland, K. (1983). Parents' beliefs about child socialization. In I. E. Sigel & L. M. Laosa (Eds.), *Changing families* (pp. 137–166). New York: Plenum.

von Cranach, M., Thommen, B., & Ammann, R. (1988). *Handlungsorganisation durch soziale Repräsentationen. Welchen Einfluß haben therapeutische Schulen auf ihre Mitglieder? [The organization of action by social representations. What influence do therapeutic schools have on their members?]* Bern, Switzerland: Huber.

Walter, W. (1993). *Vom Familienleitbild zur Familiendefinition. Familienberichte und die Entwicklung des familienpolitischen Diskurses [From the "Leitbild" of the family to the definition of the family. Family reports and the development of the discourse on family policy].* Konstanz, Germany: Forschungsschwerpunkt "Gesellschaft und Familie." Arbeitspapier Nr. 5 [Research program Society and Family working paper No. 5].

18

The Bioecological Model From a Life Course Perspective: Reflections of a Participant Observer

Urie Bronfenbrenner

I n expounding the defining properties of the bioecological model, I typically take pains to point out that the biopsychological characteristics of the
individual appear on both sides of the equation; they are at once the product
of prior developmental processes and the partial producers of the person's future developmental course. As if to put both parts of this proposition to the
test, I have been requested by the editors of this volume to undertake a dual
task: First, to recall and record those features of my own life course that may
have influenced the form and substance of the kind of developmental theory
that I subsequently produced and, second, to indicate what I see as the most
scientifically promising extensions of the theory as a basis for future scientific
work. In this penultimate chapter, I turn to the first of these tasks.

REMEMBRANCE OF THINGS PAST

My reflections from a developmental perspective begin with those of a
small child. To call them *reflections* is to endow them with more clarity
and awareness than they possessed. But they were reflections nevertheless,
and although I did not know it then, they were already those of a participant observer. As you will see, I had no other choice.

At the time, I could not have been more than 5 years old, for I was still in Russia. It was my mother who I first remember using the word *psychologist*. She always said it in a two-word tandem, as in a southerner's "damn-Yankee," except that with her it was no epithet, but a term of the highest respect and affection. "Veliki Psikholog!" she would say, with her voice capitalizing both words: "Great Psychologist!"

Who were these great psychologists? There were about a half dozen who merited the appellation. I heard their names almost every day and felt I knew each one personally. You, too, will recognize some of them: Pushkin, Chekhov, Turgenev, Lermontov, Tolstoy, Bulgakov.

The word *psychologist* had no other meaning for me until a couple of years later, when we were already in the United States. This time, it was said in English, in my father's voice. Nor was there any joy in the saying; rather, dismay and desperation. My father was a physician, specializing in neuropathology. On coming to the United States, he was fortunate enough to get a job at a state institution for what was then called the "feeble-minded." It was located in upstate New York in the Hudson River valley. Letchworth Village was its name.

In the late 1920s and 1930s, Letchworth had some 3,000 inmates, each institutionally labeled either as a *moron, imbecile,* or *idiot.* They ranged in age from about 6 years to 60 years or more. They lived in large cottages, each housing about 80 inmates, with 2 female matrons or male attendants responsible for their care. As a high school student, I worked summers as one of those male attendants.

I still remember vividly my father's anguish when the New York City courts would commit to our institution, out of error or sheer desperation, perfectly normal youngsters. My father had taken it on himself to examine each child on admission, and he had a way with kids. But before he could unwind the necessary red tape to have them released, it would be too late. After a few weeks in one of those cottages, their scores on the Stanford–Binet, given routinely by the staff psychologist, would prove the courts to have been right in the first place. By then, the children's IQs showed them to be mentally retarded. In those days, that meant remaining in the institution for the rest of their lives.

My father's requests and arguments to the staff psychologist for an early retest were to no avail. A child's intelligence, the psychologist told him, could not be determined through a subjective clinical impression; it required a standardized, objective testing procedure. Furthermore, research had demonstrated that the IQ remained constant through life. So there was no hurry. And indeed, there was not. It was a self-fulfilling prophecy. I had learned a child's lesson. In America, psychologists are not people who tell stories; they measure things.

There were more lessons to come. Soon, our home became a kind of halfway house for immigrants from Russia who had some connection, however remote, with our family. Among them were some psychologists. They were Russian, but had come by way of Germany, where they had obtained their graduate or postgraduate training. They, too, talked about "great psychologists" with respect and admiration. But their psychologists were not writers; they were real. To me, they had strange names—Köhler, Koffka, Wertheimer, Stern, the Bühlers, and the one our visitors seemed to respect and love most, Kurt Lewin, except for one Russian who, they said, was the greatest psychologist of them all, a man named Vygotsky.

As usual, the conversation was in Russian, but they kept sticking in German words. One of them was *Gestalt.* I asked my father what that meant. It means *pattern,* he said. "How do you measure a pattern?" I queried. "You don't," he replied, "you just observe it."

The word *psychology* does not appear in the next set of reminiscences, but it was there in the making. Outside our home, my father lived in three worlds: his laboratory, the wards and cottages in which the inmates lived, and the outdoors. Dad's main responsibility in his new position was to establish and direct a laboratory for doing basic research on the etiology of feeblemindedness. To pursue this goal, he adopted a dual strategy—one that looked for relationships between laboratory findings and information on the inmates' behavior. That was one of the reasons he did admissions examinations. He would then follow up particular cases with observations and interviews on the ward and elsewhere. Afterward, he would ask me what I had noticed. It was not much, but whatever it was, he always related it to other things that I had missed, but made it seem as if I had noticed them, too. "You see, little one," he would say, "there's a pattern [that word again]; patterns of behavior reflect patterns in the brain, and the other way around. The inside becomes outside, and the outside becomes inside." It was no idle remark. My father's particular interest was in the origins and manifestations of brain dysfunction. His research publications, which were just beginning to receive recognition, were all on that topic.

Brain and behavior were not his only scientific preoccupation. Along with a medical degree, he had a doctorate in zoology, and he was a field naturalist at heart. The institution grounds offered a rich biological terrain for his observant eye. There were over 3,000 acres of farmland, wooded hills, moss-covered forest, and fetid swamp—all teeming with plant and animal life. That, too, was the world of my childhood. My father took me with him on innumerable walks from his laboratory through the wards, shops, and farmland (where he preferred to see and talk with his patients) and beyond the barbed wire fences into the woods and hills that began at our doorstep. Wherever we walked, he would alert my unobservant eyes to the workings of nature by pointing to the functional interdependence between living organisms and their surroundings.

But one fine, sunny day, when I was a junior in high school, all of these experiences came to an end. Upon his own diagnosis, my father was hospitalized with tuberculosis and soon was transferred to a state sanitarium in the Adirondacks. There would be no more research papers for him, no more walks together for me. It was in the days before the wonder drugs, and the prognosis was poor. Fortunately, we could live on my father's pension, and I won a scholarship to enter Cornell. That was in the fall of 1934. For reasons I did not understand myself until many years later, I decided to major in psychology.

Those reasons relate not only to the world of my family. There was another world I was leaving behind. Among the photographs my father took during our first months in the United States is one of me as a beginning first grader, surrounded by a dozen or more of my friends. It was taken on the so-called "playground" of the Minersville School in a working-class neighborhood of Pittsburgh, PA. There was "our gang"—boys of different ages and ethnic backgrounds, with their arms around each other—diversity and solidarity rolled into one, my first introduction to *e pluribus unum*, not as an abstract principle, but as an everyday reality. It was this same peer group who, in a matter of a few weeks, turned me into an American kid. And it was I, in turn, who, as a result of this experience, found myself engaged in the slow and far-from-successful process of Americanizing my parents. Not only had I learned English much faster than they but also, with my new peer group as source and vehicle, I was learning about the neighborhood and its way of life—the American way of life that so puzzled my parents. They often could not answer my questions, but they soon discovered that I could answer some of theirs. As a result, at an early age, I found myself in the role of an interpreter to my parents, not only of the new language, but also of the new culture in which we lived and about which I was learning from my friends.[1]

When a half-year later, we moved to Letchworth, the pattern continued. The one-room schoolhouse just down the lane from where we lived had been closed down only a few years before, so the few local children attended a school in a small town on the banks of the Hudson. Its main industry, hardly thriving, was brick making from the river's clay deposits. As in Minersville, most of the families were Irish, Italian, Blacks, southern Whites, a few East Europeans, plus a cluster of Presbyterians and Methodists living in stately older houses up on the hill. I soon found the equivalent of my old peer group from working-class families, and it was with them that I spent most of my day (it was a 5-mile walk home for lunch). For me, they were a source not only of needed information but also of adventure and acceptance. It was not until many years later that I realized they were also something more: My American identity was mainly that of the American peer group.

That, too, was a world I thought I was leaving behind when I departed for Cornell, but in fact, I took it along with me, just as I had my family.

---

[1] In retrospect, I recognize that in this process of social learning, I had unconsciously developed a strategy to avoid mistakes of interpretation, both for myself and for my parents; namely, I would check the validity of my new knowledge or understanding against the perceptions of my peers. It is a strategy that has stayed with me in my scientific work. Repeatedly, I impose on colleagues, asking them to criticize early and successive drafts before submitting any manuscript for publication. Hence, the typically lengthy acknowledgments. Already, here is one point on the side of the life course hypothesis, though we are barely into the first quarter of the inquiry.

As I see it now—and as I shall endeavor to show the reader—both of those worlds, family and peers, were to shape my subsequent life course, not only in my personal life but also in my work as a researcher, theorist, and teacher in developmental science.

When I arrived at Cornell in the mid-1930s, the psychology department had a distinguished faculty, but its most renowned and influential member was a ghost. His name was Edward Bradford Titchener. Titchener had obtained his doctorate with Wilhelm Wundt, acknowledged as the father of experimental psychology. It was Titchener who, at Cornell around the turn of the century, detached psychology from philosophy and philosophers and established it as a laboratory science.

I wish I could take the time to tell you what it was like to be a psychology major at Cornell in those days. In the first year or two, we had to repeat Titchener's experiments (most of them based on Wundt) and get the same results. Until you did, you had to do them over. I did not, and I did. In the process, I learned three things about my chosen field. First, psychologists, like other scientists, measured, observed, and did experiments—especially the last. Second, psychology was psychophysics. Mind–body was not just a philosophical problem; it was a psychological reality. Third, there was not just one psychology, but half a dozen or more—separate chapters, and even separate books, on sensation, perception, thinking, emotion, motivation, comparative physiology—in short, it was the faculty psychology of an earlier era—something like what we are experiencing today, but also different. I will reflect on that in due course.

Then, in my sophomore year, I discovered that there were other psychologists at Cornell. They were the descendants of those whom Titchener had banished from the department because they did not meet his strict definition of the science. I experienced a feeling of nostalgic déjà vu when I was told, on inquiry, that two of them were Gestaltists. The first, Robert M. Ogden, had earned his degree with Külpe at Würzburg. The second, Frank S. Freeman, after obtaining his PhD at Harvard, had gone on to work with Kurt Lewin in Berlin. Ogden, later joined by Freeman, had written the first American psychology textbook based on Gestalt theory and research (Ogden, 1926; Ogden & Freeman, 1932). I found the notion that psychological processes should be thought of in terms of evolving configurations and patterns elusive but intriguing.

There was more intrigue to come. In the spring, I enrolled in Freeman's course on the psychology of individual differences, based on the book of the same name that he had published the year before (Freeman, 1934). To me, the course and the book were a pivotal experience. Suddenly, the field of psychology began to come together. In the book (and in the corresponding course discussions), there were no separate chapters on the various psychological faculties. Instead, after a historical introduction, the author turned to his main concern: a critical review of research evidence regarding the forces through which individual differences were produced, sustained, or altered through the life course. In each chapter, genetics and environment were there together.

I had not heard or read anything like this in my courses in Morrill Hall, where the science of psychology proudly reigned and with which I took pride in identifying. But there was something that troubled me even more: In Freeman's (1934) book, there were a lot of measurements (he was the senior author of a text on psychological testing) but practically no experiments. Back then, for me, a psychology without experiments was missing a vital link (and, for me today, it still is). But Freeman's book did have a lot of something else: what I later called "experiments by nature," rather than contrived by an experimenter. What is more, such experiments also met my father's definition of science. Back when I was a high school student, he once said to me (as always, it was in Russian), "Little one, there are many ways of knowing; science is just one of them. There's philosophy, religion, literature—you can gain knowledge from all of them. What distinguishes science from all of the others is analyzing observations in such a way that you can prove yourself wrong." In short, science is proof by disproof.

After taking Freeman's course, I put my two psychological worlds together by deciding that in my chosen discipline, I needed both. So, in the next semester, I took a reading course with Freeman. His first assignment was characteristic. He handed me his copy of the recently published first edition of the *Handbook of Child Psychology* (Murchison, 1931). I was to compare and contrast three chapters in the volume and give him a written report. The three he had picked for me to integrate were by Jean Piaget, Anna Freud (summarizing her father's theory), and Kurt Lewin. This time I had 3 weeks.

From Cornell, Freeman sent me on to Harvard to do graduate work with his own mentor, Walter Fenno Dearborn, whose 1928 book on intelligence was years ahead of its time, and in some ways still is. But one learned much more than that from Dearborn, sometimes a whole lesson in a single sentence: "Bronfenbrenner, if you want to understand something, try to change it."

It was from Dearborn that I learned the most important role of experiments in science: not to verify hypotheses, but to discover new ones, by proving yourself wrong. It was at Harvard, too, in a graduate seminar, that I first encountered Clark Hull's logicodeductive theory of learning and the elegant experiments generated by the theory that were carried out by Hull and his associates. That seminar brought home yet another lesson about my chosen discipline. Psychologists not only did experiments, they also thought—rigorously and systematically—both before and after each experiment.

A year later, as a doctoral student at the University of Michigan, I attended a symposium on learning theory at the meetings of the Midwest Psychological Association, in which Hull and several of his colleagues participated. They forced me to think again. And it was only then I realized that learning theory filled what for me had been a frustrating gap in a paper of Lewin's that I had regarded as a classic: his 1931 article entitled "The Conflict Between Aristotelian and Galileian Modes of Thought in Contemporary Psychology." In that seminal paper, Lewin drew what he regarded as a fundamental distinction between two kinds of scientific paradigms. The first he referred to as *Aristotelian* or *class-theoretical*. In such formulations, phenomena are explained by the categories to which they are assigned, as with Aristotle's four elements (earth, air, fire, and water). In opposition to such static concepts, Lewin argued for *Galileian* or field-theoretical paradigms that specified the particular processes through which the observed phenomenon was brought about. Scientific progress in a given field, Lewin argued, required moving from the former to the latter. Physics was an example of a discipline that had achieved that goal; it was time for psychology to do the same.

I found it a compelling argument. The only problem was that Lewin never gave any concrete illustrations of what a process might look like in the field of psychology. For me, learning theory, and its operational models, provided a first example, namely, Hull's mechanism of contingent reinforcement. It was a process through which psychological behaviors and characteristics could be induced, sustained, weakened, or extinguished.

As a doctoral student at the University of Michigan, I, too, received some contingent reinforcement. There—by location, by concept, and by execution—psychology was defined as a natural science. My now chosen specialty of child development was called *genetic psychology*, and in one of the many "rat labs" in the Natural Science Building, Norman R. F. Maier was conducting experimental simulations of Nazi society.

Even more consequentially, Freeman's initial push toward mastery of statistical designs led to a minor in mathematical statistics in Michigan's superb mathematics department. There we learned, at our peril, that tests of Type I error cannot be used as tests of Type II error. Or, to give the principle its operational definition: Any graduate student who so much as intimated that a finding should be dismissed from scientific consideration because it was not statistically significant was in for big trouble. We were also warned repeatedly against the fuzziness of correlation coefficients, whose magnitude could vary substantially as a function of the standard deviation of either the independent or the dependent variable. Increase the former, and the correlation will become larger; raise the latter, and it will drop. As a corrective, always look at slopes. But beware, because the line of best fit is usually not straight but a curve, especially if one is studying living organisms.

As you can see, the intellectual environment I encountered during my years of formal training included elements not only of theory but also of research design. And with that addition, almost all of the key pieces that were to form the foundation for my own future work were already in place. From my perspective as a participant observer, it was also a turning point. The day after I completed my final examination for the doctoral degree, I received a postdoc: I was inducted into the U.S. Army as a private. From PhD to pvt in 24 hours!

What I did not know at the time was that my real doctoral training was about to begin. But before I turn to that story, I need to fill in some gaps in the preceding picture that, in retrospect, had much to do with what followed. The first was the steady exchange of letters between me and my father during my university years. Every new idea, whether of substance or of method, got discussed in both directions. Because he was in the sanitarium, with time on his hands, more of the letters were from him than from me. But his mind was agile as ever, and as before, he used it mainly to pose questions, asking me to consider alternative views to those I had encountered or expressed. My responses, however, were not confined to my letters to him, but were also expressed in exchanges with those in the second of my two worlds: classmates and friends. These were still a prominent part of my life but had now changed in character. For the first time, I was able to share with my peers the scientific, literary, and cultural interests around which my family life had been centered. The need for adventure, acceptance, and identity had discovered new ground for sustenance.

This new fusion also found expression in my first research publication, based on my doctoral dissertation. It was a study, combining both statistical and ethnographic techniques, of the development of young children's peer groups and friendship patterns (Bronfenbrenner, 1945). At the time, I had no way of knowing that at least one paragraph in the thesis foreshadowed my theoretical work. But many decades later, Robert B. Cairns confounded an audience of developmental researchers by projecting on the screen the following passage and then challenged those present to identify both its date and its author:

> In sum, the proper evaluation of social status and structure requires the envisagement both of the individual and the group as developing units. Piecemeal analysis, fixed in time and space, of isolated aspects is insufficient and even misleading, for the elements of social status and structure are interdependent, organized into complex patterns, and subject both to random and lawful variation.

No one in the audience came anywhere close to guessing the date, let alone the author's name—not even the author himself. The passage was from a journal article based on what was to become the first part of my doctoral dissertation. The article had been published in 1944 (Bronfenbrenner, 1944, p. 75). This and other excerpts are cited in chapter 12 in this volume by Robert and Beverley Cairns, entitled "Social Ecology Over Time and Space," in which, *inter alia*, they trace the origins of my theoretical ideas. I cannot deny the authorship of the excerpts cited, but I certainly did not recognize their implications at the time. The fact that Cairns was able to do so is more a tribute to his scientific prescience than to my own. His account also provides independent evidence for a gradual evolution of scientific ideas as yet unrecognized by the investigator himself.

FROM THE PAST TOWARD THE PRESENT

World War II transformed psychological science. It did so by placing psychologists and other behavioral and social scientists in positions in which they had to confront unfamiliar and highly complex practical problems, often extending beyond the bounds of the discipline in which they had been trained. Indeed, exploiting the climate of that time, not a few actively sought, found, and even created such opportunities. In short, consistent with today's theory and research in this domain, they were able to shape their own life course (Clausen, 1986; Elder, 1985).

In this respect, I was one of the lucky ones. Over a series of diverse military assignments, I had the privilege of working with some of the leading figures in American behavioral and social science.[2] As a result, after

---

[2]Particularly influential for my own later theoretical and empirical work were Kurt Lewin and Edward C. Tolman (the brilliant experimentalist and author of the classic book, *Purposive Behavior in Animals and Men*, 1932). We first came to know each other when I was assigned to the junior staff of Station S, a unit of the Office of Strategic Services (OSS; now the Central Intelligence Agency) responsible for the psychological assessment of volunteer candidates for classified overseas missions, including espionage. Besides psychologists, members of the staff, in and out of uniform, included outstanding psychiatrists (Henry A. Murray and David M. Levy), sociologists (Theodore M. Newcomb), and anthropologists (Junius Hanks). After work, Lewin and Tolman, who were close friends, stayed up late into the night waging heated arguments about psychological theory and the design of critical experiments, interrupted by impromptu sessions of song and dance. Lewin knew more songs in more languages than anyone I have ever met (with the possible exception of my mother), and Tolman, who was the oldest member of the group, improvised accompanying dance movements with a wild abandon that would have put a teenager to shame. With due respect to the fine teachers I had during my university years (of whom Ted Newcomb was one), it was during World War II at the OSS Assessment Center that I truly received my doctoral training in psychology and related fields.

the war, I had my choice of several attractive university positions. But against the advice of some of my distinguished recommenders, after 2 years at the University of Michigan, I returned to Cornell to accept a joint appointment: One-quarter time in psychology and three-quarters time in what was then still the New York State College of Home Economics. The reason: I had already decided that my main scientific interest was in the forces and conditions shaping human development in the actual settings in which human beings lived their lives.[3]

From the perspective of the theoretical framework that I was to introduce more than 40 years later, the decision represented an "ecological transition" in my own scientific development. Although I remained identified with the root discipline in which I had been trained, I had also moved beyond it. At first glance, the nature of this expansion appears to be reflected only in empirical work.[4] A retrospective review of its content reveals a systematic effort simply to identify real life conditions and forces that are statistically associated with particular kinds of developmental outcomes. The analyses are not conducted within the framework of any explicit general theoretical model, or even of specific hypotheses about particular necessary or sufficient conditions. Rather, the overall purpose of the studies in this initial phase was to identify the empirical relationships that merited the formulation of hypotheses of scientific interest. It is this strategy that explains the long refractory period between the announcement of the endeavor and any delivery on its promised theoretical product.

But what forces determine the selection of the particular empirical relationships to be examined for their hypothesis-generating potential? If the general thesis under consideration in this chapter is indeed valid, then the answer to that question, too, should be sought and found in my own personal history.

It was only by accident that I was able to discover that connection, for

---

[3]Although I knew that this was also the college that had given Kurt Lewin his first faculty position in the United States, I doubt that this had any significant weight on my decision.

[4]Indeed, as late as the 1960s, my longtime colleague and friend Professor Kurt Lüscher (then at the University of Bern and now at the University of Konstanz) commented wryly, "The only models I see in your work are experimental and control groups and analysis of variance."

I had been looking for it in the wrong place, namely, in my research publications. But working late one evening, I happened to notice, on a high shelf of older books, two with my name on them that I had forgotten about. They were successive editions of a book of readings I had prepared for the introductory course in human development that I had taught regularly for most of my academic career. Although I am mainly known as a developmental researcher (with a corollary interest in the reciprocal relation between basic science and social policy), I have throughout my career devoted an equal measure of energy and time to teaching. Moreover, irrespective of whether the course is a small seminar or a class of several hundred, my strategy has always been the same: to ask questions, beginning at what I judge to be the upper limit of where students' level of understanding at the given stage of their learning might be (i.e., Vygotsky's, 1990, "zone of proximal development"). If there is no response, I give a hint, and then another, until an answer comes. For example, I present the results of a study and ask students to suggest what the underlying hypothesis (or hypotheses) might be.[5]

In my experience, once students learn the rules of the game, most can and do play it reasonably well. Even those who do not volunteer nevertheless pay close attention, play their cards silently, but then, after the fact, reveal their bet in visible (and sometimes audible) expressions of success or disappointment. (The same also holds for me when, as not infrequently happens, a perceptive student "tags me out at first" or—even worse—just before I'm about to cross home plate.)

What has all this to do with theory development? In my case, it turns out to provide a crucial missing link. Although my empirically oriented Socratic teaching method may have some propaedeutic advantages, it takes a great deal of preparation time. One has to know the material under discussion thoroughly and be ready with appropriate responses to a range of legitimate alternative hypotheses that motivated students can generate. Surrounding me as I write here in my study are some 20 file drawers con-

---

[5]As the reader will recognize, I had learned the strategy long before I read Vygotsky. It was during those walks with my father, where he combined the Socratic method with Aristotle's focus on the realities of nature.

taining my play-by-play teaching notes on the studies I have been presenting as bases for discussion in the courses I have taught over the past
four decades.

I have been looking through those notes, and what do I find? Already
in the late 1950s and early 1960s, one can see clearly the precursors of the
constructs and hypotheses that were to become the core of the ecological
model that was first formally presented in the late 1970s and early 1980s. In
sum, the same forces, whatever they were, that had shaped my work as a developmental scientist had also motivated and directed my activities as a
teacher in such a way that the two domains became inextricably intertwined.

FROM INDIVIDUAL LIFE COURSE TO
SCIENTIFIC LIFE COURSE

The necessary data are now at hand to address the general thesis under
consideration in this chapter—namely, to explore whether the roots of my
work as a developmental theorist, researcher, and teacher can be detected
in my own personal developmental history. Note the infinitive used; it is
not *to test*, or even *to investigate*, but only *to explore*. The choice of the verb
is deliberate because, from the perspective of research design, we have a
somewhat limiting case: a sample size of 1. I say "somewhat" because nevertheless something can be learned, namely, whether the general hypothesis is at all worth pursuing.

Before proceeding, it is important to recognize that science operates
in two modes. One is the mode of discovery; the other, the mode of ver-
ification. The first is the more important but carries a far greater risk of
failure.

With that unwelcome possibility well in view, I turn to the second and
more critical stage of the task I have undertaken. I begin with the first formal definition of the ecological model of human development, published
in 1979:

> The ecology of human development involves the scientific study of
> the progressive mutual accommodation between an active, growing
> human being and the changing properties of the immediate settings

in which the developing person lives, as this process is affected by relations between these settings, and by the larger contexts in which the settings are embedded. (Bronfenbrenner, 1979, p. 21)

One has but to look at any one of the preceding pages to recognize that in my own life course, I experienced far more than my share of exposure to "changing properties of the immediate settings" in which I lived, "relations between settings" that were quite diverse, and even greater contrasts between the "larger contexts" in which the settings were embedded. What happened in the first systematic exposition of the ecological model was that these hierarchical, nested structures constituting the environment merely received scientific-sounding names—*micro-, meso- exo-,* and *macrosystems*—the common suffix underscoring that all of them operated as systems both within themselves and in relation to each other. Indeed, virtually the entire 1979 book was devoted to a more detailed description of the structure and function of these systems and their interrelationships, and of ways to investigate specific hypotheses about these functions and relationships in the context of rigorous "experiments by nature and design" (the book's subtitle).

With respect to the life course source of this dual definition of scientific method, I need only to allude to the walks in the woods with my father, the hours spent by his side in the laboratory, his role as a Socratic mentor, and Dearborn's characteristically succinct injunction: "Bronfenbrenner, if you want to understand something, try to change it."

There were some other key elements in the 1979 book. One was the concept of *ecological transition,* defined as occurring "whenever the person's position in the ecological environment is altered as the result of a change in role, setting, or both" (Bronfenbrenner, 1979, p. 26). Once again, I certainly had more than my share of "both," at least during my formative years. But note that no mention was made of transitions occurring as the result of a change in the characteristics of the developing person. That was still to come.

Another core concept was *reciprocal activity,* originally borrowed from Vygotsky (1990). Its role in development was defined in the following hypothesis, which also invokes an element from a different psychological domain, that of *emotional relationship*, a concept primarily of Freudian origin:

> Learning and development are facilitated by the participation of the developing person in progressively more complex patterns of reciprocal activity with someone with whom that person has developed a strong and enduring emotional attachment, and when the balance of power gradually shifts in favor of the developing person. (Bronfenbrenner, 1979, p. 60)

Once again, there is no need to document the case for the high salience of all of these elements in my own life course experience. At the same time, the formulation imposes an unstated limit on the sphere in which developmentally fostering activities can operate. Activities are confined by default to the domain of interpersonal interaction, a restriction never imposed in the theoretical formulation of the construct by Vygotsky and his disciples (Leontiev, 1959; Vygotsky, 1990). Recognition of this unwarranted limitation in my own work was still to come.

Finally, one other distinctive feature of the original ecological model merits attention. Its importance is telegraphed by the repeated references to "Leontiev's Law": the distinguished Russian psychologist's statement contrasting the principal focus of Vygotskian developmental theory with that of developmental psychology in the United States.

> It seems to me that American researchers are constantly seeking to explain how the child came to be what he is; we in the U.S.S.R. are trying to discover not how the child came to be what he is, but how he can become what he not yet is. (Bronfenbrenner, 1979, p. 40) The principle becomes operationalized as a transforming experiment, formally defined as follows:
>
> > A transforming experiment involves the systematic alteration and restructuring of existing ecological systems in ways that challenge the forms of social organization, belief systems, and life styles prevailing in a particular culture or subculture. (Bronfenbrenner, 1979, p. 41)

In my own work, this principle was reflected in a strong emphasis on the importance of social change, not only as a key to understanding the origins of contemporary patterns of development, but even more as an imperative for social policy and action (e.g., Head Start). In the scientific realm, the source of this emphasis lies more with Kurt Lewin and his concept of *action research* (Lewin, 1948) than with the more abstract formulations of the Vygotsky school.

But where are the roots of this commitment to action in my personal life course? For me, one answer stands out clearly: For my parents, and for myself as well, the American Dream was an American reality. The sense of gratitude that we all felt was periodically rekindled by the stories told by my parents and others of how terrifying life had been for family and friends both before and after the Revolution, compared with the acceptance and security that we enjoyed in the United States. From early on, I felt I owed my country a personal debt. Those feelings were reinforced when I first went to the Soviet Union as a visiting scientist in the early 1960s, and it was after my return home that I first became active on issues of child and family policy in the United States.

THE THESIS CHALLENGED: SOME QUALIFYING COROLLARIES

Thus far, it would appear that the general thesis of thematic links between personal and scientific life course finds substantial support for this particular sample size of 1, and—I hasten to add—in a particularly well-matched field of inquiry, namely, developmental science. How likely is it that, ultimately, the thesis will be shown to apply to other researchers in the same field, let alone in other disciplines? Or is the thesis specific, even across disciplines, to particular stages of the scientific process, such as the construction of theoretical models for science in the discovery mode? Or— the most sobering and perhaps most likely of all—is the documented relationship, in this instance, the product of one investigator's selective memories, accompanied by a too fertile imagination?

Alas, none of the data that I have presented can speak to these questions. But I can report some further information that qualifies the original thesis even for this single case. The qualification arises from the fact that the exploratory trial of the thesis is not yet over. Only a few years after the *Ecology of Human Development* was published, I consciously and deliberately altered my scientific course. I use the word *altered* advisedly, for the change did not involve a departure from the original goal. Rather, it was a corrective recommitment that has already resulted in some new theoretical formulations and research findings. But will I be able to show, with equal face validity, that this reorientation, too, has its roots in my personal life experience?

I turn first to the nature of the scientific shift. It was in the early 1980s, at a symposium on contemporary theories of human development, that I myself first called the ecological model into question for failing to fulfill not only its own stated purpose but also that of psychological science as a whole. The symposium presentation was subsequently published. Here are some excerpts:

> One might think that I have good reason to rest content. Studies of children and adults in real-life settings are now common-place in the research literature on human development. . . . Clearly, if one regards such scientific developments as desirable, there are grounds for satisfaction. Yet, along with feelings of gratification, I must confess to some discontent. . . . It is an instance of what might be called "the failure of success." For some years, I harangued my colleagues for avoiding the study of development in real-life settings. No longer able to complain on that score, I have found a new *bête noir*. In place of too much research on development "out of context," we now have a surfeit of studies on "context without development." (Bronfenbrenner, 1986, pp. 287–288)

I then went on to acknowledge some responsibility for this wayward course:

> Anyone who takes the trouble to examine my 1979 monograph will discover . . . that it has much more to say about the nature and developmental contribution of the environment than of the organism

616

itself. Moreover, this was the result of a deliberate decision; in the preface to that volume, I expressed "the conviction that further advance in the scientific understanding of the basic intrapsychic and interpersonal processes of human development" (p. 12) must wait upon the formulation and implementation of a more differentiated and dynamic conception of the environment. I then, with some reluctance, undertook what I regarded as the necessary prior task, deferring—for the time being—my primary interest in the psychological development of the individual. (Bronfenbrenner, 1989, pp. 188–189)

It is this primary interest that has been the lodestar of my scientific and scholarly work for the past decade. Viewed as a whole, the new task called for a further explication and specification of the original theoretical model, so that it went beyond the sphere of development in context to incorporate domains and component elements previously present only in abstract form, or completely absent. Some parts of this task are already accomplished and appear in print, others are in press, and others are still in process. All of these developments are summarized and discussed in the chapter that follows.

However, before the chapter ends, I feel obligated to prepare the reader for a qualified conclusion. Thus far, each newly evolving domain in my theoretical work has had its recognizable precursors in the distinctive patterns of my own personal life course. Will the past continue to prefigure the future? The answer to that question turns out to be both yes and no. Although the next chapter presents a number of new concepts, hypotheses, and even research findings, all of these "innovations" fall well within the scope of the already documented principal domains traversed on my personal life journey. If one is willing to generalize from a single case, it would appear that the past may set the stage for theoretical work, but, eventually, the play takes on a life of its own. More concretely, if the individual life course can set the course for theoretical development in science, it is primarily in the *discovery mode*, that is, in defining the general scope, structure, and direction of the theoretical pursuit. Thereafter, science follows its own rigorous deductive and inductive logic.

It is a testable hypothesis. Whether it should have priority in future research depends on its significance within the broader, newly evolving theoretical context in which the present hypothesis now stands. It is this emergent paradigm that is the focus of the chapter that follows.

REFERENCES

Bronfenbrenner, U. (1944). A constant frame of reference for sociometric research: Part II. Experiment and inference. *Sociometry, 7*, 40–75.

Bronfenbrenner, U. (1945). *The measurement of sociometric status, structure, and development.* New York: Beacon House.

Bronfenbrenner, U. (1979). *The ecology of human development: Experiments by nature and design.* Cambridge, MA: Harvard University Press.

Bronfenbrenner, U. (1986). Recent advances in the research on human development. In R. K. Silbereisen, K. Eyferth, & G. Rudinger (Eds.), *Development as action in context: Problem behavior and normal youth development* (pp. 287–289). Heidelberg, Germany: Springer-Verlag.

Bronfenbrenner, U. (1989). Ecological systems theory. In R. Vasta (Ed.), *Six theories of child development: Revised formulations and current issues* (pp. 185–246). Greenwich, CT: JAI Press.

Clausen, J. A. (1986). *The life course.* Englewood Cliffs, NJ: Prentice Hall.

Dearborn, W. F. (1928). *Intelligence tests: Their significance for science and society.* Boston: Houghton Mifflin.

Elder, G. H., Jr. (1985). *Life course dynamics.* Ithaca, NY: Cornell University Press.

Freeman, F. S. (1934). *Individual differences.* New York: Holt.

Leontiev, A. N. (1959). *Problemi razvitiya psikhiki [Problems in the development of the psyche].* Moscow: Academy of Pedagogical Sciences RSFSR.

Lewin, K. (1931). The conflict between Aristotelian and Galileian modes of thought in contemporary psychology. *Journal of Genetic Psychology, 5*, 141–177.

Lewin, K. (1948). *Resolving social conflicts.* New York: Harper.

Murchison, C. (Ed.). (1931). *Handbook of child psychology.* Worcester, MA:

Ogden, R. M. (1926). *Psychology and education.* New York: Harcourt, Brace.

Ogden, R. M., & Freeman, F. S. (1932). *Psychology and education* (Rev. ed.). New York: Harcourt, Brace.

Tolman, E. C. (1932). *Purposive behavior in animals and men.* New York: Century.

Vygotsky, L. S. (1990). *Mind in society: The development of higher psychological processes.* Cambridge, MA: Harvard University Press.

19

Developmental Ecology Through Space and Time: A Future Perspective

Urie Bronfenbrenner

The contributions to this volume are primarily accounts of research in process and prospect rather than retrospective reviews. Taking the cue from my colleagues, in this final chapter, instead of following the easier and safer path of recapitulating recent theoretical and empirical work (Bronfenbrenner, 1992b, 1993a, 1993b, 1994, Bronfenbrenner & Ceci, 1994), I choose the riskier course of proposing as yet untried theoretical and operational models for exploring less familiar terrain. The choice rests in the belief, or at least the hope, that these models will yield scientific insights and information untapped by today's more established modes of conceptualization and analysis. This more uncertain undertaking is prompted not only by the substance of the preceding contributions but also by the creative spirit of the symposium at which they were first presented.

It is, of course, characteristic of venturesome endeavors that as they proceed they build up feelings of suspense, ultimately to be relieved at the adventure's outcome. The reader should be warned in advance, however, that although I do everything in my power to maximize the former, there is no hope for relief of suspense in the immediate future. The proposed research designs, though doable, will remain undone. At least within the covers of this volume, there will be no denouement.

By now, my not-so-subtle intent is surely all too clear. I am counting on Kurt Lewin's discovery of the motivating power of uncompleted tasks to impel others to seek closure at some future time, in particular younger colleagues whose access to that inevitably limited resource is now ever greater than my own.

There is yet another qualification. Although the models I am proposing are indeed as yet "untried," strictly speaking, they are not new in the sense of previously unformulated constructs. Rather, they represent an integration, within each projected research design, of conceptual elements successively introduced into ecological systems theory since its initial formulation in the 1970s (see References). Accordingly, before presenting concrete examples of models for investigating particular research domains, it becomes necessary to summarize for the reader the basic elements of what I now refer to as a *bioecological paradigm*. The defining properties, in their most recent form, of that paradigm are specified in the following two propositions:

Proposition 1
Especially in its early phases, and to a great extent throughout the life course, human development takes place through processes of progressively more complex reciprocal interaction between an active, evolving biopsychological human organism and the persons, objects, and symbols in its immediate environment. To be effective, the interaction must occur on a fairly regular basis over extended periods of time. Such enduring forms of interaction in the immediate environment are referred to as *proximal processes*. Examples of enduring patterns of proximal process are found in parent–child and child–child activities, group or solitary play, reading, learning new skills, studying, athletic activities, and performing complex tasks.

A second defining property identifies the three-fold source of these dynamic forces.

Proposition 2

The form, power, content, and direction of the proximal processes effecting development vary systematically as a joint function of the biopsychological characteristics of the developing person; of the environment, both immediate and more remote, in which the processes are taking place; and the nature of the developmental outcomes under consideration.

Propositions 1 and 2, when expressed in the form of concrete hypotheses, are subject to empirical test. A research design that permits their simultaneous investigation in the form of specific hypotheses is referred to as a *process–person–context–time (PPCT) model.*

The main body of this chapter is devoted to a more detailed exposition of the nature of the model and its four major components. In each case, after one or more concrete research examples, most of the attention is focused on the application of the model in exploring as-yet-uncharted domains that offer promise for enhancing the scientific understanding of the conditions and forces shaping human development through the life course. The exposition is divided into five sections. The first deals with the structure of the bioecological model as an integrated system. The remaining four sections examine each of the components in greater detail, but with the primary focus on its functional role in the system as a whole.

THE BIOECOLOGICAL MODEL AS A SYSTEM

It is my hope to persuade you that, once applied, the bioecological model turns out to be scientifically productive, both theoretically and substantively. Its most distinguishing characteristic, however, is not its scientific power, but its rarity. In a search of the literature (Bronfenbrenner, 1992b; Bronfenbrenner & Ceci, 1994), I have been able to find only three or four examples, and even in these, one or another of the quadruple criteria receives only token representation. Why so? One reason is that in none of the examples I have found is the conceptual model expressly stated; rather, it remains implicit in the research design—a phenomenon I have referred to elsewhere as the "evolution of latent theoretical paradigms" (Bronfenbrenner & Crouter, 1983, p. 360). Even so, it took some time for the latent to be made manifest. Thus, the present formulation is not to be found in the original exposition of ecological systems theory (Bronfenbrenner, 1979), and when it did first see the light of day 4 years later, it appeared in truncated form as a "person–process–context model," with the critical component of "time" still missing (Bronfenbrenner & Crouter, 1983, p. 374).

The reasons for this slow, almost reluctant emergence lie deeper than the slow-wittedness of its protagonist. In this instance, they are to be found in the historical roots of the discipline in which I was trained— psychology, in its evolving dominant, and even domineering, role in research on human development; and in the concurrent fragmentation of psychology itself into a multiplicity of specialized fields, each with its own conceptual models, modes of analysis, and sets of research findings often unrelated to their counterparts in other domains of the discipline.

Countering this dissociative trend, however, is another that is both integrative and interdisciplinary in its thrust, and the ecology of human development is one of its most explicit theoretical and empirical manifestations. In principle, it draws on, and posits relationships among, concepts and hypotheses drawn from the biological, behavioral, and social sciences—ranging from behavioral genetics and neurobiology; through psychology, sociology, and cultural anthropology; to history and economics—with an organizing focus on the conditions and processes shaping human development through the life course. In practice, however, applications of the model continue to reflect the particular biases and blind spots of each researcher's root discipline (including my own). In other words, no less in developmental science than elsewhere, every investigator inherits the strengths and shortcomings of his or her own scientific socialization. Here, in my judgment, lies the principal reason for the rarity of research designs incorporating more than two of the critical elements of the PPCT model.

This obstacle can be overcome, however, by focusing attention on the potential scientific yield of the kinds of research questions that are generated by the general bioecological model and by proposing concrete research designs for investigating possible answers. That is what I undertake to do in the pages that follow. Specifically, I present a series of theoretical and operational models bearing on what I view as important challenges and opportunities in contemporary developmental science. All of them speak to a common theme, appearing in this volume's title: "linking lives with contexts." In this context, however, the term *lives* connotes more than biography; it pertains as well to living organisms whose biopsychological characteristics, both as a species and as individuals, have as much to do with their development as do the environments in which they live their lives.

In this, as in all of my theoretical work, I use a dual strategy that relies as heavily on the research findings and formulations of others as on my own ideas. The approach involves a series of progressively integrative, deductive–inductive iterations that begin with a conceptual formulation, which is then checked against, and successively revised, in the light of available empirical findings. In the present instance, the initial sequence is reversed. In each case, I start with a specific empirical work (often one contained in or referred to in the present volume) and then introduce one or more additional components of the PPCT model, either to permit a more definitive test of the original hypothesis or of new, more differentiated hypotheses generated by the bioecological paradigm.

Before presenting specific conceptual and operational models that have still to confront the rigors of an empirical trial, I provide an example that illustrates what the final product might be like. Among the few such examples that exist, I chose one that I have described before (Bronfenbrenner, 1994), because it best illustrates both the nature of the model and its scientific promise.

The study was carried out more than three decades ago by Drillien (1964), a professor of child health in the medical school of the University of Edinburgh. The purpose of the investigation was to assess factors affecting the development of children of low birth weight compared with those of normal birth weight. The total sample size for the study was 164. The results, shown in Figure 1, depict the impact of the quality of mother–infant interaction at infant's age 2 on the number of observed

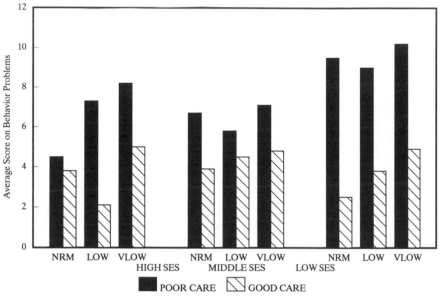

NRM = normal birth weight; LOW = between 5.5 and 4.5 lb; VLOW = 4.5 lb or less.

Figure 1

Problem behavior at age 4 by birth weight, mother's care, and social class.

problem behaviors at child's age 4, as a joint function of social class and three levels of birth weight: designated by VLBW (very low—$4^1/_2$ lb or less), LBW (low—more than $4^1/_2$ up to $5^1/_2$ lb), and normal (NRM—over $5^1/_2$ lb). As can be seen, in keeping with Proposition 1, a proximal process, in this case mother–infant interaction across time, emerges as an especially powerful predictor of developmental outcome. In all instances, good maternal treatment appears to reduce substantially the degree of behavioral disturbance exhibited by the child. Furthermore, as stipulated in Proposition 2, the power of the process varies systematically as a function of the environmental context (i.e., social class) and of the characteristics of the person (i.e., weight at birth). Note also that the proximal process has the general effect of reducing or buffering against environmental differences in developmental outcome; specifically, under high levels of mother–child interaction, social class differences in problem behavior become much smaller.

Unfortunately, from the perspective of ecological systems theory (Bronfenbrenner & Ceci, 1994), the greater developmental impact of proximal processes in poorer environments is expected (and has thus far been found) only for indexes of developmental dysfunction. With respect to outcomes reflecting developmental competence (e.g., mental ability, academic achievement, and social skills), proximal processes are posited (and have thus far been found) to have greater impact in more advantaged and stable environments. Note also that the moderating effects of person and context on the proximal process of mother–infant interaction are not symmetrical. For instance, whereas the process has its greatest impact in the most disadvantaged environment, within that environment it is most effective for the healthiest organisms (i.e., those of normal birth weight). By contrast, in the most favored social class group, it was the low-birth-weight infants who benefited most from maternal attention.

More detailed analysis of the original data suggests a possible explanation for such asymmetries. For example, it turns out that, although the percentage of mothers providing quality care was much lower in the most disadvantaged environment, most of that care was focused on low-birth-weight babies. However, in more advantaged environments, where problem behaviors were neither as frequent nor as severe, maternal attention was distributed more equally; nevertheless, as can be seen in Figure 1, in contrast to the results for the lowest socioeconomic status group, the low-birth-weight infants benefited most. In short, the characteristics of the infant influence the quality of maternal care with corresponding effects on developmental outcome, but the pattern of these relationships varies systematically as a function of the quality of the environment in which the family lives.

With the foregoing example before us as a frame of reference, I turn to the task at hand. What follows is a series of proposed research designs, each representing an extension of conceptual and operational models used in studies described in this volume and elsewhere, that permit a test of specific hypotheses addressing this general issue. The examples are organized in the context of several central themes that identify the most promising directions for the application of the bioecological paradigm in future research.

PROXIMAL PROCESSES AS MECHANISMS OF DEVELOPMENT

Perhaps the most important implication of the findings shown in Figure 1 is their demonstration of the key role of the element of proximal process in a PPCT design. Without it, much invaluable information is lost not only with respect to the developmental power of proximal processes themselves, but also with regard to the ultimate effect of the characteristics both of the person and of the environment on the subsequent course and outcome of development. Because the influence of their characteristics is primarily indirect, operating through their impact on proximal processes, their effect is underestimated in models in which such processes are not included. For example, when Drillien's data are analyzed in what is called a *person–context* design (in which the process component is omitted), the results are not very informative. All they show is that both social class and birth weight have about equal, comparatively modest, and essentially additive effects, with the highest levels of problem behavior appearing for infants with the lowest birth weight in families living in the most disadvantaged environments.

What is most revealing about proximal processes, however, is not the gain in predictive power that they provide, but their substantive and theoretical significance as the mechanisms of organism–environment behavioral interaction that drive development, and the profound ways in which these mechanisms are affected by characteristics of the developing person and of the environmental context in which the interaction takes place.

As yet, however, little is known about the operation of these processes and their effects, for the simple reason that, to date, they have seldom been incorporated in the kinds of research models that are required for their investigation. The first step for remedying this situation is to formulate concrete hypotheses and corresponding analytical models. Toward that end, I offer the following examples, in which existing research studies are expanded to incorporate a process component.

Proximal Processes in Controlled Experiments

Although Drillien's research is one of the very few to demonstrate the developmental effect of proximal processes in a full PPCT model,[1] there are many more that document a significant, and often substantial, relation between various forms of parent–child interaction and subsequent developmental outcomes. All of them, however, are subject to an alternative interpretation; namely, that the observed relationship is primarily the product of genetic rather than of environmental forces. This view has been most clearly articulated and advocated in the work of Scarr and her colleagues (Scarr, 1985, 1992; Scarr & McCartney, 1983). Scarr contends that parents construct environments for their children, and children construct their own environments primarily in response to their shared inherited predispositions. This would imply that proximal processes, which are reciprocal in nature, necessarily carry a significant genetic loading. This is certainly true; the question is, to what extent? In Scarr's (1992) view, the "environment–genetics correlation [is so strong that] environments that most parents provide for their children have few *differential effects* on their offspring" (p. 3; emphasis in original).

So extreme a position is most effectively challenged by a controlled experiment designed to test her hypothesis, and such an experiment in fact exists, although it is still little known in the United States.[2] Almost two decades ago, a Dutch developmental psychologist, Riksen-Walraven (1978) carried out an intervention experiment that had as its aim "raising the responsiveness of parents and enhancing the amount of stimulation provided by them to their infants" (p. 111). The sample consisted of 100 nine-month-old infants and their mothers living in the city of Nijmegen, The Netherlands. Because previous studies had indicated that "working class parents are less responsive to their infants . . . all subjects

---

[1]For other examples, see Bronfenbrenner and Ceci (1994).

[2]I am indebted to my Cornell colleague Rick Canfield for bringing this study to my attention.

came from working class families" (Riksen-Walraven, 1978, p. 111). The mothers and their infants were randomly assigned to four groups of 25 dyads each. Mothers in what Riksen-Walraven (1978) called the "responsiveness" group were given a "workbook for parents [stressing the idea that] the infant learns most from the effects of its own behavior" (pp. 112–113). Specifically,

> Caregivers were advised not to direct the child's activities too much, but to give the child opportunity to find out things for himself, to praise him for his efforts, and to respond to his initiations of interaction. (Riksen-Walraven, 1978, p. 113)

By contrast, mothers of infants in the so-called "stimulation" group received a workbook that emphasized the importance of providing the infant with a great variety of perceptual experiences of all kinds, "to point to and name objects and persons, [and] to speak a lot to their infants" (Riksen-Walraven, 1978, p. 112).

The experimental program for the third group was a combination of materials from that of the first and second programs. Finally, a matched control group did not receive any special treatment.

Follow-up observation and testing conducted in the home 3 months later revealed, first of all, that the instructions provided to the parents on the first day of the experiment had a substantial effect. The behaviors of the mothers in the several treatment groups differed not only significantly, but markedly in accord with the orientation to which they had been exposed at the outset of the experiment. More important, infants of mothers who had been encouraged to be responsive to their baby's initiatives exhibited higher levels of exploratory behavior than any other group and were more likely to prefer a novel object to one that was already familiar. These babies also learned more quickly in a contingency task.

Note that in keeping with Proposition 1, the most successful experimental treatment engaged subjects in activities that required initiative and reciprocal interaction with their environment. Moreover, such engagement was not short-lived or ephemeral but continued on an everyday basis over a fairly extended period of time.

I went into some detail in describing this experiment because of the vistas that it opens for future research. Note, first of all, that in contrast to most intervention experiments and programs, in this instance, the successful experimental treatment was very brief (and, what is now especially relevant, also very cost-effective). It involved only a single home visit during which the staff member conducted the baseline observations and tests and then gave the mother a booklet and explained its use. The working-class mother did all the rest. As I have documented elsewhere (Bronfenbrenner, 1958, 1974, 1985), there is a modest but persuasive body of evidence that the information provided to (or sought out by) parents can change their behavior toward their children in significant ways.[3] If so, then this raises the possibility of providing parents with easily understood information about what I have called "proximal processes" and, thus, creating opportunities for conducting the much needed further research on their nature, operation, and developmental effects, not only in infancy, but also at later ages. Moreover, it would not be difficult to add this experimental component, with randomized variations, to ongoing programs of research or of health and social services.

Proximal Processes Across Generations

Most developmental studies that include proximal processes in their research design have been carried out with children and adolescents; almost none have been conducted with adults. One of the few exceptions is found in Kohn's contribution in the present volume (chapter 5). It constitutes the latest report from a remarkable research program, now extending across more than three decades (e.g., Kohn, 1969; Kohn & Slomczynski, 1990). The investigators document empirical support for a hypothesized causal chain, beginning with the social class position of their subjects in adulthood that then extends across two generations. First, they demonstrate that the adults' socioeconomic position, as reflected in their

---

[3]Especially noteworthy in this regard is Wolfenstein's (1953) study, in which she analyzes the content of successive editions of the Children's Bureau bulletin on *Infant Care* and then relates the observed changing patterns of advice to subsequent, corresponding shifts in modal patterns of child care.

employment status, affects their subsequent intellectual development and child-rearing values. They then show how these values are transmitted from one generation to the next. The crucial explanatory link turns out to be job conditions, more specifically, the extent to which the social structure of employment allows access to jobs that permit greater self-direction at work. The exercise of such self-direction (representing an example of proximal processes operating within the adult work setting) is shown to produce enhanced cognitive competence, as measured by standardized psychological tests, as well as greater self-direction in other aspects of the adult's psychological functioning. Even more striking, however, is the demonstration of corresponding changes in modes of thought, values, and attitudes about child-rearing expressed by other members of the nuclear family, including both the worker's spouse and his or her children. Finally, these same effects were shown to generalize both across gender (i.e., female workers) and culture (i.e., the findings were replicated in Poland before its subsequent transformation from socialism to capitalism).

Although, in my judgment, the work of Kohn and his colleagues represents a landmark contribution to the study both of psychological development in adulthood and of cross-generational transmission, from the perspective of a bioecological model, there are two missing links in the proposed causal chain. Both of these lie in the sphere of proximal processes, specifically, the mechanisms through which values are acquired and transmitted. In Kohn's research, the first link in this process is reasonably clear, namely, that job structures that permit and encourage worker initiatives tend to evoke corresponding behaviors within the work setting. These, in turn, generate attitudes and personality structures that place a high value on self-direction. An accompanying set of findings, equally if not more impressive, demonstrates that similar changes in value orientation occur among the workers' spouse and children, but, in these domains, the operating mechanisms are left implicit. Is it that the workers themselves begin to act in more self-directed ways at home, or that they encourage such behavior in *other* family members, or both? And to what extent does the process of generational transmission to the children operate primarily through the mother, as the authors imply? Finally, and perhaps most critically, is it the values or the behaviors that constitute the more critical carriers of cross-generational transmission?

Clearly, these questions can be answered only if the research design is expanded to include assessment of proximal processes not only as they occur in the work setting but also as manifested in the home through the interactions that take place among family members. Moreover, such expansion invites intriguing research possibilities in a still broader sphere.

Linking Beliefs to Behaviors in a PPCT Design

As I indicated elsewhere (Bronfenbrenner, 1988), the inclusion of both beliefs and corresponding behaviors in the same research design considerably enhances the explanatory power of analytic models in developmental science. For example, Tulkin (1977; Tulkin & Kagan, 1972) found that middle-class mothers were distinguished from their working-class counterparts not only by higher levels of reciprocal interaction with their infants, but also in their views about what a 10-month-old could do and about their own ability to influence their baby's development. Specifically, the more advantaged mothers attributed greater potentials both to their infants and to themselves. In addition, the correlations between maternal behavior and attitudes were substantially greater in middle-class than in lower-class families. Later, Tulkin and Covitz (1975) reassessed the same youngsters after they had entered school. The children's performance on tests of mental ability and language skills showed significant relationships to the prior measures of reciprocal mother–infant interaction. Regrettably, no information is reported on the corresponding relation between maternal beliefs and child outcomes or on the joint or interactive effects of both beliefs and proximal process as antecedent factors. Nor is social class any longer included in the design. Hypotheses based on the bioecological model predict that processes will emerge as the more powerful vector, but that the magnitude of this power will be systematically reduced or enhanced as a joint function both of the mother's beliefs about her own and her child's competence and of the family's social class status. But these hypotheses remain to be tested.[4]

From the perspective of Kohn's research, yet another relevant question arises: To what extent do proximal processes in early childhood foster the transmission of belief systems across generations? Clearly, by the time the children are in school they will have begun to develop beliefs about their own competence (or lack thereof); does prior mother–infant interaction provide the basis for the child's internalizing the mother's beliefs about his or her competence, which in turn affects the child's performance in school? A test of this hypothesis would require an additional datum, not difficult to obtain: a measure of self-concept in relation to school learning.

I mention the foregoing research possibility not only for its own sake, but also because it moves us to unexploited scientific opportunities focused around the second component of the PPCT model: the influence of the biopsychological characteristics of the person on his or her future development.

WHO DEVELOPS, WHO DOES NOT?

By and large, today's developmental science is the science of average trends. We know very little about the exceptions, and perhaps even less about the characteristics of those members of the sample to whom the findings in fact apply. Indeed, the ultimate paradox is that the more "scientific" the study, the less we are likely to discover which human beings are subject to its results. The reason for this paradox is that psychological science took physics as its model, and physics seeks to discover universal principles: those that apply to all physical phenomena across time and space. But hu-

---

[4]The number of cells in the matrix poses the problem of obtaining sufficiently large numbers of cases in each. This difficulty may be obviated to some extent by three considerations. First, if it is true, as hypothesized, that higher levels of proximal process will produce substantial changes in the value of h^2, then significant differences may emerge even among subsamples of modest size. Second, although twins represent a comparatively small fraction of the total population, other types of consanguineous contrasts (e.g., full siblings versus half or adopted siblings) are becoming much more frequent, because of the rapid changes in family structure occurring in contemporary societies (Bronfenbrenner, 1992b). Finally, the use of a controlled experiment with random assignment appreciably increases the statistical power of the design.

man beings, like all living creatures, are widely variable in their biopsychological characteristics and, as a result, are differentially susceptible to the external conditions and forces to which they are exposed during their lifetime. Of course, this does not mean that such variation is unsystematic and, hence, not amenable to scientific investigation; what it does mean is that the research models we use must take such variation into account, and not simply in the form of random error.

Thus, to discover which persons are, or are not, affected by a particular experience requires, in the first instance, the formulation of concrete hypotheses about how particular developmental effects are likely to differ for subjects exhibiting contrasting biopsychological characteristics but who have been exposed over time to similar environments and proximal processes. Translated into operational terms, this means using research designs that incorporate the second component of the PPCT, that is, systematic variation in the personal characteristics of the subjects in the sample.

Among such qualities, those currently receiving the most research attention include differences in the following domains: temperament and personality (e.g., the Big Five); neurobiological and biochemical makeup (e.g., electroencephalographic patterns and dopamine levels); indexes of cognitive functioning in infancy (e.g., habituation, attentional behavior, speed of response, activity levels, and degree of self-regulation); and from early childhood onward, measures of intelligence, academic achievement, self-concept, role expectations, self-efficacy, values, and goals.

There are, of course, many studies in which such characteristics are investigated as developmental outcomes, but comparatively few in which they are examined as sources of variation in the person's susceptibility to the developmental effects of environmental conditions and of enduring patterns of interaction between the person and his or her immediate environment (i.e., proximal processes). Furthermore, most investigations of this kind that do exist are confined to two personal characteristics of limited explanatory power: age and gender. In short, we are confronted with a largely uncharted terrain. Moreover, with so many person characteristics to choose from, on what basis does one make the final choice? Which should receive highest research priority?

The bioecological model suggests a theoretically based answer to this question. In an invited address to the Jean Piaget Society (Bronfenbrenner, 1993a), I drew a distinction between two broad types of person characteristics especially relevant in shaping the individual's future development. On the one hand, there are the familiar measures of ability, achievement, temperament, and personality typically assessed by psychological tests. All such assessments can be thought of as indexing existing psychological *resources and liabilities*. But there is another, more dynamic set of person attributes that also affect the course and character of psychological functioning and growth. These attributes share a feature incorporated in the first defining property of the bioecological paradigm; namely, they reflect a conception of the human organism as *an active agent in, and on, its environment.* This active orientation is manifested in strong dispositional proclivities to set in motion, sustain, and enhance processes of interaction between the organism and particular features of persons, objects, and symbols in its environment. I refer to such selective, dispositional orientations toward the environment as *developmentally instigative characteristics*. As I have documented elsewhere (Bronfenbrenner, 1993a; Bronfenbrenner & Ceci, 1994), such dynamic dispositions are operative from early infancy onward, evolve over the life course, and are still manifested in old age. In the newborn, such dynamic tendencies are expressed through selective response to stimuli presented in different modalities and, shortly thereafter, to variations in stimuli introduced within the same modality. Beyond infancy, initiatives become increasingly guided by evolving conceptions of the environment and the self and are expressed through differential interests, values, belief systems, and goals in relation to persons, objects, and symbols in the environment and in relation to the self.

I suggest that the proposed dichotomy between two general types of person characterisitics, biopsychological resources versus directional dispositions, provides an initial strategy of choice for analyzing how differences in psychological makeup influence the effectiveness of proximal processes and their resultant outcomes. By introducing measures of both domains in the same PPCT design and then anaylzing their joint, synergistic effect, we can obtain a more complete estimation of the contribution of the person to his or her own development. To assess the one without the other treats the developing person as devoid of either psychological substance or psychological force. I refer to PPCT designs that meet the above dual requirement as *force–resource* models.

I recognize that what the reader now expects is some concrete examples of the use of such force–resource combinations in psychological research. But, alas, to date I have not been able to find any. The best I can do is to offer a hypothetical case set within the framework of a more general research design. In that design, subjects are simultaneously stratified along the two dimensions of force and resource, for example, three levels of IQ and three levels of personal efficacy (i.e., perception of self as an active agent vs. a victim of circumstance). In this instance, the design makes it possible to test hypotheses about the extent to which personal ability and motivation can reinforce, compensate for, or undermine *each other* in shaping the course of future development.

Finally, the biopsychological characteristics of the person, in fact, play a dual role in the PPCT model; namely, they appear twice. The second time is easily overlooked because it is not included in the acronym. I refer to the developmental outcomes under investigation. The reason for their reappearance is that the developmental outcomes at one age become the person characteristics that influence the outcomes of development at a later age. However, upon their reentry on the stage in what amounts to the last act of a particular developmental drama, these characteristics are typically given a far more restricted role. Behind this metaphor lies a research reality that, in my judgment, seriously limits the scope of contemporary developmental science.

BEYOND A SCIENCE OF
SINGLE-VARIABLE OUTCOMES

One of the consequences of the progressive specialization in science in general, and in psychological science in particular, is a return to the "faculty psychology" of an earlier era. Increasingly, there are separate scientific organizations, journals, and edited volumes devoted exclusively to research in a particular area: cognition, emotion, motivation, personality, developmental psychopathology, or social behavior and development. Seldom does a published study cross a border between two, let alone more, of these domains. Yet every scholar and researcher concerned with human behavior and development will agree that the human organism functions as an integrated system, in which the various psychological domains interact with each other. One of the scientific virtues of the proposed force–resource model is that it focuses attention on the interaction between different spheres of psychological functioning and growth, both at the level of theory and of research design.

Such a model, however, has yet to be implemented. As of now, it is difficult to find an investigation in which different kinds of outcomes are assessed in combination for the same research subjects. Rarer still among these investigations are studies that include measures of proximal processes in the model. As a result, it is not known whether a proximal process operating in a given environment may, in fact, enhance psychological functioning simultaneously in several domains or have a greater effect on some outcomes than on others. Here lies yet another opportunity for articulation and integration across the disciplines and subdisciplines that can contribute to contemporary psychological science. To put the question in its most challenging form, How are we to conceptualize the psychological characteristics of the individual in a way that permits the scientific investigation of her or his interrelated and integrated structure?

I confess at the outset that my proposed suggestions to meet this challenge are quite crude, but, at least, they may open the way to more sophisticated formulations. I start from what may be a mistaken assumption, namely, that as yet we do not have a theory about how psychological characteristics of human beings are organized that is sufficiently compelling to be taken as a firm basis for generating and testing concrete hypotheses. Under these circumstances, the only alternative is to resort to the age-old first stage of all scientific endeavors: To observe and describe patterns as they occur in nature using such crude conceptual tools as may be available. My choice for this purpose is the construct I have already presented: the force–resource model. It rests on the assumption of a synergistic effect. Let us see if such an effect, in fact, emerges but at the same time make no assumptions about the precise form that the synergy may take (i.e., whether the nonadditive escalation be linear, quadratic, or otherwise).

How can that be done? Consider a specific research question: What will be the effect of the quality of parent–child interaction at age 3 on the child's subsequent levels of mental ability and of exploratory behavior assessed at age 6? The first outcome is measured by a standardized test; the second, in a controlled laboratory experiment. In terms of the force–resource distinction, mental ability is a psychological resource; exploratory behavior, an index of motivational disposition.

Here are some hypothetical results. At the younger age, three contrasting patterns emerge: (a) subjects for whom levels of ability and motivation were both high to start with, (b) those for whom motivation was higher than ability, and (c) the reverse, with ability exceeding motivation. Over the next 3 years, proximal processes had a greater effect in increasing exploratory behavior than in increasing mental ability, but the group that showed the greatest gain in intellectual functioning was the one who had the lowest mental test score to start with but showed the strongest level of motivation. Bear in mind that these are purely imaginary findings presented to illustrate the nature of the model and to fit the as-yet unfounded hypotheses that in general, proximal processes exhibit greater power in enhancing motivation than in raising the level of cognitive development, but, in the latter sphere, are especially effective with persons who had showed lower levels of intellectual functioning to start with.

We turn next to the third component of the bioecological model: the environmental contexts in which development takes place.

HOW DO ENVIRONMENTS
INFLUENCE DEVELOPMENT?

In the first systematic exposition of the ecological paradigm, the environment was conceptualized as a set of nested structures at four successively more encompassing levels, ranging from the micro to the macro (Bronfenbrenner, 1979). I do not review that exposition here, but focus instead on the more important subsequent reconceptualizations and the hypotheses and research designs that they have generated. As I have described elsewhere (Bronfenbrenner, 1993a), paradoxically, most of these innovations have emerged as a result of "the effort to conceptualize developmentally relevant characteristics of the person" (p. 15). I begin with those reformulations that pertain to the microsystem.

The Microsystem Reconceptualized

In response to the question of how the environment influences development at this immediate face-to-face level, Proposition 1, tells us where to look first. Thus, it stipulates that proximal processes, what we have called the "engines" of development, involve interaction with three features of the immediate environment: persons, objects, and symbols. To refer to *other* people in the environment (as distinguished from those whose development is under immediate consideration), we adopt Mead's (1934) term: *significant others.*

Significant Others as Environmental Influences

The same force–resource model that captures the developmentally relevant characteristics of the developing person can be applied as well to the developmentally relevant features of significant others. As I documented elsewhere (Bronfenbrenner, 1993a, 1993b), the belief systems of parents, teachers, mentors, spouses, and close friends and associates may be especially important in this regard. Depending on their dynamic content, the belief systems of such "others" can function as instigators and maintainers of reciprocal interaction with the developing person. The previously cited example of Tulkin's (1977) research is a case in point. There, the value orientations of the mother, the principal person in the young child's environment, became a potent force affecting the child's future cognitive development.

At a more general level, the application of a force–resource paradigm across the domain of both person and other generates a kind of dyadic typology for characterizing interpersonal relationships as contexts of human development susceptible to systematic investigation. A particularly promising focus of such inquiry would be the effect of different types of dyads on the nature and power of the proximal processes that take place within them and, thereby, on the kinds of developmental outcomes that they foster.

Person–Context Models in Search of Proximal Processes

One of the most promising directions for future research in the framework of a bioecological model involves expanding a fairly common type of research design that I have called a person–context model, that is, a design that examines the joint interactive effects of characteristics of both the person and the environment on the individual's development. The scientific power of such models is significantly advanced through the addition of a longitudinal component, thus expanding it into a person–context–time model. Here are some examples.

Cross-generational relationships. A number of studies showed that the quality of husband–wife relationship before the birth of the first child predicts the subsequent quality of the parent–child relationship, as well as the resulting child outcomes (Crockenberg & Smith, 1982; Moss, 1967; Moss & Robson, 1968; Robson, Pedersen, & Moss, 1969). Viewed from the perspective of a full bioecological model, such findings raise the question of what proximal processes mediate the effect of the former relationship on the latter.

A related research question arises in the sphere of adult development. Several investigations examined the effects of marital dissolution on the subsequent long-term psychological development of women, particularly in relation to the stresses arising from competing demands of family and work. Insofar as I have been able to discover, however, no comparable studies have been conducted of the long-term consequences of such separations for men, particularly those who do not establish a new, stable relationship with another partner. The question bears on the broader phenomenon of so-called "male vulnerability," that is, the general finding that males are more likely to be affected by stressful experiences than females, with the effects on subsequent development being more extreme, more lasting, and more pervasive in other aspects of life.

Environmental stability. Another extension of the original ecological model of the environment takes as its point of departure a qualifying condition specified in Proposition 1. The proposition stipulates that, to be effective, proximal processes must occur on a fairly regular basis over extended periods of time. But suppose the environment in which such processes occur is not sufficiently stable? Under such circumstances, one would expect the effectiveness of proximal processes to be reduced, with corresponding disruptive effects on psychological functioning. I have summarized elsewhere (Bronfenbrenner, 1994; Bronfenbrenner & Ceci, 1994) some indirect evidence that lends support to this expectation. It is indirect because it is incomplete. Even though it can be shown that the effectiveness of proximal processes is greater in some environmental contexts than in others (e.g., more advantaged socioeconomic levels or two-parent biological families), it is not yet clear that instability and interruptedness of the environment are the critical factors in reducing the power of the process.

The example of social class has already moved us . . .

Beyond the Microsystem

Despite the sweep of the subtitle, it turns out to be an easy task for me to identify the most promising research developments across the full range of expanding environmental systems. All I need to do is to refer the reader to Steinberg et al. (this volume, chapter 13). As indicated by their own subtitle, Steinberg et al. take the reader on "an ecological journey" that traverses every environmental domain from the micro to the macro. The design also includes a longitudinal component (across 3 years of high school), which qualifies it on all four of the defining components of a PPCT model. All that remains is for me to encourage the reader both to imagine and to ruminate on the inviting destinations that should be pursued, not only by Steinberg, but by all of us, as his journey continues into the future.

SPACE THROUGH TIME: ENVIRONMENT IN THE THIRD DIMENSION

Considerations of time and timing as they relate to features of the environment, as opposed to characteristics of the person, have only recently begun to receive systematic attention in developmental research. The principal advances in this regard have been made by sociologists working in the life course perspective (e.g., Clausen, 1986, 1993, this volume, chapter 11; Elder, 1974, 1985, this volume, chapter 4). To date, there has been no single integrated exposition of the theoretical propositions underlying this perspective. As a result, its basic tenets have to be inferred from the empirical investigations carried out by its protagonists. This is the task my colleagues and I undertook in a graduate seminar that we conducted at Cornell a year ago. The following are what we presumed to infer as the basic tenets of the "life course perspective".

Life Course Principle 1
The individual's own developmental life course is seen as embedded in and powerfully shaped by conditions and events occurring during the historical period through which the person lives.

In short, history is exploited as an experiment of nature. The corresponding research design compares groups similar in other respects who have been exposed, versus not exposed, to a particular hisorical event; for example, Elder's studies of the Great Depression (Elder, 1974); military service and actual combat in World War II, Korea, and Vietnam (Elder, 1986; Elder, Shanahan, & Clipp, 1994); the Iowa farm crisis (Conger & Elder, 1994; Elder, King, & Conger, in press); urban inequality (Elder, Eccles, Ardelt, & Lord, in press); and, Elder's most recent work, research on youth sent to the countryside during China's cultural revolution (Elder, Wu, & Jihui, 1994).

Life Course Principle 2
A major factor influencing the course and outcome of human development is the *timing* of biological and social transitions as they relate to the culturally defined age, role expectations, and opportunities occurring throughout the life course.

The corresponding research design is one that compares early versus late arrivals at a particular transition with respect to their subsequent life course. For example, Elder, Shanahan, and Clipp (1994) reanalyzed follow-up data on subjects from Terman's classic *Genetic Studies of Genius* (all subjects with very high IQs) and were able to show marked differences in subsequent adult development depending on early versus late entrance into military service during wartime. Here are some of the costs of late entry:

- A higher risk of divorce and separation.
- A work life of disappointment and loss of lifetime income.
- An accelerated decline of physical health, most notably after the age of 50.

On the opposite side:

- For many men, and especially those who entered at an early age, military service was a recasting experience. It provided a bridge to greater opportunity and an impetus for developmental growth up to the middle years.

One is reminded of Brutus's fateful choice in response to Cassius's urgings:

> There is a tide in the affairs of men
> Which, taken at the flood, leads on to fortune;
> Omitted, all the voyage of their life
> Is bound in shallows and in miseries.
> —Shakespeare, *Julius Caesar* (III, 118–222)

Life Course Principle 3
The lives of all family members are interdependent. Hence, how each family member reacts to a particular historical event or role transition affects the developmental course of the other family members, both within and across generations.

The basic research design corresponding to this principle involves examining the differential impact of historical events and role transitions on different members of the same family experiencing these same events and transitions. For example, in a study of mother–daughter dyads in the broader historical context of the societal changes in gender roles that have taken place since World War II, Moen and Erickson (this volume, chapter 6) offered the following concluding comment, on the basis of their statistical analysis of data across two generations:

> Conventional mothers embracing traditional gender roles may find themselves with daughters who are in the vanguard of the women's movement. Some mothers may even push their daughters to achieve what was impossible for themselves. The fact that mothers and daughters experience historical events and social changes from different vantage points means that their lives are differentially touched by them and that their perspectives may well diverge. (p. 180)

Environmental changes across historical time can produce significant developmental changes in either direction. On the one hand, they can disrupt the timing and duration of normative transitions during the life course, thus interrupting the sequence of learning experiences that are essential for meeting societal expectations as one gets older. On the other hand, they can offer to the person new, at once more stable and more challenging opportunities that enhance psychological growth or even reverse a previously downward course (e.g., Elder's, 1974, studies of effects of military enlistment on young men from poverty backgrounds).

In sum, historical events can alter the course of human development, in either direction, not only for individuals, but for large segments of the population.

OUT OF THE PAST, INTO THE FUTURE

The foregoing conclusion has special significance for our own times. For more than three decades, I have been citing systematic evidence suggesting a progressive decline in American society of conditions that research increasingly indicates may be critical for developing and sustaining human competence through the life course (e.g., Bronfenbrenner, 1958, 1960,

1975, 1985, 1992b; Bronfenbrenner & Neville, 1994). At the most general level, the evidence reveals growing chaos in the lives of families, in child care settings, schools, peer groups, youth programs, neighborhoods, work-places, and other everyday environments in which human beings live their lives. Such chaos, in turn, interrupts and undermines the formation and stability of relationships and activities that are essential for psychological growth. Moreover, many of the conditions leading to that chaos are the often unforeseen products of policy decisions made both in the private and in the public sector. Today, in both of these arenas, we are considering profound economic and social changes, some of which threaten to raise the degree of chaos to even higher and less psychologically tolerable levels. The most likely and earliest observed consequences of such a rise would be reflected in still higher levels of youth crime and violence, teenage pregnancy, and single parenthood, as well as in reduced school achievement, and, ultimately, a decline in the quality of our nation's human capital.

Thus, we have arrived at a point where the concerns of basic, increasingly interdisciplinary science are converging with the most critical problems we face as a nation. That convergence confronts us, both as scientists and as citizens, with new challenges and opportunities.

REFERENCES

Bronfenbrenner, U. (1958). Socialization and social class through time and space. In E. E. Maccoby, T. M. Newcomb, & E. Hartley (Eds.), *Readings in social psychology* (3rd ed., pp. 400–424). New York: Holt.

Bronfenbrenner, U. (1960). The changing American child: A speculative analysis. In *Reference papers on children and youth*, prepared for the Golden Anniversary White House Conference on Children and Youth, Washington, DC. (Reprinted 1961 in *Merrill-Palmer Quarterly, 7*, 73–84)

Bronfenbrenner, U. (1974). The origins of alienation. *Scientific American, 231*, 53–61.

Bronfenbrenner, U. (1975). Reality and research in the ecology of human development. *Proceedings of the American Philosophical Society, 119*, 439–469.

Bronfenbrenner, U. (1979). *The ecology of human development.* Cambridge, MA: Harvard University Press.

Bronfenbrenner, U. (1985). Freedom and discipline across the decades. In G. Becker

& L. Huber (Eds.), *Ordnung und Unordnung: Hartmut von Hentig* (pp. 326–339). Weinheim, Germany: Beltz Verlag.

Bronfenbrenner, U. (1988). Interacting systems in human development: Research paradigms. Present and future. In N. Bolger, A. Caspi, G. Downey, & M. Moorehouse (Eds.), *Persons in context: Developmental processes* (pp. 25–49). New York: Cambridge University Press.

Bronfenbrenner, U. (1992a). Child care in the Anglo-Saxon mode. In M. E. Lamb, K. Sternberg, C. P. Hwang, & A. G. Broberg (Eds.), *Child care in context: Cross-cultural perspectives* (pp. 281–291). Hillsdale, NJ: Erlbaum.

Bronfenbrenner, U. (1992b). Ecological systems theory. In R. Vasta (Ed.), *Six theories of child development: Revised formulations and current issues* (pp. 187–249). London: Jessica Kingsley.

Bronfenbrenner, U. (1993a). The ecology of cognitive development: Research models and fugitive findings. In R. H. Wozniak & K. Fischer (Eds.), *Development in context: Acting and thinking in specific environments* (pp. 3–44). Hillsdale, NJ: Erlbaum.

Bronfenbrenner, U. (1993b). *Generationenbeziehungen in der Ökologie menschlicher Entwicklung [Generational relationships in the ecology of human development]*. In K. L. Lüscher (Ed.), Generationenbeziehungen in postmodernnen Gesellschaften (pp. 51–74). Konstanz, Germany: University of Konstanz Press.

Bronfenbrenner, U. (1994). Ecological models of human development. In T. Husten & T. N. Postlethwaite (Eds), *International encyclopedia of education* (2nd edition pp. 3–27). Oxford, England: Pergamon Press.

Bronfenbrenner, U., & Ceci, S. J. (1994). Nature–nurture reconceptualized in developmental perspective: A bioecological model. *Psychological Review, 101,* 568–586.

Bronfenbrenner, U., & Crouter, A. C. (1983). The evolution of environmental models in developmental research. In P. H. Mussen (Series Ed.) & W. Kessen (Vol. Ed.), *Handbook of child psychology: Vol. 1. History, theory, and methods* (4th ed., pp. 357–414). New York: Wiley.

Bronfenbrenner, U., & Neville, P. R. (1994). America's children and families: An international perspective. In S. L. Kagan & B. Weissbourd (Eds.), *Putting families first* (pp. 3–27). San Francisco: Jossey-Bass.

Clausen, J. A. (1986). *The life course: A sociological perspective.* Englewood Cliffs, NJ: Prentice Hall.

Clausen, J. A. (1993). *American lives.* New York: Free Press.

Conger, D., & Elder, G. H., Jr. (1994). *Familes in troubled times.* Hawthorne, NY: Aldine de Gruyter.

Crockenberg, S. B., & Smith, P. (1982). Antecedents of mother–infant interaction and infant irritability in the first three months of life. *Infant Behavior and Development, 5,* 105–119.

Drillien, C. M. (1964). *Growth and development of the prematurely born infant.* Edinburgh, Scotland: E. & S. Livingston.

Elder, G. H., Jr. (1974). *Children of the Great Depression: Social change in life experience.* Chicago: University of Chicago Press.

Elder, G. H., Jr. (1985). Perspectives on the life course. In G. H. Elder. Jr. (Ed.), *Life course dynamics* (pp. 23–49). Ithaca, NY: Cornell University Press.

Elder, G. H., Jr. (1986). Military times and turning points in men's lives. *Developmental Psychology, 22,* 233–245.

Elder, G. H., Jr., Eccles, J. S., Ardelt, M., & Lord, S. (in press). Inner city parents under economic pressure. *Journal of Marriage and the Family.*

Elder, G. H., Jr., King, V., & Conger, D. (in press). Attachment to place and migration prospects: A developmental perspective. *Journal of Research on Adolescence.*

Elder, G. H., Jr., Shanahan, M., & Clipp, E. C. (1994). When war comes to men's lives: Life course patterns in family, work, and health. *Psychology and Aging, 9,* 5–16.

Elder, G. H., Jr., Wu, W., & Jihui, Y. (1994). *State, initiated change, and life course in Shanghai: Project report.* Chapel Hill, NC: Carolina Population Center.

Kohn, M. L. (1959). Social class and parental values. *American Journal of Sociology, 64,* 337–351.

Kohn, M. L. (1969). *Class and conformity: A study in values.* Homewood, IL: Dorsey.

Kohn, M. L., & Slomczynski, K. M. (1990). *Social structure and self-direction: A comparative analysis of United States and Poland.* Oxford, England: Basil Blackwell.

McClanahan, S., & Sandefur, G. (1944). *Growing up with a single parent.* Cambridge, MA: Harvard University Press.

Mead, G. H. (1934). *Mind, self, and society.* Chicago: University of Chicago Press.

Moss, H. A. (1967). Sex, age, and state as determinants of mother–infant interaction. *Merrill-Palmer Quarterly, 13,* 19–36.

Moss, H. A., & Robson, K. S. (1968). Maternal influences in early social visual behavior. *Child Development, 39,* 401–408.

Riksen-Walraven, J. M. (1978). Effects of caregiver behavior on habituation rate and self-efficacy in infants. *International Journal of Behavioral Development, 1,* 105–130.

Robson, K. S., Pedersen, F. A., & Moss, H. A. (1969). Developmental observations of diadic gazing in relation to the fear of strangers and social approach behavior. *Child Development, 40,* 619–627.

Scarr, S. (1985). Constructing psychology: Making facts and fables for our times. *American Psychologist, 40,* 499–512.

Scarr, S. (1992). Developmental theories for the 1990's: Development and individual differences. *Child Development, 63,* 1–19.

Scarr, S., & McCartney, K. (1983). How people make their own environments: A theory of genotype–environment effects. *Child Development, 54,* 424–435.

Tulkin, S. R. (1977). Social class differences in maternal and infant behavior. In P. H. Leiderman, A. Rosenfeld, & S. R. Tulkin (Eds.), *Culture and infancy* (pp. 495–537). New York: Academic Press.

Tulkin, S. R., & Covitz, F. E. (1975). *Mother–infant interaction and intellectual functioning at age six.* Paper presented at the meeting of the Society for Research in Child Development, Denver, CO.

Tulkin, S. R., & Kagan, J. (1972). Mother–child interaction in the first year of life. *Child Development, 43,* 31–41.

Wolfenstein, M. (1953). Trends in infant care. *American Journal of Orthopsychiatry, 23,* 120–130.

The Published Writings of Urie Bronfenbrenner

Compiled by Kurt Lüscher and Gerri Jones

BOOKS

1985

Developing character: Transmitting knowledge. Posen, IL: ARL.
(A Thanksgiving Day statement by a group of 27 Americans)

1982

Individualism en socialism: Opvoeding in Amerika en de Sovjet unie [Two worlds of childhood: U.S. and U.S.S.R.]. Deventer, The Netherlands: Van Loghum Slaterus.

1981

Sosialisaatiotutkimus [Ecological socialization research]. Espoo, Finland: Weilin & Goos.

1980

Opvaeskt og miljo: Okologisk socialisationsforsknig [Upbringing and milieu: Ecological research on socialization]. Copenhagen, Denmark: Gyldendals Paedagogiske Bibliotek.

1979

The ecology of human development: Experiments by nature and design. Cambridge, MA: Harvard University Press. (Translated into Spanish, Italian, German, Korean, Japanese, and Polish)

1976

Ökologische Sozialisationsforschung [Ecological socialization research]. Stuttgart, Germany: Ernst Klett Verlag.

1975

(Authored with 11 others). *Report of the social and behavioral development interdisciplinary cluster.* Washington, DC: President's Bio-Sciences Medical Panel.

(Edited with W. Kessen et al.). *Childhood in China.* New Haven, CT: Yale University Press.

(Edited with M. Mahoney). *Influences on human development* (2nd ed.). Hinsdale, IL: Dryden Press.

1974

Is early intervention effective? A report on longitudinal evaluations of preschool programs (Vol. 2). Washington, DC: U.S. Department of Health, Education, and Welfare, Office of Child Development.

Wie wirksam ist kompensatorische Erziehung? [Is early intervention effective?]. Stuttgart, Germany: Ernst Klett Verlag.

1972

(Edited). *Influences on human development.* Hinsdale, IL: Dryden Press.

1970

Two worlds of childhood: U.S. and U.S.S.R. New York: Russell Sage Foundation. (Published in 12 other languages)

1964

(Edited with M. Ainsworth, L. Eisenberg, J. Richmond, A. Riesen, & B. Spock). *Colloquium on maternal deprivation* (Vols. 1 & 2). New York: Excerpta Medica Foundation.

1958

(Authored with D. C. McClelland, A. L. Baldwin, & F. L. Strodbeck). *Talent and society.* Princeton, NJ: Van Nostrand.

1945

The measurement of sociometric status, structure, and development. New York: Beacon House.

ARTICLES AND CHAPTERS

In Press

The ecology of developmental processes. In W. Damon (Vol. Ed.) & R. Lerner (Series Ed.), *Handbook of child psychology: Vol. 1. Theory* (5th ed.). New York: Wiley.

Japanische Kindheit als Grundlage einer Lernkultur: Folqerungen für Forschung und Praxis [Japanese childhood as a foundation for learning: Lessons for reality and research]. In D. Elschenbroich (Ed.), *Anleitung zur Neugier. Grundlagen Japanischer Erziehung (es 1934)*. Frankfurt, Germany: Suhrkamp Verlag.

The process–person–context model in developmental research: Principles, applications, and implications. In R. Tessier, C. Bouchard, G. M. Tarabulsy, & C. Piche (Eds.), *Enfance et famille: Contextes de developement [Child and family: Contexts for development]*. Quebec City, Quebec, Canada: Les Presses de L'Université Laval.

A world for Baby XXI: Dreams and realities. In J. K. Nugent (Ed.), *The baby in the 21st century.*

1994

Ecological models of human development. In T. Husen & T. N. Postlethwaite (Eds.), *International encyclopedia of education* (2nd ed., Vol. 3, pp. 1643–1647). Oxford, England: Pergamon Press/Elsevier Science.

Foreword. In R. A. LeVine, S. LeVine, P. H. Leiderman, T. B. Brazelton, S. Dixon, A. Richman, & C. H. Keefer. *Child care and culture. Lessons from Africa* (pp. xi–xvii). Cambridge, MA: Cambridge University Press.

Jobs and psychological development: A new sociological perspective (review of M. L. Kohn & M. Slomczynski, Social stress and self direction: A comparative analysis of the United States and Poland), *Contemporary Psychology, 39*, 803–805.

A new head start for Head Start. In *Translating research into practice: Implications for serving families with young children* (pp. 1–7). Washington, DC: U.S. Department of Health and Human Services, Administration on Children, Youth and Families.

(Authored with S. J. Ceci). Nature–nurture reconceptualized: A bioecological model. *Psychological Review*, *101*, 568–586.

(Authored with S. J. Ceci). Towards a more developmental behavioral genetics. *Social Development*, *3*, 64–65.

(Authored with S. J. Ceci & J. Baker-Sennett). Cognition in and out of context: A tale of two paradigms. In M. Rutter & D. F. Hay (Eds.), *Development through life: A handbook for clinicians* (pp. 239–259). Oxford, England: Blackwell Scientific Publications.

(Authored with S. J. Ceci & J. Baker-Sennett). Psychometric and everyday intelligence: Synonyms, antonyms, and anonyms. In M. Rutter & D. Hay (Eds.), *Development through life: A handbook for clinicians* (pp. 260–283). Oxford, England: Blackwell Scientific Publications.

(Authored with P. R. Neville). America's children and families: An international perspective. In S. L. Kagan & B. Weissbourd (Eds.), *Putting families first* (pp. 3–27). San Francisco: Jossey-Bass.

(Authored with T. White). *Youth and nationhood: An international challenge*. Battle Creek, MI: International Youth Foundation.

1993

Developmental pathways to and from the urban underclass: Commentary from an ecological perspective. New York: Social Science Research Council.

Distancing theory from a distance. In R. R. Cocking & K. A. Renninger (Eds.), *The development and meaning of psychological distance* (pp. 63–77). Hillsdale, NJ: Erlbaum.

The ecology of cognitive development: Research models and fugitive findings. In R. H. Wozniak & K. Fischer (Eds.), *Scientific environments* (pp. 3–44). Hillsdale, NJ: Erlbaum (condensed version in *Zeitschrift für Sozialisationsforschung und Erziehungssoziologie, 10*, 2, 1990, 101–114; and Kognitivisen kehityksen ekologia: Tutkimusmalleja ja pakenevia toloksia, *Psykologia*, 4, 1991, 1–15).

Foreword. In T. Luster & L. Okagaki (Eds.), *Parenting: An ecological perspective* (pp. vii–ix). Hillsdale, NJ: Erlbaum.

Generationenbeziehungen in der Ökologie menschlicher Entwicklung [Intergenerational relation in an ecological perspective]. In K. Lüscher & F. Schultheis (Eds.), *Generationenbeziehungen in "postmodernen" Gesellschaften* [Intergenerational relations in "postmodern societies"] (pp. 51–74). Konstanz, Germany: University of Konstanz Press.

Living through societal chaos: Developmental risks and rescues. In *Newsletter of the International Society for the Study of Behavioural Development, 1,* 1–2.

(Authored with S. J. Ceci). Heredity, environment, and the question "How?" A new theoretical perspective for the 1990's. In R. Plomin & G. E. McClern (Eds.), *Nature, nurture, and psychology* (pp. 313–323). Washington, DC: American Psychological Association.

1992

Advisor's foreword. In L. A. Sroufe, R. C. Cooper, G. B. DeHart, & M. E. Marshall, *Child development: Its nature and course* (2nd ed.). New York: McGraw-Hill.

Child care in the Anglo-Saxon mode. In M. E. Lamb, K. J. Sternberg, C. P. Hwang, & A. G. Broberg (Eds.), *Child care in context* (pp. 281–291). Hillsdale, NJ: Erlbaum.

Ecological systems theory. In R. Vasta (Ed.), *Annals of child development. Six theories of child development: Revised formulations and current issues* (pp. 187–249). London: Jessica Kingsley. (Original work published 1989)

Espacio Lewiniano y contenido ecológico [Lewinian space and ecological content]. *Psicología Comunitaria, 1,* 3–11.

Evolution de la famille dans un monde en mutation [Evolution of the family in a changing world]. *Apprentissage et Socialisation, 15*(3), 181–193.

Foreword. In R. Myers, *The twelve who survive* (pp. xii–xvi). New York: Routledge & Kegan Paul.

Forum interview: Urie Bronfenbrenner. *Human Ecology Forum, 20,* 16–19.

Gibt es Universalien in der Kindererziehung [Are there universals in child rearing?]. *Diskurs, 1,* 51–52.

National Center for Clinical Infant Programs: Achievement and challenge. Remarks upon receiving the Dolley Madison Award. *Zero to Three, XII*(3), 31–33.

1991

"The American Parent": NCFT 1991 conference proceedings. *Television and Families*, *13*(2), 30–33.

The nurture of nature. *Behavioral and Brain Sciences*, *14*, 390–391.

Rush-hour children. *Charlotte Observer*, March 29, 1991.

What do families do? *Family Affairs*, *3*(4), 1, 3–6.

(Authored with S. J. Ceci). On the demise of everyday memory. *American Psychologist*, *46*, 27–31.

(Authored with others). Voices from the war. *Cornell Alumni News*, *94*(5), 14–25.

1990

Las ciudades son para las familias (Cities are for families). *La Ciudad Educadors* (Proceedings of the First Congress for the Educating City), pp. 221–231. Barcelona, Spain: Ajuntament de Barcelona.

Discovering what families do. In D. Blankenhorn, S. Bayme, & J. B. Elshtain (Eds.), *Rebuilding the nest* (pp. 27–38). Milwaukee, WI: Family Service America.

Ökologische Modelle in der Jugendforschung: Anspruch und Wirklichkeit. In W. Melzer, W. Ferchhoff, & G. Neubauer (Eds.), *Jugend in Israel und in der Bundesrepublik* (pp. 33–54). Munich, Germany: Juventa Verlag.

Ökologische Sozialisationsforschung [Ecological socialization research]. In L. Kreuse, C.-F. Graumann, & E.-D. Lantermann (Eds.), *Ökologische Psychologie. Ein Handbuch in Schlüsselbegriffen* (pp. 76–79). Munich, Germany: Psychologie Verlags Union.

1989

The dangers of no day care. Unpublished manuscript, Cornell University, Ithaca, NY.

The developing ecology of human development: Paradigm lost or paradigm regained. Paper presented in the Symposium on Theories of Child Development: Updates and Reformulations, biennial meeting of the Society for Research in Child Development, Kansas City, MO.

Early childhood education programs: Needs and dangers. Testimony presented at a hearing of the Subcommittee on Education and Health of the Joint Economic Committee of the House and Senate, May 1, 1989, on the subject of "The Economic and Social Benefits of Early Childhood Education" (Published as "Investing in our children," *Research*, Oct.–Nov. 1989, *9* [4], 5–8).

Ecological models for youth research. Paper prepared for presentation at the conference on Jugendforschung in Israel und in der Bundesrepublik. Sozialisationsbedingungen Jugendlicher im Kulturvergleich [Youth research in Israel and the German Federal Republic Conditions for the socialization of youth in Israel and the Federal Republic of Germany viewed in cross-cultural perspective], The University of Bielefeld, West Germany, June 26–28, 1989.

Foreword. In M. Cochran, M. Larner, D. Riley, L. Gunnarsson, & C. Henderson, Jr., *Extending families: The social networks of parents and their children* (pp. ix–xx). New York: Cambridge University Press.

Who cares for children? Invited address to UNESCO (Bilingual Publication No. 188). Paris: Unit for Co-operation with UNICEF and WFP. (Reprinted in Research and Clinical Center for Child Development, annual report, 1988–1989, No. 12. Sapporo, Japan, Hokkaido University, pp. 27–40. Also reprinted in H. Nuba, M. Searson, & D. L. Sheiman [Eds.] [1994]. *Resources for early childhood* [pp. 113–130]. New York: Garland.).

Youthful designs for research on aging: A response to Lawton's theoretical challenge. In K. W. Schaie & C. Schooler (Eds.), *Social structure and aging: Psychological processes* (pp. 85–93). Hillsdale, NJ: Erlbaum.

1988

Alternatives to a deficit model for American families and children. In A. B. Grinols, *Critical thinking. Reading and writing across in the curriculum* (pp. 218–225). Belmont, CA: Wadsworth.

Foreword. In J. A. Calhoun, *Violence, youth and a way out* (p. 1). Washington, DC: National Crime Prevention Council.

Foreword. In A. R. Pence (Ed.), *Ecological research with children and families.* New York: Teachers College Press.

Interacting systems in human development. Research paradigms: Present and future. In N. Bolger, A. Caspi, G. Downey, & M. Moorehouse (Eds.), *Persons in context. Developmental processes* (pp. 25–49). New York: Cambridge University Press.

Strengthening family systems. In E. F. Zigler & M. Frank (Eds.), *The parental leave crisis. Toward a national policy* (pp. 143–160). New Haven, CT: Yale University Press.

Urie's message: Save the child. *Cornell Alumni News*, June 12–13.

(Authored with S. J. Ceci & J. G. Baker). Prospective remembering, temporal calibration, and context. In M. M. Gruneberg, P. E. Morris, & R. N. Sykes (Eds.), *Practical aspects of memory: Current research and issues. Volume 1: Memory in everyday life* (pp. 360–365). New York: Wiley.

1987

La cambiante ecología de la infancia. Implicaciones en el terreno de la ciencia y de la acción [The changing ecology of childhood: Implications for science and action]. In A. Alvarez (Ed.), *Psicología y educación. Realizaciones y tendencias actuales en la investigación y en la práctica* (pp. 44–56). Madrid, Spain: Visor Distribuciones.

Foreword. Family support: The quiet revolution. In S. L. Kagan, D. R. Powell, B. Weissbourd, & E. F. Zigler (Eds.), *America's family support programs: Perspectives and prospects.* New Haven, CT: Yale University Press.

1986

Alienation and the four worlds of childhood. *Phi Delta Kappan, 67,* 430–436.

Dix années de recherche sur l'écologie du développement humain. In M. Crahay & D. Lafontaine (Eds.), *L'art et la science de l'enseignement* (pp. 283–302). Bruxelles: Editions Lapor.

Ecology of the family as a context for human development: Research perspectives. *Developmental Psychology, 22,* 723–742.

Foreword. In E. Greenberger & L. Steinberg, *When teenagers work: The psychological and social costs of adolescent employment* (pp. xiii–xvii). New York: Basic Books.

A generation in jeopardy: America's hidden family policy. Testimony presented at a hearing of the Senate Committee on Rules and Administration on a resolution to establish a Select Committee on Families, Youth and Children, Washington, DC, July 23, 1986 (Published in *Newsletter of the Division of Developmental Psychology,* Division 7, American Psychological Association, Fall, 47–54).

Recent advances in research on the ecology of human development. In R. K. Silbereisen, K. Eyferth, & G. Rudinger (Eds.), *Development as action in context: Problem behavior and normal youth development* (pp. 287–309). New York: Springer-Verlag.

The war on poverty: Won or lost? America's children in poverty: 1959–1985. *Division of Child, Youth and Family Services Newsletter,* Division 37, American Psychological Association, *9*(3), 2–3.

(Authored with F. Kessel, W. Kessen, & S. White). Toward a critical social history of developmental psychology. *American Psychologist, 41,* 1218–1230.

1985

Contextos de crizanza del niño. Problemas y prospectiva. *Infancia Aprendizaje, 29,* 45–55.

Families and education in the U.S. and other countries. *Innovator, 16,* 3–6.

1984

The changing family in a changing world: America first? In The legacy of Nicholas Hobbs: Research on education and human development in the public interest. Part II. *Peabody Journal of Education, 61*(3), 52–70.

Continuity of values in a changing world. Commencement address, Brigham Young University, August 20, 1983. In D. Grunewald (Ed.), *"I am honored to be here today . . ."* (pp. 35–42). New York: Oceana.

The ecology of human development in mid-passage. In I. Bo (Ed.), *Barn I Milijo: Oppvekst i en utviklingsokologisk sammenheng* (pp. 36–69). Oslo, Norway: J. W. Cappelens Forlag A.S.

Foreword. In G. Eckardt, W. G. Bringmann, & L. Sprung (Eds.), *Contributions to a history of developmental psychology* (pp. 1–3). New York: Mouton.

Freedom and discipline across the decades. In G. Becker, H. Becker, & L. Huber (Eds.), *Ordnung und Unordnung. Hartmut von Hentig zum 23. September 1985* (pp. 326–339). Berlin: Beltz Verlag, Weinheim und Basel.

The graphic analysis of moderating effects. Unpublished manuscript, Cornell University, Ithaca, NY.

Kagaku to nigen no hattatsu: Katusarete iru henkaku [Science and human development: The hidden revolution]. *Jido Shinri, 38,* 155–174.

Midtveis i den menneskelige utviklings okolog. In I. Bo (Ed.), *Barn i miljo* (pp. 36–69). Sweden: J. W. Cappelens Forlag.

The mirror image in Soviet–American relations: A social psychologist's report (revised). In H. G. Shaffer (Ed.), *The Soviet system in theory and practice* (pp. 122–128). New York: Ungar.

Organism–environment interaction from an ecological perspective. Paper presented at the Symposium on Organism–Environment Interaction at the Biennial Meeting of the Society for Research in Child Development, Toronto, Ontario, Canada.

The parent/child relationship and our changing society. In L. Eugene Arnold (Ed.), *Parents, children, and change* (pp. 45–57). Lexington, MA: Heath.

Three worlds of childhood linking home, school and community. *Principal, 64*(5), 6–11 (Reprinted in B. D. Keepes [Ed.], *First years of school in perspective: Conference papers and recommendations* [pp. 35–49]. Adelaide: Education Department of South Australia).

(Authored with W. F. Alvarez & C. R. Henderson, Jr.). Working and watching: Maternal employment status and parents' perceptions of their three-year-old children. *Child Development, 55,* 1362–1378.

(Authored with S. J. Ceci). "Don't forget to take the cupcakes out of the oven": Prospective memory, strategic time-monitoring, and context. *Child Development, 56,* 152–164.

(Authored with P. Moen & J. Garbarino). Child, family and community. In R. D. Parke (Ed.), *The family: Review of child development research* (Vol. 7, pp. 283–328). Chicago: University of Chicago Press.

1983

The changing American family. *Forecast, 28*(5), pp. 45, 48.

The context of development and the development of context. In R. M. Lerner (Ed.), *Developmental psychology: Historical and philosophical perspectives* (pp. 147–184). Hillsdale, NJ: Erlbaum.

Family policy and family life: Friends or enemies? *Bulletin der Schweizer Psychologen*, Mai, 140–141.

Foreword. In G. L. Staines & J. H. Pleck, *The impact of work schedules on the family* (pp. ix–xi). Ann Arbor: The University of Michigan Survey Research Center, Institute for Social Research.

Ökologische Perspektiven zur Kinder- und Familienpolitik [Ecological perspectives on policies for children and families]. *Neue Praxis*, January 5–13.

On making human beings human. *Discovery YMCA*, *1*(12), 8–10, 26–28.

Our schools need a "curriculum for caring." *Children's Learning Project: A collection of readings.* Adelaide: Education Department of South Australia.

(Authored with A. C. Crouter). The evolution of environmental models in developmental research. In P. H. Mussen (Vol. Ed.) & W. Kessen (Series Ed.), *Handbook of child psychology: Vol. 1. History, theory, and methods* (4th ed., pp. 357–414). New York: Wiley.

(Authored with H. B. Weiss). Beyond policies without people. In E. Zigler, S. L. Kagan, & E. Klugman (Eds.), *Children, families, and government: Perspectives on American social policy* (pp. 393–414). Cambridge, England: Cambridge University Press.

1982

Child development: The hidden revolution. In *The National Research Council: Issues and studies* (pp. 41–55). Washington, DC: National Academy Press.

New images of children, families, and America. *Television and Children*, 5, 3–16.

What is an indirect effect? Unpublished manuscript.

(Authored with A. C. Crouter). Work and family through time and space. In S. B. Kamerman & C. D. Hayes (Eds.), *Families that work: Children in a changing world* (pp. 39–83). Washington, DC: National Academy Press.

1981

Children and families: 1984? *Society, 18*(2), 38–41; the *Grapevine Weekly*, October 7–13, 1980, VII(39), 6–8.

L'écologie experimentale de l'education [The experimental ecology of education]. In A. Beaudot (Ed.), *Sociologie de l'école pour une analyse des établissements scolaires* (pp. 19–50). Paris: Bordas.

Physiognomy, phrenology and other nonsense. (Review of *The mismeasure of man* by S. J. Gould). *The Washington Post*, Book World, November 8, 1981, pp. 4, 9.

Portrait of Urie Bronfenbrenner. *Options in Education*, National Public Radio.

Soziale Umweltzerstörung [Social environmental destruction]. *Neue Sammlung, 3*, 176–185.

Who cares for American children? In E. Goldberg, *How to write an essay*. Glenview, IL: Scott, Foresman.

Who is getting cut? Some unintended effects. Unpublished manuscript.

(Members of the 15th Anniversary Head Start Committee). *Head Start in the 1980's: Review and recommendations*. A report requested by the president of the United States.

1980

Intelligence in Black and White (Review of *Bias in mental testing* by A. R. Jensen). *The Washington Post*, Book World, April 20, 1980, pp. 1–2, 8–9.

On making human beings human. *Character, 2*(2), 1–7.

Recreating human ecology for families. *Human Ecology Forum, 10*(3), 32–34.

Toward improving the human ecology. *The North American Montessori Teachers Association Quarterly, 5*(3), 1–6.

U.S. families need public support. New York State Consumer News Service, Cornell University.

Who cares for America's children? In L. Rubin (Ed.), *Critical issues in educational policy: An administrators overview* (pp. 171–189). Boston: Allyn & Bacon.

(Authored with J. Garbarino). Forschung im Bereich Eltern-Kind-Beziehungen und im Zusammenhang mit der Sozialpolitik: Wer braucht Wen? [Interventions in the field of parent–child relations and this relation to social policy: Who needs whom?]. In K. A. Schneewind & T. Herrmann (Eds.), *Erziehungsstilforschung: Theorien, Methoden und Anwendung der Psychologie elterlichen Erziehungsverhaltens* (pp. 281–304). Stuttgart, Germany: Huber.

1979

Beyond the deficit model in child and family policy. *Teachers College Record, 81*, 95–104.

Class in a classless society (Review of *Stratification dynamics in social and individual development in Iceland* by S. Bjornsson & W. Edlestein). *Harvard Educational Review, 49*, 387–389.

Contexts of child rearing: Problems and prospects. *American Psychologist, 34*, 844–850.

Head Start, a retrospective view: The founders. In E. Zigler & J. Valentine (Eds.), *Project Head Start: A legacy of the War on Poverty* (pp. 32–34). New York: Free Press.

On families and schools: A conversation with Urie Bronfenbrenner. *Educational Leadership*, April, 458–463.

Our schools need a curriculum for caring. *Instructor, 7*, 34–36.

Reality and research in the ecology of human development. In D. G. Gil (Ed.), *Child abuse and violence* (pp. 230–273). New York: AMS Press.

Recreating human ecology. Address at the Symposium on Human Ecology: The Next Ten Years, Cornell University, Ithaca, NY.

Support systems for working parents: Some problems and proposals. Testimony presented to the Speakers Council on Government Reform of the New York State Assembly at a meeting held in New York City, November 7.

What shapes children: Enduring irrational involvement. *Penneys Forum*, Spring/Summer, 12.

Who cares for children? *Delta, 25* (New Zealand Education Department, Massey University, Christchurch), November 2–15.

(Authored with M. Cochran). *Social policy implications of "The comparative ecology of human development."* Unpublished manuscript.

1978

Children in America: The roots of alienation. In L. Rubin (Ed.), *Education reform for a changing society: Anticipating tomorrow's schools* (pp. 1–56). Boston: Allyn & Bacon.

The social role of the child in ecological perspective. *Zeitschrift für Soziologie, 7,* 4–20.

Who needs parent education? *Teachers College Record, 79,* 767–787. (Reprinted in H. J. Leichter [Ed.], *Families and communities as education.* New York: Teachers College Press).

(Authored with M. Cochran). Childrearing, parenthood, and the world of work. In C. Kerr & J. M. Rosow (Eds.), *Work in America: The decade ahead* (pp. 245–278). Scarsdale, NY: Work in America Institute.

(Authored with S. Nerlove, K. Blum, J. Robinson, & A. Koel). *Transcultural code of molar activities of children and caregivers in modern industrial societies.* Unpublished manuscript.

1977

Doing your own thing—Our undoing. *MD, 21*(3), 13–15.

The ecology of human development in retrospect and prospect. In H. McGurk (Ed.), *Ecological factors in human development* (pp. 275–286). The Netherlands: North Holland.

Lewinian space and ecological substance. *Journal of Social Issues, 32,* 513–531.

Nobody home: The erosion of the American family. *Psychology Today,* May, 40–47 (Reprinted in *New Dimensions in Head Start, 2*(2), 31–45).

Our system for making human beings human is breaking down. In B. Gross & R. Gross (Eds.), *The children's rights movement* (pp. 251–254). New York: Anchor Books.

The social role of the child in ecological perspective. In K. Lüscher (Ed.), *The child in contemporary society, Wolfsberg Bulletin Number One* (pp. 8–30).

Strengthening families through flexible work schedules. Testimony submitted to the Subcommittee on Employee Ethics and Utilization Committee on Post Office and Civil Service, May 26, 1977 (pp. 25–31). Washington, DC: U.S. Government Printing Office.

Toward an experimental ecology of human development. *American Psychologist, 32,* 515–531.

(Authored with A. Avgar & C. R. Henderson, Jr.). Socialization practices of parents, teachers, and peers in Israel: Kibbutz, moshav, and city. *Child Development, 48,* 1219–1227.

1976

The American family: Who cares? Human Ecology Institute, Cornell University, Ithaca, NY.

The disturbing changes in the American family. *Search, 2*(1), 4–10.

Ecological validity in research on human development. Paper presented at the 84th Annual Convention of the American Psychological Association, Washington, DC.

Ein Bezugsrahmen für ökologische Sozialisationsforschung [A frame of reference for ecological socialization research]. *Neue Sammlung, 3,* 235–249.

Epilogue. *Principal, 55*(6), 62–65.

The experimental ecology of education. *Teachers College Record, 78,* 157–204.

The family circle: A study in fragmentation. *Principal, 55*(5), 11–25.

Is early intervention effective? Facts and principles of early intervention: A summary. In A. M. Clarke & A. D. B. Clarke (Eds.), *Early experience: Myth and evidence.* London: Open Books.

Meeting the needs of families with young children: A research program. Unpublished manuscript, Cornell University, Ithaca, NY.

The next generation of Americans: An international perspective. International convocation sponsored by the Board of Foreign Scholarships, J. William Fulbright, Chair. Washington, DC: Smithsonian Institution.

Research on the effects of day care on child development. In *Towards a national policy for children and families* (pp. 117–133). Report of the Advisory Committee on Child Development, Appendix A. Washington, DC: National Academy of Sciences/National Research Council.

Who cares for America's children? In V. C. Vaughan & T. B. Brazelton (Eds.), *The family—Can it be saved?* (pp. 3–32). Chicago: Year Book Medical Publishers.

(Authored with J. Belsky & L. Steinberg). *Day care in context: An ecological perspective on research and public policy.* Review prepared for the Office of the Assistant Secretary for Planning and Evaluation, U.S. Department of Health, Education and Welfare.

(Authored with J. Belsky & L. Steinberg). *Day care research and social policy.* A report to the U.S. Department of Health, Education and Welfare, Federal Interagency Day Care Requirements Policy Committee, Washington, DC.

(Authored with J. Garbarino). The socialization of moral judgment and behavior in cross-cultural perspective. In T. Lickona (Ed.), *Morality: A handbook of moral development and behavior* (pp. 70–83). New York: Holt, Rinehart & Winston.

(Authored with S. Kav Venaki, N. Eyal, E. Kiely, & D. Caplan). The effect of Russian versus Hebrew instructions on the reaction to social pressure of Russian-born Israeli children. *Journal of Experimental Social Psychology, 12,* 70–86.

1975

Alienation and the American psychologist. *APA Monitor, 6,* 9–10.

The challenge of social change to public policy and developmental research. Paper presented at the President's Symposium on Child Development and Public Policy at the Annual Meeting of the Society for Research in Child Development.

The changing American family. Paper prepared for the National Academy of Sciences/National Research Council Advisory Committee on Child Development.

Child-watching in a Chinese classroom. *The Holy Cross Quarterly, 7,* 99–101.

Chinas Kinder. *Die Grundschule, 1,* 38–42.

The ecology of human development: A research perspective. Invited master lecture at the 83rd Annual Convention of the American Psychological Association, Chicago.

An interview with Urie Bronfenbrenner: Public policy and the survival of families. *Voice for Children, 8,* 1–4.

Nature with nurture: A reinterpretation of the evidence. In A. Montagu (Ed.), *Race and I.Q.* New York: Oxford University Press.

The next generation of Americans. Address at the Annual Meeting of the American Association of Advertising Agencies, Dorado, Puerto Rico.

Reality and research in the ecology of human development. *Proceedings of the American Philosophical Society, 119,* 439–469.

Who cares for America's children? Testimony before Joint House/Senate Hearings on the Child and Family Services Act of 1975, Cong. Rec., 1798.

(Authored with R. Shouval, S. Kav Venaki, E. C. Devereux, Jr., & E. Kiely). The anomalous reactions to social pressure of Israeli and Soviet children raised in family versus collective settings. *Journal of Personality and Social Psychology, 32,* 477–489.

1974

Developmental research, public policy, and the ecology of childhood. *Child Development, 45,* 1–5 (Also in J. M. Romanyshun [1974]. *Social science and social welfare* [pp. 159–182]. New York: Council on Social Work Education).

Examining American values. *Social Education, 38,* 154–155.

Experimental human ecology: A reorientation to theory and research on socialization. Paper presented at the 82nd Annual Convention of the American Psychological Association, New Orleans.

From another planet: Urie Bronfenbrenner on childhood in China. *Human Ecology Extra.* Ithaca, NY: New York State College of Human Ecology.

The origins of alienation. *Scientific American, 231,* 53–61 (Published version of *The roots of alienation.* Dale Richmond Memorial Lecture, American Academy of Pediatrics, Chicago, 1973).

The split-level American family. In S. Coopersmith & R. Feldman (Eds.), *The formative years: Principles of early childhood education* (pp. 73–85). San Francisco: Albion.

Television in the classroom. In P. L. Klinge (Ed.), *American education in the electric age* (pp. 158–167). Englewood Cliffs, NJ: Educational Technology Publications.

Three worlds of childhood. Ithaca, NY: Cornell University, Department of Communications Arts (film, video).

(Authored with E. C. Devereux, Jr., R. Shouval, R. R. Rodgers, S. Kav Venaki, E. Kiely, & E. Karson). Socialization practices of parents, teachers, and peers in Israel: The kibbutz versus the city. *Child Development, 45,* 269–281.

(Authored with E. H. Erickson). Examining American values: Two perspectives. *Social Education, 38,* 154.

1973

The American family is changing. *Saturday Review of Education, 32.*

Children, families and social policy: An American perspective. The family in society: Dimensions of parenthood. Report of a seminar held at the All Souls College, Oxford, England, pp. 88–104.

Families, schools, and alienation. *Scholastic Teacher,* 10–14.

Making children human. *Event, 13,* 13–16.

Open classrooms versus open schools. In T. Lickona, R. Nickse, D. Young, & J. Adams (Eds.), *Open education: Increasing alternatives for teachers and children* (pp. 53–64). Cortland, NY: Open Education Foundation.

Social ecology of human development. In F. Richardson (Ed.), *Brain and intelligence: The ecology of child development* (pp. 113–129). Hyattsville, MD: The National Education Press.

Testimony before the United States Senate Subcommittee on Children and Youth. *Congressional Record, 19*(142), (pp. 128–140). Washington, DC: U.S. Government Printing Office.

A theoretical perspective for research in human development. In H. P. Dreitzel (Ed.), *Childhood and socialization: Recent sociology, No. 5* (pp. 338–363). New York: Council on Social Work Education.

(Edited with H. Robinson, N. Robinson, M. Wolins, & J. Richmond). Early child care in the United States of America. *International Monographs on Early Child Care, 2,* 359–581.

1972

The case for genetic determinism. Paper prepared for the Advisory Committee on Child Development, National Research Council.

College students in the 1970's: Alienation vs. idealism. Unpublished manuscript. Cornell University, Ithaca, NY.

(Authored with J. Bruner). (January 31). The president and the children. *The New York Times,* 41.

1971

Another world of children. *New Society, 19,* 278–286.

Childhood: The roots of alienation. *The National Elementary Principal, LII,* 22–29.

Day Care USA: A statement of principles. *Peabody Journal of Education, 48,* 86–95.

On making human beings human. *Merrill-Palmer Institute.*

Parents: Bring up your children! *Look, 35,* 45–46.

Raising your children. *Today's Health, 50,* 36–39.

Reunification with our children. *Inequality in education, 12,* 10–20.

Statement to the Sub-Committee on Children and Youth of the United States Senate, April 26, 1971, 33–61.

Television as a constructive force in the lives of children. *Children's Programming Workshop,* ABC Television, New York.

Umwelt und Aggression [Environment and aggression]. *Neue Sammlung, 4,* 296–310.

Who cares for America's children? *Young Children, 26,* 157–163.

1970

Children and parents. Report of Forum 15, White House Conference on Children (U. Bronfenbrenner, Chair), pp. 241–255. Washington, DC: U.S. Government Printing Office.

Czynniki spoleczne w rozwoju osobowosci. *Psychologia Wychowawcza, 13,* 1–19.

The dependency drive as a factor in infant learning and development.

Schweizerische Zeitschrift für Psychologie und ihre Anwendungen. Revue Suisse de Psychologie Pure et Appliquée, 29, 218–223.

Does technology mechanize man? An experiment on live vs. televised instruction. Unpublished manuscript.

Motivational and social components in compensatory education programs— Suggested principles, practices, and research designs. Statement to the Committee on Education and Labor of the U.S. House of Representatives on Needs of Elementary and Secondary Education for the Seventies, *Congressional Record,* 53–71. Washington, DC: U.S. Government Printing Office.

Preface. English translation of A. V. Zaporozhets & D. B. Elkonin (Eds.), *The psychology of preschool children.* Cambridge, MA: MIT Press.

Reaction to social pressure from adults versus peers among Soviet day school and boarding school pupils in the perspective of an American sample. *Journal of Personality and Social Psychology, 15,* 179–189.

Statement, Hearings on the Subject of Social Security and Welfare Proposals at the Committee on Ways and Means of the U.S. House of Representatives, November 6, 1969, *Congressional Record,* 1837–1849. Washington, DC: U.S. Government Printing Office.

Some reflections on "Antecedents of optimal psychological adjustment." *Journal of Consulting and Clinical Psychology, 35,* 296–297.

Testimony on the Comprehensive Preschool Education and Child Care Act of 1969, Hearings of the Select Subcommittee on Education of the Committee on Education and Labor of the U.S. House of Representatives, December 2, 1969, (pp. 146–166). Washington, DC: U.S. Government Printing Office.

Who lives on Sesame Street? *Psychology Today,* 17–18.

1969

Dampening the unemployability explosion. (January 4). *Saturday Review,* 108–110.

Dream of the kibbutz. (September 20). *Saturday Review,* 72–85.

Introduction. In H. Chauncey (Ed.), *Soviet preschool education: Program of instruction.* New York: Holt, Rinehart & Winston.

Motivational and social components in follow-through programs: Suggested principles, practices and research designs. In E. Grotberg (Ed.), *Critical issues and research related to disadvantaged children* (pp. 1–34). Princeton, NJ: Educational Testing Service.

On the making of new men: Some extrapolations from research. *Canadian Journal of Behavioural Science, 1,* 4–24.

Social factors in personality development. *Megamot, 16,* 348–363.

Theory and research in Soviet character education. In A. Simirenko (Ed.), *Social thought in the Soviet Union* (pp. 269–299). Chicago: Quadrangle Books.

(Authored with E. C. Devereux, Jr., & R. R. Rodgers). Child rearing in England and the United States: A cross-national comparison. *Journal of Marriage and the Family, 31,* 257–270.

1968

The changing Soviet family. In D. Brown (Ed.), *The role and status of women in the Soviet Union* (pp. 98–124). New York: Teachers College Press.

Early deprivation: A cross-species analysis. In G. Newton & S. Levine (Eds.), *Early experience and behavior* (627–764). Springfield, IL: Charles C Thomas.

Effects of social intervention on psychological development. In *Perspectives on human deprivation: Biological, psychological, and sociological.* Washington, DC: U.S. Department of Health, Education and Welfare.

Ethnic prejudice in England, France, and West Germany: Similarities, differences, and alternative interpretations. In M. Tumin (Ed.), *A cross-cultural study among youth in three European nations.* Paris: UNESCO.

Implications of follow-through programs for the American school system. *Poverty and Human Resources Abstracts, 3,* 3–15.

The making of the new Soviet man: Soviet and American. In *The quality of life* (pp. 123–134). Ithaca, NY: Cornell University.

Methods of child rearing in the Soviet Union and the United States: A comparison. In *The acquisition and development of values: Perspectives of research* (pp. 8–13). Bethesda, MD: National Institute of Child Health and Human Development.

Soviet methods of upbringing and their effects: A social–psychological analysis. Paper prepared for the Conference on Studies of Acquisition and Development of Values, National Institute of Child Health and Human Development.

The split society: Children versus adults. *Cornell Alumni News,* 8–17.

When is infant stimulation effective? In D. C. Glass (Ed.), *Environmental influences* (pp. 251–256). New York: Rockefeller University Press.

(Authored with E. C. Devereux, Jr., & R. R. Rodgers). Standards of social behavior among children in four cultures. *International Journal of Psychology, 3,* 31–41.

(Authored with J. Harding & M. Gallway). A review and theoretical framework for the study of interpersonal perception. In L. S. Wrightman, Jr. (Ed.), *Contemporary issues in social psychology* (pp. 103–109). Belmont, CA: Brooks/Cole.

1967

The impact of peers. Recorded presentation, Department of Child Development and Family Relations, Cornell University.

Makarenko and the collective family. Preface to A. Markarenko, *The collective family.* New York: Doubleday.

A new morality. (July 1). *Saturday Review,* p. 47.

The psychological costs of quality and equality in education. *Child Development, 38,* 909–925.

Response to pressure from peers versus adults among Soviet and American school children. *International Journal of Psychology, 2,* 199–207.

The split-level American family. (October 7). *Saturday Review,* 60–66. 7,

1966

Institutional approaches to cultural deprivation—American and Soviet. Paper prepared for the Third International Scientific Symposium on Mental Retardation, Joseph P. Kennedy, Jr. Foundation, Boston.

The national need for research on factors affecting human development. A statement prepared for the Sub-Committee on Labor and Public Welfare, U.S. House of Representatives.

The needs of America's children. Unpublished manuscript.

A report on institutional methods of upbringing in the U.S.S.R. Unpublished manuscript.

Testimony, House of Representatives Committee on Appropriations, March 22, 1966, *Congressional Record*, 101–116. Washington, DC: U.S. Government Printing Office.

(Authored with E. C. Devereux, Jr., & R. R. Rodgers). *Cross-cultural studies of child rearing.* Unpublished manuscript.

1965

An achievement creates a need. *Contemporary Psychology, 10,* 65–68.

Report of the National Planning Committee for Project Head Start. R. E. Cooke, Chairman. Washington, DC: Department of Health, Education and Welfare.

1964

Allowing for Soviet perceptions. In R. Fisher (Ed.), *International conflict and behavior science: The Craigville Papers.* New York: Basic Books.

Psychology as a core discipline in home economics. Paper presented at the meeting of the Association of Land Grant Colleges and Universities, Washington, DC.

Social perception and international affairs. In *Proceedings of the 15th International Congress of Applied Psychology*, Symposium on Psychology and International Affairs, Lyublyana, Yugoslavia.

Upbringing in collective settings in Switzerland and the U.S.S.R. In N. Bayley (Chairman), *Social development of the child* (pp. 159–161). Proceedings of the 18th International Congress of Psychology, Washington, DC. Amsterdam: North Holland.

1963

Developmental theory in transition. In H. W. Stevenson (Ed.), *Child psychology.* Chicago: University of Chicago Press.

Parenthood and child rearing. In *Encyclopedia of mental health*. New York: Franklin Watts.

Why Russians plant trees. *Saturday Review, 46*(95), 96.

1962

The challenge of the new Soviet man. *New York Times Magazine*, August 27 (Reprinted in H. Schwartz [Ed.], *The many faces of Communism*. New York: Berkeley; and in E. Josephson & M. Josephson [Eds.], *Man alone*. New York: Dell).

The role of age, sex, class, and culture in studies of moral development. *Religious Education, 57*, 545–561.

Secrecy. A basic tenet of the Soviets. *New York Times Magazine*, (April 22).

Some possible effects of a large-scale American shelter program on the Soviet Union and other nations. Report submitted to the U.S. House of Representatives Armed Services Committee, Washington, DC.

Some possible effects of national policy on character development in the United States of America and the Soviet Union. In H. D. Lasswell & H. Cleveland (Eds.), *The ethic of power*. New York: Harper.

Soviet methods of character education: Some implications for research. *American Psychologist, 17*, 550–564.

Soviet studies of personality development and socialization. In R. Bauer (Ed.), *Some views of Soviet psychology* (pp. 63–86). Washington, DC: American Psychological Association.

Zum Verhalten der Eltern in den Vereinigten Staaten und in der Bundesrepublik [On parental behavior in the United States and the Federal Republic of Germany]. In L. von Friedeburg (Ed.), *Jugend in der modernen Gesellschaft* (pp. 335–358). Cologne, Germany: Kiepenheuer und Witsch.

(Authored with E. C. Devereux, Jr., & G. J. Suci). Patterns of parent behavior in America and West Germany: A cross-national comparison. *International Social Science Journal, 14*, 488–506.

1961

Discussion. In A. E. Siegel & L. M. Stolz (Eds.), *Research issues related to the effects of maternal employment on children* (pp. 37–40). University

Park, PA: Social Science Research Center, Pennsylvania State University.

The mirror image in Soviet–American relations. *Journal of Social Issues*, *17*, 45–56.

Parsons' theory of identification. In M. Black (Ed.), *The social theories of Talcott Parsons* (pp. 191–213). Englewood Cliffs, NJ: Prentice Hall.

Preliminary summary report of observations as a member of the U.S. Medical Ecology Mission to the U.S.S.R. Report submitted to the U.S. Public Health Service, Washington, DC.

Section 2: Discussion. In *Behavioral approaches to accident research* (pp. 136–144). New York: The Association for the Aid of Crippled Children.

Some familial antecedents of responsibility and leadership in adolescents. In L. Petrullo & B. L. Bass (Eds.), *Leadership and interpersonal behavior* (pp. 239–271). New York: Holt, Rinehart & Winston.

Some problems in communicating with Americans about the Soviet Union. Unpublished manuscript.

A tour through Russia. *Cornell Countryman*, May 6–7.

Toward a social ecology of childhood accidents. Unpublished manuscript.

Toward a theoretical model for the analysis of parent–child relationships in a social context. In J. C. Glidewell (Ed.), *Parental attitudes and child behavior* (pp. 90–109). Springfield, IL: Charles C Thomas (Reprinted in E. P. Hollander & R. G. Hunt [Eds.], *Current perspectives in social psychology*. New York: Oxford University Press, 1963).

1960

An achievement creates a need (Review of J. W. Atkinson's [Ed.], "Motives in fantasy, action, and society: A method of assessment and study"), *Contemporary Psychology*, *5*, 65–68.

The changing American child: A speculative analysis. In *Reference papers on children and youth*, prepared for the Golden Anniversary White House Conference on Children and Youth, Washington, DC. (Reprinted in E. Ginsburg [Ed.], *Values and ideals of American youth*. New York: Columbia University Press, 1961; *Merrill-Palmer Quarterly*, 1961, *7*, 73–84; Der Wandel in der amerikanischen Kindererziehung [The change in

American child rearing: A speculative analysis]; L. von Friedeburg [Ed.], *Jugend in der modernen Gesellschaft* [pp. 321–334]).

Freudian theories of identification and their derivatives. *Child Development, 31,* 15–40 (Reprinted in C. B. Stendler [Ed.], *Readings in child behavior and development* [2nd ed.]. New York: Harcourt Brace World, 1964).

(Authored with E. C. Devereux, Jr.). *Family authority structure and adolescent behavior.* Proceedings of the XVI International Congress of Psychology, Bonn, Germany (Reprinted in *Acta Psychologia,* 1961, *19,* 415–417).

(Authored with E. C. Devereux, Jr., & J. Harding). Leadership and participation in a rural community. *Journal of Social Issues, 16,* 1–84.

(Authored with H. Ricciuti). The appraisal of personality characteristics in children. In P. H. Mussen (Ed.), *Handbook of research methods in child development* (pp. 770–817). New York: Wiley.

1959

In dispraise of fact. *Contemporary Psychology, 4,* 114–115.

1958

Socialization and social class through time and space. In E. E. Maccoby, T. M. Newcomb, & E. Hartley (Eds.), *Readings in social psychology* (3rd ed., pp. 400–424). New York: Holt.

The study of identification through interpersonal perception. In R. Taguiri & L. Petrullo (Eds.), *Person, perception, and interpersonal behavior* (pp. 110–130). Stanford, CA: Stanford University Press.

1957

Review of Brody's "Patterns of Mothering." *Contemporary Psychology, 2,* 37–38.

(Authored with J. Harding & M. Gallway). The measurement of skill in social perception. In D. C. McClelland, A. L. Baldwin, U. Bronfenbrenner, & F. L. Strodtbeck (Eds.), *Talent and society* (pp. 29–111). Princeton, NJ: Van Nostrand.

1956

Review of Soddy's "Mental Health and Infant Development." *Contemporary Psychology*, 2, 37–38.

1953

Personality. *Annual Review of Psychology*, 4, 157–182.

1952

Principles of professional ethics. *The American Psychologist*, 7, 452–455.
What makes for effective citizenship? *Farm Research*, XVIII(2), 16.
(Authored with E. C. Devereux, Jr.). Interdisciplinary planning for team research in constructive community behavior. *Human Relations*, 5, 187–203.

1951

Toward an integrated theory of personality. In R. R. Blake & G. V. Remsey (Eds.), *Perception, an approach to personality*. New York: Ronald Press.

1948

(Authored with M. Newcomb). Improvisions: An application of psychodrama in personality diagnosis. *Sociatry*, 4, 367–382.

1947

Research planning in neuropsychiatry and clinical psychology in the Veterans Administration. *Journal of Clinical Psychology*, 3(1), 33–38.

1944

A constant frame of reference for sociometric research: Part II. Experiment and inference. *Sociometry*, 7, 40–75.
The graphic presentation of sociometric data. *Sociometry*, 7, 283–289.

1943

A constant frame of reference for sociometric research. *Sociometry*, 6 363–397.

Author Index

Numbers in italics refer to listings in the reference sections.

Abel, T., 564, *591*
Aber, J. L., 472, *513*
Abolafia, J., 230, *257*
Achenbach, T. M., 474, 497, *509*
Acock, A. C., 172, *202*
Adams, B. N., 179, *202*
Ainsworth, M., *650*
Alberch, P., 308, *341*
Alexander, K. L., 280, *298*, 497–498, 503, *509*
Altheide, D., 586, *591–592*
Alvarex, W. F., *658*
Alwin, D. F., 216–217, 220, 223, 225–227, 231–235, 237, 239, 241–242, 244, 246, 251, *254–257, 260–261*
Ammann, R., 582, *597*
Anderson, E., 355, *363*
Andersson, T., 20, 45, 48, *57*
Angoff, W. H., 32, *51*
Anthony, V. Q., 62, *93*
Antonucci, T. C., 121, *137*
Ardelt, M., 112, *135*, 641, *646*
Asendorpf, J. B., 50, *51*, 224, *256*
Astone, N. M., 477, *516*
Avgar, A., *663*

Bach, R. L., 119, *138*
Backett, K., 284–285, *298*
Baker, J., *342*
Baker, J. G., *656*
Baldwin, A., 481, *517*
Baldwin, A. L., *650*

Baldwin, C., 481, *517*
Baldwin, J. M., *51*, 398, 412, *418*
Baltes, P. B., 36, *51*, 104, *134*, 239–240, 251, *261*
Bandura, A., 36, *52*, 63, *89*, 105, 111, *134*, 170–172, 174–175, *202*, 383, *388*, 535–536, *542*
Bane, M. J., 484, *515*
Barker, R. G., 35, *52*, 274, *298*
Barocas, R., 481, *518*
Barrett, B., *516*
Barrett, G. V., 305, *341*
Barton-Henry, M., 432, *465*
Barton, S., 41, *52*
Basar, E., 25, *52*
Bateson, P. P. G., 51, *52*
Bauer, C., 502, *511*, *516*
Baumrind, D., 64, *89*, 220, *256*, 425, 431–432, *461*, 571, *592*
Bayder, N., 473, 484, *509–510*
Belle, D., 67, *89*
Bell, R., 440, *461*
Bell, R. Q., 586, *596*
Belsky, J., 555–556, 560, *560–561*, *664*
Belt, P., *516*
Bem, D. J., 175, *203*, 234, *257*
Benasich, A., *510*
Benasich, A. A., 504, *510–511*, *516*
Bengtson, V. L., 118–120, 127, *134*, 172, 180, *202, 204*
Bennett, C., 352, *364*
Bennett, F., *516*
Bennett, F. C., 502, *511*

677

Subject Index

noncognitive abilities, 335–336
North American research, 312–320
  baking cupcakes–charging batteries, 313–314
  capturing butterflies, 312–313
  day at the races, 314–316
  stocks and bonds, 316–320
physical and social notions, 310
physical milieu and emotional/affective environment, 307
South American research
  class inclusion, 324–326
  conservation, 326–328
  proportional reasoning problems, 321–324
theory of proximal processes, 328–330
translation of genotypes into phenotypes, 308, 328–330
Cohort effect, 230
Cohort replacement, 232
Cohort succession, personality and social change, 231–233
Collective efficacy, 536
Collective socialization, 492
Community, influences on adolescent adjustment, 427
Community resources, 471–472
  young children's development and, 491–495
  accumulation, 493–494
  early intervention and, 505–509
  intersection with child characteristics, 494
  intersection with family resources, 494–495
  pathway of influence on children, 503–505
  role, 491–493, 497–499
Compensation, functional community effects on children, 451–453

Connections
  adult, resilience and, 179–180
  between children, parents, and the state, 271–272
  within households, 272
Conservation, 326–328
Context, 367, 523–524. See also Social contexts
  biological effects of early maturation in females, 410
  Bronfenbrenner's emphasis, 545–546
  cross-sex, adolescence, 353
  multiple, 265–268
  role in ecology of development, 549–550
  types, 309–311
Contribution, spirit of, 286–289
Convenient groupings, 323
Cross-national research, 152–158
  class structure and social stratification hierarchy effects on personality, 153–155
  differences and inconsistencies, 155
  occupational self-direction, 155–157
  relationship between social structural position and occupational self-direction, 162
  social structural position, 156–157
Cross-sex contacts, between children, 352
Cross-sex contexts, adolescence, 353
Culture, role differentiation of parents, 359

Depression Scale, Center for Epidemiologic Studies, 431
Development. See also Community resources; Family resources
  adolescents, 425–526
  in context, 5

Life course paradigm (*continued*)
  sociocultural environment as point
    of departure, 103
  timetable, 124
  timing of lives, 114–116
Life course principles, 641–642
Life cycle, opportunities for change in
    personality, 242–247
  exposure to occupational experi-
    ences, 246–247
  occupational status, 243–245
Life satisfaction, 385–386
Life-stage principle, 115
Linked lives. *See also* Life course para-
    digm
  models, 201–202
Log-linear analysis, 186–187

Marriage, as turning point, 377–380
Maturation, early, norm-breaking be-
    havior and, 16–17, 29
Mediation, moderated, ecology of de-
    velopment, 550
Mental processes, as activities, 30
Mental system, holistic perspective,
    30–31
Microsystem
  beyond, 640
  reconceptualization, 638
Models in process, 2–3
Molar stability, 234
Money
  defining expectations about rights
    and obligations, 292–296
  pocket, for children, 294–295
Moral development, 24
Mother–infant interaction, behavioral
    problems and, 623–625
Multivocalism, 276

Narrative approach, 369
Nature–nurture issue, 23

Neighborhood
  disintegration, 537–538
  influence on adolescents, 436–437
  potential effects on children, 492–495
  social organization, importance,
    528–531
  structural characteristics, effects on
    parenting, 454–459
    social integration, 456–457
    value consensus, 457–459
  with weak social controls and moni-
    toring, 538
Neurons, overarborization, 332

Obligations, studying, 285–289
Occupational complexity, 243–244
Occupational status, 243–244
Operating factors, patterning, 41–43

Panel Study of Income Dynamics, 469
Parallelism, cause and, 145–148
Parental identification, timing of, 176
Parent–child relations
  effects of ethics and politics, 571
  types of households, 433–434
Parenthood, social systems, 358–363
Parenting, 423–461
  Acceptance/Involvement scale, 432
  authoritative, 431–435, 438–440
    ethnicity and, 443
    power of, 437–441
    transcontextual validation, 441–444
  changes in, 145–146
  effect on adolescents' personality,
    447–448
  indulgent, 434, 438, 440
  interpretation of ideas, 586
  neglectful, 434, 438, 440
  over-time impact, 440–441
  Psychological Autonomy Granting
    scale, 432
  research

About the Editors

Phyllis Moen, PhD, is the Ferris Family Professor of Life Course Studies, as well as the professor of human development and family studies and professor of sociology at Cornell University. She serves as the founding director of Cornell's Bronfenbrenner Life Course Center and codirector of its Applied Gerontology Research Institute, one of six of the Edward Roybal Centers funded by the National Institute on Aging. Moen received her doctoral degree from the University of Minnesota in 1978. While on leave from Cornell, she spent several years as director of the sociology program at the National Science Foundation. She is the author of *Working Parents: Transformations in Gender Roles and Public Policies in Sweden* (1989) and *Women's Two Roles: A Contemporary Dilemma* (1992) and has published widely on women's roles, health and well-being, families, aging and the life course, and social policy. Professor Moen is currently conducting a federally funded study of retirement and postretirement activities, health, and well-being.

Glen H. Elder, Jr., PhD, is Howard W. Odum Distinguished Professor of Sociology and research professor of psychology at the University of North Carolina at Chapel Hill, where he directs a research program on the life course and social change. His longitudinal studies began in the early 1960s at the University of California, Berkeley (Institute of Human Development), and he has continued such work up to the present through faculty appointments at Cornell University and the University of North Carolina, Chapel Hill. Professor Elder is the author of *Children of the Great Depression* (1974), in addition to numerous articles and chapters providing the conceptual and theoretical underpinnings of a life course approach, as well as empirical studies drawing on this perspective. He is currently codirector of the Carolina Consortium on Human Development.

Kurt Lüscher, Dr. rer. pol., is professor of sociology at the University of Konstanz (Germany), where he directs the research program, Society and Family. He has held previous positions at the University of Bern (Switzerland) and, as a visiting associate professor, at the University of North Carolina (Chapel Hill). His major research interests include intergenerational relations, family rhetoric, and family politics. He is a member of policy advisory committees both in Germany and in Switzerland. Professor Lüscher's most recent book *Generationenbeziehungen in "postmodernen" Gesellschaften* (1993) is an edited volume based on a symposium on Intergenerational Relations in Post Modern Societies held at the University of Konstanz in 1991.